D1432965

MUIRHEAD LIBRARY OF PHILOSOPHY

An admirable statement of the aims of the Library of Philosophy
was provided by the first editor, the late Professor J. H. Muirhead, in his description of the original programme printed in
Erdmann's *History of Philosophy* under the date 1890. This was
slightly modified in subsequent volumes to take the form of the
following statement :

'The Muirhead Library of Philosophy was designed as a contribution to the History of Modern Philosophy under the heads :
first of different Schools of Thought—Sensationalist, Realist,
Idealist, Intuitivist ; secondly of different Subjects—Psychology, Ethics, Aesthetics, Political Philosophy, Theology. While
much had been done in England in tracing the course of evolution
in nature, history, economics, morals and religion, little had
been done in tracing the development of thought on these
subjects. Yet " the evolution of opinion is part of the whole
evolution".

'By the co-operation of different writers in carrying out this
plan it was hoped that a thoroughness and completeness of
treatment, otherwise unattainable, might be secured. It was
believed also that from writers mainly British and American
fuller consideration of English Philosophy than it had hitherto
received might be looked for. In the earlier series of books
containing, among others, Bosanquet's *History of Aesthetics*,
Pfleiderer's *Rational Theology since Kant*, Albee's *History of
English Utilitarianism*, Bonar's *Philosophy and Political
Economy*, Brett's *History of Psychology*, Ritchie's *Natural
Rights*, these objects were to a large extent effected.

'In the meantime original work of a high order was being
produced both in England and America by such writers as
Bradley, Stout, Bertrand Russell, Baldwin, Urban, Montague
and others, and a new interest in foreign works, German,
French and Italian, which had either become classical or were

attracting public attention, had developed. The scope of the Library thus became extended into something more international, and it is entering on the fifth decade of its existence in the hope that it may contribute to the mutual understanding between countries which is so pressing a need of the present time.'

The need which Professor Muirhead stressed is no less pressing today, and few will deny that philosophy has much to do with enabling us to meet it, although no one, least of all Muirhead himself, would regard that as the sole, or even the main, object of philosophy. As Professor Muirhead continues to lend the distinction of his name to the Library of Philosophy, it seemed not inappropriate to allow him to recall to us these aims in his own words. The emphasis on the history of thought seemed to me also very timely; and the number of important works promised for the Library in the near future augurs well for the continued fulfilment, in this and in other ways, of the expectations of the original editor.

H. D. LEWIS

MUIRHEAD LIBRARY OF PHILOSOPHY

General Editor : Professor H. D. Lewis

Professor of History and Philosophy of Religion in the University of London

THE ANALYSIS OF MIND By Bertrand Russell. *8th Impression.*

ANALYTIC PSYCHOLOGY By Professor G. F. Stout. *Two Vols. 5th Impression.*

COLERIDGE AS PHILOSOPHER By Professor J. H. Muirhead. *2nd Impression.*

CONTEMPORARY AMERICAN PHILOSOPHY Edited by G. P. Adams and W. P. Montague.

CONTEMPORARY BRITISH PHILOSOPHY Edited by Professor J. H. Muirhead.

CONTEMPORARY INDIAN PHILOSOPHY Edited by Radhakrishnan and Professor J. H. Muirhead.

CONTEMPORARY BRITISH PHILOSOPHY Third Series. Edited by Professor H. D. Lewis.

DEVELOPMENT OF THEOLOGY SINCE KANT By O. Pfleiderer

DIALOGUES ON METAPHYSICS By Nicholas Malebranche. *Translated by Morris Ginsburg.*

ETHICS By Nicolai Hartmann. *Translated by Stanton Coit. Three Vols.*

THE GOOD WILL : A STUDY IN THE COHERENCE THEORY OF GOODNESS By Professor H. J. Paton.

HEGEL : A RE-EXAMINATION By J. N. Findlay.

HEGEL'S SCIENCE OF LOGIC *Translated by W. H. Johnston and L. G. Struthers. Two Vols. 2nd Impression.*

HISTORY OF ÆSTHETIC By Dr. B. Bosanquet. *4th Edition. 5th Impression.*

HISTORY OF ENGLISH UTILITARIANISM By Professor E. Albee.

HISTORY OF PSYCHOLOGY By Professor G. S. Brett. Edited by R. S. Peters. *Abridged one volume edition.*

HUMAN KNOWLEDGE By Bertand Russell. *3rd Impression.*

A HUNDRED YEARS OF BRITISH PHILOSOPHY By Dr. Rudolf Metz. *Translated by Professor J. W. Harvey, Professor T. E. Jessop, Henry Sturt. 2nd Impression.*

IDEAS : A GENERAL INTRODUCTION TO PURE PHENOMENOLOGY By Edmund Husserl. *Translated by W. R. Boyce Gibson. 2nd Impression.*

INDIAN PHILOSOPHY By Radhakrishnan. *Two Vols. Revised 2nd Edition.*

THE INTELLIGIBLE WORLD METAPHYSICS AND VALUE By Professor W. M. Urban.

INTRODUCTION TO MATHEMATICAL PHILOSOPHY By Bertrand Russell. *2nd Edition. 8th Impression.*

KANT'S FIRST CRITIQUE By H. W. Cassirer.

KANT'S METAPHYSIC OF EXPERIENCE By Professor H. J. Paton. *2nd Impression.*

KNOW THYSELF By Bernardino Varisco. *Translated by Dr. Guglielmo Salvadori.*

LANGUAGE AND REALITY By Wilbur Marshall Urban.

MATTER AND MEMORY By Henri Bergson. *Translated by N. M. Paul and W. S. Palmer. 6th Impression.*

MODERN PHILOSOPHY By Guido de Ruggiero. *Translated by A. Howard Hannay and R. G. Collingwood.*

THE MODERN PREDICAMENT By Professor H. J. Paton.

MORAL SENSE By James Bonar.

NATURAL RIGHTS By D. G. Ritchie. *3rd Edition. 5th Impression.*

NATURE, MIND AND MODERN SCIENCE By E. Harris.

THE NATURE OF THOUGHT By Brand Blanshard, B.Sc., Ph.D. *2nd Impression.*

ON SELFHOOD AND GODHOOD By A. C. Campbell.

PERSONALITY AND REALITY By E. J. Turner.

THE PHENOMENOLOGY OF MIND By G. W. F. Hegel. *Translated by Sir James Baillie. Revised 2nd Edition. 3rd Impression.*

PHILOSOPHY AND POLITICAL ECONOMY By J. Bonar. *4th Impression.*

THE PLATONIC TRADITION IN ANGLO-SAXON PHILOSOPHY By Professor J. H. Muirhead.

THE PRINCIPAL UPANISADS By Radhakrishnan.

THE PROBLEMS OF PERCEPTION By R. J. Hirst.

SOME MAIN PROBLEMS OF PHILOSOPHY By E. G. Moore.

TIME AND FREE WILL By Professor Henri Bergson. *Translated by F. G. Pogson. 6th Impression.*

THE WAYS OF KNOWING : OR, THE METHODS OF PHILOSOPHY. By Professor W. P. Montague. *4th Impression.*

CONTEMPORARY INDIAN
PHILOSOPHY

CONTEMPORARY
INDIAN PHILOSOPHY

by

M. K. GANDHI
RABINDRANATH TAGORE
SWĀMI ABHEDĀNANDA
HARIDAS BHATTACHARYYA
K. C. BHATTACHARYYA
G. C. CHATTERJI
ANANDA K. COOMARASWAMY
N. G. DAMLE
BHAGAVAN DAS
RAS-VIHARY DAS
SURENDRANATH DASGUPTA
D. M. DATTA
HIRALAL HALDAR
M. HIRIYANNA
HUMAYUN KABIR
S. K. MAITRA
G. R. MALKANI
A. C. MUKERJI
T. R. V. MURTI
S. RADHAKRISHNAN
P. T. RAJU
R. D. RANADE
M. M. SHARIF
V. SUBRAHMANYA IYER
A. R. WADIA

Edited by

S. RADHAKRISHNAN, D.Litt., F.B.A.
and
J. H. MUIRHEAD, LL.D., F.B.A.
*Late Professor Emeritus of the
University of Birmingham*

LONDON
GEORGE ALLEN & UNWIN LTD
MUSEUM STREET

FIRST PUBLISHED IN 1936
REVISED SECOND AND ENLARGED EDITION, 1952
THIRD IMPRESSION, 1958

PRINTED IN GREAT BRITAIN BY
BRADFORD AND DICKENS
LONDON, W.C.1

CONTENTS

PAGE

FOREWORD by the GENERAL EDITOR
of the LIBRARY OF PHILOSOPHY 13

M. K. GANDHI 21

RABINDRANATH TAGORE
THE RELIGION OF AN ARTIST 25

SWĀMI ABHEDĀNANDA
HINDU PHILOSOPHY IN INDIA 49

HARIDAS BHATTACHARYYA
THE PRINCIPLES OF ACTIVISM 67

K. C. BHATTACHARYYA
THE CONCEPT OF PHILOSOPHY 105

G. C. CHATTERJI
COMMON-SENSE EMPIRICISM 129

ANANDA K. COOMARASWAMY
ON THE PERTINENCE OF PHILOSOPHY 151

N. G. DAMLE
THE FAITH OF AN IDEALIST 175

BHAGAVAN DAS
ĀTMA-VIDYĀ, or THE SCIENCE OF THE SELF 197

RAS-VIHARY DAS
PURSUIT OF TRUTH THROUGH DOUBT
AND BELIEF 231

SURENDRANATH DASGUPTA
PHILOSOPHY OF DEPENDENT EMERGENCE 251

D. M. DATTA
KNOWLEDGE, REALITY AND THE UNKNOWN 289

HIRALAL HALDAR
REALISTIC IDEALISM   317

M. HIRIYANNA
THE PROBLEM OF TRUTH   335

HUMAYUN KABIR
FREEDOM, AUTHORITY AND IMAGINATION   357

S. K. MAITRA
OUTLINES OF AN EMERGENT THEORY
OF VALUES   379

G. R. MALKANI
FREEDOM THROUGH KNOWLEDGE   409

A. C. MUKERJI
SUGGESTIONS FOR AN IDEALISTIC THEORY
OF KNOWLEDGE   431

T. R. V. MURTI
THE SPIRIT OF PHILOSOPHY   457

S. RADHAKRISHNAN
THE SPIRIT IN MAN   475

P. T. RAJU
THE INWARD ABSOLUTE AND THE ACTIVISM
OF THE FINITE SELF   509

R. D. RANADE
THE EVOLUTION OF MY OWN THOUGHT   539

M. M. SHARIF
DIALECTICAL MONADISM   565

V. SUBRAHMANYA IYER
MAN'S INTEREST IN PHILOSOPHY:
AN INDIAN VIEW   593

A. R. WADIA
PRAGMATIC IDEALISM   623

INDEX   643

FOREWORD

THE contribution of India to the philosophical literature of the world may by this time be said to be an open book to English readers. For the last sixty years, since Max Müller began the publication of the Sacred Books of the East in 1875, the great scroll of its story has been gradually unrolling itself before their eyes. Within the last few years comprehensive and scholarly histories of Indian philosophy in all its many schools by Professor Das Gupta and Sir S. Radhakrishnan and many monographs and handbooks by less-known writers have been published both in India and in England. Even the slightest acquaintance with these sources is sufficient to convince the reader of the justice of the claims put forward on their behalf,[1] that "there is hardly any height of spiritual insight or rational philosophy attained in the world that has not its parallel in the vast stretch that lies between the early Vedic seers and the modern Naiyāyikas," who with their analytic and critical methods may be said to stand to the Vedānta in somewhat the same relation as Kant and his followers stand to the great neo-Platonic and Patristic tradition of the West.

While we may thus well be convinced that Indian thought in the past represents a chapter in the history of the human mind that is full of vital meaning for us and well fitted by its profound sense of a Spiritual Presence brooding over the world of our ordinary experience to wean us from too exclusive occupation either with secular life or with the temporary formulations, in which Western theology has too often sought to imprison religious aspiration, it may still be asked whether in India itself all this exists to-day as a mere tradition or has formed the soil and supplied the seed for fresh developments. It was in the conviction that in present-day philosophy there is more than a tradition, and that, owing partly to the inherent genius of the race, partly to a fructifying contact with Western thought, the tree of philosophical knowledge has recently put forth fresh flower and fruit that the idea of this volume as a continuation

[1] *Indian Philosophy*, S. Radhakrishnan, Vol. I, p. 8.

of the series on Contemporary British and Contemporary American Philosophy, when suggested by an Indian friend, was welcomed by the Editor of the Library of Philosophy. Coming as it did at a moment when, on the eve of the gigantic political experiment legislated for in the Indian Act, the need of a fuller understanding of the mind of the leaders of thought in that country, some of whom are certain to be called to take a prominent part in the new administration, is above all things desirable, the proposal seemed to be one of more than theoretic interest. What are the ideas of these men as to the ends of human life and the form that should be given to it through education and "the spirit of the laws" so as to make it seem to the present and future generations of this vast continent to be truly worth living? It was our own Berkeley who said: "Whatever people may think, the man who has not deeply meditated on the human mind and on the *summum bonum* may possibly make a thriving earthworm, but will undoubtedly make a sorry politician and statesman." Is there ground for the faith that among the leaders of thought in India there are men who belong to the type that Berkeley had in view, and who possess the kind of insight which can be trusted to guide their people through the desert of political experimentation and controversy that lies between them to the land which seems both to them and to most of us so full of promise? It is because it is believed that some reassurance on this head will be derived from the essays in this volume that, apart from technical value in the field of philosophy, a certain political importance and timeliness may be claimed for it.

Going beyond any temporary political bearing its publication may, it is further hoped, contribute to a better mutual understanding between the whole mind of East and West. It is surely with justice that one of the contributors has pilloried the verse "East is East and West is West and never the twain shall meet" as "an utterance of abysmal ignorance and the deepest discouragement," and has set against it the power of that "intellectual wisdom, which is one and the same at all times and for all men and is independent of all environmental idiosyncrasy," to provide an effective *entente* between them. It may therefore not be inappropriate in this Foreword to mention one or two of the points in which many Western thinkers will, it is believed, find themselves in profound agreement with the spirit that animates most of the writers.

Contrary to what is usually thought of the remoteness from practice of Indian Philosophy, what here strikes one is the lively sense of its practical value. As one of the writers has quaintly put it, "its chief concern has not been to conceive of a philosophical scheme like a toy machine to play with, but to make of it a chariot in which man could ride."

Another equally striking feature (again contradictory to popular views) is the spirit of tolerance that breathes in their teaching—the conviction that it is one truth that is expressed in all forms of anything that can be called in a true sense religion. "If we study religions," we are told by the same writer, "with a view to discovering, not how much of error, but how much of truth, each embraces, we shall be far more impressed by their similarities than by their diversities." And again: "In Hindu philosophy a man is regarded as a true teacher who gives to any individual a better access to that individual's own scriptures, for 'the path men take from every side is Mine' . . . There is always a natural manifestation of the one Almighty God amongst all right-thinking men."

Surprising too (to mention only one further point) to many who have accused Indian philosophy of a prevailing note of pessimism is the tone of hopefulness that pervades one and all of the contributors, and for which the authority of the whole course of Indian philosophy is claimed. "No Indian seer," writes another, "has allowed himself to be overpowered by a sense of evil." We hear much indeed of philosophy as a call to transcend the narrowness of egoism and identify ourselves with something greater than ourselves as the way of salvation, but this is not in order to escape from the ineradicable evil of existence but in order to find ourselves in things that give to existence its only true value. For "in the man who transcends his narrow self and merges it in the life of the whole philosophy as truth, religion as devotion and morality as goodness meet."

The Editors had hoped that Mr. Gandhi, the leader of Indian religious reformers, might have been tempted by the questionnaire sent to him to give a fuller statement than we have as yet had of the philosophy underlying his political teaching, but perhaps we ought not to regret that he has refused to devote even a small portion of his time to anything less important than the great mission he has undertaken to redeem his country from the most deeply rooted of the evils it has inherited from the past. He has, however, sent a condensed statement of the answers he would be prepared to give to the editorial questions, and we print it with gratitude below.

Owing to the necessity to impose some easily understood limit to the range of choice, the essays which follow are all written by philosophers of or about forty-five years of age. They fall into two main groups: those in which the writer devotes himself chiefly to the exposition of the great Vedic tradition as he has apprehended it and made it the basis of his own life's work; and those in which the writer, while on the whole remaining true to the spirit of that tradition, has sought to give new interpretations of it, either by instituting comparisons of it with the Western doctrines most closely allied to it or by treating of modern problems in a way which, though suggested by what he has learned from the West, is yet stamped with the mark of his own racial sympathy. Western readers will naturally find the latter group more attractive; but this volume will have failed of its purpose if it does not give them some sense of the truth that underlies even the essays with which, owing to the presuppositions on which these are founded, they find themselves least in sympathy.

Whichever of the two groups attracts the reader, it is well that he should remind himself that, as in politics so in philosophy, India stands at the opening of a new era in her history which requires above all things, along with an abiding admiration of her past achievements, a forward-looking faith in the power of the soul of her people to rise as high as, and perhaps even to excel the greatest of them.

One conspicuous omission in the essays contained in this volume requires a word of explanation. It was hoped that it might be possible to include contributions from adherents of both the great traditions represented in Indian religious thought. With this view, besides philosophers known to be attached to Hinduism, several Moslems were approached, but for different reasons excused themselves, and it has been found necessary to proceed with this, which it is hoped may be merely a first edition, without further attempt to fill the gap.

The order of the contributions is alphabetical with the exception that Gandhi and Rabindranath Tagore have been given the place of honour at the beginning in consideration of their world-wide fame in fields other than that of technical philosophy.

GENERAL EDITOR
of the LIBRARY OF PHILOSOPHY

PREFACE TO THE SECOND EDITION

In this edition a serious gap of the first edition mentioned by the late editor of the Library of Philosophy, Professor J. H. Muirhead, a noble and generous friend of Indian thought, has been filled. We have now contributions from the adherents of the different religious traditions of India, Hindu and Muslim, Christian and Zoroastrian.

I am indebted to Professor D. M. Datta of the Patna University for his assistance in collecting the new material for this edition.

S.R.

M. K. GANDHI

Born October 2, 1869

M. K. GANDHI

I HAVE been asked by Sir S. Radhakrishnan to answer the following three questions:

(1) What is your Religion?

(2) How are you led to it?

(3) What is its bearing on social life.

My religion is Hinduism which, for me, is Religion of humanity and includes the best of all the religions known to me.

I take it that the present tense in the second question has been purposely used instead of the past. I am being led to my religion through Truth and Non-violence, i.e. love in the broadest sense. I often describe my religion as Religion of Truth. Of late, instead of saying God is Truth I have been saying Truth is God, in order more fully to define my Religion. I used, at one time, to know by heart the thousand names of God which a booklet in Hinduism gives in verse form and which perhaps tens of thousands recite every morning. But nowadays nothing so completely describes my God as Truth. Denial of God we have known. Denial of Truth we have not known. The most ignorant among mankind have some truth in them. We are all sparks of Truth. The sum total of these sparks is indescribable, as-yet-Unknown-Truth, which is God. I am being daily led nearer to It by constant prayer.

The bearing of this religion on social life is, or has to be, seen in one's daily social contact. To be true to such religion one has to lose oneself in continuous and continuing service of all life. Realisation of Truth is impossible without a complete merging of oneself in, and identification with, this limitless ocean of life. Hence, for me, there is no escape from social service, there is no happiness on earth beyond or apart from it. Social service here must be taken to include every department of life. In this scheme there is nothing low, nothing high. For, all is one, though we *seem* to be many.

THE RELIGION OF AN ARTIST

by RABINDRANATH TAGORE

Born 1861

THE RELIGION OF AN ARTIST

I

I was born in 1861: that is not an important date of history, but it belongs to a great epoch in Bengal, when the currents of three movements had met in the life of our country. One of these, the religious, was introduced by a very great-hearted man of gigantic intelligence, Raja Rammohan Roy. It was revolutionary, for he tried to reopen the channel of spiritual life which had been obstructed for many years by the sands and debris of creeds that were formal and materialistic, fixed in external practices lacking spiritual significance. People who cling to an ancient past have their pride in the antiquity of their accumulations, in the sublimity of time-honoured walls around them. They grow nervous and angry when some great spirit, some lover of truth, breaks open their enclosure and floods it with the sunshine of thought and the breath of life. Ideas cause movement and all forward movements they consider to be a menace to their warehouse security.

This was happening about the time I was born. I am proud to say that my father was one of the great leaders of that movement, a movement for whose sake he suffered ostracism and braved social indignities. I was born in this atmosphere of the advent of new ideals, which at the same time were old, older than all the things, of which that age was proud.

There was a second movement equally important. Bankim Chandra Chatterjee, who, though much older than myself, was my contemporary and lived long enough for me to see him, was the first pioneer in the literary revolution, which happened in Bengal about that time. Before his arrival our literature had been oppressed by a rigid rhetoric that ⋅choked its life and loaded it with ornaments that became its fetters. Bankim Chandra was brave enough to go against the orthodoxy which believed in the security of tombstones and in that finality which can only belong to the lifeless. He lifted the dead weight of ponderous forms from our language and with a touch of his magic wand aroused our literature from her age-long sleep. A great promise and a vision of beauty she revealed to us when she awoke in the fulness of her strength and grace.

There was yet another movement started about this time called the National. It was not fully political, but it began to give voice to the mind of our people trying to assert their own personality. It was a voice of impatience at the humiliation constantly heaped upon us by people who were not oriental, and who had, especially at that time, the habit of sharply dividing the human world into the good and the bad according to the hemispheres to which they belong.

This contemptuous spirit of separatedness was perpetually hurting us and causing great damage to our own world of culture. It generated in our young men a distrust of all things that had come to them as an inheritance from their past. The old Indian pictures and other works of art were laughed at by our students in imitation of the laughter of their European schoolmasters of that age of philistinism.

Though later on our teachers themselves had changed their mind, their disciples had hardly yet fully regained confidence in the merit of our art. They have had a long period of encouragement in developing an appetite for third-rate copies of French pictures, for gaudy oleographs abjectly cheap, for the pictures that are products of mechanical accuracy of a stereotyped standard, and they still considered it to be a symptom of superior culture to be able disdainfully to refuse oriental works of creation.

The modern young men of that period nodded their heads and said that true originality lay not in the discovery of the rhythm of the essential in the heart of reality but in the full lips, tinted cheeks and bare breasts of imported pictures. The same spirit of rejection, born of utter ignorance, was cultivated in other departments of our culture. It was the result of the hypnotism exercised upon the minds of the younger generation by people who were loud of voice and strong of arm. The national movement was started to proclaim that we must not be indiscriminate in our rejection of the past. This was not a reactionary movement but a revolutionary one, because it set out with a great courage to deny and to oppose all pride in mere borrowings.

These three movements were on foot and in all three the members of my own family took active part. We were ostracised because of our heterodox opinions about religion and therefore we enjoyed the freedom of the outcast. We had to build our own world with our own thoughts and energy of mind.

I was born and brought up in an atmosphere of the confluence of three movements, all of which were revolutionary. My family had to live its own life, which led me from my young days to seek guidance for my own self-expression in my own inner standard of judgment. The medium of expression doubtless was my mother tongue. But the language which belonged to the people had to be modulated according to the urge which I as an individual had.

No poet should borrow his medium ready-made from some shop of orthodox respectability. He should not only have his own seeds but prepare his own soil. Each poet has his own distinct medium of language—not because the whole language is of his own make, but because his individual use of it, having life's magic touch, transforms it into a special vehicle of his own creation.

The races of man have poetry in their heart and it is necessary for them to give, as far as is possible, a perfect expression to their sentiments. For this they must have a medium, moving and pliant, which can freshly become their very own, age after age. All great languages have undergone and are still undergoing changes. Those languages which resist the spirit of change are doomed and will never produce great harvests of thought and literature. When forms become fixed, the spirit either weakly accepts its imprisonment within them or rebels. All revolutions consist of the fight of the within against invasion by the without.

There was a great chapter in the history of life on this earth when some irresistible inner force in man found its way out into the scheme of things, and sent forth its triumphant mutinous voice, with the cry that it was not going to be overwhelmed from outside by the huge brute beast of a body. How helpless it appeared at the moment, but has it not nearly won? In our social life also, revolution breaks out when some power concentrates itself in outside arrangements and threatens to enslave for its own purpose the power which we have within us.

When an organisation which is a machine becomes a central force, political, commercial, educational or religious, it obstructs the free flow of inner life of the people and waylays and exploits it for the augmentation of its own power. To-day, such concentration of power is fast multiplying on the outside and the cry of the oppressed spirit of man is in the air which struggles to free itself from the grip of screws and bolts, of unmeaning obsessions.

Revolution must come and men must risk revilement and misunderstanding, especially from those who want to be comfortable, who put their faith in materialism, and who belong truly to the dead past and not to modern times, the past that had its age in distant antiquity when physical flesh and size predominated, and not the mind of man.

Purely physical dominance is mechanical and modern machines are merely exaggerating our bodies, lengthening and multiplying our limbs. The modern mind in its innate childishness delights in this enormous bodily bulk, representing an inordinate material power, saying: "Let me have the big toy and no sentiment which can disturb it." It does not realise that in this we are returning to that antediluvian age which revelled in its production of gigantic physical frames, leaving no room for the freedom of the inner spirit.

All great human movements in the world are related to some great ideal. Some of you may say that such a doctrine of spirit has been in its death-throes for over a century and is now moribund; that we have nothing to rely upon but external forces and material foundations. But I say, on my part, that your doctrine was obsolete long ago. It was exploded in the springtime of life, when mere size was swept off the face of the world, and was replaced by man, brought naked into the heart of creation, man with his helpless body, but with his indomitable mind and spirit.

When I began my life as a poet, the writers among our educated community took their guidance from their English textbooks which poured upon them lessons that did not fully saturate their minds. I suppose it was fortunate for me that I never in my life had the kind of academic training which is considered proper for a boy of a respectable family. Though I cannot say I was altogether free from the influence that ruled young minds of those days, the course of my writings was nevertheless saved from the groove of imitative forms. In my versification, vocabulary and ideas, I yielded myself to the vagaries of an untutored fancy which brought castigation upon me from critics who were learned, and uproarious laughter from the witty. My ignorance combined with my heresy turned me into a literary outlaw.

When I began my career I was ridiculously young; in fact I was the youngest of that band who had made themselves articulate. I had neither the protective armour of mature age, nor enough English to command respect. So in my seclusion of contempt and qualified encouragement I had my freedom. Gradually I grew up in years—for which, however, I claim no credit. Steadily I cut my way through derision and occasional patronage into a recognition in which the proportion of praise and blame was very much like that of land and water on our earth.

What gave me boldness when I was young was my early acquaintance with the old Vaishnava poems of Bengal, full of the freedom of metre and courage of expression. I think I was only twelve when these poems first began to be reprinted. I surreptitiously got hold of copies from the desks of my elders. For the edification of the young I must confess that this was not right for a boy of my age. I should have been passing my examinations and not following a path that would lead to loss of marks. I must also admit that the greater part of these lyrics was erotic and not quite suited to a boy just about to reach his teens. But my imagination was fully occupied with the beauty of their forms and the music of their words; and their breath, heavily laden with voluptuousness, passed over my mind without distracting it.

My vagabondage in the path of my literary career had another reason. My father was the leader of a new religious movement, a strict monotheism based upon the teachings of the Upaniṣads. My countrymen in Bengal thought him almost as bad as a Christian, if not worse. So we were completely ostracised, which probably saved me from another disaster, that of imitating our own past.

Most of the members of my family had some gift—some were artists, some poets, some musicians and the whole atmosphere of our home was permeated with the spirit of creation. I had a deep sense almost from infancy of the beauty of Nature, an intimate feeling of companionship with the trees and the clouds, and felt in tune with the musical touch of the seasons in the air. At the same time, I had a peculiar susceptibility to human kindness. All these craved expression. The very earnestness of my emotions yearned to be true to themselves though I was too immature to give their expression any perfection of form.

Since then I have gained a reputation in my country, but till very late a strong current of antagonism in a large section of my countrymen persisted. Some said that my poems did not spring from the national heart; some complained that they were incomprehensible, others that they were unwholesome. In fact, I have never had complete acceptance from my own people, and that too has been a blessing; for nothing is so demoralising as unqualified success.

This is the history of my career. I wish I could reveal it more clearly through the narration of my own work in my own language. I hope that will be possible some day or other. Languages are jealous. They do not give up their best treasures to those who try to deal with them through an intermediary belonging to an alien rival. We have to court them in person and dance attendance on them. Poems are not like market commodities transferable. We cannot receive the smiles and glances of our sweetheart through an attorney, however diligent and dutiful he may be.

I myself have tried to get at the wealth of beauty in the literature of the European languages, long before I gained a full light to their hospitality. When I was young I tried to approach Dante, unfortunately through an English translation. I failed utterly, and felt it my pious duty to desist. Dante remained a closed book to me.

I also wanted to know German literature and, by reading Heine in translation, I thought I had caught a glimpse of the beauty there. Fortunately I met a missionary lady from Germany and asked her help. I worked hard for some months, but being rather quick-witted, which is not a good quality, I was not persevering. I had the dangerous facility which helps one to guess the meaning too easily. My teacher thought I had almost mastered the language, which was not true. I succeeded, however, in getting through Heine, like a man walking in sleep crossing unknown paths with ease, and I found immense pleasure.

Then I tried Goethe. But that was too ambitious. With the help of the little German I had learnt, I did go through *Faust* I believe I found my entrance to the palace, not like one who has keys for all the doors, but as a casual visitor who is tolerated in some general guest-room, comfortable but not intimate. Properly speaking, I do not know my Goethe, and in the same way many other great luminaries are dusky to me.

This is as it should be. Man cannot reach the shrine if he does not make the pilgrimage. So, one must not hope to find anything true from my own language in translation.

In regard to music, I claim to be something of a musician myself. I have composed many songs which have defied the canons of orthodox propriety and good people are disgusted at the impudence of a man who is audacious only because he is untrained. But I persist, and God forgives me because I do not know what I do. Possibly that is the best way of doing things in the sphere of art. For I find that people blame, but also sing my songs, even if not always correctly.

Please do not think I am vain. I can judge myself objectively and can openly express admiration for my own work, because I am modest. I do not hesitate to say that my songs have found their place in the heart of my land, along with her flowers that are never exhausted, and that the folk of the future, in days of joy or sorrow or festival, will have to sing them. This too is the work of a revolutionist.

If I feel reluctant to speak about my own view of religion, it is because I have not come to my own religion through the portals of passive acceptance of a particular creed owing to some accident of birth. I was born to a family who were pioneers in the revival in our country of a religion based upon the utterance of Indian sages in the Upaniṣads. But owing to my idiosyncrasy of temperament, it was impossible for me to accept any religious teaching on the only ground that people in my surroundings believed it to be true. I could not persuade myself to imagine that I had religion simply because everybody whom I might trust believed in its value.

My religion is essentially a poet's religion. Its touch comes to me through the same unseen and trackless channels as does the inspiration of my music. My religious life has followed the same mysterious line of growth as has my poetical life. Somehow they are wedded to each other, and though their betrothal had a long period of ceremony, it was kept secret from me. I am not, I hope, boasting when I confess to my gift of poesy, an instrument of expression delicately responsive to the breath that comes from depth of feeling. From my infancy I had the keen sensitiveness which always kept my mind tingling with consciousness of the world around me, natural and human.

I had been blessed with that sense of wonder which gives a child his right of entry into the treasure-house of mystery which is in the heart of existence. I neglected my studies because they rudely summoned me away from the world around me, which was my friend and my companion, and when I was thirteen I freed myself from the clutch of an educational system that tried to keep me imprisoned within the stone walls of lessons.

I had a vague notion as to who or what it was that touched my heart's chords, like the infant which does not know its mother's name, or who or what she is. The feeling which I always had was a deep satisfaction of personality that flowed into my nature through living channels of communication from all sides.

It was a great thing for me that my consciousness was never dull about the facts of the surrounding world. That the cloud was the cloud, that a flower was a flower, was enough, because they directly spoke to me, because I could not be indifferent to them. I still remember the very moment, one afternoon, when coming back from school I alighted from the carriage and suddenly saw in the sky, behind the upper terrace of our house, an exuberance of deep, dark rain-clouds lavishing rich, cool shadows on the atmosphere. The marvel of it, the very generosity of its presence, gave me a joy which was freedom, the freedom we feel in the love of our dear friend.

There is an illustration I have made use of in another paper, in which I supposed that a stranger from some other planet has paid a visit to our earth and happens to hear the sound of a human voice on the gramophone. All that is obvious to him, and most seemingly active, is the revolving disk; he is unable to discover the personal truth that lies behind, and so might accept the impersonal scientific fact of the disk as final—the fact that could be touched and measured. He would wonder how it could be possible for a machine to speak to the soul. Then if in pursuing the mystery, he should suddenly come to the heart of the music through a meeting with the composer, he would at once understand the meaning of that music as a personal communication.

Mere information of facts, mere discovery of power, belongs to the outside and not to the inner soul of things. Gladness is the one criterion of truth as we know when we have touched Truth by the music it gives, by the joy of the greeting it sends forth to the truth in us. That is the true foundation of all religions, it is not in dogma. As I have said before, it is not as ether waves that we receive light; the morning does not wait for some scientist for its introduction to us. In the same way, we touch the infinite reality immediately within us only when we perceive the pure truth of love or goodness, not through the explanation of theologians, not through the erudite discussion of ethical doctrines.

I have already confessed that my religion is a poet's religion; all that I feel about it, is from vision and not from knowledge. I frankly say that I cannot satisfactorily answer questions about the problem of evil, or about what happens after death. And yet I am sure that there have come moments when my soul has touched the infinite and has become intensely conscious of it through the illumination of joy. It has been said in our Upaniṣads that our minds and our words come away baffled from the supreme Truth, but he who knows That, through the immediate joy of his own soul, is saved from all doubts and fears.

In the night we stumble over things and become acutely conscious of their individual separateness, but the day reveals the great unity which embraces them. And the man, whose inner vision is bathed in an illumination of his consciousness, at once

B

realises the spiritual unity reigning supreme over all differences of race and his mind no longer awkwardly stumbles over individual facts of separateness in the human world, accepting them as final; he realises that peace is in the inner harmony which dwells in truth, and not in any outer adjustments; and that beauty carries an eternal assurance of our spiritual relationship to reality, which waits for its perfection in the response of our love.

II

The renowned Vedic commentator, Sayanāchārya, says:

Yajñe hutaśishtasya odanasya sarvajagatkaranabhūta
brahmabhedena stutih kriyate.

"The food offering which is left over after the completion of ·sacrificial rites is praised because it is symbolical of Brahma, the original source of the universe."

According to this explanation, Brahma is boundless in his superfluity which inevitably finds its expression in the eternal world process. Here we have the doctrine of the genesis of creation, and therefore of the origin of art. Of all living creatures in the world, man has his vital and mental energy vastly in excess of his need, which urges him to work in various lines of creation for its own sake. Like Brahma himself, he takes joy in productions that are unnecessary to him, and therefore representing his extravagance and not his hand-to-mouth penury. The voice that is just enough can speak and cry to the extent needed for everyday use, but that which is abundant sings, and in it we find our joy. Art reveals man's wealth of life, which seeks its freedom in forms of perfection which are an end in themselves.

All that is inert and inanimate is limited to the bare fact of existence. Life is perpetually creative because it contains in itself that surplus which ever overflows the boundaries of the immediate time and space, restlessly pursuing its adventure of expression in the varied forms of self-realisation. Our living body has its vital organs that are important in maintaining its efficiency, but this body is not a mere convenient sac for the purpose of holding stomach, heart, lungs and brains; it is an image—its highest value is in the fact that it communicates its personality. It has colour, shape and movement, most of which belong to the superfluous, that are needed only for self-expression and not for self-preservation.

This living atmosphere of superfluity in man is dominated by his imagination, as the earth's atmosphere by the light. It helps us to integrate desultory facts in a vision of harmony and then to translate it into our activities for the very joy of its perfection, it invokes in us the Universal Man who is the seer and the doer of all times and countries. The immediate consciousness of reality in its purest form, unobscured by the shadow of self-interest, irrespective of moral or utilitarian recommendation, gives us joy as does the self-revealing personality of our own. What in common language we call beauty which is in harmony of lines, colours, sounds, or in grouping of words or thoughts, delights us only because we cannot help admitting a truth in it that is ultimate. "Love is enough," the poet has said; it carries its own explanation, the joy of which can only be expressed in a form of art which also has that finality. Love gives evidence to something which is outside us but which intensely exists and thus stimulates the sense of our own existence. It radiantly reveals the reality of its objects, though these may lack qualities that are valuable or brilliant.

The *I am* in me realises its own extension, its own infinity whenever it truly realises something else. Unfortunately, owing to our limitations and a thousand and one preoccupations, a great part of our world, though closely surrounding us, is far away from the lamp-post of our attention: it is dim, it passes by us, a caravan of shadows, like the landscape seen in the night from the window of an illuminated railway compartment: the passenger knows that the outside world exists, that it is important, but for the time being the railway carriage for him is far more significant. If among the innumerable objects in this world there be a few that come under the full illumination of our soul and thus assume reality for us, they constantly cry to our creative mind for a permanent representation. They belong to the same domain as the desire of ours which represents the longing for the permanence of our own self.

I do not mean to say that things to which we are bound by

the tie of self-interest have the inspiration of reality; on the contrary, these are eclipsed by the shadow of our own self. The servant is not more real to us than the beloved. The narrow emphasis of utility diverts our attention from the complete man to the merely useful man. The thick label of market-price obliterates the ultimate value of reality.

That fact that we exist has its truth in the fact that everything else does exist, and the "I am" in me crosses its finitude whenever it deeply realises itself in the "Thou art." This crossing of the limit produces joy, the joy that we have in beauty, in love, in greatness. Self-forgetting, and in a higher degree, self-sacrifice, is our acknowledgment of this our experience of the infinite. This is the philosophy which explains our joy in all arts, the arts that in their creations intensify the sense of the unity which is the unity of truth we carry within ourselves. The personality in me is a self-conscious principle of a living unity; it at once comprehends and yet transcends all the details of facts that are individually mine, my knowledge, feeling, wish and will, my memory, my hope, my love, my activities, and all my belongings. This personality which has the sense of the *One* in its nature, realises it in things, thoughts and facts made into units. The principle of unity which it contains is more or less perfectly satisfied in a beautiful face or a picture, a poem, a song, a character or a harmony of interrelated ideas or facts and then for it these things become intensely real, and therefore joyful. Its standard of reality, the reality that has its perfect revelation in a perfection of harmony, is hurt when there is a consciousness of discord— because discord is against the fundamental unity which is in its centre.

All other facts have come to us through the gradual course of our experience, and our knowledge of them is constantly under- going contradictory changes through the discovery of new data. We can never be sure that we have come to know the final character of anything that there is. But such a knowledge has come to us immediately with a conviction which needs no arguments to support it. It is this, that all my activities have their sources in this personality of mine which is indefinable and yet about the truth of which I am more certain than anything in this world. Though all the direct evidence that can be weighed and measured support the fact that only my fingers are producing marks on the paper, yet no sane man ever can doubt that it is not these mechanical movements that are the true origin of my writings but some entity that can never be known, unless known through sympathy. Thus we have come to realise in our own person the two aspects of activities, one of which is the aspect of law represented in the medium, and the other the aspect of will residing in the personality.

Limitation of the unlimited is personality: God is personal where he creates.

He accepts the limits of his own law and the play goes on. which is this world whose reality is in its relation to the Person. Things are distinct not in their essence but in their appearance; in other words, in their relation to one to whom they appear. This is art, the truth of which is not in substance or logic, but in expression. Abstract truth may belong to science and metaphysics, but the world of reality belongs to Art.

The world as an art is the play of the Supreme Person revelling in image making. Try to find out the ingredients of the image —they elude you, they never reveal to you the eternal secret of appearance. In your effort to capture life as expressed in living tissue, you will find carbon, nitrogen and many other things utterly unlike life, but never life itself. The appearance does not offer any commentary of itself through its material. You may call it *Māyā* and pretend to disbelieve it, but the great artist, the *Māyāvin,* is not hurt. For art is *Māyā*, it has no other explanation but that it seems to be what it is. It never tries to conceal its evasiveness, it mocks even its own definition and plays the game of hide-and-seek through its constant flight in changes.

And thus life, which is an incessant explosion of freedom, finds its metre in a continual falling back in death. Every day is a death, every moment even. If not, there would be amorphous desert of deathlessness eternally dumb and still. So life is *Māyā*, as moralists love to say, it *is* and *is not*. All that we find in it is the rhythm through which it shows itself. Are rocks and minerals any better? Has not science shown us the fact that the ultimate difference between one element and another is only that of rhythm? The fundamental distinction of gold from mercury lies merely in the difference of rhythm in their respective atomic constitution, like the distinction of the king from his subject which is not in their different constituents, but in the different metres of their situation and circumstance. There you find behind the scene the Artist, the Magician of rhythm, who imparts an appearance of substance to the unsubstantial.

What is rhythm? It is the movement generated and regulated by harmonious restriction. This is the creative force in the hand of the artist. So long as words remain in uncadenced prose form, they do not give any lasting feeling of reality. The moment they are taken and put into rhythm they vibrate into a radiance. It is the same with the rose. In the pulp of its petals you may find everything that went to make the rose, but the rose which is *Māyā*, an image, is lost; its finality which has the touch of the infinite is gone. The rose appears to me to be still, but because of its metre of composition it has a lyric of movement within that stillness, which is the same as the dynamic quality of a picture that has a perfect harmony. It produces a music in our consciousness by giving it a swing of motion synchronous with its own. Had the picture consisted of a disharmonious aggregate of colours and lines, it would be deadly still.

In perfect rhythm, the art-form becomes like the stars which in their seeming stillness are never still, like a motionless flame that is nothing but movement. A great picture is always speaking, but news from a newspaper, even of some tragic happening, is still-born. Some news may be a mere commonplace in the obscurity of a journal; but give it a proper rhythm and it will never cease to shine. That is art. It has the magic wand which gives undying reality to all things it touches, and relates them to the personal being in us. We stand before its productions and say: I know you as I know myself, you are real.

A Chinese friend of mine, while travelling with me through the streets of Peking, suddenly, with great excitement, called my attention to a donkey. Ordinarily a donkey does not have any special force of truth for us, except when it kicks us or when we need its reluctant service. But in such cases, the truth is not emphasised in the donkey but in some purpose of bodily pain exterior to it. The behaviour of my Chinese friend at once reminded me of the Chinese poems in which the delightful sense of reality is so spontaneously felt and so simply expressed.

This sensitiveness to the touch of things, such abundant delight in the recognition of them is obstructed when insistent purposes become innumerable and intricate in our society, when problems crowd in our path clamouring for attention, and life's movement is impeded with things and thoughts too difficult for a harmonious assimilation.

This has been growing evident every day in the modern age, which gives more time to the acquisition of life's equipment than to the enjoyment of it. In fact, life itself is made secondary to life's materials, even like a garden buried under the bricks gathered for the garden wall. Somehow the mania for bricks and mortar grows, the kingdom of rubbish dominates, the days of spring are made futile and the flowers never come.

Our modern mind, a hasty tourist, in its rush over the miscellaneous, ransacks cheap markets of curios which mostly are delusions. This happens because its natural sensibility for simple aspects of existence is dulled by constant preoccupations that divert it. The literature that it produces seems always to be poking her nose into out-of-the-way places for things and effects that are out of the common. She racks her resources in order to be striking. She elaborates inconstant changes in style, as in modern millinery; and the product suggests more the polish of steel than the bloom of life.

Fashions in literature that rapidly tire of themselves seldom come from the depth. They belong to the frothy rush of the surface, with its boisterous clamours for the recognition of the moment. Such literature, by its very strain, exhausts its inner development and quickly passes through outer changes like autumn leaves—produces with the help of paints and patches an up-to-dateness shaming its own appearance of the immediately preceding date. Its expressions are often grimaces, like the cactus of the desert which lacks modesty in its distortions and peace in its thorns, in whose attitude an aggressive discourtesy bristles up suggesting a forced pride of poverty. We often come across its analogy in some of the modern writings which are difficult to ignore because of their prickly surprises and pardoxical gesticulations. Wisdom is not rare in these works, but it is a wisdom that has lost confidence in its serene dignity, afraid of being ignored by crowds which are attracted by the extravagant and the unusual. It is sad to see wisdom struggling to seem clever, a prophet arrayed in caps and bells before an admiring multitude.

But in all great arts, literary or otherwise, man has expressed his feelings that are usual in a form that is unique and yet not abnormal. When Wordsworth described in his poem a life deserted by love, he invoked for his art the *usual* pathos expected by all normal minds in connection with such a subject. But the picture in which he incarnated the sentiment was unexpected and yet every sane reader acknowledges it with joy when the image is held before him of

> . . . a forsaken bird's nest filled with snow
> Mid its own bush of leafless eglantine.

On the other hand, I have read some modern writing in which the coming out of the stars in the evening is described as the sudden eruption of disease in the bloated body of darkness. The writer seems afraid to own the feeling of a cool purity in the star-sprinkled night which is *usual*, lest he should be found out as commonplace. From the point of view of realism the image may not be wholly inappropriate and may be considered as outrageously virile in its unshrinking incivility. But this is not art; this is a jerky shriek, something like the convulsive advertisement of the modern market that exploits mob psychology against its inattention. To be tempted to create an illusion of forcefulness through an over-emphasis of abnormality is a sign of anaesthesia. It is the waning vigour of imagination which employs desperate dexterity in the present-day art for producing shocks in order to poke out into a glare the sensation of the unaccustomed. When we find that the literature of any period is laborious in the pursuit of a spurious novelty in its manner and matter, we must know that it is the symptom of old age, of anaemic sensibility which seeks to stimulate its palsied taste with the pungency of indecency and the tingling touch of intemperance. It has been explained to me that these symptoms mostly are the outcome of a reaction against the last century literature which developed a mannerism too daintily saccharine, unmanly in the luxury of its toilet and over-delicacy of its expressions. It seemed to have reached an extreme limit of refinement which almost codified its conventions, making it easy for the timid talents to reach a comfortable level of literary respectability. This explanation may be true; but unfortunately reactions seldom have the repose of spontaneity, they often represent the obverse side of the mintage which they try to repudiate as false. A reaction against a particular mannerism is liable to produce its own mannerism in a militant fashion, using the toilet preparation of the war paint, deliberately manufactured style of primitive rudeness. Tired of the elaborately planned flower-beds, the gardener proceeds with grim determination to set up everywhere artificial rocks, avoiding natural inspiration of rhythm in deference to a fashion of tyranny which itself is a tyranny of fashion. The same herd instinct is followed in a cult of rebellion as it was in the cult of conformity and the defiance, which is a mere counteraction of obedience, also shows obedience in a defiant fashion. Fanaticism of virility produces a brawny athleticism meant for a circus and not the natural chivalry which is modest but invincible, claiming its sovereign seat of honour in all arts.

It has often been said by its advocates that this show of the rudely loud and cheaply lurid in art has its justification in the unbiased recognition of facts as such; and according to them realism must not be shunned even if it be ragged and evil-smelling. But when it does not concern science but concerns the arts we must draw a distinction between realism and reality. In its own wide perspective of normal environment, disease is a reality which has to be acknowledged in literature. But disease in a hospital is realism fit for the use of science. It is an abstraction which, if allowed to haunt literature, may assume a startling appearance because of its unreality. Such vagrant spectres do not have a proper modulation in a normal surrounding; and they offer a false proportion in their features because the proportion of their environment is tampered with. Such a curtailment of the essential is not art, but a trick which exploits mutilation in order to assert a false claim to reality. Unfortunately men are not rare who believe that what forcibly startles them allows them to see more than the facts which are balanced and restrained, which they have to woo and win. Very likely, owing to the lack of leisure, such persons are growing in number, and the dark cellars of sex-psychology and drug-stores of moral virulence are burgled to give them the stimulus which they wish to believe to be the stimulus of aesthetic reality.

I know a simple line sung by some primitive folk in our neighbourhood which I translate thus: "My heart is like a pebble-bed hiding a foolish stream." The psycho-analyst may classify it as an instance of repressed desire and thus at once degrade it to a mere specimen advertising a supposed fact, as it does a piece of coal suspected of having smuggled within its dark the flaming wine of the sun of a forgotten age. But it is literature; and what might have been the original stimulus that startled this thought into a song, the significant fact about it is that it has taken the shape of an image, a creation of a uniquely personal and yet universal character. The facts of the repression of a desire are numerously common; but this particular expression is singularly uncommon. The listener's mind is touched not because it is a psychological fact, but because it is an individual poem, representing a personal reality, belonging to all time and place in the human world.

But this is not all. This poem no doubt owed its form to the touch of the person who produced it; but at the same time with a gesture of utter detachment, it has transcended its material —the emotional mood of the author. It has gained its freedom from any biographical bondage by taking a rhythmic perfection which is precious in its own exclusive merit. There is a poem which confesses by its title its origin in a mood of dejection. Nobody can say that to a lucid mind the feeling of despondency has anything pleasantly memorable. Yet these verses are not allowed to be forgotten, because directly a poem is fashioned, it is eternally freed from its genesis, it minimises its history and emphasises its independence. The sorrow which was solely personal in an emperor, was liberated directly it took the form of verses in stone, it became a triumph of lament, an overflow of delight hiding the black boulder of its suffering source. The same thing is true of all creation. A new drop is a perfect integrity that has no filial memory of its parentage.

When I use the word creation, I mean that through it some imponderable abstractions have assumed a concrete unity in its

relation to us. Its substance can be analysed but not this unity
which is in its self-introduction. Literature as an art offers us the
mystery which is in its unity.

We read the poem:

> Never seek to tell thy love
>   Love that never told can be;
> For the gentle wind does move
>   Silently, invisibly.
>
> I told my love, I told my love,
>   I told all my heart;
> Trembling cold in ghastly fears
>   Ah, she did depart.
>
> Soon as she was gone from me
>   A traveller came by;
> Silently, invisibly,
>   He took her with a sigh.

It has its grammar, its vocabulary. When we divide them
part by part and try to torture out a confession from them the
poem which is *one*, departs like the gentle wind, silently, invisibly.
No one knows how it exceeds all its parts, transcends all its
laws, and communicates with the person. The significance which
is in unity is an eternal wonder.

As for the definite meaning of the poem, we may have our
doubts. If it were told in ordinary prose, we might feel impatient
and be roused to contradict it. We would certainly have asked
for an explanation as to who the traveller was and why he took
away love without any reasonable provocation. But in this
poem we need not ask for an explanation unless we are hopelessly addicted to meaning-collection which is like the collection
mania for dead butterflies. The poem as a creation, which is
something more than as an idea, inevitably conquers our attention; and any meaning which we feel in its words, is like the feeling
in a beautiful face of a smile that is inscrutable, elusive and
profoundly satisfactory.

The unity as a poem introduces itself in a rhythmic language
in a gesture of character. Rhythm is not merely in some measured
blending of words, but in a significant adjustment of ideas, in a
music of thought produced by a subtle principle of distribution

which is not primarily logical but evidential. The meaning which the word character contains is difficult to define. It is comprehended in a special grouping of aspects which gives it an irresistible impetus. The combination it represents may be uncouth, may be unfinished, discordant; yet it has a dynamic vigour in its totality which claims recognition, often against our wishes for the assent of our reason. An avalanche has a character, which even a heavier pile of snow has not; its character is in its massive movement, its incalculable possibilities.

It is for the artist to remind the world that with the truth of our expression we grow in truth. When the man-made world is less an expression of man's creative soul than a mechanical device for some purpose of power, then it hardens itself, acquiring proficiency at the cost of the subtle suggestiveness of living growth. In his creative activities man makes nature instinct with his own life and love. But with his utilitarian energies he fights Nature, banished her from his world, deforms and defiles her with the ugliness of his ambitions.

This world of man's own manufacture with its discordant shrieks and swagger, impresses on him the scheme of a universe which has no touch of the person and therefore no ultimate significance. All the great civilisations that have become extinct must have come to their end through such wrong expression of humanity; through parasitism on a gigantic scale bred by wealth, by man's clinging reliance on material resources; through a scoffing spirit of denial, of negation, robbing us of our means of sustenance in the path of truth.

It is for the artist to proclaim his faith in the everlasting YES—to say: "I believe that there is an ideal hovering over and permeating the earth, an ideal of that Paradise which is not the mere outcome of fancy, but the ultimate reality in which all things dwell and move."

I believe that the vision of Paradise is to be seen in the sunlight and the green of the earth, in the beauty of the human face and the wealth of human life, even in objects that are seemingly insignificant and unprepossessing. Everywhere in this earth the spirit of Paradise is awake and sending forth its voice. It reaches our inner ear without our knowing it. It tunes our harp of life which sends our aspiration in music beyond the finite, not only in prayers and hopes, but also in temples which are flames of fire in stone, in pictures which are dreams made everlasting, in the dance which is ecstatic meditation in the still centre of movement.

PRINCIPAL PUBLICATIONS

Gītāñjali. Macmillan & Co.
Sadhanā. Macmillan & Co.
Creative Unity. Macmillan & Co.
Personality. Macmillan & Co.
Greater India. Macmillan & Co.
The Relgion of Man. George Allen & Unwin.
The Child. George Allen & Unwin.
Letters to a Friend. George Allen & Unwin.
The Golden Boat. George Allen & Unwin.

HINDU PHILOSOPHY IN INDIA

by SWÂMI ABHEDÂNANDA

Born October 2, 1866; Educated Oriental Seminary, Calcutta

BIOGRAPHICAL

I was born in Calcutta, October 2, 1866. My father, late Rasick Lal Chandra, was a student of philosophy and teacher of English in the Oriental Seminary in Calcutta, for twenty-five years from 1838 to 1863. I was educated first in a Sanskrit School, then in a Bengali Vernacular School and afterwards in the Oriental Seminary, from which I successfully passed the Entrance Examination at the age of eighteen.

From my childhood I wanted to know the cause of everything and used to ask questions about the "Why" and "How" of all events. When for the first time I read in Wilson's *History of India*, that Śaṁkarācārya was a great philosopher, I had a thrilling sensation, and I wanted to become a philosopher and to study his philosophy. At that time, I was a student in the drawing class of the Seminary and was learning to paint from nature. Suddenly, a thought came to my mind that I did not want to be a painter but I would be a philosopher; and so I gave up the study of the art of drawing and painting.

When I was in the preparatory class I studied Sanskrit, which was my second language. At home, I studied "Mugdhabodha," the Sanskrit Grammar, throughly, and acquired such a command of the Sanskrit language that I could compose verses in it.

At that time, I found a copy of the *Bhagavat Gītā* in my father's private library and began to study it. When my father saw me reading that book, he took it away from me, saying that the *Bhagavat Gītā* was not for boys: "It would make you insane." But his remarks could not stop me from reading it.

In my youth, I was fond of listening to discourses on Hindu philosophy and used to hear lectures on various phases of different religions. I attended the sermons on Christ and Christianity by Christian missionaries like the Rev. Dr. Macdonald, the Rev. Kali Charan Banerjee and others, who spoke regularly, every Sunday, at the Beadon Square on Chitpur Road in Calcutta. There, I also heard many anti-Christian lectures which were based upon the higher criticism of the Bible and free thought. I had the privilege of hearing Keshab Chandra Sen and Protap Chandra Mazoomdar, the celebrated leaders of the Brahmo Samaj.

In 1883 the noted Hindu philosopher, Pundit Sasadhar Tarkachudamani, delivered a series of public lectures on the six Systems of Hindu philosophy at the Albert Hall, under the presidentship of late Bankim Chandra Chatterjee, the great scholar and writer. I attended the lectures on *Vaiseshika* and *Sāmkhya* philosophies in which the Punditji explained the atomic theory of Kaṇāda, and the evolution theory of Kapila, and compared them with similar theories of the ancient Greek philosophers as well as with the modern theory of Evolution. Those discourses aroused my interest in the study of Western philosophies of ancient and modern Europe. Furthermore, when I heard Panditji's lectures on "Yoga" philosophy of Patañjali, I became interested in Hindu Psychology as well as in the practical methods of the Yoga system.

I studied Patañjali's system under the direction of the great philosopher, late Kalibara Vedantavagish, who at that time was translating the Yoga Sutras and was making an elaborate commentary on them in Bengali. After completing the study of the Yoga Sutras of Patañjali, I turned to analyse my own mind, to gain self-control and to enter into *Nirvikalpa Samadhi* through the practice of Hatha Yoga and Raja Yoga.

Then, I studied *Śiva Saṁhitā*, a treatise on the practical methods of Rāja Yoga. But I was told not to practise any of those methods described in the Yoga Sastras without being instructed by a competent Yogi preceptor (Guru). Then my great anxiety was to find a suitable teacher or guru. My class-fellow, Jajneswar Bhattacharya, directed me to go to the great Rāmakrishna Paramahamsa who lived at Dakshineswar, a suburban town about four miles north of Calcutta.

One Sunday morning, I reached the Temple Garden at Dakshineswar, where I met the great Yogi, Rāmakrishna Paramahamsa, and asked him whether he could teach me the practical methods of "Yoga Philosophy." He replied,"Yes, " and after reading of my past life, he said, "You were a great Yogi in your past incarnation. Come, my boy! I will teach you how to practise Yoga." Then, he initiated me and gave me instructions in concentration and meditation. He touched my chest and aroused my "Kundalini," the "Serpent Power" at the base of my spinal column, and I went into Sāmadhi, the state of superconsciousness. In him I found the embodiment of the Absolute Truth of the highest philosophy, as well as of the Universal Religion which underlies all sectarian religions of the world, and became his humble disciple. I had the good fortune to be with him and to serve for two years. There, I met his other disciples, among whom Swami Vivekānanda was the most brilliant. I was attracted to him and became his close companion. Frequently, I used to discuss with him various abstruse points of Epistemology, Ontology and Metaphysics of India and of Europe.

At that time, I began to devote myself to self-education and studied Ganot's *Physics*, Herchel's *Astronomy*, John Stuart Mill's *Logic*, and *Three Essays on Religion*, Herbert Spencer's *First Principles* and *Psychology*, Hamilton's *Philosophy*, Lewes' *History of Philosophy* and attended the courses of lectures at the "Science Association," which had been established by Dr. Mohendra Lall

Sircar, the famous Homoeopath. With Swami Vivekānanda I studied the Buddhistic Philosophy as well as the principles of the *Advaita* or the non-dualistic philosophy of Vedānta.

From Sri Rāmakrishna I learnt that "Dwaita," or Dualistic philosophy, leads to the Visista-Advaita philosophy of Rāmānuja in search after the Ultimate Truth of the universe, which is one and the absolute (Brahman); and that the search after Truth ends in the realisation of the oneness of the *Jīva* (individual soul), Jagat (World), and Isvara (God) in Brahman as taught in the Advaita philosophy of Vedānta; and that they are the different steps in the path of the realisation of the absolute Truth or Brahman.

In 1886, after the departue of Sri Rāmakrishna, I renounced the world and became a *Saññyāsin* monk along with Swāmi Vivekānanda and other co-disciples (*Gurubhais*). As this was our second birth, we gave up our former names. From that time I have been known by my present name. I continued my self-education by studying Panini's grammar, six systems of Hindu philosophy, the Upaniṣads and Vedānta Sutras, with the commentaries of Śamkara, Rāmānuja, Sribhāṣya, Nimbārka, Vallabhāchārya and others.

I travelled bare-footed from place to place, depending entirely on alms cooked or uncooked, whatever chance would bring to me. I always held in my mind the thought that the phenomenal world was transitory and unreal; that I was a spectator like the unchangeable Ātman of Vedānta which always remains a witness (Sākshi) of the games which the people were playing in the world. In this manner I endured all sorts of privation and hardship, practised austerities of all kinds, walked up to the sources of the Jamuna and the Ganges, where I stayed for three months in the caves of the Himalayas at the altitude of nearly 14,000 feet above the sea level, spending most of my time in contemplation of the Absolute, I realised that the phenomenal world was like a dream. Thus wandering for ten years all over India, and visiting sacred places like Kedarnath and Badarinarayana, Dwāraka and Rāmeswaram, Jagannāth and Puri, etc., I met great sages and saints like "Trailainga Swāmi," "Swāmi Bhāskarānandā" at Benares, Pavahari Baba at Gazipur, many Vaishnava saints at Brindāban and great Vedānta philosophers at Rishikesh, where I studied monistic Vedānta Philosophy under the great scholar "Dhanaraj Giri," who was the eminent Advaita Vedāntist of those days.

In 1896 Swāmi Vivekānanda, who after his successful lectures in U.S.A. on Vedānta and Raja Yoga, given in the three years following his appearance at the Parliament of Religions in Chicago in 1893, had come over to London and had delivered several lectures on Jñāna Yoga and Rāja Yoga in that great city, invited me to assist him in his work there.

I accepted his invitation and sailed from Calcutta to London in

August, 1896. My first lecture was before the Christo-Theosophical Society of London, on the Advaita philosophy of "Pañcadaśi." Swāmi Vivekānanda entrusted me with the charge of conducting his classes on Vedānta and Rāja Yoga there, and left for India in 1897. I continued my class lectures on Jñāna Yoga, Rāja Yoga, and delivered public lectures in churches and before religious and philosophical societies in London and its suburbs for one year. When I was in London Swāmi Vivekānanda took me to meet Professor Max Muller and Professor Paul Deussen of Kiel University, who had translated sixty Upaniṣads into the German language and who was the author of the *Philosophy of the Upaniṣads*. I had conversations with them in Sanskrit. But Professor Max Muller could neither speak in Sanskrit nor understand Sanskrit words when spoken, because, as he said, his ears and tongue were not trained in the sounds of Sanskrit utterances. So, I exchanged my views with him in English. He was deeply interested in the life and teachings of Rāmakrishna and said, "Rāmakrishna was an original thinker, for he was never brought up within the precincts of any university and, therefore, his teachings were new and original." This remark created a deep impression upon my mind. Later on, he published the *Life and Sayings of Rāmakrishna*.

In 1897, at the request of Swāmi Vivekānanda, I crossed the Atlantic and landed at New York, to take charge of the Vedānta Society which he had started in New York City. There, in six months I delivered ninety public lectures before large audiences on Vedānta Philosophy and Yoga Philosophy of Patañjali; organised the Society, and held regular classes on *Bhagavat Gītā, Katha Upaniṣad*, and various other Upaniṣads on the *Secret of Death, Self-Knowledge*,[1] *Sāṅkhya* and *Yoga Philosophy*, for nearly twenty years under the auspices of the Vedānta Society of which I was the president.

In 1898, Professor William James held a discussion with me in his house on the problem of the "Unity of the Ultimate Reality." This discussion lasted for nearly four hours, in which Professor Royce, Profesor Lanman, Professor Shaler and Dr. James, the Chairman of Cambridge philosophical conferences, took my side and supported my arguments in favour of "Unity."

I travelled extensively all through the United States, Canada, Alaska and Mexico, and delivered addresses on various phases of the Vedānta Philosophy in all the principal cities of those countries. I delivered a series of public lectures on "Krishna and His Teachings";

---

[1] "Self-Knowledge" includes the following subjects: Spirit and Matter Knowledge of the Self; Prana and the Self; Search after the Self; Realisation of the Self; Immortality of the Self.

These were afterwards published by the Vedānta Society of New York, U.S.A.

"Zoroaster and His Teachings"; "Taoism"; "Laotze and His Teachings"; "Lamaism in Tibet"; "Shintoism in Japan"; "Buddha and His Teachings"; "Christ and His Teachings"; "Mahomet and His Teachings"; "Rāmakrishna and His Teachings"; under the title of the "Great Saviours of the World."

In 1921, I sailed from San Francisco and crossed the Pacific Ocean, breaking my voyage at Honolulu, where I was a delegate from India at the Pan-Pacific Educational Conference. Then, I came to Japan and studied Japanese culture, philosophy and religion, stopping at Shanghai, Hongkong, Canton, Manila and Singapore, where I delivered the message of Vedānta Philosophy in popular lectures. From Singapore I was invited to Kuala-Lumpur in Malaya States where I gave a series of lectures on "Confucianism", "Buddhism", and "Taoism" before Chinese and Hindu audiences. From there I was invited to Rangoon, whence, after delivering several public lectures on the "Message of Buddha" and on "Religion of the Hindus", I returned to Calcutta.

In 1922 I went to Tibet from Kashmere, crossing the Himalayas on foot, to study the manners, customs and Buddhistic philosophy and Lamaism which prevail among the Tibetan Lamas. I went along Yarkand Road, the highway to Europe, and stopped at "Leh," the capital of Ladak, in western Tibet. My destination was "Hemis Monastery," about twenty-five miles north of the City of "Leh."

In 1923, after returning from Tibet, I established "The Rāmakrishna Vedānta Society" in Calcutta of which I am the President. In 1924 I opened a branch of this Society at Darjeeling under the name of "Rāmakrishna Vedānta Ashram."

This short sketch of my life will give the reader some idea of the different influences which have moulded my convictions.

HINDU PHILOSOPHY IN INDIA

WHAT IS VEDĀNTA?

THE popular belief is that "Vedānta philosophy" means the "Philosophy of the Upaniṣads" confined exclusively to the Vedas or the sacred Scriptures of the Hindus in India. But the term "Veda" in the present case is used to signify, not any particular book, but "Knowledge," being derived from the Sanskrit root verb "vid" to know; while the English word "end" is derived from Sanskrit "Anta." Vedānta, therefore, implies literally "End of knowledge"; and the philosophy is called "Vedānta" because it explains what that "End" is, and how it can be attained. All relative knowledge ends in the realisation of the unity of the individual soul with the ultimate truth of the universe, which is the infinite ocean of absolute knowledge, the universal spirit of Brahman. As rivers running from various sources ultimately end in the ocean, so the rivers of relative knowledge starting from various view-points and flowing through different stages of the phenomena, ultimately end in the infinite ocean of absolute Existence, and infinite knowledge—*Satyam, Jnānam, Anantam Brahma*—the ultimate Reality of the universe. It is the absolute Substance which is beyond subject and object, which is the infinite Source of knowledge, of consciousness and blissfulness, and which is not many, but one. It is the same as the "Good" of Plato, the "Substantia" of Spinoza, the "Ding-an-sich" of the transcendental thing-in-itself of Kant, the "Over-soul" of Emerson, and the "Unknowable" of Herbert Spencer. It is the Noumenon which pervades the phenomena of the universe.

The system of Vedānta is more critical than the Kantian system, because it shows the phenomenal nature of the Kantian ego, of his forms of intuition and of his categories of thought. It is also more sublime than the philosophy of Kant, because it recognises and proves the identity of the objective reality of the universe, and proves the identity of the objective reality of the universe with the subjective reality of the ego. Kant did not realise that the Thing-in-itself (Ding-an-sich) of the objective world and the "Ding-an-sich" of the subjective world are one. In no other philosophy has this oneness been so clearly explained and so strongly emphasised as it is in Vedānta. "This constituted the unique character of Vedānta, unique compared with every other philosophy of the world which has not been influenced by it, directly or indirectly."[1] In Europe there have been many idealistic philosophies which have denied the existence of the external world, but not one of them ventured to deny the apparent reality of the ego, of the senses, of the mind and of their inherent forms. In this respect, Vedānta holds a unique position among the philosophies of the world. The self or ātman, the true nature of the ego or *Jivātma* is one with the essence of Divinity (Brahman) which is absolutely pure, perfect, immortal, unchangeable and one. No philosopher, not even Plato, Spinoza, Kant, Hegel or Schopenhauer has reached that height of philosophic thought.[2]

Starting from the ultimate conclusions of ancient and modern science, Vedānta says that the absolute Truth is one and not many, yet there can be varieties of expressions and manifold manifestations of the one Truth. Furthermore, it maintains that the aim of the higher philosophy is not merely to ascertain the established conjunctions of events which constitute the order of the universe, or to record the phenomena which it exhibits to our observation and refer them to the general laws, but also to lead the human mind from the realm of the knowable to that which is beyond knowable. We are now living in the realm of the knowable, but that which teaches simply the laws which govern the knowable phenomena is not the highest kind of philosophy. We must know the laws of the knowable, yet at the same time we should aspire to go beyond the knowable and plunge into

---

[1] *The Six Systems of Indian Philosophy*, p. 223, by Professor Max Müller.

[2] Professor Max Müller declares: "None of our philosophers, not excepting Heraclitus, Plato, Kant or Hegel, has ventured to erect such a spire, never frightened by storms or lightnings. Stone follows on stone in regular succession after once the first step has been made, after once it has been clearly seen that in the beginning there can have been but One, as there will be but One in the end, whether we call it Ātman or Brahman." *The Six Systems of Philosophy*, p. 239

the realm of the Infinite. If any philosophy can help us in this attempt, then it must be higher than the ordinary system which keeps us within the limits of time, space and causalty of these knowable phenomena. The monistic Vedānta philosophy guides us above all knowable objects of perception and directs our soul toward the Eternal absolute Being, where we find the solution of all problems and the answer to all questions. Its attempt is to trace the origin of all phenomena objective and subjective, physical and mental, not by any unscientific method, but by the most rigorous processes of logic and reason starting from the ultimate generalisations of the various branches of science.

TRUE PHILOSOPHY

True philosophy must construct a theory which will be the simplest in its nature and yet at the same time will explain all the vital problems which the science of the phenomenal can never explain and which will harmonise with the highest form of the universal religion without destroying the loftiest aspirations of the human soul. True philosophy in the widest sense must perform three great functions. First, it must co-ordinate the ultimate results arrived at by special branches of knowledge which we call sciences, and taking up those conclusions, it must form the widest generalisations possible. When it does this, it is called Phenomenology. Herbert Spencer's philosophy performs this function, but it leaves out the vital problems which perplex the minds of the greatest philosophers as unsolvable mysteries. Secondly, true philosophy must investigate the realm of knowledge and trace its source. A philosophy which does this is called Epistemology. The philosophy of Kant, Hegel, Fichte and others has sought to perform this function. George Croom Robertson says: "Epistemology is just philosophy, because it deals with things, deals with beings; it deals with things going beyond bare experience, but it treats them in relation to the fact of knowing. Thus an Epistemologist cannot help being an Ontologist because this theory of knowledge must treat about things also as being. He must also be a metaphysician, because he is concerned with the whole range of things beyond the physical; he must be a philosopher in being other and more than a man of science, or concerned with things in a way to which science is not."[1]

The third function which true philosophy performs is that of leading our minds into the realm of the Absolute or the Unknown, and then it solves the problems of life and death. It explains the origin of the universe and of individual existence and the purpose of evolution. On the plane of relativity, the perfect solution of these vital problems can never be found. Furthermore, when this phase of true philosophy directs our minds towards the Infinite, it helps us in becoming free from all limitations of ignorance and selfishness. These limitations are the greatest bondages that we are now suffering from, and by performing this function, true philosophy lays the foundation of the highest form of monistic religion. No philosophy in the world performs these three functions so satisfactorily as the Vedānta philosophy. Hence we may say that Vedānta is the most complete system.

Philosophy and religion must always be in perfect harmony. Ernest Haeckel, in his *Riddle of the Universe*, tried to give a foundation to monistic religion, but his monism is one-sided, because he says that the ultimate substance of the universe is unintelligent. His insentient substance may be compared with Kapila's *Prakriti* which is eternal and unintelligent. According to Vedānta, however, the final reality of the universe is Brahman which is Sat-Chit-Ānanda, or absolute Existence-Intelligence-Bliss. It teaches that that which is the substance of our souls must possess intelligence, consciousness and blissfulness. Thus, Vedānta lays the true foundation of a universal religion which is monistic or non-dualistic.

RELIGION OF VEDĀNTA

The monistic religion of Vedānta does not admit the Sānkhyan theory of the plurality of individual souls, which are eternal and infinite by nature, but on the contrary, by following the strict rules of Logic, it establishes that the Infinite must be one and not many. From one many have come into existence, and the individual souls are but so many images or reflections of the Absolute Brahman. From this Absolute Brahman the phenomenal universe rises and in the end returns into the Brahman.

[1] *Elements of General Philosophy.*

The religion of Vedānta admits that Brahman has two aspects, the one without any attribute "Nirguṇa" and the other is with attributions "Saguṇa," who is called Īśvara or the Ruler of the universe. He is the personal God, who is the first-born Lord of the universe, who starts the evolution of *Prakriti* which forms His Body. The God of Vedānta is both the efficient and the material cause of all phenomena. He loves all living creatures who live and move and have their being in Him, and can be loved and be worshipped in return. In Vedānta the *Prakriti* of the Sānkhya philosophy is called *Māyā*, which is the divine energy of the Absolute Brahman. Māyā does not mean illusion, as some scholars think, but it is that power which produces time, space and causation, as also the phenomenal appearances which exist on the relative plane. Thus we see that the system of Vedānta is both philosophy and religion. Of the tree of knowledge, true philosophy is the flower and "religion" is the fruit, so they must go together. Religion is nothing but the practical side of philosophy and philosophy is the theoretical side of Religion.

In India, a true philosopher is not a mere speculator but a spiritual man. He does not believe in certain theories which cannot be carried into practice in everyday life; what he believes he lives up to; and, therefore, practical philosophy still exists among the Hindus in India. The followers of Vedānta live spiritual lives and strive to attain God-consciousness. In India, if anyone writes voluminous speculative philosophy and lives a worldly life, he is not considered a true philosopher.

The philosophy and religion of Vedānta embrace all the sciences, philosophies and religions of the world by accepting their ultimate conclusions, and classifying them according to their order of merit. Consequently, the universality of Vedānta is unique and unparalleled. The religion of Vedānta teaches: "That which exists is one, men call it by various names"—Rig Veda. No other philosophy or religion is based upon this fundamental truth of the unity of existence under a variety of names and forms than Vedānta, and therefore it offers, as can no other, an adequate foundation of all the different phases of dualistic, qualified-non-dualistic and monistic systems of religious thought. Thus it establishes a "Universal Religion" which embraces all the special religions of the world. It has many phases.

The dualistic phase of Vedānta includes the fundamental principles of all the dualistic or monotheistic systems, such as Zoroastrianism, Judaism, Christianity, Islam and all other systems that advocate the worship of the personal God under any name or form, or devotion to any divine ideal.

The qualified non-dualistic phase embraces all the systems which teach the immanency and transcendency of God. It includes all such ideas as "God dwells in us as well as in the universe"; "The Kingdom of Heaven is within you"; "We live and move and have our being in God"; "He is the soul of our souls, and the Life of our lives"; "We are parts of one stupendous Whole"; "We are the sons of God, the children of Immortal Bliss", etc.

The monistic phase of Vedānta is the most sublime of all. Very few thinkers can appreciate the grandeur of spiritual oneness. Yet, herein lies the solution of the deepest problems of science, philosophy and metaphysics and the final goal of all religions. It alone explains how it is possible for one to say, "I and my Father are one"; "I am He"; "That thou art"; "*Analhaq*", as a Mahommedan Sufi says.

The system of Vedānta harmonises with the religious ideals of the human mind and shows the various paths by which a man may attain to God-consciousness and emancipation from the bondages of ignorance, selfishness and all other imperfections, and eventually becomes as perfect as the Father in Heaven is perfect. Its notable feature is that it does not prescribe to all one special path by which to reach the ultimate goal of all religions. On the contrary, it recognises the varying tendencies of different minds, and guides each along the way best suited to it. It classifies human tendencies into four great divisions which together with their subdivisions cover almost all classes of people; and then it sets forth the methods which may be helpful to everyone. Each of these methods is called in Sanskrit "Yoga."

First is "Karma Yoga"—the path of work. It is for the active man; for those who like to work and are always ready to do something for the help of others. In short, it is for the busy, everyday working man or woman. Karma Yoga reveals the "Secret of Work" and opens the way to complete Self-Mastery.

The next method is "Bhakti Yoga." It is for such as are of

devotional and emotional nature. It teaches how ordinary emotions can bring forth spiritual unfoldment of the highest kind and lead to the realisation of the ultimate ideal of all religions. In a word, it is the path of devotion and love.

The third is "Rāja Yoga"—the path of concentration and meditation. The field of Rāja Yoga is very vast. It covers the whole psychic plane and describes the processes by which the psychic powers are developed, such as thought-reading, clair-voyance, clairaudience, the evolving of finer perceptions, the communication with departed spirits, the going out of the body, the curing of diseases through mental power and the performing of all such acts as are ordinarily called miracles. All psychic powers which were displayed by Jesus of Nazareth and his followers, and which have been manifested by the Yogis of India from time immemorial, are described rationally in Rāja Yoga. Furthermore, the marvellous powers achieved by the practice of *Prānāyāma*, the control of breath, and by the awaken-ing of the "Serpent power," or "Kundalini," are scientifically explained in this system of Rāja Yoga. The principal aim of Rāja Yoga is to lead the seeker after Truth through the path of concentration and meditation to the highest state of superconsciousness, where individual soul communes with the universal Spirit and realises the unity of both on the spiritual plane.

Jñāna Yoga is the fourth method. It is the path of right know-ledge and discrimination. This is for those who are intellectual, discriminative and of a philosophical nature. He who travels through this "Path of wisdom" burns the vast forest of the trees of phenomenal names and forms (Nāma Rūpa) by starting in it the fire of right knowledge. All these names and forms are produced by Māyā, the inscrutable power of Brahman. It is inseparable from Brahman as the power of burning is inseparable from fire. A Jñāna Yogi, in his search after the Absolute Truth, should reject all names and forms by saying "Not this," "Not this" (*Neti, Neti*), until he realises the one nameless, formless and absolute Being of the universe, where the subject and the object, the knower, knowledge and its object losing their relativity merge into the ocean of the absolute Brahman. Thus, we see how universal is the scope of Vedānta.

ETHICS OF VEDĀNTA

Standing on the rock of the spiritual oneness of the universe, Vedānta explains the basis of Ethics. If we injure, hate or cheat others, we injure, hate or cheat ourselves first. For this spiritual oneness we should love our neighbours as ourselves. Because love means the expression of oneness. When we begin to love others as we love our own self, we are truly ethical. Then we do not think that we have fulfilled the highest end and aim of life by eating, drinking and begetting children like lower animals, but that the fulfilment of the purpose of life consists in loving others disinterestedly without seeking any return of love as we love our own self. Animal nature, which is extremely selfish, must be conquered by moral nature through unselfish love for the real Self of others. Moral perfection consists in the destruction of selfishness. Having attained perfect freedom from the limitations of the animal self, the individual soul must strive to gain spiritual perfection which is the ultimate goal of evolution.

Spiritual perfection is the manifestation of the true nature of Spirit or Ātman which is immortal, free, divine and one with the Universal Spirit or God. Evolution attains to the highest fulfilment of its purpose when the Spirit manifests itself in its pristine purity and full glory. Each individual soul according to Vedānta is bound to become perfect in the end. As this cannot be gained in one life we shall have to admit the truth of the theory of Reincarnation.

Reincarnation explains the gradual evolution of the soul from the minutest *amoeba* to the highest man, through many lives and various forms until perfection is reached. The theory of Reincarnation is a logical necessity for the completion of the theory of evolution. They supplement each other. The Vedāntic theory of Reincarnation rejects the one-birth theory of Christianity, Islam and other religions. It is not the same as the theory of Metempsychosis or Transmigration of Souls, which was accepted by the Greek philosophers like Pythagoras, Plato and their followers. In the Platonic theory the idea of progress, growth or gradual evolution of the soul from lower to higher stages of existence, is entirely excluded, and the law of *Karma* is ignored. The theory of Reincarnation on the contrary admits the gradual evolution of each soul which is potentially divine, and which rises higher and higher in the process of the unfoldment of the latent powers, passing through various births and rebirths, always reaping the results of its own actions, being governed by the *Law* of *Karma*.

The Law of Karma includes the laws of causation, of action and reaction, of compensation and of retribution. Through this Law of Karma, Vedānta explains rationally the inequalities and diversities of nature which the theory of heredity has failed to explain. The doctrine of Karma denies the dogma that God punishes the wicked with eternal damnation and rewards the virtuous with celestial felicity. This is a dogma which makes God partial and unjust. In the doctrine of Karma there is no room for a Satan, the creator of Evil.

According to Vedānta all evil proceeds from ignorance, which is the mother of all sins and wickedness. God never punishes the wicked, nor rewards the virtuous, but the wicked punish themselves and the virtuous reward themselves by their own thoughts and deeds. The law of Karma, eternal as it is, pre-destines nothing and no one; but on the contrary making every soul a free agent for action, shows the way out of the world of misery through unselfish thoughts and good deeds.

We create our own destiny, mould our future, determine our character by our own thoughts and deeds. We cannot blame God or Satan for our own misery and sufferings for which we ourselves are responsible; because what we deserve we have got now, and what we shall make, we shall receive in future. Our present was determined by our past and our future will be determined by our present. This is the eternal Law.

PRINCIPAL PUBLICATIONS BY SWĀMI ABHEDĀNANDA

Reincarnation (1900).
Spiritual Unfoldment (1902).
Philosophy of Work (1903).
How to be a Yogi (1903).
Divine Heritage of Man (1903).
Self-Knowledge (1905).
The Gospel of Rāmakrishna (1905).
India and Her People (1905-6).
Nine Lectures (Parts 1 and 2) (1909).
The Sayings of Rāmakrishna (1910).
Great Saviours of the World (1912).
Human Affection and Divine Love (1912).

Published by the Vedānta Society of New York, U.S.A.

Lectures and Addresses in India (1906).
Travels in Kashmere and Tibet (Bengali, 1922).

THE PRINCIPLES OF ACTIVISM

by HARIDAS BHATTACHARYYA

Born November 7, 1891; Retired Head of Department of Philosophy
and Provost, Jagannath Hall, Dacca University

THE PRINCIPLES OF ACTIVISM

It is a privilege to be born in a cultured society and it is a greater privilege still to have a learned father. I was fortunate in being born, with the double equipment of academic environment and ancestral learning, in a scholarly family of Vaidika Brāhmaṇas in the village of Bhātpārā (Skt. Bhaṭṭapallī, the village of learned men) in the district of 24 Perganas in Bengal on 7th November, 1891. For over a century Bhātpārā had been the home of Sanskrit learning and the citadel of Hindu orthodoxy near Calcutta, and students from far and near had flocked to its many *tols* (Sanskrit schools) in search of higher knowledge in Philosophy in general and Nyāya philosophy (Logic) and Legal literature (Smṛti) in particular, while local youths filled to capacity its many classes in Grammar (Vyākaraṇa) and Literature (Kāvya). My father, the late Paṇḍita Rāmaprasanna Śrutiratna Bhaṭṭā-chāryya, though a great Sanskrit scholar himself, widely read, however, the signs of the times and sent all his wards to the village English school, thus initiating a tradition of western learning for the children of the family. I was very soon removed, however, to Calcutta where from one of the oldest schools of Bengal, the Oriental Seminary, I passed the Entrance (Matricula-tion) Examination of the Calcutta University in 1908. I then joined the Intermediate class in Arts at the Scottish Churches College, Calcutta, which had just come into being by the amalgamation of the Duff College and the General Assembly's Institution (which was one of the oldest Colleges in Bengal), and here I remained all through my University career, passing successively the Intermediate Examination in Arts (1910), the B.A. Honours Examination in Philosophy (1912) and the M.A. Examination in Philosophy (1914). I can look back with some satisfaction at my academic career at the Calcutta University, and as my father had died while I was still at school I had need of all the scholarships that I won at different examinations to tide over very difficult days for some years. The greatest single influence on my life has been the memory of a devout and learned father who had an inimitable gift of lucid and interesting exposition and also of establishing intimate contact with children.

To my teachers at the missionary college I owe a deep debt of gratitude. My love and knowledge of the Bible I got from two ordained ministers of the Scottish Church—Rev. A. B. Bruce and Rev. A. Tomory. Rev. W. S. Urquhart, my teacher in Philosophy, taught me the habit of careful preparation for class work. But the greatest academic influence on me came from the saintly Professor Henry Stephen who taught three generations of young men in Bengal successively in the Duff College, the Scottish Churches College and the Calcutta University. His learning was fabulous as he was equally at home in Mathematics, Biology, Philosophy and English and he knew at least four living and three dead languages. But greater than his learning and power of clarifying abstruse subjects were the humility and kindly benevolence of the saintly bachelor whose faith in Hegelian idealism permeated his life as a whole and whose character touched the lives of his students and colleagues to finer issues. To him I owe not only my love of Philosophy and broad based culture but also whatever sympathetic understanding of other people's viewpoints and capacity of speech I may have developed in the course of my teaching career and extensive tours throughout the length and breadth of India. My love of research was quickened by association with Dr. (later Sir) Brajendranath Seal, then George V Professor of Mental and Moral Philosophy at Calcutta University and later Vice-Chancellor of Mysore University, who taught me also the habit of helping aspiring juniors in their effort at self-expression through original writings.

A short spell of service at my own college (1915-1917) as Professor of Logic and Philosophy was followed by a slightly longer tenure of teaching at the Calcutta University (1917-1921) as Lecturer in Philosophy and Experimental Psychology. Then I was drafted into the service of the newly started University at Dacca (1921) as Reader in Philosophy and was in charge of the Psychological Laboratory which I founded there. From this position I rose successively to be the Head of the Department of Philosophy, the Dean of the Faculty of Arts and the Provost of the Jagannath Hall in the same University. I retired from University service on 30th June 1947, and immediately took up the work of

General Editor of *The Cultural Heritage of India* (2nd edition), an encyclopaedic work on Indian culture which is to be published in seven volumes by the Ramakrishna Mission Institute of Culture, Calcutta.

My migration to Dacca which is predominantly Muslim in composition and outlook completed the trinity of my cultural association with Hinduism through birth, Christianity through education, and Islam through service. Western education, training in Philosophy, intimate association with people of diverse faiths and the rapid change in social outlook among the Hindus in recent years have naturally affected me intellectually and inevitably raised problems in my personal life and modified my social practices to some extent. I cannot claim to have completely outgrown orthodox habits or the deep-seated convictions and traditional customs of my childhood days—in fact, liberal education has not bred in me any disrespect for my ancestral beliefs or torn me between conflicting loyalties to any appreciable extent. My increasing knowledge of other creeds and customs has made me tolerant towards others from a conviction that truth is not in the sole possession of any religious community and that temperaments have much to do with attitudes in life when not absolutely dominated by a conscious desire to be socially accommodating. This has enabled me to cultivate a habit of intellectual detachment in all matters where there might be scope for adverse emotional reaction and of not thrusting my way of life and thought upon those over whom I have any kind of supervising authority.

The Bachelor's degree in Law that I took at Calcutta from the University Law College in 1917 helped me to appreciate intellectual analysis and to understand the basis of ordered social existence and fundamental rights and obligations incidental to political and civic life. The specialised courses in Philosophy of Religion and Psychology that I took in my M.A. gave me some insight into the workings of the group mind as well as of individual minds. When by a chance accident I was initiated into the mysteries of experimental and abnormal psychology through my association with the Experimental Psychology Department of the Calcutta University in 1917, not only did I become better posted in psychological matters but I was drawn increasingly to the company of psychologists in India, who conferred on me the distinction of being elected as the President of the Psychology section of the Thirteenth Indian Science Congress (1926) and the signal honour of the Presidentship of the Indian Psychological Association (1945-47), in addition to associating me in the editing of the *Indian Journal of Psychology* for a number of years.

To my interest in Indian Philosophy, Western Metaphysics, Religion and Psychology was added that in Biology when I competed successfully in 1919 for the Premchand Roychand Studentship of the Calcutta University with a thesis on the Evolution of Individuality, different chapters of which have since been published in the *Philosophical Quarterly*[1] and the *Scientia*[2]. My main conclusions I would summarise in the following manner:

If one were to start with experience, one has to admit that plurality is an obtrusive phenomenon from which it is not possible to get away. This plurality, again, is characterised by two features —distinctiveness of units and some similarity of qualities among them. These units are further of different orders of existence, the main types being material, vital and sentient. In the inorganic world external relation holds supreme sway so that parts are loosely connected with one another and retain their original character even when separated from one another. The possession of certain spatial properties (size, shape, density, position, etc.), and certain secondary qualities in a more or less stable group serves to identify a material thing, and although its temporal location, environmental condition and motion are also material conditions of its identification, these are not generally supposed to affect its inner constitution. The chemical elements, howsoever derived, behave uniformly according to their classes under similar condition, and, except in the case of the radioactive substances which also obey definite laws about emanation and transformation, do not vary in any way though some may have isotopic forms of similar behaviour. Inorganic things are subject to the law of growth by accretion, and even though the crystals sometimes

---

[1] Individuality, *Philosophical Quarterly*, ii; Mechanism and Life, *Philosophical Quarterly*, v; also The Concept of Individuality, *Indian Philosophical Congress Proceedings*, i.

[2] Germ-Cell Constitution and Specific Ontogeny, *Scientia*, 1929.

imitate some of the features of a living organism and give an inkling of the stresses and strains that are responsible for growing a
uniform structure in each class of living things, they lack the
fundamental qualities which make a thing living. Time has no
visible effect on their nature as ageing has no meaning for things
that do not grow or decay, get differentiated in organs or reproduce themselves. They are subject to mathematical time in the
Bergsonian sense, obey mechanical laws and are therefore
externally controlled.

Life with its powers of assimilation and self-maintenance,
unforseeable growth and differentiation, regeneration of parts and
restitution of functions, retention of characteristics form in spite
of change of materials, and variation, multiplication and
reproduction together with irritability, organic memory, power
of adaptation and tendency to evolve higher forms is so radically
distinct from matter that it must be conceded the right of being
considered as an independent principle. Its holistic activity in
organising the parts into a single organism through their reciprocal
influence upon one another reveals the existence of an internal
relation and a power of unification and co-ordination which are
lacking in matter. Even though the vitalists are not agreed
amongst themselves about the real nature of life, the time and
condition of its appearance on this earth and the mode of its
operation upon matter, they have succeeded in establishing its
originality as an empirical quality of the real and the impossibility
of reducing it without remainder to physico-chemical forces,
which it utilises for its own advancement when growing and to
which it succumbs when its power of organisation fails. But life
is tethered to matter only as an immanent principle of organisation and so its survival as an independent transcendental entity,
like that of the soul, has not been claimed, and organic memory,
which Hering ascribes to all living matter, has not been considered sufficient to constitute a claim for persistence outside
the body.

Plants with their direct dependence upon inorganic matter for
nutrition developed in the direction of bulk, rapid and extensive
multiplication, long persistence in time and fixity of location,
thereby admirably fulfilling their task of supplying the food
material of the animal world. Animals that attempted a similar

mode of life, on the other hand, either failed to develop or went down in the struggle for existence or receded into a safer but lower form of adjustment. Individuality in the world of plants is subject to great limitations. For one thing, plants have very often a colonial form of life within a single organism; multiplication by cutting, budding, grafting shows that parts inside a vegetable organism, though normally forming integral portions of a bigger whole, can be made to start a new and independent system of relations after detachment from the parent body—a fact which is true only of very low animals like sponges, hydras and planarians and of blastomeres separated from one another accidentally or artificially (as in Driesch's experiments) in the early stages of the segmentation process. Then, again, sexual dimorphism is not pronounced in the plant world as it is in the world of animals, this being probably necessitated by the fact that plants do not move about as animals do, and this also affects the development of individuality proper.

When animals evolved (whether unilinearly with plants or on a divergent line), they developed individuality on a different plan. Relations of the parts became more intimate—these developed greater co-ordination with one another and began to be controlled by a central mechanism, at first on the segmental, then on the oesophagus-ganglionic, then on the thalamic, and finally on the cortical level. In addition, co-ordination by means of chemical correlation and intercellular bridges continued to function. Even micro-organisms behave somewhat distinctively and differently according to intraorganic conditions and, even where conscious memory can be safely ruled out of court, behaviour is modified by experience. As we pass on to higher animals, the senses attain greater diversity and fineness of sensibility, the range of adaptation increases and the body develops greater capacity of varied adjustment under varying conditions of life. When consciousness evolves and memory and volition make their appearance, the animal does not merely interpret and anticipate happenings but it begins to interfere in the affairs of the world so that instead of fitting itself to the environment it begins to make the environment suited to its needs. Imaginative function, conceptual ability and power of drawing inferences increase the range of the field of action and adaptation and bring into being a world of ideals to which the real is made to conform within the limits of the animal's volitional capacity and physical ability. Instantaneous reaction gives place to delayed response in the pursuit of ideals, novelty displaces routine, and the mental horizon is extended in space and time in an attempt to transcend the limitations of finitude. The foundation is thereby laid of a philosophic view of the world as a whole.[1]

But there are certain things worth noticing in the process of evolution. The first is the rule of structural and functional similarity which lies at the basis of all species-formation. The world of life, in spite of the very large number of specific types among plants and animals, is not bewilderingly fluxional and infinitely varied in character and each individual is not a type unto itself. Each type is ruled by its own racial laws in ontogeny and each individual is dominated by the laws of its own heredity on account of a germinal specificity in respect of cytoplasm, nucleus, extra-nuclear chromatin or their combination. Homology, convergence and kindred similarities in the earlier stages of segmentation among different species are soon eclipsed by divergent development when unequal division, invagination and differentiation set in. Even zygote follows a bee-line towards a characteristic ultimate form, and even centrifugation, pressure, isolation of blastomeres, enucleation, etc., fail to arrest typical growth. In fact, the evidences supplied by filial regression to the type and atavistic reversion to earlier ancestral forms, the death-roll of monstrosities and the infertility of many hybrid forms point to the operation of conservative factors in evolution which prevent the viability of extreme variations from the type. From Plato and Aristotle down to Alexander and Whitehead, philosophers have rightly urged the recognition of the formal cause or space-time configuration in the evolutionary process without which species-formation in reality and class-formation in thought by abstraction and generalisation would have been equally impossible. The evolutionary urge without which variation and progress would have been impossible must not be understood as a centrifugal tendency to pulverise the universe into absolutely dissimilar individuals. That would stop all

[1] The Case of the Philosophical Approach, *The Aryan Path*, 1948.

interbreeding on the level of life and all intercommunication on the level of thought.

The second noticeable fact is that evolution does not mean the total supersession of lower forms in course of time. Though some species of plants and animals have become extinct these have not always belonged to the lowest classes nor has the evolution of higher forms meant the extinction of all lower forms. Life is still obliged to the material world for sustenance and animals continue to draw their food supply from the world of plants. The different phyla, genera, orders, etc., of plants and animals continue to thrive and evolve without any sign of quitting their hold on being and, conversely, higher types get degenerated and occasionally become extinct.[1] Absolute uniformity either on a higher or on a lower level is not, therefore, the objective of the procession of life; even inside each species or group the individuals are definitely distinguishable by some criterion or other, as if each individual, even when sharing qualities with other individuals, has them in a different number, degree and arrangement. If Nature is careful of the type, she is not callous towards the individuals either. This would substantially support the Leibnitzian view of the identity of indiscernibles and perfection as synonymous representation of all grades in a continuous series without a gap or a duplication anywhere but without endangering the possibility of their comparison in respect of some qualities. Indirectly this would mean that the worldly symphony is generated by the co-existence of the high and the low, the beautiful and the ugly, the good and the evil, side by side and that imperfection would be conquered asymptotically but not absolutely at any time, thus ensuring the continuity of the world process by preventing a maximal entropy of values. In fact, even in man evolution has not meant equal progress in perfection of all the faculties. The intellect has outstripped the moral faculty in development presumably because the former has reference to the forces of the external world which must be reckoned with if the animal is to live and the latter to the demands of social life which are objects of deferred consideration for purposes of living; the cunning of reason has often operated without the control of

[1] The Philosophical Implications of Evolution, *Indian Philosophical Congress Proceedings*, xii.

morality and the habit of dealing with insensate things has often been carried over to dealings with one's fellow men with their attendant callousness and cruelty as evinced in successive recent wars.[1]

The third fact worth noticing is that individuals have no ultimate significance in the living world. Nature is solicitous of the race and not of the individuals which it passes on to the next generation with a new heredity in case of germinal variation. The individual is literally used as a bridge and none can claim finality of perfection or the right to persist. This has a moral for the world of minds also. It would not mean a violent break in thought if we believe, as did the Buddhists, that minds can improve the social heredity without being entitled to eternal persistence. There would also be a pragmatic justification for such a belief as individuals could then discard the notions of personal improvement and individual salvation when engaged in social service—in fact, with improved social sense they might be more careful in their conduct when they know that the sufferers from their lapses would not be themselves but the whole human race. As a corollary to this, the transcendental destiny of the individual would cease to exercise curiosity and cause anxiety and men would bend to the task of ameliorating social conditions and improving social relations so that peace and good will might prevail on earth. Each individual's achievements would be redistributed in the whole to which he belongs, thereby enriching the latter's contents like the aroma of faded flowers, as Bosanquet would say.[2]

In the Principal Miller Foundation Lectures of 1938-39 which I delivered at the Madras University I tried to establish the thesis that personal survival after bodily death need not be insisted upon as the indispensable objective of individual progress and that the ultimate world-ground need not be conceived in personal terms in order to explain social progress. I put down my *credo* categorically as belief in the existence of an over-ruling impersonal spiritual principle operating according to law and the ultimate incapacity of man to interfere in the happenings of nature or of individuals to deviate radically from the type. I have

[1] The Psychology of Nations, *Indian Journal of Psychology*, xx.

[2] Personal and Impersonal Persistence, *Philosophical Quarterly*, xviii; Individual and Social Progress, *Journal of the Madras University*, xi.

suggested, in fact, that the cunning of the world reason seems to use man and his impulses and ideals as tools for realising its own ends by widening his social contact to enable him to transcend the limits of his personality, and even his communal and national outlook, by cultivating habits of cosmic thinking, universal sympathy and disinterested action for the benefit of all. These basic ideas about the spirituality of the universe, the necessity of the religious attitude in addition to the moral,[1] the imperativeness of transcending the limitations of space, time and grouping when planning social relations,[2] the selfishness involved in pursuing the ideal of personal perfection and individual immortality, the illogicality of claiming infallibility and finality for any particular institutional religion,[3] the recognition of diversity in the methods of approach to religion according to constitutional make-up, the obligations of helping the intellectual quickening of people to enable them to develop their own religion, the futility of religious discussions without acknowledging the possibility of truth being shared by different creeds,[4] the need for toleration when dealing with alien beliefs and practices,[5] and the advisability of adjusting social philosophy to changed, if not changing, social outlook, attitude and composition[6] I tried to emphasise in my books and articles. I have also tried to establish the thesis that in the process of evolution the intellect has grown out of proportion to the moral faculty with the effect that low cunning had thrived in place of wisdom, scientific inventions have often been disseminated and utilised without reference to human happiness, and individuals and groups have been used as pawns in the game of self-seeking personal and national life.[7] Incidentally I have indicated in what direction the path of social progress lies and also the indispensable

[1] Has Religion any practical value? *Dacca University Journal*, 1926; Morality or Religion? *Dacca University Journal*, 1935. *Vedānta Kesari*, 1937; The Determinants of Morality, *Prabuddha Bharata*, 1945; Reason and Religion, *Philosophical Quarterly*, vi.

[2] Conquering Time, *Philosophical Quarterly*, xx.

[3] *The Foundations of Living Faiths*, i, Calcutta University, 1938; Ibid, *Philosophical Quarterly*, iv.

[4] The Basis of Religious Discussion, *Prabuddha Bhārata*, 1939.

[5] Some Obstacles to Toleration, *Prabuddha Bhārata*, xlii.

[6] Our Changing Social Relations, *Dacca University Journal*, 1936. Social Disintegration, *Indian Science Congress Proceedings*, xxii.

[7] Industry and the Philosophical Discipline, *Eurasia*, i; India's Psychological Reaction to the War, *Indian Journal of Psychology*, xvi.

conditions of developing cosmic ideals. But I have not attempted to hide my belief that till human nature undergoes radical alteration, *ahimsā* (non-injury) would never be realised as a universal principle of social and international conduct and that all that saints, prophets and moral preachers can hope to achieve is to enlarge the scope of self-control, fellow-feeling, and considerateness among men and nations. I have adduced instances of "moral holiday" which men in different walks of life take sometime or other, in order to show how thinly ethical culture covers our personality and how powerful the instinctual and anti-social selfish tendencies are in every one of us.[1] Social injustice I have traced to greed, love of power, selfishness, partiality, bigotry and shortsightedness of powerful individuals and dominating groups. I believe that the Buddhistic doctrine of the self as an integration which can be dissolved back into non-personal constituent elements (*skandhas*) and the Advaita-Vedānta view that in the ultimate analysis individual selfhood has no reality have this much in common that they cut at the root of that craving for personal aggrandisement and individual immortality which is the basis of much misery in this world and much social apathy.

Consistently with this view I have tried to understand the psychological basis of personal identity.[2] I have pointed out how a knowledge of biology and physiology is indispensable for understanding human psychology. I have suggested further that temperamental reactions and habits of will are more racial than individual peculiarities and that because of this it is easier to make generalisations about the intellectual operations of the human mind than about its affective and volitional operations. Sex- and age-differences in mentality may similarly be traced to differences in bodily constitution, mainly glandular in character. No wonder that organic sensations play an important part in fixing the nature of our personality, whether directly or indirectly through their selective activation of certain trains of thinking. In this way they imitate the functions of the impulses and the emotions which are partly innate and partly acquired. Abnormal Psychology has abundantly proved that an affective constellation

[1] Some Moral Holidays, *Calcutta Review*, xxiii.
[2] The Psychological Basis of Personal Identity, *Indian Journal of Psychology*, vi; *Philosophical Quarterly*, vii.

must connect memory states to weld them into a single personality and that in mental dissociation complementary affective
constellations may operate to fix the character of the different
personalities. Mood, temperament and sentiment have a profound
effect upon our character and largely determine our attitudes
towards, and reactions to, men and things. A change in their
nature may radically alter our personality and our scale of values.
Impartial memory is an abstraction and none of us can hope to
possess the entire past consciously even if it is retained, for we
are never free from instincts, tendencies and desires and it is their
operation that determines what personality we shall consciously
possess at any given time. External and internal stimuli which
initiate certain affective and volitional reactions get interpreted
according to the prevailing mood and are themselves instrumental
in developing certain aspects of the personality through resuscita-
tion of certain types of memory in keeping with their hedonic
character. We may very well suppose that if there is any post-
mortem persistence at all, heaven is that condition of existence
where only euphoric memories are revived and that conversely
hell is that state where departed souls chew the cud of bitter
memories.[1]

All these facts involve a radical alteration in our conception
of human personality. The conception of a rational soul as an
indestructible atomic unit must be abandoned in favour of that
of mind as a principle of organisation and selective action
standing in close relation to the physical constitution of the
organism concerned and swayed powerfully by emotional factors.
Our racial, familial, sexual and temperamental constitution is
powerfully influenced by bodily factors, principally the endocrine
organs.[2] Even our intellectual capacity depends to a large extent
upon sex, remote and near ancestry and maturity, operating as
factors in our reaction to the environment. The ensemble of
bodily and physical factors must be taken into account to understand aright the sense of personal identity—the logical ego of
Kant being sufficient to satisfy those who must have a unitary
physical principle to explain the sense of unity, which however,

[1] Personal and Impersonal Persistence, *Philosophical Quarterly*, xviii.
[2] The Psychologist and His Science, *Indian Science Congress Proceedings*,
xiii.

may not be infallible as cases of multiple personality, whether spontaneously generated or artificially induced, amply show. Psychical unity is more formal and functional than material and structural; and hence so long as certain formal similarities persist, the self at any two moments feels the continuity of its self-same nature. One such similarity would be the constellation of bodily feelings proceeding from the working of the organism. If coenaesthesis is anyhow altered materially, our sense of personal identity is profoundly modified and even depersonalisation may ensue. As anaesthesia and amnesia generally go together, early experiences may suffer an eclipse and fail to return to consciousness with profound alteration in or organic sensations and thus the sense of continuity may be lost. A butterfly will not feel its psychical continuity with its caterpillar state of existence. Those eschatologies that insist upon a continuance of the bodily elements in some form (whether bodily resurrection or persistence of the *liṅgaśarīra*, i.e. attenuated etheric sign-body) have stumbled upon the truth that organic persistence does have a share in determining personal identity.

The operation of the mnemic factor is the other element in the causation of the sense of psychic continuity. Organic memory, activation of neurograms, whether as instinctive reaction or as individual habit, and memory proper with the accompaniment of mental imagery and sense of recognition form a connected series, the lower stages supplying the emotional core and the higher stages the intellectual shell of the sense of identity. Emotional unity is more tenacious than intellectual continuity. That is why intellectual integrations are less stable than emotional ones and our systems of thought more liable to alteration than our complexes and sentiments. Traditional attitudes outrun cultural reactions and instincts and impulses swamp intellectual adaptation and rational behaviour. Intellectual people are less amenable to lasting control, do not easily develop a homogeneous mob mentality and therefore form bad party-supporters. In multiple personalities the emotional core varies from personality to personality and gathers relevant materials from past experience to form its sheath and alternating personalities with reciprocal amnesia sometimes prove complementary to each other in point of emotional equipment. In fact, very often emotional shock starts the process of psychic fission and submerges those elements of past experience which are responsible for the shock. Psychic changes during ontogenetic development, again owe their origin to the activation of different instincts and their emotional counterparts at different ages of the individual concerned with profound effect upon attitudes and beliefs.

If these facts are true, it is obvious that speculations about ultimates will be materially affected by emotional factors and the conative impulses that are roused to restore the mental equilibrium disturbed by emotions. Satisfaction may be either real in the sense of an actual experience following upon a prehension of entities and an adaptation thereto by some kind of physical action, or ideal in the sense of an actual experience proceeding from an adjustment by way of speculation to a world of phantasy or ideals, i.e. of imagination or conception. In the realm of the empirical we seek correspondence with facts, while regarding the elements of the transcendental or noumenal world we aim at the coherence of our thoughts and this second method we follow also when dealing with the world of abstractions. Science, therefore, is tolerant of idealism while religion and philosophy fight shy of realism; the former aims at objective verification through observation and experiment while the latter two aspire after universal agreement based on logical consistency among the elements of thought. It is soon discovered, however, that fundamental differences crop up because the subjective equipment may not be identical in all cases, specially the emotional elements, and that interpretation of experience is not always, perhaps never, based upon the intellectual factor alone.[1] We may go further and assert that the nature of the categories used to interpret sense-materials will differ from type to type, the lower types apprehending less and the higher types more than what the ordinary human type understands and appreciates. Some features of reality both animals and men apprehend, but there are other features which men alone apprehend, and there are still other features which only the best among us in any spiritual field apprehend—to poets, for instance, are revealed features which are denied to the prosaic minds. There is a minimum number of characters which living things must apprehend to be viable at all;

[1] The Voluntaristic Conception of the World, *Philosophical Quarterly*, vi.

but there are others which are not necessities but luxuries, as it were, for the purpose of living and these are not enjoyed at all stages of the evolutionary process. Similarly, what is unconscious at one stage may attain to consciousness in another—the sense of value, for instance, may be presumed from sexual selection and choice of food among animals but is consciously present only among those who can judge the relative merits of things according to a standard of perfection. It would be possible, in fact, to work out a rough parallelism between the instinct of self-preservation and the evolution of logical value or truth (in the form of a correct knowledge of the qualities and relations of things), the instinct of race-preservation and aesthetic valuation (in the shape of an appreciation of the more attractive mate. and of an effort to make oneself attractive), and the instinct of societal existence and moral valuation (in the form of a sense of rightness and wrongness in one's dealings with others or of mutual accommodation without which society cannot survive). When transcendental factors are taken into consideration, complex valuations like the religious may be added to the list and there may be a veritable transvaluation of all values in that etherial light just as colours seen in an artificial light undergo material transformation in broad daylight.

It is possible, however, to ask more basic questions. Can there be any valuation without the operation of the conative factor?[1] Feelings register success and failure by their pleasant and unpleasant characters respectively and are supposed to determine values and unvalues because pleasure and pain are their own witnesses to a desirable and an undesirable state of existence respectively. But it would be difficult to defend on this hypothesis the pursuit of ideals in the face of trying pain and the sense of contrition even when enjoying lawful pleasure. What we set our heart upon is what is considered to be valuable. A thing that does not interest us in any way has no value for us; conversely, even the most insignificant thing may acquire value when it is viewed as an instrument of fulfilling an interest or achieving a purpose. A piece of stone may ordinarily be a worthless object, but when we want to fell fruit from a roadside tree or drive away a mad dog it at once becomes valuable for the time being. Contributory

[1] Values, *Indian Philosophical Congress Proceedings*, iii.

values cease to be of worth when the primary values cease to interest us. Food is valuable so long as we are interested in life, a wife is valuable so long as we are interested in race-preservation, and friendship and company we prize so long as we are interested in social life. When life, love and friendship cease to interest us, we turn to suicide, a misogynist and a misanthrope respectively. Similarly, the sweetness of stolen pleasure may not bestow upon them any value if compunction sets in during enjoyment; conversely, the sufferings of a martyr may be suffused with a glow of worth when viewed as planting the seed of a Church. Thus feelings and ideals may work adversely to one another in any given case, thereby making values dependent not upon positive pleasures or the qualities of things and events but upon the dominant interest of a subject at any given time. The passing away of interest will mean the disappearance of value. When we make the best of a bad bargain, we may not be really interested in any of the alternative choices and yet a pseudo-value emerges because we are temporarily interested in the least unsatisfactory alternative. Here we are forcibly reminded of the view that even if there be no good there is always a better than the rest. Belief in the objectivity of values, whether as indefinable or as tertiary qualities are as begotten of the compresence of mind and some undefinable quality of objective facts or as realisations of some objective ideals, is generally associated with intuitionism or intellectualism of some sort, while their being a subjective imposition is the creed of those who are voluntaristically inclined. Those that claim an affective origin for values would insist upon the presence of pleasant feeling as an index of valuation. My sympathies are with the voluntarists who rightly insist that what the will aims at becomes a value and remains so as long as the interest lasts and that the achievement of an object may be accompanied by pleasure (which is valuable so long as it is consistent with some ideal, conscious or unconscious) but not by value consciousness, the indispensable condition of which is the dissociation between the real and the ideal. Reality becomes valuable only as judged against the background of the ideal.

My interest in voluntarism has led me to discourse at some length on the meaning of Voluntarism,[1] the need of a voluntaristic

[1] The Voluntaristic Outlook, *Philosophical Quarterly*, ii.

epistemology[1] and the dependence of value-judgments on the conative aspect of our mental life and not on the apprehension of any objective quality in things, events and situations.[2] Voluntarism which finds the key to the problems of reality and knowledge in the will-aspect of the human mind may develop both an ontology and an epistemology. Schopenhauer may be cited as the clearest exponent of the realistic aspect of voluntarism inasmuch as he tries to show that different types of beings are really modes of manifestation of the World-Will and in this he was followed by Hartmann and others though with certain modifications in his doctrine. We need not discuss how far they succeeded in presenting a better view of reality than realism and rationalistic idealism; but possibly change, motion and process, all of which take time more seriously than Absolutistic speculations, are better explained by voluntaristic assumptions as these attribute the necessity of abandoning an existing state to the operation of the impulsive factor of our personality—the innate dissatisfaction which prompts life and mind to sally forth into the unknown and the unrealised. In fact, of the four elements of causation efficient and final causes are more congruent with voluntarism than with idealism, material cause is equally important in both, and formal cause alone is more idealistic in character than voluntaristic if we believe that form and matter can be separated, and priority can be assigned to the former in some shape as by postulating the existence of Platonic Ideas or Space-Time configurations. But I have not attempted to adjudge the issue between Voluntarism and Idealism on the ontological level.

What I have tried to emphasise is that the neglect of the conative aspect in the interpretation of experience has created difficulty in epistemology. It is not suggested that philosophy can be anything but "a thinking consideration of things"; but it may still be contended that pure intellect does not alone do the work of interpretation and that without a due recognition of the contribution of the conative factor certain features of our philosophical interpretation cannot be properly explained. Activity, purpose and value are qualities that cannot be based on

---

[1] The Need of a Voluntaristic Epistemology, *Philosophical Quarterly*, vii.

[2] Existence and Value, (1); Value as Quality, *Review of Philosophy and Religion*, iii.

mere cogitation, and causality and progress depend upon conation for their meaning. To a pure intellect all these concepts are unmeaning; and yet without these attributes what an uninteresting ghostly world do we know! We shall not press the thesis that perception itself at all its stages is an act of interest and that apathy is responsible for withdrawal from all knowledge activities. Sleep, swoon, suicide, schizophrenia and kindred apathetic attitudes towards the world owe their existence to the loss of interest in things. Conversely our set or attitude profoundly affects our apprehension and appreciation and, in addition, the way in which we attend to things is responsible for investing the world of experience with definite categorical features. This fact did not escape the notice of Kant who pointed out how the different categories were schematised according to the ways in which we looked at time, the universal form of human experience. It has also been noticed that where the intellect fails to get a sure foothold the will may still try to posit something on which life activities may be based. The world of postulates and assumptions, which is the creation of the will, supplements the world of facts and probabilities which is the creation of the intellect; and even the wonder to which philosophical enquiry owes its origin may at bottom be an expression of the restlessness and dissatisfaction in which the will finds itself on failing to adjust itself to a novel situation. Even intellectual discord prompts fuller enquiry only because otherwise the will becomes torn between conflicting lines of action and fails to take up a definite attitude in pursuit of ends. If no action is going to be influenced by them, alternative or conflicting theories have the same value or lack of value for the individual concerned. Right and wrong, true and false have no essential difference where actionlessness has set in, for where adjustment is not an objective, success and failure have no meaning. After all, a philosphical speculation is an intellectual or ideal process of adjustment to the world—a plan of action which may be executed at suitable times and places if need arises. It provides its own corrective in the shape of frustrated satisfaction and want of social confirmation, which in their turn lead to further planning and fresh attempts at adjustment in order to secure social harmony and personal satisfaction through cessation of conflict. A philosophical theory cannot hang in mid-air or be equally valid with any other, for every intellectual construction has both bearing and dependence upon life-situations and no two theories are likely to coincide entirely in their significance for life at all stages.

But it is with the epistemological contributions of will that we are concerned here. It is indeed true that it is difficult to say where analogy ends and categorising begins; but it has been felt that the dynamic of change is supplied by something akin to will and is best understood with the help of the latter. Will may be supposed to supply, as Pfleiderer has suggested, the material element of change while the intellect may be supposed to supply the formal element. It is the restlessness or dissatisfaction of the will that is responsible for all changes and motions that are ushered in with a view to bringing about quiescence through satisfaction; hence the intellect, of which the primary function is passive reception, flounders when trying to understand continuous change or process which looks like the welling up of unsatisfied impulses. Leibniz had to invoke the aid of appetite to explain the spontaneous evolution of monads as the power of representation is not inconsistent with a static universe. In Alexander motion and nisus towards the Deity disturb the complacence of the space-time matrix, and similar principles have been invoked by Whitehead in his *Process and Reality*. The intellect delights in taking instantaneous snapshots while the will functions like a cinematograph camera picturing the process of a dynamic world. Naturally, therefore, the moving, the changing, the growing and the progressing features of reality get better appreciated when viewed through the eye of the will than through the eye of the intellect. In fact, to one endowed with will even kaleidoscopic changes of static pictures assume the form of pseudo-motion and a succession of impressions generates an impression of succession, as Hume suggested but could not properly justify on sensory grounds alone. Naturally, in pseudo-motion the continuity of the process which genuine change involves is lacking and the motion has got to be imported from outside as in a cinematographic exhibition of moving forms out of the still pictures of a reel.

When change itself cannot be intellectually understood except as an alteration in the qualitative grouping of the contents of the mind, it is no wonder that activity, causality, creativity, force and power should be denied in this or that psychological or philo- sophical speculation. Intellect would give us what Whitehead calls presentational immediacy, but for causal efficacy in Whitehead's sense of the term we must turn to the will. If causal relation cannot hold between simultaneities as in a presentational immediacy, it is because the aspect of time in which changes take place is not present in contemporaneous events. Unless one thing can be known to pass away or be transformed into another without completely losing its identity, it cannot stand for a cause or exercise power, and this knowledge is attached to our will-activities where later stages grow out of earlier ones and produce the moving equilibrium of conscious life with a push from behind and a pull from before. Will is the faculty of tackling events in a connected fashion, the emotional basis supplying the element of unity needed for persistence in endeavour. Intellect, on the other hand, is the faculty of detached response even when it is endowed with memory of the past and anticipation of the future. Hence highly intellectual men are best fitted to take a detached view of things but are at the same time bad lovers in every field—social, political, religious and even philosophical, as they do not develop sentiments easily and can change views and alliances quickly without being harassed by remorses and regrets, and cannot be relied upon to prove devoted and persistent party adherents (whether as leaders or as followers). Those that pursue ideals cannot, however, be deflected from their plan of action and all acts tending towards the realisation of ideals rise in a connected series by way of causal generation. When, therefore, events are looked upon as continuous, connected and caused, we are taking the help of the conative aspect of our mental life. On a purely intellectual basis process would be merely a succession of detached, qualitatively different experiences with no discernible bond of continuity in between and no ascertainable progression towards an end-state. Hence causality will be reduced in intellectualistic systems, as in those of Hume and Kant, to invariable succession without inner connection; the irreversibility of the causal sequence alone gives an inkling that the intellectual apprehension of man is not the final arbiter of the causal con- junction which seems to follow a hidden law of connection of which man is conscious when exercising will. The intellect revels in space where reversibility is possible, but the will takes time more seriously as being akin to its own nature by virtue of its necessary unfoldment in a process of realisation and progression from the present to the future. The agency of a cause need not necessarily involve deliberate action prompted by a conscious pursuit of end; but it does involve production or a communication of a portion of one's own being to later happenings and thus ultimately a continuity of one's own self through time. In intellect the transgredient reference is to another—hence its poles are of subject and object, the remembered past and the contemplated future being both objects of disinterested contemplation like things of the physical world. But in will the transcendence is of the self of one moment to the same self of another moment, the object being merely an auxiliary or instrument for the realisation of the later psychic state. Hence action of the will on the external world is designed to bring about a desirable change in the subjective state with the proximate intention of attaining repose; but actually one activity follows another in a never-ending series to reach a higher goal with every advance.

This leads to the second contribution of will to our understanding of events. To the intellect change is qualitative difference; but to the will change is progression towards an ideal. Degeneration and progression are both processes, but the former is a regression from the ideal while the latter is an approach towards it. To an intellectual scheme of the universe facts are equally valuable or equally valueless; the intellect has no partisan spirit and so it does not admit levels of existence or excellence. Its impartiality is, however, not that of the judge who is not biased but all the same evaluates facts in order to arrive at a just decision on the merits of the case; its impartiality is that of the advocate who is equally willing to take up the cause of either party in a dispute for consideration and to whom, therefore, merit is no consideration for siding with either. Plans, therefore, have no meaning for pure intellect and the world to it is a big equation where the infinite permutations and combinations of elements do not alter the value of the whole or make one state of existence a nearer approximation to an ideal than another. Intellect has no teleological perspective: its ideal philosophy is mechanism which advocates equivalence in value of all worldly happenings.

We may go a little further. We may be tempted to think that conation is spontaneous action needing no stimulus from without to start functioning. In a monadistic scheme each element of present experience may be supposed to be the end-term of a process of change initiated all from within and owing nothing to external influence. Again, mere compresence or temporal simultaneity need not imply a spatial world. Mental states that are co-existent can only be metaphorically said to occupy mental space, for the time reversed is not space but simultaneity. Unless criss-cross connections can be established among the components of any universe we do not have a world in space. A universe is a world in interaction; here units and events mutually influence one another and thereby make it a process. This means that unless reciprocity of action is understood, space cannot be conceived in its proper significance, as some interpreters of Kant have correctly pointed out. Simultaneity needs added determination from interaction to make a spatial world, and this involves the notion of activity or power, of which the source is our conative faculty. Thus ultimately will lies at the root of our sense of concrete spatiality, though not necessarily as a conscious fact. Mathematical or empty space, where nothing occurs, is an intellectual construction of detached points and reversible directions; but real or physical space presumes active mutual determination of elements and as the consequent strains are unequal in different parts no one point in this space can be substituted for another in calculating concrete results. Spatiality is shot through and through by temporality and motion.

Because will is wedded to non-equivalence while intellect is inclined towards equation, value has no meaning for intellect proper. In fact, the intellect is more at home in explaining the present with the help of the past than in using the present as the stepping stone to the future. Intellect, therefore, dissects and analyses with greater success than it initiates plans, for the urge for planning comes from dissatisfaction and dissatisfaction comes from a sense of defect. The intellect may help in the preparation of the blue print for action, but the craving for change is responsible for starting the process of planning, and the need of

maximum satisfaction for choosing one out of the many alternative possibilities pictured by the intellectual faculty. Ultimately
the need of greater harmony and proper adjustment to work off
an existing unpleasure is responsible for creating interest in our
environment, and anything that becomes an object of interest at
once becomes invested with the quality of value. No value-
judgment is, therefore, possible without taking the interest
factor into account, even though the judgment itself is an
intellectual proposition and the growth of intellect with the
attendant development of the imaginative faculty may be
responsible for creating possibilites of estrangement with the
actual. Interest must intervene before an imagined ideal state can
become a spring of action—a thought must become a wish and
then a desire before it can move us to action. But this desire which
is responsible for investing things with value-qualities need not
always be a conscious one—even sub-conscious impulse and
unconscious physiological need will make things valuable. The
adjustment of the vital series to its surroundings, so that it may
have an uninterrupted course and restore the disturbed nervous
equilibrium, has been pointed out by Avenarius and Stout as the
source of pleasure or vital satisfaction: we may very well suppose
that all habits, physiological and mental, indicate a tacit positive
valuation of the situation in which they occur and all conscious
adjustments as overt valuations of desired changes. In fact, all
qualities—primary, secondary and tertiary—may come to
consciousness at different stages of animal evolution, and even
among men the range of value-appreciation may widen with the
evolution of finer sensibility, sounder understanding and wider
social contact.

Limiting ourselves to the tertiary qualities, we may say that
there are difficulties in putting them on the level of the primary
and secondary qualities when these are realistically viewed.
It is true that subjective origin has sometimes been claimed for
these two also in different systems; but tertiary qualities are
still more subjective in the sense that universal agreement is more
difficult to achieve in their case. Seeing that they are creatures of
interest and attitude, it would be proper to admit with Bradley
and Alexander, though in a sense different from theirs, that
Reality is reality and is neither true nor beautiful nor good. It

would be possible perhaps to relate these three values to the three major drives of animal existence—self, sex and society-seeking instincts. Self-preservation would be impossible if, to use Herbert Spencer's language, the internal relations of an organism are not adjusted to external relations. A thing becomes true when it enables us to effect this adjustment; its claim to truth is then validated, to use the Pragmatic terminology. Naturally, coherence becomes the ultimate test of truth; if at any time this coherence should fail, its factual character would disappear. Why coherence should please cannot be satisfactorily explained: here we are probably face to face with an ultimate fact. The revision of theories is bound to happen when life's interests alter and incoherence sets in. If certain things seem to retain for all time their right to truth, it must be because certain interests are fundamental and abiding in character, and their universality is due to the commonness of the interests of the group. Truths of wider and of narrow denotation borrow their character from the sizes of the groups which have the interests in common. The relativity of truths will be due to the divergence of interests among different individuals and groups, and some of these divergences may be ultimately traced to differences in physiological and mental make-up. In this way one man's meat may be another man's poison, and what is sauce for the gander may not be sauce for the goose. The narrowing of interest will mean a restricted knowledge of things, and loss of interest in the continuance of the self will mean insentitiveness to nature and relations of things. Men are not generally opposed to the idea that falsity is an imposition on things *pace* our contemporary realists; but that truth also may be a similar imposition when there is no conflict with our interests does not prove so readily acceptable—the core of that imposition may be a manifold of sensibility (Kant) or sub-intuitional sensation or feeling (Croce) or past living thought now reduced from an *act* to a *fact* (Gentile), the demands of objectivity being satisfied on each of these suppositions. Truth is an affair of animal faith in most cases and we accept with natural piety the testimony of our senses because obstinate questionings and perpetual doubts would sap action and stability of conduct. But in non-sensory fields interests are more conscious and individualistic, and there agreement is difficult to attain.

We are excluding from consideration the world of conceptual symbols where agreement is achieved by abstraction from concrete personal experiences and setting up a realm of universally acceptable frame-work to facilitate social intercourse. The meaning-content of such symbols is determined not only by abstraction from personal experience but also by inter-subjective intercourse or convention or by pure definition.

Unlike Truth, Beauty seems to be passively apprehended and attached primarily to the things of the external world. On voluntaristic supposition Beauty will owe its origin to man's partiality for certain peculiarities of his bodily constitution—his bilateral symmetry and rhythmic physiological function, of which, however, he need not have a clear consciousness. That partiality determines the aesthetic sense will be evident from widely divergent standards of beauty among races of mankind. We may, again, cultivate a particular type of aesthetic taste by deliberately creating interest. Now Beauty attracts and pleases while ugliness repels and displeases. Pleasure- and pain-experience may be the rudimentary forms of appreciation of concord and conflict or primitive modes of attraction and repulsion. Life depends upon truth, but beauty-perception comes primarily in connection with the choosing of an attractive mate. Spring is both beautiful and sex-stimulating. Those that ignore truth die by natural selection; those who fail to get sexually selected for want of attractiveness and those who choose the ugly equally find that in the long run their line becomes extinct through sexual rejection at some stage. But beauty-perception is not a necessary condition of persistence among living things in which bisexual mode of reproduction is not indispensable. Why beauty should be generally perceived almost instantaneously and why aesthetic repose should lull the restlessness of will to quietude are not, however, easy to explain on any theory. Kant's formula of nature conforming easily to the needs of the understanding does not rule out the possibility that beauty is an imposition of the unconscious will on things in which the parts are so matched that the mind oscillates between equal and opposite attractions and. the will-activity is stopped as a consequence. We feel that we are not called upon to do anything in an aesthetic situation—enjoyment supplants action of all kinds except continuance in the same attitude. The ugly, however,

prompts us to interfere in the arrangement of parts and all mental
progress can be ultimately traced to this dissatisfaction with the
existing order of things and a consequent attempt to bring out
greater harmony and concord.

Unlike Truth and Beauty, Goodness depends upon society
sense. A bad man is apathetic to social disapproval of his conduct,
while one absolutely dispassionate and detached goes beyond
good and evil. The morality of masters and the morality of slaves
are differently conceived because the strong need less social aid
than the weak who must stick together in weal and woe in order
to survive. Even predatory animals, when obliged to hunt in a
pack, for food, are more considerate towards one another during
the attack than when dividing the kill. The same lupine mentality
is exhibited by war-time allies when after defeating the enemy
they begin to divide the spoils of victory.[1] The society that one
has in view determines the nature of the moral act and attitude—
a code of honour that robbers will observe in their own relations
will not be extended to other groups. Grossly immoral acts would
be done in the name of religion if one sets one's heart upon
securing the approval of imperfectly moralised gods through such
acts. While the form of morality will be imposed on any situation
needing social adjustment of any sort on our part, the content
or material of duty will depend upon the society in which we are
interested, and also upon the position we occupy in that society.
This sense of moral goodness is intimately linked up with the
capacity of choosing one course of action in preference to another;
hence a feeling of approbation or disapprobation comes in the
wake of choosing or rejecting any particular line of action, the
rejected motive acting as a foil to the chosen one and colouring
its affective quality. Mere herd-instinct or gregariousness may
produce in an unconscious fashion among animals a colony or
hive, a swarm or flight, a pack or flock, a shoal or crowd with such
mutual accommodation as may be demanded by the necessity
of space or mutual safety; but deliberate adjustment to a social
condition would demand a consciousness of others' convenience
as well as of an ideal arrangement of social components which
would be acceptable to all. Morality is socially coherent action
just as truth is socially coherent knowledge. Needless to add that

[1] The Psychology of Nations, *Indian Journal of Psychology*, xx.

the extension of the social group to include a Divine agent will materially affect the conception of morality and make it a function of religion. Any attenuation of the religious factor will tend to make the moral law autonomous, as in the Indian law of Karma, or reduce it to a mere principle of social coherence.

In this way the three tertiary values can be shown to be related to the three instincts of self-preservation, race-preservation and herding and form a hierarchy in worth. All these judgments of value are prompted by interest, though in the logical value the intellectual element is most prominent, in the aesthetic value the affective element is overwhelming, and in the moral value the conative element comes most prominently into consciousness. Mere intellect does not distinguish values, and to it all facts are of equal significance. In fact, even dreams, illusions, hallucinations, not to speak of memory images and fanciful ideas, are in no way inferior to perceptions as mental states. Their unvalue depends upon their failure to secure social confirmation and to sustain action. In a world of inaction all mental states are valueless—they form a procession of qualitatively different contents, a kaleidoscopic show in which the pictures are not graded according to worth. But once the element of value enters, procession is changed into progression or regression—a march towards or away from a state of greater perfection. Kant thought of teleology in terms of our failure to explain things mechanically, which we may put in our own language as the failure of intellect to understand the pursuit of an end without the help of will. "Better" is what brings us nearer to the goal of our will and "worse" is what takes us farther away from our objective, understanding by goal, aim, objective and such kindred terms anything on which we have set our heart and therefore not necessarily connoting any moral quality. The objectively true is what is significant for all creatures or all creatures of a certain type, the beautiful is what claims to be universal in its significance but may be only a subjective feeling, while the moral is what is socially acceptable in conduct. Universal interest would constitute objectivity in our opinion as universal validity does in Kant's system. Facts become values only when looked through the glasses of interest. Things are absolutely indifferent in their own character and are stowed away till wanted, when they assume the value according to the need, whether that be the value of truth as the subject of a judgment, or of beauty as the subject of appreciation, or of goodness as the subject of approval. With a shift in interest there may be a transvaluation of all values; the arousal of religious interest, for instance, may throw into shade all temporal values. Again, it is only in instantaneous existence that pleasure and value coincide; for when life stretches over a period of time, our immediate pleasures, in so far as they conflict with ideal pleasures, may cease to be an index of value and, conversely, a present evil, viewed in the perspective of the future, may be invested with a halo of goodness. Objective valuation is standardised social judgment upon things, processes and events that have some bearing or other on human needs and desires. The want of finality in moral judgment is due to the limitation of human knowledge about the sentient factors to be taken into consideration when planning adjustment—these may range over different extents in space and time and may even belong to a supersensuous order as in religious beliefs. The overpersonal or objective good or eternal value is the content of a standard mind which ignores the fluctuations of time, place and personality.

We conclude, therefore, that just as postulates and assumptions require the co-operation of the will-function, so also activity, causality, evolution, progress and value are concepts that cannot be explained satisfactorily on any purely intellectual basis but require the help of the will-aspect of our mental life. In fact, change, novelty, unforeseeability and growth are features, not of the intellect, but of the will, and it is to these that we owe the concepts of nisus, élan, indeterminacy and creativity with which different philosophers have familiarised us in their treatment of the dynamic aspect of the ultimately real. An idea, again, is not an intellectual picture of a possible world-situation, but an objective which is conducive to a greater satisfaction of cravings and has the power to move our will. To use Hegel's classical distinction, an ideal is not a Notion but an Idea—not a formal but an efficient cause of our action operating towards the attainment of a final state which may, however, be eternally unrealisable. We may work in the panlogistic faith that the scheme of the universe is dialectical and logical—that will add zest to our endeavours, but to be active agents in furthering the cause of civilisation we must look upon evolution as historical and temporal and as demanding the contribution of man for speedy progress and fulfilment.

In my presidential address on *Conquering Time*[1] to the Indian Philosophical Congress in 1944, I tried to make out that, though living in time, sentient beings have ever pressed forward to conquer time in a variety of ways. Retaining the impress of the past is revealed either as racial habit or as modification of behaviour or as memory image, while anticipating the future may appear in the form of instinctive preparation of home or hoarding food for self or progeny or as conscious portrayal of coming events or ideal situations. Time may further be spanned in man by a sense of personal identity stretching over the past and the present and projected into the future. The social mind effects the conquest of the past by establishing modes and traditions, developing arts and crafts and creating language and institutions, while the future is sought to be conquered by social planning and formation of social ideals. Apprehension, generalisation and idealisation represent the three stages of mental development with reaction to the actual, preparation for the anticipated and launching of the ideal as corresponding will-attitudes. Conscious possession of the past and the future has been effected slowly by mankind through the development of appropriate spoken and written language—a feat which primitive art and pictorial language could not possibly perform without the help of suitable gestures to indicate the three dimensions of time. Similarly, practical judgment and routine adjustment to the familiar antedated foresight and adaptation to the novel and the un-expected because they are akin to instinct in being responses where representation is effectively stopped by action, to use the language of Bergson. Instinct exemplifies the racial habit of con-centrating attention on the relevant point of interest in the object and ignoring the rest, while Intelligence not only ushers in a sense of plurality but also develops a relational consciousness, including subject-object discrimination, and through the power of generalisation escapes the bondage of the immediate and the subjective by establishing relations and formulating laws that are

[1] *Philosophical Quarterly*, xx.

valid for other places, times and persons. By formulating judgments that are not merely summative, i.e. merely enumerative, it takes the risk of confirmation or denial by others—a contingency from which mere personal apprehension is free. Again, by rising to the stage of mediate inference the intellect discovers the interrelations of relations or an integrated world-order and thereby moves away from mere subjective associations of ideas. Logical thinking, therefore, involves a transcendence of the present and the personal. The more far-flung the tentacles of any belief in the higher reaches of our mind and in the mind of the group the greater chance it has of resisting refutation in future. In the attempt to escape from the temporary and the personal we are increasingly drawn away from the sensuous order and make excursion at first into the realm of the imaginary and then into that of the conceptual. But the formula of eternity is discovered only by those who have that synoptic vision before which all things are revealed in their proper articulation as composing an orderly whole like the tune of a song, the scheme of a picture, the plot of a drama and the plan of a building. The planting of ideals that would stand the test of time is possible only when intervention in worldly affairs is preceded by an insight into the nature of ultimate values and the condition of orderly progress in civilisation, comfort and cultivation of freedom, by a deepening of sympathies and a chastening of morals. The reconstruction of the world can be successfully undertaken only by those who have the artist's sense of symmetry and harmony, the moralist's conception of human justice and equality, the philosopher's spirit of detachment and capacity of generalisation and the saint's conviction of the transcendental basis of human relationships. There would be no abiding peace on earth unless people are trained up in the art of comprehensive thought, world-wide sympathy and global planning on a spiritual basis. Matter conquers time through self-preservation or persistence of elemental stuff; life triumphs over time through race-preservation; but mind conquers time through conceptual thought, discovery of laws and planting of spiritual social ideals.

I have suggested in my presidential address on *Nature and Man* at the sectional meeting of the Conference on Culture, Religion and Morals in 1949, that unless certain fundamental concepts of

Indian philosophy are accepted as principles of social reconstruction human misery would never show any sign of abatement. The Indian traced all afflictions to *Avidyā*—ignorance or confused thinking in which the distinction between the self and the not-self, the pure and the impure, the pleasurable and the painful, the eternal and the evanescent is lost, and, mistaking the one for the other, we pursue personal and social objectives regardless of spiritual danger and worldly suffering. Our habit of dealing with matter for our own practical benefit, to which an industrial mode of life makes us increasingly prone, we carry over to our dealing with man. No wonder, therefore, that we become cruel and callous, thinking of men as only lumps of flesh that can be killed inch by inch to satisfy our capitalistic greed, or outright to further our imperialistic ambitions, and not as sparks of the divine capable with suitable opportunities of contributing materially to the development of culture and advancement of civilisation. By a kind of "apathetic fallacy" we obliterate the distinction between man and nature, using the former as means and field of domination like the latter and never as an end in himself. Even when we want to be considerate, we are more anxious to pamper his body with material comforts than to elevate his soul with intellectual pursuits, moral surroundings and spiritual ideals. As we wish to continue our domination in society and the state, we see to it that the submerged and backward sections do not develop in intellectual stature, begin to think independently and refuse to act as pawns in our social, political and international games. Similarly, our international sympathies closely follow the alignments of race and colour as we refuse to recede from our positions of political and economic vantage secured when the backward races were dowerless, disunited and ignorant. Though protesting theoretically and outwardly against the Nietzschean distinction between the morality of masters and the morality of slaves, inwardly and practically we follow that distinction in our personal, national and international lives. Here, again, the Indian emphasis on duties towards, rather than on rights over, other beings might prove a powerful solvent of class conflicts, party struggles and international rivalries. Payment of debts to gods and to seers and saints, to ancestors and to guests, to one's own highest unborn

D

self and to the brute creation, detachment from worldly affairs and conquest over the lower impulses constitute the prerogative of man. An optimistic faith in the goodness of human nature would remove much of the mistrust and jealousy which unfortunately generate such strained relations among men and groups.

In my Stephanos Nirmalendu Ghosh Lectures (1933-34) on the *Foundations of Living Faiths* at the Calcutta University I have tried to appraise the qualities by which the existing major faiths of the world have lived and thrived, and to bring out the point that finality in any matter of belief cannot be claimed by any existing institutional religion. Though all living religions advance more and more towards coherence in doctrine, morality in conduct and spirituality in outlook when they shake off the traditional, the local and the temporary element, a single religion to satisfy the spiritual cravings of all types of minds would never evolve, and religion would never be so rationalised as to amount to Philosophy nor could the scriptures be so successfully twisted as to yield anticipations of scientific truths discovered at a much later time. I have admitted, however, that the mysteries of the universe are revealed diversely to different types of genius and that, like a poet and a musician, a prophet or a saint may be born and not made and that to his gaze the book of nature may reveal aspects which are hidden away from the drab vision of the non-elect. Incidentally I have complimented the Indian prescription of advancing understanding as the surest method of ensuring a critical acceptance of religious beliefs and encouraging the development of a personal religion in keeping with the level of spiritual culture attained. The method of strictly regimenting the faiths and practices of an entire community according to a uniform pattern and of winning converts by threat or violence, appeal to the baser instincts or economic greed, without providing the requisite intellectual basis of imbibing the spirit of an improved culture and in utter disregard of the spiritual status of their old faith, as has been followed in the past by some proselytising religions, has not paid proper respect to the dignity of individual human life. I have been constrained to think that the empirical and the magical have still a large appeal to the followers of all faiths[1] and that the danger of an intellectual approach to

[1] Empiric Faith, *Philosophical Quarterly*, ii; also *Calcutta Review*, xxii.

religion is not altogether imaginary, as is evident from the polite atheism of many Indian philosophical systems.[1] I have attempted to lay down the conditions under which toleration can thrive[2] and periodical religious discussion can be of any value.[3]

My studies in Psychology have centred most round certain character traits that distinguish personalities from one another.[4] But in some recent articles I have drifted into a consideration of the psychology of nations that is responsible for so much conflict and misunderstanding[5] and I have suggested here also that unless in fixing social and international relations we plan for the world as a whole there would be no abiding peace.

The cumulative effect of my studies in Science and in Eastern and Western Philosophy and Religion has been this that I am now persuaded that to man, who embodies in his own constitution the mysterious conjunction of Body and Mind, the assumption of the physical world can never become superfluous and that matter is neither an idea of the Mind (Mentalism) nor itself spiritual (Monadism) nor absolutely amenable to mental control (Finalism).[6] Again, the primary characteristic of Matter is repetition of behaviour in an infinite number of representatives, that of Life variation and adaptation, and that of Mind spontaneity and idealisation. The spirituality of the universe consists not in Divine Providence, personal and spasmodic, but in the rule of law which can be apprehended by diverse faculties and different individuals in unique ways and which can be communicated by one spirit to another. Impersonality would be quite consistent with my conception of the nature of this ultimate spirituality and immortality may also be similarly conceived as contribution to social heritage. That life and speculation are indissolubly connected together and that in no interpretation of the universe can the intellect do without the conative-affective element of human nature together constitute one of my major beliefs.

[1] The Polite Atheism of Indian Philosophy, *Dacca University Studies*, i.

[2] Some Obstacles to Toleration, *Prabuddha Bhārata*, 1937.

[3] The Basis of Religious Discussion, *Prabuddha Bhārata*, 1939.

[4] The Ways of Sex, *Indian Journal of Psychology*, iii; The Sense of the Incomplete, *Calcutta Review*, xxiii; The Sadistic Trend, *Indian Journal of Psychology*, iv; Inferiority Complex, *Calcutta Review*, xxii.

[5] Psychology of Nations, *Indian Journal of Psychology*, xx.

[6] Idealism and the Physical World, *Indian Philosophical Congress Proceedings*, ix.

In Indian thought the problem that has attracted me most is the question of Human Freedom in the context of the law of Karma together with the allied problem of Human Destiny. In a series of papers I have discussed at great length the meaning of Dharma,[1] the multiple origin of the law of Karma[2] and the bearing of the Karma Doctrine on the capacity of the soul to grow in spiritual stature.[3] I have discussed the sources of the vitality of Hinduism,[4] its spiritual legacy,[5] and its system of spiritual discipline.[6] The value and validity of certain Hindu mortuary rites[7] and the various conceptions of salvation as advocated in different Indian philosophical and religious systems I have also discussed at some length.[8] I have tried to show how experience, imagination and wish-fulfilment have all entered into our picture of the Hereafter.[9] To what extent varying situations, changing faith and growing knowledge can affect mythological belief I have illustrated by the romantic history of Sarasvati the Goddess of Learning through a period of about three thousand years.[10] But I have made it quite clear that in all such speculations, beliefs and imageries the human mind only manifests its unbounded curiosity, transcendental craving and impatience of limitations incidental to its own finitude without hoping to remove finally the unsolved riddles that assail it from all sides. With his gaze fixed at an ever-receding horizon Man becomes an eternal wayfarer swayed by the spinning double star of Quest and Conquest.

---

[1] The Meaning of Dharma, *All-India Oriental Conference Proceedings*, ix.

[2] Was there a unitary Karma Doctrine?, *Vedānta Kesari*, xix; The Vicissitudes of the Karma Doctrine, *Madan Mohan Malaviya Commemoration Volume*.

[3] The Doctrine of Karma, *Philosophical Quarterly*, iii.

[4] The Vitality of Hindu Religion, *Philosophical Quarterly*, i.

[5] The Legacy of India; Spiritual Contribution, *Prabuddha Bhārata*, liii.

[6] Yoga Psychology, *Cultural Heritage of India*, i.

[7] The Mortuary Beliefs of the Hindus, *Calcutta Review*, xxxi.

[8] The Concept of Salvation, *Philosophical Quarterly*, iii.

[9] The Psychology of Heaven and Salvation, *Philosophical Quarterly*, v; The Psychology of Post-Mortem Existence, *International Congress of Psychology*, ix.

[10] Sarasvatī the Goddess of Learning, *K.B. Pathak Commemoration Volume*.

•

PRINCIPAL PUBLICATIONS

The Foundations of Living Faiths, I Stephanos Nirmalendu Ghosh Lectures in Comparative Religion—1933-34. Calcutta University, 1938.

Individual and Social Progress. Madras University, 1939.

·

THE CONCEPT OF PHILOSOPHY

by K. C. BHATTACHARYYA

Born 1875; Professor of Philosophy in Calcutta University

THE CONCEPT OF PHILOSOPHY

1. AN explication of the concept of philosophy appears to me more important than the discussion of any specific problem of philosophy. The possibility of philosophy as a body of knowledge distinct from science is nowadays called in question. I may indicate my general position by stating wherein I differ from the Kantian view of the subject.

I. ORIENTATION TO KANT

2. With regard to the knowability of the self as a metaphysical entity, Kant holds that the self is a necessity of thought and is the object of moral faith, but is not in itself knowable. My position is, on the one hand, that the self is unthinkable and on the other that while actually it is not known and is only an object of faith, though not necessarily only of moral faith, we have to admit the possibility of knowing it without *thinking*, there being a demand, alternative with other spiritual demands, to realise such knowledge. This is practically reopening the entire epistemological question of the meaning of thought and knowledge.

3. In taking the self to be unthinkable, I understand Kant's Idea of the Reason to be not only not knowledge, but to be not even thought in the literal sense. The so-called extension of thought beyond experience and the possibility of experience means to me only the use of the verbal form of thought as a symbol of an unthinkable reality, such symbolising use not being thinking. I go further and hold that a form of thought as understood by itself in logic and apart from its symbolising use is not literally thought. Some present-day positivists who deny not only metaphysical knowing, but also metaphysical thinking, would not go so far as to deny logic itself to be a body of thought. They rely in fact on logic, which they take to be pure thinking, in order to deny metaphysical thinking. I take logic to be a philosophical and not a scientific subject: the logical forms are shadows of metaphysical symbolisms and are as such themselves to be understood as symbolisms.

4. On the negative side then I go much further than Kant. On the positive side, however, I would tone down his agnosticism. That the self is believed in and is yet actually unknown is itself to me ground for holding that it is knowable without thinking and has to be so known. The self or freedom is taken to be a moral postulate, but why is a moral postulate formuated at all? Neither morality nor metaphysical theory gains anything by the formulation in theoretic form. A moral postulate is not simply an Idea of the Reason, nor is it a construct of the aesthetic imagination. It appears to me to be formulated for the contemplation of it not as a moral good or as an enjoyable value but as a truth to be known. Such contemplation cannot be a spiritual luxury or make-believe, but must have behind it the faith that it is just the process of reaching the truth without thinking. It is not indeed a duty to contemplate, but the contemplation being already there, it demands fulfilment in knowledge. The contemplation of the self as truth may start from consciousness other than the moral, nor need moral consciousness develop into it. A distinctively spiritual activity comes spontaneously and has no necessary origin. The contemplation of the self as truth demands fulfilment in knowledge only by one in whom this activity has already started. It is an absolute demand co-ordinate with other absolute demands.

5. What applies to the self applies with necessary alterations to other metaphysical entities. Metaphysics, or more generally, philosophy including logic and epistemology, is not only not actual knowledge, but is not even literal thought; and yet its contents are contemplated as true in the faith that it is only by such contemplation that absolute truth can be known.

II. GRADES OF THEORETIC CONSCIOUSNESS

6. Whether philosophy is knowledge or embodies literal thinking may be open to dispute. But in any case it presents beliefs that are speakable or systematically communicable and is like science an expression of the theoretic consciousness. Theoretic consciousness at its minimum is the understanding of a speakable. What is spoken must be in the first instance believed. What is disbelieved must be, to start with, a believed content. The meaning of a sportive combination of words like the "hare's horn" or

"square circle" is only not believed and cannot even be said to be disbelieved. Nor is such combination said to be spoken except as an example of what is not spoken. To speak is to formulate a belief. Even imperative or exclamatory speech expresses some kind of belief of the speaker, though the belief is not primarily intended to be communicated. A lie which is not believed by the speaker is not felt by him to be informatively spoken, being felt to be spoken only as incorporated in the implied prefix of all speech, viz. the imperative "believe me." It is believed content that is spoken and it is the understanding of what can be spoken that constitutes the theoretic consciousness.

7. Such understanding may not be knowledge, but it involves belief in something as known or to be known. The belief may not be explicitly an awareness of the actual or possible known-ness, but it can always be made explicit as such. The belief in knowledge may be implied in the explicit awareness of unknown-ness. The agnostic or the anti-rationalist or the absolute sceptic is primarily conscious of unknown-ness, but to be conscious of unknown-ness is to be conscious of known-ness also. They may not be said to *know* the unknown as such but they *believe* it and impliedly believe also in something as known, even though it may be speakable only as unspeakable. They are said to present a philosophy so far as they express the theoretic consciousness which implies belief in something as known.

8. All forms of theoretic consciousness as involving the understanding of a speakable are sometimes called thought. Of these, as will appear presently, only one form is literal thought, the others being symbolistic thought which should not be called thought at all. Four forms or grades of thought may be distinguished. They may be roughly called empirical thought, pure objective thought, spiritual thought and transcendental thought. Empirical thought is the theroetic consciousness of a content involving reference to an object that is perceived or imagined to be perceived, such reference being part of the meaning of the content. There are contents that are objective but have no necessary reference to sense-perception and the consciousness of such contents may be called pure objective or contemplative thought. The content of spiritual thought is no object, nothing that is contemplated in the objective attitude, being subjective

in the sense of being appreciated in a subjective or "enjoying" attitude. Transcendental thought is the consciousness of a content that is neither objective nor subjective, the further characterisation of which will come later. The contents of the four grades of thought may be provisionally called fact, self-subsistence, reality and truth. Science deals with fact, the content of empirical thought. Philosophy deals with the last three, the contents of pure thought in the objective, subjective and transcendental attitudes.

9. All contents of the theoretic consciousness are speakable. The so-called grades of thought are really grades of speaking. Fact in science is spoken of as information and understood without reference to the spoken form. It is what need not be spoken to be believed. Speakability is a contingent character of the content of empirical thought, but it is a necessary character of the content of pure philosophic thought. In philosophy, the content that is spoken is not intelligible except as spoken. Pure thought is not thought of a content distinguishable from it and is accordingly sometimes regarded as a fiction, philosophy being rejected as a disease of speech. Philosophical contents are indeed believed to be self-evident and the self-evident means what is independent of the spoken belief of an individual mind. This independence of speaking is, however, a part of their meaning. It is not part of the meaning of a scientific content which is understood without reference at all to the linguistic expression of it.

10. Now a believed content that has necessary reference to the speaking of it is not spoken of as information. Self-subsistence or enjoyed reality or truth is not assertable as fact. Belief in it may be expressed in the form of a judgment, but the form would be only artificial or symbolic. Fact is always expressible as a judgment of the form "A is thus related to B," this being the only judgment-form that is literally intelligible. A judgment of the form "X is," if it expresses belief in a fact of science, is only a periphrasis for a judgment of the above relational form. In "X is," if X stands for "A as related to B", the assertion means either only that A is related to B or that A that is thus related is related to something else. Fact is always a fact related to facts. If anywhere "X is" means something other than the

relational assertion, it means that X is self-subsistent, real or true, which is only an apparent judgment. The subject is here understood as presupposing the predicate. The predicate does not, as in a judgment proper, amplify or explicate the meaning of a subject that is already believed. The subject is here believed as a self-evident elaboration of the predicate that is already believed to be self-evident.

11. Philosophy is such self-evident elaboration of the self-evident and is not a body of judgments. The self-evident is spoken, but is not spoken *of*. Of what is only spoken and contains a necessary reference to the speaking of it there are three forms according as it is spoken in the objective, subjective or trans-cendental attitude. The difference between the first two forms is the difference between the imports of the apparent judgments "The object (-in-general) is" and "I am." In a judgment proper "A *is* thus related·to B," if the word *is* by itself means anything, if in other words the assertion means any content more than "A related to B," the content as isolated would be objectivity. It may be expressed as an apparent judgment "the relation of A and B is." In a judgment proper, the word "is" expresses only the objective attitude of the subject, but in this apparent judg-ment, "is" means an objective content which is self-subsistent but not fact. To express or formulate this content is still, to retain the objective attitude. The attitude is explicitly dropped in saying "I am." The content here also is spoken and not spoken *of*, but it is explicitly understood as not objective and as only apparently objective or symbolised by objectivity. What the word "am" means is not contemplated in the objective attitude, but is subjectively enjoyed and only spoken *as though* it were objectively contemplated. If fact is spoken of and the self-subsistent object is only spoken—both being spoken as *meant*, reality is spoken not as meant but as only *symbolised*.

12. All the three are literally speakable. To say that the object is not the subject and that the latter is symbolised by the former is still to speak literally. The word that is used as symbol is not indeed literally understood, but what is symbolised by it (and that it is symbolised) is literally spoken. The subjective is a positive entity through which the objective is understood. The concept of the object is not reached through a generalisation

of the objective facts of science. Were it not for the direct consciousness and speakability of the subject *I*, the concept of the object would never be precipitated. The first person *I* is the primary instance of a content that necessarily refers to the speaking of it. It is in fact the spoken that is understood as the same as the speaking function. In "I am" then, the predicate is a symbol of a literally spoken subject. What is taken as self-subsistent or real is literally spoken and understood. What, however, is taken as true is not literally understood.

13. How then is truth as beyond reality spoken? To answer the question, the connection between the notions of fact, self-subsistence and reality has to be further elucidated. The denial of each of these is possible. The judgment "A is thus related to B" may be denied in the form "that A is so related is not fact," "That A is so related" is no judgment, but what is nowadays called a proposition. The enunciation and denial of it are possible because we have already a belief in the self-subsistent. If the proposition is understood as not fact, it is because we cannot deny it self-subsistence.[1] So we may deny the self-subsistent in the form "object is not," meaning "What is other than the subjective is not a definite or self-identical content for contemplation"—a recognised philosophical view that is not *prima facie* meaningless. The denial is possible because we already believe in the subjective as enjoyed reality. We may also deny reality in the form "I (as individual subject) am not." This too is *prima facie* intelligible and it represents a new grade of negation, for the individual subject is understood to be real as subject and not as object though it may be individual through some sort of identification with the object. Even as individual, the *I* is enjoyingly believed and the denial of such a content is possible because we have already the notion of truth beyond reality.

14. Taking a sentence of the form "X is," it is a judgment proper if "X," "is" and their combination (or the judgment-form) are each literally understood. Where X stands for the self-subsistent, both X and *is* are literally understood but the

---

[1] The term self-subsistence instead of subsistence is used because we *mean* only in reference to a belief. The believed subsistent is the self-subsistent as meant. A meaning that is not a believed content of one grade is a believed content of a higher grade.

combination is not, since X is intelligible only through *is*. Where
X stands for the (individual) self as enjoyed, it is literally understood, but the word *is* is only an objective symbolism for enjoyed
reality and the combination therefore is also symbolic. Where
X stands for the negation of the (individual) self, it is not literally
understood, because no positive is understood as equivalent to
it. The self is unintelligible except as the subject *I* or as what the
subject *I* is not. There is no consciousness of an absolute or
transcendental self without reference to the subject *I*. If such
a self is understood, it is only as the implication of the enjoyed
I and never by itself. It is indeed positively believed, but there
is no positive formulation of it independent of the notion of *I*.
Thus here X is only symbolically understood and consequently
the word *is* and the judgment-form also are symbolically understood. "Object is" is no judgment, being tautologous as a judgment and "I am" is no judgment because *am* is only symbolism,
but both are literally spoken because the subject is literally
understood as positive. But the sentence "the absolute self is"
is not only no judgment but is not even literally spoken. Still,
it is not meaningless, and symbolises what is positively believed,
viz. truth. What is believed and is not literally speakable (and
is as such undeniable) is truth.

15. So there are the four grades of speakables. There is the
primary distinction between what is only symbolically speakable
and what is literally speakable. The literally speakable comprises
what is spoken of as information and what is only spoken and
not spoken *of*. Of these, what is only spoken is spoken either as
symbolised or as meant. Truth is only symbolically spoken,
reality is literally spoken as symbolised and the self-subsistent
is literally spoken as meant. None of these are spoken *of* as
information, while fact is spoken of as information. These
correspond to what were roughly called empirical, contemplative,
enjoying and transcendental thought. It is only what is spoken
of as information or fact that is or can be meant literally. In
contemplative, enjoying and transcendental thought, the content
is not spoken *of* but is only spoken. If it is put in the judgment
form "X is," the form is only symbolical. In the first two, X
being literally understood, the content though not literally
thought is still said to be literally spoken. In contemplative

thought, the judgment-form is only symbolical, even in enjoying thought, the word *is* is also used symbolically. In transcendental thought, X also being symbolical, "X is" is not only
not literally thought but not also literally spoken.

16. A content that can be literally spoken of is the content
of a judgment. The content of a judgment is information or
fact that is intelligible without reference to the speaking of it. A
content that is necessarily understood in reference to the speaking
of it is in some respect at least symbolically understood and
is not information, fact or content of judgment. Beliefs in science
alone are formulable as judgments and literally thinkable. If a
content is literally thinkable in a judgment, the belief in it
as known is actual knowledge. If it is only symbolically
thinkable, it is said not to be known but to be only believed
as known.

17. Theoretic consciousness was said to be belief in a speakable
content involving belief in a content as known. When the content
is spoken symbolically, it may not be believed as known, but is
at least understood as pointing to what is believed to be known.
In science, the content is spoken literally, and is just the content
that is believed to be known and is a such actually known. In
philosophy, the content is spoken as at least partially symbolised.
The self-subsistent content meant by "object is" where the
judgment-form is symbolical is not actually known and demands
to be known in absorbed contemplation (or intuited) as simply
"object." The real *I* similarly demands to be known not only
without the judgment-form, but also without the objective
intuitive attitude, i.e. in pure enjoyment. Yet in all these cases
something is literally spoken and there is no demand to know
the content without the speaking attitude. Truth, however,
which is not literally speakable at all demands to be known
without even the speaking attitude. The speaking function is
the final form of individual subjectivity and even the pure
form of spiritual thought implies it. Transcendental consciousness
starts by regarding all speaking as only symbolising, and is
accordingly conceived as completed when this symbolising speech
also is dispensed with. What transcendental consciousness
amounts to and whether it remains consciousness at all when
it frees itself from speech or individual subjectivity we do

not know, for absolute or impersonal consciousness is only conceivable in a negative way. All that can be said is that truth which consciousness starts by symbolising continues to be believed and becomes more and more self-evident as the symbolising accomplishes its purpose.

18. Theoretic consciousness is embodied in science and philosophy. Science alone speaks in genuine judgments, the content of which is fact intelligible without reference to speaking and is alone actually known and literally thought. Philosophy deals with contents that are not literally thinkable and are not actually known, but are believed as demanding to be known without being thought. Such contents are understood as self-subsistent object, real subject and transcendental truth. We have accordingly three grades of philosophy which may be roughly called philosophy of the object, philosophy of the subject and philosophy of truth.

III. SCIENCE AND METAPHYSICS

19. The philosophy of the object requires to be further distinguished from science. Both deal with the object understood as what is believed to be known in the objective attitude as distinct from the subjective, enjoying or spiritual attitude. The object in science, however, is understood as fact and not as self-subsistent. By fact is meant what is perceivable or has necessary reference to the perceivable, is speakable in the form of a literal judgment and is believed without reference to the speaking of it. The self-subsistent is an object that has no necessary reference to the perceivable, is not literally expressible in a judgment and is believed only as it is spoken. A speakable is understood in necessary reference either to sense-perception or to the speaking of it. What is believed and understood in necessary reference to the speaking of it is, however, believed as self-evident or independent of the belief of any individual mind. As understood in the objective attitude, the self-evident is the self-subsistent. Fact in science is not believed as self-subsistent, as what would be even if no one believed it.

20. The self-subsistent object is a concept of philosophy, and it is not only not a concept of science, but may be even denied by science. Science has no interest to formulate the concept of

the self-subsistent object; and it apparently believes that the object *must* be knowable or usable. The self-subsistence of the object implies that the object *may be* in its very nature inaccessible to the mind. To contemplate the object as what would be if there were no subject to know it is to believe that it may be unknowable, that in any case it is not known as of right. Science would not only take this suggestion to be gratuitous but would positively deny it. The notion that truth freely reveals itself and is in itself a mystery or even that it is its very nature to reveal itself would be scouted by science as obscurantist or anthropomorphic. To science, there is nothing in the object to make it known; it is just what is known and though it may be unknown, there is no question of its being unknowable.

21. The implicit belief of science then is that the object is knowable and usable *as of right*. This belief is at least questioned in philosophy to which it is an expression of solipsistic self-sufficiency on the part of the subject. In normal practical life, nature is not consciously exploited as a tool but is negotiated in the primitive spirit of sociableness. It is the arrogant exploiting attitude of science towards the object that provokes a self-healing reaction of the spirit in the form of philosophy or some cognate discipline. The spiritual demand is that nature should be contemplated and not merely used or manipulated. Science even as theory is evolved in a practical interest. What is more significant is that its very intellectual method is practical, being the use of actual or ideal *contrivances*. It is the wrong spiritual attitude of science towards the object rather than the so-called contradictions and problems left unsolved in scientific theory—as imagined by the philosopher but never felt by the scientist—that suggests the need for a speculative theory or the object. The concept of the self-subsistent object is the first corrective that philosophy offers of the predatory outlook of the scientific intellect. Realism is a philosophical faith among faiths: the creed of science, if formulated, would be a pragmatist form of solipsistic idealism.

22. The relation between science and the philosophy of the object may be brought out by a reference to certain problems which have been wrongly taken to be philosophical. There is the problem of piecing together the results of the sciences into

a world-view. The synthesis wanted is sometimes imagined to be the generalisation of the primary laws of the sciences into more comprehensive laws. To suppose, however, that it can be accomplished by philosophy without the employment of the distinctive technique and methods of science would be nothing short of a presumptuous folly. If a law as distinct from a loose descriptive concept could be thus established, philosophy might well take in hand the entire work of science. All that can be achieved in this direction is an imaginative description of the world, which would be not only not actual knowledge, but not even a hypothesis that is intended to be turned into knowledge. Nor could it claim the *a priori* certitude of a theory of logic or of metaphysics. Philosophical contents, if not known, are at least theoretically believed, but a world-view of this kind cannot even be claimed to be believed. It can be only an aesthetic view, having at best a suggestive value for science and an illustrative value for philosophy.

23. As an example of such speculation, I may refer to what is called evolutionary philosophy as distinct from the scientific account of evolution. Metaphysics may discuss the general concept of evolution which is but the concept of life and its materialistic, spiritualistic or other interpretations. For this, however, it does not require to piece together the results of science, all the data needed—matter, life and mind—being presented in the knowledge of oneself as in the body. The details and specific generalisations of science are utilised in the so-called philosophy of evolution not as evidence but as only illustrative material intended for visualising the metaphysical theory on the subject. The scientific account of evolution is knowledge or hypothesis, the metaphysic of life in relation to matter and mind is believed, if not known, but the so-called philosophy of evolution, so far as it is different from either, is only an organised presentation of the known or supposed facts of evolution *as though* they constituted the history of a single cosmic life. Cosmic life is not known as a fact, but may still be believed as self-subsisting. The single significant history of this life, however, as rounding off the jagged groupings of facts in science and bridging over the gaps left by it, is only imagined, and is understood to be neither self-evident nor verifiable. The significant

story of cosmic evolution then is neither science nor philosophy, but only a species of imaginative literature.

24. There is another problem, viz. the formulation of the postulates or structural concepts of science, which used to be regarded as a philosophical problem. Pure physics, for example, was taken by Kant as a branch of knowable metaphysic established by deduction from the *a priori* principles of synthetic knowledge. There is a similar confusion of thought at the present day in the romantic philosophy that has sprung up round the physico-mathematical theory of relativity, although here the confusion is of science with philosophy and not of philosophy with science as in the other case. In both the impassable gulf between fact and the self-subsistent is ignored. The so-called axioms of science are but postulates, the formulation of which is the work of science itself. The postulates are hypotheses of a kind which are intended not for the anticipation of facts, but for the organisation of them into a system. They admit of rival hypotheses and may be rejected though not as contradicted by fact, but only as clumsier and less expeditious to work with than the rival hypotheses. Again there is no passage from a postulate of science to a concept of the object in itself. Whether the real world is four-dimensional or is intrinsically indeterminate in its behaviour can never be determined from the basic conceptual devices that happen to organise the facts of science at the present day. The postulates of science neither lead to nor are deducible from any metaphysical conception of the object.

IV. PHILOSOPHY OF THE OBJECT

25. What then has philosophy to say about the object? The objective attitude is understood only in contrast with the subjective or enjoying attitude. What is believed in the objective attitude, viz. the object, need not, however, be understood in reference to the subject. Where the reference to the subject is no part of the meaning of the object, the object is called fact and is dealt with in science. Philosophy deals with the object that is intelligible only in reference to the subject. By subject is meant the individual subject or *I* which is understood in the theoretic consciousness as the speaking function that is symbolised by itself as spoken. The object that has necessary

reference to the speaking of it is the self-subsistent object for philosophy.

26. Philosophy formulates and elaborates the concept of the self-subsistent object. What is common to such object and scientific fact is objectivity which is itself no fact, being only the circumstance of being understood in the objective attitude. This is just the form of the object, the self-subsistent form that is elaborated in logic. It is indeed the form of spoken fact, but as it is the form of the self-subsistent object also, it cannot be said to have necessary reference to fact or the perceivable. Logic as the study of this form is thus no science, but a branch of the philosophy of the object. The form is itself a pure object and is also the form of pure object. The pure object of which logic is the form or shadow is the metaphysical object. The two branches of the philosophy of the object then are logic and metaphysics.

27. Logical form or objectivity is not a concept reached by a comparison of the objects or facts of science. The concept of the object is reached in the first instance by contrast with the subject as the self-evident content of the spiritual consciousness. It is in the theoretic consciousness of the spiritual grade that one is first explicitly conscious of the object as such. In the consciousness of "I am," one appreciates the objective attitude of judgment as distinct from the enjoying attitude and understands it to be assumed only as a necessary make-believe. The consciousness of the asserted being (*am*) or object as such here emerges as the consciousness of a necessary symbol of the subject *I*. That object is symbol of subject implies that object is not subject. The consciousness of negation as such in fact emerges only in this symbolising consciousness. One may be conscious of the object without being explicitly conscious of the subject, but object has no meaning except as the negation and the symbol of the subject. The symbolism here is necessary, and hence when the reference to the subject is only implicit, the object appears as the immediacy of the subject, as implicitly real. Thus object is understood as self-subsistent before fact is understood as object. Hence objectivity or the form of the object is intelligible in reference to the object that is taken to be implicitly real or what is called metaphysical object. Logic in this sense presupposes metaphysics.

28. Metaphysics is philosophy of the object and involves theoretic consciousness in the objective attitude. There is properly speaking no metaphysic of the subject. What passes as such is either the metaphysic of the mind understood as a particular type of object or is no metaphysic but a self-symbolising form of spiritual activity. Metaphysics elaborates the concept of the object in reference to the subject. The rationale of any distinction of metaphysical contents is to be found in an introspectively appreciable distinction within spiritual experience. Even the crude division of the object into matter, life and mind is not intelligible as an inductive classification of fact. That these are *all that is* can at least never be known by induction. The notion of the objective universe is that of an infinite singular and not of a universal; and an *exhaustive* division of such a singular into items that are *all positive* can only be reached if the singular self-evidently unfolds itself in them, if in other words each item means every other item or means the entire system. Such a system is self-evident only as the symbol of an introspective or enjoyed content, as the symbolic analysis of the simple or unitary consciousness of oneself living in the body. The analysis is symbolic because the so-called constituents of the content—matter, life and mind—are intelligible not by themselves but only in reference to this consciousness. Their difference is such as is immediately felt and every apparently factual characterisation of them is understood in reference to this feeling.

29. No metaphysical concept is intelligible without reference to the subject or spirit which itself goes beyond metaphysics. The characteristic abstractions of metaphysics which are supposed on the one hand to be of an "extra high grade," and on the other to be only diseases of speech are really symbolic meanings which derive their whole value for belief from the spiritual experiences that they symbolise. There are no judgments, accordingly, in metaphysics and, paradoxical as it may sound, the metaphysical beliefs are not reached by inference. The elaborate parade of deductive proof in metaphysics is only a make-believe, unless proof is taken, as it is sometimes taken, as the exposition of an unperceived tautology. Metaphysical reasoning is only the *systematic exposition of symbolic concepts*, concepts that are

implicitly taken as symbols of contents that are enjoyingly believed.

30. Fact and the self-subsistent are both literally spoken and in both the believed content is figured by being spoken. Fact is understood as independent of this figuration while the self-subsistent is presented as constituted by it. What is common to these spoken contents is this speech-created form. There are accidental forms of speech, but there are also certain structural forms that are unavoidable in the communication of belief and which are believed to belong to the understood content and not to the speech only. When a fact is spoken, there is a peculiar dualism in the understood content of the meant and the believed, the latter being meant as beyond meaning or as perceivable. When a self-subsistent is spoken, the dualism lapses, the meant and the believed being coincident. The unavoidable forms of speech are constitutive of the meaning. Logic presents a system of speech-created forms of meaning. There may be alternative systems, for logic presupposes metaphysic which presents alternative theories. The fundamental disputes in logic are unavowed metaphysical disputes. Apart from the question of accidental inconsistency within a logical system, whether one logical system is better than another is settled not by logic but by metaphysic. Metaphysical dispute, however, is not settled by logic, for apparently every metaphysical system has its distinctive logic.

31. The suspicion that the subject is not believed in in the same sense as the metaphysical object does not arise within metaphysics. Metaphysics is unaware of the distinction between the self-subsistent and the real. There seems to be nothing wrong, for instance, in the characterisation of matter or mind as real. The distinction is suggested by a contrast of logic with metaphysics. The forms of meaning as discussed in logic are a kind of entity that must be said to be believed in, but it would be absurd to say that they are real. They are believed in as not real and yet not nothing or in other words as self-subsistent. If logical form or objectivity is self-subsistent, has the object of metaphysics any higher status? The distinction of abstract and concrete has meaning only within fact and hence the object cannot mean anything more than objectivity. The metaphysical

object is defined, in contrast with fact, as objectivity or self-subsistent meaning. Metaphysic defines itself into logic.

V. PHILOSOPHY OF THE SPIRIT

32. The suggested distinction of self-subsistence and reality is explicitly verified in the spiritual or enjoying consciousness of objectivity as a symbol of the real subject. As already pointed out, in "I am," *am* meaning self-subsistent being as understood in the objective attitude is the symbol of *I* as understood in the subjective attitude. Enjoying understanding of a content in fact is the consciousness of it as symbolised by an objectively contemplated meaning. Without such a symbolism, the subject would be enjoyed but not enjoyingly understood. It is not only understood like the self-subsistent in necessary reference to the speaking of it: it is understood further as symbolised by its spoken form. This enjoying understanding is what we mean or should mean by introspection. Introspection proper is a form of the theoretic consciousness that implies an abjuration of the objective attitude. Its content is not understood as objective fact nor even as self-subsistent object. The content is not the "interior" of the body which is fact nor is the "mental" which as unintelligible without reference to the speaking of it is a self-subsistent object. The content is *I* or implies *I*, and although it is spoken as though it were an object, it is understood as what object is not, as the speaking subjectivity.

33. To introspect is actually or ideally to speak in the first person. To speak in the first person may not be to be explicitly conscious of the *I* as what the object is not. When it involves such consciousness, it amounts to introspection. Again introspective speaking may or may not involve the explicit consciousness of *being* what is spoken. When it involves such consciousness, it may be called spiritual introspection. The consciousness of being what is spoken (*I*) is itself a new achievement of the subject, its realisation or deepening of being. All introspection involves such achievement: introspection cannot be like the knowledge of objective fact, which leaves the fact unaffected in being. But there is a form of introspection which *apparently* leaves the content thus unaffected, where really there is an alteration of subjective being which is enjoyed only in the non-theoretic way.

This may be taken to be an implicit form of spiritual introspection. Sometimes there is a conscious suspension of theoretic consciousness about such alteration, a deliberate exclusion of it from introspection. In such a case, introspection tends to degenerate into objective consciousness of the mind as distinct from the *I*—what is ordinarily called psychological introspection.

34. The subject *I* is never accepted by itself in spiritual introspection. Something else is always enjoyed along with the subject and enjoyed in reference to it. This may be of three grades. There is in the first place the explicit consciousness of the subject as *unaccountably* embodied, this being the same as the consciousness of the subject as what the object including the mind is not. Next there is the consciousness of personal relation to other selves. Lastly there is the consciousness of the over-personal self. The over-personal self is enjoyingly understood not only in reference to the subject *I* but as implying the specific experience of communion, the felt form of identity with the *I*. Such enjoying identity is what is called concrete identity or identity-in-difference, a relation that is unintelligible in the objective attitude. Identity in the philosophy of the object is conceived as abstract identity of the form "A is A" and there is no place for the *relation* of identity in the sphere of fact. The consciousness of the over-personal self as thus one with the *I* is the religious form of the spiritual consciousness. The study of all contents enjoyed in explicit reference to the subject *I* may be called the philosophy of the spirit.

35. Spiritual consciousness is not mere consciousness of reality but is reality itself. Except in the specifically religious form of it, however, it involves some consciousness of reality as distinct from what may be called empty subjectivity. In the enjoying consciousness of the self as embodied or symbolised by the object, the object is conceived not as self-subsistent, but only as a shadow or symbol of the *I*, the consciousness of the shadow as such being said to be empty. In the consciousness of personal relations—the moral consciousness, for example—*I* and the other person are each not the other, each the symbol of the other, there being an alternation of symbolisms. The other person is to me "another *I*" which taken literally is a contradiction through which alone, however, he is understood. Or I (first person) am

aware of being "this person" (third person) to him, which too is symbolising by a contradiction. Each alternative is real in being but contradictory or empty in meaning or theory. The experience of religious communion or worship is the consciousness of the over-personal reality as symbolised by *I*. The conscious symbolising by *I* is a non-theoretic experience of self-abnegation: it is consciously *being* nought and not consciousness *of I* as nought. What emerges to theoretic religious consciousness is the over-personal reality alone. In this sense the religious consciousness is said to outgrow all empty subjectivity and to be the enjoyed fulness of being.

36. Religious experience as conscious fulness of being is simple and admits of no variation within itself. There is, however, an infinite plurality of unique religious experiences. Their relation is determined by themselves and not by any external reflection. Each experience by its self-deepening gets opposed to or synthesised with other experiences. One experience may enjoy another as a stage outgrown or as in absolute conflict with it, where a third experience may emerge as adjusting them to one another. There is no possibility of systematising them by secular reason and so far as they systematise themselves, they present themselves in many alternative systems. Each experience in fact is a revelation and we believe in a system only so far as it is actually revealed. Extensive internally coherent systems with indefinite boundaries are actually revealed, though there is no *a priori* necessity of a system and still less of a system admitting of no alternative systems. The Hegelian notion of a single and exclusive gradation of religions would appear from this standpoint to be intrinsically irreligious.

37. The theoretic form of a religious system is a philosophy of religion, there being as many forms of this philosophy as there are religious systems. This form expresses itself in the lower grades of philosophy—in the theory of the sub-religious spirit, in the metaphysic of the object and even in logic. Every system of religious philosophy has its distinctive theory of the spirit, metaphysic and logic. The fundamental differences within logical theory are, as has been suggested, implicitly metaphysical, those in metaphysic are implicitly spiritual and those in the theory of the secular spirit are implicitly religious. Religions may

indefinitely multiply and indefinitely get synthesised. So is there indefinite scope for differences and syntheses in philosophical theory in general. There is no question of philosophy progressing towards a single unanimously acceptable solution. All philosophy is systematic symbolism and symbolism necessarily admits of alternatives.

VI. PHILOSOPHY OF TRUTH

38. In religion, there can be no theoretic denial of the subject *I*. In worship, indeed, the subject abnegates itself but the abnegation is there an affair of enjoyed being and not of theory. There is, however, a theoretic consciousness of "I am nought," of the possibility at any rate of the subject or the individual self being unreal. The denial of the *I* is possible because we already believe that the absolute is. The absolute is not the same as the over-personal reality that is enjoyed in religion. It means what the subject *I* is not, but the reality of religious experience while it is enjoyed and symbolised by *I* does not mean such theoretic negation of *I*. What is called the absolute is a positively believed entity that is only negatively understood. It is an entity that cannot be understood as it is believed, and is speakable only by way of symbolism. Reality as apprehended in religion is indeed symbolised by *I*, but so far as it is expressed as a self, it is expressed literally. The positive character of the absolute, however, is expressible only by the negation of *I* (or more accurately by "what I am not") and as such is not literally expressible at all. If then we say that the absolute *is*, we mean by *is* not reality but truth. Reality is enjoyed but truth is not. The consciousness of truth as what is believed in but not understood either in the objective or in the subjective attitude, as not literally speakable at all but speakable only in the purely symbolistic way, is extra-religious or transcendental consciousness.

39. What is believed in and understood as literally unspeakable may be said to be self-revealing. Reality is still literally speakable and may be taken to depend on the speaking for its revelation, though the speaking (which means the *I*) is not there empty subjectivity. Truth is believed or revealed *as* independent of it, as *self*-revealing, what is true being spoken as what the speaking *I* is not. At the same time, to be even symbolically spoken, it

has to be believed as a distinct. As a positive to which even the *I* is but a symbol and therefore nought in itself, it has nothing to be distinguished from and is absolute. If, then, truth as absolute is distinguished, it can only be distinguished from itself. The self-distinction of the absolute cannot mean self-identity as it appears in the religious consciousness in which the identity-in-difference is conceived to be necessary. There is no necessity in this self-distinction. The absolute may be truth or it may be what truth is not or it may be their mere distinction without any unity in the background, which means their indeterminate togetherness which cannot be denied to be either of them. What truth is not and is yet positive is the absolute freedom beyond being (the absolute freedom of the will) and what is indeterminately either truth or freedom is absolute value. There is no sense in speaking of the absolute as the unity of truth, freedom and value. It is *each* of them, these being only *spoken* separately but not *meant* either as separate or as one. The theoretic consciousness of truth, then, is the consciousness of truth as distinct from itself as freedom and from this identity-less self-distinction or value. The absolute as transcending the enjoyed reality of religion is positive being (truth) or positive non-being (freedom) or their positive indetermination (value). The absolute is conceived rigorously as truth in (Advaita) Vedānta. What is loosely called nihilistic Buddhism apparently understands the absolute as freedom. The Hegelian absolute may be taken to represent the indetermination, miscalled *identity*, of truth and freedom which is value. All these views belong to what may be called the transcendental grade of philosophy.

40. This triple absolute is apparently the prototype of the three subjective functions—knowing, willing and feeling. These functions are primarily the self-distinction of the transcendental consciousness. The distinction of the functions does not emerge in the spiritual consciousness. Spiritual experience is simple and integral in its very nature. The consciousness of *I* is not only not the consciousness of a complex unity of these functions, it is not even the consciousness of a unity revealing itself in each of them. It not only does not analyse itself: it supplies no motive for such analysis. The tripartite elaboration of consciousness is not introspective but transcendental. The absolutes reveal them-

selves and the *I* appears trinal only as their shadow or symbolism. As the absolutes are not related into a unity, neither can their subjective shadows be said to be related. The simple *I* has no enjoyed elements or aspects to be related. Nor are the so-called functions intelligible as pure acts or interests *of the I*. They cannot be defined in subjective terms nor can they be taken as unique subjective experiences, being not presented as distinct to introspection at all. Their whole meaning is derived from the self-revealed absolutes.

41. The theory of truth is the theory of the other two absolutes also. At the same time it recognises the possibility of elaborating a primary theory of each of them in reference to the other absolutes. We have shadows of these primary theories in the lower grades of philosophy. The theory of truth, for example, as conceived in its explicit transcendental form has its shadow in the theory of knowledge which belongs to the philosophy of the spirit and in the theory of objective categories which is somewhere intermediate between metaphysics and logic in the philosophy of the object.

COMMON-SENSE EMPIRICISM

by G. C. CHATTERJI

Born March 4, 1894. Professor of Philosophy, Government College,
Lahore

COMMON-SENSE EMPIRICISM

AFTER some twenty years during which one's main intellectual concern has been the study and teaching of Philosophy, one should have thought that one would have worked out a fairly complete and well-rounded system of Philosophical beliefs. When I take stock of my philosophical knowledge, I find that I have nothing like a complete and systematic Philosophy to offer, but instead only a few disconnected and disjointed bits of doctrine, which perhaps can hardly be strung together into a common fabric, and which in any case will leave large gaps and openings through which the cold blast of doubt, and the frost of scepticism, can easily penetrate my philosophic soul. This lack of anything like a philosophical system is not the outcome of mere indolence of spirit and temperamental inaptitude, but is largely the outcome of the course of philosophical study and training I have undergone, and the general trend in which philosophical doctrines themselves have tended to move during the last twenty years that I have been interested in them. But more than anything else it is the experience of my own life and of the world in which my daily lot has been cast, which has helped to shape and mould my attitude on general philosophical problems.

In my early days of philosophical study I was attracted to Pluralistic Theism under the influence of James Ward and William James. Later the study of Bradley's *Appearance and Reality* made me a convert to the doctrine of the absolute, and I was an adherent of this school when at the age of 21 I went to Trinity College, Cambridge, and came under the influence of the great triumvirate of Cambridge, McTaggart, Moore and Russell. Of these three McTaggart was my director of studies for three years and I naturally saw a great deal of him. These were the years of the Great War in which McTaggart seemed to be immersed in intellectual coma, induced by excess of patriotism. He was more concerned to perform his duties as a special constable with zeal and so contribute his share to the national endeavour than to pursue either his own speculations about the nature of existence, or to encourage the youthful philosophical enquiries of a young disciple. McTaggart's mental apathy, more than amply compensated for by his later *Nature of Existence* which came out soon after the war, sent me with a rebound to the opposite camp of Moore and Russell, who, each in his own way, seemed to uphold for me the ideal of philosophical integrity. Moore seemed to be wholly unconcerned with the war, and went on investigating the status of sense-data with a meticulous care which made you doubt that there was a great war in progress, or that only last night a contingent of German aeroplanes had passed over the hooded lights of Cambridge on their way to London. Russell on the other hand was as much absorbed in the war as McTaggart was, only in a different way. He was publishing his essays on *Justice in War Time*, organising the Union of Democratic Control, championing the cause of conscientious objectors, and in a hundred other ways bringing his philosophical learning and analytical genius to the study of social problems, and allaying the fever of patriotism which seemed to threaten the mental balance of war-time England. It was thus that my young soul was weaned from Philosophical Idealism to Realism, for in actual practice the Idealist's Philosophy seemed to me less concerned with ideal ends than the Realist's, and the future not only of Philosophy but of a better life for the individual seemed to lie with them.

The loyalties then engendered have never been shaken, for though I no longer believe that Moore's defence of common sense is either very common or very intelligible, or that Russell's Logical Atomism is anything but a series of barren formulae, I can never return to a faith in a timeless Absolute whose logical perfection can lull us to a spirit of happy acquiescence in the intellectual, social and moral muddle in which man from his finite point of view appears to be involved.

This brief sketch of my own philosophical development is only appended here in order that it may help to throw some light on the all too incomplete fragments of my own Philosophy which I wish now to introduce to my readers. What, then, are the cardinal principles of my own Philosophy?

Philosophy, I believe, springs from some abiding human need or purpose. There is some deep-laid desire, need or craving in man to reflect upon the world and his experience, and to form some sort of a general intelligible plan or explanation of it. By this I do not mean to posit any so-called philosophical instinct in man, nor do I suggest that all men need to be, or even attempt to be philosophers. The prime need or function of life is living itself. At first man is so occupied with the mere maintenance and continuance of life, that he cannot be supposed to squander any of his fitful intelligence on solving the problem of the universe or on his place and destiny in its midst. But as he advances and does not need to spend all his waking hours in the search for food, or sexual satisfaction, or clothing and warmth, he has periods in which his mind is no longer occupied with practical concerns, and he turns his intellectual powers to two main pursuits, Art and Philosophy. Art is the product of the free imagination, Philosophy that of the freed intellect. Between these there is no hard-and-fast distinction or separation, for in Art the imagination makes subsidiary use of the intellect, and in Philosophy the intellect frequently seeks the aid of the imagination. But they are different in their goal or purpose chiefly, for Art seeks to create the beautiful, whereas Philosophy seeks to apprehend the true.

Philosophy, as I understand it, is thus a natural activity of man which springs from the actual conditions of his being and which is intended to satisfy some abiding and permanent need of his nature. This need is theoretical, the need to know and understand himself and the world of which he is a part, and is different from other needs which are practical in character or spring from the free play of imagination.

If this be accepted, it follows that Philosophy cannot divorce itself from life, without risk of becoming a series of sterile formalisms, the indulgence in which becomes mere mental gymnastics. The most fruitful periods of philosophic thought have been those in which Philosophy has remained in intimate contact with life, as witness the great days of Greek Philosophy, whereas Philosophy has always fallen into disrepute wherever it has divorced itself from the real problems of life and devoted itself to artificial subtilities of the intellect, as in the scholasticism of Mediaeval Europe. Much of modern philosophic thought seems to me to be a species of barren formalism, which has no bearing whatsoever on the essential task of Philosophy, which is to reflect upon life and seek to guide and illumine it. I believe that Philosophy is more and more called upon to fulfil this purpose as traditional faiths decline and customary morality loses its hold on the new generation.

The foregoing remarks must not be interpreted as implying any Pragmatic or Humanistic standpoint in Philosophy. I believe that Philosophy is essentially theoretic activity. It is human need and human interest which set the problems which Philosophy must attempt to solve, but any consideration of the nature of the need or interest, and of what will most satisfy that need, has no bearing upon the actual solution of its problems. Philosophy begins in concrete experience, and must return to concrete experience in the character of guide or mentor, but in the actual solution of its problems it must remain unbiased by considerations of utility or subjective satisfaction.

I believe that experience is not only the starting-point of Philosophy, but in a certain sense it is also the criterion and touchstone of every Philosophy. By experience here and elsewhere I mean the actual concrete experience of some finite individual or subject of experience and primarily the philosopher's own and not some Absolute or Universal experience, to the assumption of which he may be led from an analysis and examination of his own experience or by some abstract process of logical construction. Even if such an absolute experience is posited by Philosophy, it is my contention that the starting-point for such an hypothesis is the philosopher's own experience, and the test and criterion of its validity is again his own immediate experience. For if such an hypothesis implies that something which is an actual experience of mine cannot really be what I experience it to be, but something totally different, I contend that such an hypothesis is thereby finally condemned and declared unwarranted. Philosophy cannot legislate to reality, for its business is to examine and investigate the nature of reality, not to create it, out of some supposed imperative of Reason. I reject the Hegelian dictum that the Real is the Rational, if this dictum is interpreted to mean that by examining the supposed requirements of Reason we can arrive at any solution of the problem as to what reality actually is. Hegel calls his

Metaphysical system Logic, implying thereby that it is an *a priori* system, built up through the sole force of Reason. My contention is that Logic supplies the skeleton into which any metaphysical system must be fitted, but that it cannot supply the material, the body of metaphysics, which experience alone can yield.

While I believe that my own experience supplies the raw material for my philosophical speculation and also acts as the criterion or test by which my philosophical constructions have to be finally judged, I do not for a moment believe that my experience is itself the sole Reality, or even that Reality itself can consist of nothing but experiences or physical matters of fact. In other words, I am neither a subjective nor an objective idealist. I believe that Reality does not consist solely of my own experience, because my experience itself is sufficient warrant for the belief that there are other realities besides itself. Every experience that I have is related to some object other than itself, and in the absence of such another could not be what it is. If I am perceiving, or remembering, or desiring, or having an emotion, there is always something that I perceive, or remember, or desire, or have an emotion towards. My experiences are not self-contained or self-generated, but directed towards some object other than themselves, with which they are related by the subject-object relation. I believe that such a theory as that of Hume, which resolves all reality into a flux of immediate experiences, is totally false to experience itself, for every immediate experience contains a reference to something outside itself, in the absence of which the experience itself could not be what it is. What exactly that object or entity is with which each concrete experience of mine brings me in contact, varies with the nature of each individual experience, and it is the business of Philosophy and scientific enquiry to examine and explore the nature of those varied realities. But that such extra immediate realities do exist is warranted by each and every experience. The objects that I cognise, which stir me emotionally, or towards which I strive or aspire, are not constituted by the acts of my cognising, feeling or striving. For if this be denied, then I can neither cognise nor feel, nor strive after, and my experience cannot possess the character which it does, as a matter of fact, actually possess. If I am perceiving a blue patch of colour, then the analysis of my perpetual experience cannot merely consist of the actual content of my act of awareness, for in that case I would not be perceiving a blue patch of colour, but my awareness of it, which is a totally different thing. Further, I can never express the difference between my perception of a blue patch of colour and a red patch of colour merely in terms of awareness. The difference between those two acts lies, not in the nature of character of the acts themselves but in the objects to which each is directed. If there are no patches of blue and red colours, but merely my awareness of them, then I can never have an experience of now perceiving blue, now red, and now some other colour. What distinguishes one act of perception from the other is not the mental processes involved but the variety of objects to which they are directed. Perception thus itself implies the existence of extra-immediate entities or objects.

What I have attempted to demonstrate about perception can equally be demonstrated with regard to other forms of experience, but I will take specially the case of feeling, as it is chiefly to this form of experience that self-sufficiency and immediacy have generally been ascribed. For example, Bradley and others who have admitted the duality of subject-object have urged that this is a peculiar defect of the finite consciousness, and have in fact employed it as a ground for rejecting that consciousness as a mere appearance and not an ultimate reality. They have posited an Absolute consciousness in which the distinction of subject and object has disappeared, and to which they have ascribed a state of consciousness analogous to feeling in ourselves, in which they contend that subjectivity or immediacy is practically obliterated. I do not know what feeling as experienced by the Absolute may be like, but as experienced by myself I am absolutely certain that it is invariably directed towards an object, and in the absence of such an object it simply could not exist. In the first place I would like to urge that philosophical discussions about feeling are generally directed towards some abstract feeling of pure pleasure or pure pain, which it has not been my privilege to experience. All the feelings that I experience are usually extremely complicated and confused, and though they may have elements of pleasure and pain mixed up in them, are never solely constituted by what is called pure feeling tone. I prefer, therefore, to speak of emotions rather than of feelings. The emotions I experience are very varied in range, extending from the primitive instinctive emotions of fear, anger, disgust and so on, to highly complex and derivative emotions such as those which are generally described as aesthetic, moral and religious emotions. In every case, whether the feelings be primitive or derived, there is always some object in relation to which I have that emotion, and in the absence of which I could not continue to have that emotion. If I am angry, it is always someone or something which has made me angry, and if you could only convince me that such a person or thing does not exist, my anger must of necessity evaporate. If I could only believe that no person or circumstance is obstructing the gratification of my wishes, the consummation of my ambitions, anger would be a passion wholly unknown to me. Similarly, if there was nothing besides my own immediate consciousness, I could experience neither love nor hate, nor aesthetic appreciation, nor moral indignation or fervour, nor religious ecstasy and devotion. Such a consciousness would indeed be an evaporation of experience itself, an absence of consciousness, a state of nothingness, "a dreamless sleep and a forgetting," which indeed I am told is the goal and ambition of many a mystic especially in the East, but which at any rate I have never experienced, and which, if it does exist, must indeed be mute, unutterable, unponderable, and that of which Philosophy can have no cognisance. It is not for me to deny the existence of such obscure and abnormal experiences, whether generated artificially by the administration of certain drugs, or the practice of certain religious exercises and rites, or occurring spontaneously without external aid, but I would urge that unless such experiences can be brought under the scope of scientific psychology for investigation and explanation, they cannot be cited as evidence in support of any particular theory of the general nature of reality. Philosophy at the present moment can only take into account such experiences as are the common possession of ordinary humanity, and it is on the basis of such experiences alone that any rational or scientific theory of the world can be constructed. Experience then gives us sufficient warrant to escape from the coils of solipsism, or subjective idealism. On the basis of my experience I am entitled to believe that a world extraneous to my own consciousness exists, for at each point of my consciousness this larger world of external reality breaks in upon the chamber of my inner consciousness, disturbs and determines its flow, and it is towards this that my own emotions and strivings are constantly directed. What is the nature of this trans-subjective world, and in what manner the world of my own subjective experience is related to it, is the essential problem of Philosophy.

A little earlier in this paper I made two denials, firstly that reality consists solely of my own experience, and secondly that the world of external reality consists solely of other psychical matters of fact. It is to this second denial that I must now turn. No theory has been so generally held in Philosophy as the theory of Idealism, which holds that Reality is essentially spiritual in character, and that nothing but spirits and their experiences exist. Such Idealistic theories have been either singularistic, like those of Hegel, Bradley and others, or Pluralistic, such as that of Leibniz, while others seem to have adopted a midway position difficult to define, such as Lotze and Ward, who have attempted to build a bridge between Singularism and Pluralism. Into the various controversies between the different schools of Idealism I do not propose to enter, since what I am concerned to deny is the assumption which all schools of Idealism make in common, namely, that reality is mental, or psychical matter of fact and nothing which is not mental can ever be real. Arguments urged in support of this view in the past were generally directed against the doctrine of materialism as held by eighteenth-century mechanical science. These may be called negative arguments for Idealism. There are also certain positive arguments for Idealism which do not merely rely upon the alleged non-existence of matter, but also bring forward certain positive considerations in favour of the belief that nothing but mind can exist. Most Idealists, however, make use of both types of argument, and in what follows I shall make no hard-and-fast distinction between them. We may take the arguments used by Berkeley as typical of one school of Idealists. He urges that what I directly know in perception are merely sensations, and sensations being mental, I have no direct knowledge of any supposed physical reality which may be accepted as their cause. He admits that sensations are not spontaneous or self-caused, but holds that their cause cannot be a non-mental material substance which Locke had described as a "We know not what," but must also be mental, viz., ideas in the mind of God. He does not deny an objective world order but holds that this order and arrangement is nothing, but the ideas which God is presenting to finite minds. But Berkeley's argument if strictly enforced leads to Hume's Phenomenalism and not to his own pan-psychism. It starts with a fundamentally wrong analysis of perception, namely that any act of perception is to be simply analysed into a mental content and implies no reference to an object external to itself. It is true that Berkeley contradicts himself when he proceeds to posit an external cause or source of sensations, even though he regards this cause to be mental. Against his view I can only urge that when I perceive a blue patch of colour, what I am perceiving is a patch of blue colour, and that this is quite different from my act of perceiving, and also totally different from any act of perception on the part of any other being. I do not perceive, as Berkeley seems to imply, an idea of a blue patch of colour in the mind of God. I have ideas myself, and I am some-times aware that other people also have certain ideas. But neither my own ideas nor those of other people when known to me appear as "this patch of colour" which I am now seeing, "this hard surface" I am now touching, and so on. It is con-ceivable that a Being such as God exists, it is conceivable, further, that God has experiences similar to my own, but if God perceives the world, I would contend, as I did in the case of my own experiences, that God could only do so if the world as a fact extraneous to his act of awareness of it actually existed. If the world of nature is identified with God's act of perceiving it, then it follows that there is no world which he can perceive, and consequently there cannot even be the act of perceiving it, and so God's mind is empty, which contradicts the assumption from which we began. Berkeley's argument, therefore, fails to prove that the world of nature which I perceive is really mental. Certain other philosophers, such as Hegel, and, following him,

Bradley, Taylor and others, have urged that Reality must be mental or spiritual, because the very concept of matter, space, time and other categories in terms of which we try to interpret an extra-mental reality are self-contradictory. These contentions seem to me unconvincing, because not only are the contradictions pointed out by these philosophers largely of their own invention, but what is more, they condemn with equal emphasis the categories in terms of which we seek to interpret mental and spiritual phenomena in so far as they come within the range of our own experience. Bradley, for example, by pointing out contradictions in our concept of time, of discursive reasoning, of self and not-self, good and evil, and so on, arrives at the conclusion that finite experience and the finite self also are mere appearances. I consider, therefore, that in his Philosophy Matter and Mind are really on a par, and the Absolute which he posits is no more a spiritual or psychical Being than he is a chunk of boundless space. I have already urged that I am not prepared to accept any such hypothesis which constrains me to regard my own experience as an illusion and to substitute in its place some supposed reality for which I can find no warrant in my experience. In the present connection I would only urge that Absolute Idealism is not a Pan-Psychical theory but one which is indifferent alike to Materialism and Idealism, and really more akin to what Mr. Russell calls Neutral Monism.

My denial of Idealism must not be interpreted as implying any adherence to the opposed doctrine of materialism. I believe that experience reveals to me in Perception that external nature exists, but that the very variety and richness of this experience also implies a plurality of attributes in the objects of nature, which cannot be reduced either to my own ideas or to those of some other mind or minds, nor merely to qualitatively simple atoms behaving in accordance with simple mechanical laws. The determination of the exact properties and laws of external nature I believe is the task of Physical Science, and Philosophy has no direct concern with it. Philosophy is concerned with Physical Science only in the sense in which it is concerned with each and every science. This concern is twofold: firstly in a formal respect, since every science must conform to certain logical standards, which standards are arrived at after philosophical analysis of the concepts and categories employed by a science, and secondly in a more material respect, since Philosophy must interpret the generalisations and conclusions of every science in terms of the actual experience from which their scientific investigation first originates. Each phase of my concrete experience, therefore, gives rise to certain scientific as well as to certain philosophical problems. In every phase of my experience I am in contact with some reality extraneous to my own experience, and it is the business of the several sciences to investigate in detail the nature of these realities, and the business of Philosophy to interpret the conclusion of each individual science, as well as to form a synthesis of the conclusions of the different sciences so as to form some consistent and harmonious theory of my experience as a whole. The philosophy of Nature, therefore, is really the Philosophy of Physical Science, and can only be built upon the body of detailed knowledge which physical science is accumulating from day to day. Since scientific knowledge is itself progressive and unstable, any Philosophy of Nature which we build upon this foundation must itself be tentative and capable of adjustment to new discoveries.

What I have said with regard to external nature applies equally to the world of Mind. Just as perceptual experience reveals that there exists a world of nature extraneous to itself, so do I know through experience that other selves similar to my own exist, influence my experiences, and in turn are influenced by what I experience. The knowledge of other minds has involved Philosophy in difficulties even greater than those connected with external nature. It has been urged that if I know nature at best at second-hand, my knowledge of other minds is still more remote, for I know them only through their bodies, which are part of the already doubtful world of external reality. The problem has become still more complicated by difficulties with regard to the relation of body and mind, for it has been urged that since body and mind are totally divergent from each other, and interaction between them inconceivable, it is still more impossible that the knowledge of my neighbour's body could convey to me any knowledge with regard to his mind. I believe, however, that all those difficulties are of the philosopher's own making.

I will begin by admitting that so far as my experience goes, my knowledge of other minds is dependent upon knowledge of their bodies. Your bodies are the media through which I know that you are here, that you are listening to me, approving or disapproving of what I say. It is true that if there was a remitting apparatus here, others whose bodies I cannot see could be "listening in" to what I am saying. But in this case also the communication of one mind with another is through some bodily organ or other, and through the aid of some external agents. It is my lips which utter my thoughts, the air waves which communicate the movement to the transmitting and receiving apparatus, and the listener's ears which in the last resort convey my thoughts to his mind. It has been urged that there are instances in which one mind can communicate with another without the intervention of any bodily media, such as is claimed in telepathy or alleged communications received from disembodied spirits. Such phenomena, however, are admittedly outside the range of normal everyday experience, and still await the verdict of scientific psychology. At any rate, they do not afford any solution of our ordinary knowledge of other selves, for we all claim to possess such knowledge, while we do not lay any claim to telepathic or other forms of supernatural contacts with living or departed spirits. If we believe that we know other minds we must admit that we know them through our own and their bodies and consequently that minds can act upon bodies and vice versa. I believe, therefore, that the difficulties urged against interaction of body and mind are imaginary, and result from false abstractions with regard to the nature of body and of mind, and a misconception with regard to what is really meant by interaction in this connection. I contend that we ought to make our start from the fact of inter-action of body and mind and so proceed to conceive of body and of mind, as to permit of such interaction. In other words, the experience of body and mind relation is the datum from which we should start and proceed to form our notions of the living body and the human mind. Why philosophers have found the Body-Mind problem insoluble, is because they have started from an abstract conception of what physical bodies are and what mind is, and have so defined each of them, that their interaction is made impossible. At all grades of its manifestation, mind so far as it comes within human ken, be it the mind of a frog or that of a philosopher, seems to be embodied, and it is only through the medium of its body that it can communicate with other minds or receive communications from them.

I believe that the hypothesis of Emergent Evolution does enable us to approach the problem of body-mind interaction in a more hopeful attitude than under the guidance of the old-fashioned theories of materialism or Idealism. If we conceive of nature as a procession of events beginning with simple elements, we can conceive how, at different stages of nature's evolution, new characteristics should emerge in complex wholes which were not discernible nor predictable from a mere consideration of the simple elements, of which such wholes are composed. We can then regard life as an *emergent* property of inorganic nature and mind as an *emergent* property of organic nature.

Such a view of nature is fully in harmony with the teachings of modern Physics, which no longer conceives of matter as inert homogeneous stuff distributed at various points in space, possessing indestructible properties, to which time can bring neither dissolution nor change. In place of this static world, modern science conceives of nature as a realm of ceaseless activity, with no passive substratum, composed of self-identical bits of matter. Instead of a space which is empty, and time which is irrelevant, it regards nature as a progression of events in space-time, which may be isolated for purposes of observation and abstraction, but which are woven together in an indissoluble stream pressing forward to eternity. Science merely takes cross sections of this eternal stream of moving events, isolating a set of agitations which betray a superficial stability and in the observation of which it can ignore the influence exerted upon them by environmental conditions.

Emergence of new attributes is a common feature of our everyday experience. The butterfly emerges from the cocoon, the completed house from the bricks and mortar, the finished symphony from the conflicts and struggles of the composer's soul. Here is indeed the creative evolution of Bergson, but not conceived as a process of pure change somehow entangled in an illusory matter, but more after the pattern of Aristotle where form is something which emerges in matter, and without matter would remain unrealised and merely potential.

I use the concept of *emergence* as descriptive rather than explanatory. That new and unpredictable properties emerge in nature through the intermingling of previously known elements is a conclusion forced upon us by the facts observed in experience. But as to why such properties as *life* and *mind* should emerge in the evolutionary progression of nature, we are not in a position to explain. It is true that Lloyd Morgan and others who have introduced the conception of Emergence and emphasised the creative element in nature have used it as an argument for the teleological character of the universe as a whole, and have urged that such a universe must necessarily imply the existence of a Creator who is himself outside the evolutionary process, but whose purpose the universe embodies. Such a conclusion seems to me very inadequately grounded on the extremely narrow range of phenomena actually observed, and further to gloss over fundamental difficulties inherent in the very conception of a timeless reality, which is yet indissolubly bound up with the spatio-temporal order. Given the Deity eternal and immutable, there seems no reason why the world of finite experience should exist at all. The inevitable consequence of such an assumption is the rejection of my own immediate experience as illusory, thus destroying the very foundation on which all philosophical construction must necessarily rest. The concept of Emergence, while it does not close the possibility of some form of Theism as a possible hypothesis of the origin of the universe, does not logically imply any Theistic assumptions, and in any case would involve a complete recasting of Theological Dogma, just as it requires a modification of the categories of Physics and Psychology.

In what manner the theory of Emergent Evolution requires us to modify our previous notions of space, time, matter, mind and evolution are problems of supreme importance which cannot be touched upon here. I give preference to it only because, unlike its alternatives, it does not require me to reject the verdict of my experience, but merely to modify the concepts in terms of which I have been wont to explain that experience.

The detailed study of Mind is the subject matter of Psychology, just as the detailed study of nature is the subject of Physical Science. Psychology I regard as an independent science, but one which gives rise to philosophical problems similar to those of other sciences. But Psychology is in a sense more intimately connected with Philosophy, since its subject matter is that experience which is also the starting-point of philosophical reflection and the criterion of philosophical construction. But Psychology cannot take the place of Philosophy, for it deals merely with the mental life of the individual, while experience implies realities beyond and outside that experience and of which Philosophy must take note.

I turn now to a third aspect of the world of my experience, the aspect of value. My experience not only convinces me that there is an external nature which I contemplate, and other selves with whom I communicate, but I also *approve* or *disapprove* of things which I experience, persons whom I know, acts which I perform, or observe others performing. This attitude of appraisement is quite distinct from the attitude of contemplation or cognitive awareness. When I ask does "X" exist, I am asking a question which is quite different from the question, ought "X" to be, or is "X" good or bad. The attributes of value in terms of which I appraise things are moral as well as aesthetic. I attribute goodness to certain things, badness to others, beauty to certain things, ugliness to others. With regard to these value judgments of mine, there are two points which I wish to make clear from the very beginning. In the first place I do not believe that value is in any way derivative from existence. That is, I do not believe that if a thing really exists it follows from the fact of its existence that it is good or beautiful. Conversely, I also believe that existence is not derivative from value. If I hold that something is good, and rightly hold that it is so, it does not follow from this that therefore that thing necessarily exists. If I believe that "X" exists, it does not follow from this that "X" is good. If on the other hand I believe that "X" is good, it does not follow from this that "X" necessarily exists. To take a concrete illustration, Mill believed that all men do as a matter of fact always desire pleasure. He proceeded to infer from this that therefore all men ought to desire pleasure. But because all men do actually desire pleasure, it does not follow that they ought to do so. I can admit the first part of Mill's so-called proof of Hedonism, while totally denying his conclusion. Following Professor G. E. Moore, we may call this kind of fallacy the Naturalistic Fallacy. But many philosophers have committed an opposite fallacy, which is to infer existence from goodness. That is, they have tried to show that such and such a conclusion about reality is very good if true, and have proceeded to assume that therefore reality must actually be so, or that such and such a conclusion about reality is extremely bad, and must therefore be false. Thus it has been argued that if human life does not survive after death, the world would be a very bad place, and therefore we are entitled to believe that human life does survive after death.

The attempt to ground existential conclusions in value premises is parallel with the Naturalistic Fallacy and might be called the Ethical Fallacy. Just as moralists have often committed the Naturalistic Fallacy, so have metaphysicians frequently committed the ethical fallacy.

The second point which I wish to make clear is that when I attribute goodness or beauty to anything, the goodness or beauty is not something in my mind, but in the object which I judge to be good or beautiful. That is, I believe that value is an objective and not a subjective property. Many philosophers have held that value is subjective, in the mind of the person who makes the judgment and not in the things which he values. Many kinds of arguments have been used by philosophers in support of this view, but they have chiefly relied upon the variability of Ethical and Aesthetic standards. That a Zulu's idea of what ought to be done or not done, what ought to be admired or not admired, is very different from that of a civilised man, is too obvious to be denied. But even in the same age and clime, and what is more, very often with the same individual, judgments of taste and approval show considerable variations. But this variability of value judgments does not prove that value is merely a subjective attitude, and connotes no objective properties in things.

It is admitted that man's Ethical and Aesthetic consciousness undergoes a process of evolution, just as his sensory consciousness has been gradually evolved through his prehuman ancestors.

But just as the colours I see, the sounds I hear, are not merely mental contents, but objects apprehended by me, so also the goodness I approve of, or the beauty I admire, are not mere subjective feelings, but objective realities. To reduce value to a subjective state or feeling of the mind is to contend that valuation is an illusion, and that there is no sense in saying that Jesus Christ was a better man than Nero, or the Taj Mahal of Agra more beautiful than the latest excrescence of commercialised architecture.

Such a theory seems to me wholly false to that individual experience which I hold to be the starting-point and the criterion of all philosophising.

It has been urged that value is something which belongs to consciousness alone, and nothing but some experience, or person as the subject of experiences, can in the last resort be judged to be good or bad. Obviously such a theory cannot apply to beauty, for beauty is frequently ascribed to corporeal things, such as pictures, statues and other objects of art. It is, therefore, goodness alone which it is intended to confine to sentient experience. The question is to some extent purely academic, for I believe that the things at any rate of great intrinsic value are all connected with experience or are the subjects of experience, but at the same time I hold that the mind is itself embodied, and if the corporeal aspect of mind is divorced from it, I believe that the value of such wholes would greatly diminish if it did not altogether disappear. For example, I believe that love between persons is one of the greatest good, but all the persons whom I love have a body, and I cannot myself differentiate between my love for their bodies and my love for their spiritual personalities. That I should love a person's spiritual being and at the same time hate or be indifferent to that person's physical being seems to be an impossibility.

The analysis and examination of men's evaluating experiences I regard as the subject matter of the sciences of Ethics and Aesthetics, and conceive the relation of these sciences with Philosophy on lines analogous to those I have already indicated with regard to the other sciences.

I will conclude with a brief reference to man's religious experience. By religion I mean the attitude which the individual adopts with regard to the ultimate reality of which he conceives himself to be a part, and with which he is related in all aspects of his being, be they cognitive, conative or affective. The object of Philosophy and of religion is the same, but whereas Philosophy is merely my theory of Reality, Religion is the total response of my whole personality towards this same reality.

This definition would include every positive religion, for all religions have a credal element, that is, consist of dogmas with regard to the nature of reality, inculcate an emotional attitude towards that ultimate reality, and evoke a particular conative attitude in relation to it. It would include also the attitude of many of those who while not adhering to any positive religion, yet claim that they have a religious life of their own. It would, however, exclude all people whose religion merely consists of conformity to certain traditional ritual and social practices, but whose thoughts, feelings and emotions are in no way deeply affected by such observances.

There are many who believe that religion can provide a short cut to reality which enables us to dispense with the devious and uphill path to which Philosophy points. In religion, it is claimed, we have an intuitive and immediate knowledge of that ultimate reality which Philosophy seeks. Such a claim may rest either on a direct experience of the protagonist of this view, or a claim on behalf of a religious leader or founder, to whom such truths are said to be revealed. I do not myself believe in the validity of such claims. I admit the place of intuition in my apprehensions of reality. But intuition is the starting-point for philosophical reflection, not its culminating and completing point. Perceptual experience is thus an intuition of external reality, and communication between minds an intuition of other selves. But such intuitions need to be analysed by the respective sciences of Physics and Psychology, and then interpreted by Philosophy before man's theoretic interest in the external world or in the world of mind can be satisfied. So also with religious intuitions. That there are specifically religious experiences which are genuine, must be admitted by all unbiased observers, but that the interpretation placed upon those experiences by the person experiencing them is necessarily valid is an extravagant claim which every adherent of any particular religion himself denies to all his rivals. I place religious experience on a par with the other aspects of human experience, so far as it claims to bring me knowledge of a reality extraneous to itself. It supplies the raw material of scientific and philosophical knowledge, but cannot dispense with their aid, any more than perception can dispense with the aid of physical science or a philosophy of nature. Religious experience, according to my view, is thus a fit subject for psychological study and investigation, after which the findings of the psychology of religion must be fitted into our synthetic view of reality as a whole, as in the case of the other sciences.

What then is the religious attitude I can maintain consistently with the Philosophy I have been advocating? Taking my start from my own experience, I have contended that experience brings me in contact with three phases of objective reality, which I have called external Nature, other Minds and Values. I have urged that our knowledge of these is the problem of special sciences, which themselves are incomplete, and that their interpretation and synthesis, which is the special task of Philosophy, must therefore itself be tentative and progressive. Our Philosophy must therefore be lacking in finality, for while rejecting certain theories as most decidedly irreconcilable with the dicta of experience, it can only express a provisional preference in favour of others which seem more in conformity with that experience. Thus we cannot offer any explanation of the origin, destiny and future of our own lives, or of that of the universe of which we are a part. Our knowledge is everywhere incomplete, and both the world of inner experience, as well as the world of external nature, are like great books, of which humanity has as yet only scanned a few scattered pages somewhere in the middle. The cardinal dogma of our religion must therefore be a suspense of judgment on final issues, an ardent search for the advancement of that little knowledge of the great unknown which we already possess, and a determination to hold fast to whatever of truth we have perceived, whatever of goodness or of beauty our souls have grasped. Ours is but a little day, for out of the great unknown we come, and into a still vaster unknown we pass away. But in our little fitful day the gods have given us the gift of laughter, of human friendship, and the vision of beauty both in Nature and in Art. What if we ourselves are mortal, our laughter but the prelude of tears, love's brief transport the herald of approaching doom, and beauty but the echo of a dying song? Shall we refuse the gifts which the gods bring us, for brief must be the time in which we can enjoy them and mortality the fate of all we prize! Shall not our own mortality teach us to treasure all the more the good things that life brings us, and the very niggardliness of fortune enhance the value of its gifts? And if sorrow, or grief, or loss be our portion these also we shall bear with what of fortitude we can summon, for these also are but transitory, and in any case rebellion and false expectation will but enhance our own afflictions. And if we have wooed with any ardour that coy maid, Philosophy, she also will come to our aid, and by teaching us to lose the personal in the impersonal pursuit of remoter ends, help us to preserve that sanity and forbearance, in the face of good fortune or ill fortune alike, which has been from times immemorial her reward to her devotees.

ON THE PERTINENCE OF PHILOSOPHY

by ANANDA K. COOMARASWAMY

BORN 1877, in Ceylon, of an English mother and Hindu father (the late Sir Muthu Coomaraswamy). Educated in England, graduated at London University (D.Sc. in botany and geology), Fellow of University College, London; was Director of the Mineralogical Survey of Ceylon, 1903-6, and for the last seventeen years a member of the staff of the Museum of Fine Arts, Boston, being now "Fellow for Research in Indian, Persian and Muhammadan Art," and also a Vice-President of the India Society, London, the Indian Society of Oriental Art, Calcutta, and of the American Oriental Society, U.S.A., and a correspondent of the Archaeological Survey of India.

ON THE PERTINENCE OF PHILOSOPHY

"Wisdom uncreate, the same now as it ever was, and the same to be for evermore."—St. Augustine, *Confessions*, ix. 10.

"Primordial and present Witness."—Prakāśânanda, *Siddhāntamuktāvali*, 44.

I. DEFINITION AND STATUS OF PHILOSOPHY, OR WISDOM

To discuss the "problems of philosophy" presupposes a definition of "philosophy." It will not be contested that "philosophy" implies rather the love of wisdom than the love of knowledge, nor secondarily that from the "love of wisdom," philosophy has come by a natural transition to mean the doctrine of those who love wisdom and are called philosophers.[1]

Now knowledge as such is not the mere report of the senses (the reflection of anything in the retinal mirror may be perfect, in an animal or idiot, and yet is not knowledge), nor the mere act of recognition (names being merely a means of alluding to the aforesaid reports), but is an abstraction from these reports, in which abstraction the names of the things are used as convenient substitutes for the things themselves. Knowledge is not then of individual presentations, but of types of presentation; in other words, of things in their intelligible aspect, i.e. of the being that things have in the mind of the knower, as principles, genera and species. In so far as knowledge is directed to the attainment of ends it is called practical; in so far as it remains in the knower, theoretical or speculative. Finally, we cannot say that a man knows wisely, but that he knows well; wisdom takes knowledge for granted and governs the movement of the will with respect to things known; or we may say that wisdom is the criterion of value, according to which a decision is made to act or not to act in any given case or universally. Which will apply not merely to external acts, but also to contemplative or theoretical acts.

Philosophy, accordingly, is a wisdom about knowledge, a *correction du savoir-penser*. In general, philosophy (2)[2] has been

---

[1] It is not pretended to lay down a final definition of philosophy.

[2] Our numbering of the philosophies in inverse order as (2) and (1) is because Aristotle's First Philosophy, viz. Metaphysics, is actually prior in logical order of thought, which proceeds from within outwards.

held to embrace what we have referred to above as theoretical or speculative knowledge, for example, logic, ethics, psychology, aesthetic, theology, ontology; and in this sense the problems of philosophy are evidently those of rationalisation, the purpose of philosophy being so to correlate the data of empirical experience as to "make sense" of them, which is accomplished for the most part by a reduction of particulars to universals (deduction). And thus defined, the function of philosophy contrasts with that of practical science, of which the proper function is that of predicting the particular from the universal (induction). Beyond this, however, philosophy (I) has been held to mean a wisdom not so much about particular kinds of thought, as a wisdom about thinking, and an analysis of what it means to think, and an enquiry as to what may be the nature of the ultimate reference of thought. In this sense the problems of philosophy are with respect to the ultimate nature of reality, actuality or experience; meaning by reality whatever is in act and not merely potential. We may ask, for example, what *are* truth, goodness and beauty (considered as concepts abstracted from experience), or we may ask whether these or any other concepts abstracted from experience have actually any being of their own; which is the matter in debate as between nominalists on the one hand and realists, or idealists, on the other.[1] It may be noted that, since in all these applications philosophy means "wisdom," if or when we speak of philosophies in the plural, we shall mean not different kinds of wisdom, but wisdom with respect to different kinds of things. The wisdom may be more or less, but still one and the same order of wisdom.

As to this order, if knowledge is by abstraction, and wisdom about knowledge, it follows that this wisdom, pertaining to things known or knowable, and attained by a process of reasoning or dialectic from experimental data, and neither being nor claiming to be revealed or gnostic doctrine, in no way transcends thought, but is rather the best kind of thought, or, let us say, the

[1] This is, for example, the matter in debate as between Buddhist and Brahmanical philosophers. For the nominalist, the ultimate forms, ideas, images or reasons are merely names of the counters of thought and valid only as means of communication; for the realist (idealist) the ultimate forms are "realities" dependent upon an inherent in being, i.e. real in their being and nominal only in the sense "only logically distinguishable."

truest science. It is, indeed, an excellent wisdom, and assuming a good will, one of great value to man.[1] But let us not forget that because of its experimental, that is to say statistical basis, and even supposing an infallible operation of the reason such as may be granted to mathematics, this wisdom can never establish absolute certainties, and can predict only with very great probability of success; the "laws" of science, however useful, do nothing more than resume past experience. Furthermore, philosophy in the second of the above senses, or human wisdom about things known or knowable, must be systematic, since it is required by hypothesis that its perfection will consist in an accounting for everything, in a perfect fitting together of all the parts of the puzzle to make one logical whole; and the system must be a *closed* system, one namely limited to the field of time and space, cause and effect, for it is by hypothesis about knowable and determinate things, all of which are presented to the cognitive faculty in the guise of effects, for which causes are sought.[2] For example, space being of indefinite and not infinite extent,[3] the wisdom about determinate things cannot have any application to whatever "reality" there may or may not belong to non-spatial, or immaterial, modes, or similarly, to a non-temporal mode, for if there be a "now," we have no sensible experience of any such thing, nor can we conceive it in terms of logic. If it were attempted by means of the human wisdom to overstep the natural limits of its operation, the most that could be said would be that the reference "indefinite magnitude" (mathematical infinity) presents a certain analogy to the reference "essential infinity" as postulated

[1] Common sense is an admirable thing, as is also instinct, but neither of these is the same as reason, nor the same as the wisdom that is not about human affairs, but "speculative," i.e. known in the mirror of the pure intellect.

[2] When a cause is discovered, this is called an explanation. But each cause was once an effect, and so on indefinitely, so that our picture of reality takes the form of a series of causes extending backward into the past, and of effects expected in the future, but we have no empirical experience of a now, nor can we explain empirically how causes produce effects, the assumption *post hoc propter hoc* being always an act of faith.

[3] As is very elegantly demonstrated by St. Thomas, *Sum. Theol.*, i, q. 7, a. 3, cf. q. 14, a. 12, *ad.* 3; his "relatively infinite" being our "indefinite" (*ananta*). incalculable (*asaṁkhya*) but not placeless (*adeśa*) nor wholly timeless (*akāla*).

in religion and metaphysics, but nothing could be affirmed
or denied with respect to the "isness" (esse) of this infinite
in essence.

If the human wisdom, depending upon itself alone ("rationalism"), proposes a religion, this will be what is called a "natural
religion," having for its deity that referent of which the operation
is seen everywhere, and yet is most refractory to analysis,
viz. "life" or "energy." And this natural religion will be a
pantheism or monism, postulating a soul (*anima*, "animation")
of the universe, everywhere known by its effects perceptible
in the movements of things; amongst which things any distinction of animate and inanimate will be out of place, inasmuch
as animation can be defined rationally only as "that which is
expressed in, or is the cause of, motion." Or if not a pantheism,
then a polytheism or pluralism in which a variety of animations
("forces") is postulated as underlying and "explaining" a
corresponding variety of motions.[1] But nothing can be affirmed
or denied as regards the proposition that such animation or
animations may be merely determinate and contingent aspect
of a "reality" indeterminate in itself. Expressed more technically,
pantheism and polytheism are essentially profane conceptions,
and if recognisable in a given religious or metaphysical doctrine,
are there interpolations of the reason, not essential to the religious
or metaphysical doctrine in itself.[2]

On the other hand, the human wisdom, not relying on itself
alone, may be applied to a partial, viz. analogical, exposition
of the religious or metaphysical wisdoms, these being taken
as prior to itself. For although the two wisdoms (philosophy (2)
and philosophy (1)) are different in kind, there can be a formal
coincidence, and in this sense what is called a "reconciliation

---

[1] Science differs from animism only in this respect, that while science
assumes forces in the sense of blind wills, animism (which is also a kind
of philosophy) personifies these forces and endows them with a free will.

[2] Pantheism is more commonly predicated of a given doctrine merely
by imputation, either with unconsciously dishonest intention or by
customary usage uncritically perpetuated. In every case the observer
presumed to be impartial should consider the doctrine itself, and not what
is said of it by hostile critics. On the general impropriety of the term
"pantheism" in connection with the Vedānta, see Lacombe, Avant-propos
to Grousset, *Les Philosophies Indiennes*, p. xiv, note 1, and Whitby,
Preface to Guénon, *Man and his Becoming*, p. ix.

of science and religion." Each is then dependent on the other, although in different ways; the sciences depending on revealed truth for their formal correction, and revealed truth relying upon the sciences for its demonstration by analogy, "not as though it stood in need of them, but only to make its teaching clearer."

In either case, the final end of human wisdom is a good or happiness that shall accrue either to the philosopher himself, or to his neighbours, or to humanity at large, but necessarily in terms of material well-being. The kind of good envisaged may or may not be a moral good.[1] For example, if we assume a good will, i.e. a natural sense of justice, the natural religion will be expressed in ethics in a sanction of such laws of conduct as most conduce to the common good, and he may be admired who sacrifices even life for the sake of this. In aesthetic (art being *circa factibilia*) the natural religion, given a good will, will justify the manufacture of such goods as are apt for human well-being, whether as physical necessities or as sources of sensible pleasure. All this belongs to "humanism" and is very far from despicable. But in case there is not a good will, the natural religion may equally be employed to justify the proposition "might is right" or "devil take the hindmost," and in manufacture the production of goods either by methods which are injurious to the common good, or which in themselves are immediately adapted to ends injurious to the common good; as in the cases of child-labour and the manufacture of poison gas. Revealed truth, on the contrary, demands a good will *a priori*, adding that the aid of the rational philosophy, as science or art, is required in order that the good will may be made effective.[2]

There is then another kind of philosophy (1), viz. that to which we have alluded as "revealed truth," which though it covers the whole ground of philosophy (2), does so in another way, while beyond this it treats confidently of "realities" which may indeed be immanent in time and space tissue, and are not wholly incapable of rational demonstration, but are nevertheless said to be transcendent with respect to this tissue, i.e. by no

[1] St. Thomas, *Sum. Theol.* i, q. 1, a. 6, *ad.* 2.
[2] Prudence is defined as *recta ratio agibilium*, art as *recta ratio factib ilium*

means wholly contained within it nor given by it, nor wholly amenable to demonstration. The First Philosophy, for example, affirms the actuality of a "now" independent of the flux of time; while experience is only of a past and future. Again, the procedure of the First Philosophy is no longer in the first place deductive and secondarily inductive, but inductive from first to last, its logic proceeding invariably from the transcendental to the universal, and thence as before to the particular. This First Philosophy, indeed, taking for granted the principle "as above, so below" and vice-versa,[1] is able to find in every microcosmic fact the trace or symbol of a macrocosmic actuality, and accordingly resorts to "proof" by analogy; but this apparently deductive procedure is here employed by way of demonstration, and not by way of proof, where logical proof is out of the question, and its place is taken either by faith (Augustine's *credo ut intelligam*) or by the evidence of immediate experience (*alaukika-pratyakṣa*).[2]

Our first problem in connection with the highest wisdom, considered as a doctrine known by revelation (whether through ear or symbolic transmission), consistent but unsystematic, and intelligible in itself although it treats in part of unintelligible things, is to distinguish without dividing religion from metaphysics, philosophy (2) from philosophy (1). This is a distinction without a difference, like that of attribute from essence, and yet a distinction of fundamental importance if we are to grasp the true meaning of any given spiritual act.

We proceed therefore first to emphasise the distinctions that can be drawn as between religion and metaphysics with respect to a wisdom that is one in itself and in any case primarily

[1] E.g. *Aitareya Brāhmana*, viii. 2.

[2] "Metaphysics can dispute with one who denies its principles, if only the opponent will make some concession; but if he concede nothing, it can have no dispute with him. . . . If our opponent believes nothing of divine revelation, there is no longer any means of proving the articles of faith by reasoning" (St. Thomas, *Sum. Theol.*, i, 1. q, a. 8 c.); and *ib.*, q. 46, a. 2: "The articles of faith cannot be proved demonstratively."

Similarly in India it is repeatedly and explicitly asserted that the truth of Vedic doctrine cannot be demonstrated but only experienced. "*By what* should one know the Knower of knowing" (*Bṛhadāraṇyaka Up.*, iv. 5. 15).

directed to immaterial, or rationally speaking, "unreal" things. Broadly speaking, the distinction is that of Christianity from Gnosticism, Sunnī from Shi'a doctrine, Rāmânuja from Śaṁkara, of the will from the intellect, participation (*bhakti*) from gnosis (*jñāna*), or knowledge-of (*avidyā*) from knowledge-as (*vidyā*). As regards the Way, the distinction is one of consecration from initiation, and of passive from active integration; and as regards the End, of assimilation (*tadākārata*) from identification (*tadbhāva*). Religion requires of its adherents to be perfected; metaphysics that they realise their own perfection that has never been infringed (even Satan is still virtually Lucifer, being fallen in grace and not in nature). Sin, from the standpoint of religion, is moral; from that of metaphysics, intellectual (mortal sin in metaphysics being a conviction or assertion of independent self-subsistence, as in Satan's case, or envy of the spiritual attainments of others, as in Indra's).

Religion, in general, proceeds from the being in act (*kāryâvasthā*) of the First Principle, without regard to its being in potentiality (*kāraṇâvasthā*);[2] while metaphysics treats of the Supreme Identity as an indisseverable unity of potentiality and act, darkness and light, holding that these can also and must also be considered apart when we attempt to understand their operation in identity in It or Him. And so religion assumes an aspect of duality,[3] viz. when it postulates a "primary matter,"

[1] Throughout the present essay it is assumed that sensibility means the perception of things by the senses, not a cognition but a reaction; reason, the activity of the intelligence with respect to the causal series of accidents, sometimes called the chain of fate, or in other words an intelligence with respect to things phenomenally known in time and space and called "material"; and intellect, the habit of first principles.

[2] Thus *Chāndogya Up.*, vi. 2. 1 asserts a religious point of view, as distinct from the metaphysical point of view that prevails in the Upaniṣads generally, e.g. *Taittirīya Up.*, ii. 7. Christian philosophy maintains that God is "wholly in act." Metaphysics concurs in the definition of perfection as a realisation of all the possibilities of being, but would rather say of God that "He does not proceed from potentiality to act" than that He is without potentiality.

[3] Duality, as of "spirit and matter," "act and potentiality," "form and substance," "good and evil." This is avoided in Christianity metaphysically, when it is shown that evil is not a self-subsistent nature, but merely a privation, and can be known to the First Intellect only as a goodness or perfection *in potentia*. It is avoided in Sufī metaphysic by considering good and evil as merely reflections in time and space of His essential attributes of Mercy and Majesty.

"potentiality" or "non-being" far removed from the actuality of God, and does not take account of the principal presence of this "primary matter" in, or rather "of" the First, as its "nature."[1]

Religions may and must be many, each being an "arrangement of God," and stylistically differentiated, inasmuch as the thing known can only be in the knower according to the mode of the knower, and hence as we say in India, "He takes the forms that are imagined by His worshippers," or as Eckhart expresses it, "I am the cause that God is God."[2] And this is why religious beliefs, as much as they have united men, have also divided men against each other, as Christian or heathen, orthodox or heretical.[3] So that if we are to consider what may be the most urgent *practical* problem to be resolved by the philosopher, we can only answer that this is to be recognised in a control and revision of the principles of comparative religion, the true end of which science, judged by the best wisdom (and judgment is the proper function of applied wisdom), should be to demonstrate the common metaphysical basis of all religions and that

[1] "Matter" here must not be confused with the "solid matter" of everyday parlance; in Christian philosophy, "primary mátter" is precisely that "nothing" with respect to which it is said *ex nihilo fit*. Such "matter" is said to be "insatiable for form," and the same is implied when in the *Jaiminīya Up. Brāhmaṇa*, i. 56, it is said that "In the beginning, the woman (= Urvaśī, Apsaras) went about in the flood seeking a master" (*icchanti salile patim*).

[2] The physical analogy is represented in the assertion of the anthropologist that "God is man-made"; a proposition perfectly valid within the conditions of its own level of reference.

[3] That is mainly, of course, in Europe from the thirteenth century onwards. In Hinduism, a man is regarded as a true teacher who gives to any individual a better access to that individual's *own* scriptures; for "the path men take from every side is Mine" (*Bhagavad Gītā*, iv. 11). Clement of Alexandria allows that "There is always a natural manifestation of the one Almighty God amongst all right-thinking men" (*Misc.*, bk. v); Eckhart says almost in the words of the *Bhagavad Gītā*, cited above, "In whatever way you find God best, that way pursue," Dante will not exclude all the pagan philosophers from Heaven; in the Grail tradition, Malory says that "Merlyn made the round table in tokenyng of the roundenes of the world for by the round table is the world sygnifyed by ryghte. For all the world crysten and hethen repayren vnto the round table" (*Mort d' Arthur*, xiv. 2); these may be contrasted with the position taken in the Song of Roland where, when Saragossa has been taken, "A thousand Franks enter the synagogues and mosques, whose every wall with mallet and axe they shatter . . . the heathen folk are driven in crowds to the baptismal font, to take Christ's yoke upon them."

diverse cultures are fundamentally related to one another as being the dialects of a common spiritual and intellectual language; for whoever recognises this, will no longer wish to assert that "My religion is best," but only that it is the "best for me."[1] In other words, the purpose of religious controversy should be, not to "convert" the opponent, but to persuade him that his religion is essentially the same as our own. To cite a case in point, it is not long since we received a communication from a Catholic friend in which he said "I've been ashamed for years at the superficiality and cheapness of my attempt to state a difference between Christians and Hindus." It is noteworthy that a pronouncement such as this will assuredly strike a majority of European readers with a sense of horror. We recognise in fact that religious controversy has still generally in view to convince the opponent of error rather than of correctness in our eyes; and one even detects in modern propagandist writing an undertone of fear, as though it would be a disaster that might upset our own faith, were we to discover essential truth in the opponent; a fear which is occasioned by the very fact that with increasing knowledge and understanding, it is becoming more and more difficult to establish fundamental differences as between one religion and another. It is one of the functions of the First Philosophy to dissipate such fears. Nor is there any other ground whatever upon which all men can be in absolute agreement, excepting that of metaphysics, which we assert is the basis and the norm of all religious formulations. Once such a common ground is recognised, it becomes a simple matter to agree to disagree in matter of details, for it will be seen that the various dogmatic formulations are no more than paraphrases of one and the same principle.[2]

Few will deny that at the present day Western civilisation is faced with the imminent possibility of total functional failure

---

[1] The "best for me" need not be "truest absolutely" as judged by absolute metaphysical standards. Nevertheless, the metaphysician will not suggest that the follower of a "second best" religion should abandon it for another (cf. *Bhagavad Gītā*, iii. 26, *na buddhibhedaṁ janayed ajñānam*), but rather that he go *farther in* where he already is, and thus verify as "true" his own images, not by those of another pattern, but rather by the prior form that is common to both.

[2] "Diverse dogmatic formulations," i.e. *dharma-paryāya* as this expression is employed in the *Saddharma Puṇḍarīka*.

nor that at the same time this civilisation has long acted and still continues to act as a powerful agent of disorder and oppression throughout the rest of the world. We dare say that both of these conditions are referable in the last analysis to that impotence and arrogance which have found a perfect expression in the dictum "East is East and West is West, and never the twain shall meet," a proposition to which only the most abysmal ignorance and deepest discouragement could have given rise. On the other hand, we recognise that the only possible ground upon which an effective entente of East and West can be accomplished is that of the purely intellectual wisdom that is one and the same at all times and for all men, and is independent of all environmental idiosyncrasy.[1]

We had intended to discuss at greater length the differentia of religion and metaphysics, but shall rather conclude the present section by an assertion of their ultimate identity. Both, considered as Ways, or praxis, are means of accomplishing the rectification, regeneration and reintegration of the aberrant and fragmented individual consciousness, both conceive of man's last end (*puruṣârtha*) as consisting in a realisation by the individual of all the possibilities inherent in his own being, or may go farther, and see in a realisation of all the possibilities of being in any mode and also in possibilities of non-being, a final goal. For the Neo-Platonists and Augustine, and again for Erigena, Eckhart and Dante, and for such as Rūmī, Ibnu'l Arabī, Saṁkarâcārya, and many others in Asia, religious and intellectual experience are too closely interwoven ever to be wholly divided;[2] who for example would have suspected that the words "How can That, which the Comprehending call the Eye of all things, the Intellect of intellects, the Light of lights, and numinous

---

[1] In this context the reader is recommended to René Guénon, *L'Orient et l'Occident*, Paris, 1932.

[2] Cf. Erigena, *De div. naturae*, i. 66, *Ambo siquidem ex una fonte, divina scilicet sapientia, manare dubium non est*, and *Bhagavad Gītā*, v. 4-5, "It is the children of this world, and not the men of learning who think of gnosis and works as different. . . . He sees in truth who sees that gnosis and works are one" (for Sāṁkhya and Yoga as meaning gnosis and works respectively, see *ib.*, iii. 3). That the Way of Gnosis and the Way of Participation have one and the same end becomes evident when we consider that love and knowledge can only be conceived of as perfected in an identity of lover and beloved, knower and known.

Omnipresence, be other than man's last end," "Thou hast
been touched and taken! long has thou dwelt apart from me,
but now that I have found Thee, I shall never let Thee go,"
are taken, not from a "theistic" source, but from purely Vedāntic
hymns addressed to the Essence (*ātman*) and to the "impersonal"
Brahman?

II. HOW DIVERS WISDOMS HAVE CONSIDERED IMMORTALITY

Let us now consider the application of different kinds of wisdom
to a particular problem of general significance. The pertinence
of philosophy to the problem of immortality is evident, inasmuch
as wisdom is primarily concerned with immaterial things, and
it is evident that material things are not immortal as such
(in *esse per se*), nor even from one moment to another, but are
continually in flux, and this is undeniable, regardless of whether
there may or may not be in such perpetually becoming things
some immortal principle. Or to regard the matter from another
angle, we may say that whatever, if anything, there may
be immortal in phenomenal things must have been so since
time began, for to speak of an immortal principle as having
become mortal is the same thing as to say it was always
mortal.

It needs no argument to demonstrate that human wisdom,
rationalism, our philosophy(2), will understand by "immortality,"
not an everlasting life on earth, but an after-death persistence
of individual consciousness and memory and character, such
as in our experience survives from day to day across the nightly
intervals of death-like sleep. Rational wisdom then will take
up either one of two positions. It may in the first place argue
that we have no experience of nor can conceive of the functioning
of consciousness apart from the actual physical bases on which
the functioning seems to rest, if indeed consciousness be in itself
anything whatever more than a function of matter in motion,
that is to say of physical existence; and will not therefore
conceive the possibility of any other than an immortality in
history, viz. in the memories of other mortal beings. In this
sense there can also be postulated the possibility of a kind of
resurrection, as when memory is refreshed by the discovery

of documentary proofs of the existence of some individual or people whose very names had been forgotten it may be for millennia. Or human wisdom may maintain, rightly or wrongly, that evidences have been found of the "survival of personality," viz. in communications from the "other world," of such sort as to prove either by reference to facts unknown to the observer, but which are afterwards verified, or by "manifestations" of one sort or another, a continuity of memory and persistence of individual character in the deceased who is assumed to be in communication with the observer. If it is then attempted to rationalise the evidence thus accepted, it is argued that there may be kinds of matter other and subtler than those perceptible to our present physical senses, and that these other modalities of matter may very well serve as the suppositum of consciousness functioning on other planes of being.

It will be readily seen that no spiritual or intellectual distinction can be drawn between the two rationalistic interpretations, the only difference between them being as regards the amount or kind of time in which the continuity of individual character and consciousness can be maintained in a dimensioned space and on a material basis, theories of "fourth dimensions" or of "subtle matter" changing nothing in principle. Both of the rationalistic interpretations are rejected *in toto*, equally by religion and metaphysics.

Not that the possibility of an indefinite perdurance of individual consciousness upon indefinitely numerous or various platforms of being and in various temporal modes is by any means denied in religion or in metaphysics (it being rather assumed that individual consciousness even now functions on other levels than those of our present terrestrial experience),[1] but that a persistence in such modes of being is not, strictly speaking, an immortality, this being taken to mean an immutability of being without development or change and wholly uneventful; while that which is thus presumed to subsist apart from contingency, viz. the soul, form or noumenal principle (*nāma*) of the individual, by which it is *what* it is, must be distinguished alike from the subtle and the gross bodies (*sūkṣma*

---

[1] "Even we ourselves as mentally tasting something eternal, are not in this world." St. Augustine, *De Trin.*, iv. 20.

and *sthūla śarīra*) which are equally phenomenal (*rūpa*), as being wholly intellectual and immaterial.[1]

For example, "things belonging to the state of glory are not under the sun" (St. Thomas, *Sum. Theol.*, iii., Sup., q. I, a. I), i.e. not in any mode of time or space; rather, "it is through the midst of the Sun that one escapes altogether" (*atimucyate*), (*Jaiminīya Up. Brāhmaṇa*, i. 3), where the sun is the "gateway of the worlds" (*loka-dvāra*), (*Chānd. Up.*, viii. 6. 6), Eckhart's "gate through which all things return perfectly free to their supreme felicity (*pūrṇânanda*) . . . free as the Godhead in its non-existence" (*asat*), the "Door" of John X, "Heaven's-gate that Agni opens" (*svargasya lokasya dvāram avṛṇot*), (*Aitareya Brāhmaṇa*, iii. 42).[2] It is true that here again we shall inevitably meet with a certain and by no means negligible distinction of the religious from the metaphysical formulation. The religious concept of supreme felicity culminates as we have already seen in the assimilation of the soul to Deity in act; the soul's own act being one of adoration rather than of union. Likewise, and without inconsistency, since it is assumed that the individual soul remains numerically distinct alike from God and from other substances, religion offers to mortal consciousness the consolatory promise of finding there in Heaven, not only God, but those whom it loved on earth, and may remember and recognise.

Nor will metaphysics deny even in a "Heaven," on the farther side of time, there may be, at least until the "Last Judgment," a knowledge-of (*avidyā*) rather than a knowledge-as (*vidyā*), though it will not think of him whose modality is still in knowledge-of as wholly Comprehending (*vidvān*) nor as absolutely Enlarged (*atimukta*). Metaphysics will allow, and here in formal agreement with religion, that there may or even must be states of being by no means wholly in time, nor yet in eternity

---

[1] Therefore incapable of "proof," whether the phenomena adduced be "scientific" or "spiritualistic."

[2] While it is shown here how the formulations of different religions may express the same conceptions in almost verbal agreement, it must not be supposed that we therefore advocate any kind of eclecticism, or conceive the possibility of a new religion compounded of all existing religions. Eclecticism in religion results only in confusion and caricature, of which a good example can be cited in "Theosophy."

(the timeless now), but aeviternal, "aeviternity" (Vedic *amṛtatva*) being defined as a mean between eternity and time;[1] the Angels, for example, as conscious intellectual substances, partaking of eternity as to their immutable nature and understanding, but of time as regards their accidental awareness of before and after, the changeability of their affections (liability to fall from grace, etc.), and inasmuch as the angelic independence of local motion (because of which Angels are represented as winged, and spoken of as "birds"),[2] whereby they can be anywhere, is other than the immanence of the First, which implies an equal presence everywhere. Nor is it denied by religion that "Certain men even in this state of life are greater than certain angels, not actually, but virtually" (St. Thomas, *Sum. Theol.*, i, q. 117, a. 2, *ad.* 3), whence it naturally follows that "Some men are taken up into the highest angelic orders" (Gregory, *Hom. xxxiv in Ev.*), thus partaking of an aeviternal being; all of which corresponds to what is implied by the familiar Hindu expression *devo bhūtvā*, equivalent to "dead and gone to

---

[1] St. Thomas, *Sum. Theol.*, i, q. 10, a. 5. He says "states of being" in the plural deliberately (cf. René Guénon, *Les États multiples de l'Être*, Paris, 1932), although for purposes of generalisation it has been necessary to speak only of three, viz. the human, angelic and divine, that is those to which the literal, metaphorical and analogical understandings pertain respectively.

With the Christian "aeviternity," Indian *amṛtatva*, and the traditional concept of "humanity" and "Perfect Man" (e.g. Islamic *insanu'l kamil*), cf. Jung, *Modern Man in Search of a Soul*, p. 215: "If it were permissible to personify the unconscious, we might call it a collective human being combining the characteristics of both sexes, transcending youth and age, birth and death, and from having at its command a human experience of one or two million years, almost immortal. If such a being existed, he would be exalted above all temporal change . . . he would have lived countless times over the life of the individual, or the family, tribe and people, and he would possess the living sense of the rhythm of growth, flowering and decay. It would be positively grotesque for us to call this immense system of the experience of the unconscious psyche an illusion." Here it may be noted that "unconscious" presents an analogy with "Deep-Sleep" (*suṣupti* = *samādhi* = *excessus* or *raptus*); on the other hand, the use of the word "collective" betrays a purely scientific, and not a metaphysical conception.

[2] "Intellect is the swiftest of birds" (*manaḥ javiṣṭam patayatsu antaḥ*, *Ṛg. Veda*, vi. 9. 5). It is as birds that the Angels "celebrate in the Tree of Life their share of aeviternity" (*yatra suparṇā amṛtasya bhāgam . . . abhi svaranti*, *ib.*, i. 164. 21). The traditional expression "language of birds" (which survives in "a little bird told me") refers to angelic communications

Heaven." Precisely this point of view is more technically
expressed in the critical text, Bṛhadār. Up., iii. 2. 12, "When
a man dies, what does not forsake (na jahāti) him is his 'soul'
(nāma),[1] the soul is without end (ananta, 'aeviternal'), without
end is what the Several Angels are, so then he wins the world
everlasting" (anantam lokam). Cf. Rūmī (xii in Nicholson's
Shams-i-Tabrīz), "Every shape you see has its archetype in the
placeless world, and if the shape perished, no matter, since
its original is everlasting" (lāmkān-ast); and St. Thomas, Sum.
Theol., ii-i, q. 67, a. 2 c, "as regards the intelligible species, which
are in the possible intellect, the intellectual virtues remain,"
viz. when the body is corrupted. This was also expounded by
Philo, for whom "Le lieu de cette vie immortelle est le monde
intelligible,"[2] that is to say the same as the "Intellectual Realm"
of Plotinus, passim. If we now consider the implications of these
dicta in connection with Böhme's answer to the scholar who
enquires, "Whither goeth the soul when the body dieth?" viz.
that "There is no necessity for it to go anywither. . . . For . . .
whichsoever of the two (that is either heaven or hell) is manifested
in it (now), in that the soul standeth (then) . . . the judgment
is, indeed, immediately at the departure of the body,"[3] and in
the light of Bṛhadār. Up., iv. 4. 5-6, "As is his will . . . so is
his lot" (yat kāmam . . . tat sampadyate) and "He whose mind
is attached (to mundane things) . . . returns again to this
world . . . but he whose desire is the Essence (ātman), his
life (prâṇāḥ) does not leave him, but he goes as Brahman unto
Brahman," it will be apparent that although the soul or intellect
(Vedic manas) is immortal by nature (i.e. an individual potentiality that cannot be annihilated, whatever its "fate"), nevertheless the actual "fate" of an individual consciousness, whether

[1] Nāma is the correlative of rūpa, being the noumenal or intelligible
part and efficient cause of the integration nāma-rūpa, viz. the individual
as he is in himself; and therefore to be rendered not by "name" (for this
is not a nominalist but a realist doctrine), but by "idea," "archetype,"
"form" or "soul" (as when it is said "the soul is the form of the body");
ātman on the other hand being "essence" rather than "soul" (essentia,
that by which a substance has esse in whatever mode).
[2] Bréhier, Les Idées philosophiques et religieuses de Philon d'Alexandrie,
1925, p. 240.
[3] Böhme, On Heaven and Hell (in Everyman's Library, volume entitled
Signatura Rerum, etc.).

it be destined to be "saved" or "liberated" (*devayāna*), or to enter into time again (*pitṛyāna*), or to be "lost" (*nirṛtha*), depends upon itself. And therefore we are told to "Lay up treasure in Heaven, where neither moth nor rust corrupt"; for evidently, if the conscious life of the individual be even now established intellectually (or in religious phraseology, "spiritually"), and the intellectual or spiritual world be aeviternal (as follows from the consideration that ideas have neither place nor date), this conscious life cannot be infringed by the death of the body, which changes nothing in this respect. Or if the consciousness be still attached to and involved in ends (whether good or evil) such as can only be accomplished in time and space, but have not yet been accomplished when the body dies, then evidently such a consciousness will find its way back into those conditions, viz. of space and time, in which the desired ends can be accomplished.[1] Or finally, if conscious life has been led altogether in the flesh, it must be thought of as cut off when its sole support is destroyed; that is, it must be thought of as "backsliding" into a mere potentiality or hell.

Space will not permit us to discuss the theory of "reincarnation" at any length. The fundamentals are given in the *Ṛg*. Veda, where it is primarily a matter of recurring manifestation, in this sense for example, Mitra *jāyate punaḥ* (x. 85. 19) and Usas is *punaḥpunar jāyamāna* (i. 92. 10). An individual application in the spirit of "Thy will be done" is found in v. 46. 1, "As a comprehending (*vidvān*) horse I yoke myself unto the pole (of the chariot of the year) . . . seeking neither a release nor to come back again (*na asyāḥ vimucaṁ na āvṛttam punaḥ*), may He (Agni) as Comprehender (*vidvān*) and our Waywise Guide lead us aright." The individual, indeed, "is born according to the measure of his understanding" (*Aitareya Āraṇyaka*, ii. 3. 2), and just as "the world itself is pregnant with the causes of unborn things" (Augustiue, *De Trin.*, iii. 9) so is the individual pregnant with the accidents that must befall him; as St. Thomas expresses it, "fate is in the created causes themselves" (*Sum. Theol.*, i, q. 116, 2), or Plotinus, "the law is given in the entities upon whom it falls . . . it prevails because it is within them

---

[1] It is the good purpose, for example, which operates in the return of a Bodhisattva, who is otherwise fit for Nirvāṇa.

. . . and sets up in them a painful longing to enter the realm to which they are bidden from within" (*Enneads*, iv. 3. 15); and similarly Ibnu'l 'Arabī, who says that while being is from God, modality is not directly from Him, "for He only wills what they have it in them to become" (Nicholson, *Studies* . . ., p. 151). On the other hand, it may be taken as certain that the Buddhist and still more the modern Theosophical interpretations of causality (*karma*) or fate (*adṛṣṭa*), which assert the necessity of a return (except for one who is *mukta* or has "reached" *nirvāṇa*) to the very same conditions that have been left behind at death, involve a metaphysical antinomy; "You would not step twice into the same waters, for other waters are ever flowing in upon you" (Heracleitus). What is really contemplated in Vedic and other tradional doctrines is the necessity of a recurrent manifestation in aeon after aeon, though not again within one and the same temporal cycle,[1] of all those individual potentialities or forces in which the desire to "prolong their line" is still effective; every Patriarch (*pitṛ*) being, like Prajāpati himself, *prajā-kāmya*, and therefore willingly committed to the "Patriarchal Way" (*pitṛyāna*).

What is then from the standpoint of metaphysics the whole course of an individual potentiality, from the "time" that it first awakens in the primordial ocean of universal possibility until the "time" it reaches the last harbour? It is a return into the source and well-spring of life, from which life originates, and thus a passage from one "drowning" to another; but with a distinction, valid from the standpoint of the individual in himself so long as he is a Wayfarer and not a Comprehender, for, seen as a process, it is a passage from a merely possible perfection through actual imperfection to an actual perfection, from potentiality to act, from slumber (*abodhya*) to a full awakening (*sambodhi*). Ignoring now the Patriarchal Way as being a "round about" course, and considering only the straight Angelic Way (*devayāna*), with which the Ṛg. *Veda* is primarily

---

[1] In *Bhagavad Gītā*, vi. 41, for example, *śāsvati samā* is very far from implying "forthwith." We doubt very much whether any Aupaniṣada passage could be cited as implying a re-embodiment otherwise than at the dawn of a new cycle, and then only as the growth of a seed sown in the previous aeon, or as a tendency with which the new age can be said to be pregnant.

and the individual *mumukṣu* specifically concerned, we may say that this Way is one at first of a diminishing and afterwards of an increasing realisation of all the possibilities intrinsic to the fact of being in a given mode (the human, for example), and ultimately leads to the realisation of all the possibilities of being in any or every mode, and over and beyond this of those of being not in any mode whatever. We cannot do more than allude here to the part that is taken by what is called "initiation" in this connection; only saying that the intention of initiation is to communicate from one to another a spiritual or rather intellectual impulse that has been continuously transmitted in *guru-paramparā-krama* from the beginning and is ultimately of non-human origin, and whereby the contracted and disintegrated individual is awakened to the possibility of a reintegration (*saṁskarana*);[1] and that metaphysical rites, or "mysteries" (which are in imitation of the means employed by the Father to accomplish His own reintegration, the necessity for which is occasioned by the incontinence of the creative act), are, like the analogous traditional scriptures, intended to provide the individual with the necessary preparatory education in and means of intellectual operation; but the "Great Work," that of accomplishing the reunion of essence with Essence, must be done by himself within himself.

We have so far followed the Wayfarer's course by the Angelic Way to the spiritual or intellectual realm; and here, from the religious point of view, lies his immortality, for indeed "the duration of aeviternity is infinite" (St. Thomas, *Sum. Rheol.*, i, q. 10, a. 5, *ad.* 4). But it will be maintained in metaphysics, or even in a religion or by an individual mystic such as Eckhart (in so far as the religious experience is both devotional and intellectual in the deepest sense of both words) that an aeviternal station (*pada*), such as is implied in the concept of being in a heaven, is not the end, nor by any means a full return (*nivṛtti*), but only a resting place (*viśrāma*).[2] And likewise, it will be

[1] See *Aitareya Aranyaka*, iii. 2. 6; *Aitareya Brāhmana*, vi 27; *Satapatha Brāhmana*, vii. 1. 2. 1 and *passim*. Cf. also Guénon, "L'Initiation et les Métiers," *Le Voile d'Isis*, No. 172, 1934.

[2] *Saddharma Puṇḍarīka*, v. 74. Similarly, the true end of the ritual acts and appointed sacrifices of the Veda is not the attainment of a temporary heaven, but the awakening of a desire to know the Essence

maintained that to conceive of the intellectual realm itself as a place of memories would be a derogation, for as Plotinus says of its natives, "if they neither seek nor doubt, and never learn, nothing being at any time absent from their knowledge . . . what reasonings, what processes of rational investigation, can take place in them? In other words, they have seen God and they do not recollect? Ah, no . . . such reminiscence is only for souls that have forgotten" (*Enneads*, iv. 4. 6);[1] and still more must we say respecting mundane memories (*vāsanā*) that "when the soul's act is directed to another order, it must utterly reject the memory of such things, over and done with now" (*ib.*, iv. 4. 4. 8).

The metaphysical concept of Perfection, indeed, envisages a state of being that is, not *in*human since it is maintained that such a state is always and everywhere accessible to whoever will press inwards to the central point of consciousness and being on any ground or plane of being, nor "heartless" unless we mean by "heart" the seat of soulfulness and sentimentality; but assuredly *non*-human. For example, in *Chānd. Up.*, v. 10. 2 it is precisely as *amānava puruṣa*, "non-human person," that the Son and aeviternal *avatāra*, Agni,[2] is said to lead onward the Comprehending one who has found his way through the Supernal Sun to the farther side of the worlds, and this is the "pathway of the Angels" (*devayāna*) as contrasted with that of the Patriarchs (*pitṛyāna*) which does not lead beyond the Sun but to re-embodiment in a human mode of being. And it is foreseen that this *devayāna* must lead, whether sooner or later, to what is expressed in doctrinal mysticism as a "final death of the soul," or "drowning," the Sūfī *al-fanā an al-fanā*; by which is implied a passage

---

(*ātman*) (*Siddhàntamuktāvali*, xxxiii, with Venis' note "Paradise is as it were but the half-way house").

[1] Similarly in Dante, *Paradiso*, 29. 79-81, "their sight is never intercepted by any new perception, and so there is no need of memory, for thought has not been cleft."

[2] Agni(-Prajāpati), who in the Vedas is the Herdsman of the Spheres (*gopā bhuvanasya*). Waywise Leader (*vidvān pathaḥ puraeta*), Messenger and Herald (*dūta arati*), and stands as the Pillar of Life at the Parting of the Ways (*āyor ha skambha . . . pātham visarge, Ṛg. Veda*, x. 5. 6) in cosmic crucifixion (*dharuṇeṣu sthitaḥ, ib.*), corresponding to the "dogmatic" Buddha, Christ as distinguished from Jesus, and to the "Idea of Muḥammad."

beyond even consciousness in deity as act, to a Supreme (Skt. *para, parātpara*) beyond all trace of even an exemplary multi-plicity, nor in any way "intelligible." And there, so far that is from any possible "reminiscence" of any that have been known or loved in otherness, in the words of Eckhart, "No one will ask me whence I came or whither I went," or in Rūmī's, "None has knowledge of each who enters that he is so-and-so or so-and-so."[1]

If this appears to be a denial of ultimate significance to human love, the position has been altogether misunderstood. For all metaphysical formulations, assuming that an infallible analogy relates every plane of being to every other, have seen in human love an image of divine felicity (*pūrnānanda*), imagined not as a contradiction of but as transformation (*parāvtrti*) of sensual experience. This is the theory of "Platonic love," according to which, as Ibnu'l Farīd expresses it, "the charm of every fair youth or lovely girl is lent to them from Her beauty"; a point of view implicit too in Erigena's conception of the world as a theophany, and in the Scholastic doctrine of the *vestigium pedis*, the trace or footprint of divinity in time, which has its equivalent in Vedic and Zen symbolisms. What this means in actual tradition is that the beloved on earth is to be realised *there* not as she is in herself but as she is in God,[2] and so it is in the case of Dante and Beatrice, Ibn'l 'Arabī and an-Nīzām,[3] and in that of Chandīdās and Rāmī.[4] The beauty of the Beloved *there* is no longer as it is here contingent and merely a participation or reflection, but that of the Supernal Wisdom, that of the One Madonna, that of the intrisic being of the Bride, which "rains down flames of fire" (*Convivio*) and as *claritas* illuminates and guides the pure intellect. In that last and hidden station (*guhyam padam*), nature and essence, Apsaras and Gandharva, are one and indivisible, knowing nothing of a within or a without

---

[1] Nicholson, *Shamsi-i-Tabrīz*, p. 61.

[2] Cf. *Tarjumān all-Ashwāg*, xl. 2, "She was exalted in majesty above time"; and Rumī, " 'Tis love and the lover that live to all eternity" (xiii, in Nicholson, *Shams-i-Tabriz*).
Another example could be cited in the *Shepherd of Hermas*.

[3] Whom Ibnu'l Arabī met at Mecca in 1201, see Nicholson, *Tarjumān al-Ashwāq*, 1911.

[4] Cf. "Sahaja" in our *Dance of Śiva*, 1917.

(*na bāhyaṁ kiṁcana veda nāntaram, Bṛhadār.* Up., iv. 321),
and that is their supreme felicity, and that of every liberated
consciousness.

All this can only be described in terms of negation, in terms
of what it is *not*, and therefore we say again that metaphysics
can in no way be thought of as a doctrine offering consolations
to a suffering humanity. What metaphysic understands by
immortality and by eternity implies and demands of every
man a total and uncompromising denial of himself and a final
mortification, to be dead and buried in the Godhead. "Whoever
realises this, avoids contingent death (*punar mṛtyu*), death gets
him not, for Death becomes his essence, and of all these Angels
he becomes the One" (*Bṛhadār. Up.*, i. 2. 7). For the Supreme
Identity is no less a Death and a Darkness than a Life and a
Light, no less Asura than Deva: "His overshadowing is both
Aeviternity and Death" (*yasya chāyā amṛta, yasya mṛtyuḥ, Ṛg.
Veda*, x. 121. 2).[1] And this is what we understand to be the
final purport of the First Philosophy.

---

[1] Similarly, *Śatapatha Brāhmaṇa*, x. 4. 3. 1-3 *Eṣa vai mṛtyur yat
samvatsaraḥ . . . prajāpatiḥ,* "He, the Father, who is the Year and likewise
Death."

The Darkness and the Light, belonging to His *asuratva* and *devatva*
respectively, remain in Him, who is both *asura* and *deva*, Titan and angel,
sarpa and *āditya*; at the same time that from Wayfarer's point of view
their reflections in time and space are evil and good. In Hinduism, "the
Darkness in Him called Rudra" (*Maitri Up.*, vi. 2), and is represented
in the names and hues of Kālī and Kṛṣṇa; in Christian *yoga*, the Dark
Ray or Divine Darkness, Eckhart's "sable stillness" and "motionless
dark that no one knows but He in whom it reigns" (cf. the "Clouds and
thick darkness" of Deut. iv. 11), is spoken of already in the Codex Brucianus
and by Dionysius, and become the subject of the *contemplatio in caligine.*
Regarding the propriety of the expression "Christian *yoga*," we need only
point out that St. Bernard's *consideratio*, and *excessus* or *raptus* correspond
exactly to *dhāraṇa, dhyāna* and *samādhi.*

PRINCIPAL PUBLICATIONS

Mediaeval Sinhalese Art (1908).

Rajput Painting (1916).

The Dance of Siva (1917).

History of Indian and Indonesian Art (1927).

A New Approach to the Vedas (1934).

The Transformation of Nature in Art (1934).

Articles in the *Encyclopaedia Britannica* and *National Encyclopaedia.*

Editor of Indian words in *Webster's International Dictionary* (1934).

Recent articles include a series on "Early Indian Architecture" in *Eastern Art*; "*Kha* and other words for zero, in connection with the metaphysics of space," in *Bulletin of the School of Oriental Studies*; and "The technique and theory of Indian Painting," in *Technical Studies.*

THE FAITH OF AN IDEALIST

by N. G. DAMLE

Born 1893. M.A., Bombay University.
Professor of Philosophy, Fergusson College, Poona.

INTRODUCTORY

It is with considerable hesitation that I accepted the invitation of the Editor to contribute a paper to this volume, giving an account of my philosophical position and the circumstances and influences that have led me to it. I hesitated because I did not consider myself worthy of a place by the side of such highly gifted and eminent contributors as—Rabindranath Tagore and Mahatma Gandhi, Dr. S. Radhakrishnan and Dr. R. D. Ranade, who have illuminated with their own light their special spheres of thought and activity. I hesitated further because I had no definite and comprehensive philosophical system of my own to propound in this paper. I overcame this hesitation by arguing to myself that the firmament of thought is not reserved for the stars of the first magnitude, but there is room also for those of lesser magnitude; nor is it reserved for those heavenly bodies which are self-luminous but there is room also for those that shine by borrowed light. I found consolation and encouragement in the following words of Jñāneśwara, the great mystic-philosopher-poet of Mahārāṣtra "If God is pleased with the flowers of Vyāsa, would He refuse the little Dūrvās that I may offer to Him? If large elephants come to the shores of an ocean, is a small swan prevented thereby from coming? . . . if the swan walks gracefully on the earth, does it forbid any other creatures from walking? . . ."[1] Without transgressing the limits of modesty I may say that I have devoted thirty years of my life to the study and teaching of Philosophy, which has helped me cultivate a general philosophical outlook and gain some insight into the fundamental problems of life. During this period as a result of reading and discussion, reflection and meditation, I have come to entertain certain philosophical opinions and religious beliefs. I cannot, however, claim any novelty or originality for them, since their ingredients may, directly or indirectly, be traced to the writings and utterances of some of the world's greatest thinkers, saints and prophets. To all of them I express my deep sense of obligation. I have studied in many "Schools", drawn from many sources; and I am not quite sure whether the various opinions and beliefs I

---

[1] Jñāneśwara: xviii, 1711-14.

hold can be harmonized and designated by a simple and appropriate label. When, however, for the purpose of this paper I began to review my philosophy as a whole and to define to myself its general character, four labels suggested themselves to me, viz. "Integral Idealism", "A Mystical View of Life", "The Faith of an Idealist", and "Science, Humanism and Religion". Out of these I have selected "The Faith of an Idealist" as the most suitable title for this paper. In this short paper I have followed the example of certain American and English philosophers and attempted, if I may say so, a sort of "intellectual auto-biography". It should be noted that facts as recalled in memory and recorded in such "intellectual auto-biographies" are always selected and may be unconsciously coloured by our present outlook. The biographical details have been so selected and arranged that they should acquaint the reader with the circumstances which have moulded my philosophical views and beliefs.

INTELLECTUAL AUTOBIOGRAPHY
OR
THE FAITH OF AN IDEALIST

I WAS born in 1893, and according to the Hindu Calendar on the ninth day of the second fortnight of the month of Māgha. I have often felt that the year and the day have a special significance in my life, for as I review the evolution of my thought I find that, besides the orthodox family in which I was born and the religious atmosphere in which I was brought up, the two outstanding influences in my early life were Rāmadāsa and Vivekānanda. The year 1893 is associated with Vivekānanda's memorable speech in the World's Parliament of Religions at Chicago, in which he delivered the inspiring message of the unity of religions and universal toleration. The ninth day of the second fortnight of the month of Māgha is observed throughout Mahārāṣṭra as a sacred day in memory of Rāmadāsa, the exponent of activistic mysticism and the spiritual adviser of Śhivājī the Great, the liberator of Mahārāṣṭra. I admired and revered Rāmadāsa and Vivekānanda because they practised what they preached, and they preached love of God and service of mankind. They did not lead a life of mere contemplation caring only for their own salvation but actively worked for the uplift and freedom of the people.[1] While a young student I could not understand the pros and cons of their philosophical theories or the meaning of their mystical experiences, but I could follow, however vaguely, the tenor of their fundamental principles and their application to life. That indeed produced, above everything else, an attitude of mind which I may now describe as a wholesome *spiritual outlook*. This outlook, to use the words of a poet, "true to the kindred points of heaven and home," has survived many early doubts and occasional difficulties and sustained me throughout my life.

By the middle of 1910 when I had almost completed my school education, I remember I had often dreamt that I was flying in

[1] Ātmanah mokṣārtham jagatah hitāya ca.

the air like a bird above hill and dale, surmounting all obstacles, with a peculiar feeling of exhilaration. Again, I had a wonderful experience, repeated two or three times for which it is difficult to offer a satisfactory explanation. It was mid-day. I was relaxing. My eyes were half-closed, and I had a very dim consciousness of external objects, when all of a sudden my mind was filled with an exceedingly vivid and compelling but a mysterious sense that I was living in an unreal world, a world which is only a dream of God, myself being a dreamer in God's dream, a world none the less full of light and delight! I did not understand the significance of these experiences then, but later on I took them to be a harbinger of the luckiest event in my life, which occurred by the end of 1910 at Jamkhandi, then a State in Southern Maratha Country. There, through the kindness of my uncle, Mr. R. D. Ranade, now Emeritus Professor of Philosophy, Allahabad University, I came in contact with the Saint of Umadi (a village in Karnatak). His blessings ushered in the *dawn of spiritual life.*

Philosophy always had a special attraction for me, but my mind hesitated for a while between Sanskrit, Mathematics and Philosophy in view of the prospective career, before I finally decided to offer Philosophy for the B.A. and M.A. degrees of the University of Bombay by enrolling myself as a student in the Fergusson College, Poona. And I am glad to record that I have never regretted the choice. When I thus entered the next stage of my intellectual career, I had to devote a good deal of my time and energy to the study of the more technical and theoretical aspects of the different branches of Philosophy. But now and then my mind was diverted to the study of such subjects as social and political philosophy with reference to Plato and Green, Hobhouse and MacIver, and English literature, my favourite authors in those days being Carlyle, Ruskin, Emerson, Wordsworth, Tennyson and Browning. I was led to the study of Browning by Henry Jones's excellent little volume on "Browning as a Philosophical and Religious Teacher". This diversion and my interest in ethical and religious problems prevented me from indulging in mere abstract speculation and logic-chopping. I regarded *philosophy as a way of life* and not merely as a way of thinking. Much time could have been saved, had there been a satisfactory system of professorial and tutorial guidance in vogue in those days. The value of "stimulation, direction and illumination" which students can derive from their contact with the right type of teachers can hardly be over-estimated. But as such valuable contact was possible to a very limited extent, I had to rely mostly on myself. During this period I did a lot of reading, gathering material from the writings of many eminent thinkers, past and present, Western and Indian. But as I look back I have to confess to a sense of dissatisfaction that though there was great "accumulation", there was very little of "illumination". The mind tended to become more receptive than critical and it could hardly put forth any novel or original ideas or points of view. There was, however, a relieving feature even in this situation. I could derive some illumination and stimulus to critical and constructive thinking from reading Gītānjali and Sādhanā of the poet-philosopher, Tagore, Gītārahasya of the patriot-philosopher, Tilak, and Lectures on Upaniṣads, delivered at Bangalore in 1915, later revised and published as "A Constructive Survey of Upaniṣadic Philosophy" in 1926, of the mystic-philosopher, Ranade. They revealed to me, each in his own way, the treasure of philosophical wisdom of the Upaniṣads and the Bhagavadgītā. A new light was thrown on old problems, and the importance of approaching vital philosophical problems in a critical and constructive spirit was impressed on my mind.

Having come under the fascinating influence of Plato and Spinoza, the Upaniṣads and the Bhagavadgītā, I felt that philosophy could not really be divorced from life, and that its outlook must be comprehensive and not partial or one-sided. I believed then, as I feel convinced now, that *the characteristic attitude of philosophy is synoptic, which duly considers all the aspects and levels of reality in their inter-relations, all forming together a unified spiritual whole.* Analysis and criticism play an important role in philosophical investigation but they cannot usurp the place of construction; and the construction of a world-view is the main task of philosophy. In addition to these critical and constructive aspects of philosophy we have to recognize a third aspect, viz. the practical and moral. With the construction of an intellectual edifice the work of philosophy is not completed; it finds its consummation in the vision of the Good, in the intellectual love of God, in freedom from ignorance and bondage, in free, creative, blessed life. Here may be found *the beginning of my faith as an idealist.*

My study of Sanskrit and my experience as Assistant Editor of *Sanskrit Research*, a quarterly journal conducted under the auspices of Sanskrit Academy, Bangalore, brought me into contact with eminent orientalists, and I was offered the post of the Curator of the Bhandarkar Oriental Research Institute, Poona, giving me an opportunity of actively associating myself with the critical edition of the Mahābhārata, the great epic of India. I was also offered at the same time a position in the Philosophy Department of the Fergusson College, and Life-membership of the Deccan Education Society which conducts that College. Whether I accepted the first or the second alternative, it meant *a life of dedication*[1], either to the cause of oriental learning and research, or to the cause of higher education in the Province of Bombay. Impelled by love of philosophy, liking for the teacher's profession and patriotic sentiment, I chose the latter and took the pledge on March 17, 1920 to serve the D. E. Society as a Life-member and the Fergusson College, my *alma mater*, as a teacher of Philosophy. March 17 is observed as "Chiplunkar Day", and I began my career by addressing a meeting of students and teachers that very day on the life and teaching of Vishṇu-shāstri Chiplūṇkar, one of the founders of the D.E. Society. This address was considered to be a good augury for the future. In my address I referred to his unbounded love of Marāthī, his ardent patriotism and his advocacy of Indian culture, and concluded by observing that nothing would please the departed soul more than the establishment of a University in Poona, teaching all subjects through the medium of Marāthī. After the lapse of twenty-eight years the Poona University has now been established and it is earnestly hoped that before long it will decide to use Marāthī as the medium of instruction and examination.

During the first ten years or so in the Fergusson College, with a break of two or three years partly due to my illness and partly due to the great political upheaval caused by Mahatma Gandhi's agitation for India's freedom, I applied my mind far more intently than I ever did before in my college days to the study of the various branches of philosophy in which I had to

[1] āyuh yajñena kalpatām.

offer instruction to under-graduate and post-graduate students. I familiarized myself with the philosophical classics and systems of philosophy, both Indian and Western, and also with the different types of ethical theory and schools of psychology. I realized the difference between learning for oneself and teaching others, especially young minds in their formative stage. It is true that a man learns while teaching through contact with younger minds, and that a teacher to be successful must possess in addition to a thorough grasp of his subject an ability to express his ideas in a lucid and skilful manner. But my desire at that time (in conformity with the prevailing examination-ridden system of education to which even some of the most senior and renowned professors had to yield) to make my teaching directly useful to students preparing for their degree examinations led me to attach greater importance to exposition than critical examination, to learning than independent thinking. At the instance of my educationist friends I interested myself in educational problems and accepted the Joint-editorship of the periodical, *The Progress of Education.* I was called upon to serve as Joint Secretary of "The Academy of Philosophy and Religion" and as Joint Editor of its journal *The Review of Philosophy and Religion.* I was also elected a member of the Regulating Council of the Bhandarkar Oriental Research Institute to which I have continued my attachment all these years.

All this resulted in widening rather than deepening the basis of my thought. I, therefore, tried to conserve my energy for specializing in certain select branches of philosophy and developing, as far as possible, a fairly definite point of view. A study of the principal systems of Indian philosophy and their comparison with similar thought sytems in the West, I thought, would also further the object I had in view. In such a comparative study it is necessary to guard against the tendency to exaggerate the points of similarity, and to account for them, somewhat hastily, on the hypothesis of "borrowing" by the one side or the other. We should not magnify or over-stress or be misled by the superficial, verbal or apparent points of resemblance, say, for example, between Jainism and Leibniz's monadism, Buddhism and Comte's positivism, Sāṁkhya and Spencer's evolutionism and Yoga and Freud's psycho-analysis. The following extract from my paper on *Fichte and his Idealism* will illustrate my attitude in such matters: "Fichte's life and writings do not indicate any acquaintance with or direct influence of Indian philosophy on his doctrine. They only reveal his indebtedness to Western philosophers, specially to Spinoza and Kant. Fichte (who lived from 1762 to 1814) may have been indirectly and unconsciously influenced by Indian thought and outlook through the intellectual atmosphere of his age. In this connection we may refer to the German translation of Kālidāsa's Śākuntala by Georg Förster (1791) which had deeply impressed Herder and Goethe, and through the Schlegels the Romantic Movement in Germany; to the first German translation of the Bhagawadgītā (1802); to Anquetil Duperron's Latin translation of the Upaniṣads, which had acquainted Schiller and Schopenhauer with the profound wisdom of the Indians (about 1805) and to Friedrich Schlegel's "The Language and the Wisdom of the Indians" (1808). Though Fichte had no direct relation with Indian philosophy, we find some resemblance between his theory and the Vedānta of Indian idealists like Śaṁkara. Scholars like Bhandarkar, Otto and Shrinivasachari have pointed out Fichte's affinities with the Sāṁkhya of Kapila, the Yogācāra school of Buddhism and the Bhedābheda theory of Bhāskara. But the points of similarity should not be stretched too far. It is necessary to view them in proper perspective, in relation to their psychological back-ground and historical setting."

Though as a member of the Senate and other Bodies of the Bombay University I have had my share in promoting the cause of psychology and encouraging its study for the Degree Examinations, I preferred to put ethics and religion in the forefront of my philosophical thought. Far from denying the importance of psychology, I even emphasize like Wallace, McDougall and Ross the need of the psychological approach to the study of human affairs, without over-estimating the part of instincts and emotions and with a due recognition of the influence of reason and will in shaping the course of social life and institutions.[1]

[1] Reference may be made to the sections on "Civics and Psychology," "Psychology of Private Property," and chapter on "Social Life and Institutions" in my book on *Civics* (Macmillan and Co., 3rd Edition, 1948), which is intended to serve as an introduction to social and political philosophy.

I was at first attracted by certain modern developments in psychology, such as Watson's Behaviourism and Freud's Psycho-analysis, but my enthusiasm soon dwindled, because I found that psychologically they were very one-sided and that their philosophical implications were far from satisfactory. Behaviourism ignores consciousness and dispenses with introspection and makes behaviour the exclusive field of study, relying upon external observation and experiment; regards human beings as mere machines; explains the whole mental life in terms of stimulus and response, describing thinking as "silent talking"; and ends in materialism and mechanism. Psycho-analysis exalts the unconscious, utterly forgetful of the super-conscious and explains "the higher lights by the lower obscurities"; accounts for dreams as wish-fulfilment; exaggerates the role of the irrational impulses and instincts, particularly the sex-instinct; undermines the traditional basis of moral life by denying freedom and decrying reason as a mere tool of instincts and suggests as a substitute the *ignis fatuus* of what passes as "new morality"; and lands in atheism by discarding religion as an illusion and as "a way of escape" from the realities of life. Such mechanistic and soul-less, irrational and God-less theories did not find favour with me. My studies and experience have led me to believe that a psychology without a soul is like the play of Hamlet without the Prince of Denmark, and that a full and clear understanding of the conscious is possible only in the light of the highest transformation of which it is capable, namely, the Super-conscious or pure Self-consciousness. Psychologists who eliminated altogether the soul and the Super-conscious from the purview of their science seemed to me therefore to grope in darkness and fail to touch reality behind its appearances. The Gestalt psychology in general, however, attracted me on account of its affinities with the synoptic and "holistic" attitude which I have found very helpful in philosophical as also in educational, political and ethical inquiries, in tackling problems of one and many, whole and parts, society and individual. I appreciated its criticism of brick-and-mortar psychology of the nineteenth-century associationists, its introduction of the notion of pattern in psychology and its emphasis on organized wholes. Analysis of an experience or performance, it tells us, cannot take us far; it must be studied as a whole and in its setting. A melody, for example, is not present in the notes taken singly as independent units, but only in their arrangement in a certain pattern. The same notes may give rise to different melodies. Personality is not a mere sum of its different traits but a gestalt; and, as Miss Calkins puts it, even the Absolute may be described as the Supreme Gestalt!

Now, in reviewing the relations of ethics to psychology and also to religion and metaphysics, leaving aside for present purposes other references and considerations, I appealed from Taylor, the author of *The Problem of Conduct* (1901) to Taylor, the author of *The Faith of a Moralist* (1930), from his psychologism, relativism and secularism to his ethical and metaphysical theism. In his earlier work he maintains, as against Green, that ethics is a purely empirical science with its roots fixed in psychology and sociology and advocates its independence of metaphysics and religion. His empirical theory of morals is based on the psychological analysis and sociological survey of moral ideas and sentiments and modes of behaviour in the context of concrete human situations. But it fails to furnish, on that basis, any universally valid principles of right conduct and to reach final solutions of perplexing ethical problems, thus leading to relativism and scepticism. In his later work, he unites ethics to metaphysics, the temporal and secular good to the eternal and the divine. Morality, he holds, cannot be completely autonomous, but it requires support from and finds culmination in religion, in natural theology as completed by super-natural revelation. Moral perfection can be attained not through personal effort alone, however strenuous and devoted it might be, but through "the initiative of the eternal", through the grace of God. Analysis and description of moral phenomena are indeed exceedingly valuable, but they cannot be a substitute for their interpretation and evaluation which is possible in the light of the *summum bonum*. Origin cannot decide validity. "The significance of the lotus is not to be found by analysing the secrets of the mud from which it springs."

Logic and epistemology have an importance all their own as propaedeutic to metaphysics. It was even specially stressed by Indian philosophers belonging to the "systematic period" though they held divergent views. But I had no liking for merely formal and barren logical and epistemological discussions, such as we come across in the works of Indian logicians like Gaṅgeśa and Gadādhara expounding Navya Nyāya (new logic) and also in the works of neo-realists and critical realists and exponents of mathematical logic or logistics and in their technical articles in philosophical journals like Mind. Besides, some of these discussions were beyond me because they demanded a good deal of training and proficiency in mathematics and physics. The mathematical or symbolic logic, which is opposed to the formal logic of Aristotle, the empirical logic of Mill, the metaphysical logic of the idealists like Hegel, Bradley and Bosanquet and the psychological logic of the pragmatists like Schiller, has been developed into a highly specialized science with its exact language of signs and symbols. Within its own limited field it has achieved a triumph in pure, formal and precise thinking, but it does not cover the whole province of logic and it has little metaphysical significance. Further, in its development as Logical Positivism it has become anti-metaphysical, affirming that all metaphysical propositions are nonsensical and condemning all metaphysical, moral and religious controversies as utterly futile. The distinctive contribution of the new realistic movement lies in its clever and detailed analytical investigation of special problems like perception and in its refutation of subjective idealism. Its representatives have employed the microscopic as against the telescopic method of the idealists and, as against the pragmatists, they have kept theoretical understanding rather than practical utility as the goal of their philosophical inquiry. They have conducted their investigations on logical and scientific lines without introducing ethical and religious considerations or striving after a comprehensive metaphysical[1] system. They are thus generally inclined to ignore the speculative and constructive, ethical and religious aspects of philosophy. There are, however, a few distinguished exceptions like Whitehead, who, it may be observed, illustrate *The Meeting of Extremes* (realism and idealism) *in Contemporary Philosophy*.[2]

A comparative study of Indian philosophy and a critical survey

---

[1] Mr. C. E. M. Joad's remark that "Modern Realism is a movement of metaphysical renunciation" is, in a sense, amply justified.

[2] The name of the book by Bosanquet.

of the new trends in psychology, logic and epistemology which limited the scope of my studies mainly to ethical, metaphysical and religious problems, supported, directly or indirectly, the idealistic view of the world that was gradually shaping in my mind. I was greatly impressed though not logically convinced by the idealistic and purposive trend of the recent developments in physics and biology, as represented by scientists like Einstein and Planck, Eddington and Jeans, J. A. Thomson and J. S. Haldane, Bergson and Lloyd Morgan.[1] With all my appreciation of the triumphs of science and technology, my mind could find no rest in its materialistic and mechanistic implications as usually understood. I have come to discern more and more clearly the limitations of science (how it is analytical in its method and sectional in its outlook, how its data are "phenomenal" and its laws statistical in character and how as a result of convenient abstraction, it excludes active mind and higher values from its purview, taking, as it were, "the juice out of reality") and to realize more and more keenly the supreme need and importance of attaining, as far as possible, philosophical synthesis and spiritual illumination, whereby one may obtain an insight into the ultimate nature of reality in its wholeness and in regard to its various aspects and levels as indicated by such terms as matter, life, mind and spirit.

I should also mention in this connection the benefit I have derived from thought-provoking discussions with the research students working under my guidance for the Doctor's degree and with the Professors of philosophy in different Universities attending the sessions of the Indian Philosophical Congress where I have read papers on *Some Aspects of Modernism in Philosophy* (as President of Logic and Metaphysics Section), *Fichte and his Idealism, Property and Improperty, Ultimate Truth and Perennial Philosophy*, etc. What has, however, largely determined the direction and development of my thought is the influence (sometimes only indirect and negative) of thinkers like Plato, Spinoza and Hegel, Bradley, Bosanquet and Royce, Bergson, Croce and

---

[1] Briefly discussed in my *Scientific Outlook—its Evolution,* a series of six radio talks broadcast from Bombay and in my paper on *Lloyd Morgan's Philosophy of Emergent Evolution* in the Proceedings of the Indian Philosophical Congress.

Whitehead, Ward, Inge and Taylor. I have found their works not only exceedingly instructive, shedding a flood of light on vital philosophical problems, but also highly suggestive and stimulating. I feel most deeply indebted, above all, to the Vedānta[1] of which the Upaniṣads, the Bhagavadgītā and the Brahma-sūtras form the triple foundation (Prasthānatraya); to the great truths of Perennial Philosophy as taught and practised by the wise and holy of all faiths, Hindu and Christian mystics, Mohammedan Sufis and devotees of Taoism and (Mahāyāna) Buddhism; to the mystical poetry and sayings of the saints of Ālandī and Dehu, of Dakṣineśwara, Nimbargī and Umadī. Among the living Indian philosophers whose scholarly and brilliant writings have considerably influenced my views, I specially mention the names of Sri Aurobindo Ghosh, Professor R. D. Ranade and Radhakrishnan. I am indebted to them for the integral, mystical and moral aspects of my idealistic philosophy. To Professor Ranade in particular who has profoundly influenced my life, I owe in large measure what little spiritual insight I may have.

The above account will give the reader a fair idea of the general background of my philosophical credo and some of its important aspects. A fuller and more explicit statement of my views has to be left for some other occasion.

[1] The following are the main Vedāntic threads which along with others selected from Western sources are rather freely woven into the somewhat complex fabric of my faith as an idealist, which, if I may say so, is a faith that enquires and gathers: One alone absolutely Real—Existence-Consciousness-Bliss (ekamevādwitīyam Brahma—Sat-Chit-Ānanda). Two kinds of knowledge—transcendental (Parā) and empirical (Aparā). Three orders of existence—Imaginary, Phenomenal and Real (trividhasattā —Prātibhāsika, Vyāvahārika and Pāramārthika). Four ends of life— Duty, Wealth, Pleasure and Salvation (chaturvidhapuruṣārtha—Dharma, Artha, Kāma and Mokṣa). Five sheaths of the soul—Physical, Vital, Mental,I ntellectual and Beatific (pañcakoṣas—Annamaya, Prāṇamaya, Manomaya, Vijñānamaya and Ānandamaya).

The possibility of an aspirant attaining salvation here and now even while alive (jīvanmukti), which means Self-realization (ātmasākṣātkāra or Swarūpadarśana) or realization of the identity of the Absolute and Self (brahmātmaikyānubhava), when he is blessed by Divine Grace (prasāda), the land-marks in his progress being indicated by spiritual visions and auditions (of unlit light and unstruck music of the Infinite, for example), resulting in ecstatic delight, and finally in perfect peace or settled calm of spirit.

Here, in the meanwhile, I shall content myself with giving the following extracts with slight alterations from my papers, except the one on "Integral Idealism" which is largely rewritten, in elucidation of certain points in my idealistic philosophy.

SCIENCE, HUMANISM AND RELIGION :

Science has indeed developed our intellect and given us knowledge of the external world and mastery over it. But the inner world has remained unsubdued. Knowledge has grown from more to more, but "more of reverence" has not come to dwell in us. Science touches but a part of our life and its problems. Spiritual values escape the meshes of our intellect. Humanism has a wider outlook on life and includes in its purview such higher values as æsthetic and moral, for example, which embellish and elevate human life. But in its over-emphasis on the human and secular side of life, it ignores the Cosmic and Divine. It cannot lift us from the finite to the infinite, from the temporal to the Eternal, and cannot satisfactorily solve the deepest problems of life. It is true that humanism regards man as mind, not as mere body, but it does not duly consider the essentially spiritual nature of man. Science is partial not "Whole," Humanism is secular not "Holy." Hence, their light is broken and dim and their guidance of limited value. It is only religion, the religion of Spirit, which, with its gaze fixed on the Whole and the Holy, the Infinite and the Eternal, can bless humanity groping in darkness with steady light and unerring guidance. Such a religion stands for the ideal of Self-realization and disinterested service of humanity flowing therefrom. It is through such religion which, without belittling the services of scientific rationalism and large-hearted humanism, only points out their insufficiency and limitations, that mankind will be saved. . . .

INTEGRAL IDEALISM :

. . . By integral idealism then we may understand a synthetic philosophy of Spirit. It includes a recognition of different orders of being and ways of knowing, of different ends of life and means of fulfilling them and also their evaluation on the basis of the supreme reality of Spirit.

. . . Integral idealism does not criticize the search for unity as the last infirmity of philosophic minds; on the contrary, it propounds a frankly monistic theory. Only it does not stand for any abstract or exclusive form of monism, whether materialistic or spiritualistic, which it finds philosophically untenable as representing a very partial and one-sided view and morally undesirable as leading either to sensualism or asceticism. It is opposed to "the airy subjectivism of the solipsist who thinks that he can destroy the world by going to sleep," and also to spiritual pluralism of the personalist who revolting against the static philosophy of the all-devouring and impersonal Absolute, attaches supreme importance to the category of personality and holds that reality consists of a plurality of persons having intrinsic dignity, uniqueness and freedom which they maintain to the last even by the side of God, who is only the chief among them and needs their co-operation. Such a conception of God, finite and personal, and of persons as absolutely unique and distinct, is logically unsound and shows little insight into the most essential aspect of religion, viz. the mystical. God to the mystic is absolutely real, eternal and infinite, the alpha and omega of all being; and knowledge of God by identity, supernal bliss of unitive experience and acting as the mouthpiece of God and doing His will, the highest ideal of his life. Personalism however is justified in its criticism of abstract monism and the conception of a "block universe." Integral idealism itself, in fact, stresses the doctrinal and practical importance of paying special attention to the concrete and dynamic aspects of Reality.

. . . The familiar world of sense and the scientific world of conceptual knowledge are phenomenal appearances of noumenal reality. Though Reality and appearances are thus distinguishable, there is no dualism between them. Whatever its practical utility, the dualistic way of thinking (and it assumes different forms) is found to be theoretically superficial and liable to be criticized as being generally based on "the fallacy of misplaced concreteness." Reality is a concrete, spiritual whole in which all differences are reconciled and all dualities are transcended. It is beyond the pale of sense and understanding but can be grasped by intuition, in which the subject-object relation is transcended. It may be pointed out here that it is Self-consciousness that supplies the best clue to Reality.

. . . Reality is infinite and it is in and beyond appearances which are finite. It is thus both immanent and transcendent. Reality manifests itself in diverse forms (material, vital and mental, for example) which are not all on one plane but exhibit a hierarchy or "climbing stairs of perfection." Far from overlooking these differences, integral idealism acknowledges their relevance and adjudges their value by ascertaining their place in the scheme of Reality. When we speak of ascent from the lower to the higher steps in the ladder of perfection we find that it is determined by the principles of continuity and emergence. Emergence which implies discontinuity, surprise and Grace is opposed to continuity which implies gradual and inevitable unfoldment. But integral idealism finds it possible to reconcile them. . . . It will be seen from the above that integral idealism regards existence and value as inseparable, and finds continuity and emergence as compatible, both being necessary to account for "rising higher and higher in the scale of Reality."

. . . If Spirit (Ātman) thus as distinguished from matter, life and mind, is absolute reality, and intuition (svānubhava) as distinguished from perception, inference and testimony, is the most direct and convincing way of knowing, liberation (Mokṣa) constitutes the supreme end of life. Among the three subordinate ends moral integrity stands first, pursuit of wealth and pleasure being allowed so far as it does not contravene the claims of inward purity and social justice. Now, liberation is the ideal of God-realization, of perfect knowledge, complete freedom and supreme bliss, overflowing in loving kindness to the whole of mankind. This ideal, rightly understood, does not lead to an other-worldly, pessimistic or anti-social life. If there is liberation, it is "here or nowhere." It is liberation *in* this world and not *from* this world in order to find a dwelling-place in some other. There is no other world; it is only this world seen under the form of eternity by the eye of the soul when it turns round from darkness to light. The life of a liberated soul is not self-centred but it centres round God and all his actions radiate from that centre. They are inspired and supported by the clear vision and joyous strength which he obtains through deep, inward meditation and they contribute to the relief of man's estate and proclaim the glory of God. His life, in fact, is a rhythm of withdrawal and return, withdrawal into solitude for quiet contemplation and return to society for translating that vision into disinterested service of humanity. In the words of Eckhart, "What a man takes in by contemplation, that he pours out in love." He thus lives in this world without being entangled in it, and cheerfully discharges all his moral and social duties in the living present without losing sight of the Eternal, that is to say, by cultivating the true spirit of other-worldliness, of which discrimination (Viveka) and detachment (Vairāgya) constitute the essential features. There is thus no running away from life as it is or seeking an easy or sentimental escape therefrom, but facing it with knowledge, courage and cheer. Integral idealism with its doctrine of liberation is opposed to escapism whether it assumes the form of archaism, or futurism, or asceticism. It stands for transfiguration . . . Its highest ideal is the realization of eternal life here and now in this world, the realization of a thoroughly integrated life in Spirit in all its aspects and phases.

TIME AND ETERNITY :

We are advised to "take time seriously." There is much truth in this advice. But without a faith in the Eternal, we shall not be able to understand what time really is, much less shall we be able to take it seriously. Unless we have faith in the values that we are realizing in time as being really grounded in the Eternal and Uncreated, we shall be depriving them of their fullest, perhaps of all their meaning. Values which are merely a function of time to be realized at some future date and which are not sustained and vitalized by some eternal reservoir upon which they draw, are lifeless things, such stuff as dreams are made of . . . In creative activities, in the creation of a beautiful work of art, for example, there must be *"reception" from region beyond*. As Browning says, it is not a creation so much as an effluence. The difference between a seer and an artist on the one hand and ordinary men on the other is that while the latter are engrossed in the ephemeral objects that meet their eyes, the former gaze on the eternal ocean of values and thus get a foretaste of immortality. . . . We misunderstand the nature of Eternity if we look upon it as endless time, as present time indefinitely prolonged in both directions, past as well as future. We do not reach Eternity by going backward or forward. It is to be realized, as the seers and saints tell us, *here and now*. . . . Time may be described in the picturesque language of Plato as "a moving image of Eternity." But the image is a true image.

CREATION AS PLAYFULNESS OF THE ABSOLUTE :

The spiritual unity of the Absolute is not a dead, monotonous, static unity, for then it would cease to be spiritual. The Spirit is essentially active. Modernism in philosophy is, in a sense, as much justified in its attack on the changeless and motionless character of the Absolute as in its revolt against the featureless, abstract unity of the Absolute. . . . The world is a dynamic expression of the Absolute, which spontaneously and eternally reveals the inner wealth of its fulness in newer and yet newer manifestations. This revelation is change or creation as understood in the time-sense . . . In all its manifestations the Absolute does not transform itself into something else but freely gives out what it contains in itself in fulness . . . There is nothing outside the Absolute which can compel or obstruct its free revelation in varied forms. It is pure freedom or spontaneity. . . . The very nature of the Absolute is to overflow and this spontaneous overflow is called the creation[1] of the world. It may indeed be described as an act of "playfulness" (Līlā) of the Absolute or its self-delight! Though stress is here laid on the transcendence of the Absolute, its immanence can never be lost sight of. These are only two aspects which are, as Miss Underhill happily puts it, enshrined in the Greek and Latin names of God, *Deus* (the Transcendent Light) and *Theos* (the Inward Love) which blend into one in the integral experience of the mystic.

INTELLECT AND INTUITION :

We distinguish between intellect and intuition; but we do not construe that distinction into an entire disparateness or an irreconcilable opposition. The great Indian tradition has not committed

[1] "Those who regard God (Absolute Self) as building up a world from an ever-lasting inert matter, like a vessel made by human hands, or ascribe to Him the creation of the world out of nothing, know neither the world nor Him."—Fichte.

that mistake. It has tried to complete the account of reason by the revelation of intuition, which is wisdom gained by the whole spirit. Intellect is not despised as giving a totally distorted or false picture of Reality. Its account is true so far as it goes; but it does not go far and deep enough. It tries to give us a cogent and coherent account of Reality but it is more or less external and it does not penetrate into the heart of Reality. Its thought-constructions are more or less abstract and lacking in directness and emotional warmth and intimacy which characterize intuition. The predominantly analytical, discursive and vacillating nature of intellect rquires to be corrected and supplemented by the wholeness, directness and utter certainty of intuitive experience. All that may be dark or dim to intellect becomes radiant to intuition. Intellect may show us the temple of God; it may take us near the temple; it may even help us enter it; but it itself remains outside. It is intuition that takes us inside the temple and enables us to see God face to face and be one with Him. It is in intuition ultimately that the synoptic view of the rational philosopher blends with the beatific vision of the religious mystic. . . .

According to our idealistic theory, it is the Absolute Self that is ultimately real, in which the finite self and not-self are grounded and from which they derive their reality. The Absolute Self, popularly called God, is beyond the ken of discursive reason or "inquisitive understanding which has heard of Thee but seen Thee not." In this sense our theory is agnostic. It is mystical because it believes that God can be intuitively apprehended. According to our theory, reason criticises itself, and recognizing its own limitations it points beyond itself to intuition.[1] It implies disagreement with the view that identifies Thought and Being, Real and Rational, and is thus opposed to Pan-logism. But this does not mean that it implies misology[2] any more than misanthropy. On the contrary, it regards "distrust of logic or reason" and "hatred of man" as the greatest danger to philosophic sanity and moral integrity. Let us not forget that he who attempts to overthrow reason ends by overthrowing himself, and that he who hates man shatters the very foundation of moral life!

ULTIMATE TRUTH :

There are certain thinkers who deny the reality of Ultimate or Absolute Truth. According to them, it is only a fiction of the human mind or at best only its fond hope. There are some others who while

[1] Intuition thus transcends reason. But to transcend is not to reject or ignore but to transfigure.

[2] Fawcett, the exponent of "Imaginism," for example, in extreme opposition to Hegel's "Pan-logism," carries his dislike of reason to the point of proudly exclaiming, "Thus we have got rid of reason!"

recognizing its reality yet regard it as unknowable. But our idealistic theory considers such sceptical and agnostic theories as untenable, the former whether implying dogmatic denial or teaching "caution's excess" and the latter whether assuming the Kantian or the Spencerian form. It holds that there *is* Ultimate Truth and that it is attainable, though its full attainment is extremely difficult . . .

Just as appearances are grounded in Reality and permanence is implied in all change, Absolute Truth is pre-supposed in all partial and relative truths. . . . All truths except the last are fragmentary and shine by borrowed light. They are true in their own kind and true only so far as they go. Ultimate Truth is the truth of truths. It is universal and eternal. It is self-valid, carrying its certainty and validity within itself and needing no external criterion. It is self-luminous like the sun which shines by its own light and in whose light we see the sun itself and everything else.

Science may welcome any truth however fragmentary, but our idealistic theory has for its aim the attainment of that Truth which is the source and test of all truths and which refers to the first principle of being in all things. In the last analysis, Truth coincides with Reality. It is knowledge by identity or integral experience of Reality which we may call Ātman or Brahman. We call it Ātman when we discover it within us by penetrating the different sheaths, physical, vital, mental, intellectual and beatific, and by going beyond the states of wakefulness, dream and deep-sleep to the state of Pure Self-consciousness. We call it Brahman when we discover it without us by probing the manifold, fluent world of appearances and discerning its one, abiding, substantive Ground. Ultimate Truth is not perceived by sense nor understood by thought but it is intuitively apprehended. It is a matter of immediate, spiritual experience. It is ineffable. "The eye goes not thither nor speech nor mind." The Absolute Truth satisfies a man's spiritual yearning by establishing his contact, and finally by uniting him, with Godhead or Brahman. This contact, this union, is liberation which is beatitude. With the attainment of such Truth, all doubts and difficulties are removed, all discords and discrepancies vanish and our life is transfigured and we live in blissful eternity . . .

If the Ultimate Truth is attainable, what is the way, we may ask, that leads to its discovery and realization? Why is it that "Truth is the cry of all but the game of the few?" All men desire truth but only those rare souls who pay the required price can attain it. The price is indeed very heavy. They have to undergo a severe intellectual and moral discipline. Certain conditions are laid down in the Upaniṣads and emphasized by Śaṃkara which a seeker after truth must satisfy. He must have, in the first place, an inquiring spirit, a desire to know what is Real. He must learn to discriminate between the eternal and the ephemeral and must not allow himself to be deluded by appearances. Further, he has to see that his mind is

G

kept free from all prejudice and attachment to the fruit of action. Again, it is necessary for him to acquire self-knowledge by turning the eye inward and to purify his heart by practising virtues such as tranquillity, self-control, charity and compassion. And lastly, he must not only have a keen desire for knowledge but also an intense yearing for liberation. But it should be remembered that for the attainment of Truth which means spiritual illumination or Ātmajñāna, intellectual discipline and moral purity, however indispensable, are by themselves not enough. They only prepare the ground. For spiritual illumination prayer, meditation and Divine Grace are necessary. Such prayer is more than an out-pouring or an entreating. It is silent communion with God. It is not of the nature of petition, intercession or even adoration, but of contemplation. Such contemplation to be positively fruitful and illuminating must, as emphasized by saints and seers of India in particular, take the form of meditation on the Name of God as imparted by a Spiritual Teacher who has realized his identity with God. The surest, the safest and the best pathway to spiritual illumination or Self-realization is constant and one-pointed meditation on the Divine Name with unswerving faith and whole-hearted love and devotion. But with all our knowledge and morality, prayer and meditation,we shall not reach the heights and enjoy the fulness of spiritual experience unless we are blessed by God with His abounding Grace.

ĀTMA-VIDYĀ, OR THE SCIENCE OF THE SELF

by BHAGAVAN DAS

Born January 1869

ĀTMA-VIDYĀ, OR THE SCIENCE OF
THE SELF

PRELIMINARY

IN the year 1880 A.D. a boy was studying in the Matriculation
Class of the School attached to the Queen's College of Benares.
From time immemorial Benares has been and continues to be
the greatest publicly known centre of Saṁskṛt learning and the
religious capital of India. In that same year, 1880, when the boy
was in his twelfth year, he witnessed his dearly loved and loving
grandmother pass away. He followed her bier to the funeral pile,
wondering deeply what it all meant. Then came into his hands
casually papers which spoke of holy men, Rishis, Yogis, possessed
of sacred, mystical and philosophical knowledge, as if they were
still to be found. He also happened to have some conversations
with benevolent Saññyāsins and spiritual-minded persons. In
earliest childhood he had greedily absorbed story portions of
the purànas, the Rāmāyana, and the Mahābhārata, sitting
beside his grandmother, when the Pandit recited and expounded
them in the afternoons; the philosophy with which they were
saturated passed over his mind, leaving behind only sub-conscious
traces, if any. But now some sleeping germinal tendencies
(*samskāras*) awoke, though the boy of twelve understood but
little of the things that he read and heard.

A curious sense of the futility of this earthly life came into
his sensitive boyish mind. Mixed with the usual distractions
and engagements, play and school, of boy-life, vague mystical
achings, yearnings for something better, "The desire of the moth
for the star, of the night for the morrow, The devotion to something afar from the sphere of our sorrow," seized him off and
on. Gaining strength as he grew older, these questionings took
definite shape as the ever-present wish to understand the "why"
of the misery within and without, the "how" of its cure. All
subordinate questions were inseparably connected with the great
question of the "why" and the "how" of the Universe. No part
can be understood unless its articulation with the whole in the

ways of co-ordination, subordination, super-ordination is worked out. Part and whole, individual and society, society and the universe, finite and infinite, can be understood and dealt with only in relation to each other. To convince Arjuna, distraught with a sudden compassion and a horror of the slaughter of cousins, that it was his duty to war against his sinful kinsmen, Krishna had to compress into seven hundred verses an explanation of the whole scheme of the Universe and the meaning of all life.

The boy took up courses of psychology, ethics, metaphysics in the College; thought, discussed with sympathetic friends, and read all he could in English and Sanskrit. The disadvantage of two unfamiliar languages ultimately proved an advantage, for the times required that the invaluable ideas enshrined in the old Sanskrit medium should be interpreted in the new counters of thought. Only so could they help towards a *rapprochement* between Eastern and Western, ancient and modern, thought and life.

The longing to find out the "why" and the "how" became a psychic fever. Consciously, subconsciously even more, this was the mood of the youth up to 1887. In that year he somehow found satisfaction; an answer arose in his mind, which summed up, in itself, answers to countless subordinate queries. The fever abated. Aspiration for a better, a holier life, remained—and remains, unfulfilled unfortunately, to this day. But his mind is more or less at peace at the centre, though there is not and cannot be peace on the surface.

That boy, that youth, is the present writer, now in his sixty-seventh year waiting patiently to cast off his nearly worn-out body, wishing well to all, praying with all his heart that other hearts may find much greater peace, at least no less, than he has found.

In humble endeavour towards this great object, by inner compulsion, and even more by the wish of kind friends, who liked his reinterpretations and presentations in fresh forms of the eternal truths recorded in the scriptures by the ancients, the writer has compiled a number of books to be of service to such readers as may be more interested in the modern ways of thinking, to express them livingly, since the old ones have become hackneyed with much use.

The writer may mention here at once that he is a believer in
(1) infinitely countless individual selves or souls; (2) their rebirths,
evolution and involution, in and through evolving and involving,
integrating and disintegrating, forming and dissolving, material
bodies and surroundings; the passing of each self, through all
possible experiences, in infinite time, space and motion; in (3)
cycles and circles of time and space on all possible scales of
duration and extent, in which the processes of rhythmic evolution
and involution manifest themselves; in (4) One all-including,
all-pervading, ever-complete, timeless, spaceless, Universal Soul
or Spirit or Self, which is Absolute and Changeless, which is
also identical with and includes within It-self all the countless
individual selves, and whose eternally changeless, and yet also
ever-changing, Ideation the entire world-process of all souls and
bodies is.

Reasons for this faith, expounded in his books, as fully as
was possible for the writer's very feeble powers, may appear
briefly in the course of the present paper.

THE PSYCHIC FEVER OF SPIRITUAL ADOLESCENCE

Psychic fever seems to be a normal event in the evolution of
the human soul, somewhat like adolescence in that of the
physical body, and frequently, though not always, coincides
with it in time. A certain dissatisfaction with the ever-disappoint-
ing, fleeting, painful, deathful world seems to be the main
emotional characteristic of it; and a disinclination for the
apparently futile daily duties of life, the actional characteristic.
If the intellectual characteristic of enquiry into causes is weak
(as it is in the earlier stages of the soul's evolution), and the
frustration of wish and hope and consequent fear and anger
and despair are very severe, then, in extreme cases, physical
suicide may be the result. If both enquiry and distaste are
weak, the mood passes, and the individual settles down to the
routine of life quietly. But if the intellectual enquiry is keen,
persistent, invincible; if the passion of revolt against the cruelties
and injustices of life which inspires that enquiry is compassion
for fellow-sufferers; if the revolt is against the sufferings of not

only oneself but of all selves—as it is when the soul has arrived at a certain stage, as every soul must, and is turning from egoism to conscious altruism, on the way back to Universalism in the great cycles of the World-process—then the result is an Understanding, a philosophy, a theory of who am I, what am I, whence and whither and wherefore am I; who, what, whence, whither, wherefore, are all these other I's; what, why, how, is all this, i.e. the world of objects and its incessant process; what the meaning and purpose of life with all its pains as well as all its pleasures.[1] The result of the successful passing through this experience seems intended by Nature to be the strengthening of the individual body, soul and spirit, in action, emotion and intellect, for the discharge of the duties of life, physical, super-physical and metaphysical.

VAIRĀGYA AND ITS CONSEQUENCES—OF DIFFERENT KINDS

Vairāgya (dis-passion, dis-taste), if it is predominantly (*rājasa* and *tāmasa*) inspired by "egoistic restless or clinging passions," leads in its extreme form to "physical" suicide, whereby the unhappy soul destroys the outer apparatus through which it experienced misery, under the false belief that it will thereby destroy the real source of misery (*kleśa*); a source which, however, is fundamentally internal, and only superficially external; for the outer apparatus itself is created by it and will be fashioned by it anew, again and again, until it, the internal cause, has been diagnosed and cured. But when the dis-affection is intelligent (*sāttvika*), enlightened, philanthropic, accompanied by intense intellectual seeking for cause and remedy, is guided by discrimination (*viveka*) between the permanent and the transient, the lasting True and the fleeting False, when it is combined with the "cardinal virtues" (*sādhana-shatka*) which are the opponents and vanquishers of the six "deadly sins" (*ṣadṛpu*), and is motived by poignant "yearning for freedom" (*mumukṣā*), not only for oneself but for all selves, freedom from that quint-essence of all pains, viz. the fear of pain and death, the feeling of being at the mercy of another, the doubt of Immortality

---

[1] See the opening chapters of the writer's *The Science of Peace, Tales from the Yoga Vāshishta; The Science of the Emotions;* and two pamphlets, *Psychology of Conversion* and *The Fundamental Idea of Theosophy.*

and Self-dependence—then the result is Realisation of the True Universal Self (*Ātma-bodha*), Spiritual Knowledge, Theosophia, God-Wisdom, Metaphysical knowledge of "that which is beyond the physical" but yet includes the physical; conviction of the Immortality and invulnerable Self-dependence of the Self, the Universal Self with which all selves are identical; the destruction of Error, Delusion, Nescience, False Belief (*avidyā-nāśa*), the "meta-physical" "suicide" of the inner egoistic selfish self, under the compulsion of the True Knowledge (*Vidyā*) that separative egoism (*ahamkāra*) is the final internal root of all misery; then the result is the realisation, by the person, of the identity of his individual self (*jivātmā*), personal ego, with the Supreme Self (*Paramātmā*), the Absolute Ego, and consequent freedom from all fear and sorrow, extinction of the sense of separateness, the uprising of the Bliss of the sense of non-separateness; the conviction that All is One-Self, that All is I, unto I, by I, for I, from I, of I, in I; that all possible relations expressible by any prepositions are ever-present between I and not-I.

The far-reaching nature of this sense of non-separateness is seen in the awful consequences of its opposite, race-separatism, nation, class, creed, colour, sex, age-separatism; consequences from which the human world has been and is suffering, in the shape of war, pestilence, social convulsions, perpetual semi-starvation in intensive and extensive forms, since the beginning of the twentieth century.

Sensitiveness to the sorrows of others, sympathy, is the sensing of the Universal Self in all selves and things, round which every atom, every orb of heaven, the breath in the lungs, the blood in the veins and arteries, every manifestation in every department of Nature, revolves in cycles, and in which all duality, all opposites, are "turned into one" (uni-versed). Such compassionate passion of dis-gust (*vairāgya*) with the heartless iniquities of life, and such indomitable faith that the secret of the universe is powerless to withstand the might of thought are indispensable for the kindling of "the Light that lighteth every man."

Buddha, in his divine madness, abandoning wife and child, takes the oath: "I will not enter these gates again until I have won the secret of life and death to help my fellow-sufferers."

The secret he wins and teaches all who care to learn is that "we suffer from ourselves, none else compels"; there *is* none else to compel.

THE UNITY OF LIFE AND THEREFORE OF THE SCIENCE OF LIFE

In Indian tradition the culmination of philosophy is the same as that of pragmatic ethics, science, art, religion—in the sense of ultimate principles, or rather one final principle. Nature, God's nature, Nature's God, is a breakless continuum. The bodily-mental life of man, with all the varied organs and functions involved, is the life of an organic unity. The laws and the facts of all the sciences, arts, philosophy, the religion of God—Nature —Man are all at work simultaneously in that life, in the body and mind of man, as indeed in everything everywhere, in varied degrees. Indian philosophy, Vedānta, the "final knowledge," is not only a theory, a body of knowledge, a set of beliefs; it is a philosophy which arises in, and in turn gives stronger rise to, philanthropic aspiration, and inspires and guides beneficent action. It is eminently emotional, devotional, humanitarian also, for it sees and worships the One in all animate and seemingly inanimate Nature. It is Jñāna-bhakti-karma, knowledge —devotion—works, all in one. Its purpose is to maximise human happiness and to abolish sorrow; to satisfy not only intellectual curiosity but also emotional hunger and actional craving; to reconcile and balance and give scope to head, heart and limbs; to give duly apportioned equal opportunity to the man of knowledge, the man of desire, the man of action, the undeveloped man, one and all. It is called darśana (insight), vision, view, because it enables us to see the heart of all things.

THE LOGION WHICH SUMS UP THE SCIENCE OF LIFE

In the exalted mood which followed the "sudden flash" of insight that lighted up the darkness and brought the answer the writer composed a little poem in the manner of the aphoristic and ecstatic utterances; the last lines were:

Out of the storm rose calm the thought—
I (am) This not, I (am) This not.

These words, slight though they look, enclose all the philosophy which the present writer has been able to achieve. The soul must crave to discover the true nature of God, of Self, as frantically as the suffocating man struggles for air, before it finds the Truth. The spiritual preceptor of the Upaniṣads imparts the "commonplace" knowledge by a solemn, earnest, tenderly affectionate whisper into the ear of the equally earnest and devoted listener, in psychical conditions which transmute the common lead into exceedingly uncommon gold; and a mental, a spiritual, miracle is performed; *Tat tvam asi*: *So'ham*, Thou art That which thou seekest; Thou hast been seeking thine own True Self; I am That; the I is That; "That I (which Thou and I are, that I is, and am) not this." For the requirements of the writer's mind, the Upaniṣad teaching, "That am I," was completed by the thought, "Not this." Positive and Negative together make up the Absolute, the Whole Truth, of the Relatives abolishing, neutralising, each other.[1]

THE STRUGGLE FOR THE LOGION

Failing to find satisfaction in the current philosophies of the East and the West—very likely because of his imperfect understanding of them—and having struggled on till he arrived at this great word, this Logion, his quest ended, though the unending routine of duties remained. After this glimpse, the hidden word began to shine out clearly from the pages of the Scriptures.[2] Recapitulating the progress to the logion, the following steps can be traced. The popular theory of causation (*ārambha-vāda*), that an extra-cosmical personal God makes and unmakes the world at will, fails to convince lastingly. The scientific theory of causation (*pariṇāma-vāda* or *vikāra-vāda*), that the world-process is a continuous transformation or creative evolution which is the result of the interplay of two infinites, indestructible matter and indestructible force—this is only a description, not an explanation. Two infinites are illogical. The metaphysical theory of causation, that the world is an unreal dream-idea (*māyā-vāda ābhāsa-vāda*), is the ideation, the willed-imagination

---

[1] See the writer's *Science of Peace*.

[2] See quotations in *Science of Peace* and other works of the writer.

of My-Self (*Param-ātma*, Brahma), the Infinite Universal Self, comes nearer home.

But some difficulties remain. Why should the Self dream at all? And such a very painful dream! Why any change—which means desire, incompleteness, imperfection? And what after all is change? Every change means the passing of something, some being, into nothing, and of non-being into some being, something; this violates the very fundamentals of ordinary logic. How can we reconcile Change with the Changeless, Brahma with Māyā, and Joy of Self-dependence with Misery of Life—this is the ultimate trouble with this last theory of causation.

"I am" is the most unquestionable eternal fact. "Cogito ergo" is superfluous. "Sum" is enough. But "This," the world of objects, the opposite of "I" (*vivarta*), this "Other-than-I," this "Not-I," this "Else-than-Subject," all the mass of objects which consciousness looks at as "This"—this is also an indubitable though utterly changeful, ever passing, fact. If we succeed in reconciling the two in such a way that the not-I shall be at the will of the I and not the other way round; such a way that the I, while doing what it pleases with the not-I, shall still not lose its eternal fulness and completeness; such a way that disorder, arbitrariness, shall go hand in hand with law and order; then we shall have found the consolation and the peace that we are seeking. The insistent question, why this process, why this posing and opposing, this mutual limitation, remains the crux. The incomprehensibility is admitted; the synthesis seems partial, almost superficial. But if anything remains incomprehensible, all remains such; the chain is no stronger than its weakest link. The unquestionable fact of Becoming, of change is utterly illogical and impossible to understand, so that we want to feel that there is *no* change in reality. As regards Being and Non-Being or Nothing, the only real, ultimate, permanent Being that we are aware of is "I am"; and the non-real Being, the No-thingness that we are simultaneously aware of, is that of the transient, evanescent, "This," the not-I.

We must try again. The secret lies hidden somewhere between "I" and "This." If we can discover the precise nature of the relation between these two, which are the only things that interest us, which fill our whole life and make up and exhaust the whole universe, we will surely have discovered the secret.

Instead of saying "Being is Nothing" (as Hegel said), it seems more readily intelligible to say, "Being is Not Non-Being, Not Nothing, or rather Not-any-particular-thing"; better than that, "Ego is not non-Ego"; better than that, "I is not not-I"; better than that, "I (am) Not Not-I"; and, finally, better than all else, "I (am) not-This," or in the Samskṛt order, "I-(am)-This-Not" (*Aham-Etat-Na*).

In this sentence we gain the reconciliation we sought, the all-comprehensive synthesis which includes both thesis and antithesis within itself. The contrast between "I" and "not I" is so utterly complete that any thought of mutual identification (*anyonyā-dhyāsa*), complete or partial (in the way of mutual limitation), is not possible. But if we use the word "This," the impossibility disappears. Our body is clearly "This" to us. We say: "This body is mine," as we say, "his coat is mine"; "mine," not "me" but different, only belonging to me. And we obviously feel identified also with our body when we say "I am coming," "I am going," "Here am I." Mine is not I. Yet it is an extension of "I," a part of "I."

In the awareness "I (am) Not This," or "I-This-Not," the whole of all possible not-I's is affirmed, is present here, now, all at once, and, at the same time, the being, the existence, the reality, the truth of them all is denied. Affirmation and negation, supposition and opposition, are simultaneous in it. In the Logion (*Akam-Etat-Na*) we have the Motion, the movement, of the endless, everlasting, pseudo-infinite rhythmic swing of Self-heterisation and Self-establishment, both compressed into one successionless, timeless, spaceless, notionless, Uniform Awareness of the I as Not-Not-I. Such is the transcendental view (*param-ārtha-drishti*), the view from the standpoint of the Infinite, the Whole, the Unmanifest yet Ever manifest, the Unlimited and Unconditioned I.

But from the experiential standpoint (*vyavahāra-drishti*), the point of view of the conditioned This's—to the eye of the "This," the simultaneous All-consciousness of "I" and of all possible "not-I's affirmed and denied in the same breath appears as the Illusion of the alternating swing of to and fro, inbreathing

and outbreathing, which is motion, of *first* affirmative identification and *then* negative rejection in the *succession* which is Time,
amidst the *co-existence* of "here and there and side by side" of
pseudo-infinite not-I's, which is Space. The successive appearance
and disappearance of every "This" is its supposition and opposition by the I.

THE SIGNIFICANCE OF THE LOGION

The complete dialectic process of the full and final synthesis
thus appears to be—not merely a positing or posing of the I,
an opposing to itself by the I of a not-I, and then a composing
of the two by mutual limitation (which can be understood only
as partial identification), but—a posing of the I, an imposing,
upon it-self, by the I, of an opposite of it-self, then an opposing
and deposing of that imposture, and finally, a reposing, the
repose, of it-Self in its own pure Infinity (*Své mahimni sthitih*).
But the perpetually recurrent, superficial, incomplete, unreal,
synthesis of endless particular compositions of I and not-I's is
also a fact, an illusory fact; it *appears* as the unending spiral
circling of the Self in and through a pseudo-infinite number of
individual selves, all recurrently first connecting and then
disconnecting themselves with pseudo-infinite "this's," bodies,
mineral, vegetable, animal, human, superhuman, etc., on all
possible scales of time and space and motion in an endless
World-process of evolution and involution, "cycles in epicycles"
all "inveterately convolved."

Because the Supreme I is one, infinite, eternal, motionless,
attributeless, differenceless, conditionless, and the This is Its
opposite in every respect, yet inseparable from It, and imitative
of (because falsely identified ·with) It, therefore the This is
Many, is pseudo-infinite or illimitably extensive in space, everlasting or pseudo-eternal in time, never-resting, full of all sorts
of particular qualities, differences, conditions. The One I is
individualised, personalised, particularised, into pseudo-infinitely
many selves by the pseudo-infinite bodies with which it is
associated and dissociated.

Because each I is the One I, therefore each soul asserts and
achieves its indefeasible immortality by and in a pseudo-eternity
of endless rebirths. When it becomes tired of being an actor

in the drama, it becomes a silent spectator of the cinema. When it tires even of that, it can retire into deep slumber, of (*mokṣa, nirvāṇa*) freedom from all particular limitations, extinction of all distinctions, for as long as it pleases. When it is tired of slumber it can wake again, in a new world, a new system, if it so wills. Heavens and purgatories are no less and no more real than the fair and foul places of the waking world, the vivid glad-visions and nightmares of dream-life; our near and dear, as also objects of our hate and fear, are always present and close to us, according as we deeply wish and so deserve; so also is profound slumber wherein we and friend and foe all are One. All is ever-present in God's Memory, Supra-Conscious Omniscience; our memories are infinitesimal parts of That, as are our pleasures and pains and peace. We have whatever we really want. To really want is to will and deserve.

Since there is only One Self manifesting itself in all, there is no limitation of Its Will possible. Limitation is by an-Other; there is no-Other. Compulsion is by an antagonist; the adversary of the Self, viz. Not-Self, is within the Self, and ever-slain. All sorts of opponents are willed by the Self itself, in hostile pairs, and are destroyed by internecine war. The World-process, with all its loves and hates, laughs and sobs, friends and foes, weals and woes, lights and shades, is Its Will (*Līlā, Krīḍā, Nāṭaka*), play, drama. The reflection in, the imitation by, all selves, of this Supreme Wilfulness, "My Will there is none to dispute," is the illusion, the fact, but illusory fact, of "Free-will" in the individual. But the Supreme Will *necessarily* wills *opposites* which abolish each other; hence the contra-illusion of "Predestination."

From the Own-Being (*Svabhāva*), the very Nature of the Supreme Self, as expressed by the Logion, it follows that all proposings and imposings of not-I's *must inevitably* be neutralised, counter-balanced, contradicted, by equivalent opposings and deposings, in rhythmic swing, on the two half-circles, the arcs, of (*Pravṛtti* and *Nivṛtti, bandka* and *mokṣa*) birth and death, growth and decay, "pursuit" and "renunciation," "bondage" and "deliverance," descent and ascent, putting on of bodies and putting off of them. All plusses, additions, multiplications, must necessarily be nullified by equal minuses, subtractions, divisions, so that, taken together, they may be always making up the Absolute Zero, the Endless Circle, Vacuum-Plenum. Thus the Absolvedness from all particularities, the Ab-solute-ness, of the Supreme remains ever undisturbed.

Because the One Self, from the transcendental standpoint, includes at one, here, now, in utterly restful peace, all space, time, motion, therefore each self, from the empirical standpoint, in order to prove the identity of the Son with the Father, the Part with the Whole, seeks to encompass all time, space, motion, and accomplish its Parent's Perfectness, by perpetual procession, on all scales of these three, in and through all sorts of bodies and all possible kinds of experiences connected with those bodies. Witness the everlasting rush of the orbs of heaven through space, and of the living beings that may be on those orbs—all seeming separate from each other, in pseudo-infinite multiplicity, yet all also perpetually interlinked with each other into a Unity of "cycle in epicycle, orb in orb," system in system, individual and species and genus within and without one another, atoms within worlds and worlds within atoms, without end. Consider also the "inveterately convolved" and limitless *spiral* traced in empty space by the *circling* and *rolling* of these globes, these dead and living planets and bright and dark stars.

If we get firm hold of and are satisfied with the distinction between the transcendental standpoint of the Infinite and the experiential standpoint of the Finite, we still realise that to the former view there is *no* change, that "all is every-where and every-when and all-ways" (*sarvam sarvatra sarvadā sarvathā*); and where there is no change there can be no questioning of why and how. If we are convinced that the five senses which "prove" the existence of material objects do not cognise and prove themselves, that the eye which sees sights does not see itself, the ear which hears sounds does not hear itself, nor the skin, tongue, nose, touch, taste, smell themselves, but that they all are cognised and "proved" by the I, that "I" feel, am aware, am conscious, that they exist and see and hear, that the I-Consciousness is the Ultimate Fact which proves all other-facts, and is not proved by any other-fact, that is the locus of all experiences, good and evil, pleasurable and painful, that it is also Universal and the *Same* wherever there is an I-Consciousness, that "there is another" is also "*my*-consciousness" and the "other" is within "my-consciousness," that "within" and "without" are both "within," "thing" and "thought" both "thought," "subjective" and "objective" both "subjective," then too, we would see that our curses and sorrows, as much as our blessings and joys, are all within us, all equally the creations of that I My-Self. It creates them all by Its own Will, of Its own pleasure. Why have you done this? "Because of so-and-so"; Why that? "Because of such-and-such other reason." Finally the answer comes, "Because it was my pleasure to do so, because it pleased me to do so, even to inflict pain upon myself"; and therewith the questioning ceases. Things are proven by their opposites. The I proves Itself by opposing an imaged, imagined, Non-ego. If we wish to taste pleasure we must feel and contra-distinguish pain also. Pain, limitation, cramping, finitising, is prime incentive to search for remedy in the Infinite, and its inseparable bliss of freedom and self-dependence. But the final answer to all possible ·questioning, the abrogation of all enquiry, complete satisfaction and peace, seems possible only by means of the transcendental stand-point of the Logion and the negation and abolition of change itself.

RECONCILIATION OF ALL VIEWS

In the light of these principles, we may find the means of reconciling different views if we only substitute for their "only" —"this view *only* is the true view"—the word "also" and explain in what sense and with what qualifications and reserva-tions each and every view is true. Thus, since the grades of evolution stretch endlessly either way, "above and below," souls of very high grade and power may well occupy the places of personal Gods, of planets, of suns, of systems, Brahmas, Vishnus, Shivas, and Saraswatis, Lakshmis, Gauris, Archangels, Elohim, Ilaha, of higher and higher grades, as the Puranas and the scriptures of all religions say, and rightly be objects of devotion and worship to subordinate souls; in this sense, to this extent, theism is justifiable. Again, since I and Not-I, Spirit and Matter, are inseparable, in the general metaphysical sense, it may well be said that there is no strictly inanimate matter, that "the Universe is one stupendous whole whose Body Nature is, and God the Soul"; in this sense, pantheism is justified. Similar is the case with the views of transformation, of creative evolution, ever-new, "nothing is ever repeated"; also ever-old, "there is nothing new under the sun"; also chance, fate, and so on. Absolute Monism, as expressed by the Logion, explains and synthesises them all.

TRINITY

The word-sound made of three letters, A, U, M, may be regarded as the elemental sound-continuum which can yield all the sounds of animate and inanimate nature. This sound-word reverberating through space is the prime manifestation of the Unmanifest. It represents the Primal Trinity of the Self, the Not-Self, and the affirmative-negative Relation between the two. The World-Process has been described as made up of pairs of opposites, the ultimate opposites being self and Not-Self; these together with the Nexus between them make a triad. The Nexus is itself dual, assertion—denial. The Unity of the One in the Many gives rise to the Law of Uniformity, of "similarity in diversity," the seeing of which is science, as the culmination of such seeing, the seeing of Unity in Multiplicity, is metaphysics, completed science, completely organised or unified knowledge. The opposition of the "I" and the "not-I" generates the law of duality in its static aspect; in the dynamic aspect it engenders pairs of activities like progress and regress, evolution and involution.

The relation between the One and the Many sets the stamp of triplicity upon the Universe and its processes.[1] All triads spring from the Primal Trinity, which is an unbroken Unity or Zero. Groups of these triads form the subject matter of the several sciences, all interlinked, by the law divine embodies plainly in the Logion.

Since the whole nature of the I (sva-bhāva) requires and includes, for self-realisation, by contrasts, a pseudo-infinity of not-I's, we have the appearance of arbitrariness, disorder, if we look at any one particular not-I from the empirical standpoint. But since that same Nature requires that every not-I *must be*

[1] See *Praṇava-Vāda or the Science of the Sacred Word*, by Bhagavan Das.

contradicted by an opposite not-I, we have law and order. Desire is the element of arbitrary whim; reason is the element of law and system.

This unavoidable perpetual cyclical return of the Finite to the Infinite is the basis of all logical and mathematical necessity and world-order. All the fundamental concepts root back in this Primal Trinity of Spirit (*Puruṣa*), Matter (*Prakṛti*) and the positive-negative Force (*Sakti*), which constitutes the Relation between them. The *facts* of science reflect the arbitrariness of each affirmation; the *laws* the necessity of the perpetual negation.

A FEW IMPORTANT TRIADS

All these triads may be grouped into three Sciences[1] of (*a*) the **I** (*Paramātma, Puruṣa*), the Infinite Spirit; (*b*) the Not-I (*Anātma, Mūlaprakṛti*), Matter, the Finite, the pseudo-infinite; (*c*) the Nexus (*Sakti*) Energy.

I. In the Science of the Infinite Ego we may see the triad of (*a*) the Impersonal Absolute Ego, including (*b*) all limited, personal egos and individualised by (*c*) mind-bodies; thus we distinguish metaphysics, psychology and psycho-physics. When the Ego posits the Non-Ego, three moments or aspects develop in that single act, fact, or moment.. It *knows* the non-ego; it *desires* to attach or absorb the non-ego; it *identifies* itself with the non-ego. In the individualised Ego, these three functions are known as cognition, desire and action (*jñāna, icchā, kriyā*).

The abstract universal aspects of these three concrete functions of the soul, psyche, or mind, are known in Sanskrit as Chit, Ānanda and Sat, respectively. They are the principia of Omniscience, Omnipotence and Omnipresence. The objective aspects of the Pure Ego, corresponding to these subjective potencies, are the True (*Satyam*), the Beautiful (Priyam), the Good (*Hitam*); or Śāntam, Sundaram, Sivam, the Restful, the Lovely, the Auspicious. The object of knowledge is the True, the one changeless fact amidst endlessly restless and changing illusions; the Self is the only such sure and constant friend that will not, cannot, ever abandon us. The object of desire is the Beautiful;

---

[1] A full discussion of the classification of sciences is found in *The Science of Social Organisation*, i, pp. 264-274.

the Self is the ultimate heart's desire of all hearts, the One object of all longing; all Else is dear for Its sake; It is dear for Its own sake. The Good is the object of action; self-realisation, in and through and by love and service of the higher Self in all selves is the *summum bonum*, greatest good (*niś-sreyasa*).

The properties in the Non-Ego (*Prakṛti*) corresponding to these attributes or potencies of the Ego (*Purusha*) are cognisability, desirability, movability (*sattva, rajas, tamas*). In a concrete piece of matter they become quality, substance, movement (*guṇa, dravya, karma*). Though strictly belonging to matter, our living bodies are identified with our souls; hence these three words, sattva, rajas, tamas, are used to express functionings of the soul.[1] A sāttvika soul is the luminous soul of the man of wisdom truly cognising the qualities of things; a tāmasa soul is full of inertia and tenacity, clinging to objects; a rājasa soul is the man of action, restless, ever-moving.

When the Ego begins to turn away from the Non-Ego and wishes to de-pose it, to put if off, what it formerly regarded as True it now regards as false, what was Beautiful and Joyful as Ugly, painful; what was Good becomes ill, Evil; cognition as true becomes cognition as false, desire takes on the form of aversion, action turns into reaction.

II. In the Science of the Relation which connects the other two Sciences, we see that the Nexus has two aspects: a negative and a positive. The negative appears as the triple condition of all experience—Time, Space, Motion. The positive manifests itself as causal Energy and yields the triad, Action, Reaction, and the connecting Causation. The Mathematics of Time is Arithmetic with its triplet of one, many, connected by the rule of three, ratio and proportion. The numbers and the cipher are all metaphysical concepts never exactly reproducible and fixable in the concrete. The Mathematics of Space is Geometry, with its triplet, the point, the radii, included in the sphere; another triplet is that of definitions, axioms, postulates. Similar features may be distinguished in the Mathematics of Motion, Dynamics.

Since Time, Space and Motion constitute the triple condition of all experience of the World-Process, mathematics runs

---

[1] See note to Chapter XI of *The Science of Peace*.

through all sciences. None can be perfectly known unless the connected mathematics is also known. Hence to know well and fully (*samyak-khyānam*) is to know in terms of (*sankhyā*) numbers. Sānkhya, in the days of the Gītā, seems to have meant the same thing as Vedānta.

III. The Science of the Non-Ego may be said to be the History of the Universe, i.e. of a relatively complete cosmic system. Our solar system makes the unit for our purposes. In such cosmic History, the leading triad of Sciences would be (*a*) Chemistry, dealing with atoms (*anu-s*), super-atoms (*param-ānu-s*), and other primal forms of matter; (*b*) Physics dealing with forces of different kinds; (*c*) Astronomy, dealing with the formation and the movements of "eggs of the Infinite" (*Brahm-ānda*), the orbs of Heaven, the globes of the stars, suns, planets, their action and interaction. It has always to be borne in mind that all things and therefore all sciences intermingle, overlap, permeate one another in overt or subtle ways; that if atoms make up worlds, worlds are stored away in atoms; that infinitesimal and infinite are both equally infinite; that space, time, motion are relative illusions created by the moods of the seer.

Under Astronomy in the large sense would fall Geology, Physiography, and Biology; the last may be subdivided into Mineralogy, Botany, Zoology and Anthropology. Under the last we may distinguish Psychology, Physiology and Sociological History, corresponding broadly to the Ego, Non-Ego, and the Nexus, Mind, Matter, Life. Thus, we come back full circle to the principles noted in connection with the science of the Ego. The more our consciousness expands and our faculties extend, the more does that which was distant and appeared useless come near and become utilisable—on the Path of Pursuit and Power and self-assertive Egoism, for purposes of selfish enjoyment; and on the opposite and complementary Path of Renunciation and Peace and self-effacement in Altruistic Universalism, for purposes of philanthropic service.

In History, chronology is the time feature; Geography is the space feature; Narrative, the march of events, is the Motion-feature.

Physiology is also full of triads: (*a*) Functional Physiology, (*b*) Morphological Physiology or Anatomy, and (*c*) Medicine;

the last can be distinguished into the triad of sciences of health, pathology and treatment. In the human body any number of systems are discernible, all arrangeable into triplets, traceable to the primary triplet of entoderm, mesoderm, ectoderm.

Psychology naturally divides into (a) the Science of Cognition, (b) the Science of Desire, (c) the Science of Action. The psycho-physics of the human body as the indispensable apparatus of all physico-mental experience has to be dealt with alongside of Psychology proper. In cognition we may discern three kinds: (a) of the present fact, sensation, perception; (b) of the past fact, memory, recognition, recollection; (c) of the future fact, expectation, pro-cognition, pro-gnos-tication. All processes and moods of the intellectual aspect of the mind would seem to be compounds of these three factors in various degrees.

THE SCIENCE OF COGNITION

The practical aspect of the Science of Cognition is Logic, the science or rather the Art of sifting Truth from Falsehood. The triad of the Science of Reasoning is (a) correct observation of facts, (b) correct generalisation or induction as to the relation between facts, and (c) correct inference as to similar relation between other things newly seen to be of the same kind. This triad takes the well-known forms of concept, judgment and inference. The inductive generalisation in the form of one of the premises represents the memory of the past; the particular new fact stands for the present cognition; the conclusion connects the two and extends them into the expectation of the future.

Indian Nyāya does not make the distinction between Deductive and Inductive Logic. In deduction, strictly speaking, there appears to be no proper inference, no expectation, no advance from the past and the present to the future, but only axiomatic self-evidence, clearer understanding of the present, as in pure mathematics. The reasoning of Nyāya proceeds by inductive generalisation (vyāpti-graha). All the tests of truth are ultimately based on the first, viz. direct experience (Pratyakṣa). A remarkable consequence follows. Inference proceeds from directly observed particulars to some other similar particulars, in a conclusion, which by the very fact of similarity, is capable of being *verified* by direct observation, as the first particulars were. But Consciousness is always "My"-consciousness, "I"-consciousness; it is *unique*; there is nothing else, *No Other*, like it.

Na tat samas ca abhyadhikasca drsyate. (Śvetāśvatara Upaniṣad.)

We can never cognise an-other-consciousness. We can cognise only My-or-I-consciousness. Hence a real *inference* that others have souls, are *selves*, like mine, is not possible; because such an inference is impossible to verify by direct observation. Other *bodies* like mine by all means. They are observable, and inferrible, and verifiable. Consciousness, the Self, can be and is cognised, recognised, only directly. Hence we instinctively, intuitively, directly cognise and recognise the One and only Self in "My-" self and body, as well as in all other bodies.

The method of making sure of the generalisation is that of agreement and difference or concomitant variation (*anvaya-vyatireka*). The Nyāya explanation of generalisation from one single observation is that when we cognise any (*viśeṣa*) *particular* object and its qualities, we simultaneously cognise (the *sāmānya* or *jāti*) the *genus* included by (*samavāya*) *inherence* in it. The Vedānta explanation of this inherent genus would be that the Infinite One inheres in each particular one and gives it a pseudo-infinite generality which is expressible by the affix "ness" (*tva* or *tā*). This is the element of law. Variation is introduced by other *ones*, other particulars, the progeny of Multiplicity, which is inseparably included in the Primal Unity. Repeated observations are not necessary, though they often help to make the generalisation more precise, within the limits of given times, places and circumstances. From the standpoint of Final Knowledge (*Vedānta*), the Ultimate and Sole Truth and Reality as well as Ideality is the Absolute, and the relative or comparative truths and falsehoods distinguished by scientific logic are both Unreal, Illusory (*Mā-yā*).

THE SCIENCE OF DESIRE

The next department of Psychology is the Science of Desire. The triad of Desire may be said to be (*a*) simple elementary Wish, primarily for food, (*b*) Emotion, (*c*) complex Sentiment, as that of cognition is sensation, memory-expectation and reasoning. What is the nature and meaning of desire? The Infinite Self, having made itself finite, as individual self identified with a finite body, tries to recover its lost Infinity and appurtenant attributes by encompassing all experience and thereby proving itself possessed of all power, omnipotence. The feeling of its smallness, the nisus towards greatness, this "lack," this "want" appears as the state of mind which we call desire. Pain is the feeling of smallness; the feeling of the removal of such smallness, the feeling of greatness, is the feeling of pleasure.[1]

The final surcease of pain and the gain of infinite pleasure is the realisation that I am the greatest, that "I al-one am," that "there is non-else" to hinder Me, My freewill and play. But this pleasure is no longer pleasure. It is transformed into the bliss of peace which includes and abolishes both pain and pleasure into which it was broken up. Desire is the motive-power, the energy, the potency that vitalises and keeps going all living things and therefore all the World Process. This pair of pain-pleasure, which is the heart-beat of desire, is more important than any other pair. Desire subdivides into two kinds: that which causes pain causes hate, the desire to thrust away; that which causes pleasure creates love, the desire to bring near and foster. The connecting third, peace, may be said to be indifference of many forms, grades and shades. Self-preservation, self-increase, and self-multiplication are the three main forms of desire.

The simplest physical "wish to be" is hunger for food; hence the industrial arts; intellectual wish is curiosity for knowledge, the food of the "mental body," hence educational institution; spiritual wish is longing for eternal being, by union with the Eternal, hence religion. "Wish to be much and more" on the physical plane is ambition for wealth, whence property; on the intellectual plane it is ambition for possession of valuable things, whence art galleries, museums, libraries; on the spiritual plane, it is the desire to realise that "All is I and I am All," whence renunciation of all separative limitations. "Wish to be many" in the body is the wish for spouse, progeny, followers,

---

[1] *Nālpe sukham asti, bhūma-eva sukham:* (*Upan.*) "There is no joy in the small; greatness is happiness."

power, whence the institutions of marriage, family, dynasty, inheritance; in the mind it is the wish to make discoveries, write books, create works of art; in the spirit it is the wish to love and serve all beings and identify oneself with them all, and manifest in them all.

EMOTIONS

Inclination and aversion for things which being pleasure and pain, when they become connected with living beings, become the emotion of love and hate. Love, with consciousness of the (a) superiority, (b) equality, (c) inferiority of the object, respectively, becomes (a) respect, (b) affection, (c) compassion. So hate becomes (a) fear, (b) anger, (c) scorn. All other emotions are derived from these in combination with other cognitional facts. Love emotions become permanent, appear as virtues in the character; hate emotions, as vices. Of the six "internal enemies" (ṣad-ṛpu), lust, greed, and infatuated clinging may be regarded as excesses or perversions, by attachment to wrong objects, of love-emotions; while hatred, pride and jealousy are forms of hate-emotions. The six "enemies" running to extremes become "manias," which may be named as eroto-, avaritio-, pholbo-, cido-, magalo- and zelo-manias. The social forms of these, which are making a madhouse of the world, are sensualism, mammonism, mutual terrorism, militarism, imperialism and diplomatism. All abnormal psychology, psychiatry, psycho-analysis has its origin in the perversion and unbalancing of the emotions. All health in the social life means balance in them. The changing and moving life which surrounds us is formed by the "hearts" of human beings.[1]

As the practical aspect of the science of cognition is the art of ascertaining the truth, so that of the science of desire is the art of cultivating the right desires and emotions and achieving the highest virtue of character and the ability to respond, in every situation of life, to every demand, with only the appropriate benevolent emotion.

The Rishis and prophets of the world brood over the human race, yearning that all may attain, in their turn, the majority of the soul, that higher second birth, regeneration, which will

[1] Full treatment of these matters is given in *The Science of the Emotions*.

enable them to stand upon their feet and help the next generation of young souls forward on the path of evolution.

The life of the spiritual "office-bearers" (*adhikārins*) is a life of awful sadness as well as of sublime gladness. They have realised their oneness with the whole, and in their hearts the sin and sorrow of the world have to be sublimated and transmuted in the fire of ever greater self-sacrifice. The Buddha's ears ever do hear the whole world's cry, and his mouth ever speaks the words which bring the only and perfect consolation: "Ye suffer from yourselves; none else compels. Would you be free from pain? Then give up selfish pleasure, come to me, enter the glorious path of sacrifice and find the final peace." Every teacher and consoler of mankind has said the same.

THE SCIENCE OF ACTION

Life, mind, has three aspects or functions. Every civilisation has therefore the same three: (*a*) its characteristic body of knowledge, its science; (*b*) its ideals, aspirations, culture, art; (*c*) its enterprises, ways of living, social structure, external conduct towards other nations. Religion has the same three: (*a*) jnāna, basic truths; (*b*) bhakti, devotion, worship; (*c*) karma, sacraments, works.

Metaphysical and psychological "Scientific Religion" (the literal meaning of Vaidika Dharma) applies itself expressly to the administration of human affairs and enjoins a "social organisation" (*Varṇa-dharma*) interwoven with an orderly "planning of individual life" (*Āśrama-dharma*), which are to philosophy as practical or applied science is to pure or theoretical science. The Individuo-Social organisation of India is Applied Metaphysic and Psychology.

"None who knows not the science of the Self can carry action to fruitful issue" (Manu). The quintessence of the Ethic of Action[1] has as its indispensable motive power the desire enshrined in the golden rule: "Love others as yourself and do as you would be done by." The cognition behind this desire is the fact that the "others" are your-self, and yourself and all other selves are *in* God and *are* God, the Universal Self.

But life and surroundings are simple only in principles; they

[1] See the writer's *The Essential Unity of All Religions* for texts.

are very complex in details because of the proliferations and convolutions of the duads and triads.

Desa-kāla-nimittānām bhedair-dharmo vibhidyate. "Duty must perforce vary with time-place-circumstance." Hence guidance is needed. The divine law of the golden rule has to particularised and fitted to the situations and relationships of life by human law. Dharma, law, binds together rights and duties, and by means of these mutual rights-and-duties binds together human beings into a society "wherein all individuals move forward and progress together," advance towards clearly recognised "ends of life" in co-operation, by regulated, balanced, egoism subordinated to collective altruism, not trying to outrace one another in blind suicidal competition driven by unregulated egoism.

To be made practicable, the golden rule is provided with a technique, a social structure, with well-defined temperamental vocations, rights and duties, work and renunciation, distinct means of livelihood, incentives to best egoistic as well as best altruistic work within the capacities of the different psycho-physical temperaments.

APPLIED PHILOSOPHY, i.e. ADMINISTRATION

Accordingly, philosophy and psychology are applied by Manus and Rishis, the patriarchs and lawgivers of the race, to establish a system in which the life of each individual and the life of society as a whole are both organised and interwoven as warp and woof to subserve clearly visualised "ends of life." Individualism and socialism are duly combined and balanced. Co-operation and competition are properly regulated. Class co-operation is maximised, class conflict is minimised. The means of doing all this is the clear defining and equitable partitioning of the hardships and the prizes of life in accordance with the laws and facts of human nature.

This system of Socio-Individual organisation is known as Varṇāśrama Dharma. In it each individual life is divided into four natural stages, and the total social life into four main vocations, according to natural temperaments.[1] This ancient system can be appreciated only if the relation between society and the individual is realised in its true nature. The governing

[1] Fuller treatment can be found in the writer's *The Science of Social Organisation* and *Ancient Versus Modern Scientific Socialism.*

principle of the arrangement is the end or final cause which the organism subserves. Organisation is practical reason, fulfilment of intelligence. To organise wisely individual and social life, it is necessary to know their meaning, purpose, origin and destiny. The purblind leaders of the blind, the statesmen, politicians, economists, who have no thought for these ultimate values, can lead themselves and their willing followers or unwilling serfs only into the bottomless pit. Metaphysic tells us of the penultimate values and the supreme value, viz. self-expression and self-realisation (a) first in and through and by identification with a body, and then (b) by separation from and negation and transcendence of that limiting body; (a) happiness here, and (b) hereafter or rather in the Eternal—happiness, the essence of which is the feeling of Self-existence and Self-dependence, i.e. Self-allness.

THE ENDS OF LIFE

The end and aim of life of the individual and therefore of society is dual: (a) the fulfilment of bodily, physical, material, sensuous desire, (b) the realisation of spiritual desire which is desire-lessness, the perfection of Allness. These two are known as Kāma and Mokśa. At the human stage of evolution, material desire has to be refined by wealth (artha), artistic possessions; such possessions have to be regulated by Law and Religion (dharma, means both human and "divine" law). Law and Religion, property and family are thus the fundamenal institutions of human life in its first half. In its second half should prevail the other part of the summum bonum (Brahm-ananda Mokśa). Herein is achieved the complete transcendence of individualism and separatism and the culmination of socialism and collectivism.

Men and women at this different-sexed stage of evolution are patently incomplete, each without the other; both without the relating third, the child, God and Nature need man to embody and express both. Hence the family is the true unit of society and not the individual. For family life parity of temperament between the mates is necessary—a matter for psycho-physical testing and ascertaining before marriage. Earning of sufficient livelihood, possession of sufficient property, vocations suited to temperament and ability are necessary. This is matter for wise legislation. How to harmonise and synthesise the conflicting elements of human nature, antagonistic temperaments, so as to make the social organism healthy, how to organise society for peace and obviate organisation for war on the one hand, and, on the other, to have the social organism ready for self-defence at need is told us by unsurpassable Vedic Metaphor.

INDIVIDUO-SOCIAL ORGANISATION

Society is made up of individuals; the purpose of its life can be nothing else than the attainment of the *summum bonuum* by each individual life in its proper time; therefore it also should be organised like the individual. Head, trunk, limbs subdivided into arms and legs, in the body; cognition, desire, action, inchoate plasm of consciousness in the mind; nervous, nutritive, muscular, skeletal systems, in the body; intellectual, emotional, volitional, sub-conscious systems, in the mind; these give us the principles of social organisation and the four main organs thereof, the four natural psycho-physical types or classes of human beings, viz. the man of knowledge, the man of desire, the man of action, the man of unskilled or little-skilled labour and of undifferentiated, unspecialised, comparatively un-educable child-like mind, who has no initiative of his own and can do mostly only what he is told by others of the other three types.

(*a*) The first quarter of life, devoted to the stage of education discipline, (*b*) the second given to the stage of householder, family life, and the earning of income, (*c*) the third quarter given to the stage of retirement from busy competitive life, practising renunciation of possessions, doing honorary public service, engaged in study of the deeper sciences of the spirit; (*d*) the last quarter set apart for laying aside all worldly things, immersed in spiritual exercise and prayer for the well-being of others—these four stages correspond with the two halves of growth and the two halves of decay and indicate the principles which govern the organisation of the individual life. The first two show decreasing egoism and the last two increasing altruism. The new-born baby is one lump of pure selfishness; the grandfather, ready to give up his body, should be the acme of unselfishness. In the moment the baby appears as essence of selfishness, the parent becomes the "mother," unselfishness incarnate. Thus, in the individual life, in family life, in social life, God's nature, if reverently understood and obeyed by man, balances and gives due scope to both egoistic individualism and altruistic socialism.

This socio-individual organisation has four main departments: (a) Educational organisation by means of the wise men of knowledge, "the learned professions" (brāhmaṇas); (b) Protective, defensive (political), organisation by means of the valorous men of action (kshattriyas), "the executive professions" who protect the weak and enforce the law; (c) Economic organisation by the settler on the land, the supplier and nourisher, the manager of wealth, production and distribution, "the business professions" (vaishyas); (d) Industrial or labour organisation by means of the worker, the man of helpful unspecialised labour, "the labouring professions" (shūdras).

These four vocational classes are constituted into Guilds (Sreṇis), each elastically self-governing but inter-dependent with the others, all presided over by the Presidium (Dharma-pariṣad) of "holy" men and women, chosen from all the four, after their retirement from family life, who possess special knowledge and experience. Such holy persons would have no personal ambitions to gratify; they would be patriarchs chosen to legislate by universal acclaim, because they are philanthropic; they would not represent antagonistic interests and would have no need to fight with each other in the legislative hall, as in a gladiatorial arena with tongues for weapons; they would represent different and mutually supplementary departments of knowledge and experience in harmony with one another as organic parts of a whole; they would disinterestedly wish well to all just interests and would make good and wise laws for the promotion of all such equally. The form of government is a comparatively minor matter; the right structure and organisation of society is all-important. The four-fold social organisation has remained the ideal, and the undisputed duty of all political forms of (Hindu) government has been, by tradition, throughout Indian history, simply to maintain it. The chief executive head should be an heroic man of action ever ready to risk his own life to protect every one in the exercise of his proper rights and duties. The sole duty of the Guild of Executors (which in most countries now has become the "State" and the "Government") is to see that none encroaches upon the rights of others, that no person belonging to one profession is allowed to usurp the functions of others. By this arrangement the always disastrous consequences of concentration, in the same bureaucratic or autocratic hands, of all the four main kinds of power, science-power, arms-power, bread-power, labour-power, is avoided; balance of power and peace between the four main vocational classes can be maintained within each nation and therefore between all nations. The marvellous pencil of the Puranic artist limns forth in permanent colours for all time in a few great broad strokes the type of the all-grasping autocrat in the description of such imperial despots as Nahuṣa and Rāvaṇa.

The two main functions of the State, (a) prevention of evil (dushta-nigraha). (b) promotion of good (shishta-sangraha), would be discharged separately yet interdependently by the four guilds. The preventive or constituent function is discharged by the Guild of Executors. The promotive or ministrant function sub-divides into (a) education, (b) provision of necessaries and comforts, (c) supply of unskilled assistance by and through the other three Guilds, viz. of Educators, of Suppliers, of Helpers. Each Guild has its own special means of earning livelihood prescribed. This way equitable distribution is promoted.

Necessaries would thus be ensured to all; comforts and luxuries would have to be won by special competitive achievement; special honour, as heart-nourishment and incentive, to the man of science and art; special power of authority to the man of valorous action; more private possessions, property, wealth, to the man of desire; extra dose of amusement to the man of labour. The Guild of Educators (brāhmaṇas) would see to it that all members of society received appropriate cultural and vocational education; the Guild of Defenders (kshaṭṭriyas) would see to it that none offended by commission or omission, would redress wrongs, ensure enjoyment of rights and duties; the Guild of Feeders and Suppliers (vaishyas) would ensure that all are supplied with necessaries; the Guild of Workers (shrūḍas) would supply all the unskilled help needed by the other guilds.

Thus, the Book guides the Sword, the Sword guards the Granary, the Granary feeds the Plough, the Plough supports the weight of all. Without the Plough all the others would

crash down, as head, arms, trunk must all fall from their respective positions in the standing body, and roll in the mud
and mire, without legs. This in the waking condition; in sleep,
head, trunk, arms, legs are all on the same level, without difference
of function. It must be reiterated and carefully noted that all
are always inter-dependent, always balanced in power, within
each nation, and therefore making peace between all nations.
No swelled-head, no muscle-bound-arm, no pot-belly, no all-
calves are permitted. All the parts of the social organism, as
of the family organism, are equally loved and nourished; the
junior are more carefully loved and looked after and not despised.
Such "moral equivalent of war" as is necessary for the satisfaction of the ineradicable "aggressive" instincts is amply
provided by the difficulties, the hardships, the risks to limb
and life, that have to be perpetually contended against in even
the most normal discharge of the duties of each guild.

CONCLUSION

Thus may each individual of all human society, generation
after generation, in country after country, life after life, progress
steadily to the goal, along the two paths of (*Pravṛtti* and *Nivṛtti*)
pursuit and renunciation, connected and unified by (*Ānuvṛtti*)
cyclic revolution, casting off his body eagerly when it is worn out,
triumphing over death by realisation of the deathlessness of the
Spirit. At the turning-point between the two paths, the two arcs,
God who had forgotten Himself into man, begins to remember
again that He is God, in the body-temple of the soul that has
arrived at that stage. In this sense is true man's instinctive
feeling that "the crown of creation is man," the western philosopher's belief that "the Absolute becomes conscious of itself
in man."[1]

> [1] *Sṛiṣṭvā parāṇi vividhāny-ajay-ātma-śaktyā,*
> *Vrikṣān, sariśripa-paśūn, khaga-ḍamsa-matsyān,*
> *Tais-ṭair-atuṣṭa-hridayo, Manujam vidhāya,*
> *Brahm-āvaloka-ḍhiśaṇam mudam āpa Devaḥ.*
> (*Bhāgavata*)
> House after house did God make for Himself,
> Mineral, plant, insect, fish, reptile and bird,
> And mammal too. But yet was He not pleased.
> At last He made Himself the shape of Man,
> Wherein He knew Himself the Infinite.
> And then the Lord of All was satisfied.

In the stages and the conditions of the "forest-dweller" and the "renouncer" are the possibilities of developing (*Yoga-siddhis*) superphysical powers, extensions of faculty (*Ātma-vibhūtis*), spiritual perfections. One of these is the power to concentrate the consciousness in the (sūkshma-sharira, the mano-maya and higher koshas) "subtle-body," "mind-body," made up of subtler "mental" matter, and leave and re-enter the (*sthūla sharira*) "dense physical body" at will, as a person his clothes.

Tam svat sharirat prabrihen-munjad-ishikam iva dhairyena.
(Katha Upaniṣad)

"Let him draw the subtle soul from out of the physical body by patient, persistent, and undaunted endeavour, as the core is drawn out from the sheaths of the thatching-grass," as the butterfly draws itself out from the chrysalis.

He who has attained this power becomes literally, technically, "super-physically" (*jivan-mukta*) "free while living," free from terror of death of the physical body, for he has experienced and mastered the death of this body while yet alive;[1] but not necessarily free from fear of death of all bodies, fear of annihilation. He who has attained to the conviction, in thought, of the Universality of the Self, is "spiritually" "meta-physically" "free," free from all fear of annihilation. The former freedom is the (*kāryā vimukti*) "to be achieved" by difficult processes of psychophysical yoga-concentration, and has higher and lower grades; the latter is the (*citta-vimukti*) "freedom of the consciousness" from the sense of separatist limitation, which is gained by steady unflinching labour of persistent thought and the yoga of introspection; and it also has higher and higher degrees. The two kinds, it is so indicated, are not necessarily inseparable.

Thus does the Science of the Self, metaphysical psychology, help the orderly conduct of the individual life within the social life, and bring material as well as spiritual happiness within the reach of all.

Within this well-proportioned and well-balanced system of (*Sāstra* and *Vyavahāra*), Theory and Practice, this (*Ātmavidyā* and *Varṇāsramadharma*), scientific code of individuo-social and

---

[1] The Prophet Muhammad gives the same advice to his advanced disciples, in a Hadis-saying: Muto qablun tamuto, "Die before you die."

materio-spiritual life, given to mankind by the eternal spiritual wisdom (embodied more or less fully in the Scriptures of all the races) through its exponents, the primal patriarchs, out of their love for their progeny—within this scheme, degenerations set in and deformities grow, from time to time, because of the Law of Decay. Then regenerators and reformers arise, whenever and wherever there is need, to re-proclaim the self-same ancient truth in its purity, but in new words and forms and ways. Avatāras, Messiahs, Messengers, Prophets, Saintly Sages, have come in the past and will come again in the future, whose grand figures loom and names of might echo through the haze of the ages. They have come, and will come, to close effete epochs and open fresh ones, to call to birth new civilisations out of the ashes of that self-same Phoenix, the Human Race. One lays greater stress on some one aspect of the total (*Brahma* and *Dharma*) Truth and Duty, another on some other, and thus gives to the religion and civilisation which he founds a distinctive predominant characteristic, though all other features must be present also in subordination. All the glories of the Infinite cannot be equally manifested in one time and place. Also, when any one function of human nature runs to excess and so breeds evil of a special type, an opposite quality has to be emphasised by the Guardian—Lovers of Humanity to restore the balance which means health and happiness.

But the one burden of the teaching of all, the innermost truth and the principal purpose and duty of all life has ever been and evermore shall be, by ever deeper Yoga-Vedānta to realise ever more fully the Infinite Glory of the Eternal Self.

Sarvéshām api chaitéshām ātma-jnānam param smritam;
Tad hy-agryam sarva-vidyānam prāpyaté hy-amritan tatah.
(*Manu*)

Ijyā-chāra-dam-ahimsā-dāna-svādhyāya-karmaṇām
Ayam tu paramo dharmo yad-yogén-atma-darśaṇ am.
(*Yājñavalkya*)

Etadh-hy-ev Aksharam Brahma, etad-hy-ev-Aksharam Param,
Etad-éva viditvā tu yo yad-ichchhati tasya tat.
(*Katha Upaniṣad*)

Sarvas-taratu durgāṇi, sarvo bhadrāṇi paśyatu,
Sarvaḥ sad-buddhim āpnotu, sarvaḥ sarvatra nandatu.

"Greater than all other truths and duties is the truth and duty of Self-realisation, for it bringeth the certainty of immortality. The essence, the final purpose of all rites and ceremonies, all virtuous conduct and sacrifice, all self-control and harmlessness, all charity and all study, is to achieve, by Yoga, the Vision of the Self, Knowing It, whatsoever one desireth, that is his."

"May all cross safely beyond the places that are difficult to cross; may all see happy days; may all achieve Right Knowledge: May all attain the Peace."

Aum—Āmīn—Amen.

PURSUIT OF TRUTH THROUGH DOUBT AND BELIEF

by RAS-VIHARY DAS

Born 1897; Lecturer in Philosophy, Post-graduate Department,
University of Calcutta.

PURSUIT OF TRUTH THROUGH
DOUBT AND BELIEF

I AM not a philosopher, if by "a philosopher" is meant one who has achieved a well-reasoned systematic view of the universe, in the light of which he can explain every fact of experience, whether theoretical or practical. I am a philosopher only in the modest sense that I take interest in some of the problems discussed by recognised philosophers of the past and of the present day, and have hesitatingly come to hold certain views in regard to these problems. I do not claim, and, indeed, would repudiate the suggestion, that these views are original or novel in any sense. My philosophical position, such as it is, is thus defined by my views on certain philosophical questions.

But it is very difficult, if not impossible, to give a satisfactory account of the way which led me to these views. Certain considerations no doubt weighed with me in my coming to a particular view, but it cannot be claimed that the logical strength of these considerations is always sufficient to support the view which is supposed to be based on them. I am inclined to think that our views are not always arrived at through a logical process of reasoning, and that although they must have causes which are sufficient for them, these causes are often hidden in the depth of our personality, and may not appear before our consciousness. At any rate, our personality is a dominant factor in determining our philosophical and other views, and nobody can bring before his consciousness his own (or anybody else's) personality in its fulness and depth. If therefore I am unable to indicate clearly and truly how I was logically or historically led to the views I have come to hold, I hope my failure is not due to any particular defect of my nature or education.

However, I can state certain facts in connexion with my philosophical education which may conceivably be connected with my present views. After a brief statement of these facts, I shall proceed to give an account of some of my philosophical views to which I seem to attach some importance. I shall also try to indicate, wherever possible, the relevant considerations which have prevailed with me in determining my views in question.

Even before I began a formal study of philosophy, I had become acquainted with certain philosophical ideas from my miscellaneous studies. But I got my real teachers of philosophy when I came to the M.A. class. I read Hegel's *Logic* (smaller) with Dr. H. Haldar, Lotze's *Metaphysics* with Dr. B. N. Seal and Kant's *Critique of Pure Reason* with Prof. K. C. Bhattacharya. I learnt more from personal discussions with my teachers than from the books on which they lectured.

I am particularly indebted to Dr. B. N. Seal and Prof. K. C. Bhattacharya. The wide sweep of Dr. Seal's mind and the breadth of his views impressed me, and it was probably from him that I derived an interest in knowledge of all kinds as well as an interest in free speculative thinking. He was an enthusiast for Indian Philosophy and introduced me to Śaṁkara and Rāmājuja. I easily followed him in his sympathy for the latter's teaching.

The acuteness and subtlety of Prof. K. C. Bhattacharya at once humbled and captivated my mind. It was a wonder and delight to see how deeply he probed any philosophical question and brought to light many new aspects, of which we had no idea before. It was he who first made me conscious how enormously difficult it is to return a confident answer to any serious philosophical question. It was very fortunate that my great teachers never sought to thrust any of their philosophical views on me, but allowed me to grow in my own way. I believe I could have learnt more from Prof. K. C. Bhattacharya than I did, if my sympathies were not already engaged in other quarters.

The course of philosophical· studies, even from the undergraduate stage, at the Calcutta University, during my student days, was dominated by Hegelian ideas, and by way of reaction I was drawn to realistic writers.

After passing the M.A. examination, I joined the Indian Institute of Philosophy at Amalner, where I remained for 26 years. I had splendid opportunities there of studying Indian Philosophy under orthodox pundits and of discussing philosophical questions frequently with my colleagues. The official philosophy at the Institute was *Advaita Vedānta*, and there too by reaction my mind fell back upon *Nyāya-Vaiśeṣika*, which represents the robust realistic trend of Indian Philosophy. Thus although I lived in an idealistic atmosphere, it has tended to harden my inner realism. This does not mean that I do not appreciate, or have failed to learn from idealistic writers. On the contrary, generally speaking, I find more depth in idealistic writers than in the realists, though the latter seem to attract me more by their greater clarity.

A. BELIEF AND KNOWLEDGE

It will be generally agreed that philosophy is concerned with knowledge, and it seems desirable that I should make clear at the outset what I understand by "knowledge." An answer to this question has seemed necessary because of the lack of unanimity that seems to exist among philosophers as to the meaning of the term "knowledge." Some philosophers hold (i) that knowledge is indefinable, and (ii) that it is always infallible and has therefore to be distinguished from belief which is fallible. I shall consider only these two points here.

(i) I admit that there is an essential element in knowledge which is indefinable. I call it consciousness. If anyone does not directly understand what is meant by consciousness, I cannot make him understand it by any number of words. Consciousness again involves the idea of something else which may be called its object. Whenever I am conscious, I am conscious of something. The something in question may be vague or obscure to any extent, but it can never be altogether absent. Some philosophers have conceived the possibility, and have even asserted the actuality, of objectless consciousness. I seem to find no meaning in such consciousness. For me consciousness is always of an object.

Now the object of consciousness may be of any kind whatever. Psychologists have analysed consciousness into different modes, such as cognition, volition and feeling. The object in each case seems to be characteristically different, especially as regards its relation to the corresponding mode of consciousness. The object of feeling (e.g., a pleasure) cannot exist apart from our feeling of it. The object of willing is seen in the future and comes into existence through the operation of willing. The object of cognition, on the other hand, does not owe its existence to it. I mean by knowledge a form of cognition. (I am not sure whether the psychologist's analysis of consciousness into three distinct modes is quite correct. I have made use of his analysis merely to explicate my view of knowledge).

Knowledge for me is a mode of consciousness in which the object is taken to exist apart from, and independently of, the act of consciousness of which it is the object. Further, the object of knowledge must be an existent object and in it we can distinguish two aspects which may be described as the thing and its character, otherwise called existence and essence or *that* and *what* by some philosophers. By the term "thing" here I mean the object as merely existing, viewed abstractly as distinguished from its character, which in fact is never separated from it. We may sometimes fix our mind on a character, ignoring the thing of which it is a character. In that case we have a cognition of which the object is the character apprehended. I seem to think that there is sometimes such apprehension of a mere character. But I am not sure whether there is any apprehension of a mere thing apart from any character. If there be any, it will not be a case of knowledge, as the apprehension of a mere character also is not knowledge, since the full object of knowledge is constituted by a thing or a substantive characterised by an adjective. Apprehension of a mere character (or a mere thing) is also cognition, not feeling or willing, but is not knowledge in my, or, as I take it, in the ordinary, sense of the term "knowledge." Knowledge in my view thus appears to be definable as a form of cognition (which is a mode of consciousness) of which the object is an existent thing with a character. Sometimes a character is falsely ascribed to a thing which does not possess it. Knowledge in that case, in which such false characterisation takes place, is called false. True knowledge means knowledge in which a character is asserted of a thing to which it really belongs. Since the case of false knowledge, until its falsity has been found out, cannot be distinguished from a case of true knowledge, I hold, following a very common usage, that knowledge may be either true or false. But I am ready also to respect the other view, according to which knowledge must always be true, because what we seek and what is really worthy of its name is knowledge which is true. I now pass on to consider the second point.

(ii) It is not my purpose here to arrive at a correct and independent analysis of belief. I am willing to accept the analysis which is sometimes given and which discovers in it two distinguishable elements, viz., (1) the entertaining (understanding) of a proposition, and (2) the assenting to or adopting that proposition. It appears that the process of assenting further consists of two factors, one volitional and the other emotional. When we assent to a proposition, we seem to decide in favour of it, we make up our mind that something is so and so. Our attitude is the same as when we decide to do something. This is the volitional factor. Further when we assent to a proposition we have the feeling of confidence, of sureness about it. Now the question is whether knowledge as we have it, or are likely to attain in this world, goes any further than what is called belief. I seem to think that it does not, and although we are sometimes able to make a distinction between knowledge and belief (as when we say "I don't know who made this noise, but I believe it was so and so"), it is not possible to distinguish subjectively knowledge from confident belief.

I am strengthened in my opinion by the fact that in every case of knowledge the object appears (is known) as characterised by some adjective, but whether the adjective (i.e., the assigned character) is really present in the object known cannot be made out in the very act of knowledge, which therefore remains always theoretically questionable. That is, it is fallible like belief.

Moreover the volitional and emotional elements which are said to characterise belief, as distinct from knowledge, appear by no means to be absent in the case of knowledge also. Mere emergence of a content in consciousness of apprehension of a character is not knowledge, unless the content is posited in reality or the character is asserted of something existent. This position or assertion appears volitional in character. Also when we are said to know a thing we cannot help feeling a degree of certainty about it.

Nevertheless we are bound to recognise some difference in meaning between knowledge and belief. By knowledge proper we mean knowledge which is true. If anything is to pass as knowledge it must claim to be objectively valid. A belief on the other hand refers especially to our feeling of certainty and volitional acceptance. Hence a belief may be strong or weak whereas it gives no good sense to speak of knowledge as strong or weak. To know is merely to recognise some fact as evident. Thus it appears that knowledge should be entirely exempt from error. But such knowledge is more ideal than actual. What passes for knowledge with us is in most cases no better than belief. And it may be one of the functions of philosophy to make us aware of the uncertain character of much of our accepted knowledge. What then is Philosophy?

B.   PHILOSOPHY AS CRITICAL REFLECTION

In formulating my view of philosophy, I am guided by certain assumptions to which I hope no serious objections will be taken. I assume that philosophy is an affair of knowledge, such as science and history. Secondly, I assume that it is teachable by rational means. Certain conclusions seem to follow from these assumptions. One of them is that philosophy is not mysticism and is not a matter of intuition, because mysticism or intuition, as I take it, cannot be taught, far less by any rational means. The question about the nature of philosophic knowledge is a difficult one. We seem to have only one meaning for knowledge and if science gives all the attainable knowledge about reality, there seems nothing left for philosophy to do.

It is said that science studies only parts or aspects of reality, while philosophy studies reality as a whole. But can there be a study of a whole which is exclusive of the study of the parts? If not, then philosophy should include all the sciences. It was, therefore, thought at one time that philosophy was the science of sciences or that it unified the results of different sciences. This is obviously an impossible idea, because no philosopher can be found who combines in himself all the available scientific knowledge; and moreover it makes philosophy entirely dependent on the sciences and leaves nothing distinctive to it.

Those who think that knowledge must be of one kind only and

are also convinced that science undoubtedly gives us knowledge are sometimes led to suppose that we get no knowledge in the other hand, that we get knowledge in philosophy and also that philosophy is different from science. I have, therefore, to distinguish between scientific and philosophic knowledge.

A scientific judgment may be expressed in the form "S is P", where S stands for a substantive and P for its character. This may be said to express a fact constituted by the thing and its character (together with their relation). Supposing I know this fact and know it truly, and assert "I know that S is P," what seems to be asserted is the original fact as also its knowledge. But when we assert true knowledge of an object, we seem to assert not *knowledge* either as a character or as a substantive, but merely the *object* as known. By true knowledge we mean knowledge which is unaffected by any subjective factor, and, in asserting true knowledge, the subject may be left out of account, though for the purposes of common speech, it has always to be mentioned. Thus I am led to suppose that when (1) I know a fact and when (2) I know the fact as known, I am knowing the same thing. Only in the second case my knowledge is self-conscious, and in the first case it is not so. The distinction between scientific and philosophic knowledge appears analogous to the distinction between consciousness and self-consciousness. In my view, knowledge is not ordinarily self-conscious, but it becomes self-conscious only when it is challenged by any doubt or question. Scientific knowledge may be said to be already reflective in character, as it is based on the reflection on our perceptual experience, which is a conscious process. But scientific knowledge is always expressed in objective judgments, in which there is no clear reference to the knowing subject or to knowledge itself. Such reference comes in when scientific knowledge is made further reflective and raised to the philosophical level. This appears to be the only difference in respect to those cases of scientific knowledge which are cases of ideal knowledge and are absolutely true. Being absolutely true and true of reality, it cannot be improved upon by philosophy, except in the sense of being made reflective.

But, as a matter of fact, our scientific knowledge is highly tinged with imaginative construction and involves many assumptions. The function of philosophy, in regard to this kind of knowledge, is to subject it to critical reflection with a view to discovering what the underlying assumptions are, how far they are justified and whether they are mutually consistent. In fact philosophy means for me little more than critical reflection. We may describe it as critical reflection on life, understanding "life" in the most comprehensive sense, as inclusive of experiences of all kinds, not excluding our higher rational activities, such as science, art, morality, etc.

In our ordinary moods, we are not reflective; our minds are turned to objects, mostly outward objects. But when we meet with some failure in the pursuit of objective ends, our mind is then turned back upon itself, and we begin to consider things with a questioning mind. Most often such consideration seems to start with a sense of disillusionment, which means a sense of having been under an illusion. Thus the roots of philosophy or critical reflection seem to lie in failure and illusion and consequent doubt regarding things and values.

I have described philosophy as critical reflection, but what exactly this critical reflection is and how it has to be carried on, we can learn only from a study of philosophy. Philosophy itself must teach us what philosophy is. When we profess to teach philosophy, we merely try to teach critical reflection, either by explaining the classical examples of it, as we find them in the works of recognised philosophers, or by giving a demonstration of it ourselves in the class-room. The particular opinions held by a philosopher, or the conclusions arrived at by him, are not of primary importance. The really important matter to consider is how they arrived, or what exactly they did in arriving, at those conclusions. To learn what opinions certain remarkable individuals called philosophers held in the past is to learn mere history, but to learn how they arrived at their conclusions is to take an object-lesson in philosophising, and to consider critically their ways of philosophising or their philosophical opinions is to practise philosophy. Opinions differ from philosopher to philosopher, but critical reflection, I believe, is more or less the same in all philosophers and it appears to be teachable in the way suggested above.

C. COMMONSENSE REALISM

When we philosophise on any kind of experience, we subject certain beliefs involved in that experience to critical reflection, which may have the effect of dissipating or modifying or even, sometimes, of confirming those beliefs. Our commonsense beliefs appear to be the natural starting point of all philosophising, and we are frankly realistic to start with. My critical reflection, probably because it is neither very deep nor sufficiently critical, has left my commonsense beliefs more or less unaffected. But although it has not changed my commonsense, it has at least made it self-conscious. I shall try to make it here plain why and in what sense I have remained a realist. I think realism needs no justification to establish itself, since we all naturally begin as realists, and realism is already in possession of the field. What needs justification is the rejection of realism, but I have not yet met with any complete or satisfactory refutation of realism. I shall not, therefore, try to give here any reasons in positive support of realism, but I may briefly indicate some of the reasons which have weighed with me in my not accepting certain types of idealism which find favour with many philosophers.

By idealism I here mean generally the type of theory which makes the objects of knowledge dependent for their existence on our knowledge of them. The object which is dependent on my knowledge is clearly an imaginary or illusory object. And *Advaitism* unequivocally says that the object is an illusion. I can well understand how a particular object may be an illusion, because I can think of a real object (or real objective situation) in place of the illusory one. But that the object as such should be illusory I cannot conceive at all, because such illusion would require the judgment that there is no object at all, and this judgment seems to have no significant content of meaning. Moreover by illusion we understand a presentation which is condemned in the light of some other knowledge which refers to the same object. And I do not know how our knowledge of object as such can ever be condemned. It cannot be condemned by unobjective knowledge (if such there be), because it is irrelevant, not having the same reference, nor can it be condemned by objective knowledge, because being itself objective, it cannot invalidate objective knowledge as such.

I cannot also accept the position of those who do not openly declare the object to be an illusion, but still hold that the object is a construction of the mind. They seem to conceive knowledge as a form of doing. I, on the other hand, understand knowledge as purely revelatory in character. Knowledge seems utterly incapable of doing or making anything. True, we sometimes bring together certain ideas and conceive a new thing. But all this is in imagination, and when the product of imagination is taken to be an object of knowledge, we have a clear case of illusion. For a Kantian the object of knowledge is not illusory, but an appearance, while the real thing-in-itself is unknown and unknowable. It is no doubt sense to call an object appearance, in the light of the real object, which is known, and is in some way different from it. But to call the entire realm of objects appearance, while nothing else is known with which it can be contrasted, seems to bring no clear sense to me.

Those who do not leave the real object outside, but bring it wholly within knowledge, and make it entirely correlative to the subject, may seem to occupy an easier position. But I do not think I understand their position any better. We can understand two entities as correlative to each other in certain of their aspects. But they must each have a nature of their own, other than their correlative aspects. When we do not know them except as correlative, we cannot be said to know them in their ultimate reality. To call them correlative is to describe them as relative. But their relativity or relation, far from exhausting their entire being, cannot even be intelligently asserted, unless we have some sense or meaning for their independent character.

To say that the ultimate reality is neither subject nor object, but their unity does not seem to improve the position much. First, because by the conception of unity, which appears to be a relation, we get no appreciable new light about the nature of the things united; secondly, because we can form no idea how both subject and object (which are apparently opposed to each other) are to be combined into a single unity. To cite the instance of self-consciousness is not very helpful either, because the notion of self-consciousness, in the sense intended here, is itself full of difficulties.

Those who reduce the object frankly to a function of the

subject do not have to face these difficulties, but they seem to falsify the very notion of the object. A subjective function which is an act or way of *knowing* has never the meaning of an object which is *known*. Yet the former is equated with the latter and the equation seems illegitimate and incomprehensible.

These are some of the considerations which have led my mind away from idealism to realism.

My realism consists principally in my view that the object of knowledge exists independently of the act of knowing, but knowledge is not possible without some object being given to it. I can conceive the object apart from any subject, but I cannot conceive the subject except in relation to some object. I do not consider this ability or inability to be a merit or a defect of my mind, but an obvious consequence of my notion of knowledge, which I take to be quite legitimate and proper.

I like to describe my view as commonsense realism, in distinction from certain other forms of realism. The distinction is based on my view of perception and of physical objects. I regard perception as a direct and primary form of knowing, and so, differ from those realists, who do not recognise perception strictly as a form of knowing, or, even recognising it as knowledge, do not take it to be either a direct or a primary form of knowing. In the sphere of knowledge, I do not find anything more primary than perception and in perception I seem to cognise directly an object with a certain character. Supposing we call the peculiar character of a table "tabularity," then I admit that in order to learn what tabularity is, I may have to compare and contrast tables with other objects. But once I have learnt what this character is, I can directly cognise it in any object which is a table. My previous knowledge of tabularity may be a condition of my perception of a thing as a table, but the condition being fulfilled, the perception seems to take place quite simply and directly without involving any elaborate process of comparison.

Many philosophers say that the so-called secondary qualities like colour, smell, etc., are due to the affections of our sense-organs and cannot, therefore, be regarded as resident in objects. I admit that I have to open my eyes before I can see a colour and it may be true that certain changes occur at the time in the optic nerves, which are part of my physical eye. But I do not see the eye or its affection, when I see a colour, and I cannot think that the particular colour I see is a gift of my eye. The function of my organism is a condition of my knowledge, and, being a condition of knowledge, it should not make knowledge impossible. If the character colour could not be asserted of an object, because of the accompanying function of the organism, then, since the organism is bound to function in any act of knowing, no character whatever could be asserted of anything. This would make knowledge impossible. It will not do to say that ultimately we know the functions of the organism only, because, on the present hypothesis, we should not know that there is any organism at all. This is surely an intolerable position. I find it easier to think that the colour really belongs where I actually find it.

Some modern thinkers have discovered a new kind of entities called sense-data, which are said to be directly known, and out of which the physical objects are supposed to be constructed. I must confess that I find it difficult to believe in the existence of such back-less superficies, as the sense-data are sometimes described to be. I do not also think that there can be a common class of objects, which are indifferently present in veridical perception as well as in illusion. Lastly, I fail to discover any such entities in my actual knowledge. I never apprehend a coloured patch, whose entire being is exhausted in the mere sensible quality. I see a coloured thing which, as I take it, exists at a definite place and possesses many intelligible qualities besides the sensible ones. What seems to be given first, in actual knowledge, is the physical object, the obvious of ordinary perception, and it is only by an effort of abstraction that we can formulate the concept of a sense-datum.

The commonsense character of my realism will probably appear also in the fact that I regard myself as one with my body. It appears common sense to say that I am thin and short. I accept this statement literally and this is possible when I understand myself as identified with my body. Some kind of material organisation seems indispensable to life and consciousness, and I do not think it possible to have any experience except in and through the body.

I do not think that the phenomena of consciousness can

be adequately described or explained in purely materialistic terms. A feeling or thought is utterly distinct in kind from heat or colour or the movement of material particle. Consciouness in my opinion is absolutely *sui generis* and is not like anything else in the universe; and although I think it inseparable from the body, I do not pretend to understand how it is connected with the body. By reflection I am no doubt made aware of consciousness, but I find it to be entirely unobjective. In fact it is not anything *found* but is another name for *finding* itself. It cannot be equated with any objective modification, nor can it be conceived as resulting from an objective process. My consciousness, then, is not anything *in* my body, nor is it the result of any bodily process, although some kind of bodily process seems to accompany it always. The body, or my self as embodied, is conscious from the beginning, and the changes in my body are reflected in the changes in the content of my consciousness. The relation between consciousness and its content seems as difficult to understand as the relation between consciousness and the body. But somehow they seem to be most intimately connected. The relation between consciousness and body seems analogous to the relation between beauty and a statue which is beautiful. Beauty is not a material attribute of the statue, although it is inseparable from it. Just as the beauty vanishes with the destruction of the statue, so, I think, my personal consciousness will cease with the death of my body.

D.   SCEPTICISM

I understand knowledge as revelatory of the object. In all our efforts to know, our sole object is to see the object revealed as it really is. This, however, is an ideal which it is always difficutt to realise in practice, because we have to know the object through the instrumentality of our senses and the mind, and although they are meant to help the revelation, they often distort it. We may suppose that the senses commit no mistakes (though they certainly do, when they are not healthy, and it is difficult to be sure when they are perfectly healthy), but in interpreting the material presented by the senses, we often go wrong, as is clearly proved by numerous instances of error and illusion. What we actually see or hear is not wholly given by the senses, but is made up to some extent by imaginative interpretation. And it is not possible to distinguish in an object, at the time of knowledge, what is given by the senses from what is added by our subjective interpretation. I cannot say that imaginative interpretation is necessarily wrong; it is, I suppose, meant to aid our perception of objects. But one has to recognise the fact that what is added by imagination has never any guarantee of its objective validity. Though imagination working in the interest of knowledge is never quite free, yet it seems evident that it cannot operate without some scope for freedom, and when this fact is once recognised, we cannot but recognise also that there is no necessity that what is given by imagination should entirely coincide with what is in fact presented to the senses. At any rate the numerous instances of error and illusion, with which we are familiar, make it abundantly clear that what is taken to be knowledge in any particular instance may not be real knowledge, that the character asserted in knowledge may not be actually present in the object of knowledge. That is, although our assertions are meant to reach the fact, there is no necessary connexion between assertion and facthood, and the factuality of an objective assertion is accepted on faith only. This means that we can never free ourselves from the doubt that our so-called knowledge may prove wrong.

Thus an element of scepticism seems inseparable from all our endeavours of knowledge. Critical reflection with which I have identified philosophy, proceeds from a feeling of doubt and is maintained in being by the same sceptical spirit. Philosophy, thus, which is free enquiry and is not based on any dogmatic faith, is and will always remain to some extent sceptical.

They say sometimes that scepticism refutes itself. This does not seem to be the case. Scepticism, as I understand it, is not a positive theory which may be affirmed or denied, but an attitude of mind which is essential to all genuine critical enquiry. If I am asked whether even when I doubt, I am not *certain* that I doubt, I have only to point out that although I *know* that I doubt, my secondary or reflective knowledge does not alter or falsify the primary fact which is doubting. Far from supposing that scepticism refutes itself and stands self-condemned, I am inclined to think that is is irrefutable and should be recognised as a valuable element in our life and thought. I think it irrefutable in the sense that it is quite unavoidable for a mind which is at once honest and intelligent. If a mind is sufficiently intelligent, it will recognise that all our so-called knowledge is hedged in by various beliefs and assumptions, and there is besides a degree of uncertainty and obscurity attaching to almost every judgment which we make or imply in the name of knowledge. If it is honest, it is bound to recognise how uncertain must be our hold on truth claimed under such conditions. About every objective judgment, we may raise the question, Is it true? To admit the significance of this question is to admit some room for doubt. When we realise that there is an element of belief (or volitional acceptance) in our ordinary knowledge, we realise at the same time that it is open to doubt. Paradoxically, if a little loosely, I may say, I believe and, therefore, I doubt.

The value of scepticism for knowledge will be easily recognised. It opens the path to free enquiry and loosens the roots of prejudice which is a hindrance to knowledge. There is also a sense in which scepticism may be pursued as an intellectual ideal. We may make it an aim of our intellectual efforts to become conscious of the elements of uncertainity, obscurity and vagueness, which are to be discovered by careful analysis in various kinds and instances of our accepted knowledge. The moral value of scepticism cannot also be overlooked. As it works against bias and prejudice, it tends to make men impartial and tolerant of each other's faith.

E.   PRACTICAL IDEALISM

I am often sceptical; but my scepticism does not run so far as to paralyse my thought and will. It does not bar out all beliefs, but only recommends that they should be held rather lightly, so that, on the discovery of any conclusive contrary evidence, they may be given up without much difficulty. So I find no difficulty in believing in certain ultimate values. I have already expressed my belief in scepticism itself. But scepticism is not an ultimate value, i.e., it has no value in itself. It is valuable only for its moral and other consequences. I seem to recognise certain values which are intrinsic and ultimate.

I do not know whether the concept of value is definable. I may indicate what sort of thing I mean by the term. Value means for me something which is desirable (considered worthy) on its own account, is necessarily appreciated by our reason and sought to be realised by us. We understand value in relation to our feeling and will. That is, if anything is conceived as a value we cannot but desire its realisation and regard it with a feeling of appreciation. If anything is to be an object of our rational willing, it must appear to us as a value, although in many cases we may find, on reflection, either that it is not desirable at all or desirable for the sake of something else, in which case it would be considered a dependent value and not an ultimate one.

Truth appears to be an ultimate value. By the term "truth" we describe the character of knowledge which is perfectly accordant with its object and is absolutely clear and certain, leaving no room for doubt and uncertainty. Knowledge in this ideal form is also called truth, and is the ultimate objective and ideal for all our cognitive efforts.

I conceive freedom to be another such ideal or value. Just as truth is the ideal of knowledge, freedom is the ideal of will. Just as perfect knowledge is true knowledge, perfect willing is free willing. Freedom seems unintelligible except in terms of willing. (Political freedom ultimately means capacity for free willing on the part of the citizens of a state).

What freedom positively means I confess I do not exactly know. Negatively it means the state of not being bound. Willing is a function of reason and it seems at present to be controlled by the solicitations of sense. Freedom which we seek as a rational ideal is emanicpation from the insistent demands of sensibility. Our will is free when it is no longer dominated by the thought of any sensible object.

I like to describe the ideal of feeling as love. I do not here mean by love any kind of physical attachment or psychical impulse. I mean by it the feeling of unalloyed joy together with a sense of unity. Pure joy of course appears desirable for its own sake and is to be realised in feeling. I associate it with a sense of unity also, which seems desirable and is realisable only in feeling. The object of cognition is quite distinct from cognition; the object of willing is ahead of willing and is not one with it. Only in feeling can we realise our unity with the object.

There may be other ideals, but I seem clearly to recognise these three, corresponding to the three functions of reason, cognition, willing and feeling. We may conceive these three as forms of the Good, which represents the common form of the ideal. (In place of the traditional forms of ultimate value, truth, goodness and beauty, I would have truth, freedom and love. In the conception of love I have sought to combine both charity and beauty. Delight and harmony, associated with beauty, appear in my conception as joy and unity).

I cannot regard these ideals as subjective fancies; they present themselves to my consciousness as objective, as veritable determinants of my rational being, and I feel bound to recognise them as supremely real in some sense. I am thus an idealist in the sense that I believe in ideals as having supreme importance in the scheme of things.

The distinction between a realist and an idealist turns, in my opinion, ultimately upon the relative importance attached by them respectively to the objective facts and subjective functions or ideas. They recognise in a sense both these factors, objective and subjective, but whereas the realist considers the objective as prior, and in a sense superior, to the subjective, the idealist holds the opposite view. In matters of knowledge I have to recognise the dominant rôle of the object, and so, I am a theoretical realist. But as I would have my will or practical reason completely determined by the subjective (which includes for me both ideas and ideals), I may be called a practical idealist.

Further, I think that it is in our concern for inactual ideals, as against the actualities of our physical and psychical being, that we rise above animality and realise our spiritual being. There appears to be a general upward trend in nature from matter towards life, mind and consciousness. In our concern for the ideal of truth, freedom and love, we aspire to rise above mere consciousness, which we share in common with animals, and in so rising, become truly spiritual. I take spirituality to be the supreme concern of the universe. My physical organism and psychical being will no doubt perish in course of time, but in my concern for spiritual ideals, I seem to escape from the particularity and finitude of my physical and psychical being and become identified with what is universal, infinite and eternal. This seems to be the only kind of immortality that can be achieved by mortal men.

PRINCIPAL PUBLICATIONS

The Essentials of Advaitism (The Punjab Sanskrit Series, Lahore, 1931).

"The Theory of Ignorance in Advaitism" (in *Ajñāna: the Theory of Ignorance*, Luzac, 1933).

The Self and the Ideal (Calcutta University Press, 1935).

The Philosophy of Whitehead (James Clarke & Co., 1937).

"In Defence of Substance" (*Proceedings of the Indian Philosophical Congress*, 1934).

"Relations in Modern Indian Logic" (*Calcutta Review*, 1932).

"Our Knowledge of Physical Objects" (*The Monist*, 1932).

"On Knowledge" (*The Philosophical Quarterly*, 1940).

PHILOSOPHY OF DEPENDENT EMERGENCE

by SURENDRANATH DASGUPTA

Born October, 1887. Principal Sanskrit College, Calcutta.

PHILOSOPHY OF DEPENDENT
EMERGENCE

I COME from a family of Eastern Bengal where Sanskritic study especially in literature and medicine continued for upwards of one hundred and fifty years without any break. The family is known by the illustrious title "Kavīndra" of one of my ancestors. My father was the only person who broke away from the traditional pursuits of the family, acquired a working knowledge of English and became a surveyor. There were certain occurrences in my childhood which desrve mention in order to throw some light upon my temperamental background. During the ages of five to eight, when I had a very elementary vernacular education and no knowledge of Sanskrit or English, I could, in some intuitive manner, explain the purport of the Sanskrit verses of the Gītā. I could also demonstrate the various Yogic postures (*āsanas*) and also give practical instruction to people regarding the complicated processes of internal and external washings technically known as the *dhouti* by the Yogins. I could also give pretty satisfactory answers in a simple manner to most questions on Indian philosophy and religion. As a result therefore my house was crowded from morning till night with ardent enquirers seeking instruction on Indian religion and philosophy. English and vernacular papers at the time in Calcutta were always busy in narrating many episodes about me, whom they branded as "the wonderful boy." Three saintly persons then living in Calcutta, Bijoy Krishna Goswāmi, Sibnārāyan Paramahamsa and Jagadbandhu of Faridpur, were my special friends and associates. At the age of seven I also delivered a lecture before a large gathering in the Theosophical Society Hall in Calcutta. My occupation at the time was the answering of questions from early morning till late at night, excluding the intervals for meals.[1] I also often spontaneously entered into a

[1] The sorts of questions that I used to answer are as follows. These questions and answers are collected from a daily newspaper of 1894, a copy of which I have been able to preserve. *Q*. What is the relation between knowledge and devotion? *A*. It is through knowledge that devotion springs. *Q*. What is the nature of God? *A*. He is a spiritual illumination which

meditative trance condition as I gazed on the Ganges from one of the ghats (landings) or when I sat in front of the temple-deity at Kalighat.

I was employed as the senior professor of Sanskrit in the Chittagong College in 1911, and since then I have worked on Indian philosophy devotedly and also carried on my studies in European philosophy. As I conceived the plan for writing a comprehensive history of Indian philosophy and worked assiduously, it occurred to me that the outlook of Indian philosophy was obstructed in some directions by certain fundamental limitations. The impressions of a super-conscious trance-state which I had in my childhood never left me, and as they were being continually revived in me in my maturer years, it was impossible for me to deny the existence of the mystical state of self-absorption so much referred to in the Upaniṣads. When I went to Cambridge and worked for a thesis on *Contemporary Idealists and Their Critics* under the illustrious Dr. McTaggart and came in contact with personalities like Moore and Ward, my mind became more critical not only towards European philosophy but also towards Indian philosophy as a whole. I had thrown off the shackles of Hegel long before I went to England, but Einstein's theory of relativity, the *anekānta* relativism of the Jains, and the realists with whom I came in contact in England, finally drew my mind away from all sorts of Absolutism in philosophy. I was getting sick of Absolutism for a long time but lacked the initiative to make an open revolt. My life in Cambridge invigorated me, and the main fruit that I reaped there was courage.

Indian philosophy is like a tropical forest, where almost all types of thought, that have been current in the West since the days of the Greeks, can be found. The writings of the commentators through successive generations abound in logical precision of thought and true philosophical acumen, whch are almost unparalleled. The note of ethical purity, religious contentment and inwardness of mind, with which Indian philosophy cannot be compared with any physical illumination. Q. What is the relation between *Prakṛiti* (primordial-nature-cause) and *Puruṣa* (the soul)? A. The creation happens spontaneously from the Prakṛiti under the direction of the Puruṣa and both are intimately associated with each other, like a lame man sitting on the shoulder of a blind man and directing him.

rings, and the practical harmony between life and philosophy that forms the central theme of almost all systems of Indian philosophy, mark them out from systems of European philosophy, where philosophy is looked upon more as a theoretic science than as a science of practice. The chief concern of the philosophers of India in the past was not to conceive a philosophical scheme like a toy-machine to play with, but to make it a real chariot on which they could ride. But life here on the earth was sorrowful and was only a life of probation. The real life consisted in the ushering in of a life of emancipation, which would absolutely extinguish this life. Philosophy should be brought into practice for conducting this life to that end. Philosophy was never blended in harmony with the present life as we experience it without subordinating the latter to some other higher forms of existence. In this view, philosophy was the guide for the attainment of a permanent state of being from which there is no fall, no change.

Indian philosophy, in spite of its magnificent outlook, thoroughness of logical dialectic, its high appreciation of moral and religious values, is closed all round by four walls of unproved dogmas: (1) the dogma of the infallibility of the Vedic wisdom, (2) the dogma of emancipation and bondage, (3) the dogma of the law of Karma, (4) the dogma of rebirth. Of these, the first is the primary dogma which is associated with the corollary that reason is unable to discover the truth—a creed which is almost suicidal to any philosophy in the modern sense of the term. According to this view, reason is only useful for biological or sociological purposes, but is impotent to give us any glimpse of the nature of truth. Reason must always be a hand-maid to scriptural testimony and must always, therefore, be used for discovering the import of such testimony and for persuading us to believe it. A student of Indian philosophy knows well how reason entered into the Vedic circle like the camel in the fable and ultimately practically dislodged the Vedic dogma professing only a lip-loyalty to it. Different interpreters of the Upaniṣads have always treated the Vedic texts like noses of wax and twisted them differently to suit the convenience of each specific type of reasoning. If reason is the interpreter, the infallibility of the Vedic wisdom becomes only nominal.

An ineffable super-conscious state is often described in the Upaniṣads, and in some passages there is a tendency to regard it as an unchangeable condition or state from which there is no fall. This has often been interpreted as the doctrine of emancipation. It has been argued that, if there be an unconditional state, that must be no state but the pure self as pure consciousness. If that is the only reality, its associations with appearances of diverse contents must be in some sense false or illusory. Relation of identity, or rather the identity itself, is the only reality. The act of relationing implied in identity, which is responsible for the notion of difference, is the nescience (*avidyā*) somehow subsistent in the identity. So long as the identity remains in the ineffable state, there is no relationing; but as soon as it descends into the knowable, it can only do so through the extraneous association of a relationing implied in its very nature. Relying on the unrelational ineffable state as the ultimate reality, the relationing factor implied in it is regarded as false. Others, however, such as the followers of the Sāṁkhya, while admitting the existence of the unconditioned as the ineffable super-consciousness (the *puruṣas*), could not restrict the concept of reality to it alone, and were obliged to admit another order of reality as an indefinite complex (the *prakṛti*), which somehow evolved from itself, varied forms of mutual relations, and through them, qualities and their appearances. They thus admitted the concept of identity-in-difference as determining reality. In the realm of world-phenomena, they admitted a spontaneous evolution of difference and change and the emergence of new categories of existence at different levels. The emergents are not regarded there as mere additive resultants, but as emanations somehow coming into being from the structural complexes. But in the field of knowledge they admitted a different order of causality, that certain mental complexes being there in co-presence with the unconditioned—the self—there was the phenomenon of knowledge. This was a contradiction of the doctrine *ex nihilo nihil fit*, for if knowledge was not already there, it could not have come into being. It is further unable to explain why in spite of the same co-presence with the unconditioned, the phenomenon of knowledge should cease at emancipation. Thus the assumption of the unconditioned either as the only reality or as a parallel reality made it difficult either to explain change or the return from the change to the changelessness. Had it not been for the dogma of emancipation, the systems would not have been fettered in this way, and a more rational explanation might have been effected.

On the moral side, the assumption of the unconditioned as emancipation led to the view that all our experiential states are states of bondage. Bondage, thus considered, has to be regarded as the natural tendency of some mental states to flow towards other mental states (which in the moral terminology is called "*tṛṣṇā*" or desire), and the actual flow of it and its resultants are called Karma. But as the hypothetical emancipation is never experienced by any one of us and as its reality cannot be denied on account of the scriptural testimony, the only way left was its indefinite postponement.Such a postponement necessitated the postulation of a practically endless series of succeeding lives, through which the relational mental structure persisted. The cause of this rebirth is *tṛṣṇā* or Karma, which represents the relational tendency and the actualisation of it, which is inherent in the very structure of the mind. The possibility of emancipation necessitated the postulation of the possibility of the destruction of mind and this implied the assumption of an inherent contra-diction in mind, such that, while at certain stages in co-presence with the unconditioned it would produce relational groups, at other stages it would cease to produce them. This is the so-called "teleology" which appears explicitly in the Sāṃkhya and implicitly in the Vedānta.

Without going into an examination of other systems of Indian philosophy, I can say that the principal lesson that I derived from my study of it is that extraneous assumptions of any kind, which do not directly explain experience, but which are brought in from outside, are bound to hamper the progress of philosophical speculations and blur the philosophical out-look. Philosophy, if it is to grow, has to be founded on experience, either direct or indirect. The word experience is very difficult to define. Definition implies that the term to be defined has to be explained by a reference to the underlying relations subsisting between simpler but yet constitutive notions. I do not mean that the constitutive notions are in themselves sufficient for the purposes of definition. But at least the relations

subsisting between the constitutive notions should be sufficient
to indicate the nature of the emergent idea to be defined. The
word experience covers for us all possible mental facts. Facts,
again, are not necessarily expressible in propositions. They are
the possession of one or more qualities or relations by an appearance or by an existent. By a mental fact, again, I do not mean
the mere inward occurrence in the mind, but I mean by it
anything that is revealed in the mind either through the inward
workings of the mind or by the outward relationing that it may
have with the objective world or the minds of others. All sense-
occurrences, feelings, desires, willing, the logical and the reflective
phenomena, images or the imaginings, *a priori* faiths, all stock
of ideas derived from social intercourse, all promptings of value,
hopes and aspirations of men (civilised or uncivilised), psychological experiences of all descriptions, the inheritance of knowledge that we have through the works of other people, are all
included within experience. Experience also includes the mystical
experiences of religious men, the aesthetic experiences of the
artists, the emotional experiences of the devotees and the
supernormal trance experiences of the Yogins. Science, in
the ordinary acceptance of the word, restricts itself to the
study of facts in an inter-related system in special departments of the workings of Nature. As soon as discoveries
are made or anticipations achieved, they ·become parts of
human experience. When the poet, the dreamer or the
lover fills his mind with his mental creations, throbbing
and pulsating with emotions, with the vague and indefinite
wanderings of his mind and with conflicting oscillations of pangs
and happiness, we have a field of human experience which has
its law and order as much as the experience of an insane person.
The fanatic, the contemplating Yogin on the banks of the
Ganges at Hardwar, the ecstatic devotee forgetting himself in
the divine communion, have all their experiences; and the non-
relational or the supra-relational state into which a man slowly
passes inward far beyond the threshold of consciousness—a
state which is inexpressible by any logical propositions, but
can be felt in its uniqueness—is also experience. But all these
experiences are concrete occurrences in the human mind,
howsoever they may or may not be related with the objective

world. But if any philosopher imagines that there is an ultimate experience in which all the special experiences have commingled together indistinguishably like the rivers in the ocean, then since it exists as a philosophical supposition, but is not directly the content of any apperceived concrete human realisation, I would not call it direct experience because it is not a human fact. The Absolute of Bradley, which he describes as "Experience," is no experience at all, as it is never felt or realised. The conception of such an Experience, however, is an experience inasmuch as it is a mental fact. If, however, a hypothetical metaphysical entity, such as Bradley thought he discovered, can explain our various concrete experiences in their varied relations, I should admit it as an indirect experience. All that is felt, perceived or realised, forms the content of our individual experience, whereas all that is gathered or learnt from the direct experiences of other people forms the content of human experience in one. The totality of this human experience must always remain unknown to us to a large extent. In acquiring all individual concrete experiences also we are helped in an indirect manner by the experiences of others. For, though an experience may be concretely realised in us, it may appear like a fleeting phantom on which we are slow to put our reliance, unless its existence in others is somehow demonstrated to us. It is only in the case of experiences, relating to biological self-preservation and race-preservation, that we are primarily sure; but in these cases also the surety of our convictions arises through a long process of other experiences associated with our physical activity and the achievement of the end. This idea appealed to some Indian philosophers to such an extent that they defined right knowledge as that which leads to the fulfilment of objective ends. The cognitive operation is described by them as beginning with an awareness, impelling the person to action and ultimately leading him to the attainment of the object signified or presented by the awareness. Such a definition of experience can only be true to some extent regarding our experiences in relation to the biological satisfaction of ends. The word "biological" is of course used here in a very wide sense. It proves, however, that an experience, appearing in the mind, has to be rehabilitated by a reference to other sets of experiences which cannot be so

I

rehabilitated by a reference to the fulfilment of objective ends. In a major portion of such cases through social intercourse with our fellow-beings, through mutual communication with those around us, by putting ourselves in touch with other minds far removed from us in time and space through the medium of books and through the observation of the behaviour of persons around us, we are always comparing notes about what we feel with the similar ideas and feelings of others, and thereby gravitate towards a common level of experience. In such operations our minds behave more as automatic machines than as free agents responding and reacting in the environment. Language itself is a great machine with which we must work for getting ourselves levelled down to the experiences of our compatriots. In every turn of expression that we use or hear we are forced to adapt ourselves to the thoughts and feelings of others. This forced adaptation, on the one hand, quickly draws us up to the high level of the experience of civilised man, and on the other, looked at from a different angle, it curbs free spontanetity of the mind which has to create anew by reacting on the environment of the mind. The natural result of this process is that we are habituated to take as valid only those experiences of ours which are found in consonance with the experiences of others. Moreover, there grows a tendency in us to shut out and discourage all such experiences as are not likely to be compatible with the experiences of others. Ordinarily the validity that we ascribe to the experiences which we hold in common with others arises out of a sense of a relation of consonance that we feel with regard to our own experiences. The doctrine of self-validity of knowledge that each cognitive state carries with it a sense of its own validity, as preached by some Indian philosophers, is false. Such philosophers draw a distinction between validity and invalidity, and suppose that invalidity arises out of incompatibility, whereas validity is a natural character of all cognitions. This is a misconception of the whole situation. Validity means the consonance of an awareness with what it professes to be. Whenever an awareness refers to a field of experience, related to the objective world or to the objective experience that we have in common with our fellow-beings around us, such awareness carries with it implicitly a history of previous references by virtue of which it automatically asserts its right. This history of references is the average resultant of previous experiences with a predilection towards validity or invalidity, as the case may be. Thus, when on an April noon a motorist perceives water flooding in the Red Road at the maidan of Calcutta, such knowledge does not carry with it any sense of validity. Moreover, it is a matter of common knowledge that an element of doubt is often associated with our sense-experiences regarding the objective world, unless the history of previous experiences associated with it renders them indubitable. Such doubts are more largely associated with the experiences that we have in social or psychological intercourse with other minds. Our notion of validity in such field of experience is merely the appearance of the apex of a triangle of which the base is at the moment hidden from our view, but is apparent on closer analytic inspection.

Regarding the experiences of feelings and emotions, it is only those which proceed from compatible or incompatible inner biological relations of the brute man, that may be said to be somewhat independent of common human experience, woven through mutual intercourse. But most of the other feelings and emotions of a civilised man proceed from the compatibility or the incompatibility of the relations that individual mental states have with the bigger human experience from which they have bubbled up. Our experiences of value, moral, aesthetic or religious, are also largely dependent on this social intercourse. As the horizon of this intercourse gets larger and larger the parochial and the limited characteristics of the experiences, the associated joys and sorrows and the sphere of the value-sense get broader and broader, which may bring a man in conflict with his immediate social surroundings and yet make him confident of the validity of his experiences. Yet we are not entirely bound to the experiences of our immediate social surroundings or to the most distant human horizon of thought; for there is always a scope, in at least some minds, for the creation of new relations and new experiences as newly emergent forms with which they particularly identify their personalities. There they may be absolutely lonely and may come in such a conflict with their immediate social surroundings that they may be smashed into pieces as it were, but still they maintain their confidence in their newly emergent forms of knowledge, feeling or belief. In such cases the validity of their beliefs does not depend upon a previous history of reference, but upon the new forms that have emerged out of such a reference and in their uniqueness possess special history. Their history is dominated by the creative process of their own thought.

It will now be seen that there are two forms of validity: (1) that which establishes its right by an implicit or an explicit history of reference to the structure of our experience woven out in association with the experiences of others, (2) that which emerges out by itself borne on the shoulders, as it were, of a previous mental history of a different order. This second form of validity attaches to experiences, which appear in this or that mind for the first time, but later may, through communication, become the common property of human experiences as a whole. Even if they ar incommunicable for their uniqueness, they may yet by sufficient description serve as light-posts for the guidance of others having similar experiences. This applies to various kinds of religious and ecstatic experiences which are often unique and the history of which can only be traced to the temperamental background of the individual.

At this point a relevant question may be raised as to whether there is any such concrete reality as the social mind, German mind, English mind or the mind of humanity. To this our answer is at once yes and no. I do not believe in the existence of any experiential whole, the parts of which are not directly amenable to any individual experience. In this sense the word "social mind" or any other like expression is merely a convenient phrase to denote the idea of numerous experiencing individuals working towards a common purpose. But we shall see later on that different relational groups, when they co-operate together in the same direction, may behave like an individual. In that sense it would not be unwise to admit the existence of a separate social mind. Even parts of the social mind may, in this sense, be taken out separately and regarded as an individual having its growth and career towards a particular goal. Thus we may speak of the growth and development of the political mind, or of the religious mind of India. I wish to make it clear that I do not use the word in a figurative sense. I wish to lay stress on the fact that particular relational groups co-operating together behave as an individual. Converting the proposition, in another way, I may say that an individual manifests itself wheresoever the relational groups of one or more different orders co-operate for a harmonious end.

It is unfortunate that language should practically be the only mode by which we can express our experiences to others or in a very large measure deal with them ourselves. Experiences are dynamic, concrete and showing themselves in different shades of tone and colour in association with other experiences, whereas language is static, abstract, definite and lacking in the wealth of reality. The growth of language has hardly been able to keep pace with the ever-growing experiences. In the very structure of language there is a false logic which has to be wedded to experiences of all descriptions, in order to keep going their currency either with us or with others. Even the mathematicians, who deal with merely abstract ideas, had to invent a language of their own for giving precision and perspicacity to their investigations. If this is so in the case of Mathematics, how much more should the difficulty be felt in giving expression to experiences or in pinning them down in our minds with a few inadequate terms. Joy, bliss, happiness, gladness, pleasure are some of the terms to denote the mental sense of elation which occurs in myriads of forms, each one of which has its own specific uniqueness. This difficulty of expression reserves for us to a very great extent the privacy of our individual experiences. It limits the sphere of general communicability to such an extent that in a large measure communication in a proper sense is only possible between individuals having similar kinds of experiences. This makes possible the formation of such new relational groups among like minds, that what is real to them may be false to others. Closely allied with the language difficulty there is a difficulty, associated with the general structural relation of our mental states, which may be designated as the *a priori* logical mode. It is by no means certain that the facts, which our experience denotes and which our language expresses, obey in all respects the peculiar structures or relations of our experiences. We must, therefore, have to rest satisfied with the anticipation that our experience may not be able to denote facts and relations of all orders. There may be facts and relations of all orders. There may be facts and relations which would for ever remain undiscoverable by human experiences.

It has been said above that experiences may be direct and indirect. What we mean by direct experience is similar to what Bertrand Russell means by "knowledge by acquaintance." Our indirect experience seems to have a wider scope. It means, firstly, knowledge attained by descriptive communication or by inference. Secondly, it also implies the knowledge by implication or of any hypothetical fact or entity which, though not directly perceivable, may be regarded as explaining the phenomena of nature and of mind denoted by our experiences. All scientific theories, and laws of nature explaining the attested facts, and also almost the whole of pure Mathematics and a very large portion of mixed Mathematics, are examples of this indirect experience. The assumption of more dimensions of space than what are directly perceived by us, so necessary for explaining the truths of Mathematics and Physics, may also be regarded as examples of indirect experience. So also metaphysical assumptions that may serve to explain a philosophical system may be regarded as matters of indirect experience. The validity of indirect experiences is to be tested by their logical cogency in explaining facts or by attestation by direct acquaintance.

The aim and purpose of philosophy is to give a connected and systematic explanation of all our experiences in their mutual connection and relatedness and, through them, of the phenomena which they denote. Philosophers must, therefore, gather all possible facts in different departments of nature and also the various kinds of relevant human experiences. New facts are being discovered every day, and the discovery of one little fact which may not fit in with a particular philosophical scheme may upset it or endanger its existence. A philosophy which starts from certain *a priori* notions and seeks to deduce or distort all phenomena according to them, or which merely occupies itself with dealing with one or a few special kinds of experience, does not deserve the name of philosophy in our sense of the word. As an illustration of the former, we can refer to the philosophy of Hegel or of Spinoza, and as an illustration of the latter we can take the philosophy of the Vedānta. But philosophers should not claim to be omniscient, and it will be a training for them in humility if, instead of twisting facts for a supposed explanation, they would simply confess their ignorance where they fail to know, or where the nature of things is such that no knowledge of the situation is possible. By the very nature of our definition of philosophy it would appear that philosophy is a growing science. It is not correct, however, to think that philosophical systems worked out by the great masters of the past are mere fanciful creations. They are genuine attempts to discover the truth, and even though they may have failed in the entirety of their conceptions, they have always made some discoveries, and even in their failures have demonstrated the hollowness of philosophical investigations in particular lines, and have thus forewarned the future traveller. Thus both in their positive and negative results they have aided humanity in paving its way towards its destined goal of progress. The history of science is also a history of errors and misconceptions, and also a history of the discovery of truth which had to be purged of its impurities by the untiring work of later investigators. Both in science and in philosophy, each important investigator has put in a brick by which the temple of knowledge is being constructed. But, while science collects facts only in a particular department of study, philosophy, in its most comprehensive sense, has to collect facts from all possible departments of knowledge, not only of nature but also of mind. All sciences and human experiences—moral, religious, aesthetic, social, psychological, mystic and the like—form the data for the constructive work of philosophy. The data of philosophy increase with the growth of human knowledge and attempts at systematisation may fail at the most crucial points in failing to explain facts. Both philosophy and science have thus to move forward together. It has been the belief of the past philosophers that the purpose of philosophy is to discover the nature of reality, though the term has been used in very different senses by different writers. With me reality means all that can be experienced directly or indirectly, all that appears and the immediate pre-suppositions of such appearances. Philosophy must remain silent about bare dreamy possibilities. With the growth of knowledge new realities may dawn upon our vision which it would be the business of future philosophers to deal with. A dream, a mirage, a hallucination are also reality so far as they are experienced. A dream may be called unreal in the sense that it has no connected relation with other dreams of other days or with the experiences of the waking life. It is this break of connection, the impossibility of relating it with other experiences at other times, that makes us call it unreal. So far as it is an occurrence as an experience at a particular time, it has a definite aetiology and is in that way connectible with other facts and experiences, and is thus within the scope of philosophical investigation. Freudian attempts in this direction are an illustration to the point. The older idea that reality can be equated with the non-relational has so well been challenged by many other philosophers, that it is needless to attempt a fresh refutation of it. The belief that reality is something behind the phenomena, behind the experience and behind the relational outlook of things, seems to me to be a positive superstition. If there are facts, entities or relations behind the phenomena as determinants of them, they are no doubt real. But that does not take away the reality of what is experienced; since we shall have to deal only with what is experienced; that alone has supreme importance for us. It is only through what is experienced that what is not experienced will gradually come in our view in an indirect manner. The view that, because experiences are real and are related, only the relational whole of experiences is the real, is also a gratuitous assumption. Such a totality is never given in experience, and in attempting to affirm the whole as the real the philosopher denies the reality of parts and brands them as illusory. Such a point of view also ignores the most fundamental part of reality and of knowledge consisting in the passage of experience to experience through relations which is the very structure of knowledge. It, therefore, ends in denying the reality of knowledge, feeling and willing which constitute our concrete experience.

The method of philosophy is that of science. It analyses experiences and the facts denoted by them, collects them, and arranges them in order, forms hypotheses and theories to explain them in relation to other experiences. It thus uses both the deductive and the inductive methods of science and attempts a systematisation of all known facts and experiences. Its difference from other sciences consists in the fact that while other sciences are busy at the work of systematisation and the discovery of new facts and relations in their own specific departments, philosophy takes the results of those sciences and other facts arising out of human relations and tries to bring them together in such a system of relations that it may discover a common ground-plan which holds them all; or if facts in a special universe cannot be harmonised with facts of other universes, philosophy would show the extent to which explanation is possible and what are its natural limits. Thus Physics, Chemistry, Biology, History, Sociology, Anthropology, Aesthetics, moral experiences, psychological experiences, mystic experiences, are all the feeders of the science of philosophy. Philosophy deals with all the objective, the subjective, and the supra-subjective facts in their broad outline of relationships, leaving the study in the specific and special relationships and facts in charge of special departments of science.

I cannot leave off here without saying a word about what I mean by explanation. The word explanation is used in a variety of senses. When a fact is subsumed under a general law, or when it is deduced from one or more axiomatic principles, or when the various relevant conditions which invariably precede an occurrence are enumerated, it is said to be explained. When universal laws cannot be discovered, a reference to occurrences of a similar nature may also serve as an explanation. A man gets influenza in October and it is explained by saying that such fevers are very common in October. Again the explanation of an occurrence of a complicated fact of nature, such as the formation of dew-drops, is to be found by a close analysis of the occurrence itself in various fields. Thus we have not only dew-drops in the early morning on the leaves of grass, but on the sides of a glass pane also. It required also a knowledge regarding the presence of moisture in the air and the conditions under which such moisture is retained or given up. By piecing together the various bits of information and by comparing the different occurrences on analogical grounds, an explanation of the occurrences may be available. Explanation of the origin of the biological species is sought in different ways, e.g. the climate, the locality, the environment, the conditions of life, the comparative anatomy and modes of life of analogous animals. Explanation of historical events is sought in the socio-political and the economical conditions of the country, the socio-political and economical history of the people, traditions, customs, religions and other kinds of beliefs, temperamental and the general psychological characteristics of the people together with the exciting events that led to a crisis, such as those of the French Revolution. All these events, which are facts of entirely different orders, are connected up in our minds as co-operating towards one final result. Analogies in history fail to be instructive when any of the relevant conditions or facts, positive or negative, is omitted. Explanation of a literary passage has first to clear up the anticipations or allusions which are implicitly contained in it, but, even then, the peculiar charm and emotional suggestions may be entirely missed unless the person to whom the explanation is offered is already initiated in those kinds of experiences. It is needless to multiply examples in such a short paper; but from what has been said, it will be evident that explanation consists in relating a particular fact or occurrence either with kindred other occurrences or with other previous occurrences which more or less invariably precede it or with the component events or facts which give it its structure. When a fact is subsumed under a general law, we also follow the same process, for a law is only a symbolic statement of certain similar occurrences under similar conditions, and, as such, all deductions imply the relating of a particular fact or occurrence with similar other occurrences in a particular and definite manner. Explanation by reference to axioms or *a priori* principles also refers to the fact in question as being an instance of the axiomatic statements. Analogy plays a great part in explanations, and the enumeration of causal conditions serves as the vehicle of explanation by a backward reference to history and also by implicitly relating the fact in question to similar other facts limited by similar causal history. The demand for explanation is the most natural demand of the mind which reveals its very nature.

The word "mind" is a symbolic term for what is in reality a

process of weaving experiences together in a definite and systematic order, which transforms a denotation of objective presentation into an experience, by associating it with meaning. In one sense, therefore, mind is not an entity, it is a series of relationing processes, not in a lineal order but in a structural order. When anything is presented to the mind it is not introduced at a particular point (using a spatial imagery) but in interconnected waves and processes of inter-relationing. That being so, anything that cannot fit itself with these inter-relationing processes has virtually to be rejected by the mind. Truth consists in the subsistence or non-subsistence or the affirmation and denial of one or more relationships between determinants and relational complexes or between them and relations or qualitative emergents to the extent or in the order or manner in which such relationships subsist or do not subsist or exist or do not exist (restricting the word "existence" to objects of non-denotative experience and "subsistence" to objects of denotative experience or their pre-suppositions). Error, however, may be defined as a subject-object polar occurrence which, though denotable in a particular character under proper relations by any dimension or dimensions of knowledge, is not denoted by it or them as such, under the said conditions, though it is denoted by one or more other dimensions of knowledge. Such errors are rejected by the mind, because they could not have a place in the mind. So also the dream-experiences are rejected. It is for this reason that wise instructions or scientific truths may be rejected by a wrongly-bent or prejudiced mind. This relationing activity of the mind may be called the economic activity by which the mind refuses to entertain lonely individuals in their separatedness; these must be bound together in family-ties of relationships and be taken together along with other similar or dissimilar members, in order that they may have a place in the mind. By the expression "economic activity" I mean that activity which is pertinent to the mind as a relational complex by which it integrates separate facts into the wave-structure of other facts, and makes them co-operate in unison with them. When facts of the same order are integrated, we have universals; when facts of the same or different orders are integrated in the same time-instant in a specific relation, we have the interpretation of facts as propositions of a factual order; and when different time-instants are involved in an invariable relation, we have what is called causality. When such integration is implicitly mediated by other facts, we have what is called conditions. The super-vention of such a condition modifies the relation of causality. When facts or events that are qualitatively different are integrated together in universal time-relation of occurrence or non-occurrence, we have what may be called laws. The notion of law is, thus, closely related with the notion of causality. In our ordinary notion of causality we apprehend that the cause somehow impels or necessitates the effect. But, as many philosophers have pointed out, there is no such notion of necessitation involved in causality. It may well be asserted that a causal proposition has no idea of force in it. The application of the idea of universality is also not correct in any scientific sense. The idea of universality is only present in deductions where what was implicit is made explicit, and no new element is introduced. The relation that the whole state of the universe bears to the next instant cannot be definitely predicted even if we could know the whole state of the universe at any particular instant. Causation, thus, is only an approximation of anticipation from a large number of individual instances of the sequence of partial states of the universe with regard to another individual instance, where such a sequence is expected to turn out. If under certain conditions an eclipse is predicted in 1937, it is because under similar conditions eclipses have occurred in all observed cases of the past. It is, thus, merely an anticipation or expectation of one particular event from innumerable series of sequential events that occurred in the past. This expectation may turn out to be true or false, but the affirmation of its probability in all such future cases would be hazardous and unscientific. There is, thus, no causality in a universal sense. Causality, thus viewed, is a relational integration from individuals to individuals. Excepting the case of assertion of causation regarding pure mathematical quantities, where the word "causality" is used in a sense of deduction, making explicit what was implicit, probably no case of cause explains the structural quality of the so-called effect as a mere resultant of it. Causality, thus, is a study in history which explains the aetiology of an occurrence by noting down its fairly large number of invariable antecedents. When causality is used in the sense of analysing the structural components of a qualitative complex, then also it cannot explain the concrete qualitative fact which is more than a resultant of the components. Where the complex is merely a resultant of the components, we have a case of deduction and not causation. No true case of causation, therefore, explains the "why" of a situation; it merely records the "what" in temporal order. In some Indian systems it has been assumed that the emergence of qualities through a causal process is an inexplicable extraneous affair and emphasis has been laid on the identity of the causal entity with the effect, and the process as such has been denied, whereas in others causal process has been regarded as making explicit what was implicit, and thus causality has been treated as a case of deduction. Others such as the Nyāya and the Buddhist, however, have regarded the effect as a new emergence. The concept of the emergence of new qualities or relational complexes does not involve as a necessary pre-condition that the causal elements or the processes leading to emergence should persist as an integral part of the emergents. The function of the causal conditions in a causal process consists in the fact that they co-operate together towards the appearance of emergent qualities or relations. When causal elements or the diverse relations involved in a causal process lead up to an emergent quality or relation or relational com- plexes, they may be called, for the sake of convenience, the "basis" of the emergents. The use of this term does not imply that any part of it is a constituent of the emergent qualities or the emergent relational complexes. In a certain class of such emergents the "basis" may, however, be a constituent of them, but that is not necessarily so. But even when the basis is not a constituent, it may remain as co-operative factor in inducing the emergent qualities or complexes such that the modes of the modification of the basis should have its counterpart in the emergent quality or complex. The relation between the basis and the emergent qualities or the complex may be designated as an emergent relation as distingushed from the analogous resultant or the deductive relations. the emergent relation being a unique and inscrutable relation, the converse relation subsisting between the emergents and the basis should also be regarded as unique and inscrutable, and may be designated as a converse emergent relation. The relation between an emergent and other relational complexes through the medium of the basis may be designated as the translated emergent relation. A basis may also itself be an emergent of other causal complexes. Two emergents may also come in direct relation as two original relational complexes and produce further emergent qualities or relational complexes.

The concept of mind and of the ego or the perceiver is indeed a difficult one. Idealists in India and in the West have some-times maintained that the object of awareness, being given in awareness, is nothing but awareness, and, therefore, that there cannot be an object unless there is the awareness of it. The fallacy of this position was shown by Moore in a brilliant paper in which he showed that awareness and its object are two different things. The Buddhists argued that the two are one since they are given simultaneously. They regarded it as a deduction from a supposed general truth that things realised at the same instant of time are identical in nature. The fallacy is obvious. The image of orange is co-present with the word "orange," and no one would think for a moment that the word "orange" is identical with the round yellow object. Again, it has been held that the subject and the object are given in and through knowledge. The term in-and-through is ambiguous; for if it means a relation, two terms S and O must be present before the relation can occur; and if it means that knowledge alone exists and the subject and object are both its modes and a sort of extraneous imposition on it, then also the reality of knowledge as such, independent of such bi-polar modification, must be demonstrable to us in experience, and some justification ought to be available as to why such bi-polar modification should occur. It is a peculiar situation that nothing can be denoted or referred to except through knowledge, but yet it is un-fortunate that the situation be so exploited that knowledge should be regarded as the only reality. The word "knowledge" is used in a variety of senses. The knowledge of a blue patch of colour in front of me is very different from the know-ledge that I suppose I have of the n-dimensions of space, or the knowledge that I may have of a tense pain, or an ecstatic state which is more or less unrelational. The use of the word "I" is also very ambiguous when used as a subject of the verb "to know." Had it not been for the crude conditions of grammar, the situation might just as well have been described as "there is a knowledge of such and such." One may as well say "there is knowledge of such and such at such a centre at such an instant." The spatio-temporal limits are just as much necessary for knowledge as for any other event in the world, though on account of the peculiarity of the phenomenon of knowledge its spatial location is not possible. Again, it is said that both the subject and the object are revealed in and through knowledge. In that case the subject, being revealed in knowledge, is as much an object of knowledge as any other object. Unless the existence of pure objectless knowledge is demonstrable, it seems irresistible that there is only knowledge, and object or objects are denoted by it. The existence of subjects as such cannot be proved. The existence of knowledge as such cannot also be proved. Furthermore, there is no characteristic appearance of the subject with which I can directly be acquainted. The knowledge of the subject, if we have it at all, is only a knowledge by description or a fiction of linguistic construction. It is difficult to discover if there is a special content of "I," the knower, as a mere perceiver, what the Vedāntists would call the "Sākṣi." If there were such an unchangeable perceiver, this entity would have a character and would be perceived as such. On the other hand, we know that in the consciousness of a new-born babe, who is unaware of a linguistic construction, there is hardly any apperception of "I," and it is extremely doubtful whether his knowledge ever takes the subject-object form. As the individual grows through experience, there are special associations of meaning attached to the "I." He not only says " 'I' perceive" but he also says "I am good," "I am powerful," "I am the hero in battle-fields," "I am unconquerable." All these expressions point to a growing association of meaning with the "I" which not only characterises the subject but also the nature of the perceived object. A common man perceives certain symmetries in a picture and a master artist also perceives them, and even others; the perception is common to them both, but yet the two apperceptions are poles asunder. The apperception of the master artist is associated with the whole history of the "I" as the perceiver, as the creator of many beautiful pictures appreciated by his fellow-beings throughout the world. This shows that though we cannot refer to any particular unchanging entity as the "ātman" or the "self" as the perceiver, we find that in each case of adult perception the apperception of any particular fact or object refers to a history which it modifies and by which it also is modified. According to our theory (the details of which cannot properly be elaborated and justified in this brief paper), there is no sensation, no image, no appearance, no apperception which appears as a singular unitary atomic fact. It appears in a background of a mental complex which has as its counter-part a pretty large area of physiological happenings and processes. Using physical imagery, I may say that as we grow in experience, the area that is determined by and determines an apperception also enlarges, and the relational processes involved therein also become more and more complicated. This complex area is structurally intimately connected with the entirety of the mental complex; but at any particular time-instant the excitation involved in the mental complex on the occasion of an apperception is in a comparatively limited field. It is these processes excited in a limited field which, being in themselves relational complexes, behave as an indivdual that is referred to as "I" in "I perceive." The "I" is thus referred to not through indirect acquaintance as such but through implication. This implication involves the operation of a part of the mental whole in relation to the apperceived object. Such a self is neither a bundle of perceptions nor an entity which has perceptions as its body, but is an integrated whole, as a part of the bigger mental whole. It, therefore, not only grows but may change its nature at different times as a result of the mental history, as also on account of environmental influences, and on the occasion of diverse kinds of apperceptions. The mental history is composed of four elements: (1) the original tendency of mutual operations of the mind-complex which is an emergent from the physiological complex, which determines its emergent relations, (2) the environmental history, (3) the history of the manner in which emergent qualities and facts are integrated in the mind-complex, (4) the integrations that have actually been effected. Though the mind-complex is described as a co-relation of diverse relational processes, and though it has been said that there may be groups of relational areas, which may appear to be separable from the rest of the mind-complex and may behave as individuals at different time-instants, yet such a separation takes place only in the interest of the practical activity of the mind, as it is impossible that all relational processes should show themselves at any particular time-instant. But this should not, on any account, be interpreted to mean that any mental field is not connected and integrated with the whole history of the mind complex, or that an individual mind-complex, which has grown in association with other mind-complexes, should be wholly or even largely separable from them. Just as an individual human body can tend to move in one direction at one instant of time, though it has the capacity to move in various directions, so the fulfilment of practical activity requires that the mental history should converge towards a particular area in consonance with the environmental requirements, which would oppose its movements in other directions. The more the mind-complex liberates itself from the environmental conditions and creates for itself more and more stable psychical environments, the more is it possible to have the activities fulfilled more freely and spontaneously in consonance with such an environment. Under proper conditions it may be possible to have glimpses of the mind-complex, as if it were an apperceivable unit separate from the body. Though the mind-complex has been described as a relational complex, such a relational complex must be viewed as one of free and spontaneous activity and, though the activity of any separable field of it may be determined by the operation of the continually evolving mental history, yet it is possible under proper conditions that the activities of any such field should grow so intense that it would not merely be a function of mental history, but, behaving as an individual, it would largely modify the mental history itself. This spontaneous activity may be designated as free-will. It is as much determined by history, as it may itself determine the history. History is not a static fact but a fact of continual mutations—

history determining spontaneity, and spontaneity determining history. The history on its cognitive side is the meaning which is the soul, as it were, of any conscious state. No state is conscious which is not referent at least to some history. The greater the reference to history, the greater the meaning and depth of consciousness.

Kant conceived a theory in which it was supposed that there were unknown things-in-themselves, the influences of which were interpreted by the minds in spatio-temporal and logical relations for the construction of experiences. Criticisms of such a theory are too well known to be repeated here. But one question naturally arises. Are the spatio-temporal and logical relationing entirely arbitrarily given by the mind or are they determined by the very nature of things-in-themselves? In the case of the latter supposition, the things-in-themselves would not be unknown, but would be entirely of a determinate character. On the former supposition, the orderliness of experience would be merely accidental, a supposition quite impossible to accept. Without the relationing activity of the mind ascribing meaning to every mental occurrence and thereby rendering it a fact of experience, it would be difficult to compute the contribution or modification that is effected by physiological processes, through which a fact of objective nature can be presented in a newly emergent form to the mind-complex. It is, therefore, extremely difficult to believe that knowledge is a relation such that the objective sense-data are present at the same time both in the external world and in the mind, and that the mind is only like a door of ingress. For, in that case, we have to ignore the modificatory contributions of the physiological medium, as also the historical contribution of the mind-complex. We know that there are different avenues of experience which I have elsewhere designated as dimensions of knowledge. There are the five senses and also the sixth sense, the muscular; in addition to these, there are the different kinds of inferential processes, the emotional, the ecstatic, the mystic and the trance-states, omitting the other super-normal processes, such as are found in hypnotism, thought-reading and the like, regarding which there are many differences of opinion. Our first start in mental life is in association with the six senses of which, again, the ocular dimension is regarded as the most important. If we take into consideration the modificatory contributions, through which the external something is presented to us, say, through our eyes, we see first of all that there is no contact between the eye and the external something. We know that the external something by itself cannot be presented to the eye. What is presented to the eye are certain reflected rays of light, which have been distorted in various manners (inter-molecular or physical) by various objects. Thus, instead of saying that the external something—the object—is presented to us, we may as well say that the external something, commonly called the rays of light, impinge on the eye in a distorted manner, yet holding a special order among them. Both this order and distortion have an orderliness imposed on them by the nature of the object, which leads to the affirmation of ocular phenomena, and the objects denoted by them. At the apex of all these processes (which are known only by scientific investigations of recent times and of which we are not directly aware) there is an emergent quality of colour-sensation, at the basis of which there are sundry physiological processes. This colour, again, in order that we may be explicitly conscious of it, must be integrated in the mental history and be subordinated to the principles of working of the mind-complex. Under the circumstances, we cannot say that the blue patch of colour, that is implicitly projected in the mind or explicitly perceived as such, exists outside of us in the self-same quality. It is an emergent quality which has as its basis the physiological processes acting in unison with certain other physical facts. But it has a certain co-variant relation, firstly, directly with the physiological processes which form its basis, and, secondly, with the physical stimulus which roused the physiological processes. This co-variant relation is a determinate relation of an unalterable nature. Even when the colour-image passes through the fourth order of transformation by its integration with mental history, the co-variant relation remains true to a pretty definite extent. The exact nature of the relationship cannot be determined on account of the fact of new emergence at each of the stages. But, though the nature of the relationship cannot be estimated, the co-variant relation has such definiteness that, howsoever the nature of the external world may vary as related to our experience of it, our awarenesses of it stand in a definite co-variant relation with it, such that our awarenesses may be said to denote real objective facts, and this is the basis of our commerce or intercourse with the external world. This is what I may call the denotative theory of knowledge. Our knowledge does not correspond with the object, nor is it a fact of such a nature that it means a modification of the entire state of the universe, nor is it a mystic history-less illumination or a mere product of co-operating collections, but it is such that we have one to one relation with the so-called external object and also with our mental history. It is a function of them both. The word "orange" has no similarity with the round yellow object, though it denotes it by a specified type of relationship; so our knowledge is related to the so-called objects which have no nature in themselves except in relationship with other relational complexes. Relation is a word the connotation of which is ultimate and indefinable. The relations may be of different orders and types. Oue of the distinctions that are observed regarding relations is that they are either symmetrical or asymmetrical; with reference to the relation that holds between the sensory acquaintance and the external fact denoted by it, it may be said that it is asymmetrical, that is, the relation between the external fact and the internal acquaintance is different from the relation between the sensory acquaintance and the fact. It is on account of this fact that while a sensory acquaintance projects itself as an external fact, the external fact co-operates with other data towards the emergence of the sensory acquaintance. The contention of the ultra-idealist that there need not be an external fact but that the mind has the ideas impressed on it, or evolves them by its own activity, would render community of experiences impossible of explanation. If we were to suppose that such a community is possible on a theory of accidental harmony of illusions, it would be merely running the philosophy to bankruptcy. Thus, the external fact has to be admitted. It has also to be admitted that we cannot know it just as it is. But not to know it, just as it is, is not to have no knowledge of it. So long as the co-variant relation between the external facts, which may be regarded as the determinat at the one pole, continues through other determinants in the chain, with the determined at the other pole as the sensory acquaintance, we may say that we know the external fact. When we say that we know the number "2," all that we mean by it is that we know a number of relations that it has with other real or imaginary numbers. An object is said to be known when we know some of its relations in a variable or invariable order with other relational complexes. It is not given to us that we should know any entity whatsoever in all possible relations, and we should have to be content if any entity or complex is given to us in at least some definite relations with other entities or relational complexes. Knowledge implies the knowledge of relations. Even a sensory impression may be said to be known only so far as its relations with other things are known. A thing is nothing but a complex of relations. The question about the possible relatum will be taken up in due course. According to the explanation of knowledge given here, it will be seen that even what is called a direct acquaintance and direct experience is in fact only a mediated experience where the terms in the middle are merely jumped over and we have a direct passage from the determinants to the awareness, and *vice versa*. Awareness of relations may be regarded as the particular mode of the passage of the mind from one term to another or from one item of experience to another.

But are awareness of relation and the relation the same? Or do relations exist externally outside the mind? If they do exist, what must be their nature? The position that I have to take is that relations exist as ultimate facts, but their knowledge as imparted to us is through a relation of translated emergence. Since relations are admitted and relation of relations also admitted, and it is also admitted that we have knowledge only of relations, it will be absurd to ask if we can know any relation as it may exist outside of us without any further relation. Knowledge is possible only in the possibility of relational structures emergent from the mind-complex. No single relation *per se* can yield an acquaintance of it, for acquaintance itself consists in the emergence of certain relations as a qualitative fact in and through a relational structure, which may remain implicitly as the basis of it, but which can be made more and more explicit by a process which can be designated as deliberation. The traditional classification of logical propositions shows that the structure of knowledge consists in relations. When a particular relation is said to be known between A and B, the relation bcomes explicit and the terms remain implicit; but all the same, the terms are relational complexes, out of which a particular relation emerges as a qualitative fact, which is commonly designated as acquaintance. The qualitative nature of a fact is nothing but the emergence of one or more relations from relational complexes. When the relational complexes become extremely implicit, we have an instance of abstract logic or Mathematics where direct experience is at its minimum. Since only relational emergents arising in and through relational complexes which are constituents of mind-complex can reveal themselves in acquaintance, knowledge of relational determinants in the external order or in the other mind-complexes can only be through a co-variant order of emergence. Relational complexes or relations existing in external order are designated as relational determinants, as distinguished from our awareness of relations. If we remember that relations can only be known when they beome emergent in the mind-complex, the fear of the vicious infinite vanishes. Relations may become emergent through successive series of other relations or of relational determinants of different orders, and the whole process of such a connected series of mediation may be there without being emergent, in which case we can have no direct acquaintance of them, though we may be indirectly aware of them only as co-variant terms of determinants. Relational emergents of the mind-complex may thus be regarded as the function of other relational determinants of one or more different orders. Relational determinants may in their turn be emergents from other determinant complexes; but they cannot be known since only relational emergents of the mind-complex show themselves in acquaintance. The so-called revelation in knowledge is nothing but the emergence of relations in and through relational complexes.

A question here naturally arises whether there are any relata. This is a difficult question. Since relations can only arise in and through relational complexes, we have no experience of relations without there being any relata. But what may be the ultimate nature of relational determinants as apart from all relational emergents must remain for us doubtful. If there are such ultimate relata or terms of reference, relations must be interwoven in their very nature and structure. Thus there is no position where we can get to ultimate terms without involving relations. Even the assertion of the identity of any ultimate term involves the relation of identity; and without asserting the proposition that an ultimate term is what it is, we cannot refer to it even in the most indirect manner. From an analysis of our experience we know that relations may behave as emergent qualities and may thus behave as relata to other relations. The question, therefore, regarding relata and relations becomes only a relative one; and it may be admissible to think that there are ultimate relational determinants which behave among themselves both as the relata and relations. Our ultimate starting-point must therefore be with relations that are determinants. An analysis of our awareness of relation also shows that it consists in the passage of the mind from certain relational complexes to certain others. Such a passage may be designated as a movement of determination. Determination thus is the very nature of relations and is nothing extraneous to it. The world as such is a big mathematical equation in which most of the relations have not taken an emergent form in the mind-complex. The world that we can know is by its very nature only a small fraction of the world that is. Howsoever our knowledge may advance, it has to be admitted that there is always a limit both as regards scope and extent and as regards the ultimate levels, beyond which relational determinants must remain wholly unknown. The limit is the limit of the emergent mind-complex. Relations, in our view, are both external and internal. When they contribute to the projection of an emergent they are internal, and when they do not they are external.

In some systems of modern philosophy, space-time has been regarded as the ultimate original in nature. But, in our view, since space-time also is a relational whole, having definite properties of its own, there must be some level of which it is a product. That level is the level of our ultimate relational terms. I have intentionally used the term "product" in this connexion, as I do not at the present time feel sure whether the space-time has for its component or constituent the ultimate relational terms. When a product is a resultant of some elements, such elements may be said to be components of the latter. But when the product is an emergent fact, the elements that led to its projection may be said to be its constituents. But it seems to me quite possible that it will be gratuitous to suppose that all the determinants in the space-time structure should be emergible in the mind-complex. The mind-complex acts in harmony with our sense-organs and, as such, with the so-called matter. If there is any definite type of space-time structure which is not co-terminous with mass or matter, it is quite possible that we may not have any knowledge of it. Since space-time structure is a relational whole and since mass and force are ultimately reducible to it, the existence of force as a separate determinant cannot be admitted. The force that appears to our mind is only an emergent fact, the datum of which has to be sought in the relational field. Space-time structure being a relational whole, slices taken from it for any consideration must be of a purely relative nature. The space-time structure being the ultimate experiential basis of all emergents, at least some of its characters continue through the series of emergents up to the mind-complex. This explains the fact why mind starts with some vague notions of space-time, which get more and more explicit with training and the history of experiences.

When a relational complex leads to the projection of another relational complex, such that only some of its constituent characters are manifest in the latter and the latter has some new characters associated with it, we would call the latter an emergent of the former. It thus appears that in all cases of emergents there is, on the one hand, some loss of old characters, and, on the other, some gain in the formation of new ones; and the new ones are not explainable in terms of the old ones as a resultant of them. Thus the protons, neutrons, electrons and the ions are some of the fairly ultimate facts of the order of matter, the phenomena of which as protons are emergents in the mind-complex and the nature of the determinants of which is being discovered by the mind through complex spatio-temporal relationships of waves, corpuscles and the like. The protons, electrons and the ions are the constituents of all inorganic and organic substances—in fact, of the entire material world. The properties of different inorganic substances are due to the different spatio-temporal structure and the proton-electronic fields in them. These properties, which entitle them to their special existence as different elements, are emergent facts in consonance with our general principle of emergence. But the relational fields of these relational complexes are such that there is no specification and division of functions in them, so that the only ways of their working are in inter-molecular and inter-atomic directions, There is no selective action in them and no effort to retain their persistency or recover damages wrought on them by environmental conflict by any functional modes. They are thus not true individuals, though in a general sense electrons or protons—though constituted as a commingling point of various relational fields—may, for explanatory purposes, be taken as individual wholes.

It is only when we come to life that we come to the peculiar situation where a piece of structural matter distinguishes itself from the rest of the material world by its selective action, effort to persist, attempts at repairing damages and by a peculiar phenomenon, technically called behaviour, and reproduction. In the field of matter, some distant resemblance to selective action in living organisms can be traced in the peculiar responsive action of colloids to ions. Life, whatever it may be, manufactures the material stuff suited for its manifestation by itself from other organic and inorganic substances in a manner and to the extent that no laboratory chemist can ever hope to do. As life advances from the vegetable to the animal and from the lower animals to the highest, the human, we have a gradual advance of a multifold differentiation of functions and activities which all work in a selective harmonious manner leading to the development of the body and the reproduction of similar bodies in it in endless series. In multi-cellular animals, each cell possesses the characteristic of an independent living being and yet merely in the presence and association with other fellow-cells an entirely different individual, the animal, is projected as an emergent. Here we have a relational complex which is of an entirely different order from the relational complexes in the material order. Here we have two emergents, the life-process-complex, and the body-complex, and though body-complex is the basis of the emergent life, the body-complex is itself also an emergent of the life-process-complex. Neither of them can be said to be prior to the other. We have here a peculiar instance of two relational complexes of a different order, mutually determining each other, just as we have in man the mind-complex, determining the life-process-complex and the body-complex. No instance of this order is available in any of the lower levels. It may well be supposed that the crude beginnings of mind-complex must have begun at least with the unicellular animals. The inter-relation of the relational processes subsisting between the relational complexes, mind, the structure of the body, life-functions and the environment, cannot be considered separately except as an abstraction. They are all in one, and one in all. The different constituents that compose the living man are such that each co-operates towards the emergence of other forms in definite directions. We have already noted that in the case of man the presence of other mind-complexes is an important factor towards the development of the mental life in various grades of social life uniting the past, the present and the future. It is impossible for me now to do justice to the many problems that are associated with a study of the biological field, which are not only extremely interesting but which could have thrown a flood of light on the elucidation of the above view. One or two points may be cursorily touched.

The distinguishing feature of life is that here the relational modes are of a dynamic nature, such that the reality or existence of any particular mode is dependent on other modes of a different order and *vice versa*. We have here a situation in which a particular relation-mode or function does not exist *per se* but through others, and there is thus a mutual dependence of such a nature that it is impossible to start with any one of them as being prior to the other. We have here a circle of revolutions in which any point can be regarded either as the first or as the last. Yet the first is in the last and the last is in the first. If this relationship is such in life, it is still more so with regard to the flowing activity of the mind-complex, which is absolutely unrepresentable by any terms of physical notation, which behaves as an integrated growing whole and yet keeps its co-variant relations with life-processes, the body and the environment. Another point is that even the cellular membrane has a special selective action which attains its highest evolution and development in instinct and human intelligence. The selective action in the case of all animals beginning with the uni-cellular is to be found in the peculiar phenomenon called behaviour, which is the registration in an unknown manner of past experiences. This peculiar phenomenon of behaviour serves to destroy the barrier of time and makes the past, present and the future coalesce at any given instant, and thus starts the history of the individual as personality. In the lower grades of life where the behavour of the individual animal is largely under the control of the body-complex, the term personality may not suitably be used. But as the mind emerges out of the body and begins to assert itself in its spontaneous existence though carrying with it the peculiar body-emergents as appetitive functions, begins to show itself as a true individual, the integrated history of which, having risen above the appetitive functions, begins to reveal itself in accordance with a selective purpose, which is its own emergent as value. The appetitive functions here do not lose their existence but have a transmuted modification in consonance with the value-sense. Here the biological tendencies are not destroyed but their potency, and indeed the potency of the whole life-history, converges towards the achievement of the self-emergent purpose, the value. There is thus here a new ordering of the old existent states of previous history producing by their harmony, contentment and blissfulness associated with the progressive march of the higher man. In the lower order the conflicts between the animal and the environment are annulled by the life-process itself in a very naturalistic manner. With the evolution of mind, mental conflicts of different orders arise through our intercourse with other minds. Such conflicts are natural and obvious; and the life-process instead of annulling them often increases them. But as a new selective purpose as value emerges in man, he sets his house in order. The integrated history behaves as a person and the conflicts are annulled and the whole history becomes a history of self-realisation in the light of the value. Where the emergent value cannot exert itself as the real and constant selective purpose of the man but is in conflict with the biological selective purpose and only inconstantly shows its supremacy from time to time, we have the picture of the ordinary struggling man.

The selective action associated with life introduces us to a relational complex, which deals with purpose. The idea of purpose must be conceived as a relational order that makes for the persistence of itself by introducing only such relations into itself as are contributory to its existence and growth. When we say that the world has a purpose, we only mean that it is contributory to our being and development. To say that the entire universe is purposive is probably an exaggeration. Only those relational orders and complexes which are contributory to life may be regarded as fulfilling the purpose of life. There may exist many types of relational complexes which originate in their own law, but which are not contributory to the purpose of life. Thus, if a fragment of the world is purposeful, there is probably another fragment of it which is purposeless. When the mind emerges from the biological basis and feels itself in its integrated history as a self-subsisting unity of relational complexes in commerce with other minds, which being contributory to its development may be felt as its constituent, a new non-biological purpose arises, the whole field of vision of which is raised above the biological level. Minds separately chained to bodies can be held together as consitutents only through love. Love is thus the fundamental non-biological relationship which can cement together in a common goal of higher relationship all minds of the past, the present and the future. Such a possibility cannot happen unless and until the apperception of value as a self-emergent purpose of the mind-life is enthroned in the dominating position of a queen.

The one important fact is that the mind-complex should have such an independent existence that it may transmute the biological tendencies (used in a very wide sense) to its own order under the guidance of the emergent value-forms. When there is a beginning of it we have the beginning of saintliness. Our process, therefore, is not a process of mental annihilation but a richer process of mental growth, where mind assumes its true role of an emergent reality linked to the body as its basis but leading a life which is entirely its own. The emergent orms of value may appear as the beautiful, the good, the realisation in knowledge, the realisation in will, the realisation in higher non-biological emotions turning towards an apex as God or in any other form. The treatment of the emergent forms of value is a very wide subject by itself, and cannot be treated in the present paper. The true God is not the God as the architect of the universe, nor the God who tides over our economic difficulties or panders to our vanity by fulfilling our wishes, but it is the God who emerges within in and through our value-sense, pulling us up in and through the emergent ideals and with whom I may feel myself to be united in the deepest bonds of love. The dominance of value in all its forms pre-supposes love, for it is the love for the ideal that leads us to forget our biological encumbrances. Love is to be distinguished from passion by the fact that while the latter is initiated biologically, the former is initiated from a devotedness to the ideal. When a consuming love of this description is once generated, man is raised to Godhood and God to man.

PRINCIPAL PUBLICATIONS

A Study of Patañjali. Calcutta University Press.

Yoga Philosophy and its Relation to other Systems of Thought. Calcutta University Press.

Yoga as Philosophy and Religion. Kegan Paul (London).

Hindu Mysticism. Open Court (Chicago).

Indian Idealism. Cambridge University Press.

History of Indian Philosophy, Five volumes, four of which are already published by the Cambridge University Press.

KNOWLEDGE, REALITY AND THE UNKNOWN

by D. M. DATTA

BORN in East Bengal (Mymensingh) in 1898. Educated in Assam and Bengal, graduated from Calcutta University and received special training in Indian and Western Philosophy at the University College of Calcutta under the orthodox Pandits and University professors. After passing M.A. in 1921 did social work in villages for the education of girls and backward classes, and the production of Khadi (hand-spun and hand-woven cloth) for which received special training in the Āśrama of Mahatma Gandhi at Sabarmati. Resuming academic work, worked as senior Research Fellow at the Indian Institute of Philosophy, Amalner, Bombay (1924-25), held Basu Mallik Chair of Indian Philosophy under National Council of Education, Jadabpur, Calcutta (1925-28). Since then at Patna College, as Asst. Professor and then Professor of Philosophy, in Patna, Bihar.

KNOWLEDGE, REALITY AND THE UNKNOWN

I. THE FUNCTION OF PHILOSOPHY

There is a good deal of controversy now-a-days about the function and utility of philosophy. The best way of settling such issues, it appears to me, is to consult the long history of philosophy and the lives of the great philosophers of different times and places. If we do so, we cannot fail to notice the salient and common points that can be taken as the peculiar characteristics of philosophy. The chief among these are the insight and far-sight, the disinterested and comprehensive view of things in which persons known as philosophers have excelled others and by which they have made their lives worthy ideals for their fellow-beings. Confucius, Janaka, Buddha, Socrates, Plato, Aristotle, Sankara, Al Farabi, Al Ghazali, Spinoza, Kant, to mention only a few, illustrate this truth and at the same time remind us of the high esteem philosophers have enjoyed in human society. These facts remove also, to some extent, the doubt about the utility of philosophy.

By their insight philosophers have tried to distinguish between the real and the unreal, and grasp the inner and ultimate natures of things. By their far-sight they have tried to distinguish eternal values from transitory ones and have led their own lives and guided others accordingly. By considering all available data they have tried to form a comprehensive view of the universe. The world still needs, perhaps more urgently than ever, such persons for performing these important functions. Unfortunately, however, there are, in modern western philosophy, three undesirable tendencies—mostly born of an undue and uncritical respect for science—which would seem to challenge this view. We shall briefly consider them here.

The first of these is *the anti-metaphysical tendency*, found chiefly in Logical Positivism. It tries to show that the attempt of metaphysics to know the nature of reality underlying the phenomenal world and beyond sense experience, is a meaningless

K

task. Because, it points out, the meaning of a sentence depends on its verifiability and, therefore, any metaphysical question or statement regrading trans-empirical reality cannot be verified. The pursuit of metaphysics is thus a nonsensical affair. But this view of the positivists has evoked much criticism.[1] The chief objections raised are (1) that sense-experience is not the only kind of experience, (2) that the meaning of a statement is not the same thing as its verifiability, (3) that according to this criterion of meaning the criterion itself, being unverifiable by sense-experience, would be nonsensical and so also must be those statements of science which deal with imperceptible entities like atoms, electrons, energy, ether, force, laws, etc. Under the pressure of such criticism the logical positivists have modified their original position several times and begun to differ among themselves, in such a way that their attack on metaphysics has proved all but abortive, and it has been diverted to a part of science with which metaphysics would sink or swim. In fact, the very human inquisitiveness which led scientists to penetrate beneath the superficial and limited views of things by inventing microscopes and telescopes and to supplement perception by imagination and supposition, has also led philosophers to go still deeper into the heart of the universe and imagine the nature of reality behind and beyond sense-experience.

Another undesirable trend in modern western philosophy is to question the rationality of the attempt of philosophers to construct a comprehensive view of the universe as a whole. This attitude is mostly due to a *dissatisfaction felt against the system-building efforts* of Hegel and his followers. It is found first in British realists like Russell and Moore and their followers, the American realists. But it develops into an extreme view again in the Logical Positivists who hold that the business of philosophy is nothing but the logical analysis of scientific statements. On the whole, then, it is held by many important thinkers in the West now that the business of philosphy is analysis rather than synthesis.

I admit that analysis is very useful for philosophy. Without analysing facts, ideas and particularly the meanings of words and

[1] I have dealt with this subject in several papers read before the Ind. Phil. Congress and published in its Proceedings and the Phil. Quarterly.

sentences that constitute philosophical questions, we cannot arrive at any precise and accurate conclusion. But it is going too far to suggest that analysis is the only or the main business of philosophy. The aim of every branch of knowledge, and particularly that of science and philosophy, is to construe facts and ideas found by analysis and understand what they mean when put together. This is but the product of the basic tendency of the mind which Bosanquet calls the "wholing" tendency which is exhibited in perception, imagination and reasoning by the irresistible inclination to complete the idea of the whole when only a few parts are given. This is also shown in the undeniable monistic tendency of science to string together many facts by one law, and the many laws into more and more general laws and also in its attempt to bring all material substances under 92 chemical elements and all these again under one electrical energy of positive and negative characters. It is but natural and reasonable, therefore, that there should be an attempt, in philosophy, to discover the most universal characters present, in material and non-material phenomena and to form, with their help, some idea of the universe as a whole.

One great defect of one-sided dependence on analysis is that it often exposes us to the fallacy of composition in so far as we are apt to lose sight of the whole as a whole and think that what is found in the analysed parts is all that can be found in the whole. Another defect is that one can never feel sure that the parts found by analysis are the only ones; nothing has been left over.

It must be admitted, of course, that the finite human mind cannot form an exhaustive and adequate view of the entire universe. But in this, as in other matters, man has to be satisfied with so much as he can achieve by his best efforts. It will be instructive to bear in mind in this connection that we do not possess exhaustive knowledge of even so called finite things like a speck of dust, as sub-atomic physics is more and more bringing home to us; and yet we do not give up our effort to know.

It is natural and reasonable, therefore, that man should try to form, in philosophy, as comprehensive and adequate idea of the universe as is humanly possible and should also plan, unlike lower animals, his entire life in the light of this idea.

The third undesirable tendency in modern western philosophy, I want to point out, is the *divorce between philosophy and practical life*. Philosophy has become a mere intellectual game, like pure science and pure mathematics. The satisfaction ot intellectual curiosity and the attainment of truth are no doubt very laudable ideals. But mere intellectual satisfaction cannof satisfy the whole of man. The origin of intellectual curiosity itself may be directly or indirectly traced to some practical problem, as western pragmatists and others, who realize the biological significance of the intellect as a means to better practical adjustment, have begun to admit. Moreover, it is doubtful whether truth itself can be attained by reason without practical moral discipline of the passions and prejudices which warp human judgment. Ancient Indian philosophers rightly recognize these points and lay down courses in practical moral discipline, contemplation of philosophical truths and re-orientation of life in the light of these for the complete realization of philosophical truths. Again, in the domain of science, also, there is a growing tendency now in the West to encourage investigation more on the side of applied science than on that of pure science, to base life on science.

By a closer contact with practical life philosophy can regain the prestige it once enjoyed in the ancient world. And in a world where pride, prejudice and passions of narrow-minded political leaders have created so much of hatred, strife and misery, the influence of philosophers who have moulded their lives rationally in the light of philosophical truths and who possess the widest outlook and deepest insight, would be a great asset for society.

II PHILOSOPHICAL DIFFERENCES

The differences among philosophers have often been utilized for ridiculing philosophy and proving its futility. The basic presupposition behind such hostile criticism is that truth must be one, and, therefore, different philosophies about the same world cannot be true. The proposition, truth must be one, is ordinarily accepted by all almost as self-evident and, therefore, very little explanation and justification are found in its support. By saying that truth must be one it is perhaps meant that two contrary or contradictory propositions cannot be at the same time true of the same subject. Without entering into elaborate discussion it is possible to show the falsity of this view by showing only a few exceptions. A man seated in a car is moving and not moving at the same time with reference to outside objects and the seat respectively. He is fair and not fair, warm and not warm, tall and not tall, etc., etc., as compared with different persons and things. He is again both hard and soft in respect of different parts of his body, kind and cruel in respect of different persons. In short, what we commonly regard as the same logical subject is not the same in every part, aspect, respect and relation. It presents, on analysis, a multiple structure justifying opposite assertions, as has been recognised by Jaina logicians in ancient India. In the West, Russell has criticised the ordinary simple notion of things as the "billiard ball notion" and the neo-realists have called it the "brick-bat notion" and both have held like the Jainas that we must take a more inclusive, comprehensive view of things. The Jainas have gone further to elaborate a system of logic advocating multiple truth.

It should be clear from this that if there be alternative possible and valid judgments about what is called a single thing, the vaster and more complex the subject-matter, greater chances are there for differences of opinions. Consequently philosophy which has to deal with the entire universe in all its intricacies would admit of the greatest variation in accordance with the innumerable possible standpoints that philosophers can occupy and the different aspects of the universe which they may select for consideration in accordance with their differing interests created by divergent influences of place, time, society and personal inclinations. Even in sciences we find rival theories advocated by different scientists. The undulatory and the corpuscular theories, the theories of determinism and indeterminism in physics, the many alternative theories of evolution and extinction, in biology, astronomy, geology, etc., may be cited as examples. David Hilbert, the great German mathematician, conceives the possibility of many alternative systems of physics equally capable of explaining the physical world.

In the light of these facts, it will be realized that differences among philosophers are the necessary consequences of the great complexity and vastness of the subject-matter of philosophy and that the many alternative doctrines do not necessarily falsify one another. On the contrary if a particular system is true to its own point of view, that is, if it gives a consistent and faithful account and explanation of things as they appear from its particular standpoint it may be quite acceptable. Such different accounts may, therefore, be regarded as supplementing one another.

It should not be supposed that I am trying to maintain here that truth is altogether subjective and there is no sense in which truth must be one. On the contrary what I have been trying to maintain implies that if two persons can consider the same subject from the same standpoint, in the same aspect, respect or relation, then there ought to be unity of judgment regarding the matter and that judgment may be regarded as the only true one from that standpoint, in that aspect, etc. If, again, two persons can judge the same subject from all points of view, in all aspects, etc., then also they must agree and then their total judgments must give the total truth about the thing.

When we argue and try to convince one another we try tacitly or explicitly to make the opponent judge the subject from the same standpoint, etc., and in simple matters such agreement is roughly attained. But with the increase of complexity and vastness of the subject it becomes increasingly difficult to effect unanimity by this process. The attainment of complete unanimity remains only an ideal which we feel compelled to pursue, but fail completely to realize. Philosophers are tantalized by this ideal and the whole history of philosophy in different lands may be regarded as a series of repeated and varied attempts to reach this ideal. The different self-consistent systems may thus be regarded as supplementing one another. Notwithstanding this predicament in which the philosopher finds himself it should be his attempt to look at things from as many points of view as possible, so as to make his philosophy as comprehensive and acceptable as he can.

But the acceptability of a philosophy, I believe, largely depends also on the practical lead it can give to life and the happiness it can cause to the individual and society in the circumstances in which they are at the particular time and place.

The views expressed hereafter on the major philosophical issues of the day are the outcome of an attempt to assimiliate

Indian and Western ideas and unite them on a broad basis. To me they have been also a source of inspiration in life. But it is too much to hope that they will appeal to all.

<h3>III. THEORY OF KNOWLEDGE</h3>

Knowledge. It is customary to describe knowledge as the relation between the mind and something else and the mind as being unconscious before such relation. This description is quite true, in fact it is a truism, if by knowledge is meant consciousness of a *particular* thing and "unconscious" means unconscious of *that* "thing".

But a more important question that arises here is whether the mind is altogether unconscious (like a table or a chair) before a thing is related to it for knowledge. The customary answer is that consciousness *always* involves a relation between some subject and object and, therefore, it cannot precede such relation. The reason adduced here, namely, that consciousness is *always* a subject-object relation, may be either taken as a self-evident truth or established by induction based on observation. The first alternative is possible, so far as I can see, only if the proposition is taken as an analytic one, that is, only if it is assumed that consciousness connotes subject-object relation. But that is begging the very question which is to be solved.

The attempt to prove by induction the proposition that consciousness involves a subject-object relation, will be to point to several cases of consciousness, of table, chair, pen, etc., in each of which both the subject and the object exist. But this method of simple enumeration cannot give us any certain conclusion. We cannot claim that all kinds of cases have been exhausted. This doubt becomes more definite when we consider cases like self-consciousness, knowledge of knowledge itself, and dreamless sleep. If the mind can even partially know itself then the gulf and distinction between the knower and the known, the subject and object, vanishes in substance and becomes only a verbal distinction or at most a distinction between two different aspects of the same mind; and the idea that consciousness requires something other than the mind is found to be false. If again it is admitted that knowledge can reveal itself we have another exception to the supposed rule. If dreamless sleep is really experienced, as is implied by the memory of a person who reports after awaking that he enjoyed a dreamless sleep, then we have another case, the consciousness of a blank, that is, objectless consciousness.

Space does not permit the consideration of the many objections that have been raised against the interpretation of such cases of objectless consciousness. But I can only say that it seems to me that having, by the method of simple enumeration, generalized from the vast majority of cases, where the subject-object relation exists, that this must be good of all cases of consciousness, attempt is made afterwards to retain this fallacious belief by explaining away all cases which were previously overlooked and are now presented as exceptions.

To come back to the question whether mind can be thought to be conscious in any way before any object is presented to it, we find then that the objection that it cannot be so, because consciousness implies a necessary relation to an object, is not insurmountable. On the contrary if consciousness is altogether absent previously its sudden appearance, out of the unconscious antecedents, is extremely difficult to understand. Before I can perceive an object presented to me I must attend to it, otherwise there would be no consciousness of the object. But attention is scarcely possible without some consciousness, some inclination to know the object. This would imply a kind of consciousness before there is consciousness of that particular object. Freud's theory of the preconscious and unconscious is not incompatible with this position. His unconscious is only the lack of conciousness of specific objects; but is full of cravings and inclinations which seek fulfilment and direct the overt behaviour of persons to specific ends. The unconscious, moreover, retains all past experience. So the so-called unconscious mind is not unconscious like a table or chair.

In short, I think we can better understand the phenomenon of knowledge by accepting the pre-existence of a general consciousness which, by a gradual and continuous process of inclination, attention and selection, is directed towards specific forms and specific objects, than by thinking of the sudden appearance of consciousness out of non-conscious conditions. Leibnitz, Bergson as well as the Advaita Vedāntins of India, have emphasized the continuity among the different degrees of consciousness, and different aspects of experience and admitted some general con sciousness common to all.

The distinction between subject and object is one of office or function. After a particular knowledge arises we may analyse it and distinguish the knower and the known. But this distinction is neither universal nor fundamental. In self-consciousness, we have seen, the subject is not different from the object. It is only artificially, and in false analogy with ordinary consciousness, that two aspects of the self are distinguished, in such a case, as subject and object in a proposition like "The self knows itself." In ordinary cases also there may similarly be at first one undivided experience, a deep enjoyment of a landscape, for example, without any distinction being made between the subjective and the objective aspects of it.

If we start with two fundamentally different entities, like subject and object it is difficult to understand their subsequent inter-relation. But if they are conceived as separated aspects of one previously undivided experience or consciousness we can understand their relation more easily.

In general, then, I believe that specific knowledge of any thing may be understood as the precipitation or concentration of a pre-existing general consciousness in a particular direction. This can be understood from the following examples. I have a general awareness of my mind and by successful concentration of attention in a particular direction I may have the specific awareness or knowledge of a particular mental content, a sorrow, a disappointment, a desire, a memory image. I have a general awareness of my body and by concentration in a particular direction I may feel a tooth-ache, the existence of my little toes, a strain on the abdominal muscle, the movement of the right eye-lid. In a similar way I have first a diffuse and general awareness of the world around me and by successful attention, through the necessary organic mechanism, I become aware of a particular colour, sound, smell and the like.

Continuity of the knowledge-field. Our conception of the world and its relation to us is based mainly on visual perception which presents the world as an extended spatial field in which objects appear outside our bodies and outside one another. This generates also the vivid notion of the separateness of the knower and the objects known. It is useful for the nice adjustment of our bodies to the environment and animals possessed of vision have, therefore, a greater chance of survival.

But the visual knowledge of things generates the misleading idea of the discontinuous and discrete character of the world, and makes it difficult for us to understand their underlying unity, continuity and inter-relatedness. If we shut our eyes and suppress, if we can, the deep-rooted visual image of the world, and then try to explore the world with touch, taste, smell and sound we can feel qualitatively different touches, tastes, smells, sounds, etc., but they are not felt as away from us. Even sounds coming from different distances of the extended visual field are felt to be only louder or lower but they give no suggestion of differences in distance if we can suppress successfully their visual meanings. There is thus an intermingling mass of different experiences into which also enter our somatic feelings. Our bodies do not stand out separate from objects, nor do objects from one another. There is a felt continuity and interpenetration of the different kinds of experiences.

Vision comes very late in evolution and most animals have no visual experience. There is no reason, as Whitehead points out, why we should not believe our non-visual experiences and base our philosophical conception of the world on them if we can avoid thereby the many difficulties that metaphysics experiences as a result of accepting the discontinuous and isolated existence of things on the testimony of vision.

Realism versus Idealism. I can briefly indicate here also my attitude towards this great controversy in present day epistemology.

Twentieth century realism is a revolt against the epistemological idealist—the subjective idealist like Berkeley—who reduces objects to ideas and refuses to distinguish between the two. The German realist Brentano opposes this idealist theory by showing that knowledge involves two distinct factors, the mental act (perceiving, thinking, etc.) and an object towards which it is directed. Moore and Russell, at an early stage, accept this two-factor theory of knowledge and point out that knowing (or the mental act) does not know itself but something else, and therefore, the object known cannot be identical with the idea or the mental act. The American neo-realists follow the British lead in refuting the idealistic reduction of objects to ideas of the mind. But some of them (e.g. Holt) go to the other extreme of denying, like the behaviourist, ideas or consciousness altogether and, therefore, give up the two factor theory in favour of, what Lovejoy calls, pan-objectivism and they understand knowledge as a relation between two *objects*—the knower's body and the object perceived.

With all these realistic thinkers I agree to hold that when I perceive an *external* object, a table for example, the object is *distinct* from the act of perception or the idea of the object. Even in illusion this distinction between the act of perceiving and the object perceived outside should be admitted. The reason for this view is that the object is immediately perceived as being outside me, and we cannot disbelieve immediate consciousness so long as it is not contradicted.

But we must also admit that there are perceptions like those of pleasure, pain, tooth-ache[1] where there appear no external objects apart from the perception, and the distinction between the act and object is not certified by immediate consciousness. If in such a case a distinction is still to be made, as it is done by most realists, it would only be a verbal one, based on the analogy of external perception.

Many realists are not satisfied with merely holding that the object of perception is distinct from the perceiving act, but they also hold that (1) it is independent of the mind and (2) it possesses real existence. But none of these views is certified by immediate consciousness, neither can they be proved satisfactorily by any argument. To prove that the object is independent of the mind one must prove that no character that appears in the object, and no element that enters into the constitution of the object is in any way derived from past experience or from any *a priori* mental form or category. This is more than one can show; on the contrary, it is unlikely that at least things like the depth and solidity of a material thing, the hard look of stone, the soft one of cotton, etc., would appear to be there in the object without mind's interpretation and previous experience.

[1] A case where, even Moore now thinks, *esse* and *percipi* are inseparable.

If by "the object's independence of the mind" is meant that at least something of the object exists even when no mind perceives it, the contention is equally difficult of proof. From the nature of the case, it is not known what happens to the object then. As I have tried to show in a paper on *Stace's Refutation of Moore's Realism*,[1] both the idealist and the realist commit fallacies by making assertions, negative and positive, in a case of lack of knowledge like this, the idealist by thinking that the existence of the unperceived should be denied because it cannot be proved, and the realist by thinking that the existence of the unperceived should be admitted because it cannot be disproved. Only two considerations are there which can enable us to break this suspense and decide in favour of realism. The first is, as Hume pointed out, " practical convenience", and the other is, as Russell once said, "simplicity of hypothesis". On these grounds in every day life we believe that objects continue to exist even when they are not perceived.

The *real* existence of the object perceived does not follow from the mere perception of the object, for the simple reason that there are so many objects we perceive, the mirror image, the bent stick phenomenon, the flatness and small size of the sun, the position of the sun above the horizon during twilight and the like, which we do not admit to be existing *really* as such. This shows that objectivity (i.e., the character of being an object of perception) is not the same as reality.

The American neo-realists are forced to admit this. Holt says, for example, that his realism does not pretend to show the reality of objects, but only their subsistence. The American critical realists more frankly admit that what we perceive, the datum, is only essence, and not existence, and that on perceiving an object's essence directly we also believe that it exists, only (as Santayana following Hume says) by "animal faith" that makes life possible.

It should be noted then that most of contemporary realism, in spite of its great revolt against idealism, does not prove the reality of the object but only its subsistence or essence, and, therefore, realism is reduced to a misnomer. It can be more accurately described as objectivism, that is, the position that objects that are present to any mental act or consciousness are

[1] *Philosophical Quarterly*, 1936.

distinct from the latter. This is, so far as I can see, what is held by most of the present day realists including Moore, the neo-realist and the critical realist. I admit this position as reasonable. I may add that whenever *any* object appears to *any* mental state, imagination, conception, perception, illusion, hallucination it must be accorded objectivity.

But the pan-objectivity of some neo-realists who try to deny the mental altogether is an unbalanced reaction against sub-jective idealism, and as untenable as the latter. All kinds of consciousness, we have seen previously, do not present objects to which the former can be reduced; and even where they do, consciousness is immediately felt and it can be denied only by the suppression of attention to the background of objective experience. Moreover, by the reduction of knowledge to mere physiological processes within the knower's body, these realists fail to explain how the knower can know the external world, the past and the future. From mental solipsism there is thus a recoil into physiological solipsism. Realism is thus undermined.

Perry's famous criticism against subjectivism on the ground that it takes an unfair advantage of the ego-centric predicament is quite pertinent. But he and his pan-objectivistic colleagues fall into the opposite error, which may be caricatured by his opponents as fallacy of arguing from the *object-centric predicament*. For, from the predicament that knowledge *usually* centres round some object two conclusions are fallaciously drawn by these realists; namely (1) that *all* consciousness must have some object, and (2) that the object is the *only* thing in knowledge and the latter can be reduced completely to the former.

The obvious fallacy in the first conclusion is generalization from most cases to all; and that in the second is to treat the obvious factor as the only one. The attempt to deny conscious-ness and take the object as the sole thing in knowledge would be like denying light and thinking that only objects (lighted) exist.

IV. THE NATURE OF REALITY

Does reality mean objectivity? Objectivity in the most general sense is the character of being an object of any kind of con-ciousness; and it cannot in this meaning be said to be a sign of or synonymous with reality. Objects of imagination (e.g. a golden mountain) and those of dream (e.g. a flying horse) are not regarded as real by any one. In a narrower sense "objectivity" is used to signify the character of being an object of sense-perception. Ordinarily what is present to sense is regarded as real par excellence. But unfortunately enough one may very vividly see a pink rat or hear a sound, or smell a smell which others may perceive otherwise or not at all, and one thus doubts or disbelieves the reality of even sense objects. There is a third meaning, the narrowest, in which objectivity implies the character of an object which is public, that is present to all minds or senses. It is believed by many that such a thing must be real. But as we already saw, a mirror image, the flatness of the sun, its motion and small size, etc., are equally perceived by us all, yet, they are not accepted as real.

The meaning of reality. It is found from these examples that objectivity can neither mean, nor necessarily imply, reality. What then is the meaning of reality? The meaning of an already current word cannot be arbitrarily fixed. It must be found out inductively from usage. If we collect, compare, contrast and analyse the many instances where the words real and unreal are used, we may find out what they actually connote.

The comparison of tables, chairs, trees, which are ordinarily called real, with objects of dream and illusion, brings out by contrast the fact that while both kinds are present to some kind of consciousness and belief is present in both, belief in the latter is contradicted by some stronger experience, whereas the belief in the former is not. Unreality may thus be regarded as that the belief in which is contradicted. Reality may be said to be that the belief in which is not contradicted. It should also be noted that mere non-contradiction does not constitute reality, as some writers seem to suggest. With this negative character there is found, in what is called real, a positive and more important factor that generates belief, namely its manifestness or presence to consciousness, which is immediate in the cases of perceived objects, but mediate in the cases of entities like electrons, energy, the centre of the earth, etc., which we can conceive and believe but do not perceive.

Lest it should be wrongly generalized from this, as is sometimes done, that only objects can be real, we should remember that subjective states such as one's perceiving, imagining, thinking, are also believed as real. Belief in such states may be either based on indirect knowledge, such as inference, authority, reasonable supposition or on immediate and non-objective consciousness if the states are one's own, so that they manifest themselves.

What is common to real objects and real subjective states and what generates belief in both cases—is manifestness or obviousness, epithets which we use to characterize the nature of entities whose reality we do not doubt. Reality thus can be said to manifest itself.

The hierarchy of the unreal and the real. The self-contradictory, the square-circle, the son of a barren mother, etc., lack this power of manifesting themselves in any kind of consciousness; they cannot even appear to be. An object of conscious imagination, e.g. a golden mountain, appears before the mind, but does not claim reality and no belief is placed in it. An object of illusion appears and claims reality and there is temporary belief, but it is withdrawn when it is contradicted. In some cases the illusory object ceases to appear, in other cases (e.g., the bent-stick-phenomenon, the flat appearance of the sun) it continues to appear in spite of contradiction and disbelief.

The objects of normal perception, tables, chairs, etc., manifest themselves and belief in them is not actually contradicted, but it is possible to doubt, and actually many competent minds have doubted, whether they also may not be falsified by some future experience just as the objects of illusion and dream are.

As there is no guarantee against such a future possibility we cannot repose absolute trust even in objects of normal perception.

It is seen then that nothing can be said to be absolutely real which is not manifest and is not beyond actual as well as possible contradiction. But have we any acquaintance with such absolute reality? In reply it may be pointed out that even in cases where belief in reality is contradicted or challenged, we notice that it is only the claim of the thing as possessed of a specific kind of existence that is disbelieved or doubted, but that there is *some* existence cannot be denied. When the illusory snake or the dream object is denied, the existence of some substratum, external or internal, is not and cannot be denied. Similarly, if the objects of normal perception be abolished by some subsequent experience, it is the tablehood or chairhood or at most its externality that can be abolished, but some substratal existence, even if it be a mere idea of the mind, must remain behind, in order to make the perception possible. An utter unreality, a square circle, as we saw, cannot appear even for a moment.

It is found thus by the critical examination and evaluation of different kinds of experience that existence must be universally present in every case, and that existence is an undeniable reality. In other words if we judge any experience that it reveals pure existence, not existence of any specific character but existence as such, our judgment would be beyond actual and possible contradiction.

Pure existence real par excellence. Pure, unqualified existence is then found, by the irresistible logic of contradiction, as that belief which is not only not contradicted, but cannot be conceived to be capable of contradiction. This, therefore, can be accepted as real *par excellence.* The diverse specific forms in which existence reveals itself are either actually falsified (e.g., illusory phenomena), or falsifiable (e.g., objects of normal perception). But yet in so far as they are present to consciousness and free from self-contradiction we cannot class them with the square circle, the utterly unreal. In between the absolutely real and the absolutely unreal we can, therefore, distinguish these two orders of relative reality—the contradicted appearance of existence and the not-yet contradicted but contradictable appearance. We are thus led to recognise different grades of reality.

Existence, the absolute reality, is at the same time the most universal feature present in all kinds of experience. It is what unifies the internal and the external by showing the continuity between the two. Mental states exist and manifest themselves; and so also do the external objects. Manifestation is regarded as the essence of consciousness, in its different forms. So we can say that existence in both the internal and external world possesses the essential character of consciousness as possessing the power of manifestation. The basic and primary thing in every knowledge is revelation. We can see this in exclamations like, "A beautiful idea," "A lovely sky." The idea and the sky are manifest in these cases.

But in some cases after the revelation we split up this total, undivided presentation, into the two aspects, the subjective, and the objective, and say "I have this idea", "I see the sky". This intellectual act of differentiation of the knower and the known and also of the known into different objects and the inter-relation of the differentiated are very necessary for practical life, for the successful adjustment of the organism to the environment.

Bifurcation of existence. So long as the practical attitude does not begin to dominate we can perceive, and aesthetically enjoy, one continuous, harmonious revelation of existence, the diverse forms and aspects of which intermingle and interpenetrate. Under the pressure of the bodily needs we isolate ourselves by a kind of withdrawal from the whole of revelation to a part of it, roughly delimited by our body, identify ourselves with it and treat the rest as external to us. Yet we cannot live for a single moment without the world from which we have separated ourselves. Even the body *needs* air, food, water, temperature, the constant pull and push of the environmental forces. There is thus a series of hankerings, which really are the different attempts to be reunited with the whole from which the self is separated but without which it cannot live.

Impersonal description of this process would be that the one all pervasive Existence reveals itself in multiple form and tries to re-unite the many.

The three moments of unity, diversity and synthesis are found in our personal experience as well. The (one) wish to speak bursts forth into different successive words and then we understand them by re-uniting the word-meanings into that of a sentence. An impulse to draw a picture gives birth to a series of strokes outside one another, but when completed they make one picture. We have here also the clue to the birth of succession and extension, the schemes of time and space, out of what is non-successive and non-extended.

Body, Self and Moral Progress. Though the self of man is ordinarily identified with the body by interest and love, its range is by no means fixed, as the Vedāntins and James rightly point out. One can and does identify oneself, with one's dress, property, family, community, country, and so on; and one even sacrifices one's body for the sake of any of these. On the othe hand, it is instructive to note that man is not equally interested in and identified with every part of the body even. Moreover, his will has control over only some parts of the body, some of the most vital processes and organs are altogether beyond his conscious control, whereas he can control by some of his organs and by his thought, advice and love respectively, material objects and human beings apparently separated from his body by vast spaces and long periods of time. By the necessary practice man can develop, again, control over many muscles of the body not ordinarily subject to his will.

All these facts taken together disprove the identity of the self and the body and show the possibility of the self's expansion as well as contraction. This last fact again points to the underlying unity of the self with the rest of existence.

Our visual perception, as we saw previously, though exceedingly useful for practical life, particularly for the preservation of the body, gives us a discrete, isolated and externalized view of things. The body, as we *see* it, is confined to a position among other objects forming the extensive spatial field of vision. But this is not the only way in which the body is and can be known. If we close our eyes we can still experience the body by its different feelings—the so-called somatic feelings. This body as inwardly felt thus is not felt to be outside the environment, but continuous with it. The visually distant and external objects of the environment mingle with the bodily experience through sounds, smells, tastes and touches, and together they form an interpenetrating and intermingling whole of experience in which the idea of our separation from the world is lost, if the visual images can be successfully prevented from interfering with this experience. *The extended, bounded, solid body revealed by vision is, by this process, dissolved into a mass of sentient experience, from which the environment is not excluded.* If the former set of characters seen is called material and the latter mental, we see here clearly (1) that what is material from one point of view is mental from another; (2) that there is no fundamental opposition between the two ; (3) that it is possible to realize even through the body our inseparability from the so-called external world. Such an experience, if rightly utilized for re-orientating our ordinary superficial, visual conception of the body and the material world, can enable us to realize the inseparable unity of outer and inner existence.

If again we shift our point of view from the experiential to the behaviourist one, the body is found to be a power-house of inclinations, tendencies, cravings—samskāras—which find expression in the different kinds of activities. These form a set or system of forces by which one person can be distinguished from another just as they can be distinguished by their (visual) appearances. Ordinarily all the activities of a person aim at the preservation and well-being of his own little isolated bodily existence. But experience teaches him that even the preservation of his limited existence is not possible without rationalizing and socializing his cravings and activities—that is, without sacrificing his narrow self for a wider one in which the interest of other persons is harmonized with his own.

Moral progress is not possible, then, without a gradual expansion of the self by overcoming the barriers that separate the self from others. Philosophy which can reveal the identity of the self with the rest of existence is, therefore, a great aid to morality. On the other hand the philosophical view of the unity of all existence cannot be fully realized and made effective without a practical moral life of constant contemplation of the truth and without guiding all action in its light. Love and good will are the outcome of such a moral endeavour. The Indian systems of philosophy, in spite of great differences in theory, are almost unanimous in their moral programme. Desisting in thought, speech and action, from ill-will, hatred, injury, to all beings, and attitude of love to all, man should liberate himself from the misery that the mistaken notion of his self causes to him. This difficult moral path can be traversed only step by step; but every successful step, the removal of every bit of misconception, anger, hatred, jealousy brings its own reward, that is inward peace. This encourages the aspirant to push on until the goal is reached—the self is identified, in thought, speech and action, with entire existence; and perfect peace is attained.

It is scarcely necessary to mention that this philosophy of existence and the moral path inspired by it can harmonize not only individuals with individuals, but also societies with societies, and nations with nations.

But it should be noticed that the basic philosophy and moral discipline remaining the same there can be different alternative formulations of reality and different alternative mental attitudes of the individual to life and reality.

To surmount, for example, its limitation to the body and its cravings, the self, instead of widening its range of identification to other forms of existence, may *withdraw* from all limited appearances of existence including the body. It may thus try to remain as a disinterested witness of all appearances and rise above personal limitations. Egoism can be overcome by this method as also by the one of expansion of interest by love, charity and goodwill to other beings, described above.

V. RELIGION

It is also possible to cast the philosophy of existence into a religious frame by identifying the pure self-manifesting existence, which underlies all inner and outer forms of existence, with the God of religion who is also believed to be the ground of all beings. The manifestation of the inner and outer phenomena in a systematic manner, and in many cases by series of means and ends, enables us to identify it with creation of things by God according to law and purpose. But we understand to a greater extent the mystery of creation by looking at the phenomena within our mind and body than by looking outside. We can perceive how the existence in us rises from a state of complete detachment and forgetfulness in sleep gradually to an awareness of subtle objects in dream and thence to a wakeful life of full awareness of objects, and becomes interested in them and tries to obtain them with will and purpose ; and how again it retires to sleep every day and relaxes its clutch over objects obtained by toil and greed. Here we experience the possibility of the formless and impersonal assuming forms and personality and also renouncing them. This also enables us to understand how the transcendent absolute may be the personal God of religion. By witnessing how a mere wish to speak generates a succession of different ideas and words, and how these again take shape in a co-existent system of written symbols, we can understand how that which is itself non-successive or timeless and non-extended or spaceless can express itself in time and space.

But all these inner experiences also show the different aspects of the self as of God, and we can feel in them the manifestation of God through the self. Thus by identifying God with existence which underlies both the inner and the outer we realize that the self in us is one with the self of Nature. God thus becomes as dear as the self.

By considering again the fact that we have so little knowledge of, and control over, the bodily processes, of the brain, the senses, nerves and muscles, etc., by which our wishes are carried into actions and by which the most vital functions of breathing, circulation of blood, digestion of food, speaking, etc., take place, we feel our ignorance and helplessness and feel awe and gratitude towards the inner principle of our life which guides and regulates these activities on which our life depends. Thus the impersonal existence becomes the God of Religion and the object of different religious emotions. By self-surrender or surrender of the will of the self, constituted by ignorance into a separate entity, to the will of God the devotee can overcome his egoism and all attachment to selfish ends, and become a tool of the Divine Will. Thus the path of religion and that of morality have similar effects on the inner life of man. They can supplement other other.

VI. THE UNKNOWN

Philosophy, like every other branch of knowledge, must necessarily be limited to the discussion of what falls within consciousness, immediate and mediate. Our notion of existence is derived from what is manifest in perception, inference, imagination, etc., i.e. from the known, in the widest sense of the term. Our notion of reality is obtained, as we saw, by a further sifting of the known with the criterion of non-contradiction. Yet it will be dogmatic to conclude that the known is all. Our curiosity about the unknown remains and goads us to increase the bounds of knowledge.

Some philosophers point out that there is nothing beyond knowledge and that what is called the unknown or the unknowable must also enter the domain of knowledge in order that it may be so referred to. The reply to such a puzzling argument would be that in order to be able to refer to the unknown it is sufficient if it is known that it is not known. In other words we must at least distinguish between the knowledge of something as unknown from the ordinary knowledge of something as known, and widen thus the ordinary meaning of "knowledge". This wider knowledge, the consciousness of the known and the unknown, can, therefore, be regarded as the matrix out of which definite knowledge emerges.

It is not reasonable, therefore to deny the unknown. The unknown must be recognised as somehow marking the limit of every definite knowledge. If we carefully attend to the emergence of positive consciousness we can realize that our ideas take definite shape out of an indefinite background. Like a search-light our positive attention reveals things out of a surrounding gloom, that is, the unknown, about which we cannot make any assertion, except that it is beyond grasp.

Now, if "absolute" be the name that we may like to give to the all-inclusive that covers the known and the unknown, we cannot say that it is wholly amenable to the categories of thought. In so far as this enters the logical pale of definite and systematic thought it assumes a logical character; but even the whole of what enters definite consciousness is not logical or real, as we have previously seen.

Philosophy tries to know reality by reasoning that obeys the laws of logic. But it should only bear in mind the limits of human knowledge and logical thought. The moral effect of such an attitude on philosophy would be humility that would prepare the mind for new and unexpected revelations of the absolute and remove cocksureness which more than anything else stands in the way of the attainment of truth. As in religion so also in philosophy the self, as a knower and reasoner, has to recognise its limitations and helplessness, and ultimately surrender itself to the Absolute for sharing as much of it as the Absolute chooses to reveal.

PRINCIPAL WRITINGS

BOOKS:

The Six Ways of Knowing (A critical and comparative study of Vedānta Epistemology). George Allen & Unwin Ltd., London, 1932.

An Introduction to Indian Philosophy (in collaboration). Calcutta University, 1939.

The Chief Currents of Contemporary Philosophy (*European, American and Indian*). Art Press, Calcutta.

PAPERS:

"Objective Freedom". *International Journal of Ethics*, Chicago, 1922.

"Testimony as a method of knowledge". *Mind*, 1927.

"The conceptions of Self and God in Berkeley". *Philosophical Quarterly, Amlaner*, Bombay, 1931.

"The Objective Idealism of Berkeley". *The Monist*, Chicago, 1933.

"The Main Currents of Contemporary Indian Philosophy". *Aryan Path*, Bombay, 1935.

"The Moral Conception of Nature in Indian Philosophy". *International Journal of Ethics*, Chicago, 1936.

"The Revolt against Metaphysics". Address to Indian Philosophical Congress, Delhi, 1936.

"The Windowless Monads". *The Monist*, Chicago, 1936.

"Idealism *Versus* Realism—a criticism of Dr. Stace's 'Refutation of Realism' ". *Philosophical Quarterly*, 1936.

"Kant and the objectivity of Space and Time". *Philosophical Quarterly*, 1939.

"An Argument for the Unknown". *Philosophical Quarterly*, 1948.

"The Psychology of Culture conflict in the light of the Psychology of Insanity". Symposium, Indian Science Congress, 1947; published in *Calcutta Review*, 1948.

REALISTIC IDEALISM

by HIRALAL HALDAR

Born 1865 M.A., Ph.D., Calcutta University
Late Professor of Philosophy in the University of Calcutta
Sometime George V Professor of Philosophy

REALISTIC IDEALISM

MORE than fifty years ago, when I entered Calcutta University as an undergraduate, there was very little of what can rightly be called philosophical teaching in the University. Certain text-books, mainly on psychology and ethics, were prescribed and all that the Professors generally did was to expound them and to dictate to the students short summaries of them. Very often the exposition was wanting and the dictation of notes everything. One conspicuous exception to this method of teaching was that of Dr. William Hastie, who was Principal of the General Assembly's Institution affiliated to the Calcutta University when I became a student of the College in 1882. But I was a freshman, and as Dr. Hastie's lectures were delivered to the higher classes only, I had not the opportunity of being benefited by his stimulating teaching. Dr. Hastie was one of the few real teachers of philosophy that ever came out to this country. But by the time I reached the B.A. Classes he had quarrelled with his home authorities and resigned. The usual sort of teaching did not suit me at all. I had a perfect horror of taking down dictated notes. I longed for instructive and inspiring lectures but none was available. Under such circumstances I was forced to ignore college teaching altogether and to acquire such knowledge of philosophy as I could by means of private study only. This reliance on my own efforts probably did me a great deal of good by compelling me to think a little on my own account. At first I had not much taste for philosophy. But fortunately my attention was drawn to a series of short articles in a weekly journal of Calcutta inculcating an idealistic doctrine of the Berkeleian type. These articles awakened my interest in Berkeley and I turned to his writings. I read his *Principles of Human Knowledge* and *Three Dialogues between Hylas and Philonous* and was very much impressed by them. But I was enabled to avoid a subjectivist bias by reading almost simultaneously expositions of Kant by Stirling, Green, Caird and Adamson. The *Critique of Pure Reason* I studied a little later. Hegel I tried to read but without success. Such expositions of him as came into my hands were perfectly useless. I remember spending hours one evening over Ueberweg's account of Hegel in his *History of Philosophy*. Not a single line was intelligible and I closed the book in despair. This, I suppose, is the usual experience of those who first approach Hegel. The book which first enabled me to comprehend something of the meaning of Hegel was Edward Caird's *Hegel* in Blackwood's Philosophical Classics Series, a book which is justly described by Professor Watson as "small but golden." William Wallace's Prolegomena to his translation of the *Encyclopædia of the Philosophical Sciences* was also of immense help. By and by I managed to read the *Encyclopædia* itself. The philosophical movement known as Neo-Hegelianism was in my student days gathering strength in Great Britain and I was one of the very few, not improbably the only one, who then felt its power in India. I eagerly studied everything that appeared from the pens of J. H. Stirling, the two Cairds, Green, G. S. Morris, R. Adamson, J. Watson, A Seth, afterwards Pringle Pattison, D. G. Ritchie, F. H. Bradley, B. Bosanquet, R. B. Haldane, afterwards Viscount Haldane, Henry Jones and others. I was very powerfully influenced by these writings, particularly by those of Green and Caird. Bradley's *Ethical Studies* also very deeply impressed me. A new heaven and a new earth seemed to be disclosed to my eyes. In later years Hegel was studied with much difficulty and slowly.

I should add that in the Proceedings of the Society for Psychical Research and Myers' *Human Personality and its Survival of Bodily Death* I have found much that is informing and suggestive.

I have seen myself described as a Hegelian. The basis of my thought is undoubtedly Hegelian, but in the course of years, as this sketch may show, I have been led to modify in many ways what I have learned from Hegel. No man, however poor a thinker he may be, can exactly reproduce the views of another. The very essence of individuality is its uniqueness and therefore the angle of vision of one man is bound to be somewhat different from that of another. In the process of making my own the ideas acquired from Hegel and others, I have inevitably transformed them more or less.

Alexander Bain was perfectly right when he said that the ingenuity of a century and half had failed to see a way out of the contradiction exposed by Berkeley. The contradiction is that of supposing that the objects all around us, the things which we see, smell, taste, hear and touch exist on their own account independently of their being perceived. To be, argues Berkeley, is to be perceived. Take away from things the relations in which they stand to the perceiving mind and they lose all meaning, simply cease to be. The objective world can no more exist apart from mind than can the outside of a thing exist in isolation from its inside. The self is the very centre of being of whatever can be called real, the life and soul of all that is. The experienced world has its support in mind. This argument is by no means of modern origin and Berkeley was not the first to use it. It was well known to the sages of the Upaniṣads nearly three thousand years ago. In the *Bṛhadāraṇyaka Upaniṣad*, for example, probably the oldest of the Upaniṣads, Yājñavalkya tells his wife Maitreyi, that all things forsake him who supposes that they are separate from mind. As the sound of a musical instrument cannot be taken hold of apart from that instrument, as the sound of a conch-shell cannot be apprehended separately from the conch-shell, but if the musical instrument and the conch-shell are cognised the sounds emanating from them are necessarily cognised along with them, so none of these things issuing forth from the self can be known independently of the self. It may be said that the plausibility of the idealistic argument is due to a confusion between a thing and the thing as known. A man with whom I am shaking hands is necessarily related to the act of handshaking but this does not mean that his very existence depends on it. The food I am eating implies the act of eating, but eating is not the necessary condition of the existence of the food. So a thing *as perceived* is dependent upon perceiving, but the thing as perceived is not identical with the thing. The latter has no necessary relation to knowledge. The contention of the idealist is that no such distinction can be made between object and object of knowledge. The very essence of an object is its being known. As Yājñavalkya says all things flee from him who attempts to separate them from the self. Food which is not eaten is possible, a man with whom no one is shaking hands is possible, but a thing which no mind knows is impossible. It is the outcome of false abstraction.

But however sound and unassailable Berkeley's fundamental principle, in its essence, may be, the conclusions he draws from it are not all tenable. In the first place, he gives a too restricted meaning to it. Perception is not the only mode of knowledge and it is therefore not possible to say that what is perceived is alone real. It would have been better if he had said that the *esse* of a thing is its *intelligi*. In his earlier writings he ignores almost completely the universal forms of knowledge and takes cognisance of its contents only consisting of particular sensations and ideas. In the *Siris* this view is to some extent corrected and the importance of universality in knowledge realised. Even in the *Principles* he admits that the self is an object of thought, not of perception. In the second place, from the right premiss that nothing is real apart from mind the wrong conclusion is drawn that everything is reducible to ideas of the mind. So far from it being true that things are only ideas, ideas have no meaning, as Reid urged, without their reference to things. The *opposition* of mind to its object is the very basis of knowledge and without this duality no sort of cognition can take place. If to be is to be perceived it is equally true that to be perceived is to be. In all knowledge the distinguishable but inseparable factors opposed and irreducible to each other are the mind that knows, the object that is known and the act or process of knowing. Imagination also has this three-fold character. The imagined world is as much opposed to the imagining mind and its activity as the solid world of perception in time and space. This being so it is the images of the mind, the ideas that are to be brought into line with things and not the latter with the former. The imagined world is quite as objective as the physical world of perception to which we belong. Things therefore are not mental ideas, they are objects of mind. Instead of things being ideas, it is ideas which have the status of things. This truth is clearly realised by the idealist philosophers of India. Saṃkara, for example, who is commonly but wrongly supposed to be an illusionist, a thinker who denies the reality of the world, lays the utmost stress on the opposition of what is known to the mind that knows. In the absence of something distinguished from mind and opposed to it knowledge is no more possible than it is possible for a dancer to dance on his own shoulders. Epistemologically, Saṃkara is a thorough-going realist. He does not say that the empirical world is in any way dependent for its being on the finite mind. All that he maintains is that ultimately, from the highest point of view, it has no independent existence apart from Brahman. Both Saṁkara and Rāmānuja maintain that even illusions are not unreal and merely subjective. They are as objective as the things of ordinary perception, the only difference being that they are not common to all, but individual and last only as long as they are experienced.

The objective world then is wider and more comprehensive than the world of common cognition and contains numberless extensions in the shape of the products of the imaginative activity of the mind. What is imagined is not one whit less objective and opposed to the mind than what is perceived. It is not more mental than the latter and has no specially intimate connection with the subjective process of knowing. It is on the same footing with sensible realities and differs from them not in essence but in respect of detailed characteristics only. Imagined things are not of common experience and are peculiar only to those who conceive them. Unlike perceived substances they have no tangible qualities and do not offer any resistance to movement. They are not enduring and are in being only as long as the activity of imagination continues. The error of the subjective idealist is to suppose that images, ideas, representations are purely mental and to maintain that perceived objects are like them. The subjective processes of cognition alone are mental. The contents of the mind to which they refer, no matter whether they are perceived or only imagined, are all equally objective and antithetical to mind and constitute ingredients of different kinds of what is called the external world. It is not things that are to be reduced to ideas but ideas are to be assimilated to things. There is nothing that belongs specially to the knowing mind except its own activities.

In what has been said above, stress has been laid on the opposition of the experienced world to the mind that knows it. It stands over against the subject on its own legs and is in no way reducible to it. Its existence is not dependent upon the finite minds which are included within it except those portions of it that are the products of their imaginative activities. On the opposition of subject and object all knowledge is founded. There is no such thing as an insulated mind contemplating only its own internal states. The whole content of mind, percepts as well as ideas, belongs to objective experience. What are specifically mental are its own activities of knowing and willing. But the opposition of subject and object does not mean that they are separable from each other. The error of realism is to make this opposition absolute, just as the error of subjective idealism is to ignore or minimise it. There the opposition is undeniably, fundamentally and glaringly, but it presupposes an ultimate unity from which it arises and of which it is the other side. In the realisation of this truth consists the strength of idealism. Berkeley's doctrine is an inadequate and misleading expression of it. The South Pole is not the North Pole or a locality within it; it is diametrically opposite to it. Nevertheless the being of the one pole is implicated in that of the other and they exist only as two necessarily connected sides of the earth. Similarly the front and the back of my body do not look at each other. They are not on speaking terms with each other, but in spite of this they are the inseparable parts of my entire organism. Just in the same way mind and its object are the two opposed aspects of the one all-embracing unity which also is mind. The term "mind" has two meanings. It is the knower opposed to the object of which it is conscious. Further, it is the unity presupposed in the distinction of subject and object and manifested in that distinction. This all-inclusive spirit within which distinctions of every kind arise, which is bifurcated into subject and object is the ultimate reality—the universe in its last interpretation. It is not mere mind, not abstract matter but the source and presupposition, the truth of both.

To superficial observation nature seems to be but a vast aggregate of independent entities existing side by side with one another in space and time without being in any way essentially connected. It is by pure chance that a thing is what and where it is. Remove it from its place and there is no change whatever anywhere in the world except in itself. What necessary connection is there between the individual bricks heaped together there on the ground? May not the earth vanish into nothing to-morrow owing to some catastrophe and the rest of the universe remain exactly as it is? What modest man does not think that his coming into being and passing into nothing makes no difference whatever to the world to which he happens to belong unaccountably for a few years? Self-subsistent realities are somehow put together and to the totality thus formed we give the name of nature. This view seems to be plausible at first sight but on reflection it turns out to be quite erroneous. According to Spinoza it is imagination, not knowledge. Things exist in virtue of the relations in which they stand to one another. These relations are not external to the things. They constitute their very nature, make them possible, sustain them and are inseparable from them. Lotze has shown that if things were isolated no interaction between them would be possible. How could one thing affect another if there were a breach of continuity between them? A influences B. What is this influence? If it emanates from A then in being detached from A and passing on to B, it momentarily at least enjoys independent existence and becomes a third thing C giving rise to the problem of its relation to A and B. Bradley's argument against external relations is in spirit the same. If a relation be outside the related terms how does it get itself connected with them? The truth is that things are not self-subsistent and independent. They have being only in so far as they are essentially related to one another. It is not that things first exist separately and then casually enter into relations. Apart from the relations they are mere abstractions as unreal as the top of a thing separated from its bottom. Relations are the very pith and marrow of the related entities, their foundation and support. Science brings this truth to light. It regards the universe as a unitary system of which individual objects are constituent elements. Everything is real only in its own place necessarily connected with other things by means of definitely ascertainable relations. Everywhere in the Cosmos isolation means death.

Nothing in this world is single,
All things by a law divine in each other's being mingle.

Objects are continuous with one another and because of this continuity they are also different. They are one because they are many, many because they are one. Unity finds expression in difference and difference has its presupposition in unity.

L

Undifferentiated unity and mere difference are the products of abstract thinking. In the concrete world unity and difference go together. They are complementary aspects of the whole— the universe. If things ceased to be different they would coalesce with each other and vanish into a geometrical point. On the other hand if they absolutely flew apart from each other they would be dissipated into nothing. It is because they attract and also repel each other, are one as well as many, that they exist as integral parts of a single spatio-temporal world. The world undoubtedly looks like an aggregate of independent units. But this is superficial appearance only. In its true nature it is an organic whole realised in the difference of its members. It is the concrete reality of which finite beings and the so-called things are only fragments kept apart by false abstraction. These fragments scientific reflection shows to have being only as elements of the whole—the Cosmos.

But what is the ultimate nature of the unity of all things? Is it some form of the universe itself or some supra-cosmic essence into which the world is absorbed and from which it emanates alternately? The latter view, in spite of the support it has received in the history of thought, is untenable. The unity of the world is the world itself in its ideality, the world regarded as the spirit in which it is centred and of which it is the expression. Inter-connected things which exist in virtue of the influence which they reciprocally exert upon one another are one, not as this or that thing is one but as the universal principle that pervades them, connects them and at the same time maintains their difference. Their unity, in short, is not a numerical unity, for a numerical unity presupposes other similar unities from which it is excluded. It is ideal unity, the unity of a principle common to them, realised completely and indivisibly in each of them but limited to none of them. It is the universal mind at the root of things manifested in them and their mutual relations. In the words of the *Bhagavad Gītā* it is the supreme Brahman that "exists in the world pervading all things and having hands and feet everywhere, eyes, heads and faces in all directions and ears on all sides." It is "without and within all things and beings, the unmoving and also the moving Though undivided it yet exists as if divided in them."

We thus see that from the highest point of view the universe is spirit self-distinguished into the knower and the known, the cognising mind and its own other, namely the object-world that is cognised. The distinction of self and not-self, mind and matter, is fundamental and inescapable. It is not by obliterating but by maintaining and transcending this distinction that the Absolute is what it is. Neither can matter be evaporated into subjective impressions nor can mind be regarded as a by-product of matter. They are opposed to each other as correlated aspects of the one ultimate reality.

The mind in which the universe finds its truth and explanation is not foreign to it. It is the mind of the universe itself, its own highest form. What at a lower level of interpretation is a system of mutually determining things in space and time is at a higher level of interpretation mind—mind that does not exclude the physical world but takes it up into itself. The material world is inwardised in mind and mind is externalised in matter. They are the correlated phases of the one all-inclusive spirit. In preaching this truth idealism is in no way inconsistent with realism. It does not make it its business to deny the reality of the world. On the contrary, it strongly affirms it. It goes as far as realism does but goes farther, maintaining that the world is indeed real, even what are called ideas are component parts of it, but that in order to know that it is real it has got to have mind. What is the use of being real if mind, without which consciousness of reality cannot be, is wanting? It is not enough that you or I are aware of it. The real world ought to have its own mind so that it may enjoy the abundance of its wealth which is never completely known to any finite being. Surely the idealist who says that the objective world is spiritual without ceasing to be physical is a better realist than he who denies mind to it and thereby makes its reality worth nothing.

The spiritual whole is internally divided into subject and object, self and not-self. The object-world again as related to intelligence involves the distinction and inseparable union of the universal and the particular, the forms of thought and the contents of experience. The relation between the universal and the particular has always been a subject of controversy among philosophers. It was Plato who first realised the importance of the universals, ideas as he called them, and saw that without them neither knowing nor being is possible. But he separated the ideas from sensible phenomena and thought that they were imposed upon the latter *ab extra*. The empiricists, on the other hand, think that they consist of the common features of experienced facts obtained by means of abstraction. Kant's great achievement was to show that experience is richer than what the empiricists take it to be and involves both the categories of thought and the particulars of sense. Like Plato he separates the universal from the particular but perceives that so separated they are names only, the one empty and the other blind. The empiricists suppose that experience consists of particular phenomena only. Kant does not deny that they have independent being, but argues that they are as good as nothing unless they are subjected to the categories. He undertakes the impossible task of showing how the forms of thought and the matter of sense are brought into relationship with each other and of course fails. But the solid result of his philosophical thinking was to demonstrate that apart from the principles of the understanding experience is not possible. In actual knowledge the universal and the particular are never found cut loose from each other. Sensible phenomena are never merely discrete and disconnected but are always pervaded and sustained by universal forms of thought as connected members of the intelligible and orderly cosmos. Nature is not made by the understanding but is the outer expression of reason. A firm grasp of this truth is the merit of Hegel. In his eye, the material universe, always involving the duality but not the dualism of the universal principles of reason and the particular facts of experience, is the embodiment of the Infinite mind. It is this mind "that is the ultimate nature of life, the soul of the world, the universal life-blood which courses everywhere, and whose flow is neither disturbed nor checked by any obstructing distinction, but is itself every distinction that arises, as well as that into which all distinctions are dissolved; pulsating within itself, but ever motionless, shaken to its depths, but still at rest."[1]

[1] *Phenomenology of Mind*, Baillie's Tr., George Allen & Unwin, vol. 1 p. 157.

Kant regards the categories only as instruments used by the self for the purpose of producing knowledge out of the data of sense. In themselves they are but empty forms not essentially related to one another and to the self. Hegel, on the contrary, views them as at once forms of thought and modes of being, subjective as well as objective. They are not airy abstractions but comprehensive systems implying particularity. They are all essentially related to one another as vital parts of the whole of reality. The organised whole of which they are members is the Absolute. Each of them is implicated with and has no being apart from the rest. They form a graded system and the business of philosophy is to show how thought necessarily passes from the lowest of them step by step through the intermediate stages to the highest. Each category incorporates the immediately lower one into itself and is taken up into the immediately higher, and the highest, the Absolute Idea, therefore contains them all as necessary elements of itself. It is to them what the living body is to its members. For Hegel this view implies that the Absolute Idea is a completed and closed sytem and that human knowledge is co-extensive with reality. There cannot in his view be anything in thought or reality which has not a definitely ascertainable place in the system of the Absolute Idea.

Now it is not easy to avoid being overpowered by the persuasiveness of Hegel's argument. The methodical procession of the categories produces an immense effect on the reader's mind. But in the end few are able to accept the view that the Logic exhaustively discloses the contents of reality. The really valuable work which Hegel does is to demonstrate that the universe is an orderly and intelligible system with mind at its centre, but this does not mean that we know in detail what its constitution and contents are. If the categories specified by him were the only elements of this system, if human intelligence penetrated reality to the very core, omniscience would be the necessary consequence and there would be no room for doubt and hesitation of any kind. It sometimes looks as though Hegel actually claimed omniscience. But the revisions to which he himself subjected the arrangement of his categories, the alterations he made in their list from time to time, show that he by no means knew all that there is to be known and that reality after all very largely eluded the grasp of his intellect. The truth, of course, is that human knowledge is not co-extensive with reality and the categories of Hegel's Logic do not furnish a complete exposition of it. They are only a section of the contents of Absolute thought detached from the whole. The fragmentary character of our knowledge is obvious. It bears unmistakable marks of its narrowness and incompleteness. The breach of continuity which is everywhere apparent in the world, the abrupt manner in which facts of one order are marked off from those of another order, the immense blanks between the bright spots of knowledge, the failure of the universals of thought and the particulars of sense to fit in with each other smoothly and without hitch, the inability of time and space to attain the completeness at which they aim, the antinomies and contradictions of which experience is full, the unreason obtruding upon us on all sides in a world which theory forces us to regard as rational through and through, the evils that mar the beauty and orderliness of the cosmos, the angularities and rough sides of things, the trials and tragedies of life, all plainly indicate that the world to which we belong is not the whole, but only a fragment of the real universe the major part of which is beyond our ken. It is in Kant's words but an island in the vast ocean of reality, only the ocean is not something unintelligible but the rational whole of existents.

The categories of human knowledge do indeed express the nature of reality but only partially. They are valid so far as they go, but in the Absolute they must be supplemented by others not at present known to us. Of them organised into a complete whole the objective world, both seen and unseen, is the expression. What we call nature is only a tiny fragment of this greater universe, if we may call it so, and in it alone the Absolute mind finds its full content. The unseen world or worlds, it must be remembered, is not psychical. There is nothing purely psychical or purely physical. All the *contents* of the mind are objective and opposed to the self that knows. The unseen universe, therefore, although not material, is of a piece with what is material. It is spiritual exactly as *this* world, the material world, is spiritual. Whatever is, is the expression of mind. There is nothing which is out of relation to intelligence. As Bradley says. "Outside of spirit there is not and there cannot be any reality." All the worlds, the visible material world and the invisible immaterial but objective worlds, are parts of one stupendous whole and in this whole the Absolute mind is completely embodied. A purely spiritual or psychical world is as much a fiction as a purely material world. What is real is also ideal and the genuinely ideal must be real.

The Absolute mind is one but it is not a monadic unity. In it the minds of the things that constitute the world are fused into a single whole or, what is the same thing viewed from the other end, it is pluralised in them. The universal mind is immanent in all things. This means that it is present in each of them undivided and as a whole, which cannot be unless it is in it as its inner soul. To be a self-complete whole, to be in all parts of it equally and yet to remain a whole in each part is the prerogative of the universal. The mind for which the universe is, is not apart from it; it is its own central principle. Its relation to things, therefore, is not an external relation like that of one thing to another. It is the ideality of each of the things themselves, the very core of its being. In being externalised in the multifarious objects of the world, the Absolute mind goes forth to them and dwells in them as their own individual minds. It becomes manifold and yet remains one. Were it not so it would be external to them and being limited by them would be just like one of them. The self of the world is one and yet many. In it many minds, the minds of the myriads of objects that are comprised within the world, are gathered up and, on its part, it is diversfied in them. There is nothing unintelligible in this notion of minds being many and yet one. The self of every one of us is such. A is a distinguished statesmen, a great meta-physician and an expert player of cricket. These are distinct personalities with different characters and yet they are fused into a single whole in the self of A. Pathological cases of multiple personality prove this. In them the process of disintegration goes so far as to give rise to distinct personalities sometimes of opposite characters and very hostile to one another. The case of Sally Beauchamp is an example. We speak of the conflict of the better self and the worse self in us. Why should this be regarded as only a metaphor and not literal truth? What every man is that the Absolute itself is. Is not man made in the image of God? The self is our ultimate principle of explanation. In analogy with it we think of the Absolute. But our self is never a solitary unit. It is not only composite in itself but is never a solitary unit. It is not only composite in itself but is always a member of the social whole. The concrete actuality is the social mind. If therefore the Absolute is spirit, its nature must be analogous to the composite mind of society. It is on one side mind consisting of many minds and on another the physical world consisting of inter-related objects. There are thirty-three millions of Gods in the Hindu pantheon. This need not be denied; only it must be remembered that they are all integral parts of the supreme Brahman. An infinite number of selves, the selves of the constituent members of the objective world, go to form the Absolute mind. This is what Arjuna sees in *Viśvarūpa* (the cosmic form of the Lord) in the *Bhagavad Gītā*; "O Lord of the Universe, O thou whose form the Universe is, I behold thee of countless forms everywhere with many arms, bellies, mouths and eyes. I do not see thy end, nor thy middle, nor yet thy beginning."

Things existing in time and space and excluding each other are limited, but in their ideality, as minds, they are all-pervading and omniscient. A finite object is marked off from others, repels them, but this is possible because it is also continuous with them and includes them in its own being. Such inclusion takes the form of the consciousness of them. What is distinguished from others is in the very process of distinction joined with them. That is to say, it transcends the distinction between them and itself as inclusive mind. Nothing, therefore, as ideal can be limited to the place where it is as a reality. It encompasses all being, is everywhere. A strong point of the pluralistic systems of Indian philosophy, Jainism, the Sāṃkhya and the Nyāya Vaiśeṣika, is their conception of the many selves as omnipresent and eternal. These, however, cannot be regarded as independent and self-subsistent but must be viewed as component factors of the one Absolute mind. The many are one and the one is many. Each of the particular selves into which the Infinite mind is differentiated represents, because of its all-inclusiveness and omniscience, the whole world. But it does so in its own unique way, from its own special point of view. It is the merit of Leibniz to emphasise this truth. But unfortunately he distinguishes the ideation of the world from the world and isolates the monads from each other, thereby making the unity of the world inexplicable. The Jain doctrine of Syādvāda has a clearer perception of the truth. The one world is known by many minds, the minds of the things that constitute it, in various ways like different triangles standing upon the same base. Their world-pictures are different. The universe presents itself in different perspectives to them, but they are all fused into a composite whole. Different views of things obtained from different standpoints become complementary to one another in the final synthesis. What is seen with the right eye is also seen with the left eye in a slightly different way but the two visions are merged in one and do not remain apart from each other. See a word consisting, say, of five letters with attention mainly focused on each of the five letters successively and you will get five somewhat different appearances, but they are all amalgamated with each other in the ordinary appearance of the word. Nothing is as simple as it seems to be. A lump of sugar is no doubt sweet, but who will undertake to prove that it is sweet to me in precisely the same way as it is to you? Its real sweetness may be the synopsis of the sweetnesses felt by all those who taste it. As no two faces are alike, so it may be that no two perceptions, no two ideas of the same thing are alike. The vulture finds enjoyable repast in a rotten carcass, but to men it is noxious. This ought to give us food for reflection. The truth is that relatively things are different from different standpoints, but absolutely they combine in them all these variations. There is no contradiction in this, for the essence of contradiction is the confusion of standpoints. The Absolute cognises the world in an infinite number of ways from the standpoints of the countless things the minds of which are confluent in it without detriment to their distinctness. Its knowledge therefore is infinitely rich and complex. The universe is not only diverse in composition but knows itself in diverse ways.

Finite beings belong to nature; they are rooted in it and arise out of it. They in no sense create it. By means of their cognitive process, they merely select certain elements of reality which go to constitute the world we experience and live in. They have been regarded as partial reproductions of the Infinite mind, emanations from it conditioned by organic processes. But as the Absolute mind is a unity of many minds, finite selves can only be fragmentary expressions of these constituent minds and not of the Absolute as a whole. Except the contents of their experiences there is nothing additional in the Absolute. Human bodies are among the things whose minds enter into the composition of the Absolute. Each of it is the objective side, the outer expression of an omniscient mind having its abode in the Absolute as one of its members. Consisting of millions of cells it is itself highly composite. In one body, consequently, there are many bodies and many minds. One self has not many bodies, and many selves, as is sometimes supposed, do not belong to a single body. The many cells that compose the body are the many bodies of the many selves unified in the one mind of the whole body which is the ideality of the body itself. It is a constituent element of the Absolute mind. Finite selves are detachments from these deeper selves, assuming new forms, relatively independent and setting up their own households. They are sustained by the Absolute but not swayed by it from outside. They participate in its being, share in its freedom and are not mere excrescences upon it. Finite selves no doubt derive the materials of their life and experience from the Absolute but are not useless repetitions of what already exists. They give rise to novelties in being limited and in the course of the changes they undergo as they grow and seek to realise their purposes, to work out the ideals of their lives. They do not revolve round and round the same point but move on from freshness to freshness, from one stage of life to another and newer. They do not stagnate but alter and progress, do not perpetuate the existing but create the non-existing. In them the Absolute attains new modes of being, new outlooks on existence. In their knowledge they carve out only a small section of the whole of reality. The things we experience are not the things as they are in the knowledge of the Absolute but selections made from them for the purposes of life. Only so much of them is known as our organs of sense are fitted to take in and the sense-organs as they are at present are constructed not to reveal to us the total wealth of existence but to enable us to adapt ourselves to our existing environment and thereby to live. The table before me is not the table as it is in Absolute knowledge possessing an infinite number of properties but only the sum of a few of its characteristics that come within the range of my knowledge. Even of these characteristics a very small part only is perceived at any particular moment. What *we* perceive may therefore be said in one sense to depend on us for its existence, but as it is an ingredient of the true reality, it is in another sense independent of our cognition. Besides the features selected from the whole the perceived object may in virtue of its relation to our knowledge have new elements added to it. These, of course, exist as percepts only as long as they are perceived. But even here their support is not the human mind by itself but that mind in commerce with the object.

Finite minds necessarily seek to be the infinite that they potentially are. The Infinite immanent in them goads them on and does not allow them to rest. Even the shoemaker wants sovereignty over the whole universe. But self-realisation is not possible in isolation. Only in fellowship and co-operation with one another can human beings move forward towards the goal of life. In their ordinary lives and achievements as finite beings in time they are seldom aware of their greatness, but sooner or later they are bound to be conscious of their true nature, to be united with the source of their being in knowledge and love. God is not without man and man is not without God. The Divine spirit manifested in the community of men and the community of men rooted in the Divine spirit, God in man and man in God— this whole is the Absolute Spirit.

PRINCIPAL PUBLICATION

Neo-Hegelianism, Heath Cranton (1927).

THE PROBLEM OF TRUTH

by M. HIRIYANNA

Born 1871; Educated at the Maharaja's College, Mysore,
and the Madras Christian College
Professor of Sanskrit, Maharaja's College, Mysore (1917-27)

THE PROBLEM OF TRUTH

The logical aspect of knowledge is now commonly discussed with exclusive reference to the nature of ultimate truth. There is no doubt that this is the question with which epistemology is finally concerned, but it may be asked whether we cannot advantageously begin by having before us a less ambitious aim. Irrespective of the final solution we may arrive at about the nature of truth, there is knowledge which is distinguished as either true or false from the common-sense point of view; and we may start by asking what this distinction means. Our answer to this question may not satisfy the ultimate epistemological test, but we need not occupy ourselves with that consideration from the beginning. "Confusion often results," it has been said, "from proceeding at once to large and complex cases." If we thus restrict the scope of the enquiry, we shall be simplifying the problem to be solved; and its solution, though it may not furnish the complete explanation of the nature of ultimate truth, may be expected to throw considerable light upon it. We propose to adopt this plan of treatment in the sequel.

Let us begin by analysing an act of perception. When a person opens his eyes (say) and sees a table before him, there are, as ordinarily supposed, three elements that can be distinguished in the situation: First, the percipient who sees; secondly the object, viz. the table; and lastly the sense-data or sensa, as they are described—a certain shape, colour, etc., which he associates with the table and regards as its actual characteristics. These sensa he takes as revealing the nature of the table but partly, for, while he may be seeing only its shape and colour, he believes that it has also other qualities like hardness and weight. It may appear that the common man does not distinguish between the last two of the three elements just referred to; the fact, however, is that he only does not attend to the distinction between them particularly but passes over swiftly from the sensa to the object which is what practically interests him. The process has been compared to our overlooking the peculiarities of the print in reading, because it is the meaning of what is printed that interests us.[1] This is the

[1] *Mind.* (1921), p. 389.

popular notion of the perceptual situation; and it implies belief
in (1) the presence of the self (2) the givenness and the direct
apprehension of the object and (3) the partial revelation of its
character by the sensa, which are likewise given and directly
known. Of these, the ultimate nature of the self or the knowing
subject is not relevant to our present purpose. It is a problem for
metaphysics. All that we have to remember is that it is a factor
which enters into the cognitive situation. The same observation
holds true in the case of the final nature of the object also. The
points that chiefly matter for us now are the nature of sense-data,
their relation to the object and the manner in which they both,
viz. the sense-data and the object, come to be known.

I

According to the above analysis, the sensa are actual features or
"literal aspects" of objects; and they both are directly apprehended by the self. We should now ask to what extent this analysis
stands the test of reflection. It it be correct, it should apply to
all perceptual knowledge; but it seems that, though it may be
right as an analysis of perception that is true, it does not apply to
illusion and error[1] where we apprehend an object or some aspect
of it which is not there. Without prejudging the question, however, we shall try to find out whether errors can be at all explained
by assuming that even they do not involve a reference to anything
that is not actually given. Such a view was maintained not only
in respect of perception but also all knowledge (excepting only
memory) by certain thinkers in ancient India,[2] and it will serve
as a convenient starting-point for our enquiry. The illustrations
usually given in explaining their theory are those of a white
crystal which is mistaken for red when placed by the side of a
red flower, and of a conch which is seen yellow by a jaundiced
person. We shall select the latter for consideration, but with a
slight alteration. We shall suppose that the conch is seen through
a sheet of yellow glass instead of by the jaundiced eye, and that

[1] We shall, in what follows, overlook the distinction between errors
of perception and illusions, as the only difference between them is that
while the judgment is explicit in the former, it is implicit in the latter.
Illusions have been described as "errors in the germ."
[2] Prābhākaras.

the fact of the existence of the glass is for some reason or other
lost sight of. Here we have, according to this theory, the perception of the conch *minus* its true colour, viz. white, and the
sensation of the yellowness alone of the glass. They are two acts
of knowing, but they quickly succeed each other; and we therefore
miss the fact that they are two. Each of them is valid so far as it
goes, for neither the yellowness nor the conch as such is negated
afterwards when we discover the error. But we overlook at first
that they stand apart; and it is only this deficiency in our knowledge that is made good later when we find out our mistake. Thus
discovery of error only means a further step in advancing knowledge. It confirms the previous knowledge and does not cancel
any part of it as false, so that to talk of "rectification" with
reference to error is a misnomer. In admitting that error is incomplete knowledge which needs to be supplemented, the theory
grants that ignorance is involved in it; but the ignorance, it maintains, is purely of a negative character and does not import into
erroneous knowledge any element which is positively wrong.
In other words, it holds that the mind may fail to apprehend one
or more aspects of what is presented, but that it never *mis*-
apprehends it and that all errors are therefore only errors of
omission.

There is no need, on this view, to verify any knowledge. All
knowledge is true in the sense that no portion of what it reveals
is contradicted afterwards; and to question whether it agrees
with reality in any particular instance is therefore to question
its very nature. But truth being commonly distinguished from
error, it is necessary to give some explanation of the distinction.
The so-called error may be partial knowledge; but we cannot
characterise it as such, for human knowledge is always partial
in one sense or another. So another explanation is given, and
it is indirect. Though all knowledge is alike incomplete, error
is more so than truth. It is *relatively* incomplete, and its relative
incompleteness is determined by reference to an extrinsic
standard, viz. a pragmatic one. All knowledge, according to this
school, leads to action; and the success or failure of the activity
prompted by any particular knowledge is regarded as constituting
its truth or error. In other words, that knowledge is true which
works; and that which does not, is erroneous. Though this school

upholds a pragmatic view of truth, it should be noticed that it is essentially unlike modern Pragmatism. Epistemologically speaking, the latter amounts to a sceptical attitude, for it teaches that absolute truth in any matter is unattainable because it does not exist. Every truth is provisional—true only so long as it furthers human purposes. But here knowledge is admitted to have a logical, apart from a practical or guiding, value. Though it may be false on its purposive side, it is theoretically quite true and never fails to agree with the outside reality which it reveals. If we still speak of knowledge as sometimes false, we mean that it is not useful—thus transferring to it a feature which is significant only in reference to the practical consequences that follow from it. All knowledge in itself being thus regarded here as true, we may say that while current Pragmatism denies truth in the sense in which it is ordinarily understood, the present theory denies error.

This theory merits commendation for its simplicity as well as for its complete consistency in explaining the logical character of knowledge. It may be said to represent the extreme form of realism, for it not only upholds that external objects are independent of the knowing mind and are directly apprehended; it even denies error. But it is far from convincing. The indirect manner, for instance, in which it explains the familiar terms "true" and "false" is hardly satisfactory. But even waiving this consideration, it must be said that a purely negative explanation cannot account for error which, as a judgment, presents the two elements in it as synthesised though they may be actually unrelated. Its distinction from "doubt," which lacks such synthesis as shown by its alternative suppositions, and is not a judgment but a suspension of it, points to the same fact. In our illustration, the knowledge of the conch cannot accordingly be assumed to arise separately from that of yellowness; there is only a single psychical process, and the resulting knowledge includes a reference to a positive element which is false. Error is therefore misapprehension and not mere lack of apprehension. Such a view, we may add, is implied even in the explanation given by the school of thinkers mentioned above. It will be remembered that, according to that explanation, discovery of error means only an advance from less complete to more complete knowledge.

But there may be incomplete knowledge which we do or do not know to be so at the time; and it is only the latter that can be regarded as an error, for surely nobody that *knows* that his knowledge is incomplete can be said to make a mistake when that knowledge, so far as it goes, is admitted to be right. It will be wrong only when there is an implicit, if not an explicit, identification of it with truth or adequate knowledge. That is, if our knowledge is to be viewed as erroneous, it is not enough for us to be merely unaware of one or more aspects of the presented object; we should also take the knowledge as complete or adequate. And in so far as what is incomplete is taken for the complete or the less adequate for the more adequate, there is misapprehension. Thus the mind may not only misapprehend presented objects, but it invariably does so in error; and all errors are, therefore, errors of commission. Errors of *mere* omission in the sphere of knowledge are strictly not errors at all. There is, however, this much of truth in the previous view when it insists on the validity of all knowledge, that, so far as its perceptual form at least is concerned (to which we are now confining our attention), it always points to some reality or other, and that there can, therefore, be no complete error. That is, though a part of the content of knowledge may be false, the whole of it can never be so.

The outcome of the above reasoning is that there is always in error some element which needs to be recanted later, although it may be only the element of relation as in the above example; and, so far, the contention that no portion of what knowledge reveals is ever negated afterwards has to be given up. Before we enquire into the precise status of this element, it will be desirable to consider another type of error. We have hitherto spoken of errors in which, even after they are detected, the two elements involved, taken separately—or, to state the same in a different manner, the subject and the predicate of the propositions expressing the corresponding judgments—continue to be presented as before. Even the false localisation of the predicate ("yellow") persists, though it no longer misleads the person who has seen through the error. But there are other instances in which the predicate is contradicted—and necessarily the relation also along with it—the moment the error is discovered. This happens, for example, when we find out that we mistook a block of crystal for ice on seeing at some distance a certain shape and colour which are common to both.[1] The difference between the two cases is that in the one the predicative element ("yellow") is actually within the field of visual sensation, while in the other it ("ice") is not so. What we come to know as false in the latter case, when we fail to find that the given object is neither cool nor moist (say) as we expected, is not, therefore, merely the element of relation but also the predicate. Our perception of "ice" here, as if it were bodily present, when it does not form part of the given situation needs a satisfactory explanation. All that we know for certain is that there is *something* given, and that the sensa actually apprehended—a certain shape and colour as we have assumed—are of that something,[2] and not of the object to which they seem to pertain. Two explanations of this "presence in absence" are possible:

(1) It may be argued that the object in question, though not present in the given situation, is still to be reckoned as a physical existent because it is found elsewhere and should have been actually experienced at some other time. While the force of this argument may be admitted so far as it means that only things resembling those experienced before can be seen in such errors, it has to be observed that the question here is not merely about the *being* of the object but also about its presence at a particular place and at a particular time. In error, it is experienced as here and now; and the experience in this determinate form is contradicted later. The reality of the object *in itself* may be conceded, but it has no bearing upon this fact, and the contradiction, therefore, remains wholly unexplained by it. It may be said that what is meant by the above contention is not that the object is merely external and real but also that it somehow comes to be actually presented, though remote in time and place.[3] That would be to credit physical objects with what has been described

---

[1] The Prābhākara school, mentioned above, explained this class of errors also on the same principle, the two consecutive mental acts here being the perception of the subject and the recollection of the predicate.

[2] This statement requires modification as, for example, in the case of the moon which looks vastly smaller than it actually is. But it will be better to postpone the consideration of this point for the present.

[3] As is maintained, for example, in the Indian Nyāya-Vaiśeṣika system and, in a somewhat different form, by Professor Alexander (see *Space, Time and Deity*, vol. ii, p. 254.)

as "a somewhat surprising mobility." But even granting the
supposition, there is the difficulty of explaining how, if the object
be given, its givenness comes to be negated later. The other
element, for instance, in the error, viz. the one represented by the
subject ("this")[1] in the judgment—"This is ice"—is also given;
but it is not contradicted later. Its presence, on the other hand,
at the place where it appears is reaffirmed when we replace the
wrong judgment by the correct one—"*This* is a crystal." The
distinction in the way in which the correcting judgment affects the
two elements indicates that, although what is predicated may
be taken as out there, it cannot be regarded as real *in the same
sense* in which the subject is. The fact is that those who give such
explanations confound likeness with identity. They forget that,
while the erroneous object may be similar to what has once been
experienced, it need not be the same. They are right in urging
that knowledge is self-transcendent and always implies a content
that is known—something beyond or other than itself, and that
error forms no exception to this rule. But if the reasoning should
be free from all prepossession, the only conclusion we can draw
from it is that content here is a mere presentation, and not that
it is also physically real.

(2) If the erroneous content is merely a presentation and not
a physical reality, it may be thought that it is either a memory-
image or an ideal construction. But this conclusion again clashes
with experience. If it were a memory-image, it would involve
a reference to past time and to a distant place, and would not,
therefore, be apprehended as immediately given. In other words,
if the presentation were an ideal revival, one would realise it as
such at the time. There being no such realisation here, it cannot
be explained as a memory-image. It is not denied, we should add,
that the false "ice" would not have been presented at all, had
not real ice been experienced before. The mental disposition left
behind by past experience is, indeed, an indispensable condition
of the occurrence of such errors; but it only helps to determine the
nature of the presentation, and does not, for the reason just
stated, make it a memory-image. A similar kind of reasoning

---

[1] As we have already seen, the "this" in such cases signifies not merely
present time and proximate place, but also some sensa like shape and
colour.

applies to the second alternative of an ideal construction. The "ice" in that case would be experienced as related to the future, or it would appear without any special reference to time at all. In either case, the apprehension of it as a *present* existence would be inexplicable. The mental attitude, besides, would then be one of supposal and not of belief, as it is here.

The considerations which singly or in combination prevent us from accepting the above explanations in regard to the status of the object in error are its felt immediacy, its determinate position in the objective sphere, and its later sublation. Both the explanations possible being thus ruled out, we are obliged to regard it as a presentation which is quite unique. Its uniqueness consists in this, viz. that its nature cannot be fully expressed in terms known to logic or to psychology. A necessary condition of its emergence is that a real object should be apprehended, but only in its general aspects, and that the percipient, while being ignorant of its specific features, should be unaware of his ignorance. A sense of ignorance would perforce prevent the occurrence of error. In the case of "doubt," for instance, only the general features of the object presented are grasped; and yet there is no error, for one is *conscious* at the time that one does not know its distinctive features, as is clear from the wavering of the mind between two alternative possibilities. It is this dependence of the wrong object for its appearance upon a defect characterising an individual percipient[1] that explains why it is private to him and is not public or open to the view of others. Similarly, it is the position in the outside world of the thing mistaken, or the source from which the sensory stimulus comes, that determines the position of the wrong presentation there. The "ice" appears where the crystal is; and a change in the location of the thing mistaken would, other conditions remaining the same, result in a corresponding change in the external location of the wrong object. Ignorance, however, is not by itself sufficient to account for error; and it is always found associated in producing it with some fortuitous circumstance or other like the flash of similarity between the given thing and another.

[1] Ignorance also might be general or common to all; but the resulting misapprehension would not, in that case, be ordinarily recognised as an error by any one.

But it is difficult to detail these circumstances, for they vary so much from one instance to another. We can only characterise them generally by saying that, in the matter of giving rise to error, they are altogether subsidiary to ignorance and that their nature is such that the removal of the latter simultaneously renders them inoperative. Thus in the present case, the resemblance between the crystal and the ice is a necessary factor in producing the error; but the removal of ignorance, which means a knowledge of the specific features of the crystal, at once makes it ineffective. The resemblance, of course, continues thereafter, and may remind one of real ice; but it cannot aid the false presentation of it as before. It means that ignorance, as characterised above, is what sustains error; and we shall refer to it alone hereafter, disregarding additional causes like the one just mentioned.

Thus in all errors of the kind we are now considering, the subject ("this") and some of the sensa that characterise it are actually given; but the predicate ("ice") and the relation between it and the subject are unique presentations. The content of erroneous knowledge is, therefore, a medley of the true and the false. According to the principle on which we have explained the wrong presentation here, the element of relation in the case of the "yellow conch" also should be reckoned as unique. It is experienced immediately and as actually obtaining between two external objects; it is also later discovered to be false. Thus in both classes of error there is complete correspondence between knowledge and content. This does not imply the acceptance of the view that knowing involves a psychic medium which is *like* its object. Knowledge, on the other hand, reveals reality directly; and by its correspondence with content, we here mean that no part of what it reveals is ever sheer non-being. There may be disparity in the nature of the elements included within its content, for, while some of them are real, others may be unique in the sense explained above. But the latter, though not physically real, are felt as confronting the mind and cannot therefore be absolute nothing. There is resemblance between the two kinds of error[1] in other respects also. Both are forms of misapprehension

---

[1] Other forms of error, like dreams and hallucinations, fall under one or other of these two; or they partake of the character of both.

traceable to ignorance of the actual character of the given objects, and both are private to the erring observer. To an important difference which they exhibit, we have already had occasion to allude. In the case of the crystal mistaken for "ice," the discovery of error or the knowledge that the given reality it not ice, means the total disappearance of the wrong presentation.[1] The presentation is due to ignorance and the removal of the cause removes the effect. But in the other case, the knowledge that the conch is not yellow has no such effect, and the relation *appears* to persist even after it is contradicted. This appearance should consequently be traced to a circumstance other than ignorance which is the source of the error, viz. a particular disposition of the conch and the yellow glass relative to the point of space occupied by the observer. It is a conclusion which is corroborated by the fact that the apparent relation vanshes as soon as the disposition of the objects in question is changed.

II

True knowledge, by contrast, is that whose content is free from such unique presentations. Here also we may, and ordinarily do, go beyond the given as in error; but, on account of the apprehension of the sensa constituting the specific features of the object presented and not its general ones only, our knowledge does not become erroneous. Since sensa, according to what we have stated, are the very basis of our knowledge of the external world, they should be regarded as directly known; and it seems to follow from this that the object, of which they are the actual aspects, is also known directly. But this latter point cannot be properly argued without reference to the question of the ultimate nature of objects, which we are not considering here.

According to the description just given, knowledge is true when no part of its content has to be discarded as false. That is, it does not come in conflict with the rest of our experience, but harmonises with it.[2] This signifies that it is coherence with other experience, and not correspondence with reality, that

---

[1] The "ice" may appear there again, but it only shows that a man may fall twice into the same error.

[2] Old truths may need to be modified in the light of new experience. But we are not taking such details into consideration here.

makes it true. The rejection of the correspondence hypothesis does not mean the denial of the self-transcendent character of knowledge. It only means that since *all* knowledge, as we have pointed out, equally satisfies the condition of agreement with an objective counterpart, correspondence cannot be regarded as a distinguishing feature of truth. The conclusion that truth is coherence may be reached somewhat differently by considering the manner in which error comes to be known. Error, as we have seen, is a judgment that is self-discrepant; but its self-discrepancy remains unknown until it is revealed by another judgment which contradicts it. Now while one judgment may confirm or supplement another, it is difficult to see how it can correct or annul it, for there is no reason to prefer either of them to the other. The only circumstance in which it may do so is when it forms part of a body of knowledge which, as a whole, is, for some reason or other, regarded as well established. That is, a judgment can correct another or claim to be true, not by itself, but as belonging to, or as implicated in, a system of judgments. Since without the evidence of such a system, no one can know reality from unique presentations, we may say that error also, like a judgment which is true, becomes intelligible only in connection with a body of coherent knowledge which is taken as the standard of reference. The standard is ordinarily furnished in the case of each individual by the totality of his experience. When, however, any doubt arises and the individual's experience, even at its widest, is inadequate for settling it, an appeal to the experience of others becomes necessary. It is this collective experience or the common sense of mankind that, in the end, serves as the standard. That knowledge is true which fits into it perfectly; and that which does not, is false. Herein consists the social or general character of truth, as distinguished from error. We share truth with others; and it is therefore public, while error is private. The elements constituting the content of a true judgment are mutually compatible, since all of them are alike public. Error differs from truth in this respect, for it involves a reference not only to an object of common experience but also to unique presentations which are private and are not therefore endorsed by that experience.

We have so far assumed that all sensa correctly reveal the

character of the object given, if only partially, and are never false. But it does not seem to be always so, for we know from experience that the precise form in which they appear depends, for instance, upon the point of space occupied by the percipient with reference to the object in question. It shows that sensa are not only partial in their bearing upon the nature of the object given, but that they may also vary though the object remains the same. A coin, for example, presents a round or an oval shape according to. the position from which it is viewed. Similarly, a change in the position of an object may affect the sensa. A ship, which is seen as but a speck on the horizon, seems to increase in size as it approaches the shore, although there may be no change in the standpoint of the observer or in the objective situation as a whole. It may therefore appear that sensa also, like objects and relations, may be false. These altered sensa, it should be admitted, are not verifiable. A coin, to take one of our examples, cannot be both oval and round. But yet such appearances are not to be regarded as false; for, unlike erroneous presentations, they can be deduced from the actual sensa according to well-known physical laws. These secondary or derivative phenomena, as we may call them, may not literally qualify the object; but, owing to the fact that their altered form is determined by strict laws, they indicate correctly, though only indirectly, the nature of the object to which they refer. It is in this indirect, and not in a literal, sense that we characterise the data in such cases as true. The fact is that they are the result solely of the physical conditions under which normal human perception takes place, and do not in any manner depend upon the idiosyncrasies of the percipient mind to make them erroneous. Hence we should place these presentations on a footing which is quite different from those in error. Seeing a tree stump, which is at a distance, to be smaller than it actually is, is very much different from taking it to be something else (say), a human being. Besides, these phenomena do not commonly deceive us like erroneous presentations. A ship is not understood to undergo actual increase of bulk as it approaches the shore from a point on the horizon. All of them, no doubt, contain the seeds of error, and may therefore prove deceptive. A child may believe that the moon is really only as small as it appears, or that railway tracks actually converge towards a point in the distance. But then the essential condition of error, viz. ignorance of the true character of the objects in question, is also present; and its removal, though it shows the beliefs to be erroneous, does not lead to the removal of the presentations. In other words, they disappear as errors but persist as appearances of the real. These appearances may not, in themselves, be real; yet they are not false in the sense in which erroneous presentations, like the "ice" in our former example, are. For the same reason, the *apparent* relation also, noticed before in connection with errors of the first type like the "yellow conch," is not to be regarded as false.

We may designate these secondary phenomena as "perspectives of the real" or, briefly, "perspectives."[1] The distinction between them and erroneous presentations, as already indicated, is that the latter are rooted in ignorance which is a defect of the knowing subject, while the former are purely the result of certain physical conditions under which an object happens to be apprehended. The term "perspective," no doubt, implies relation to the standpoint of a particular observer; and, so far, the presentations are personal. The point here, however, is not that the phenomena in question are unrelated to the individual, but that they are in no way due to his oddities. In this latter respect, they are like sensa proper; but, unlike them, they do not directly belong to the objects to which they seem to belong. Hence in determining the true character of any perceived object or objects from such phenomena, we should apply a suitable correction taking into account the nature of the physical context in which they appear. In simple cases we make such corrections ourselves, as, for instance, when we see a coin as oval but interpret it as circular; in more intricate ones, however, the aid of science is necessary as in ascertaining the true magnitude of the moon from its apparent size. The truths so determined are impersonal because they reveal objects as they are in themselves, not as they appear, and are therefore independent of the point of view of the person or persons asserting them. While a part of empirical knowledge may

---

[1] This term, which is used by more than one modern philosopher (e.g. Professor Alexander), is intended here to stand, though not in every detail, for the phenomena underlying what is described as *sopādhika-bhrama* in the philosophy of Śaṁkara.

be impersonal, the whole of science is so, for the one aim of the scientist is to find out the actual features or normal aspects of things. The extent to which this difference affects the correctness of common knowledge, where the phenomena concerned are of a complicated nature, may be very great; and what are only "perspectives" and, as such, are not literally true, may often be mistaken by us for sensa or actual features of the external world. Hence empirical knowledge, as a whole, stands far lower, in point of accuracy, than the scientific. Its primary function is to subserve the purposes of everyday life, and it does not therefore ordinarily aim at greater accuracy than is needed for their fulfilment. Its value lies in its practical utility, not in its theoretical certainty; and the saying that "thought is the slave of life" is therefore essentially true here.

III

The conclusion thus far reached is that the common-sense analysis of knowledge, with which we started, requires to be modified in two important respects. There are some instances, viz. "perspectives" which only indirectly disclose the character of external objects; and there are others, viz. errors which, while they may reveal reality, also include presentations that are not genuine parts or aspects of it at all. Objects and relations may thus be erroneously presented, but never sensa. It may seem that, if proper allowance be made for these two kinds of discrepancies, the system of common knowledge, taken as a whole, will give us the final or absolute truth sought after in epistemology; but it does not, because it has other limitations. In the first place, it obviously refers only to a small portion of the whole of reality, and is therefore fragmentary. In the second place, it leaves out even from this portion a great deal as not relevant to the carrying out of common human purposes which is its pre-eminent function. Scientific knowledge is without this latter limitation, since it aims at expounding phenomena in terms of the non-human; but even that cannot be regarded as giving us the final epistemological solution, for it also is selective, though in a different way. No science treats of the whole of reality, and each is concerned only with particular aspects of it; and, since it studies these aspects apart from their concrete accompaniments, it may be said to deal more with abstractions than with reality. Moreover science, in spite of the indefinite expansion possible for it, will never arrive at an exhaustive knowledge of reality because its selective method will always leave for it a field which is still to be explored. Although the view of truth formulated above cannot therefore be regarded as final, it will yield the solution which epistemology seeks when its implications are fully worked out. We shall now point out how it does so; but, within the limits of this paper, we can do so only very briefly.

The possibility of its furnishing the final solution is contained in the conception of knowledge as a system, and of truth as coherence with it. A strict adherence to this view may seem to lead one to the conclusion that truth is relative. For there may be two or more coherent systems of knowledge which are at variance with one another, and what is true from one standpoint may not be so from another. All our so-called truths may thus turn out to be equally false relatively, not excluding the results of scientific investigation. We have explained the common notions of truth and error, it will be remembered, by reference to the body of knowledge that bears the stamp of social sanction. But it is really only one of the standards by which truth may be distinguished from error; and we should take into account the possibility of there being also other types or systems of knowledge, relatively to each of which a similar distinction can be made. These systems may be many; and every one of them, according to the view taken of knowledge here, corresponds to a self-consistent whole of objective existence—the sphere of reference, which is common to all the judgments making up that system. Hence it is not only the world in the ordinary sense that exists; there may be others also, so long as they are systematic or are wholes constituted of inter-related parts, making it possible to distinguish the true from the false in statements relating to them. The world of Shakespeare's *Othello*, for example, is such a system, since it admits of right as well as wrong statements being made about it. It would be false, for instance to represent Desdemona in it as in love with Cassio. As a consequence of such an enlarged view of objective existence, there will be not one type of truth only, but several—each order of existence, constituting the basis for a distinct type of it. "Our beds are not stained," it has been said, "by the wounds of dream scimitars"; but our dream beds may well be.

It may, on such considerations, be held that there is no absolute truth at all and that we may regard any truth as relatively false, if we choose to do so. But it appears that the very notion of *relative* truth suggests the recognition of an absolute standard by which all knowledge is judged; and we have to accept such a standard, giving up "relativist epistemology," if we are to avoid universal scepticism. Only it is necessary to further define truth, if it should be absolute. This can be done by bringing in the idea of comprehensiveness, when the systematic coherence which is our definition of truth will be perfect. The fulfilment of this new condition means the possibility of conceiving absolute truth as the expansion or development of one of the above truths such that it will, in some sense or other, include within its sphere of reference the whole of existence—not merely objective worlds but also conscious subjects. To leave out any portion of it would be to admit two or more truths, none of which, on account of their mutual exclusion, can be taken as absolute. But it may appear that there is no means of determining which of the relative truths is to be elevated to this rank. If, however, the sceptical position is to be avoided, a choice has to be made; and there is every consideration, short of logical certitude, to recommend common truth for the purpose. We may now divide all the subsidiary truths into two groups— one consisting of those that relate to the everyday world, though they may not all refer necessarily to the same aspects of it; and the other consisting of the rest which relate to the world of fiction or even to the region of dreams and illusions, so far as they are self-consistent. Of these, the former may be viewed as lying on the way to absolute truth; and since they may approximate to it more or less, we may speak of them as representing degrees of truth, a higher degree of it meaning greater completeness in the view it gives of reality. The truth of science as well as that of empirical life is of this kind. They mark relatively higher and lower stages on the path leading to ultimate truth. All such truths are integrated in the absolute one which is self-complete. The others cannot thus be integrated, owing to the divergence in their objective reference. But when we remember that, whether they refer to ideal constructions or to unique presentations, they are dependent for their subject-matter upon the reality which forms the content of the first group of truths, we find that they have their ultimate explanation, through them, in the absolute truth, even though they cannot be said to actually endure in it. They may be described as lower kinds of truth to distinguish them from the degrees of it already referred to. These two groups or classes of truth correspond to two orders of existence, one less real than the other. The world of morals implied by ethical truth, for example, belongs to the common order of existence, because of its direct bearing on actual life. But the world of art, though the truth at which it finally aims may be the very highest, stands lower than that. This is evident, for instance, from the fact that, as observed by A. C. Bradley,[1] "we dismiss the agony of Lear in a moment if the kitten goes and burns his nose."[2]

It is this absolute truth that is the goal of epistemology; and it yields a unified view of the whole of reality. All the elements of the universe—whether they be knowable objects or knowing subjects—appear in it as internally related; and each of them reveals itself there as occupying the place that rightly belongs to it within the whole. That is, the ultimate truth is entirely impersonal. Further, these elements are seen in it not merely as they are at any particular moment, but in the perspective of their entire history—as what they were in the past and as what they will be in the future. Or rather there can be no distinctions of time in it—"no future rushing to the past," but one eternal now. A temporal world when viewed in its wholeness, it has been remarked, must be an eternal one. In this concreteness and completeness it differs from scientific truth, though impersonal like it. It also differs from truth as commonly understood by us which is neither comprehensive nor wholly impersonal. There is one important point to which it is necessary to draw attention before we conclude. If the absolute truth should really comprehend

---

[1] *The Uses of Poetry*, p. 12.
[2] This preference, however, implies that we realise at the time the relative status of the two realities. There is such realisation generally in the case of art, but not in illusions.

all, it cannot exclude the self of the person that contemplates it. It will not therefore do if he stands apart, regarding himself as a mere knower and therefore distinct from what it points to. He should, on the other hand, view himself as inseparably one with it. The subject and the object would still be distinguished in his view, but there would not be that opposition or disaccord which we commonly feel between them. It means a profound transformation in the ordinary conception of the knowing self and of the objects known. Here naturally arises the question of the precise nature of the transformation in each case; but, as our present concern is with truth rather than with reality, we shall not attempt to discuss the possible answers to it. We shall only make one observation: though we left undetermined at the start the ultimate character of the self and of the object, we assumed that they were distinct. This initial dualism has to be abandoned now, for, according to the final conception of truth at which we have arrived, the knower and the known, though distinguishable, are not separable. Knowledge begins by assuming that they are different, but it culminates in the discovery of a latent harmony between them in which the difference is resolved. It is not merely the notions of the subject and the object that are thus transmuted; the knowledge also which relates them must be of a higher order than any we are familiar with—whether perceptual or conceptual. But this higher experience, which may be described as insight or intuition, is not altogether alien to us, for we get a glimpse of it whenever for any reason we rise above the distractions of personal living. Only it is too faint and fitful to enable us to understand what the exact character of the experience will be when the absolute truth is realised. All that we can say is that for one who attains to such experience, through a proper development of this intuitive power, there will be nothing that is not immediately known and that no part of what is so known will appear as external. What the means of developing intuition are, and whether the ideal of absolute truth can be completely realised, are questions whose consideration lies outside the scope of the present paper.

PRINCIPAL PUBLICATIONS

Outlines of Indian Philosophy. George Allen & Unwin (London, 1932).

Naiṣkarmya-siddhi of Sureśvara. Published in the Bombay Sanskrit Series (1925).

Iṣṭa-siddhi of Vimuktātman. Published in the Gaekwad's Oriental Series (1933).

Essentials of Indian Philosophy. George Allen & Unwin (London).

M

FREEDOM, AUTHORITY AND IMAGINATION

by HUMAYUN KABIR

FREEDOM, AUTHORITY AND IMAGINATION

I

THE experience of two World Wars within the short interval of a quarter of a century is a warning which we can ignore only at our peril. No further evidence of the world crisis through which we are living is necessary. Achievements of the human spirit built up through centuries of devotion and endeavour are crashing all around us. The tragedy of this ruin and desolation is the greater because it is so deliberate and yet so futile. If an earthquake or flood had overwhelmed us, if volcanoes had poured their molten lava on the work of man, there would be in our sorrow at least the consolation that the destruction was due to non-human agencies over which we have no control. The devastation which is taking place is, however, no visitation of nature, but an expression of the wild frenzy of men who are using all their energy and craft, all their endurance and courage for a carnage of mutual destruction.

If we want to find a way out of this impasse and discover a mode of life which may save us from the repetition of such senseless massacre and destruction, it is necessary to understand the nature of the society in which such crises can arise. An understanding of the nature of society would at the same time imply an understanding of the nature of the individuals who constitute it. It cannot be stressed too strongly that society and individual are inseparable though distinct elements of one organic fact. For purposes of analysis we often treat such elements separately but failure to recognize their indissolubility leads to error and disaster.

The concept of society as an organism is our basic fact. The analogy between social and physical organisms must not, however, be pressed too far. In the physical organism, the organism is the fact and its limbs are mere moments. The relation even in such cases can be regarded as one of interdependence, but it is obvious that the organism has a greater importance than the component units. The importance of the units is mainly, if not solely, functional, and these functions are determined by the purposes of the organism. Even where the organism and its units seem to have different functions, analysis will show that the contrariety is only apparent. It is, however, different with the social organism. Its units are centres of individuality and independence. They refuse to be regarded as mere components of the organism. Society no doubt claims the allegiance of its members, but the very fact that the claim has to be made and may in certain circumstances be refused, proves that the analogy of the relationship of the limbs to the physical organism cannot express the real relation of individuals to society.

A little reflection will show that the most noticeable characteristic of the crisis from which the world suffers today is a conflict within and between individuals and groups. Overproduction and unsatisfied demand are only one sympton of this conflict. The individual desires blindly and secures chance satisfaction only because he is at war within himself. Society produces in abundance and remains unsatisfied only because elements within society neither feel nor think nor act in unison. The result is chaos and confusion in the individual, the national and the international spheres.

We can express this conflict most simply and yet perhaps most adequately by describing it as a failure to reconcile freedom and authority. Both freedom and authority are social concepts and must be so, for man is essentially a social being. This social character is grounded in his nature itself. In spite of occasional aberrations, rationality is man's distinguishing feature, at once his crown and his cross. Rationality presupposes a transcendence of the individual point of view. Any being so far as it is rational, is social. We may arrive at the same finding in another way. Freedom and authority must be attended with self-consciousness, and self-consciousness without rationality is a contradiction in terms.

Since freedom and authority are both social concepts, and society is essentially organic, freedom and authority are distinct but not separate. Any attempt to regard one as primary is bound to lead to contradictions. Most of the problems concerning freedom and authority, and therefore conflicts and crises in human society, are due to loss of insight into this fundamental fact. The moment we try to isolate freedom from authority and base the one upon the other, we distort their true significance and misunderstand the nature of the social whole with consequences that are disastrous for society and individual alike.

The paradox may be stated as follows. Freedom and authority both represent normative claims and in purely natural happenings there is no question of either. An event either happens or does not, and there the matter ends. It is only metaphorically that the earth exercises compulsion on the falling apple. The activity and hence the freedom of the apple in such a situation are both purely metaphorical. The limbs of the human body have as little freedom as his body has authority. It is only in the realm of self-conscious, and therefore unique, individuals that the conflict between freedom and authority can arise.

Stated in this way, it becomes clear that purely economic or political explanations of the human crises are over-simplifications. Belief in purely economic action is even rarer today than that in the mere economic man. It is being more and more clearly realised that economics is not a true description of one particular kind of action but a description of all action from an abstract and arbitrary point of view. Economics abstracts from the specific characteristics of different kinds of action and concentrates on the aspect which is common to all of them. There is only one such aspect and this derives from the fact that all action is purposive. The purposes may be different, but all actions share the common characteristic of having in view some end or other. This common aspect of actions is their suitability for their respective ends. This suitability defines their utility, and hence economics is the science of utility.

Utility and satisfaction are, however, as the analysis of psychological hedonism has shown, mere abstractions. So far as economics deals with such abstractions, it shares in the fundamental abstractness of science. Satisfaction varies from individual to individual and from time to time with the same individual. What satisfies A, B abhors. Utilities which X seeks today, he repudiates tomorrow without the slightest hesitation. Conflicts within and between individuals and societies, therefore, arise not in the pursuit of abstract relational schema of *the economic*, but on account of *goods* which rightly or wrongly are believed to possess intrinsic or absolute value.

Political explanations of the human crises suffer from a similar defect. Man is not consistently a political animal. The world that is most important to him is the world he has built up round his own experiences. No two men are exactly alike. The innate uniqueness of individuality compels the ultimate separation of every man from his fellows. He may combine with others for economic or political purposes, but he cannot merge his being into that of his fellowmen. There will always be the irrational surd of his personality. The spiritual sphere of human life—interpreting the term to mean religion, philosophy and art—is the province where the unique quality of individuality finds full play. Men utter the same shibboleths and protest loyalty to the same ideals, but the white light of the abstract ideal comes to each man tinged with the colour of his own personality.

The State has in the past sought and seeks even today to dominate the private life of its members and determine the quality and texture of their experiences. It has sought and is seeking to dictate what thoughts they shall think and what belief they shall believe, under the threat of repudiation or even persecution for non-conformity to its demands. Such dictation is, however, bound to fail. Man's thought is his own and not the most dictatorial of States can take it away from him. The State can control conduct, or more accurately, behaviour—the external and observable aspects of the action of the individual. To admit this is to recognize that like economics, politics is not a true description of one kind of action, but an abstract and arbitrary description of all action. Unless we remember that this is so, both economic and political analyses are bound to lead to error. The State can, through law, maintain only the universal external conditions of social order. This, like the utility of economics, is an abstraction for which no man will fight.

Political and economic explanations of the crises in civilisation, therefore fail. They depend upon a view of man that makes him more intellectual than he actually is. Man is neither wholly nor consistently economic or political in his motive or action. His action is not a mere example of some abstract law. The irrationality or illogicality of which the economist or the politician accuses him is only the emergence of some aspect or element in his nature which the economist or the politician ignored or overlooked.

The failure of economic or political explanation of human conduct has led some thinkers to deny altogether the efficacy of thought in the management of human affairs. Instinct, not reason, they say is the basis of society. They hold that just as there is a gregarious instinct which leads to the formation of society, there is a pugnacious instinct which leads men to fight one another. For them, the basis of society is instinctual and conflicts are equally the result of instinct. So long as man is man, he will love and hate, make friends and fight. Advance of civilisation can only extend the scope and scale of his operations but cannot change his innate character.

In place of the confident rationalism of the nineteenth century, the modes of modern thought are curiously diffident about the powers of reason. The nineteenth century tended to identify reason with the discursive intellect. If the reaction had led to a wider conception of the scope and functions of reason, philosophy would have gained by it. Unfortunately, however, the tendency has been towards a growth of anti-rationalsim. The multiplication of instincts to explain the multiplicity of human action is only one instance of it. Like the invocation of instinct, the exaltation of feeling and the enthronement of the unconcious are symptoms of the malady. The emergence of fatalism in several schools of dialectical materialism—perhaps the most characteristic mode of political thought of the present century—is a fresh and damaging proof of man's pragmatic distrust in the efficacy of reason for the purposes of practical life.

Instinctual explanation of human action is, however, a confession of failure in social analysis. It brings out an instinct to explain any action for which its pre-conceived theories fail to account. The result is a multiplication of instincts to which no limit can be drawn. Votaries of the theory agree neither about the number nor about the nature of such instincts. The experiments of the behaviourists have further discredited the instinctual theory of human activity. Even those who do not accept the fundamental standpoint of behaviourism must admit that its researchers have undermined the solid stability of the instincts. If reflexes can be conditioned and elaborate modes of behaviour built out of simple responses, there is in principle no limit to the possibilities of variation in human conduct. If we know neither the number nor the nature of the instincts and further admit that both are variable, there is hardly any point in explaining individual or social conflicts in terms of them.

The instinctual theory of human conduct is, therefore, untenable; neither is it necessary. The failure of economic and political explanations is due, as we have already seen, to over-intellectualisation. They seek to apply to human conduct the methods of scientific analysis and fail because the abstract concept cannot express the individual in its infinite complexity and wealth of details.

The rejection of abstract analysis does not necessarily require the rejection of reason. That would follow only if it is held that abstract analysis is the only mode of thought. The presumption is derived from the fact that such analysis is the method of science, and science is rational. From the rationality of Science it is then inferred that there can be no rationality outside the precincts of science. This may be the case, but it is too big an assumption to make without proper examination and proof. However that be, it is undeniable that neither intellectual nor instinctual interpretations can explain adequately the causes of social malaise. Both, however, indicate that the source of the malaise is to be found in the stubborn intransigence of the individual in society.

II

An analysis of society reveals to us that social phenomena are always in a state of unstable equilibrium. This instability is the result of the conflict between freedom and authority and is aggravated by the maladjustments between social order and social content. Social order may be defined as the pattern of relations that has grown through the interplay of the forces with which the different units in the social organism are charged. It rests on the distinction of the interests of the different social elements and constitutes an attempt to achieve a harmony among the conflicting interests. Social content may be defined as the sum total of the desires and anticipations, experiences and aspirations, interests and allegiances of the mass of individuals who constitute society. At its best, the order achieved by any society is a precarious harmony that the slightest redistribution of emphasis among the different interests might upset. At its worst, the order represents the tyranny of one predominant interest, secure only as long as it can keep in check the balance of growing forces arrayed against it.

The maladjustment between social order and social content is, in a sense, inevitable. The social order is a growth determined by the interplay of interests within a given framework. Such a growth requires time but there is no guarantee that the relations between the interests constituting society will remain stable and unchanged during the period of growth. The units of society have their own laws of change. These not only may, but generally do differ from one another. By the time a social order is stabilized, it may have ceased to represent a true balance of forces between the different elements of the social content. If we take a cross-section of society at any point of time, the order revealed will be the reflection, not of the prevailing disposition of social interests, but that of the interests of the stage immediately antecedent to it. The social structure and the social content belong to different regions in the order of growth but they are juxtaposed into one another on the same temporal plane.

We have already pointed to the refusal of the individual to be submerged in social consciousness. Man is no doubt a social being, but equally he is a solitary pilgrim of eternity. If he were wholly social, there would be no problem of the relation of authority and freedom. Authority, which is the dynamic expression of the prevailing social order, would be merely a function of the social content so defined. If, on the other hand, he were completely alone, the discord between authority and freedom would equally disappear. Freedom would, in that case, be merely a function of his solitariness. It is the stubborn intransigence of the individual in society that is at the root of our problem, but the inevitable time-lag between the social order and the social content further aggravates it.

This disharmony between social order and social content is the motive force behind all social change. Conflicts whether on international or intra-national scale arise out of this disharmony. In the political field, it explains the discontent and unrest that seek to extend the system of rights till it is co-extensive with that of duties. In the field of morality and religion, it seeks to harmonize the conflict and interests within the individual till they coincide with the balance achieved by the social organism as a whole. In the sphere of social relations, it is responsible for the continuous adjustments that are required for maintaining the dynamic equilibrium of society against the stresses which particular interests impose upon it.

Such a dynamic conception of society and its order is in all essentials true, but the process of growth and change is concealed by several factors inherent in the structure of society itself. A properly organized social order would immediately respond to the minutest variation in the distribution of emphasis among the several units. A change of development in the social content would in that case be accompanied or neutralized by a corresponding variation in the structure of the social order itself. In such a society, evolution would be the natural law of growth.

This, however, is only an ideal and serves only to prescribe the end towards which social activity ought to be directed. In actual life, societies represent an unstable equilibrium achieved by the interplay of interests at any particular point of time. This instability is based upon the imperfect organisation of the forces which in their struggle and co-operation determine the structure of human society. The fusion of the conflicting interests is incomplete and varies from society to society. Where the fusion is complete, society responds easily and without conflict to the slightest change. The elasticity of the social order is thus measured by the degree of fusion. The power of adjustment and growth varies from society to society, but in no case is this power equivalent to the demands made by the incessant metabolism which characterizes all living societies.

A social form must, therefore, from its very nature, make for rigidity and permanence. Form is the universal imbedded in the nature of a particular. It is impervious to the alterations in its particularity so long as these alterations do not negate the universal imbedded in it. When such negation takes place, we are faced with a metamorphosis which seems abrupt and discontinuous. We call it a revolution, but it is a revolution to us only because we cannot translate into our conceptual patterns the continuity of alterations made possible by the contingency of the particular. This law of inertia of social forms is the first factor which conceals and, what is worse, opposes the continual alterations going on within the social organism.

The second factor, though distinct from, is closely connected with the first. We have seen that all social forms exhibit an elasticity of variation that is less than unity. This relative inelasticity is due to an imperfect fusion of the different interests which together constitute the social group. The imperfect organisation entails that some of the interests within society are weighted as against the others. The unequal weightage of some interests against the others secures to such elements of the social content a position of privilege. The consequence is that the preservation of a particular form of society, and hence a particular type of state-form, becomes identified with their group interest.

These two factors—the intrinsic inertia of all forms and the identification of the interests of society with those of a particular group within it—tend to increase the resistance of the social order to the pressure exerted upon it by alterations in the nature of the social content. Social content is and must from its nature be in a state of continual flux. The change takes place, not only through the process of time and the consequent accumulation of new experiences, but also through subtle alterations in the disposition and relation of the elements within a society. Like the slightest change of tone which yet makes all the difference in the atmosphere of a landscape, the slightest variation in the emphasis of the different elements transforms the social content almost beyond recognition.

The rigidity of form and the flux which characterizes its elements invariably tend to increase the maladjustment between social order and social content. There is danger of explosion whenever the form fails to adjust itself to the content in time. Factors which enhance the rigidity of form are to be regarded as reactionary precisely because they increase such risk. Where the social order is too rigid, it is no longer a dynamic equilibrium of conflicting forces, but a formula or pattern forcibly imposed on the multiform factors comprising society. The result is a growing tension between the rigid and static social form and the repressed and submerged elements of the social content. There can be no relief unless the social order gains in elasticity, or in the alternative, the suppressed elements gather sufficient energy to compel a violent overthrow of the prevailing social order.

Overthrow of the social order might mean either internal or external conflict. In either case, there would be an explosive social revolution. Just as an earthquake relieves the growing stress between the different strata of the earth and establishes a new equilibrium, such revolutions would tend to establish a new balance between the diverse elements of the social content. In process, it would generally destroy those aspects of the social order which make for rigidity and oppose timely adjustment to change. It may, however, in the general upheaval also destroy many of the acknowledged values in the structure of the superseded system.

The disadvantages of such violent revolution are three-fold. The concentrated energy of the repressed elements might, in certain conceivable circumstances, destroy not only the repressive elements of the social order. but in the revolt against particular dis-values, destroy the social order itself and along with it all the values which that society has painfully evolved. A revolution may destroy an equilibrium which is becoming oppressive and substitute in its place a new harmony at a higher level. There is, however, also the possibility that the disruptive forces which it unleashes may destroy all equilibrium and bring back a state of disorder that would be a falling-back even by the standards of the superseded society. This lapse towards a lower form of social order may well be described as a return to chaos, which would be the end, at least for the time being, of civilisation and culture for that society.

Even if all values are not destroyed, there is no guarantee that the revolution must necessarily set up a system of values more comprehensive and satisfying than the one it supersedes. In most cases, this will no doubt be the tendency. The tension which provokes the outburst will not be released till some more satisfactory equilibrium is established among the conflicting forces. We must, however, remember that the motive force of the revolution will be supplied by some interest or interests that have been suppressed in the past. In the natural course of events, these interests would seek for, and perhaps secure, compensation for the comparative neglect or repression from which they formerly suffered. There will thus be a very real danger that the new equilibrium will give undue weightage to the forces formerly repressed and repress those which had the freest play in the old regime. This would create, though inversely, the conditions which led to the last revolution. In other words, the harmony achieved will again be a one-sided and incomplete harmony, and hold within itself the certainty of fresh upheavals. Revolutions, almost without exception, breed new revolutions and those who take to the sword shall, through the logic of events, perish by the sword.

All this is on the assumption that the revolution will succeed, but from the very nature of the case, there can be no guarantee of success. An unsuccessful revolution, instead of releasing the strain through a more satisfactory alignment of forces, is likely to lead to acuter repression. This would drive underground the forces that seek free play and thus insure the occurrence of a further and perhaps more violent explosion.

Whether the revolution succeeds or not, it is bound to bring in its wake great human suffering and misery. This is an inevitable feature of any disruption of social harmony. Pain in itself is never good, even though it may at times have a cathartic value which compensates for its intrinsic evil. If an end is in itself supremely desirable, and if that end can be achieved only through the intermediation of pain, we may accept it as a necessary corollary to the attainment of that ideal. We must, however, be sure that there is no other way, and even then, it is something to be suffered only for the sake of the good to which it ultimately leads.

The aim of enlightened policy should, therefore, be the creation of conditions in which revolutionary changes may take place without the need of a violent disruption in the continuity of social life. The maladjustment between social form and social content inherent in the nature of a developed and complex social organism makes rapid and far-reaching changes inevitable. Revolutions can, therefore, be avoided only if the elasticity of the social form can be heightened to such an extent that it responds to the changes in the social content with sufficient rapidity and sensitiveness to avert the necessity of an explosive outburst. This is perhaps what Whitehead had in mind when he spoke of the interplay of static vision and dynamic history in the production of a type of society in which satisfaction is mated with survival.

III

The intransigence of the individual is then at the back of all conflicts of human society. It is born out of an imperfect realisation that good is either social or it is not good at all. Attempts were often made to enhance this realisation through education. Ancient Indian philosophy stressed the unity of the true and the real. Plato identified virtue and wisdom. The whole of the nineteenth century was inspired by a faith in rationalism. The change of heart which it was hoped would result from the spread of education did not, however, take place. It was intellectually grasped that if man is to live in community with his fellows—and no alternative mode of life is possible for him—what he intends and achieves must, at least in the long run, bring benefit to others as well. Intellectual recognition was not, however, accompanied by a change in the modes of conduct, and men went on fighting one another in the name of reason and the social good.

In a sense, the failure of nineteenth century rationalism was inevitable. It sought to apply the methods of abstract analysis to problems of human personality without enquiring whether such methods are applicable there. Abstract analysis is par excellence the method of science. We need not stress here the fact that even science requires constant reference to *a* particular, though it is indifferent as to *which* particular it is. It is this indifference to particularity which makes science the most fruitful field of abstract analysis. The scientific concept thus treats all its instances as indistinguishable members of a class. The essence of personality, however, is that each individual is a distinct centre of self-consciousness. Further, the concept is a function of unity used by the self-conscious subject for explaining the order and regularity of his multi-form experiences. It cannot, therefore, serve as a principle of explanation of the self. The recognition that the individual is indefinable marks a limit to the application of the scientific concept. It also demonstrates that the intellect is only an instrument of knowledge and cannot, therefore, be equated with the self which is the subject of knowledge.

We may here indicate one of the reasons why nineteenth century rationalism, in spite of its fervour and optimism, failed. The importance of science has been constantly increasing since the days of the Renaissance. This has had its effect on our conceptions of society and the State. The various forms of the social contract theory mark the efforts of the human mind to account for society on the analogy of physical science. Individuals and their contractual relations were the counterparts in political theory of atoms and gravitational relations in Newtonian physics. In a word, categories of natural science were without examination or criticism sought to be applied to problems of human action.

There was a change in the method of science itself with the rise of biology during the nineteenth century. Along with this change in scientific method, the nature of political theory also changed. Theories of social contract were gradually replaced by the concept of society as an organism. Relations between the members of society were no longer regarded as mere generalisations of individual self-interest. Social phenomena demanded explanation on a basis of mutuality transcending the limits of mechanical interaction. As a consequence, it also began to be realized that instead of saying that man *is* rational, we ought rather to say that man is *becoming* rational. This was no doubt a development in the right direction, but the fact remains that here again scientific categories were applied to social phenomena without criticism or question. The rationalism of the nineteenth century was, therefore, not so rational as it claimed to be.

The recognition of the organic character of the State and the individual did not, moreover, have any perceptible influence upon the principles or methods of education. Education continued for long to be a discipline of the intellect alone. It is only in recent times that the emphasis is being shifted to the education of the instincts and the feelings. This failure of nineteenth century rationalism to apply the results of its own findings to the solution of practical problems is not a matter of accident. It is another instance of the strain of anti-rationalism which Whitehead found to be characteristic of scientific thought. He has indicated one of its causes in science's distrust of the general law. Another cause is to be found in the divorce of the theoretical reason from the practical will to whose disastrous consequences we have already referred.

Thought is by its nature general and seeks to introduce into the variety and flux of experience an element of order and stability. Education of the intellect is therefore intended to encourage uniformity in conduct, but unless the other elements in human nature—instincts, emotions and the will—are educated simultaneously, mere education of the intellect defeats its purpose. The reason for this is not far to seek. The intellect operates through concepts, for of all types of generalisation, classification under a concept is the simplest. Emphasis on the intellect tends to conceptualise all experience and generalise still further an aspect of our nature which is intrinsically general. This can only aggravate the distinction between thought and those other aspects of our nature which are essentially unique. The result is conflict within the individual of which social conflict is both effect and magnified reflection.

The conflict can be resolved only by discovering some principle which can unify the general with the unique. If concepts were our only instrument for generalisation of experience, it is evident that such harmony could not be achieved. Man would, in that case, be doomed to inner conflicts with their disastrous repercussions on external affairs. Fortunately for us, we have instances of other types of generality. The world of feeling is just as real as the world of reason, and has an immediacy which thought often lacks. Feelings are in their nature unique, and yet under certain conditions achieve a universality which cannot be expressed in conceptual terms.

Another type of non-conceptual generality is to be found in the realm of the will. The will expresses itself in decisions each one of which is unique, and yet it is the same will which manifests itself in each one of them. It is obvious that we cannot explain the relation of the will to its decisions on the analogy of the relation of the universal to its particulars. The conceptual nexus is based on indifference to particularity. It is immaterial whether we refer to instance A or instance B. The volitional nexus presupposes the uniqueness of each instance. To suggest that one decision can be replaced by another would be to show a total misunderstanding of the nature of the will. These instances from the world of feeling and volition show that in addition to the world of concepts—where the particular is only an instance of the universal—there are other regions of experience where universality and uniqueness coalesce. In other words, in addition to the world of particulars, with which conceptual analysis deals, there is also a world of individuals whose nature cannot be revealed by abstract thought.

The considerations stated above confirm our earlier hypothesis that the problems of the modern world centre round the individual. All philosophers agree that the study of the individual is in a special sense the province of the imagination. Reason, we have seen, cannot express the nature of the individual. The essence of rationality is universality expressing itself through concepts. The individual on the other hand is what it is, not on account of the features it shares with other individuals, but on account of those which are its unique possession. Whether it be the world of art in which feelings find unique embodiment or the field of morality in which the will expresses itself in unique decisions, we have here a range of experiences whose true appreciation depends on the significance of the individual. The individual can be most briefly described as the unique universal. Imagination penetrates into the uniqueness and achieves for it aesthetic or moral universality. A critique of imagination is thus essential for a proper understanding of the central problem of our age.

This, however, is not all. Art is not only an embodiment of the individual but also the expression of emotions and instincts. In fact, it is the only expression that mankind has till now achieved. An intellectual judgment expresses little of the excitement and energy with which our instincts are charged. What are left unexpressed in such judgment, do not therefore cease to be. They recede from the foreground of consciousness and are submerged in what we often describe as the unconscious. They, however, influence our conduct from behind the scenes more than we know or care to admit. This proves that it is not quite accurate to describe them even as the subconscious. More often than not, our conscious behaviour is a projection of what remains unexpressed. Nor is it always possible to draw a line of demarcation between the different levels of consciousness.

Emotions or instincts cannot, therefore, be totally suppressed. Pushed back in one quarter, they spring back into our behaviour from another and perhaps unsuspected quarter. Besides, experience has again and again proved that nothing but unhappiness results when we seek to suppress completely any instinctive emotion. Uncontrolled and undisciplined display of the same emotions leads to equally great unhappiness. Attempts at suppression and wild orgy of emotions are therefore both harmful to the individual and hence to human society. Art which expresses emotions and at the same time introduces order into them is, therefore, one of the constituents of civilisation itself.

Freud has described the unconscious as a chaos, a cauldron of seething excitement which is impervious to the passage of time. The repressed is the region of timeless entities possessed of a vital energy which the expressed elements of human nature do not and cannot possess. This fact helps to explain a phenomenon in social behaviour that has often baffled the psychologist. It is common experience that men, who as individuals are responsible and reasonable, behave irresponsibly and unreasonably in a mob. It is not enough to say that this is due to the absence of individual responsibility. Mob action is marked by a savagery and violence which the mere surrender of responsibility cannot explain. Absence of responsibility may account for thoughtless and even foolish action, but not for the bestial frenzy which often characterizes men in a mob. The conception of the unconscious as unaltered by the passage of time offers a clue to the explanation of this phenomenon.

The function of art is the expression of the individual. Expression marks the passage from the unconscious to the conscious. Expression is, therefore, simultaneously communication, though the reverse is not necessarily true. This applies even in the case of the emotions of the individual. In expressing such emotions, the individual communicates them. Since no emotion can be expressed except through its actual experience, self-expression is in all cases self-socialisation. Expression of a feeling is, therefore, simultaneously the projection of the self into society. What was originally the emotion of the artist alone becomes through expression and communication the emotion of all those who share his experience. Expressed emotions are social emotions and as such civilised emotions.

In the case of unexpressed emotions—and they constitute what we mean by the term unconscious—the emotions are unexpressed and therefore unsocialised. Because they are unsocialised and private, they are not subject to any of the checks or counteracting influences imposed by society. Immune from public or private criticism, they change neither in nature nor intensity. Impervious to the passage of time, they possess the vitality and energy of primeval man. Precisely for that reason, they are characterized by a savagery which is absent in the case of all expressed and therefore socialised emotions. In a mob, surrender of individual responsibility is accompanied by a physical and psychical sympathy in which these repressed feelings are communicated without being expressed. Surrender of responsibility induces a state of mind which facilitiates such psycho-physical communication. Responsbility is based on self-consciousness. Surrender of responsbility results in the reduction of self-conciousness to mere sentience. The subconscious and recalcitrant elements of our nature, therefore, come to the fore when the individual loses himself in a mob.

This would also offer an explanation of the demand for novelty in art. What has been expressed is to that extent socialised and civilised. Its repetition cannot cause in us the excitement which the expression of a hitherto untamed feeling would arouse. It is the function of the artist to bring to consciousness the unexpressed instinctual aspects of our nature. The result is to socialise and civilise them, but in the process of doing so, he cannot but disturb the conventions that have already been established. It is too much to expect that wild instincts will be tamed without struggle or conflict. The process of expressing hitherto repressed feelings cannot but release forces from that deeper level of being which is hid in the subconscious regions of our personality. Art thus disturbs the even and orderly surface of the ordinary man's conception of reality. The artist is characterized as an eternal rebel. Our social self interpolates between desire and action the procrastinating factor of thought. The aim of art is to remove this buffer and bring to experience all the immediacy and vitality of free intuitions.

Plato, who was both an artist and a philosopher, but more of a philosopher than an artist, realised this. That is why he banished artists from his Republic. He wanted to introduce into his ideal State the order and precision of the abstract concept. His identification of the State with society only emphasised the tendency, but the fate of the artist was sealed the moment he sought to explain all experience in terms of Form and Appearance. The individual must conform to the social pattern and must not exhibit any features which in any way disturb the harmony and order of the ideal Form. What wonder then that he would banish from his Republic the artist who in his exaltation of the individual introduces an element of anarchy into the carefully arranged order of his picture? Plato condemned art because it is in general the expression of the unexpressed and undisciplined parts of our nature and as such must, he thought, be discouraged in the interests of rational ideals and virtues.

This, however, is precisely the reason why an analysis of the aesthetic activity has become so important today. The anarchic and unsocialised elements in human nature cannot be simply suppressed. Any attempt to do so leads to the breakdown of the very order for whose sake Plato wanted to banish art from his ideal State. The emotions which are not expressed do not die. They remain as mere brute feelings, neither mastered nor controlled. Concealed in the darkness of man's self-ignorance, they break upon him in orgies of passion that he can neither check nor understand

The failure to raise psycho-physical communication to conscious activity is attended by individual neuroses and social chaos. Both represent our failure to reconcile the claims of freedom and order. It is only such reconciliation that can assure the future of human progress. The function of art is to bring to consciousness the hitherto unconscious and instinctual intuitions and perceptions of man. In the process of expression, art weaves them into a fabric which can take its place in the organised life of conscious reality. Our fundamental problem today is the maintenance of the values of the individual in an ordered society. Art as the universalisation of the unique has successfully solved this problem in its own sphere and holds the promise of success if its technique is extended to other fields of experience.

A critique of art must, from the very nature of the case, be a critique of imagination. The function of imagination in suggesting a way out of our present crisis becomes clear if we consider one other point. Our empirical thinking is governed by the categories imposed by the social form into which we are born. Inductive generalisations based merely on the experience of the past are not, therefore, adequate to our needs. We must transcend the mentality of the age and envisage a social order whose dynamic equilibrium charges each of the social factors with its own intrinsic potency. This cannot be done so long as we conform to ways of social thinking which have evolved, as in present day society, out of the interplay of forces in which some are weighted as against the others. In science, progress is the result of the play of free imagination controlled by the requirements of coherence and logic. A method of rigid empiricism, if consistently pursued, would have left science where it found it.

Philosophy undertakes a criticism of the prevalent forms of society on the basis of the concept of a perfect and elastic social equilibrium. The accumulated experiences of the social forms of the past may contribute to the enunciation of such a concept. The concept must nonetheless be *a priori* and the result of an imaginative construction. Imagination must, therefore, penetrate beyond the encrustations of social form and discover the original ingredients out of which the social content is built. It can and must do more. It can even play with inconsistency and thus throw light on the consistent and persistent elements in experience. Reflection and analysis reveal the disastrous consequences which follow from maladjustment between social form and social content. Such maladjustments arise out of the intransigence of the individual. Imagination which fuses reason and will in the fields of beauty and morality offers a hope that the conflict can be resolved in the theoretical field as well. A critique of imagination is thus essential for a proper understanding of the central problem of our age. It is also the essential prologomena to any metaphysics that seeks to explain reality in all its manifold manifestations.

OUTLINES OF AN EMERGENT THEORY OF VALUES

by S. K. MAITRA

Born January 19th, 1887. Beneats Hindu University.

OUTLINES OF AN EMERGENT THEORY OF VALUES

I. INTRODUCTION : PERSONAL STATEMENT ON THE INFLUENCES
THAT SHAPED THE GROWTH OF MY OWN PHILOSOPHY.

I have hitherto never stated in a categorical manner my own general philosophical position, though I have expressed my views on isolated philosophical problems, such as the problem of negation or the problem of values. The reason for this, apart from a general disinclination to pose as a philosopher rather than as a student of philosophy, is that I have always thought that the philosopher's mind should grow with age and experience, and as I have so far never felt that I have had enough of these, I have thought it best to defer to a later date any statement of my general philosophical position. But now that I am in my sixty-second year, this reason is not so strong as it was before. Moreover, the feeling is also growing in my mind that if I were to wait for further experience before stating the result of my own reflection and contact with great minds, both living and dead, my gift to the world might remain undelivered.

I, therefore, welcome this invitation from the editor of this second edition of *Contemporary Indian Philosophy* to give a statement of my own philosophical views, the more so, as it gives me an opportunity of collecting my thoughts on the fundamentals of philosophy in a way in which I have hitherto not done. But before I make this statement, I must say something about my intellectual inheritance and the influences that were brought to bear upon me in the early part of my career.

I was born in Calcutta on the 19th January, 1887, in a Brahmin family. My father, who was in the educational line and served as Professor of English literature at the Dacca, Presidency and Ravenshaw Colleges, was very liberal in his views on social and religious matters, and I was brought up, therefore, in an atmosphere which was totally free from social and religious orthodoxy. He was also a great admirer of Rabindranath Tagore and used to recite to us his poems, so that I, along with my brothers and sisters, imbibed a love and admiration for Rabindranath's writings as part of the intellectural atmosphere in which we lived. This, as I shall show presently, was of great significance for the development of my philosophical thought.

My first philosophical *guru*—and I am not ashamed to own it— was the great German philosopher Hegel. In my college days the influence of Hegel was very great among the English educated classes in Bengal. My own professor was a pupil of Dr. Stephen, a great devotee of Hegel. But the greatest Hegelian in my college days was the late Dr. (later Sir) Brajendranath Seal, who was the leading figure in the philosophical world of Bengal in those days, about whom I shall speak presently. Among the leading figures in the political world in those days, I know definitely that the late Bipin Chandra Pal was a Hegelian. Be that as it may, in my college days I was a great admirer of Hegel, whom I regarded as the greatest philosopher that had ever lived. Curiously enough, Kant left me cold. In fact, I looked upon Kant as an incomplete Hegel and Hegel as the completed Kant. I simply devoured all books that I could get hold of on the Hegelian philosophy. The book, however, which impressed me most was Caird's great work, *The Critical Philosophy of Kant*. I have often wondered why it is that I have not written on Hegel, at least not written anything commensurate with my great admiration for him. The reason, as far as I can see, is that at the time when I had this devotion I had not thought of writing, and when I began to write, the old spell was gone. That is why, although I have written on Bergson and other philosophers, I have not so far written on Hegel, except a small comparative study of his philosophy and that of Sri Aurobindo.

The influence of Hegel, however, did not last very long. The first suspicion that all was not well with the Hegelian philosophy came to me when I began to study Greek philosophy. It was in connection with Heraclitus. Heraclitus was undoubtedly earlier than Parmenides. But the Hegelian logic required that Parmenides should come first and then Heraclitus. Here I discovered was an intentional distortion of an historical fact for the sake of a logical theory. Heraclitus also, I found, could not be treated as a mere philosopher of Becoming. Further doubts about the correctness of the Hegelian position arose when I made an intensive study of Śaṁkara's philosophy. I felt that it was taking too narrow a view of the Absolute to look upon It as being accessible only to Reason. At this time I made the acquaintance of the late Principal Ramendra Sundar Trivedi, of Ripon College, Calcutta, who began his career as a scientist, but later on passed from science to philosophy. It was probably his scientific training which was responsible for his giving the world a higher reality-status than what the orthodox Advaita Vedānta did. But para-doxically enough, it was his deep study of the Vedānta that enabled him to give it a reality very much higher than that given by science. For it was not the reality of a vast desert of arid facts, which is all that science gives it, but that of a fertile field irrigated by innumerable streams. Herein lay the genius of Ramendra Sundar Trivedi. He substituted for the *facts* of science the *values* which sustain life. And he could do it because of his grasping the spirit of Vedic literature. It was first in his introduc-tion to the Bengali translation of Aitereya Brāhmaṇa that he showed this standpoint from which he looked at the vast field of Vedic literature. He subsequently developed it in his books *Karma-Kathā* and *Yajña-Kathā*. He showed that the key-note of Vedic culture was its recognition of the world as a field for the realization of values and not as a wilderness of facts.

This made a profound impression upon my mind. I felt that here was a standpoint much more fruitful than that of Hegel. The Absolute of Hegel, in spite of his best efforts to give it con-creteness, was like an isolated mountain peak, grand to look at and grand to contemplate, but possessing no intimate contact with the world in which we live and move and have our being, whereas the Saccidānanda of Ramendra Sundar Trivedi was like a watershed from which arose innumerable springs fertilizing the whole valley which we call our world.

I soon discovered, therefore, that I was no longer the devotee of Hegel that at one time I was. Perhaps my admiration for Rabindranath and familiarity with his writings had also some-thing to do with this change. For if they had done nothing else, they at any rate had prepared my mind for the reception of standpoints other than that of logic or reason. But soon another event happened which accelerated the process of this change. This was my meeting the late Dr. (later Sir) Brajendranath

Seal at Darjeeling. I have already mentioned that in my college days Dr. Seal had the reputation of being one of the greatest Hegelians in India. But when I first made his acquaintance in 1913, his views had changed considerably, and from being an ardent Hegelian he had become a Vaishṇavite. But before I speak of his philosophical views, I must say something of the tremendous impression which his personality made not only upon my mind but upon the minds of all who came in contact with him.

Indeed very few people have impressed me so much as the late Dr. Seal by the breadth and depth of his scholarship, his phenomenal memory, his urbanity, and above all, by his wonderful conversational powers. His conversational powers were indeed so wonderful that I have always regretted that there was no Boswell to record his talks. One had only to mention a topic and words would flow from him like a torrent for hours. And what words! Many leading men of Bengal of the present and also of the past century—writers, teachers, statesmen, politicians—derived the inspiration of their lives from these talks. I have heard him talk in one of the common rooms of the Lowis Jubilee Sanitarium, Darjeeling, or in his room in his house in Rammohan Shah Lane, Calcutta, for hours, keeping his audience literally spell-bound.

He told me that he also, like myself, had been a great devotee of Hegel in his earlier years. On my asking him what made him discard Hegel, he said it was the weakness of the Hegelian logic. Weakness of the Hegelian logic! That struck me at that time as something very strange, for I had always considered his logic to be Hegel's strongest point. In fact, I regarded Hegel as a logical wizard. Once you got entangled in the meshes of his logic, there was no escape for you—that was what I had always thought. There were undoubtedly weak points in Hegel's philosophy, but his logic I thought was the strongest weapon in his armoury. So I was considerably surprised when Dr. Seal insisted that it was his logic which was the weak point in Hegel's philosophy. On my inquiring why he considered Hegel's logic to be defective, he replied it was because of its triadic rhythm scheme. "The triadic rhythm", he added "makes a fine musical appeal, no doubt, but ours is a hard world, too hard to be put under this musical scheme." When I asked him if he knew of any better logical scheme than Hegel's, he replied, "Certainly. Take, for instance, the Caturvyūhavāda of the Vaishṇavas. The tetradic scheme of this logic is infinitely superior to the triadic scheme of Hegel." I was of course not enamoured of the Caturvyūhavāda in spite of the brilliant exposition of it by Dr. Seal, but Dr. Seal's words led me to think that perhaps the defect of the Hegelian logic could be removed by substituting a polyadic synthesis for its triadic one. At first I thought that such a synthesis could be effected with the help of reason or logic. My paper on "The Logic of the Real", which I read before the Indian Philosophical Congress in 1926, was an attempt in this direction. Further reflection, however, convinced me that a polyadic synthesis with the help of reason alone was not possible. It could only be done in the region of values, where reason did not play the leading rôle. But more of this hereafter.

My faith in the supremacy of reason was further shaken by the philosophy of Bergson, to which I devoted several years of very close study. My introduction to Bergson's philosophy happened quite accidentally. I chanced to read a review of Bergson's book *L'Evolution Créatrice* in a philosophical journal. I was so much impressed by what the reviewer said about Bergson's philosophy that I immediately decided to get a copy of this book and read it. I had picked up sufficient French to be able to go through the original. The book made a tremendous impression upon me, and I decided to read the earlier works of Bergson also—his *Matière et Mémoire, Les Données Immédiates de la Conscience* and the famous *Introduction to Metaphysics*. My close study of Bergson revealed to me further weaknesses of the standpoint of reason. But I soon discovered that his philosophy had more a negative than a positive value, that it was very good as a corrective of rationalism, but had very little of a positive construction to offer. This was due to the vagueness of its theory of intuition. It never explained what it meant by intuition. In the same book *An Introduction to Metaphysics* there were two diametrically opposite views of intuition, one making it the cognition of what was most particular in the particular, and another identifying it with what Bergson called "an integral experience", that is to say, an integrated knowledge of the totality of things. His later work *The Two Sources of Morality and Religion* had not yet appeared. If that book had appeared, I could have got some positive ideas about what Bergson's intuition really stood for, for he has made it clear in that book that by intuition he means the mystic's intuition. But even this would not have removed all difficulty, firstly, because the mystic's intuition is a very vague term, for no two mystics have got the same intuition, and secondly, because the two types of mysticism he has described in that book, namely, the active and the contemplative, introduce further complications in the theory of intuition, for they seem to make intuition a practical faculty, whereas in the earlier works it was treated as a purely theoretical faculty.

Be that as it may, I found that Bergson's philosophy lacked the necessary positive character which a Weltanschauung that could claim to be a rival of Hegel's must possess. It was, moreover, as one-sided as the Hegelian philosophy, for if Hegel erred by making reason all in all, Bergson equally erred by ignoring reason and making intuition the sole principle of his philosophy. Truth lay midway between these extremes, that is to say, in giving both to reason and intuition their due place in the world-view.

That was the way in which the problem of philosophy presented itself to me. But I soon discovered that to put the problem of philosophy in this way was putting the cart before the horse. The type of consciousness should be determined by reference to the problem of reality and not *vice versa*. It was the bane of contemporary Western philosophy that the real problems of philosophy were lost sight of in the controversy relating to the claims of the rival human faculties to the knowledge of truth. The true problem of philosophy was: What was the nature of reality? Was it existence or was it consistency or was it something else? Bergson threw consistency to the winds, whereas, for Hegel, consistency expressed the true character of reality. The view to which I was gravitating was that there was one dimension of reality which was hidden from the gaze of both these philosophers or at least to which they had not paid sufficient attention,[1] which really

---

[1] I personally believe that it would be doing injustice to Hegel to say that he treated reality as mere consistency. What he was driving at was a view of reality as a concrete whole, which was rather the conception of it as value, though the method which he employed was the logical method of coherence or consistency. See my article *A New Approach to Bradley's Philosophy* (K. C. Bhattacharyya Commemoration Volume (in the press)), where I have shown how the standpoint of value is distinctly present in the philosophy of Hegel.

contained the essence of reality. That was the dimension of value. This was also, I felt, the central teaching of the Upanishads, which had insisted upon calling reality *satyasya satyam*, the truth of truth, thereby indicating that it was not to be identified with the surface reality of existence. So also, another explicit statement of the Upanishads, "naiṣā tarkeṇa matirāpaneyā," "this knowledge cannot be obtained by reason," expressed clearly that it could not be identified with consistency. What it was, was indicated in the systematised Vedānta by the word Saccidānanda. This conception of Saccidānanda ·was perhaps the grandest achievement of our ancient culture.

It was a condensed formula which indicated more tersely than anything else could, the essential nature of reality. It showed that there were three dimensions of reality, namely, *Sat* or the dimension of existence, *Cit* or the dimension of consciousness or reason, and *Ānanda* or the dimension of bliss or value. The whole standpoint which looked upon Reality as Saccidānanda might be called the standpoint of Reality as Value. All reality had these three dimensions. To regard reality as only Sat or existence was to take a one-sided view of it. So also, to look upon it as merely Cit was equally one-sided. Again to take it as mere Ānanda was to forget that it must be existent and must be brought into contact with our reason or logic.

The standpoint of Value emphasized the character of reality as Ānanda. But if this standpoint was to be a truly philosophical one, it must not ignore the other two dimensions of reality. In fact, both existence and reason must be treated as values, the one being the value of objectivity and the other the value of coherence.

With the help of this standpoint of reality as value, I discovered that the quarrel between intuition and reason could be easily settled. The different dimensions of reality required different types of consciousness to grasp them. For instance, perception might be looked upon as the kind of consciousness most at home in the detection of existence, reason in the detection of coherence, and intuition in the detection of value. But we must not make this division too watertight. For instance, perception alone was not competent to detect existence but required the help of both reason and intuition for this purpose. The bane of the controversy between reason and intuition was, in fact, the division of consciousness into watertight compartments.

I, therefore, realized that the most promising standpoint for philosophy was that of Value. Unfortunately, I did not get much help in my attempt to construct a philosophy of values from the avowed champions of this philosophy, such as Münsterberg, Rickert and Windelband or the psychological school of value-philosophy of Meinong and Ehrenfels. The main defects of the philosophy of values of Münsterberg, Rickert or Windelband were firstly, that it made a distinction between reality and value, thereby robbing value of its reality-status, and secondly, that it had no clear idea as to what the standpoint of value was, for one found in almost all forms of it that a sort of Hegelian Absolute occupied the ultimate position, value being relegated to a pen-ultimate one. The psychological school of value-philosophy did not attack the real problem at all. It no doubt discussed very ably the problem of valuation. It showed what factors entered into our valuation of things, but it did not touch the fringe of the problem of values, for value and valuation had no common ground. In thinking like this, I knew that I was deviating from the standpoint of Urban who, in his Book *Valuation: Its Nature and Laws*—a book which no student of the philosophy of values could ignore—very clearly stated (at page 385) that the question of validity or evaluation was bound up with the facts and con-ditions of valuation, and that the axiological problem arose directly out of the psychological, but I felt that it was essential for the philosophy of values to keep the standpoints of valuation and evaluation completely separate. My subsequent studies in the philosophy of values have confirmed me in this opinion, as will be seen in the sequel. Indeed, I hold more strongly now than ever before the view that there should be no mixing up of the philos-ophy of values with any psychological theory of valuation.

I cannot conclude this account of the development of my philosophical thought without reference to two great thinkers with whom I came in contact comparatively late in life, but who have more profoundly influenced the present direction of my thought than any of the thinkers I have already mentioned. As their influence is still continuing and as my present philosophical position is mainly the result of the direct influence of their thought upon me, as also of my reaction to their thought, I shall deal with them mainly in the second part of this paper. I refer, in the first place, to the great sage of Pondicherry, Sri Aurobindo, with whose philosophy I first became acquainted in the winter of 1939-40, when his great work *The Life Divine*, which had already appeared in the pages of the " Arya," was published in a revised and greatly enlarged form. I regret very much that I had not read this great work when it appeared in the pages of the "Arya," for if I had done so, it would have saved me a number of years of philosophical wanderings in search of a standpoint. It is difficult to estimate the influence of Sri Aurobindo's philosophy upon me, because it is still growing. Moreover his ideas have become so much a part and parcel of my own thought that it is impossible for me to say which thought is mine and which is Sri Aurobindo's.

The other philosopher who is responsible for shaping the present direction of my thought is Nikolai Hartmann, with whose great work *Ethics* I first became acquainted towards the end of the year 1933. I consider Hartmann's book the most important contribution to the philosophy of values that has appeared in this century. One result of my acquaintance with Hartmann's philosophy is that whatever leanings I may have had formerly towards psychological theories of value, have disappeared completely. But, paradoxical as it may seem, it is what I consider to be the weaknesses of Hartmann's philosophy that have had a greater effect upon the shaping of my own philosophy than what are undoubtedly his strong points.

II. OUTLINES OF AN EMERGENT THEORY OF VALUES

I. THE STANDPOINT OF PHILOSOPHY MUST BE THAT OF VALUE

I now come to my main task, which is to give as briefly as possible the salient points of my own philosophy. As I have already said, it is my firm conviction that the only correct standpoint for philosophy is that of Value. It is high time, I think, that philosophy changed its old moorings and turned definitely into a philosophy of values. I say "old" with reference to Western tradition. I might as well have said "new" with reference to our Indian tradition, for our tradition is to be value-centred, and not existence-centred as that of the West is.

Of half-hearted value philosophies we have quite a number in the West, but of thorough-going ones, we have very few. And that is why the West has so far not felt the impact of value-philosophy as it should have done. If it had felt this impact, the course of philosophy in the West would have been very different from what it has been. For one thing, there would have been less logic-chopping and a more sincere attempt to get into grips with reality.

It really seems strange to me why the West has tolerated so long the tyranny of the existential view. Due to sheer force of habit the West has readily accepted the equation Existence—Reality. Yet what a tragedy lies embedded in this equation, what a pitiful tale of philosophy's failure, what a lamentable lack of enterprise in philosophical speculation!

And here, I think, also is to be found the reason for the domination of science. For if philosophy cannot look beyond existence, it has practically already surrendered to science. It is in its predilection for values that the differentia of philosophy lies. Take away this predilection, and what remains of it to distinguish it from a train-bearer of science?

And yet the West has still a dim perception that it is those philosophers who had a point of view of their own different from the stereotyped existential standpoint, who were the masters in their field. That is why it still adores Plato, that is why it still pays homage to Descartes and Kant and to that philosophical wizard, Hegel. And that is why, coming to our own times, it has a secret reverence for Bergson, although it may outwardly be most loud in its condemnation of his doctrines.

I think the time has come for philosophy to declare itself unequivocally for the standpoint of value, leaving that of existence to science. This would settle once for all its age-long quarrel with science and would give it a viewpoint of its own from which to survey the world.

But it may be asked, what is the standpoint of value, and wherein does it differ from that of existence? There are two statements of two modern philosophers which I think can help us here. One is the statement of Bradley (*Vide Appearance and Reality*, 2nd revised edition, pp. 162-63): "If we take up anything considered real, no matter what it is, we find in it two aspects.

There are always two things we say about it; and, if we cannot say both, we have not got reality. There is a 'what' and a 'that', an existence and a content, and the two are inseparable. If we try to get the 'that' by itself, we do not get it, for either we have it qualified, or else we fail utterly. If we try to get the 'what' by itself, we find at once that it is not all. It points to something beyond, and cannot exist by itself and as a bare adjective. Neither of these aspects, if you isolate it, can be taken as real, or indeed in that case is itself any longer. They are distinguishable only and not divisible." Now this statement of Bradley's, as I have pointed out elsewhere,[1] puts him in the forefront of value-philosophers, for it shows how clearly he has grasped the truth that reality has two aspects—one an aspect of existence and the other an aspect of content. Indeed, it shows Bradley to be a much more consistent philosopher of values than many of the avowed champions of this philosophy, such as Münsterberg, Windelband, and Rickert, as these philosophers, by making a distinction between reality and value, have done great disservice to the philosophy of values. By treating the distinction between existence and value as a distinction within the framework of reality, Bradley has stated correctly the position of the philosophy of values. For what this philosophy teaches is that the nature of reality is not exhausted by saying that it is existence. Something more is needed to constitute reality. That which we call existence is only the superficial core of reality; underneath it, there is the deeper core, the core of values, without which reality is not complete. That is why in the Kenopanishad it is said, "nedaṁ yadidam upāsate" ("it is not that which people worship").

Curiously enough, Bradley is not aware that he is a philosopher of values, nor do his contemporaries regard him as such. This reminds one of the hero in Molière's play *Le Bourgeois Gentilhomme*, who is not aware that he is talking prose, although all his life he has been doing so.

Bradley's earlier statement in his *Principles of Logic:* "Judgment proper is the act which refers an ideal content (recognised as such) to a reality beyond the act", also draws pointed attention to the importance of the recognition of value, but it suffers from

---

[1] *Vide* my article *A New Approach to Bradley's Philosophy*, contributed to the K. C. Bhattacharyaya Commemoration Volume (in the press).

the serious defect that it identifies reality with existence. The contrast it makes is between value, described as ideal content, and reality. This contrast shows that primarily and essentially the ideal content or value is *not* reality. The matter is made worse by the explanations which he always thinks it necessary to offer whenever he has to show that it *also* is real. In fact, its place is always among the "also rans". Bradley's later statement in his *Appearance and Reality*, which I have discussed above, is a decided improvement upon his earlier one.

The other statement I have referred to, is that made by Windelband in his book *Präludien*, where he distinguishes between judgments of the type "The cloth is white" and those of the type "The cloth is good". The first type of judgment is what he calls an Urteil, and the second type, a Beurteilung. The first type of judgment is the judgment of fact or the existential judgment, and the second type, the judgment of value. There is a fundamental distinction between them, though they have the same grammatical form.[1] Philosophy according to him, is exclusively concerned with the second type of judgment.

This statement of Windelband's has the merit of rousing us from our "dogmatic slumber", from our complacent acceptance of the view that existence and logical categories are the only content of reality. That way it has done yeoman service. In fact, no one else has put so strongly the case for the recognition of the extra-logical and extra-existential content of reality as Windelband has done. There is, moreover, an advantage in defining a thing by the characteristics of its best type. He has, in fact, by drawing his examples of values from ethical values, followed the same method which the Gītā has done in the tenth chapter, namely, that of indicating each .type by the best of that type. For instance, when speaking of the Ādityas, the Gītā mentions only Viṣṇu, when talking of radiances, it mentions only the sun, and so forth, the idea being that the essential characteristics of each type are most prominent in the best of that type. Likewise Windelband, in speaking of values, mentions only the ethical values, where the characteristics of values are most strikingly evident.

But the very merits of Windelband's statement are also, from

[1] *Präludien*, 5th edition, Vol. I, p. 29.

the philosophical point of view, its most serious defects. For they leave us with an unreconciled opposition between value and existence, leading headlong to a dualistic philosophy, which has been the bane of most of the philosophies of values of the present day. From the point of view of philosophy, it is necessary to recognise that even existence is a value. In fact, value appears in three main distinguishable forms in human consciousness, as existence, as a logical category and as value proper or, to employ our old expressive Indian terminology, as Sat, Cit and Ānanda.

Comparing Bradley's statement with that of Windelband, we find that while the former suffers from being too wide, the latter suffers from the opposite defect, namely of being too narrow. Bradley's defect, as I have pointed out elsewhere,[1] is that he has not distinguished between different types of content but put them all under the same name "what." He has failed to point out, for instance, the essential distinction between logical categories and values proper. Windelband's defect is just the reverse. He has taken too narrow a view of values, for he has identified them with some special classes of values, completely ignoring all others.

2. THE SUBJECTIVE AND OBJECTIVE VIEWS OF VALUE

From both the statements we have examined above, emerges clearly the view that value is nothing but the content of reality. And if we accept the equation Reality—Value, as the philosophy of values asks us to do, we have to say that Reality is Content and nothing but Content.

But merely to say that reality is nothing but content does not solve all difficulties. The question arises: Is it the content as apprehended by an individual consciousness or is it independent of it? In other words, is value subjective or objective? This is the generalized form of the question with which ethics has to deal: Is rightness subjective or objective?

This is one of the main questions with which the philosophy of values has to deal, and we have valiant champions upholding the view that value is objective, and equally valiant ones upholding the other view. In fact, this is the battle royal in the philosophy of

[1] *A New Approach to Bradley's Philosophy,* already referred to.

values. There are also some who, like Urban, follow a middle path, declaring that value is both subjective and objective. They are the *mādhyamikas* in the philosophy of values. Space does not permit me to discuss the merits of this controversy. To my mind the champions of the subjective and objective views of value do not deal with the same problem. The subjectivists deal with what may be called the psychological problem of valuation, whereas the objectivists deal with the metaphysical problem of values. The two problems should be kept quite distinct. The psychological problem of discovering the mental factors that enter into an individual's valuation of things has no connection, except a very indirect one, as I shall presently explain, with the metaphysical problem of values. I am, therefore, unable to agree with Urban when he says (*Vide Valuation: Its Nature and Laws*, p. 385) "At numerous points we have seen specifically—what was stated in general terms at the beginning—that the question of validity or evaluation is in some way closely bound up with the facts and conditions of valuation. The problem of evaluation being the adjustment of the implicit claims to reality which our feelings of value with their presumptions, judgments, and assumptions make, it is necessary to interpret those claims in terms of their empirical origin and conditions." It is curious that Urban himself a few pages earlier expressed a different view, for he there showed that it was impossible to pass from the logical unity of an uncontestable value to the empirical unity of conscious ends and of felt values. To quote his own words: "That the logical presupposition of all valuation must be a single incontestable or unconditional value, follows from the logical unity of the subject of the value judgment, and from the claim of the value judgment to objectivity. But from the logical unity of the subject we cannot pass to the empirical unity of conscious ends and felt values; from the logical postulate of an unconditioned value we cannot pass to the unconditioned value of any concrete content. Such a transition is made impossible, we have seen, by the equivocal character of the actual feelings of obligation and of intrinsic appreciation or approval and disapproval in the limiting cases, and by the oscillation between the ideals of self-realisation and self-abnegation" (*Valuation: Its Nature and Laws*, P. 381). This passage makes it clear that there is a big gap between the actual "feelings of obligation and of intrinsic appreciation or approval or disapproval" and the logical pre-supposition of a single incontestable or unconditioned value. How can it be stated, therefore, that for the determination of the latter a consideration of the former is necessary?

Urban's attempt, therefore, to bridge the gulf between the subjective and objective views of value is not successful. A better attempt to connect the two views has been made by Nikolai Hartmann. He asserts that although values are objective, yet every human being has got the power to sense the values. The subjective consciousness of values, therefore, agrees with the objective character of the values. There is no distortion of the values in their passage through human consciousness. The method of discovering the values is, consequently, an empirical one. It consists in analysing the rich content of valuational experience already present in human consciousness. As he puts it, "In willing, resolving and acting, in disposition, in one's attitude towards life or in quiet participation, the principles are contained in rich abundance as the regulative factor. Accordingly, it must be possible to discern them there "(*Ethics*, Authorized English translation by Stanton Coit, Vol. I, p. 96).

But this, in my opinion, is taking too optimistic a view of human consciousness at its present level. And paradoxical as it may seem, such an optimistic view regarding present human consciousness is really a pessimistic view of human consciousness, judged from the standpoint of its potentialities. For it confines human consciousness to its present limited, incomplete state. For the possibility of human progress depends upon the progressive revelation of the values in human consciousness. If, therefore, it is maintained that the fullest revelation of the values has already taken place in human consciousness, then the very possibility of human progress is rendered impossible. Optimism of this kind, in fact, is disguised pessimism. It confines man for ever to his present condition and bars the way to his further advance. I hold, therefore, that values are objective and that at the present stage of human consciousness, it cannot be said that a complete revelation of the true nature of the values is possible through it, however exalted it may seem to be.

3. THE LADDER OF VALUES

The next important thing to remember about values is that they are a graded reality. They form a hierarchical organization: they are always distinguished as higher and lower. The terms "higher" and "lower" are also often applied to existents, but strictly speaking, they are only applicable to values. The distinctions among existents are horizontal, not vertical. In existence abstraction is made of all content, except the content of objectivity. When I say that a thing exists, I only refer to its objectivity, to its independence of my feeling or emotion or thought. But from the point of view of mere objectivity, it is not possible to say that one thing is higher than another. If, therefore, we speak of existents as higher or lower, it is because we treat them not as mere existents, but have surreptitiously clothed them with a content other than that of mere objectivity. It also proves how difficult it is for human beings to dwell on the plane of mere existence. We cannot but convert existence into value.

Be that as it may, values can be graded. There are higher values and lower values. The criterion of gradation is richness or fulness of content—what may be called *bhaga* in our expressive Indian terminology. The description of God as *Bhagavān* is a description of Him from the point of view of value. It draws our attention immediately to the truth that the highest reality is the highest value.[1] The criterion of richness of content is an axiological and not a logical criterion. It cannot be identified with the logical criterion of consistency, to which all logical criteria are reducible. What is more consistent need not be more full of *bhaga*, though consistency is undoubtedly one of the *bhagas* that go to make up the character of the Ultimate Reality as Bhagavān.

One of the best gradations of value is what we find in the Kaṭhopanishad. I have dealt with it in my book *The Spirit of Indian Philosophy*. But for the benefit of those who have not read that book, I give below a summary of what I have said there. A gradation of values is given in Kaṭh 1.3.10-11: "Higher than the senses are the objects of sense. Higher than the objects of sense is the mind (manas). And higher than the mind is the

[1] See Śrīmadbhāgavata, 1. 2. 11, where Brahman, the Ultimate Reality, is called Bhagavān ("brahmeti paramātmeti bhagāvaniti śabdyate").

intellect (buddhi). Higher than the intellect is the Great Self (Mahat Ātman). Higher than the Great Self is the Unmanifest. Higher than the Unmanifest is the Puruṣa. Higher than the Puruṣa there is nothing at all." I have shown in my book that this Puruṣa, which is the top value in the Kaṭhopanishad's scale of values, is nothing else than the Puruṣottama of the Bhagavadgītā. Now nobody can deny that the Puruṣottama of the Gītā is one of the richest and most concrete conceptions of God that exist, in any literature. The Puruṣa of the Kaṭhopanishad, therefore, is a Concrete Reality, rich in content. It is, in fact, in the best and truest sense of the term, a Person. There are two other gradations of values in the Kaṭhopanishad, and they also point to the same thing, namely, that as we rise in the scale of values, there is an increase in content, until we reach the highest value, which is the richest in content.

This is perhaps the proper place for discussing the question whether there is only one value or there is a plurality of values. This question from the axiological point of view is not so important as it is from the point of view of logic. From the logical point of view there cannot really be any room for two principles, if they are to be treated as full-fledged principles, that is, as universal truths. The second principle must be subordinated to the first. But from the axiological point of view, plurality and unity can very well go together. In fact, axiologically the relation between the highest value and the other values is somewhat similar to that between the leader and his followers. The position of the leader does not require that the followers should be reduced to mere ciphers. So also the affirmation of a highest value does not require that the lower values should be reduced to mere shadows. On the contrary, the highest value can only function as such if it is surrounded by a plurality of lower values. In the hierarchical organization of values, therefore, there must be values of all ranks, topped by a Supreme Value, somewhat in the manner of the Roman Catholic Church, where there is a hierarchy of an ecclesiastical order, on the top of which is the Pope. It will not do, therefore, to deny the existence of the lower values in our enthusiasm for the Supreme Value. Nor, of course, should we whittle down the importance of the recognition of a Supreme Value, as Hartmann has done. To deny the Supreme Value means in fact the denial of all values. No value can function without the direction of the Supreme Value. The Supreme Value is the goal towards which all the other values are moving; it is the mainspring of the whole process of evolution. That the world is evolving means nothing else than that it is moving nearer and nearer to the Supreme Value.

But this is not all. The Supreme Value is not only responsible for the evolution of the world, but also for its very existence. For, as I shall show presently, the values which make the world what it is today are themselves emergents of the Supreme Value. Over and above the axiological relationship between the Supreme Value and the lower values which I have discussed above, there is also the ontological relationship between them, according to which the former is the source of the existence of the latter. Hartmann thinks that the higher values are ontologically dependent upon the lower values, though they are axiologically independent of them. Thus he says (*Ethics*, Vol. II, p. 25, English translation by Stanton Coit), "A relation, therefore, of dependence holds between the wider and narrower spheres of values. It is unequivocal, irreversible dependence of the higher upon the lower. But the dependence is purely material, not axiological. The lower is the stuff upon which the higher works; it is merely the *sine qua non* of the latter. In every other sense the higher is independent of it; its specific quality, moral goodness, is something new, something which was not represented in the lower value towards which it stands in complete indifference." He thinks that if the lower values were ontologically dependent upon the higher, they would lose all their independence, and would be completely determined by the latter, whereas the view which he has put forward, namely, the ontological dependence of the higher values upon the lower, maintains the axiological independence of the higher values upon the lower, maintains the axiological independence of the higher values and at the same time gives the lower ontological independence. But, as I have shown elsewhere,[1] this view is extremely derogatory to the higher values, for it gives the higher values authority but no power. And authority without power is absolutely useless. In fact, this

[1] *A Critical Estimate of N. Hartmann's Philosophy of Values* ("The Vedānta Kesari," June 1946).

constitutes one of the main weaknesses of Hartmann's philosophy of values. There are other consequences of this view, which I shall presently examine.

4. VALUES AND THEIR REALIZATION

I now come to the problem of the realization of values. Perhaps of all the problems connected with values, this is the one which causes most headache to the value-philosopher. This is because there is a good deal of ambiguity about the expression "realization of values." Bradley has discussed this very fully in connection with the term "self-realization" in his *Ethical Studies*. Rashdall also in his *Theory of Good and Evil* has discussed it in connection with the ambiguity of the word "self-realization", but his discussion does not help us much, because the ambiguity which he points out appertains mainly to the word "self" and not to the word "realization", whereas, from the point of view of the philosophy of values, the main difficulty centres round the word "realization". As Bradley has pointed out in connection with self-realization, there is on the face of it a contradiction in the very idea of the realization of values. How can we speak of the realization of that which is eternally realized? Usually the value-philosopher avoids this difficulty by saying that values are not real in themselves but become real when through some agency they are "realized." This is, in fact, the view which Hartmann has elaborated. According to Hartmann, values exist in an ideal world, and are realized only through human agency. They may remain unrealized for ages; they may even never get a chance of being realized, unless some human being takes it into his head to realize them. They are, therefore, absolutely at the mercy of human beings for their realization. Man, therefore, has a great responsiblity. It is up to him either to realize the values or not to realize them. Herein lies the possibility of his moral life. He is good or bad, according as he realizes or does not realize the values which he senses.

Now this theory, as I have pointed out elsewhere, bristles with difficulties. The first and most crucial difficulty concerns its separation of an ideal world from the real world and its placing values in the ideal world. The ideal world, if it has to have any meaning, must somehow be real. To call values ideal or irreal (Rickert) is, therefore, metaphysically unsound. It is, moreover, derogatory to the position of values. In fact, it means giving up the standpoint of the philosophy of values, for that standpoint must maintain the supremacy of values. This is the fundamental weakness of the philosophies of Münsterberg, Rickert and Windelband, and Hartmann also shares it with them. Hartmann's whole theory of values is, in fact, based upon the ontological weakness of values. I have already examined this weakness in another connection, and have shown how disastrous it is for a philosophy of values. But that weakness is nothing compared with this weakness that I am talking of, this absolute helplessness of the values and their lying completely at the mercy of man for the chance of getting admission to the world of reality. Can we conceive of a greater tragedy than this, of innumerable values knocking at the door of man and being refused admission to his world? And there is no guarantee that this tragedy will ever end. Rather, if we are to accept Hartmann's theory of human freedom, so long as man enjoys freedom— and man is not man if he is not free—this tragedy can never end. It is the prerogative of man, as it is also his freedom, to allow this tragedy to continue. End this tragedy, and from Hartmann's point of view, you end man.

What a view is this of values, as well as of man! Has value-philosophy nothing better to offer? Can there be a worse condemnation of the philosophy of values than this? If, therefore, the philosophy of values is to be a presentable philosophy, it must reject *in toto* this theory of the ontological weakness of values. And if it does this, what havoc must it not make of these paltry views of man's freedom, as well as of his relation to values! I ask in all seriousness these so-called champions of human freedom: Does freedom mean persistence in evil? Does it consist in being shut out for ever from light? Is it the noblest conception of man to think that he will for ever remain the fragile, fallible creature that he is today? Has he really no higher destiny than this? And as for values, if they have supplied the great ideals which have inspired mankind through the ages and have made it possible for man to achieve whatever he has done in the realm of art, science, religion and philosophy, can they be treated as beggars shivering in the cold wind and knocking at his door for favour of being admitted to his parlour? And if we are to give a negative answer to this question, must we not say that values, by the mere fact that they are values, have got the power of realizing themselves? In fact, realization is a technical term which is employed to indicate the inherent power of all values to manifest themselves in what we call our world, but which is really the world of these values. Yes, values must possess this inherent power or they are not values at all. Better far to deny all values and worship at the altar of facts than accept values and treat them as beggars living upon human charity.

5. EMERGENT THEORY OF VALUES: VALUES AS AVATĀRAS

Values, therefore, do not require any external agency to realize themselves, but the power to make themselves manifest in the world is inherent in them. In fact, we should not talk of the realization of values, but rather of their emergence. Values emerge, and their emergence makes the world what it is. Different values have emerged at different times and have given their distinctive note to the evolution of the world. At every crucial stage in the evolution of the world, particular values have emerged, and it is this which is at the root of the cosmic, and consequently also of the human evolution. As I have stated elsewhere,[1] "What happens when we speak of the realization of values is that values *descend* into the world. The world, in fact, has come into being and has attained its present status on account of such descent. From the point of view of values there is no realization, there is only descent. But from *our* point of view and from the point of view of the world, there is realization. That is to say, we become more and more real, we come nearer and nearer to reality, as there is further and further descent of the values. Realization, therefore, means for us *ascent*, ascent to higher and higher grades of reality, and for the values it means *descent*, descent of more and more of themselves into us and into the world."

Values, therefore, are Avatāras, Avatāras of the Supreme Value or Saccidānanda. They are the successive emergents of the

---

[1] *Sri Aurobindo and Nikolai Hartmann* (Sri Aurobindo Mandir Annual, 1945).

Supreme Value, the different forms which its descent has assumed. So far the chief emergents have been Matter, Life, Mind and Soul, and, these, therefore, are the principal values which are present in the world. But other and higher values are yet to emerge. In fact, evolution means nothing else than the emergence of higher and higher values. The process will not stop until the Supreme Value or Saccidānanda has emerged.

The above is a brief outline of what I may call the Emergent Theory of Values. The most important advocate of this theory, to my mind, is Sri Aurobindo, who in his great work, *The Life Divine*, has laid the foundations of this theory. A brief summary of his theory I have given in my articles, *Sri Aurobindo and Nikolai Hartmann* and *Sri Aurobindo and Hegel* which appeared respectively in the Sri Aurobindo Mandir Annuals for 1945 and 1946. Among modern Western philosophers, S. Alexander is the most important champion of this theory. But Bradley also, as I have shown in my article, *Sri Aurobindo and Hegel*, already referred to, may be counted among its champions. The roots of this theory, however, so far as the West is concerned, go back to Plotinus. In our country, the doctrine of Avatāra, as given in the Bhagavadgītā, is the foundation of all emergent theories of values. In fact, the sketch of this theory which I have given above, is nothing but a generalized form of the Gītā's doctrine of Avatāra.

This theory, as its name, Emergent Theory indicates, is opposed to all theories of evolution based on the principle of Continuity. It is a direct challenge to that principle, the last great champion of which was Hegel. The philosophy of values is essentially a philosophy of emergence, as perennial philosophy in the West, of which the last great representative was Hegel, is the philosophy of continuity. The philosophy of values, in fact, has to fight on two fronts. On the one hand, it has to fight with the champions of the Existence Theory of Reality. This fight is, of course, its main fight; it is a fight for its very existence. On the other, it has to conduct a campaign against the advocates of the theory of continuity. But its two opponents are practically the same, for the Existence Theory of Reality and the Theory of Continuous Evolution are both essential parts of perennial philosophy.

One thing more I should like to say here. There is too much loose talk at present about the functions of reason and intuition.

For the same kind of knowledge these two faculties are sometimes employed. For instance, Bradley employs both reason and intuition to achieve the same thing, namely, consistency or coherence. For the earlier stages of this task he employs reason, and for the later stages, intuition. There is much greater justification for Bergson's demanding the employment of intuition for detecting those features of reality which reason is constitutionally incapable of detecting. I think it is high time that there was a gentleman's agreement among philosophers about the functions of reason, intuition and other faculties. The present chaos in this matter is intolerable.

6. VALUES AND DISVALUES

I now come to the last part of my task, which, in some respects, is perhaps the most important, because here we have an acid test for the validity of any theory of values. I refer to the discussion of the problem of disvalues. There are two rocks on which most theories of values have suffered shipwreck. One is the problem of the relation between existence and value, which we have already discussed, and the other is the problem of disvalues. The latter problem, stated briefly, is this: Do disvalues form a separate class by the side of values, or are they still to be regarded as values in spite of their apparent antithetical character? To accept a dualism of values and disvalues, as Hartmann has done, is, I think, tantamount to an admission of the failure of the philosophy of values to give us an acceptable philosophy. It will not do also to deny, as some value-philosophers have done, the existence of disvalues. Disvalues in the form of imperfection, suffering and evil undoubtedly exist. The only question is whether they are to be treated as separate realities or as being ultimately reducible to values of some kind.

As I have stated elsewhere[1] I dissent from the view which looks upon disvalues as forming a separate class by themselves. We must remember, in the first place, that the disvalue has a meaning only in the plane of values. It is a value which runs counter to, or is opposed to, the positive or constructive value. But it is never in a position to suppress the corresponding

[1] *Ibid.*

value. On the contrary, values have a coercive power over disvalues. If they are not in a position to force the disvalues into submission, it is due to their present ontological weakness, which is itself nothing else than a reminder that our present stage of evolution is a comparatively low one. At the stage of evolution which we have reached, there may be disvalues which we are not in a position to overcome, but this does not mean that they will never be overcome or that human beings are constitutionally incapable of overcoming them. In fact, human evolution means increasing power to overcome the disvalues.

It has also to be remembered that many of these disvalues, like superfluous organs of the body, are relics of an earlier stage of evolution when they were of considerable value. Thus, selfish instincts in man are reminders of a primitive stage of society, when for the protection of human life they were of great value. In the present stage of human society they have become disvalues, because individuals no longer require to protect their own lives by their own unaided efforts and because it is more necessary for the advancement of the individual's own interests that he should develop social instincts. There is, therefore, at present a conflict between these instincts and social duties, and consequently, they are treated as disvalues. But at a higher stage of human evolution. with a further transformation of these instincts, this conflict will disappear, and these same instincts which, in their present form, cause a disruption of our social life and are consequently treated as disvalues, will, in their transformed condition, cease to be disvalues. Even at the present stage of our evolution, these instincts have undergone some transformation—they no longer are in that crude form in which they appeared in a more primitive state of human society—but the transformation is not sufficiently great to enable them to shed their opposition to the demands of social life, and therefore, they are still treated as disvalues.

But the most important reason for the presence of disvalues is that at the stage of evolution which we have reached, the values that have emerged so far are not complete and perfect values, but there is an admixture of disvalues in them. Herbert Spencer, therefore, is right when he says that it is only in a perfect society that we can have absolute rightness. In our present state all that we can hope to attain is relative rightness. Disvalues owe their existence to the fact that none of the values at present in vogue can be regarded as complete, and that, consequently, part of their meaning has got to be expressed through disvalues. That is why the poet said, "Our sweetest songs are those that tell of saddest thought." Disvalues, therefore, are part of the process by which the meaning of our incomplete values comes into expression. They are necessary elements of our present stage of evolution. What we call pleasure, for instance, is not pure bliss. Nor is pain the complete absence of it. The value of bliss expresses itself, therefore, through both pleasure and pain. As Sri Aurobindo says (*Vide The Life Divine*, Vol. I, p. 163) "... pain and pleasure themselves are currents, one imperfect, the other perverse, but still currents of the delight of existence . . . It is because we do not seek the essence of the thing in its contact with us, but look only to the manner in which it effects our desires and fears, our cravings and shrinkings that grief and pain, imperfect and transient pleasure or indifference, that is to say, blank inability to seize the essence, are the forms taken by the Rasa." It has also to be remembered that the chief value which we at present possess, namely, mind, itself creates disvalues. As our ancient sages said, mind is the cause of both man's emancipation and bondage ("*mana eva manuṣyāṇām kāraṇam bandhamokṣayoḥ*"). Human progress owes no doubt a great deal to mind, but it cannot be denied that a great part of the evil from which we are suffering at present is also directly attributable to it. The development of science is a case in point. It is undoubtedly one of the greatest achievements of mind. But who can deny that it is also responsible for a number of evils—and some of them of the most disastrous kind—which are such a dark feature of our present civilization? There are certain fundamental limitations from which mind suffers. By its very nature it is a consciousness which cuts up and breaks asunder the forms of things from the indivisible whole in which alone they can really exist. Not only that, but it treats the parts as if they could exist independently. Now this is the origin of egoism, which is the root cause of all evil. Egoism does not arise from the mere separation of the part from the whole. But it makes its appearance when the part is treated as if it were the whole. But this is precisely what mind does. It is not content merely with breaking the unity of the whole by separating the parts from it, but it invests the parts with a self-sufficiency which gives them the appearance of wholes. Our present scientific age has produced one kind of egoism, which we may call the egoism of science. It consists in the belief that science is all in all, that it gives a body of truths which is self-sufficient, that is, which does not require the help of any other body of truths for its completeness. It is this egoism of science, and not its phenomenal progress, which is responsible for the ills which we attribute to science.

It follows as a direct corollary that some values which we very highly esteem under our present mental régime will have to be treated as disvalues when we shall pass out of the domain of mind into that of still higher values. This is particularly true of our ethical values. Great as the importance of these values is in our present mind-dominated civilization, they cannot be looked upon as the highest values, and, therefore, they will have to give place to still higher ones. That is to say, at a higher stage of human evolution they will have to be looked upon as disvalues. That is why Śrīmadbhāgavata says (11.19.45) that the discrimination of right and wrong is itself wrong and we have to rise to a condition above such discrimination ("guṇadoṣadṛśirdoṣo guṇastūbhayavarjitah"). This is what some philosophers point out when they say that the highest value is "beyond good and evil." Sri Aurobindo also has stressed this point. Thus he says (The Life Divine, Vol. I, p.14 6), ". . . ethics is a stage in evolution. That which is common to all stages is the urge of Sachchidānanda towards self-expression. This urge is at first non-ethical, then infra-ethical in the animal, then in the intelligent animal even anti-ethical for it permits us to approve hurt done to others which we disapprove when done to ourselves. In this respect man even now is only half-ethical. And just as all below us is infra-ethical, so there may be that above us whither we shall eventually arrive, which is supra-ethical, has no need of ethics." Of this supra-ethical condition we can only have faint glimmerings, we cannot have any knowledge, for to have a knowledge of it means that we have already reached it. Its nature, therefore, for us is an unfathomable mystery. That is why our Vedic sages said, "yo 'asyādhyakṣah parame vyoman so'nga veda yadi vā na veda" ("he who is the author of it in the highest heaven, he knows it or even he does not know it"). But although it is a mystery to us now, we have the surest guarantee that a time will come when it will cease to be a mystery to us, because we ourselves shall reach that condition.

PRINCIPAL PUBLICATIONS

The Neo-Romantic Movement in Contemporary Philosophy. The Book Company, Ltd., Calcutta, 1922.

The Social Organization in North-East India in Buddha's Time (Being an English Translation of Richard Fick's book *Die Soziale Gliederung im Nordöstlicher Indien zu Buddhas Zeit*). The Calcutta University, 1920.

Philosophical Currents of the Present Day (Being an English Translation of Dr. Ludwig Stein's book *Die Philosophischen Strömungen der Gegenwart*). The Calcutta University, 1918-24.

An Introduction to the Philosophy of Sri Aurobindo. First Edition, 1941: The Culture Publishers, Calcutta ; Second Edition, 1945: The Benares Hindu University.

Studies in Sri Aurobindo's Philosophy. The Benares Hindu University, 1945.

The Spirit of Indian Philosophy. Published by the Author, 1947.

Rabindranath (jointly with three others). The Book Exchange, Calcutta, 1944.

FREEDOM THROUGH KNOWLEDGE

by G. R. MALKANI

Born June 4th, 1892; Director of the Indian Institute of
Philosophy, Amalner, Bombay Presidency.

FREEDOM THROUGH KNOWLEDGE

I. FREEDOM THE GOAL OF ALL RELIGION

The goal of religion may be said to be freedom in some sense or other. The religious consciousness arises as a response to a higher reality. But what necessitates it is the feeling of our finitude, and the need to escape from it and all the ills of life that are consequent upon it. We are all pessimists in our secret and unconscious thinking to that extent. Without it, we should not need a religion; and with it, we cannot be altogether immune from religious faith. We may or may not all demand more life or abundant life, but we all do demand a life that is harmonious and free from ills of different sorts. This objective may be sought to be realised in different ways. Different religions have different answers to give. But the goal is always the same. All religions are one in this. They may differ widely in belief and practice. But they do not differ widely in the true *summum bonum* of life. Without disparaging any religion, for all religions are ways to the same goal suited to the historical and the cultural environment of each particular community, we contend that there is a pre-eminent way for realising the *summum bonum*. It is not dependent upon any historical circumstance. It may truely be called the ancient religion, or the religion of the Eternal Man. This is the way of knowledge, or the way of Truth. If philosophy is understood as the search for Truth or the highest form of Wisdom, then philosophy serves a religious purpose, and becomes in fact the best form of religion.

II. IS PHILOSOPHY THE PRODUCT OF A PURELY THEORETICAL INTEREST ?

We are accustomed to think that philosophical speculation arises out of a purely intellectual interest or out of intellectual curiosity. It arises out of the need for the co-ordination of the empirical sciences, or a review and an assessment of their achievements in terms of objective truth. Or again, it arises out of the intellectual demand for unity, or for the harmonisation of conflicting beliefs, scientific and religious. In other words, the justification for philosophical speculation is purely intellectual or theoretical. We want to know the truth for its own sake; and every level of scientific knowledge imposes upon us the obligation to construct a world-view in conformity with it.

This is, however, not entirely true. Our theoretical interest is always inspired by some purpose or some value. We seek scientific knowledge not for its own sake (for it is very imperfect as a species of knowledge), but for its practical bearing on the physical and biological needs of life. It is only in the case of philosophy that we fail to see this connection between the pursuit of truth and life. But if philosophy represents the highest form of the theoretical interest, then it could only be inspired by the highest value. Otherwise, it is not a genuine theoretical interest at all. It is only a form of intellectual dilettantism or sophism. We contend that philosophical thinking has for its objective the realisation of the highest value, which is the goal of all religions. Philosophy thus coincides with religion. We *want* to be free. We seek philosophical knowledge *in order* to be free. The motto of all real philosophy should be: Truth alone can make us free.

III. IS THERE SUCH A THING AS PHILOSOPHICAL KNOWLEDGE?

It may now be said that what goes by the name of philosophical knowledge is not real knowledge at all. There is no such thing as purely rational knowledge. All our actual knowledge is confined to empirical Science, which seeks to contact reality through known or recognised forms of knowledge and in a truly rational way. There is no other way open to reason, unless we confuse certain purely subjective structures of thought or conceptual schemes with rational knowledge. To speculate or to build up these structures, which would seem to explain certain facts of experience or to interpret them, is not to know. Such speculation is free in character, and it has no finality. Alternative schemes of concepts would appear to be equally true, or perhaps equally false. They have not even the merit of scientific hypotheses, which can be tested by the facts of sensible experience. They are never meant to be verified. They are simply taken to be true, perhaps self-evidently true. But they are nothing of the sort.

They are not based on any *objective* intuition of reality, such as the scientist can claim. They are based upon a subjective intuition, which the philosophers exalt with the name of "rational insight" or "rational intuition." Real knowledge ought to be a species of direct awareness. There is no such direct awareness to which the cogitations of the philosopher may be said to lead us. Philosophical knowledge is not knowledge at all. It is verbal knowledge at the best, relating to the use of certain words.

IV. THE DEMAND FOR A HIGHER KIND OF KNOWLEDGE

We now contend that real philosophical knowledge is possible. In fact, it is the only knowledge worth the name. Knowledge at the common-sense level, or at the level of science which is merely its extension, is only an *appearance of knowledge*. It is through and through mediated. It can be erroneous. It is always dubitable. The element of subjective interpretation in it cannot be distinguished, in a fool-proof manner, from the element of objective intuition. This gives rise to, and necesssitates, philosophical reflection. How can a piece of knowledge, which is understood to be the awareness of reality as such, be dubitable? Dubiety means subjectivity, which is inimical to knowledge. Philosophical reflection is the method of tackling the doubt with a view to resolving it, and thereby making knowledge true to itself. Indubitable knowledge is the only real knowledge. This knowledge is evidently not a gift of nature to us. It can only be the result of a mental clean-up. Such is the undertaking of philosophical reflection. It proceeds on the basis of our original intuitions of reality. There is no demand for a fresh and supernormal intuition which we do not at present possess. There is demand only for analysis, criticism and explication.

Reason of itself is not a form of intuition. There can be no direct awareness of reality on the part of reason. Reason only mediates. It interposes the idea between reality and the knowledge of reality. Reason can be intuitive only on one condition: "If reality is not unintelligent and material, if it is by its very nature intelligent, immediate and intuitive, and if reason can find its way to this reality through the negation of all the subjective and ideal elements with which this reality is loaded at the empirical level, reason can be the instrument of a direct awareness of this reality." Reason in this case brings no revealing character *to* reality. Reality is self-revealing. The true function of reason as a method of knowledge in philosophy would thus appear to be negative. It is to dissipate doubt and error, and to let reality to speak for itself and to reveal itself. Where reality is dead and inert and requires the light of reason, in the form of concepts and categories, to reveal it, we can only have insoluble, and therefore endless, problems of thought. Concepts and categories interfere with reality. They give us a purely subjective picture of it, manufactured in the mind. Thought must undo this mischief. Truth is essentially objective. The subject should make no contribution to it in knowing it. This is only possible when truth is self-revealing and self-evident to thought. Such is the presupposition of all philosophical reflection upon knowledge.

V. THE PHILOSOPHICAL IMPORTANCE OF DOUBT AND ERROR

We become philosophically reflective, the moment we recognise the subjectivity of our knowledge leading to doubt and error. The tendency to doubt has been considered a drawback in the intellectual make-up of philosophers. Philosophers are supposed to have no sense for the practical; and so they doubt and doubt endlessly. But the doubt of philosophers is theoretically inevitable. It is inspired by reason itself. It is never aimless and endless. It is pursued systematically with a view to eliminating it completely. If there is any rational scope for doubt, doubt ought to be resurrected. The difference between the ordinary man and the philosopher is that while the former is too easily satisfied, the latter is not. The philosopher accepts only one kind of truth, and that is truth which is indubitable and absolutely certain. Certainty for him is not merely a state of the mind; for the uncritical person has it most often. It is rational certainty relating to objective truth. We must be face to face with truth which is self-evidently true.

But doubt is not the only thing that gives us thought. There is also error. We suffer from illusions. It has been argued that the fact of illusion is philosophically unimportant. Science has an explanation for every illusion. If we know the appropriate laws of nature, we should cease to make a problem about an illusory appearance. A straight stick appears bent when half immersed in water, the sun and the moon look smaller than what they are, the waves of heat-radiation in a desert look like water, etc. All these are familiar instances, and all these can be completely explained on scientific grounds. But taking into account all that science has to say by way of explanation, *the fact still remains that objective reality is not as we perceive it to be.* What is not really there is perceived by us to be there, and what does not exist is perceived by us to exist. Science can give no explanation for this *error*. If science could show that what we call "illusory appearance" is really there, and that we perceive it as it is there, that would indeed be an explanation. But science does not show this. It does not show that the stick which we perceive as bent is really bent, or that there *is* a bent appearance in reality itself irrespective of our perception. What it shows is that our perception *conditions* the appearance, which is therefore an appearance *to us* only, and not a thing *in itself* which is the goal of knowledge. Science gives no explanation why a subjective appearance should be taken by us to be objective and real. There is evidently an error of judgement here which has vitiated our perception. We have, in other words, *erroneous perception*. We perceive what is not really there. We perceive water where there is no water. This water is accordingly a creation of our perception only, taken to be objectively real. But if our perception can thus play pranks with reality, where should we draw the limit? There is no theoretical limit. We have no *unconditioned* perception which contacts reality directly, and knows it as it really is, without *judging*. All perception is mediated by factors which make their varying contribution in the final product, which we call the percept. There is no incorruptible set of conditions that do not enter as factors in the perceived thing, and maintain completely their outsidedness and neutrality with regard to it.

What alone explains an illusory appearance is the error of perception. This error we can never explain. It is something irrational. We can never give any *reason* why we perceive erroneously. Where a reason could be given, perception becomes part of a real situation. We should have to admit that we *could not but perceive so.* Such perception, necessitated by a real situation, is never erroneous. What I am *obliged* to perceive, I rightly perceive. I have no freedom. Error is an indication of our freedom. I create what is really not. I perceive as existing what I should not so perceive. Correction is thus possible. It is of the very essence of error. If there is no awakened consciousness of truth, there is really no error. But if I am obliged to perceive something for *all rational* purposes, there can be no awakening from it, no consciousness of a cancelled illusion. Error involves an irrational jump from the given to the not given. It can be exposed, but never explained. As a matter of fact, it offers no problem of explanation to thought. It is in a way self-explained, as what should not be, but is. We become wiser through error, but we can never become wise over it or succeed in explaining it.

VI. THE DISTINCTION OF APPEARANCE AND REALITY

Once we admit the subjectivity of our present knowledge, the distinction of appearance and reality becomes inevitable. Appearance is something *to us* only. Reality is, and ought to be, *in itself.* The whole problem of knowledge takes the form, can we know something that really *is*, and not merely something *to us*? Can we know without the subjectivity of knowledge? This can only be the quality of self-evident truth. Self-evident truth is recognised by us as a truth in itself, that we can reject only at the peril of our rationality. If reality can assume the form of such a truth, then reality is truly known, and without subjectivity. Truth and reality become convertible terms. Such reality required no other *expression or appearance* in order to be known. It is known in itself and as it is.

It is different with the appearance. Since the appearance is something to us only, it has no place in reality. It is merely a subjective creation, falsely identified by us with reality. Accordingly, every appearance is necessarily untrue and unreal. There is no such thing as "a real appearance," which is a contradiction in terms. Every appearance is just an appearance, and nothing more. It *appears*, but never *is*. Its stuff is the stuff of known-ness, not the stuff of being. If we take away knowledge, known-ness collapses. But if we take away knowledge, being does not collapse.

An appearance, however, must be the appearance of something. Reality alone can appear, as we say. Accordingly, an
appearance implies something that lies behind it and supports it,
but which itself does not appear. It implies reality. Reality, on
the other hand, does not imply appearance. It does not require
anything beside itself in order to be. Its existence is truly unrelated and unconditioned. The existence of the appearance is
radically different. It is pseudo-existence only. The relation to
reality is fundamental to it and constitutive of it. It is the
relation of false identity. This relation is not a real relation,
which can only subsist between two real and independent
entities. The appearance is not such an entity. It is dependent
upon the relation. Thus, *while reality in itself is unrelated, a
relation has been introduced from outside in order to make appearance
possible*. The relation of false identity is only a product of the
subjective error of false identification. It is the subject that
brings about a relation which could not otherwise subsist. It is
only as I identify falsely, that there is a relation of false identity.
And even then, I can never identify, even falsely, one real thing
with another real thing, or take one real thing for another.
Indeed, at a distance, I may perceive two trees as one tree. I may
not be able to distinguish them. But I certainly do not perceive
one tree to be another tree. All I can say is that my percept is a
composite one, in which there is no distinction between appearance and reality. Where I can make this distinction, it is always
conceptual entity that I confuse with a *real entity*, never a real
entity with another real entity. Every appearance has this subjective or conceptual character, and its only relation to reality is
that of false identity.

VII. THE WORLD-APPEARANCE

The world consists of all those objects, sensible or otherwise,
that we appear to know. This world is essentially related to the
subject. It is something *to us* only. It is not known as self-
evidently true. Rather it is true only in so far as it is a recreation
of our thought and sensibility. Constituted as we are, the world
is to us what it is. It could appear differently under a different
set of subjective conditions. It is thus an appearance only. There

is nothing in the objects of our knowledge that we could un-reservedly fix as being true in itself or unconditionally true. But if that is so, it is not the reality. There must be a non-phenomenal reality beyond it, which does not appear. Only it cannot be a *transcendent object,* such as Kant conceived. A transcendent object is a contradiction in terms. Accordingly, we replace the Kantian conception of an unknowable thing in itself by the more rational conception of *transcendent reality* that cannot be known in the objective attitude, but that can, and ought to be, known as self-evidently true.

That the world of our knowledge contains elements of sub-jectivity, and therefore is an appearance in some sense or other, will be admitted by many philosophers, particularly by those who have been influenced to the least extent by the Kantian revolu-tion. What they will not admit is that this appearance is illusory. We contend that there is no *via media* between reality and illusion. There is no such thing that truly exists *and* is also an appearance. The only real existence is unconditioned. Appearance is never unconditioned. Appearance and existence can never therefore coalesce. In other words, there is no real appearance or appearance that exists. If something is an appearance, it does not exist. It can only be illusory. Being is one thing and appear-ance another. They can only be confused. They can never really be one. Reason, accordingly, cannot stop halfway, and accept as true a mixed entity, which is both appearance and reality, or which is partly appearance and partly reality. Consistency requires that we should resolve such mixed entities into their component parts, and make a radical distinction between what is and what only illusorily appears.

For the same reason, there can be no degrees of truth and falsity. Something is either true or it is false. For practical con-siderations, we may admit certain forms of error as symbolic of truth. In theory, a miss is as good as a mile; in practice, there can be greater error and less. The former is far from the truth. The latter approaches the truth, almost resembles it; so that it can be a means of pointing to it. Ultimately truth, being un-objective, can only be symbolically indicated. That is the only value of objective appearances of various grades. They act as symbols of varying value. But there is *no sense* in which appearances can be included, even after their supposed transmutation, into reality. They have got to be rejected and negated. That is how their symbolic purpose can be served. Otherwise, they only lead us into greater error—we take for reality what is not reality.

If what we have said is true, and the world of our daily intercourse is an appearance only, there is a common illusion from which we all suffer. We take for real what is not real. This error on our part is not a *theory* to be verified. It is a *fact* to be recognised. It is the real import of our experience as it is. Reflection, which is a form of rational analysis, reveals it. We fail to recognise it because it is universal, and because it does not hinder the activities of our life. But a common illusion is yet an illusion. It does not become truth, because it is socially certified. Truth does not require an outside certification. It ought to be self-certified. The world-appearance, dominated by doubt and error, is a product of our ignorance. We do not know the truth. We suffer from a cosmic illusion, called māyā.

The only explanation of an illusion is the error of perception. Error, psychologically, may be undeniable. But psychology, like all other sciences which study facts, must submit to logic; and in logic, error is a fact that is no fact. It contains within itself its own dissolution. A real entity is just itself. It may be short-lived; but it possesses its soul as long as it lives. And when it changes or dissolves, it does not cease to exist altogether. It continues under another form. Even philosophers, who do not accept change as something superimposed upon substance, or a change of form only leaving the substance unaffected, do accept objective immortality for their momentary actual entities. They seem to think that nothing that is ever real could be dismissed altogether from the totality of being. But the fact of error is a challenge to this notion of real being.

A real entity must be real at least for the time it is. An error is *never* real. It demands, *by its very nature*, its own dissolution. Or strangely enough, it achieves its errorhood through being dissolved. An error which is not seen through and recognised as error is no error; but then, it is already dissolved and dissipated.

It is only a faint shadow of this truth, when we say that error *can be* dissolved, as though dissolution were an *accident* which might occur, but which need not occur. We contend that dissolution is no accident. It is part and parcel of the nature of error. *Corrigibility* is evidently such a part. An incorrigible error is no error. *But if corrigibility is to be understood, error must be already exposed*; and an exposure of error is a dissolution of it. Paradoxically therefore, an error becomes an error only *if*, and *when*, it is dissolved. To be itself, it must be exposed, cancelled, and transcended. We can only locate it in the past as what was and what is already transcended, never locate it in the present as what simply *is* like all real entities. Thus while a real entity could never be cancelled or negated, an error is no error if it is not negatable, and in fact negated. When I contemplate an error, I only contemplate it *as negated*. In other words, to know error is to be free from error. But a cancelled error is no error. There is no challenge from it to any real fact or truth.

This is not all. There is a correlativity between the subjective act and its object. If a certain object of perception is illusory, the perception in question is illusory as well. We can never claim, after disillusionment, that we *really* perceived the object in question. We can only claim that we seemed to perceive it, or appeared to do so—and that this appearance was false. The reality of the subjective is definitely tied to the reality of the objective. If I perceive an illusory object, then I only perceive illusorily. Such then is the nature of our perception of the illusory world. It is part of the illusion. It does not really exist, and it offers no separate problem. An error of perception can be corrected, it can never be explained. It is something irrational. To explain it would be to give it a place in reality. But it has no place.

The reality of māyā, understood as the *cause* of the world-illusion, is of a piece with the reality of all illusions. It is not a non-entity, like the sky-flower. It is not a real entity like that which is never cancelled. It is distinct from both, and inexplicable in those terms. Thought ought to have no problem about it, and ought to be free from its incubus on recognising its irrational nature; but it intrudes upon thought, through the sheer lethargy of the latter, and poses as some kind of real entity that offers a standing and insoluble problem. But it cannot tolerate discriminating thought. It thrives only on unreason.

IX. THE NATURE OF TRUTH THAT WE SEEK IN PHILOSOPHY

Philosophical truth is not like scientific truth. It is no concern of philosophy to make predictions or to seek to know what is yet to be. What is yet to be must be like what is. There is no distinction of quality between them. If we have a doubt about the reality of what is, or consider it as the object of erroneous perception, the same must be said about those facts which are still only future. The whole domain of empirical knowledge stands condemned. What we are philosophically concerned with is not the nature of truth that is yet to be, but the nature of truth that is. In other words, *truth for philosophy has a timeless character.* If we can know what truth is here and now, we can know what truth always is. For the philosophical problem of truth arises from the consciousness of doubt and error that infect all facts that we ever empirically know. If we have eliminated these in one empirical setting, we have eliminated them in every empirical setting. Philosophical truth is in this sense timelessly true. It is eternal truth—or truth that was, is, and shall ever be hereafter. Moreover, since empiricity, and all that it implies, has to be transcended, we can truly say that we have known "that, knowing which all else is known." For there is simply no "all else," no differences, when empiricity as such is rejected. It is a claim to a form of *omniscience.* But it is not omniscience in empirical terms. *It is omniscience of a level of consciousness where differences are seen to be illusory, and unity grasped as true.* If no truth of this kind is possible, then we might as well take a philosophical holiday, or ascribe to philosophy no other function than that of sophistication.

X. OUR PRESENT INTUITIONS OF REALITY OUR ONLY GUIDE

We have certain intuitions of reality which are common. They have a fixed character. They simply cannot change. We may have a new intuition of reality. But it will not be new in its *form,* which alone determines its truth-value. We may develop a new power of knowledge, a sixth sense, but what it will reveal will still be something empirical, something that is merely given from outside, and therefore open to that very criticism of reason which has unreservedly condemned all present empirical facts. No new intuition of reality can escape this criticism, if it is merely an extension or an amplification of what we already do know. But if still we insist that a new intuition is possible, and that it alone can solve the problem of knowledge for us, then that intuition is at least philosophically quite valueless; for no amount of reflective thinking can ever elicit it. We enter a region of mysticism where reason is completely dethroned, and its claims ignored instead of being satisfied.

It is the *form* of intuition that counts, not the content. In fact, the content is wholly relative to the form. It is the form that gives truth or otherwise. If then we could find, in our present experience, a form of intuition which is direct and immediate in a sense that doubt and error could never assail it logically speaking, then we have *the truth* which we seek. We now contend that we have no more than two ultimate forms of intuition of reality. We have the intuition of objective fact in all its different forms, physical, mental or even spiritual. Something is a "this" to us. It is "given" in the most general sense. This intuition is recognised by the average man as well as by the philosopher. When it is contended that our only intuition of reality is sensible, we are merely referring to this general intuition in a specific form. It is common ground between the scientist and the philosopher. But if the philosopher recognises no other form of intuition, he is a dogmatist, and he is paying an unconscious compliment to the scientist. A positivist in philosophy is a scientist who has missed his vocation and turned a philosopher.

There is another intuition of reality which is not generally recognised, or only insufficiently recognised. It is the intuition of "I." Philosophers and mystics have often given the very sane advice, "know thyself." But this dictum is taken in a very specious sense in which many other elements beside the self enter into the composition of the self. In fact, the average man, no less than the most sophisticated philosopher, easily go into error, the moment they reflect upon this intuition. It is conceivable that when we reflect upon our knowledge of objective reality, we emerge out of it "chastened." We recognise the limitation of our knowledge, and the illimitable, almost mysterious, character of reality. But the moment we reflect upon the intuition of "I," we find no mystery in it. It is so simple. And yet we easily, and most naturally, walk into error. We seem to be in the right about this intuition only as long as we do not reflect. For then we do not treat the "I" as an object of any kind. No one ever consciously says, "this is I." Everyone uses the term "I" significantly, and he uses it for something that is quite immediate. It never stands for a socialised object, common to the speaker as well as to the hearer. It stands for the speaking I only, that reveals its true inwardness in the use of the term. We understand the term perfectly in this sense, and have no doubt about its correct meaning. But the moment we reflect, we distort this natural significance, and a term which is never *used* to symbolise an object or a *this*, easily lends itself, in reflection, to an objective meaning. It appears to stand for *an entity* that has no uniqueness about it, that is an *object* of a sort, and that is *common* to several different individuals. The *I* becomes *this*. In the field of intro-spective awareness, it is identified with an *actual entity* or an occurrent thought. Thought becomes the thinker. Thus a term that is never *used* to signify a "this" is contemplated, with equanimity, and almost with the pride of enlightenment, as a *this*. These realistic philosophers who are often very shy of the word "illusion" when used in respect of objective appearances, feel no hesitation in applying the term to any non-objective and enduring entity which may be claimed to be the real significance of the term "I."

It is quite evident to us that the entity signified by the term "I" is just the opposite of the entity signified by the term "this." So much is this the case, that the two can never reside together in one and the same thing, even as light and darkness cannot do so. There is no possible thing that can be both *I* and *This*. Some philosophers have admitted a neutral stuff of reality as the original stuff. But they will be hard put to it to give meaning to it. If it has the character of given-ness or presentedness, it is some kind of object. If it is never given, but always immediate, it is the true subject, *I*. There is no third alternative. The so-called neutral stuff is really conceived objectively.

Philosophers have also supposed that one and the same entity can function both as subject and as object successively. This view, too, involves confusion of thought. What is the *sameness* that continues unaffected through the subject-function and the object-function? It is only a pseudo-subject that can be contemplated as object, not the real subject. The real subject can never become the object. It is never known. It is always immediate without being known. But if that is so, all attempts of philosophers to analyse the "I" into some kind of transient object, or an objective relation, are foredoomed to failure. Their conclusion, that there is entity that deserves to be called by that name, or that the only entity that deserves to be so called is some other entity that is never really meant by the term and that is never immediate, is due to a bad type of confusion. In truth, we have here an intuition of reality which is so direct and immediate, and so self-revealing, that we can only entertain a doubt or fall into error, by first misinterpreting the original intuition and taking for an object what is never given as object and what is radically opposed to all objectivity.

XI. THE ABSOLUTE SELF

The term "I" may be taken to stand for a unique but an individualised entity. This is when *I* is distinguished from *you*. It is then literally meaningful. But like all other meaning, this meaning, too, is objective. *Only an objective content can be meant.* We have, however, in the intuition of "I" not only this meant something, this object of some kind, or the ego-function. This is only the perverted form of that which cannot be literally meant, because it is diametrically opposed to every form of the object. Thus, when I use the term "I," my meaning may be literal or it may be symbolic only. It is the latter that is all-important. For here we are face to face with a reality that cannot be the literal meaning of any word, but that can only be symbolically indicated. The symbol has a literal meaning which we here negate. It is through this negation that its symbolic character is realised. In other words, the real I or Self is the negation of the finite I that is literally meant by the word.

The true Self which is wholly unobjective and which can only be symbolically indicated is not like the traditional soul, a hidden or mysterious entity. The existence of the soul is accepted for outside reasons, never on the basis of an intuitive experience. It is accepted, apart from religious considerations, in order to provide a unifying and enduring principle for mental life. When we think of the soul, we think of an underlying and unknown substance, that is to all appearances no more intelligent by its nature than mere matter. It is no wonder that the philosophical value of this hypothesis is rated very low. My real Self on the other hand, indicated by the term I, is not an unknown entity in this sense. It is not screened from our view by any overlying or intermediate reality. It directly reveals itself in every piece of knowledge. It could not be hidden or suppressed. If we know *anything* at all, the Self reveals itself in it. It is the only knower. All things are known by it. It is not known by anything else. In fact, it is in the self-revelation of the Self that all other things are revealed. The *self-revelation* then logically precedes *other*-revelation.

This self-revelation of the Self is not the same thing as what goes by the name of self-consciousness. In self-consciousness, we objectify the self. We know it as related and as finite. It is the self fallen from its subjectivity and become an object. Its awareness is in principle not at all distinct from the awareness of all other things. But there is a knower beyond it which knows its emergence into conscious activity as well as its disappearance from it. This knower is a pure consciousness that does not emerge or disappear. It is not to be confused with any mental act. It is an actless revelation. For the same reason it cannot be *known*. We can only know an object. But who can know the knower? This knower is an immutable awareness that never ceases and never goes to sleep. It reveals sleep itself. How can we argue that this ever-present awareness is a mysterious entity? It is mysterious only if it is sought objectively. But then we are looking for it in the wrong way. What wonder that we do not find it?

Agnosticism is a respectable philosophical theory. But it is based upon the erroneous idea that reality is both objective and mysterious. The object, however, is never by its own nature mysterious. If there is any mystery about it, the key to it lies in the subject. For the object is as the subject has made it. What we do know and what we do not know, are both dependent upon the nature of our approach to reality. If our approach is external and sensuous, there will always be an aspect that we know, and an infinitely greater aspect that we do not know. We have made this division in reality, not that reality has hidden anything from us. We have created the mystery, not that reality is by itself mysterious. We can correct our approach, and reality will cease to be mysterious. But there can be no possible mystery about the Self. It is not something inscrutable, just because it is never *given*. Accordingly, we do not find it easy to adopt an attitude of agnosticism towards it. We find it easier simply to deny it. There is no reality called the Self, we think. But it is like the sun shining, and the blind see it not. The Self is ever self-revealing and self-evident, *svaprakāsa*. Doubt and error are not relevant to it, because there is no subjectivity in our knowledge of it. It is simply not known as object. It is the truest form of knowledge, if there is one. Indeed, we cannot deny all ignorance of the Self, giving rise to a problem and a perplexity. But the knowledge which would be competent to drive out this ignorance would not be knowledge in the ordinary sense, in which we know an object, and in knowing it constitute it. It would be knowledge free from every element of subjectivity, and therefore free from that idealisation of reality which is natural to thought at the empirical level. It would be a kind of non-empirical awareness in which the function of thought would be reduced to a *coincidence* and an *identity* with reality as it is in itself. Knowledge becomes reality, and the knower of *Brahman* becomes *Brahman*. It is a form of mysticism without any mystery, since the basis of it is a universal intuition.

XII. THE CHALLENGE OF MATTER

What we have said about our intution of the Self may be true in the last analysis. But this intuition is never found in its pure form. It is always found mixed with the intuition of the not-self. The Self is found *related* to the world as the knower or as the subject. If then the world is not, we think that the Self also is not. We may argue that the world is an idea only, and that what is related to the "world as idea" is the ideating subject, not the real Self, which remains unrelated. But the world reappears in another form as the necessary adjunct or part of the Self.

The external and physical world may be an idea, because it is an appearance to us. But there is the physical body which mediates this appearance, and conditions it. *That is not an idea.* This is a common argument with most materialists and realists. But all that it proves is that the body is a privileged object only, not that it is real as something independent and in-itself. We may regard the body as part of the physical world, and so completely material. In that case, it has all the given-ness of that world. But we may also regard it as part of the percipient subject. When I look at my hand, the hand is my object, but the eye with which I look is not my object. It is indistinguishable from the looker. In fact, the pure subject is quite helpless. It cannot see. It sees *with the eye.* This eye we cannot look at as object. It has achieved a new relation with the subject. It has become indistinguishable from it. There is a distinction, and yet the distinction is annulled. I am conscious of seeing *with the eye*, which proves the distinction. But in so far as I *actually see*, I see the object, I do not see the eye at all. I am not even conscious that there is an eye. Either, then, the physical body is just a part of the physical universe, and like it an appearance only, or alternatively, it has ceased to be given and ceased to be material. The subject alone is not the body. How then can we prove the reality of the body, as a physical entity, in a sense in which the physical world is not? Either it is only an idea like the latter, or it is nothing physical at all which may be said to be real in itself or unconditionally real. In both cases, its reality is the intelligent subject, without which it would be nothing at all.

The intelligent Self has different forms of the object related to it in this intimate way, or as its body. The physical body is only one form. Mind with its succession of states is another. Thought as well as the thinking *I* or the *ego* are equally forms of the body of the Self. The Self as thus embodied is our greatest illusion, and the basis of the illusion of the external world. If the former illusion could be removed through discrimination, the illusion of a world or the illusion of *otherness* as such would automatically disappear. It is our false notion of the Self, involving a confusion of two distinct and diametrically opposed intuitions of reality, that is responsible for the world-appearance. As we purify that notion and correct our error, the world-appearance is progressively cancelled. When we reach the pure Subject or Self, there is nothing left that can be *other* to it. We are left with reality that is without a second. Small wonder it is then that the ignorance of the Self is the sole cause of the appearance of a world, and the knowledge of the Self is the sole redeeming knowledge or the knowledge of Truth as such.

The traditional question of the relation of mind and body assumes a different form on our view. We mean by the term "body," not only the gross physical body, but also the subtler mental or psychical body. The latter, too, is in principle unintelligent. On the other side is the spirit, which is a pure and immutable Intelligence. The only relation which the body can have to the spirit is the relation of false identity. This is not a real relation, or a relation which can subsist between two real and independent entities. It can only subsist betwen a real entity and one that is constituted by the relation and is not real by itself. Such is the status of the body in the spirit-body relation. Since the world-appearance is a product and an off-shoot of this relation, we can truly say that the world itself is our body. Our body does not stop with the physical organism, but extends beyond it to include the whole material universe. My Self is the Self of the world—its Creator and immanent spirit.

XIII. THE WHOLE OR THE ABSOLUTE

It is natural to suppose that the Whole or the Absolute is not only great beyond all conception, but that it is inclusive of both the Self and the not-self, the subject and the object. Unfortunately, the Whole thus conceived is bound to be objective and finite. The notion of a System, a differentiated Unity, a Whole inclusive of appearances, is essentially objective. It is a construction of thought. No thought, no Whole of this kind. But an objective Whole is a spurious Whole. It can never include the *real subject*. It is only a creation of the subject. It is an appearance made by thought and informed by thought. We substitute for this Whole another Kind of Whole. It is the Whole of the pure and the absolute Subject or Self. (a) This Subject can never be

included in a larger Whole; for there is no larger Whole. The
subject that can be included is related and finite. It is an object
of a kind, and requires to be itself revealed or known. What
knows it is the real Subject, which is never in its turn known.
(b) It is essentially unrelated, and absolute. The moment we
think of it as related, it is already degraded. It has ceased to be
Itself. (c) It is the only reality that has *no other*. For the moment
it has an other, it will require to be transcended as what is only
an object of a kind and so finite.

The real Whole is the unrelated Self. It is immediate *without
being known*; for only the mediate can be known. It is unrelated
in itself; but all other things are related to it, and are real only
as they are related. It neither excludes appearances, nor does it
include them; for either course would render it limited and finite.
It includes the appearances only in the sense in which the underlying ground of reality includes the illusory appearances falsely
conceived in it. We cannot know the reality and *also* know the
illusory appearances. The knowledge of the one is incompatible
with the knowledge of the other. If we know the illusory, we
cannot know the real, and vice-versa. The only way to know the
real is through the cancellation and the negation of the illusory.
This is how the Self is known. When this knowledge arises, and
we know the Self as the Truth, we have lost our finitude, and rid
ourselves of all those ills which result therefrom. Verily, we have
seen the Truth, and become the Truth. Truth has made us free.

XIV. THE JOY THAT PASSETH UNDERSTANDING

There is joy in this knowledge. It is not the short-lived and
ephemeral joy that is incidental to some activity, and that presupposes some form of want or imperfection. Joy without joyful
activity is unthinkable to us. But it is only an appearance of joy.
It is not a pure joy. It is mixed with regret. The reasons for it
are many. It has a limit which could be exceeded. It does not
therefore quite fulfil. It lapses; and we find ourselves desiring
over again, perhaps with a keener desire. It is not truly positive.
It is due merely to the removal of a want or the fulfilment of a
desire. Its positive character lies not in it, but in the *status quo*
presupposed by all desire, out of which desire arises and into

which it finally disappears. It is boisterous in form, not restful and peaceful as perfected joy ought to be. There is an illusion even here. We think that the joy is in the activity. It is really in the *status quo* or the desireless state of being to which all pleasurable activity ought to lead.

True joy must derive not from any activity, but from the nature of reality as such. Such joy alone can fulfil. It is as stable as reality itself. It can never be lost or exceeded. It is as old and as eternal as reality itself. This is the joy of the Self, which we humanly and imperfectly catch in the various desireful activities. The joy of these activities is dependent upon the nature of our instruments and upon our capacity. Not so the joy of the Self. It is the inherent nature of the Self itself. As we cannot run away from the Self, we cannot run away from this ocean of joy. Only we do not recognise it. It expresses itself quite clearly in the love of the Self beyond which there is no greater love. Self-love is a vice, if it differentiates between *you* and *me*. But it is the highest virtue, if it has reduced these differences to unreality, and based itself upon a recognition of the unity of all being and its inherent joyfulness. We never can love anything better than the Self. We love all things for the sake of the Self. We do not love the Self for the sake of anything else beside it. It is our only unconditional love. It is the limit and the end. Being itself is joyful. We can truly say that when we know the Self, we enjoy immortality in the highest sense of that term.

PRINCIPAL PUBLICATIONS

Problem of Nothing; Ajñāna or A Theory of Ignorance; Philosophy of the Self. All published by the Indian Institute of Philosophy, Amalner, East Khandesh, Bombay.

SUGGESTIONS FOR AN IDEALISTIC THEORY OF KNOWLEDGE

by A. C. MUKERJI

Born 1890; Professor of Philosophy, Allahabad University.

BIOGRAPHICAL

I WAS born in a family of moderate means in a village of Bengal. The earlier part of my life was one of stress and struggle; but what sustained me throughout this period was my faith, derived mainly from my mother, in the efficacy of prayer and the ultimate triumph of the moral life. The otherwise inexplicable turns of some of the events of my later life have confirmed this belief. Forced by circumstances to leave Bengal after I had passed the Intermediate Examination of the Calcutta University from the Krishnath College, Berhampore (Murshidabad), I joined the Central Hindu College, Benares in 1910 as an undergraduate where afterwards I was appointed an Assistant Professor of Philosophy in 1914. This brought me into contact with some of the high-souled persons of the college whose precepts and practice left upon my mind an indelible impress the value of which cannot be too highly measured. My love of philosophy had its inception in the lectures of Dr. Hiralal Haldar which I attended in the Krishnath College; but I owe my initiatiou to Professor P. B. Adhikari, an affectionate and inspiring teacher of the then Central Hindu College of Benares. His influence upon my life and belief has been immense. While attending the lectures of Dr. Bhagavan Das of Benares, who not only professed but lived his philosophy, I was awakened to the vast possibilities of the comparative method in philosophy. I lost no time in availing myself of the facilties offered by Benares for the study of Indian Philosophy and placed myself under two reputed Sanskrit scholars of the time, late Pandit Harihar Shastri and Pandit Dinanath Vedāntavāgish. This was the most crucial stage in the development of my philosophical beliefs. I have been always impressed by Kant's thought and still believe that it, notwithstanding all that has been said against it, has an aspect of abiding value. The study of the "advaita" Vedānta not only threw further light upon some of the knotty problems of Kant's philosophy but seemed to me to open up new lines of constructive thought through the synthesis of Indian and Western traditions in philosophy. I had long cherished the desire to get an opportunity to come into personal contact with my western colleagues; but as it never materialized I sought their contact through correspondence. I wish to put on record my grateful acknowledgment of the immense help I have derived from the comments and criticism with which some of them favoured me; particularly helpful was the readiness with which Harold H. Joachim, A. S. Pringle-Pattison, and H. W. B. Joseph consented to respond to my repeated calls for discussion which sometimes led to prolonged correspondence. I may end this brief sketch with two confessions.

No serious thinker can be seriously wrong in his deepest convictions; this belief took deep roots in my mind at a very early stage of my career. I could, therefore, never reconcile myself to the attitude of those whose love of one system is purchased at the cost of their respect for another. The other confession is that Philosophy for me is not a cleverly woven-out fiction; no statement, however edifying or otherwise valuable, has any philosophical worth if it be not founded on logically solid grounds.

SUGGESTIONS FOR AN IDEALISTIC THEORY OF KNOWLEDGE

The problems arising out of "the dual nature of human experience" forced an eminent idealist, H. H. Joachim, to end his admirable and remarkably stimulating analysis of knowledge with "a confession of ignorance." Scepticism, no doubt, has a very healthy effect upon every sincere pilgrim to the Temple of Truth, and as a philosophical attitude its value is certainly far superior to the dogmatic attitude which breeds a false sense of security by inducing a condition of dogmatic slumber in which ignorance is bliss. But this does not justify inaction. It appears, however, that Joachim who thus gave himself up to scepticism was essentially correct in his demand for a fundamental reconstruction of Idealist Logic which had left Metaphysics and Logic in a state of "irreconcilable antagonism," as well as in his protest that "the metaphysician is entitled to acquiesce in logical theories, when their success demands that he should accept within the sphere of Logic assumptions which his own metaphysical theory condemns." (*The Nature of Truth, p.*179).

This anomaly in the idealistic theory of knowledge needs for its effective remedy a careful re-orientation of the idealist creed without falling into the pitfalls from which it has been the age-long endeavour of idealism to save a sound theory of experience. The remedy, that is, does not lie in completely ignoring the valuable achievements for which we are indebted to the idealists, and laying the foundation of a metaphysics *de novo* which would be entirely cut off from the idealistic moorings. But while recognising and appreciating the great insights that have inspired their analysis of knowledge and experience, we must yet apply to it the cathartic method of self-purification by hauling up and examining some of the assumptions that have led idealism to this distressing condition of internal dualism and irreconcilable antagonism between Logic and Metaphysics. Joachim's challenge, we believe, has not been satisfactorily met. In fact it cannot be met while idealism remains unconscious of the assumptions, bred by an objectivist attitude, that have poisoned its life and crippled its growth at the very start of its career. It is true that the idealists have waged a keen and protracted battle against the objectivist approaches to knowledge and reality favoured by empiricism and realism; but the revival and ramifications of empiricism in contemporary philosophy lend countenance to the presumption that the battle against the objectivist attitude has not been fought to the bitter end.

Though the outlook of contemporary thought is predominantly empirical, the apparently novel and revolutionary character of the methods and the systems it has brought into birth tends to hide their empirical lineage. The method of phenomenological reduction, that of seeking clues to the nature of the universe in the great ranges of human experience, or in the biography of creative personalities, the proposal to replace the "Critique of Pure Reason" by the "Critique of Historical Reason," and many other sensational developments of contemporary philosophy, with their anti-epistemological attitude and consequent antipathy to the detached study of the forms of thought would at first sight give the impression that contemporary philosophy has travelled far on the way to the Temple of Truth and has left far behind the spirit of pre-Kantian empiricism. But we contend that this impression, to say the least, is incorrect. Rightly interpreted, the empirical and the transcendental methods represent the only two directions in which the pendulum of human thought is capable of oscillating. The classical defect of empiricism lies in its blindness to its own presuppositions; and this, which may be called transcendental blindness, led to some of the gravest and most disastrous aberrations in the history of philosophy. It, of course, can on no account be doubted that the modern mind has given ample evidence of its power to reach staggering heights of learning and scholarship. But the most unfortunate fact is that scholarship does not necessarily go along with insight. One may be, to put it in the language of an Indian tradition, a *śāstra-vit* without being an *ātma-vit*. The general hostility to epistemology is largely due to an imperfect perception of the distinction between the principles of reason and a theory. The former are the logical implicates of all theories, and form the common ground of the warring theories, and, consequently, have a foundational character absent from the latter. The criticism of a theory may end in its partial modification or total replacement by another theory; but the need for this modification or replacement arises from the failure of that theory to conform to the demands of reason. The changes in the fortunes of a theory being dictated by the principles of reason, these are above criticism and beyond the possibility of revision or replacement. They form the solid core of knowledge which inspires and sustains the continuous search of Truth through a series of theories. A theory would not be suggested, far less recommended for serious considerations, if its sponsor had not believed that the other theories are false and that the principles by means of which their falsity is known are absolutely true. Thus the principles that determine the truth or falsity of the theories have to be presupposed by every theory of the world on pain of being reduced to a merely dogmatic and arbitrary position. Hence, as the discussion of the principles of truth forms a part of epistemology, the battle among the theories leaves unaffected their logical implicates, and the changes and re-adjustments of the theories do not decide the fortunes of epistemology.

Philosophical constructions, in so far as they are divorced from the insight into the epistemological principles, run the risk of being in fact as sterile as mere stories or finely woven fictions. Arbitrary interpretations of life and history, distaste for logical compulsion in arriving at a conclusion, unbridled freedom to fancies and prejudices, are but the necessary accompaniments of misology and hatred of epistemology. It is only when our philosophy sits loose on our life that we can despise logic and epistemology and afford the luxury of merely original and revolutionary theories or sensational constructions.

If then we were to address ourselves to the serious task of reconstruction of our philosophical beliefs, the work must begin with logic and epistemology: and the method must be that of applying to them the cathartic remedy of self-purification as distinct from the criticism of epistemology *ab extra*, and thus discovering the roots of the ultimate dualism which has left logic and metaphysics in a hopelessly irreconcilable antagonism. But as no proposal to reconstruct epistemology or metaphysics can afford to ignore a careful consideration of the original form of empiricism before Kant and thus define one's attitude towards

the analysis of experience from the empirical and the transcendental standpoints respectively, a brief review of the progress
of philosophical thought before and after Kant would unearth
the roots of dualism and the mischiefs it has created from the
very beginning of modern philosophy.

The Copernican revolution which Kant claimed to bring about
in epistemology, though mainly successful, has rendered itself
open to misapprehension and misinterpretation owing to the
very language in which he expressed himself but which failed to
convey adequately the depth of his thought. While ostensibly
engaged in effecting a compromise between the rationalist and
the empiricist, Kant laid the foundation of epistemology as a
unique discipline; but his defective intellectual legacy stood in the
way; and the result was that knowledge was sometimes regarded
from the psychological standpoint as a mental process between
the mind, on the one hand, and the object, on the other. The
experiment he launched was intended to prove that the objects
must conform to the basic principles of thought but the language
he used gave the impression that knowledge was an affair in
which the knowing mind and something external to mind were
concerned. The critics were thus justified in interpreting his
theory as dualistic: the knowing mind armed with the forms of
space, time and categories on the one side, and the sense-manifold
on the other. The mind waits, as it were, with its weapons ready-
made and complete till the sensations present themselves to it;
and when they are actually presented, the mind imposes its
forms on the sensations, much as, to put it in the language of one
of his commentators, the fisherman throws his net and catches
the fishes. That such an interpretation is favoured and encouraged
by Kant's language cannot be called in question; but none has
the key to Kant's deeper thoughts who does not see that it
would be a sheer travesty of Kant's position to identify it with
that of the subjective idealist for whom knowledge is purely a
matter of subjective or private elaboration of the sensations.
Whatever might have been the limitations of Kant's intellectual
heritage, none should underrate the fact that if unity, plurality,
causality, etc. are for him the conditions of the existence of the
material bodies, they are equally the conditions of the existence
of mind. To trace, therefore, the transcendental conditions of

knowledge to the mind would commit him to the absurd position that mind is the source of those very conditions without which it itself could not have existed.

But if we were to appreciate the theory of the subjective origin of the conditions of experience, as it is envisaged by Kant's deeper thoughts, it must be seen that all that it is intended to signify is that sense-experience cannot fully explain science. That is, science which claims to be a body of certain and necessary knowledge cannot depend entirely on the inductive and experimental method; on the contrary, all knowledge which is derived from observation and experiment is but the progressive filling in of a scheme which is not itself of experimental origin. His challenge to empiricism lay in the momentous distinction between a transcendental principle and an empirical generalization, and in demanding of the empiricist to offer an explanation of these principles in terms of any other principles which would not commit him to a *hysteron proteron*. The presence of the *hysteron proteron*, to put it from the other side, in an explanation is the proof of the transcendental nature of the principles that we are seeking to explain. In this sense, a transcendental principle is the presupposition of all ordinary proofs and disproofs; and transcendentality and irrepressibility are inseparable from each other.

If we were to trace the origin of the trouble responsible for the misinterpretations to which Kant's thoughts have been subjected, it will not do to confine our enquiry within the four walls of his works. The poison was in fact injected into philosophy at the very beginning of modern philosophy when Descartes, following the intentions of ordinary language, accepted an ultimate dualism between spirit and matter, which according to him, represents a dichotomous division of the universe. Everything, in the last analysis, is supposed to fall either under the head of mind or that of matter, so that no reality can escape their tentacular prehension. When, therefore, Locke started on an epistemological enquiry he found the dualism already established firmly in philosophical thought, and his problem reduced itself to showing that the entire furniture of the mind which had been mistakenly supposed to be innate had its origin in something external to it. All our moral and intellectual principles have been empirically derived and the mind, before this process of derivation started, had remained as a mere *tabula rass*. Neither Descartes nor Locke was seriously troubled with the paradoxes which, though coming to head at several places of their analysis of knowledge, were born of this ultimate dualism.

Descartes, having adopted uncritically the method of analysis and abstraction, set the spirit in sharp opposition to matter and stressed their self-centred individuality to such an extent that his philosophy contained the germ of a scepticism needing a little readjustment and re-orientation for its full development. Anxious to save philosophy from the region of doubtful speculations, he started with an indubitable reality which would re-assert itself in the very process of doubting. But what he failed to see was that, if such a self-established principle had to be the basis of a sound theory of knowledge, it could not be conceived as an individual standing by the side of the other individuals, because the spirit that knows must somehow transcend its own individuality and rigid self-assertion. A sharp dualism between the knower and the known, each having an exclusive and self-centred existence, cannot explain knowledge which essentially implies self-transcendence on the part of the knower. In other words, a spirit which is to be distinguished from matter by the attribute of thought must be conceived as leading an atomic existence by the side of the things that it is expected to *know*. But this it cannot do; all that it can know must be itself, much as a mirror, supposing it is miraculously invested with the power of thinking, could not know anything except its own reflections. Similarly if knowledge had been conceived as a peculiar attribute or a peculiar response of the mind *co-ordinate* with the other things which in their turn possess their peculiar attributes or responses, such a mind could never break the boundary of its subjectivity and reach out to the things different from itself, much as the table does not know the chair.

The difficulty we are considering here was vaguely felt by Berkeley, and it will be interesting to make a brief reference to the desperate effort he made to rise above the limitations of his predecessors. The spirit "who knows and perceives" the ideas, as he puts it, is "a thing entirely distinct" from the ideas. This *heterogeneity* he emphasises in different contexts. "Nothing seems of more importance toward erecting a firm system of sound and real knowledge . . . than to lay the beginning in a distinct explication of *what is meant by thing, reality, existence:* For in vain shall we dispute concerning the *real existence* of things, or pretend to any knowledge thereof, so long as we have not fixed the meaning of those words. Thing or Being is the most general name of all; it comprehends under it two kinds entirely distinct and heterogeneous, and which have nothing common but the name, viz. spirits and ideas." The distinction is so important for Berkeley that he goes so far as to remark that only that theory of knowledge "may be proof against the assaults of scepticism" which is based upon a clear recognition of the heterogeneity between the spirit and the ideas. A spirit he defines as "one simple undivided, active being" which is called Understanding as it perceives ideas, and Will as it produces or otherwise operates about them. "*I myself* am not my ideas, but somewhat else— a thinking active principle that perceives, knows, wills and operates about ideas. I know that I, one and the same self, perceive both colours and sounds; that a colour cannot perceive a sound, nor a sound a colour; that I am therefore one individual principle, distinct from colour and sound; and for the same reason, from all other sensible things and inert ideas."

It would be difficult to imagine a more brilliant instance of a thinker struggling hard to rise above the limitations of his intellectual heritage. Berkeley feels that the spirit which knows cannot belong to the same order of existence to which the things it knows belong. Yet, on the other hand, he has in his intellectual legacy no other mode of expressing the heterogeneity than by defining the spirit as a thinking and willing substance which is the support of ideas. And he is here obviously unconscious of the anomaly between the psychological and the epistemological ways of regarding the spirit. While stressing the distinction of the spirit that knows from the objects that are known, he still continues to view it as one object among other objects, as a substance by the side of the other substance. That there is "no parity of case between Spirit and Matter"; that the mind "is more distant and heterogeneous from the ideas than light is from darkness"; that "*Spirits* and *ideas* are things so wholly different, that when we say 'they exist', 'they are known', or the like, these words must not be thought to signify anything common to both natures"—such remarks are repeatedly made, but he seldom realises the serious consequences they have for his empirical philosophy and for his psychological approach to the problem of knowledge. In fact, his insight outstrips his intellectual heritage, and thus his theory of the knowing spirit might be said to hold in a state of unstable equilibrium the doctrine of spirit as the subject and that of mind as an object among other objects. When it is realised by him that the spirit which knows an idea is a thing entirely heterogeneous from the ideas that are known, or that the same self which perceives both colours and sounds can have nothing in common with the colours and the sounds which do not perceive each other, he is evidently using the term self in the sense of the subject that knows all objects. When, on the other hand, he proceeds to describe the self as something that knows and wills, he is using the term spirit or self in the sense of one kind of thing in the midst of the other kinds, and knowledge is conceived as an attribute or activity of the self.

Thus in Berkeley, as much as in Kant, there is evident a mighty struggle to express through an imperfect intellectual legacy what refused to be tortured into the forms of the language in which it was embedded. The dichotomous division of the universe into spirit and matter with which modern philosophy began was, in fact, hopelessly inadequate for expressing the subtler aspects of a type of epistemology of which, though it was the merit of Kant to lay the foundation, Berkeley, too, had an obscure presentiment. His emphasis and repeated insistence on the heterogeneity between spirit and idea was an unconscious repudiation of the Cartesian dualism along with its co-ordination of spirit with matter; yet he hardly perceived this and unhesitatingly characterised the self as a spiritual substance. Even when the anomaly forced itself upon him in the Dialogue and it was seen that, to act consistently, he must either admit Matter or reject spirit, his only answer was that whereas "I have no immediate intuition" of matter, "the being of my self, that is, my own soul, mind, or thinking principle, I evidently know by reflection." The doctrine that the self was known through immediate intuition or reflection established itself so firmly in the philosophical tradition of his time that he accepted it as a matter of course, as a truism that needed no proof. The tradition, in fact, could not be challenged till the paradoxes of an ultimate dualism would precipitate the necessity of raising philosophy from the psychological to the transcendental level.

Dualism, to revert to the main topic, implies two different items that are distinguished from each other by their respective peculiar characteristics, and which, as belonging to the same genus, are co-ordinate in their status. Thus, when spirit and matter are taken to be different from each other, each possessing its differentiating attribute, it is implied that they are members of a democracy no one possessing a privileged dignity over the other. Knowledge in that case becomes a relation of *compresence* between two things of equal status, and of equal rank. The insuperable difficulty implicit in such a dualistic theory of knowledge forces itself upon us only as we stop to answer the question how, on this supposition, spirit could ever know matter. The colour, to take Berkeley's example, does not know the sound, but the spirit knows the colour as well as the sound. This means that the spirit has the power to break through its privacy and subjectivity, and thus reach out to the colour and the sound; but this reaching out or transcendence of subjectivity is possible neither for the colour nor for the sound. A peculiar character or attribute would lose its peculiarity if it had belonged to or inhered in a thing different from that of which it is a peculiar property; it would be, in other words, a contradiction to suppose that knowledge is a peculiar attribute of the spirit as distinct from matter, and to hold at the same time that the spirit knows matter. Conceived as a quality, knowledge would necessarily be confined within the subjective life of the substance in which it inheres, and as such, could not be a relation between the knowing substance and the other substance that is known. Thus in a perfect democracy spirit must be deprived of its right to know something lying outside itself.

The process of democratization of all objects of thought, though it was started by Descartes with regard to the problem of spirit and matter, was set in operation seriously by Locke. Locke's attempt to drive the ideas of unity, cause, etc., from the same experience which, according to him, was the source of the ideas of colour and sound and all other simple and complex ideas was in fact an implicit denial of any graded dignity or hierarchy in the sphere of knowledge. Every concept has an identical genealogy with the rest, and their common progenitor is experience. There is an apparent obviousness in this position, so much so that it has continued to provide the background of many respectable theories of knowledge through a long line of philosophical adventures before and after Kant. But it never occurred to Locke that, if *ex hypothesi* all concepts are of empirical origin, the *mind* which according to him is gradually furnished with the innumerable ideas can be no exception to the general rule; it is only after the idea of mind has been derived from experience that anyone may think of the mind being the recipient of ideas from the impact of the external world of matter. In the absence of the idea of mind, the idea of matter, the idea of cause, etc., the description of the origin of the ideas would carry no meaning. If an empirical epistemology, therefore, is to be built upon a radical basis, it should be able to account for the empirical origin of all concepts; it should, in other words, make the impossible attempt of starting its analysis with no idea. Locke evidently does not begin at the beginning; his analysis begins at a highly developed stage of the mind when the ideas of mind, matter, cause, unity, etc., are already there, ready for use in showing the empirical origin of knowledge.

Locke's failure in his attempt to make his empiricism radical and self-consistent had its ultimate source in his democratizing disposition. He could not see that every empirical or psychological account of knowledge must have epistemological presuppositions without which it could not even take its departure; and, consequently, these presuppositions cannot be placed side by side with the ideas that have an empirical lineage. But this practice of levelling down the status of the presuppositions to that of the ideas they condition has been so general yet so disastrous that in the interest of easy reference we may call it *the fallacy of transcendental dislocation*. If, for instance, it is found that causality is the inescapable concept which renders an empirical theory of knowledge intelligible, then, the venture to show the empirical origin of the concept of causality would be to commit the fallacy of transcendental dislocation. This of course is not to deny that the child, for instance, may at the beginning have no idea of cause which is gradually derived from experience; this would be to confuse epistemology with psychology. All that it means is that the child who has yet no idea of cause cannot be an empiricist who has to use the concept of cause in giving an empirical account of knowledge. Whether as a matter of fact the child does or does not employ, consciously or unconsciously, the concept of cause is of no vital conern for determining the epistemological issue; but, supposing that Locke's contention is true that the idea of cause is absent at a particular stage of mental development and that it comes to be acquired at a later stage, this very description owes its intelligibility to the causal principle. Because it distinguishes between two successive stages in the development of the child's mind, one at which the concept was not present, and the other at which the concept is a part of the mind's furniture, the second following necessarily upon the first. This is to presuppose necessary succession between them; not only this, but even supposing that repeated observations have produced the illusion of causal connection, this very supposition presupposes necessary connection between the observations and the illusion. This character of the concept of causality may be called its irrepressibility. A principle, in other words, is irrepressible when it is re-asserted in the very act of deducing, doubting or refuting it. It is also transcendental inasmuch as it enters into all intelligible description of experience as its inescapable logical implicate. In his just suspicion of the reality of the innate ideas, Locke democratized all ideas and failed to distinguish between the transcendental ideas and those that are empirical; this transcendental dislocation which essentially consists in making the foundation of knowledge collateral with its superstructure has been at the root of some of the gravest errors in epistemology, and its ravages have impoverished many a carefully thought out system of metaphysics. A vague apprehension of the consequences of a radical democratization in epistemology induced Berkeley to insist on the heterogeneity of the spirit, without a clear recognition of which, as he remarked, no theory of knowledge "may be proof against the assaults of scepticism." The truth of Berkeley's observations is amply confirmed by the contemporary theories of knowledge.

After these considerations it is not necessary to analyse Hume's arguments in detail. Hume was apparently satisfied with Locke's criticism of the rationalistic approach to epistemology, and as he himself had no idea of the source of knowledge other than what was suggested by Locke he despaired of arresting the tide toward scepticism caused and nurtured by empiricism. That scepticism was the inevitable result of democratization of the foundational principles of knowledge could not suggest itself to Hume who was more conerned with making Locke and Berkeley consistent with the creed of empiricism than with examining the foundation of the empirical outlook itself. Nor did he stop to consider seriously whether consistent scepticism could stand on its own legs. In fact even the illusions cannot be proved to be false without the basis of a solid core of knowledge, and uncertainty in particular instances implies absolute certainty about the general features of the world within which the particular instances fall. Scepticism is thus a parasite which feeds upon absolute knowledge. It is true that our knowledge about the behaviour of a particular thing or about the relation between two things cannot reach the level of demonstrative certainty. But this fact does not warrant the sceptical conclusion that all knowledge is contingent and more or less probable only. Except on the basis of the belief that we know the general features of the world of reality, our ignorance of the particular things would not get a foothold. Here is the fundamental mistake of all forms of empiricism.

Hume, for instance, doubted that the sun may not rise in the east tomorrow. What he failed to see was that such a doubt could not exist except for a man who was absolutely certain that the sun of today will remain identical with the sun of tomorrow, and that the tomorrow will necessarily follow today. It is only on the assumption of the identity of the sun and of the objective necessity of the succession that the doubting mind feels justified in entertaining suspicion about the future behaviour of the sun. If, on the contrary, reality is assumed to be a perpetual, never-ceasing flux which leaves nothing identical or permanent for any length of time, if, that is, the sun had constantly changed from moment to moment, and the events were so loosely and externally connected as to be completely devoid of necessity in succeeding each other, there could arise no doubt about the sunrise; because in that case there would be neither the sun to falsify our expectation nor the tomorrow without the sunrise. From this it should be obvious that the doubt about the sunrise cannot arise except on the presupposed certainty that there is a world where things remain identical in different contexts and at different times, and where the events are so connected that one can only succeed, and not precede, the other. The sceptic has at least to accept the reality of a world in space and time in which the things maintain their identity in spite of changing environments and altered contexts. It is only within such a world that one is justified in doubting that what the past experience has taught may be untaught by the future experience.

Thus, space, time, identity, causality, etc., are presupposed by the sceptical attitude to the specific behaviours of things or the specific relations obtaining between the things. They form a sort of intellectual atmosphere sustaining the sceptical contentions; it would, therefore, be suicidal for scepticism to annihilate the very atmosphere in which it lives, moves and has its being.

The great lesson thrown into prominence by these prevarications and inner paradoxes of pre-Kantian empiricism has been that empirical generalisations rest upon a non-empirical basis. In view of the diverse ramifications, sometimes explicit and often implicit, of the empirical analysis of experience which still holds the field in metaphysics, we have been compelled to devote a considerable space to the condition of philosophical thought before Kant, to show that in spite of the many drawbacks in the Kantian analysis philosophy owes a great debt to his epoch-making discovery that our knowledge of Nature, however perfected and developed through the experimental or statistical method, is in ultimate analysis founded upon certain transcendental principles which themselves are not of empirical origin. The value of this discovery will continue to defy correct appreciation while we do not abandon the slovenly practice of using the term "mind" in the psychological as well as the epistemological sense. If, that is, the term is used in the psychological sense of a particular thing by the side of the other things, then the doctrine of the mental origin of the transcendental principles is not only false but, as we have contended above, it is a self-contradictory venture in so far as it seeks to explain knowledge in terms of a peculiar property of a class of things in the democracy of other things. If, on the other hand, the term is used in the epistemological sense of the subject, the doctrine is a momentous achievement, hardly less important than any epoch-making discovery in the field of the natural sciences. The subject then is realised as one of the universal pre-conditions of all objects of knowledge, and as such, its relation to the objects is in no way reducible to any of the inter-objective relations, much as the relation of space to the geometrical figures is irreducible to any of the relations that may exist between one figure and another. In this sense the subject may be called a foundational principle which supports the entire superstructure of the world of objects including mind and matter, the physical electron and the psychical complexes. It is, therefore, highly misleading to describe true idealism as a doctrine that reduces all reality to mind-dependent psychical states or which looks upon the world as composed of psychic entities.

The remarkable developments of idealistic metaphysics based on the recognition of the transcendental principles of knowledge should have destroyed the prospects of the extreme forms of pluralism, realism, and empiricism, for all time to come. If this has not been achieved so far, the reason, at least partly, lies in the half-hearted battle the idealists have fought against the objectivist attitude in philosophy. A full consideration of the ravages created by the objectivist outlook in the idealist's camp and of the process of revitalizing it by eliminating from its complex skeins the threads of loose texture, is not possible here. As an illustration, we may briefly refer to some of the observations the idealists are in the habit of making on the nature of thought and its role in knowledge.

That we cannot trace the origin of the transcendental principles of knowledge to the mind conceived as a member of the democracy of the universe and that the genealogy of ideas owes its intelligibility to the formative principles of self-consciousness which are not of empirical origin, have been the source of the strength and inspiration of idealism. But the value of these insights has been seriously obscured by the fatal tendency, sometimes too patent to escape detection, to dislocate and analyse these principles in the same way in which a scientist dissects a complex

substance into its component parts. But a more careful consideration of the knowledge situation should have made it clear that it
is ultimately as unprofitable to undertake a naturalistic analysis
of thought as to exhibit the feat of springing upon one's own
shoulders. As every speculative analysis presupposes thinking we
cannot turn round and make thought itself an object of analysis
in the same way in which we analyse the objects of thought.
Thought is not a mere subjective process or a particular faculty
among the crowd of other processes or faculties, but is the
universal pre-condition of all objects that are thought of. In this
sense every subjective process and in fact every item of analysis
presupposes thought as its foundational principle. From this
peculiarity of thought it further follows that whatever is
involved in thinking cannot be *co-ordinate* with the "things"
about which we think. Being the foundation of all objects thought
cannot be levelled down to the status of the superstructure it
builds up; to do so would be to commit the same fallacy of
transcendental dislocation that vitiated Locke's co-ordination
of the transcendental ideas with the empirical ideas.

Yet what is most curious is that the same philosopher who laid
the foundation of a sound epistemology by bringing out the
importance of the function of thought in knowledge should have
also prepared the way for the mistake of making thought co-
ordinate with its own object. The "I think" or the unity of self-
consciousness, according to Kant, is the ultimate transcendental
condition of experience; consequently, all objects of experience
must conform to the conditions of self-consciousness. But in
offering an analysis of self-consciousness Kant's insight became
unsteady. On the one hand it was taken to be the pre-condition
of all objects; and, on the other hand, it was held to be equivalent
to the consciousness of self as reflected back from the consciousness of object. According to the former interpretation the unity
of apperception is the transcendental condition of the object-
consciousness, whereas the latter interpretation makes it consequent upon the consciousness of object. The critics of Kant have
not been slow to recognise and regret this unsteadiness of his
insight at a most crucial point of his theory of knowledge.

The subsequent development of idealism had been marked by an
unfortunate dismissal of the more fruitful of the two alternatives

between which Kant's analysis wavered. It has since insisted upon the correlativeity of the subject-consciousness and the object-consciousness, and their inseparability has come to be one of the most persistent features of the idealistic analysis of knowledge. Self and not-self, subject and object, thought and thing, are supposed to illustrate the correlativity in the same sense in which cause is correlative to the effect or substance is correlative to the accident. Each of the correlative terms, it is contended, has a necessary relation to the other and would be unintelligible when taken in its abstract identity; it at once is itself and its other, or, as it is sometimes put, it is at war with itself and contains in itself its own negation. Thus every finite, definite object of thought has an apparently self-contradictory existence, it wavers between being and not-being. But thought cannot rest satisfied with contradiction, and the only remedy, it is urged, lies in recognising that the whole truth about an object of thought is neither in its identity nor in its difference, but it lies in its identity in difference. Following this line of analysis it has been urged that even the pure unity of thought, the pure consciousness of self, is essentially synthetic. But, it is added, the subject, though it has no meaning when divorced from the object, is yet a reality of a superior order because the correlativity of the object and subject is a correlativity for the subject. This gradually leads to the conclusion that the world is the self-manifestation of a spiritual principle which is a universal that differentiates itself and yet is one with itself in its particularity.

Some such monistic interpretation of the world would be inevitable on the suppostion that whatever is real must be clearly definable by contrast with its "other." The knowing mind accordingly has neither an atomic existence nor is it merely related to matter, but it is a self-distinguishing principle which, while distinguishing itself from its "other," over-reaches the distinction. Without this self-distinction, it is supposed, the spiritual principle would lapse into a veritable vacuum, and abstract identity empty of all contents because that which refuses mediation is too indefinite to carry a meaning. The critics of absolutism have rather too hastily, and sometimes with regrettable superficiality, dismissed this profound analysis in the interest of a cheap type of pluralism. A pluralistic metaphysics based upon the fallacy of abstract identity ought to be an anachronism. And it is considered as such by a large number of contemporary thinkers who have appreciatively viewed the great transition of thought from Kant to Hegel. And if pluralism based upon the fallacy of abstract identity is supported by a broken reed, equally ill-supported is the widely accepted doctrine which finds in knowledge nothing more than a relation of compresence.

By showing the importance and the nature of the universal in knowledge, this monistic interpretation, we believe, has definitely narrowed down the sources of error to which the realistic theories have been peculiarly obnoxious; and in its right appreciation of the function of interpreting thought it has made a valuable advance upon the rival theories of experience. Yet we venture to submit that in its just campaign against the fallacy of abstract identity, it has exaggerated the importance of the principle of identity-in-difference and failed to perceive the limits within which alone the principle is universally valid. That every object of thought must, on pain of being reduced to pure nothing, be defined against its "other" and that underlying the difference there must be a unity in order to make the difference significant, constitute the abiding contribution of idealism to epistemology. But an imperfect perception of the heterogeneity of the transcendental principles from the objects they condition have given rise to the serious error of misapplying the principles governing the *objects* of thought to *thought* itself. This erroneous application and the resulting paradoxes may be illustrated from a few observations of one of the most careful and acute idealists of the last century. Having rightly urged that every intelligible object of thought must be differentiated from what it is not and that no object of thought can be absolutely differentiated so as to exclude any identity or unity which transcends the difference, E. Caird has gone on to observe that neither things nor thoughts can be treated as simply self-identical, as independent or atomic existences. The unconscious shift of the analysis from the object of thought to thought itself is too patent in such observations to be missed by a careful student of Caird's works. That the principle of identity-in-difference is a valuable principle in the sphere of the objects of thought he has succeeded in showing with great penetration and force; but the profound fruitfulness of this

P

new discovery seems to have blinded him to the paradoxes involved in the transference of the principle from the objects to the thought itself. That the objects of thought are essentially parts of a whole and, as such, they carry us beyond themselves, may be admitted, but when we go beyond the objects and speak of thoughts and things as parts of a whole, thoughts are evidently made co-ordinate elements with the things that are objects of thought.

The paradoxes arising out of this levelling down of thought to one of the elements within a whole co-ordinate with things have remained unchallenged owing mainly to the apparently serious difficulties which would beset any other alternative theory of the relation of thought to reality. But this, of course, cannot be the justification for leaving the paradoxes unreconciled and unremoved. To make thought co-ordinate with thing, for example, clearly militates against the central and most fruitful insight of idealism that thought, inasmuch as nothing is external to it, is the universal pre-condition of the things, and as such, thought cannot be one faculty in a crowd of other faculties, or one element among a crowd of other elements. To put it from the other side, all distinctions are *within* thought; it would, therefore, be an unmitigated paradox to consider thought as one of the members of the relation of distinction. When "a" is thought to be distinct from "b," the distinction in order to have a meaning must fall *within* thought. They could not be thought as distinct if thought itself had to be distinguished from them. In fact the unrestricted application of the principle of identity-in-difference would give birth to an infinite regress. If the double movement of differentiation and unification by which thought makes its objects intelligible had to be turned upon thought itself, nothing could be intelligible in the long run.

It is a serious error, therefore, to maintain that intelligibility in every case is due to differentiation and integration. And the only way out of the paradoxes arising out of the misapplication of the characters of the objects of thought to thought itself is to recognise that thought cannot be reduced to the status of its own object; yet it is the unobjectifiable, transcendental, principle presupposed by all objects. It would not be possible here to expose all the paradoxes and prevarications to which this naturalistic tendency to treat thought as co-ordinate with the objects has given birth in the history of epistemology and metaphysics. But it may have been clear from what has been said above that epistemology and metaphysics need a fundamental reconstruction on the basis of the important recognition of the unobjectifiable factors in knowledge and reality.

The recognition of the unobjectifiable factors in knowledge and reality, however, must necessitate the abandonment of some of the doctrines that have been associated with the idealistic approach to reality, such as that the subject and the object are in perfect correlativity with each other, that consciousness over-reaches the distinction between itself and the objects, that meaning is inseparable from mediation, etc. It should be clear from our discussion that the principle of correlativity, strictly speaking, is applicable only in the sphere of the objects; it becomes misleading when used to represent the unique relation between the objects and their transcendental conditions. Similarly, the concept of over-reaching cannot correctly represent the significance of consciousness and the important role it plays in knowledge; all distinctions are presented *to* consciousness, or, to put the same thing in another language, all distinctions are *within* consciousness, or better still, revealed by consciousness; therefore, if consciousness had to distinguish itself from the object, this distinction could not be within itself or be revealed by itself.

The enormous obstacle to a correct appreciation of the doctrine that all distinctions are within consciousness or revealed by consciousness arises from the difficulty of checking the natural tendency, promoted by language and ordinary thought wedded to the forms of language, to misconceive the universal as another item alongside of the particulars and to introduce artificial distinctions in the principle that conditions all distinctions. "I think," "I know," or "I am conscious" being the universal pre-condition of the knowledge of objects, thought or consciousness, strictly speaking, cannot possess the character of self-transcendence or ideality. But this circumstance does not reduce it to an unmeaning abstraction; it would, of course, be such an abstraction in case it were one object among other objects. The trouble arises from the fact that communication is possible only through conceptual description which is the function of discursive intellect; and the result is that even an unobjectifiable principle, when communicated, is thrown into the forms needed for conceptual description. Such expressions, for instance, as "my consciousness," "my character," "my will," etc., encourage the distinction between the self on the one hand, and consciousness, character, or will on the other. And this has given rise to a number of artificial problems of ethics and metaphysics, by reason of the unconscious assumption that corresponding to the dualistic structure of language there is a distinction in reality. But as we must communicate our ideas to one another and seek the truth through mutual criticism and co-operation, the only remedy is to remember that thought or consciousness, when used in the transcendental sense, does not conform to the conditions of dualistic or conceptual mechanism of the intellect, and that the principle of *Determinatio negatio est*, though universally applicable to the finite objects of thought, is not applicable to the Infinite Ultimate Consciousness in the light of which all distinctions have their meaning.

The paradox contained in the belief that even consciousness owes its meaning to mediation and implies a synthesis may be exposed by following its conceptual description to its legitimate consequences. To *know* consciousness *as* consciousness, it must be distinguished from its "other"; again, to know knowledge *as* knowledge, knowledge has similarly to be distinguished from its "other"; and so on *ad infinitum*. The fact is that in the ultimate consciousness knowing and being are identical, and, therefore, the conceptual or mediational machinery is not applicable to it. In the light of these considerations, we may easily understand why contemporary British idealism, in analysing the place of self-consciousness in knowledge, has to swallow the paradox that the self comes into existence when it distinguishes itself from the not-self. This paradox will remain unresolved while our analysis is on the conceptual level. An important step towards a completer analysis of self-consciousness has been taken by contemporary Italian idealism, particularly by Giovanni Gentile, who has repeatedly warned against the mistake of putting "the unity of mind" and "the multiplicity of things" together and on the same plane. A resolute pursuit of the analysis on the same line would inevitably lead to the conclusion that all finite existences have for their sustaining background an infinite, unconditioned, self-revealed, consciousness which, though defying the mechanism of the discursive intellect, is ever known through a sort of indirect envisagement, much as the eye is known through the visible objects or the infinite space is known through the spatial properties of the finite things.

PRINCIPAL PUBLICATIONS

Self, Thought and Reality. The Juvenile Press, Allahabad, 1933.

The Nature of Self. The Indian Press, Allahabad, 1938.

Some Aspects of the Absolutism of Shankaracharya (A comparison between Shankhara and Hegel). The Allahabad University Studies, 1928.

The Religious Quest—Malaviya Commemoration Volume. Benares Hindu University, 1932.

Kant's Analysis of Scientific Method. The Review of Philosophy and Religion, Vol. VI. No. 1, 1935.

Knowledge and Reality. The Allahabad University Studies, 1942.

Reality and Rationality. The Review of Philosophy and Religion, 1942.

The Svayamsiddha Principles of Knowledge. The Review of Philosophy and Religion, 1943.

Presupposition and Proof. The Review of Philosophy and Religion, 1944.

THE SPIRIT OF PHILOSOPHY

by T. R. V. MURTI

Professor of Philosophy, University of Ceylon.
Born June, 1902.

THE SPIRIT OF PHILOSOPHY

PERSONAL STATEMENT

I AM grateful to the Editor, Professor Radhakrishnan, for asking me to contribute to this volume. I make no claim to formulate a system of philosophy. Certain convictions have been growing in me, largely as a study of philosophy and religion as cultivated in the East and the West. I am conscious that I approach philosophy from a standpoint that is essentially traditional. I accept many things which a western mind would find difficult to accept. As a Hindu, I had always believed in the Law of Karma. Reflection on it has induced in me a kind of conviction that it is quite a plausible explanation of the governance of the universe. The conception of the hierarchy of Values (puruṣārtha) with Freedom as the highest value has been no less a conviction. That Philosophy is not an affair of intellectual curiosity or theoretic analysis but a serious spiritual discipline (sādhanā) directed towards the attainment of Freedom is basic to Indian Philosophy, and I subscribe to it without reservation. It is difficult for me, as one brought up in the traditional Hindu atmosphere, to understand that there could be irreconcilable antagonism between Science and Philosophy or Religion. A proper appraisal of Values should, I believe, remove the conflict. These are some of the background beliefs or presuppositions with which I approach philosophy.

In the following pages I have tried to present a Philosophy of Spirit, for I consider this as the basic quest in all philosophy. I have had to content myself, in an article of this limited size, with a statement of the main features without much attempt at argument or elaboration. My exposition is generally based on the Advaita Vadānta and the Mādhyamika systems—the two finest expressions of Indian Absolutism. Among contemporary Indian Absolutist thinkers I have learnt a great deal from Professor Radhakrishnan and the late Professor Krishnachandra Bhattacharyya. Apart from their writings, I have had the inestimable advantage of receiving their personal instruction and guidance.

PHILOSOPHY is the discovery of Spirit (adhyātmavidyā). The actual progression towards this goal as well as its symbolic formulation may be comprised in the concept of philosophy. In all the strivings and speculations broadly taken as philosophy (metaphysics) and exemplified in the several systems of thought, the search for the Spirit is the underlying theme. Very often this objective is obscured by the dust of conflicts raised by different philosophies. The confusion with other pursuits, notably with science and culture, also clouds the issue. Criticism and positivism are protests against this tendency, and are valuable as guarding against this confusion.

The realisation of Spirit is not necessarily by philosophy alone. Religion, too, has the same aim. The Spiritual is the genus of which the philosophical and the religious consciousnesses are the species. On a different view, religion may be subordinated to philosophy and *vice versa:* philosophy could be understood as universal and ultimate and religion as regional and preparatory.

Science investigates the sensible world in a strictly objective way; it attempts to relate and describe objects in terms of other objects. It is a one-level knowledge. There is no occasion for raising such questions as whether the world is real or apparent, whether it is valuable or worthless. Such questions are unintelligible at the scientific level, and no conceivable scientific purpose would be affected by the kind of answer we give to these and similar questions. There is, however, no philosophy without evaluation, without reference to an attitude of the experiencing subject. Philosophy, as belonging to a different dimension, is not an extension of science; nor is it a substitute for the latter. The two just do not intercept each other.

Logical Positivism has done a service to philosophy in drawing our attention to the difference between philosophical statements and scientific propositions. The latter refer to empirical existents and are verifiable, to a certain extent, by appeal to sense-experience. Thoughtful Positivists are realising that the criterion of verifiability is not strictly true even in science. No universal proposition, and science deals only with the universal, is verifiable in principle. Knowledge of future events and of other minds present formidable difficulties.

Logical Positivism is clearly fallacious when it claims to legislate out of existence not only metaphysics but ethics and religion too. "All significant propositions are verifiable", what sort of statement is this? It is neither empirical, for there is no fact corresponding to this; nor is it tautological, for its denial does not involve contradiction. It is metaphysical in the accepted sense. What the statement really does is that it takes over the criterion of significance presumed in science and declares that this is the only criterion of meaning available. This is an arbitrary restriction of meaning. If at all, it should be stated hypothetically: if the criterion of meaning presumed in science is the exemplar of all meaning, then metaphysics is non-significant But in so far as it makes a downright universal statement, Positivism is not positivistic enough: it is metaphysical. It should simply say that the proposition as used in science and commonsense is *different from* statements in metaphysics. It should not make this difference a ground for preference; for, one might as well condemn science for not being significant like metaphysics.

Language contains words and expressions that do not signify the material or the physical realm. From words like God, Soul, Spirit, etc., we cannot directly prove the existence of these entities, as this would be a species of the ontological argument. They are, however, indications of a different realm. "Language is the actuality of culture"; it is the mirror of all our attainments.

Even the logical positivist has some acquaintance with the non-factual realm. For, he accepts, besides propositions concerning empirical matters of fact which are probable and verifiable, some others belonging to logic and pure mathematics. The function of the latter is merely to clarify, analyse and simplify complex propositions; they are tautologies. Are they propositions in any accepted sense? They make no reference to actual or possible facts. They are not even statements, but are symbols of thought-operations. They need no verification, being analytic and axiomatic. As completely containing their content within themselves and subject to their own laws of consistency, Logic and Mathematics constitute a self-subsistent realm in contrast to the factual world of empirical existence investigated by science.

The self-subsistent is by no means confined to logic and mathematics. Art and Literature belong to this autonomous universe. The difference between them is that while the former is regulative, the latter is creative. The poet or the artist creates his world of imagination, very often as an other to the real physical world. The canons of the aesthetic world are certainly not arbitrary, but they are totally different from natural laws. There is no natural necessity why the cultural should supervene on the physical. It is, however, a fact exemplified in all civilisations that the beautiful is superimposed on the merely useful. Shelter and dress must not only protect us from the rigours of the weather, but must look fine and artistic. The same tendency is observed in every detail about food, sex, etc.

Though not spirit or spiritual, the emergence of the cultural order facilitates the consciousness of the spirit. Spirit is the pervasive underlying reality. The apprehension of the universal is not possible without perceiving two or more particulars. The universal is not one more particular set side by side with other particulars. Nor does it exist separately in a different sphere by itself. Spirit is hidden because of its unobtrusive universality and non-utilitarian character. As all things, it is nothing in particular; as everywhere, it is nowhere specially. How then do we know it? The universal is disengaged from the particulars, as what is common and continuous in the differents. Both the physical and the cultural are *to a consciousness*, to the "I" which experiences and enjoys them, though in diverse ways.

The two realms—natural and cultural—stand in thorough going contrast: the first is alien to us, the other is created and sustained by our effort; the former is the world of empirical matter, the latter is a world of *a priori* self-sufficient forms. The greatest difference obtains in our mode of enjoying them. Material things have to be appropriated and their substance consumed to derive pleasure from them. Exclusiveness and rivalry are inseparable from pleasures. In this we do not differ from the animal. On the other hand, cultural pursuits, e.g. music, painting, literature, etc., elevate us; they give us joy, the joy of creation or at least sympathetic participation. There are no proprietary rights in them; they can be shared without diminution of content or quality. Such joys are not subject to limitations of time, "a

thing of beauty is a joy for ever." While an animal would con-
sume the flower to derive satisfaction from it, the deity will contemplate its beauty. Man is the meeting-point of the animal and
the divine. He thus feels in him the conflict of the "lower" and
the "higher."

The existence of the natural and the cultural orders is not
essential for the existence of Spirit. They are, however, necessary
as a step in our *discovery* of Spirit. If our experience had been
confined to one order for all time, we could not differentiate it
from the spiritual. If we had only one mental state or even one
phase of experience (e.g. the waking), we could not distinguish
the self as different from its states. It is because the self is continuous and identical amidst change and difference that we are
conscious of a self behind the states.

The existence and apprehension of the two orders provides
only the background for the discovery of Spirit; one may, however, wander from one state to another without realising the
significance of this alternation. Our attention must be drawn to
it. This happens when our normal objective attitude is reversed,
as we become subjective, reflective. Empirical illusions are
occasions, in natures that are sensitive, for this inwardisation.
What I have been taking as real turns out to be false. This throws
a challenge and presents a problem. Painful experiences act in a
similar way on the practical side. Our normal appraisal of values
receives a rude shock. Such experiences are not exceptions; in
fact, they now reveal themselves as quite the norm. The withdrawal or even suspicion of our dogmatic belief in the reality and
value of the world is the dawning of philosophical consciousness.

II. THE DIFFERENT APPROACHES TO THE REAL

It is commonly held that we start with a formal criterion of the
Real as Non-Contradiction, Coherence or Correspondence, etc.,
and then apply the criterion to things, sit in judgment over them,
accept them as real if they measure up to this criterion of ours
or condemn them as false if they do not. There are some fatal
objections to this procedure. It is not revealed how we have so
secretly and securely alighted on this criterion at the very outset of our quest. The entire procedure would in that case be

hypothetical: if we accept criterion A as the standard, then c, d, e are the consequences; but if B were accepted . . . x, y, z, would be the consequences. Why should one accept criterion A rather than B? After having accepted one or the other, however, the argument can get under way. The logic of a system is posterior to its criterion, and so cannot justify it. Our initial choice would remain arbitrary in the extreme. Besides, we have no means of deciding in favour of one criterion as against another, every criterion being equally formal. The suggested origin of the philosophical consciousness in a mere play of the imagination is artificial; it does not arise in the natural evolution of experience. There is no challenging problem before us the solution of which is provided here. The problem must be present to us in all its intensity and universality; we must be conscious of a mystery behind the entire range of things.

The most important reason for rejecting the formal mode of progression in philosophy is that we do not start with a mere idea or concept of spirit and then ask to be supplied with a concrete entity answering to it. We shall not then be able to escape the Kantian criticism. A concept can never acquire being; nor can any concept, however exalted, be identified with being. Spirit, as Pure Being, is apprehended in all experience: we are in intimate and inalienable contact with it. Philosophical analysis only serves *to disengage* it from things with which it is usually confused and to reveal its transcendence. There could also be no question of producing the consciousness of the spiritual *de novo*. Such consciousness having risen in the manner suggested before, philosophy or religion can direct and deepen it.

The real order of our discovery is that we reach the real by removing the imputed character with which it is clothed; only by breaking the outer shell of appearance do we penetrate to the kernel of reality within. Philosophy starts with the negative judgment or with the consciousness of the false. Only as a contrast is felt between what *appeared* at first to uncritical attention, but which later on turns out to be something else on close scrutiny, can the notion of the real or a quest for the truth arise.

We are here faced with a dilemma: can we negate the false without first being in possession of the knowledge of the real. For, only when we know what the thing in question really is can we be in a position to negate its imputed aspect. On the other hand, if we are already in possession of the truth, negation becomes a gratuitous procedure; it is not an indispensable instrument, a necessary movement, in our discovery of the real.

It is not always the case that we have first known what a thing really is before we negated its imputed character. The "snake" that I misperceive may be realised to be no snake at all from my shouts and cautious proddings, from a safe distance of course, not evoking any aggressive response from the "snake". In fact, my conviction that the presentation before me is not a snake at all, i.e. the negation itself, may lead me, by dissipating fear and ignorance, to the knowledge that the mistaken object is a rope. To take another instance. The extravagant claims and inconsistencies of one or several systems of philosophy may be sufficient ground to condemn them as false. No thesis can be accepted as true simply on the ground that another or a better one is not produced. The weakness of one view cannot by itself be the strength of another view. The very rejection of wrong views, on the score of their inherent flaws, may lead me, by clearing the ground of all undergrowth, to a true knowledge of the Real.

This mode of approach to the Real may be termed *dialectical*. The Mādhyamika system is a representative example of this. Speculative systems, because of their dogmatism, come into inevitable and interminable conflict with each other. If one system conceives reality on one pattern, a second system explains it on a different and opposed pattern. Such antinomical attempts of dogmatic metaphysics engender the Transcendental Illusion. Criticism is the awareness of this illusion, as it analyses and exhibits the inherent flaws infecting every system of thought. It is at once their resolution. It is not relevant to our purpose to examine whether criticism is possible without a position or whether criticism itself is not a position. A correct understanding of the function of criticism, which is the *reflective awareness* of a position, rules out its being another position; and on that very consideration, as being an impartial tribunal, criticism cannot presuppose a position. What the various systems of philosophy *say* with regard to the real may be false, for, they are mutually contradictory. But the philosophical consciousness of which they are the concrete expression cannot be questioned; what can be questioned is their *mis*direction. There are two important features in the dialectical approach to the real: one is its faith in the inner dynamism of the philosophical consciousness to take us to the real, through opposition and resolution of the opposition through criticism; the second is the purely negative function it assigns to criticism. What prevents us from having an intimate and immediate knowledge of the real is our views, thought-patterns, which obscure and obstruct our vision. Intuitive knowledge of the Real (prajñā) is the total negation of all views (dṛṣṭi).

A different analysis of the context of illusion may be made; and this would of necessity mean a correspondingly different approach to the real. In the previous analysis we depended upon the situation discovering itself, by revealing the inherent flaws through its own inner dynamism. We can, however, conceive of that illusion-situation in which a reliable passerby tells us that the thing lying before us is a rope. With this assurance, we go near and directly perceive it to be just as it was described to us. Such knowledge may further provide the ground for the negative judgement, "This is not snake."

In the Vedānta approach to the real, we start our spiritual journey with a chart or true knowledge of the real already in our possession. The Upaniṣads reveal and declare to us, through words, that the Ātman (Spirit) alone is real. Such knowledge is even stated as possible only through revelation (aupaniṣada). If we already have knowledge of the real through revelation, extra-philosophically, what is the function of philosophy, it might be asked? Two answers are possible. It might be held that the intial knowledge that sets us on our journey and guides our path is knowledge through description, verbal and therefore mediate (parokṣa); it would be necessary to convert this knowledge into a direct experience of the real by our contemplation and meditation. More properly, it may be held that there is no qualitative difference in the two stages of our knowledge of the Real; for even from the outset, the knowledge pertaining to the Self (Ātman, Brahman) is direct and immediate (aparokṣa). Our later effort does not bring about any qualitative change; but merely removes certain misconceptions and doubts, thereby deepening and intensifying our initial knowledge. The function of negation or dialectic is secondary: it does not reveal the truth, but only serves to strengthen and complete it. The Vedānta approach may be termed theological, as it depends on extra-philosophical revelation that sets philosophy on its feet. It would however, be wrong to take it as dogmatic or as subordinating philosophy to theology. The cue may be received from revelation, but the ultimate knowledge of the Real is one's intimate and intuitive realisation of it. Our attention to an innate eternal truth, like principles and axioms, may be drawn by a teacher who propounds it to us; but it is realised by us and becomes an integral possession of our self.

What is common to both the approaches is the conception of Spirit as the reality of all things, its transcendance and our non-discursive intuitive apprehension of it.

III. THE TRANSCENDENCE OF SPIRIT

There are two main stages in the discovery of Spirit. The first is the transition from things to Spirit, from appearances to their reality. The procedure is essentially negative: we literally un-cover and divest things of their apparent character to reach their inner core. This is knowledge of Spirit as what it is not. And having gained access to the real, we know what it is by penetrating to its essential nature. The first is definition of Spirit *per accidens* (taṭastha-lakṣaṇa); the second is the intrinsic, intuitional appre-hension of it (svarūpa-lakṣaṇa).

Spirit is the spirit of things, their inner essence or reality. It is not spirit and things: spirit on one side and things on the other. Conversely, the world can be conceived as the appearance of Spirit, as what it is mistaken for. The soul is apprehended as *not* the body with which it is ordinarily identified. We regain it only as we withdraw ourselves from the objects of sense and from our own body.

Though in the world of phenomena, Spirit is not of it. It is Transcendent Being. The appearance, however, is not without it. The relation between them is one-sided, not reciprocal: it is like the one obtaining between the ground and its appearance. This relation, which may be called transcendent identity, is *sui generis*. Other relational modes, e.g. substance-attribute, cause and effect, universal and particular, have to be conceived on this pattern.

The proof for the existence of Spirit as Transcendent Being (Absolute) is axiological. Without transcendence no evaluation is possible. The distinctions we make between truth and falsity and the dissatisfaction we feel with the objects of the world and our unceasing quest for something far transcending empirical things imply an absolute norm; it presupposes two orders, the higher and the lower. These are not spatial positions, nor can they be conceived as the more or the less extensive. The distinction is qualitative. The true and the false are not merely different like red and blue; there is preference or evaluation. The false is what is rejected or dispensable, and the true is the indispensable. The real and its appearance are not, therefore, mutually implicatory. To call anything appearance is to be aware of two aspects of a thing, the essential and the accidental: what a thing is in itself, absolutely, unrelatedly and what it appears to percipients under certain conditions. Again, what appears always appears *as* another; it is understandable only in the context of of illusion or mistake.

All these implications follow, it might be urged, if we employed the notion of appearance. But are we necessitated to employ that notion at all? If all our perceptions were veridical and absolute without any subjective (accidental) element in them or if they were utterly subjective without a suggestion of the independently given, there would be no need to make the distinction of the real and the apparent. Such however is not the case. The ever-present problem in all experience is the sifting of the real from mere appearance.

A proper interpretation of relation would also lead to the same result. The logic is that the two terms sustaining a relation are not of the same order, one is *higher* and the other *lower*: the two terms are neither mutually dependent nor mutually independent, i.e. relation is neither "internal" nor "external". If mutually dependent, we cannot distinguish between the two terms; as they so necessarily imply each other that one cannot exist without the other any time and in any manner. We cannot even say that there are two terms, for the basis of distinction is lacking; distinction implies difference and separability. If mutually independent, there is no basis of connection: each term is a self, a self-contained universe as it were; the two terms could not be brought together. To escape this predicament we have to conceive one term as basic and thus capable of existing apart from the other; while the other is incapable of so doing and therefore dependent. One term, the higher, is not exhausted in the relationship; it has a transcendent or non-implicatory existence which is its intrinsic nature; and this makes for its distinction from the other term. The latter, however, is entirely exhausted within the relation and has no non-relative existence; this aspect provides for the relatedness or connection of the two terms.

To illustrate this logic *in concreto*. The attribute is not anything without substance; the latter is something by itself, self-existent and self-evident. Substance is not a mere name for the cluster of qualities; for, it must be already existent in its own right for the cluster to form. Spirit may be understood as the ultimate or only Substance, the prius of all things. The cause is free from and superior to the effect; the two are not on a par. In the ultimate analysis, only the Free can be the cause. If the cause transformed itself and were exhausted in the process, there would be annihilation and replacement, but no causation. The causal sequence has to be conceived as an emanation (vivarta), production without diminution of power. Spirit is the ultimate Free Cause. The Universal is not a mere name for the totality of particulars, nor is it dependent on them. Without the universal the different particulars cannot be related; they cannot even be compared or contrasted. The differences appear and have their being on a common platform. Differences presuppose unity and identity and not *vice versa*. The particulars depend on the universal without dividing it.

Spirit is free to manifest itself in numberless ways; and the manifestations are in and through Spirit. They are not integral parts of it. They indicate Spirit without constituting it. If they constituted it, Spirit would be nothing apart from finite things that are subject to decay and dissolution; it would not be transcendent. If, however, appearances did not indicate Spirit, we could not even be aware of its reality, much less reach it. It need not be feared that what does not constitute an entity cannot also indicate it or that only the differentia can distinguish a thing. Even an assumed mark can serve the purpose of definition. The bough of the tree may well indicate the location of the moon without belonging to it. The eagle perching on the chimney does serve to mark off and single out the particular house from among several, without forming a permanent fixture therein, What is essential is that the mark should not belong to any other, though it need not belong to this entity essentially. Likewise, the world of appearance may be indicative of Spirit without constituting it; the appearance may even be said to belong to Spirit in the sense of not belonging to any other.

Appearances are not different from the Absolute Spirit, though they are not one with it. The relation is neither reciprocal identity nor utter difference. It is what we have called Transcendent Identity. If not identical, Spirit and phenomenal things would fall asunder: Spirit would not be spirit of things, their reality. If there were no transcendence, things would be all, there would be no reality behind the appearances. The distinction between the real and appearance should not then arise. The Transcendence of Spirit is not to be mistaken for the illegitimate transcendent use of the Categories of thought, substance, causality, etc., beyond phenomena. It is the freeing of Being of the empirical accretions wrongly ascribed to it; it is not investing a concept with existence. We are already in intimate and inalienable contact with Spirit as Being.

IV. THE ESSENTIAL NATURE OF SPIRIT

The first stage in the discovery of Spirit is the transition from the world of appearance to its reality. The analysis of relation and the axiological argument based on value-judgments can but indicate the presence of the Spirit. We know that it is; we still do not have any definite apprehension of what it is. A cue to the nature of Spirit could be obtained if we analysed the nature of philosophical consciousness. And this, as I have stated before, is an attitude of the experiencing subject to the object or of a content to a consciousness that enjoys and avaluates it.

We could think of three, and possibly only three, attitudes of the experiencing subject to the content: one, in which the content determines the mode of attention: attention is, as it were, lost in the object, but not *vice versa*; or second, in which consciousness determines the content and not *vice versa*; or third, that in which the determination is either way, mutual. It might be thought that a fourth alternative is possible in a situation where neither determines the other. But this is clearly tantamount to denying all relation: the two things fall asunder, and we cannot even speak of them as two. Our a priori scheme thus yields only three modes of relation between consciousness and content. And these may be identified with Knowing, Willing and Feeling.

These three spirit-functions may be formulated thus. In knowing the Truth, our attitude is one of discovery or revelation of what is already present; the given is all. The object of knowledge, as in Truth, is unconstituted by the subjective act of knowing. There may arise a demand, as the goal of spiritual discipline, to realise the Truth as what is not, and need not be, known. The Thing-in-itself, the given, must be known without the mediation of the Categories of thought, without any trace of subjectivity—empirical and transcendental. The latter usually condition experience; and while from a practical point of view the object known through them may be valid, yet for a lover of the Truth, Pure Being must be known in its undistorted form. It is not a necessary part of the Truth that it should be known and declared as the truth. Nor does it suffer either by being known and declared. It may freely condescend to reveal itself. In Willing, the willed content is *wholly through* the act of willing, not having any being without the latter. This is best exemplified in moral endeavour and in conscious imagination. The spiritual demand here will be to realise the *Pure Act* without any trace of the given, the other. In Feeling, content and consciousness, object and subject, form an indistinguishable whole or unity; the separation of the one from the other would mean abstraction or hollowness and consequent loss of the feeling tone. As no empirical emotion, physical pleasures or even aesthetic joys can come up to this ideal, the spiritual demand would be to realise a state of perfect amplitude or Fullness of Feeling as Bliss (paripūrṇatā or ānanda).

The justification for holding that the nature of philosophical consciousness defines the nature of Spirit is that philosophy is the most significant expression of the human spirit. And Spirit is not another entity but essentially identical with the human: Man shorn of his adventitious and apparent characteristics is indeed Spirit. If this were not accepted, we shall have been left with no means of understanding and appreciating Spirit. It would be utterly foreign to us.

As a point of confirmation, it may be noted that all the great philosophies and religions of the world speak of the Triune Nature of Godhead. In spite of the admitted difficulty in giving a rational (conceptual) explanation of it, the doctrine of Trinity has been held as a vital definition of Godhead in deeper Christianity. In Buddhism we have the Trikāya conception of the Buddha. And the Vedānta conception of Brahman as Sat, Cit and Ānanda stands, I venture to suggest, for the three functions of Knowledge, Willing and Feeling. Spirit is Truth or Knowledge; Spirit is Freedom or Will; Spirit is Bliss or Feeling. Each is *sui generis*, a Self: each is identical with Spirit (Brahman) wholly, and not a part or a predicate of it. It would indeed be less of a mistake to take them denotatively as things or substances. The three are not synonymous; their difference is not verbal. Pure Being, Act (Freedom) and Bliss are equally and fully Brahman. This does not mean a plurality of Absolutes, as there is no conceptual distinction; all these denote one entity, though in different ways. Brahman is their inexpressible substantial unity.

V. SPIRIT AS THE BASIC VALUE AND BASIS OF ALL VALUES

The Philosophy of Spirit is no speculative luxury. It is not for the satisfaction of a theoretic curiosity. Philosophy is not practical in any narrow sense; it would not solve any one problem in particular. But it is at the basis of every human activity, and it would solve not one but all problems. Realisation of Spirit is the realisation of all Values, as it is Truth, Freedom and Bliss. It is not only a vision of reality, but a consummation of life as well.

Even in the emprical sphere, the philosophy of spirit has great value. It is necessary to realise that our empirical differences exhibited in the political, social and cultural modes of life are but the outward expression of different ideologies or metaphysical premises. Any attempt to eliminate or stifle these basic and geuine differences succeeds in creating bitterness and competition. The cultural differences have not only to be tolerated but accepted in humility of spirit and fostered.

Owing to the phenomenal discoveries in science and their practical application, the peoples of the world have been brought together; the geographical and physical oneness of the world has been brought home to us. But our divergences and rivalries have also increased tremendously; war has become chronic and global in its proportions. The present-day world lacks unity and good-will; it has no soul or spirit to animate and unify it.

A vicious materialistic philosophy produces unrest, strife and bitterness among men, as it is based on egoistic premises—appropriation and domination. Only a spiritual philosophy can serve as the basis of a world-culture. The essence of this consists in the utter negation of all egoity and the realisation of the unity of all being. It is only Absolutism of Spirit that can make for the fundamental unity of existence and at the same time allow for the differences that are exhibited in the great cultural groups of the world. The transcendence of Spirit means its freedom from every empirical standpoint, and universality. Different ways of realising the Spirit are quite compatible with its universality.

THE SPIRIT IN MAN

by S. RADHAKRISHNAN

Born 1888; Vice-Chancellor and Professor of Philosophy,
Andhra University, Waltair
Educated at the Madras Christian College

THE SPIRIT IN MAN

I. PHILOSOPHY AND RELIGION IN INDIA

In the history of thought the problem of philosophy is approached in two different ways. There are some who take up particular groups of phenomena for investigation and leave the links to take care of themselves. Others view the world as a whole and seek to give general syntheses which comprehend the vast variety of the universe. The two ways of approach cannot be sharply separated. The universe is an interrelated changing process. When we study its parts, by separating out in thought certain aspects, we cannot help raising the question of the nature of the universe as a whole and man's place in it. In India philosophy has been interpreted as an enquiry into the nature of man, his origin and destiny. It is not a mere putting together or an assemblage of the results obtained by the investigation of different specialised problems, not a mere logical generalisation intended to satisfy the demand for all-inclusiveness. Such abstract views will have formal coherence, if any, and little organic relationship with the concrete problems of life. To the Indian mind, philosophy is essentially practical, dealing as it does with the fundamental anxieties of human beings, which are more insistent than abstract speculations. We are not contemplating the world from outside but are in it.

The practical bearing of philosophy on life became my central interest from the time I took up the study of the subject. My training in philosophy which began in the years 1905 to 1909 in the Madras Christian College, with its atmosphere of Christian thought, aspiration and endeavour, led me to take a special interest in the religious implications of metaphysics. I was strongly persuaded of the inefficiency of the Hindu religion to which I attributed the political downfall of India. The criticisms levelled against the Hindu religion were of a twofold character. It is intellectually incoherent and ethically unsound. The theoretical foundations as well as the practical fruits of the religion were challenged. I remember the cold sense of reality, the

depressing feeling of defeat that crept over me, as a causal
relation between the anæmic Hindu religion and our political
failure forced itself on my mind during those years. What is
wrong with Hindu religion? How can we make it somewhat
more relevant to the intellectual climate and social environment
of our time? Such were the questions which roused my interest.

Religion expresses itself in and discloses its quality by the
morality which it demands. While there is a good deal in Hindu
religion and practice which merits just criticism, dark aspects
of brutality, cruelty, violence, ignorance of nature, superstition
and fear, in its essence the religion seemed to me to be quite
sound. Its followers are carried along by a longing for the vision
of God which has brought some of them to the verge of a holy
perfection in which the perplexing dichotomy between the flesh
and the spirit which men for ever feel but never understand is
overcome. Hindu culture is directed towards that which is transcendent and beyond. Its great achievements in times past were
due to a high tension of the spirit to which our age has no parallel.
The purpose of religion is spiritual awakening and those who are
awakened are delivered from base delusions of caste and creed,
of wealth and power.

There is, however, a tragic divergence between this exalted
ideal and the actual life. In the first place in our anxiety to have
no temporal possessions and spend our days in communion with
spirit, the essential duty of service to man has been neglected.
Religion may start with the individual but it must end in a
fellowship. The essential interpenetration of God and the world,
ideals and facts, is the cardinal principle of Hinduism and it
requires us to bring salvation to the world. In the great days,
the burning religious spirit expressed itself in a secular culture
and a well-established civilisation. The religious soul returned
from the contemplation of ultimate reality to the care of practical
life. This fact is illustrated in the lives of the great teachers like
Buddha and Śaṁkara who shared in the social and civilising
function of religion. Hinduism strove victoriously against the
corruption of the ancient world, civilised backward people,
transformed and purified the new elements and preserved the
tradition of the spiritual and the profane sciences. Proceeding
on the assumption that all are of the same divine essence and

therefore of equal worth and entitled to the same fundamental rights, Hinduism yet hesitated to take the bold steps essential for realising this end. Exalted ideals propounded by the founders of a religion meet with obstacles imposed by social inertia and corporate selfishness and those imbued with its true spirit must get back to the ideals and by effort and example break down the obstacles. Secondly, the kingdom of spirit is an elusive thing where one is deceived by shams and illusions. There are sinister people in every land who practise a kind of sorcery and bewitch the uneducated emotional into a sort of magic sleep. Much harm is done by spiritualistic and necromantic practices in which spirit and sense, religion and the powerful seductions of life get confused. It is essential to liberate not only bodies from starvation but minds from slavery. Saintliness, when genuine, is marked by true humility and love. Religion is a search for truth and peace, not power and plenty. Thirdly, in the name of religion we are often taught that the prevailing conditions are ordained by God. Thus it had been, was now and ever would be. Rightly interpreted, religion means courage and adventure, not resignation and fatalism. The customs and institutions of a community in which moral obligations are ingrained require to be reformulated in a dynamic social order. As these give their moral education to the members comprising a community, they should not lag far behind the conscience of the community. There is such a thing as the degeneration of accepted ideas. Many of them are kept going artificially, even after life has left them. The contemplative thinkers who transmit to their generation the delicacy of old forms, reverence for the past, the breath of history, the power to feel and understand the secure and the self-contained as well as the visions of new things and vistas of a transformed age, men who know how to look upon tradition as something fluid and mobile, constantly modified and changed by the demands of life, are not among those who belong to the priestly profession today. The present class of priests, with rare exceptions have lost their good breeding, kindliness and polish and have not gained in sureness of intellect, learning or adaptability. They know only that the discipline of tradition erects a barrier against radicalism and excessive individualism. They think that they are safeguarding the community against revolutionary change but are only fomenting it. If we pull off their masks, doubters stand revealed in many cases. They are not sure of what they preach and are mere opportunists by reason of a dumb gnawing despair whose nature they themselves do not understand. They are to some extent responsible for the prevalent spiritual sluggishness. They thrust formulas into our heads which we repeat mechanically, without any real knowledge of what they mean. A few ceremonies are observed more out of regard for our reputation or our relatives or as a matter of habit than out of any inward urge or sense of community. We are Hindus simply because of the legal framework of life and the individual feeling of security within which we live and have our being. Many of us have not the slightest idea of the true nature of religion, that hidden flame, which is more active among the young whose minds are in ferment. We can hear the call and the challenge of the youth for a new emphasis in religion, a new mankind. It is of the spirit of youth that it can never entirely despair of human nature. It will debase itself rather than cease to believe in its dream visions. It is convinced that the affliction that is visited on us is the return for our common failure.

Our present political condition is the sign of an inward crisis, a loss of faith, a weakening of our moral fibre. Events happen in the mind of man before they are made manifest in the course of history. It is essential for us to get back to the old spirit which requires us to overcome the passions of greed and avarice, to free ourselves from the tyranny of a dark past, from the oppression by spectres and ghosts, from the reign of falsehood and deceit. If we do not undertake this task, the sufferings of our day would be without meaning and justification.

II. THE NEED FOR A SPIRITUAL RENEWAL

A veritable renewal is what the world and not merely India stands in need of. To those who have lost their anchorage, to our age itself which is in a great transition, the way of the spirit is the only hope.

The present chaos in the world can be traced directly to the chaos in our minds. There is division in man's soul. We assume that the intellectual and the moral exhaust the nature of man and that the world can be rebuilt on the basis of scientific or secular humanism. Man tears himself from the religious centre, discovers his own powers and possibilities and through their impetuous play tries to create a new society. The modern intellectual whose mind has been moulded to a degree seldom recognised by the method and concepts of modern science, has great faith in verifiable facts and tangible results. Whatever cannot be measured and calculated is unreal. Whispers that come from the secret depths of the soul are rejected as unscientific fancies. Since men began to think, there have always been sceptics. "The wise man," said Arcesilaus, "should withhold his assent from all opinions and should suspend his judgment." This admirable attitude for the scientific investigator is now turned to one of dogmatic denial which offers but an inadequate guide to life and action.

What are these seemingly indisputable facts on which the new world is to be built? Human life is an infinitesimal speck on a tiny planet, in a system of planets revolving round an insignificant star, itself lost in a wilderness of other stars. Life is an accident arising in some unknown fashion from inert matter. It is wholly explicable, though not yet explained by mechanical laws. It has assumed various forms through the operation of chance (variation and environment). Even the mind of man is a chance product evolved to help man to overcome in the struggle for existence. The world of nature is indifferent to man's dreams and desires. Many strange creatures, products of millions of years of evolution, have passed away and man need not be so presumptuous as to think that he alone is fated to go on for all time. He is but an episode in terrestrial evolution and his existence on earth will come to an end.

The science of anthropology tells us how relative all moral systems are, especially those relating to sexual life. To the intellectuals who were in any case gradually shaking off the traditional moral restraints and rehabilitating the rights of the flesh, Freud, without intending in the least such a result, made licence respectable. The science of psycho-analysis is said to justify the consecration of all desires and a complete liberation from all restraints.

Social groups are formed in the interests of survival. They

have no other purpose than furthering their own material good, by force and fraud, if necessary. Economic welfare is the end of all existence. The principles of evolution offer a scientific basis for militaristic imperialism. When powerful groups exploit the weaker races of the earth, they are but instruments for furthering the evolution of higher biological forms which has brought us from amoeba to man and will now complete the journey from Neanderthal man to the scientific barbarians of the modern world. The great powers constitute themselves into God's police-men for preserving law and order in all parts of the globe, into missionaries for civilizing the weaker races, who are treated as creatures of a lower order, annoying intruders with a different mental cast and moral constitution. The Jews are not the only people who called themselves the Chosen Race. Others also have faith in their mission, though this faith is based not on revelation but on historic or legendary destiny. To fulfil their destinies nations are converted into military machines and human beings are made into tools. The leaders are not content with governing men's bodies, they must subjugate their minds. They must transmit faith in their messianic mission to the community at large. Without much effort they gain the goodwill of the decadent and the discontented, the poor and the unemployed, the adven-turous and the opportunist and the young and the eager who have neither ideal nor guiding star but only erring minds and quivering hearts. The seeds of rampant nationalism find fertile soil in the unpledged allegiance of emancipated minds. An abnormal state of moral and mental tension results where free thinking is replaced by dull obedience, moral development by moral quietism, feeling of humanity by arrogance and self-righteousness.

Religion needs certainty, complete assurance, but this is just the quality which scientific naturalism has pretty thoroughly discredited. Our need to believe, we are told, cannot be a sufficient foundation for faith. Religion, as a matter of history, has crippled the free flight of intelligence and stifled glad devotion to human values. It has fostered superstition and prescribed crime. It has comforted millions of suffering humanity with illusions of extra-terrestrial solace to compensate for the barrenness of their earthly lives. Religion is only a species of poetry (Santayana), mythology

(Croce), sociological phenomenon (Durkheim), or a narcotic for a decadent society (Lenin). Spiritual life is a deception and a dream. At best we can use religion as a code of ethics. It can be reduced to a few rules of morality. When Kant defined religion as the knowledge of our duties as divine commands and made God not a present help but a future judge rewarding the good and punishing the wicked, he very nearly ousted God from human life. In his *Religion within the Limits of Reason*, Kant views moral life as a life of individual self-determination in which neither God nor man can assist but in which each individual must carry on his separate struggle by his own unaided strength. Such a view leaves little room for anything like true religious worship or for the investment of life with purpose. The men of talent, without any binding ties or true affinities, disastrously isolated, thrown entirely on their own resources, their own solitary egos, with no foothold either in heaven or on earth, but completely uprooted are the free men who have emerged from the narrow frames of creeds and sects, from the fear of popes and priests; these are the ideal heroes, the beacons for all the ages. Each man is a prophet and the result is a regular Tower of Babel where no one understands the other. Each of them understands in his own way his own ideal for the world. Confusion of tongues in the Tower will and must end in catastrophe.

"This may well be called the age of criticism," said Kant, "a criticism from which nothing need hope to escape. When religion seeks to shelter itself behind its sanctity, and law behind its majesty, they justly awaken suspicion against themselves and lose all claim to the sincere respect which reason yields only to that which has been able to bear the test of its free and open scrutiny." But what has criticism achieved? It has banished absolute truth from thought and life. In aesthetics, beauty is treated as subjective. In jurisprudence, law is declared to be an expression of social convention, not of justice. In morality a full and varied life is said to be inconsistent with a rigid moral code. Even theologians have dropped the Absolute and taken to finite, "self-educating" gods.

What is the result of this new positivist criticism on life? We have a world of rationalist prophets, of selfish individualists, of a monstrous economic system compounded out of industrialism

Q

and capitalism, of vast technical achievements and external conquests, of continual craving for creature comforts and love of luxury, of unbridled and endless covetousness in public life, of dictatorships of blood and brutality, anxious to make the world a shambles dripping with human blood, of atheism and disdain for the soul, a world in which nothing is certain and men have lost assurance. In the great cities in the East as well as in the West we meet with young men, cold and cynical, with a swagger and a soldierly bearing, energetic and determined to get on, waiting for a chance to get into a place in the front rank, men who esteem themselves masters of life and makers of the future, who think, as Byron said, they lead the world because they go to bed late. Their self-assertive, off-hand manner, their vulgarity and violence, their confident insolence and cocksureness, their debasing of the law and derisive disregard of justice show the utter demoralisation through which the world is passing. They are not merely the thin crust of the social pyramid. They lead and control the masses who in the new democracies are gifted with a capacity for reading which is out of all proportion to their capacity for thinking. Life has become a carnival or a large circus in progress, without structure, without law, without rhythm.

Let us look closer for the other side to the picture. The denial of the divine in man has resulted in a sickness of soul. To suspend our will and thought and drift whither we do not know is not satisfying. Man can never be at rest, even if his physical needs are amply met. Bitterness will continue to disturb his mind and spoil his peace. Nature cannot be completely tamed to do man's bidding. Her caprices, her storms and tempests, her cyclones and earthquakes, will continue to shatter his work and dash his hopes. The great human relationships cannot be easily freed from interference by pride and jealousy, selfishness and disloyalty. Fortune's vagaries and the fickleness of man will continue to operate. Peace of mind is a remote hope until and unless we have a vision of perfection, a glimpse of eternity to prevail against the perspective of time. Security without which no happiness is possible cannot come from the mastery of things. Mastery of self is the essential prerequisite.

The world is passing through a period of uncertainty, of wordless longing. It wants to get out of its present mood of spiritual chaos, moral aimlessness and intellectual vagrancy. Burdened and tired to death by his loneliness, man is ready to lean on any kind of authority, if it only saves him from hopeless isolation and the wild search for peace. The perils of spiritual questioning are taking us to the opposite extreme of revivals and fundamentalism in religion. These are only half-way houses to a radical reconstruction of the mind. The uncertainty between dogmatic faith and blatant unbelief is due to the non-existence of a philosophic tradition or habit of mind. The mental suffering of the thinking, when the great inheritance of mankind is concealed by the first views of science, the suffering which is due to the conflict between the old and the new values, which are both accepted, though without reconciliation, is the sign that no upheaval, no crude passion can put out the light of spirit in man. However dense the surrounding darkness may be, the light will shine though that darkness may not comprehend it. Only when the life of spirit transfigures and irradiates the life of man from within will it be possible for him to renew the face of the earth. The need of the world today is for a religion of the spirit, which will give a purpose to life, which will not demand any evasion or ambiguity, which will reconcile the ideal and the real, the poetry and the prose of life, which will speak to the profound realities of our nature and satisfy the whole of our being, our critical intelligence and our active desire.

III. INTUITION AND INTELLECT

My attempt to answer the question stated in the previous section is largely influenced by the thought of Plato and Śaṁkara. They are not concerned so much with particular religious dogmas as with the central problem of religion. Today, our trouble is not so much with the infallibility of the Pope or the inerrancy of the Bible, not even with whether Christ or Krishna is God or whether there is a revelation. All these problems have changed their meaning and are dependent on the one and only problem, whether there is or is not behind the phenomena of nature and the drama of history an unseen spiritual power, whether the universe is meaningful or meaningless, whether it is God or chance. Plato and Śaṁkara appeal to me for the other reason that they are masters in the art of tempering the rigour of their argument with that larger utterance which is the soul of true literature. Writers on philosophy sometimes require to be reminded of Landor's warning: "Clear writers like fountains do not seem as deep as they are: the turbid look most profound."

Hindu systems of thought believe in the power of the human mind to lead us to all truth. Our ordinary mind is not the highest possible order of the human mind. It can rise to a level almost inconceivable to us. Each system prescribes a discipline or a practical way of reaching the higher consciousness. Faith in the ultimate values which characterises the philosopher in Plato's Dialogues, as distinct from the pseudo-philosopher or the sceptical sophist, is not a matter of dialectics or sophistry but of spiritual awareness.

The idealist tradition both in the East and the West has asserted the supremacy of spirit in man. Mere physical desire and passion, impulse and instinct, even intellect and will do not exhaust his nature. The spiritual status is the essential dignity of man and the origin of his freedom. It is the state anterior to the divisions between intellect, feeling and will, where consciousness forms a unity which cannot be analysed. It is the presupposition, the limit and the goal of our divided consciousness. When the spirit, which is the mind in its integrity, is at work, man has the immediate intuition of his unity with the eternal, though, in the derived intellectual consciousness, he remains apart and works into the grounds of his own being and discerns his relation to and dependence upon the presence behind the trembling veil of phenomena.

This essential truth is expressed in the language of religion as the indwelling of the Logos. There is the image of God in man, an almost deathless longing for all that is great and divine. The values of the human soul are not earth-bound but belong to the eternal world to which man can rise through discipline and disinterestedness. He can transcend the old law of brute creation which gives the race to the swift and the battle to the strong and accept the principle that he that saves his life shall lose it. When, in response to the imperative voice of conscience, he renounces everything and dies, he touches infinite, lays hold on the eternal order and shares his kinship with the divine. At the centre of the soul there is a something, a spark "so akin to God that it is one with God, and not merely united to Him" (Eckhart).

Spiritual apprehension or the kind of awareness of real values which are neither objects in space and time nor universals of thought is called intuition. There is the controlling power of reality in intuitive apprehension quite as much as in perceptual acts or reflective thought. The objects of intuition are recognised and not created by us. They are not produced by the act of apprehension itself.

Ours is an age which is justly proud of its rationalism and enlightenment. But any sound rationalism will recognise the need for intuition. St. Thomas observes: "The articles of faith cannot be proved demonstratively. The ultimate truth which is the criterion by which we measure all other relative truths is only to be experienced, not to be demonstrated."[1] Descartes, though a thorough-going rationalist and admirer of the geometrical method, uses the intuitive principle. While he employs the process of doubt to free the mind from error and prejudice and insists that we should accept only what presents itself to the mind so clearly and distinctly as to exclude all grounds of doubt, he finds what is clear and distinct in his knowledge of himself as a thinking being. It alone is beyond all doubt, self-evident, dependent upon nothing else. Descartes distinguishes perception, imagination and syllogistic reasoning from intuition which he defines as "the undoubting conception of an unclouded and attentive mind, and springs from the light or reason alone. It is more certain than deduction itself in that it is simpler." While the truths intuition grasps are self-evident, training, or what Descartes calls method, is necessary to direct our mental vision to the right objects so that our mind can "behold" the objects. In so far as our minds are not creative of reality but only receptive of it, we must get into contact with reality, outward by perception, inward by intuition, and by means of intellect interpret and understand it. Logical proof is not self-complete. Certain *a priori* principles constitute limits to it. We are not referring to the psychological *a priori*. The temporal

[1] *Summa Theol.*, q.46, n. 2.

priority in an individual mind may be traced to social tradition or race memory but there are certain propositions which are presupposed in experience which can neither be proved nor disproved. These unproved first principles are known by intuition. Thus we have a sense of the organic wholeness of things while intellectual knowledge is abstract and symbolic. And again, the higher the reality the less adequate is our knowledge of it. Analytical intellect cannot give us a full understanding to the ecstasy of love or the beauty of holiness.

It is unfortunate that insistence on intuition is often confused with anti-intellectualism. Intuition which ignores intellect is useless. The two are not only not incompatible but vitally united. Plato is the classic on this question. He says in the *Symposium* (211) that we know the essence of beauty in a supreme beatific vision, which is, as it were, the consummation of the philosopher's searching enquiry. Similarly in the *Republic* (vii and viii) we are told that the world of forms is apprehended by us through the exercise of reason, though Plato is quite clear that it is not through mere reason.[1] Intuition is beyond reason, though not against reason. As it is the response of the whole man to reality, it involves the activity of reason also. The truths of intuition are led up to by the work of the understanding and can be translated into the language of understanding, though they are clearly intelligible only to those who already in some measure have immediate apprehension of them. Intuition is not independent but emphatically dependent upon thought and is immanent in the very nature of our thinking. It is dynamically continuous with thought and pierces through the conceptual context of knowledge to the living reality under it. It is the result of a long and arduous process of study and analysis and is therefore higher than the discursive process from which it issues and on which it supervenes.

Intuition is not used as an apology for doctrines which either could not or would not be justified on intellectual grounds. It is

---

[1] Cp. Burnet: "To anyone who has tried to live in sympathy with the Greek philosophers, the suggestion that they were intellectualists must seem ludicrous. On the contrary, Greek philosophy is based on the faith that reality is divine and that the one thing needful is for the soul, which is akin to the divine, to enter into communion with it."—*Greek Philosophy*, vol. i, *Thales to Plato*, p. 12. This is certainly true of Plato.

not shadowy sentiment or pathological fancy fit for cranks and dancing dervishes: It stands to intellect as a whole to a part, as the creative source of thought to the created categories which work more or less automatically. Logical reflection is a special function within the concrete life of mind and is necessarily a fraction of the larger experience. If it sets itself up as constitutive of the whole life of mind, it becomes, in Kant's words, a "faculty of illusion." The different energies of the human soul are not cut off from one another by any impassable barriers. They flow into each other, modify, support and control each other. The Sanskrit expression "samyagdarśana" or integral insight, brings out how far away it is from occult visions, trance and ecstasy.

Simply because the deliverances of intuition appear incontestable to the seer or happen to be shared by many, it does not follow that they are true. Subjective certitude, whose validity consists in mere inability to doubt, is different from logical certainty. The sense of assurance is present, even when the object is imaginary and even such objects, so long as they are believed to be actual, evoke feelings and attitudes quite as intense and effective as those excited by real ones. While religion may be satisfied with the sense of convincedness, which is enough to foster spiritual life, philosophy is interested in finding out whether the object believed is well grounded or not.

Intuition requires cultivation quite as much as the powers of observation and thought. We can realise the potentialities of spirit only by a process of moral ascesis which gradually shapes the soul into harmony with the invisible realities. Plotinus tells us that the path to the goal is long and arduous, traversing first the field of civic virtues, then the discipline of purification and then the contemplation which leads to illumination. Indian thought requires us to abstract from sense life and discursive thinking in order to surrender to the deepest self where we get into immediate contact with reality. To know better, we must become different, our thoughts and feelings must be deeply harmonised. Intuition is not only perfect knowledge but also perfect living. The consecration of the self and the knowledge of reality grow together. The fully real can be known only by one who is himself fully real.

IV. ART AND MORALITY

What we need today in our life is a breath from the spirit of another and a more abiding world. We must recapture the intuitive powers that have been allowed to go astray in the stress of life. Our contemporary civilisation with its specialisms and mechanical triumphs knows a large number of facts but not the mystery of the world in which these facts are. Other disciplines than exact sciences are required—art and literature, philosophy and religion—to quicken the perceptions of wonder and surprise, of strangeness and beauty, of the mystery and miraculousness of the world that surrounds us, if only we could see with eyes which are not dulled by use and wont. Science can dissolve the physical world into electrons and bombard the atom but cannot account for the genius who can do all these things, for the noble human countenance, for the expression of its eyes and the affections that shine through them. Man has the roots of his being struck deep into the nature of reality. On this bedrock are all his creative activities firmly based.

A great writer on aesthetics, Theodor Lipps, regards artistic intuition as an act of Einfühlung, which has been translated as "empathy" on the analogy of sympathy. If sympathy means feeling with, empathy means feeling into. When we contemplate an object, we project ourselves into it, and feel its inward rhythm. All production is an attempt at reproduction, at an approach to things seen and heard and felt. If a work of art fails, it is generally due to its lack of empathy. In a Sanskrit drama *Mālavikāgnimitra* (ii. 2), where the picture fails to bring out the beauty of the original, the failure is attributed to imperfect concentration (*śithilasamādhi*) of the painter. The mind concentrates on the material, becomes thoroughly possessed by it, gets as it were fused into it, absorbs it, and remoulds it according to its own ideals and thus creates a work of art. This act of pure contemplation is possible only for perfectly free minds which look at the objects with utter humility and reverence. This freedom is as rare as that purity of heart which is the condition of seeing God. It is a state in which all our energies are heightened, tautened and sublimated. We draw or paint, not with our brains but with our whole blood and being.

Art is the utterance of life. It is the expression of the soul's vision and is not wholly rational. It oversteps the limits of the rational and has, in Bacon's phrase, something strange in its proportion. The artist's attitude to the universe is more one of acceptance than of understanding. He sees the burden of mystery in all things, though he does not shudder in fear of it. He tries to pluck the mystery out of the thing, and present it to us. This, he is able to do, not by means of his reason, but by a riper reason, his intuitive power, which is the nexus, the connecting link, between the appearance and the reality, the flesh and the spirit. Until we have the inevitable fusion of the divine and the temporal, the subtle interpenetration of the spirit through the whole man, we will not have the quiet fire that burns, the lightning flash of vision that illuminates the darkness of the earth and the virgin apprehensions that take away the sting from the pains of mortality. All great artists, who have the subtle, spiritual appeal, convey a stillness, a remoteness, a sense of the beyond, the far away.

In my Hibbert Lectures on *An Idealist View of Life*, I complained that many of our best writers are too intellectual and did not attain to the heights of real greatness. They touch the mind but do not enter the soul. For great art, what is needed is inspiration and not intellectual power, what the Indian poet Daṇḍin calls natural genius (*naisargikī pratibhā*). Great art is possible only in those rare moments when the artist is transplanted out of himself and does better than his best in obedience to the dictates of a *daimon* such as Socrates used to say whispered wisdom into his ears. In those highest moments, the masters of human expression feel within themselves a spark of the divine fire and seem to think and feel as if God were in them and they were revealing fragments of the secret plan of the universe. Matthew Arnold said that, when Wordsworth and Byron were really inspired, Nature took the pen from their hands and wrote for them. In other words, they are activities of the pure spirit, manifestations of the human consciousness, at its highest, purified by detachment and disinterestedness. Some of our best writers skim the surface, look on it, examine it but do not take the plunge. That is why they do not feed, refresh and renew the spirit. Their works are not works of art but exercises in ingenuity. They have intellectual power, technical skill but not that rare adequacy of mind which engenders strange values from another world, through the perfect arrangement of a few colours on the canvas or a few lines of poetry.

But, let it not be forgotten that the true work of art is charged with thought. It is not the expression of mere emotion. A good deal of system and symmetry, of reflective determinateness is involved in the unfolding of the artist's experience. A Beethoven symphony or a Shakespeare play has one indivisible inspiration but its expression involves elaborate labour on the intellectual plane. This labour is the effort of man to create its embodiment.

As consistent thinking is not creative thinking, as intellectual verse is not inspired poetry, in conduct respectability is not righteousness. Mere correctitude of behaviour is not the last word of morality. It may be conventional good form but it is not creative good life. The moral hero is not content with being merely moral. When Socrates refused to escape from prison, he did not behave like the conventional good man of his age who would have wriggled out at the first chance. Jesus's behaviour before Pilate is not motived by prudential morality. Common sense and worldly wisdom tell us that if a doorway opens for a man who is in prison, he is a fool if he does not make use of it. Holiness is however different from vulgar prudence. It is an inner grace of nature by which the spirit purifies itself of worldly passions and appetites and dwells in patient, confident communion with the universal spirit. Those who have this chastity of mind and spirit which lies at the very heart and is the parent of all other good see at once what is good and hold to that and for its sake humble themselves even unto death. Well-being, comfort, luxury, all these things which mean so much to the common run of men, leave them indifferent, if they are not felt as burdensome hindrances to the heroic life of creative love. This is true not only of the well-known sages of India and Greece, the prophets of Israel and the saints of Christendom, but also of the many obscure heroes of the moral life who go below the precise formulas and get at the social aspirations from which they arise and lead humanity forward.

Most of us are slaves of impulse and emotion, habit and automatism. We are not normally aware of the large influence of automatic thinking, of mental habit and the great hold which our past experience has on our present outlook and decisions. Human nature has in it the tendency to set or harden into fixities of habit. There are habits not only of the body but of the intellect and the feelings. Anything strange or uncommon appears to be immoral, for it is contrary to the routine habits which are settled —what we may call the social conscience. We live or try to live by a code which we have not examined but have accepted without adequate consideration. We eat and drink, play and work, attend to business and adopt hobbies not because we have chosen these activities for ourselves but because the environment in which we grew up indicates them for us. We accord to society what it expects from us, fulfil the duties which our station assigns to us. This is passive acquiescence, not active creation. We do not live our lives but in a sense are lived by our conditions. But this cannot go on for long, unless we surrender our thought and will and reduce ourselves to the level of automata. Our little understood urges from within, our likes and dislikes, our passions of greed and ambition soon produce conflicts. Society makes large demands on our life and adaptation to them is not always easy. Sometimes, we may feel that we are acting as traitors to humanity, by obeying the rules which our narrow group imposes on us. Often, personal relationships happen to be unfulfilled. Life, that sphinx with a human face and the body of a brute, asks us new questions every hour. The backward or those who are still children in the game of life allow their activities to be governed by automatic attractions and repulsions but their activities are by no means free. To hold the balance between instinctive desires and cravings and social obligations is the task of the moral life. Only when man attains unity, when he has discovered his whole nature and ordered it, has he the right to say "I will." His free decisions seem then to come of themselves and develop of their own accord, though they may be contrary to his interests and inclinations. They infringe on the ordinary routine of life and bring into it a new type of power. These creative decisions cannot be foreseen, though they may be accounted for in retrospect. Though they defy anticipation, they are thoroughly rational. There is a wide gulf between mechanical repetition and free creation, between the morality of rules and the life of spirit.

Religion is, in essence, experience of or living contact with ultimate reality. It is not a subjective phenomenon, not mere cultivation of the inner life but the apprehension of something that stands over against the individual. The real is known not as the conclusion of an argument but with the certainty of a thing experienced. We cannot prove the reality of God in the same way in which we prove the existence of a chair or a table. For God is not an object like other objects in nature. God is spirit which is distinct from the knowing subject or the known object. All proofs for the existence of God fail because they conceive of God as an objective reality. Spirit is life, not thing, energy not immobility, something real in itself and by itself, and cannot be compared to any substance subjective or objective. The divine is manifested in spiritual life or experience. It is given to us in life and not established by ratiocination.

Though religious experience is analogous in some respects to the other manifestations of spiritual activity, such as scientific genius, artistic creation or moral heroism, it cannot be identified with any of them. It is unique and autonomous. The spirit is at home with itself in religion and its life satisfies every side of our being. The peace which we obtain through it is not mere emotional satisfaction. In it the mind becomes irradiated with the divine light and obstinate questions of reason find an answer. The will loses its irresoluteness as it becomes one with the divine will. Spiritual geniuses possess the highest that man can possess, constant contact with the creative principle of which life is the manifestation, coincidence with the divine will, serene calm, inward peace which no passion can disturb, no persecution can dismay.

Any philosophic account of the universe must consider all known data, our hopes and fears, our efforts and endeavours. While philosophy cannot take anything for granted, it cannot ignore the testimony of religious experience to the nature of ultimate reality which it also seeks to apprehend. If art initiates us into truth, if the object of poetry is "truth which is its own testimony" (Wordsworth), it may well be that even religious experience makes a real contribution to the understanding of the world, and possesses a profound metaphysical significance. It is our duty as seekers of truth to listen with reverence to the judgments of those seers who have cultivated the religious sense and are specially endowed with a fine discrimination in matters of spirit.

Simply because there are persons to whom religious experience is unknown, we cannot say that it is either unreal or impossible. Our limited experiences are not the standard for all. There are many for whom beauty is a word and music only a noise, but that does not mean that there is no reality in the artist's experience. Again, religious experience is exceptional only in the sense that all genius is exceptional. It does not mean that the experience cannot be verified by those who take the necessary trouble. Even though all of us may not give utterance to the voice of spirit, still it finds an echo in the depths of our soul. To suggest that men who have religious experience are mental invalids is inconsistent with the well-known fact that some of the greatest mystics are men of remarkable intellectual power, shrewd discrimination and practical ability.

The sceptics dismiss the experiences of saints and mystics as due to unsoundness of mind or psychological tricks. They are perhaps justified by the history of religious experience where it has often been confused with emotional thrills and edifying feelings. This fact only reminds us of the need for careful scrutiny and examination of what claims to be religious experience. Simply because religion has often been mistaken for what it is not and got mixed up with fantastic notions and wanton cruelties, we cannot disregard the entire field of religious experience as baseless. We are not willing to dismiss sense perception as illusory simply because we have dreams and hallucinations. Our experiences are liable to misinterpretation and our judgments are not infallible. We are nowadays reverent even to the experience of ghosts: we need not be rude to the experience of God. If we adopt a narrowly rationalist view, not merely religion but all the higher activities of mind become unmeaning and pathological. Such a view narrows the range of vision of the human mind.

Though religious experience has developed into varied doctrines and expressed itself in different intellectual notations, there is a certain kinship of the spirit among the religious geniuses who have made their mark on history, who join hands across the centuries and bid us enter into the kingdom of the spirit. They affirm that the self perceives directly the ultimate reality which is there, existing in its own right, untouched by the imperfections of the world. It is intimately present to and in ourselves. Truth, beauty and goodness are not subjective fancies but objective facts. They are not only ultimate values included in the purpose of the world but supreme realities. Their objectivity and sovereignty are sometimes brought out by calling them attributes of God. We have a consciousness that we belong to that which is ultimately real. Again, we cannot eliminate the element of mystery in religion and attempt to measure the transcendent and the eternal by finite and temporal standards. Any effort to make religion absolutely rational would be to misconceive its essential character. Baron von Hügel has a pregnant observation on this question. To expect clearness with regard to the knowledge of the Supreme, he says, "indicates a thoroughly unreasonable, a self-contradicitory habit of mind."[1] When we hear enthusiastic descriptions of ultimate reality, it is well to remember Lao Tse's dictum that he who knows the Tao may be recognised by the fact that he is reluctant to speak of it. Plato in his Seventh Epistle declares his intention of publishing nothing on his *Idea of the Good*: "There is no writing of mine on this subject nor ever shall be. It is not capable of expression like other branches of study but as the result of long intercourse and common life spent upon the thing, a light is suddenly kindled as from a leaping spark, and when it has reached the soul, it thenceforward finds nourishment for itself." The mystics appeal to us to build the ideal society, the universal republic where there is neither Jew nor Gentile, neither Greek nor barbarian, where all men *qua* men are of equal worth. Religious geniuses are devotees of the ideal of universal brotherhood, based on the conception of the sanctity of the human person.

While those who share the experience do not seek for proofs for the existence of spirit, but feel immediately certain of what is experienced, proofs have to be offered for those who do not share the experience. The rationality of the faith requires to be demonstrated. Though the famous arguments for the existence

[1] *Essays and Addresses on the Philosophy of Religion*, First Series, p. 100.

of God may not be logically conclusive, they show the inadequacy of naturalistic explanations. Nature is not its own *raison d'être*. No part of it contains its own explanation. There is in the procession of events we call nature, the emergence of higher qualities whereby, as Browning put it, "out of three sounds we frame not a fourth sound but a star." Life emerged out of the non-living when the cooling earth was able to support life. Physico-chemical explanations are admittedly inadequate for life, and for the rise of mind and personality. The characteristics of the higher level cannot be deduced from those of the lower. While science can describe the precise circumstances under which higher qualities emerge, it cannot say why they do so. Naturalistic evolution which attempts to account for the development of new species by the theory of accidental variations preserved by selection and fixed by heredity assumes a series of miracles. We must grant an intention of nature to account for the co-ordination of complementary variations in a manner beneficial to the organism and its transmissibility to its descendants. Bergson in his *Creative Evolution* suggests that the evolution of the species is not the result of the mechanical action of external causes but is the expression of a vital impetus operating in individuals, carrying them in a given direction towards ever higher complexities. The theory of vital impetus is an admission of the mystery of life and its movement. The more we examine organic evolution, the more do we find that there is very little of the random. Life grows to some end and the end is the growth of spirit. A universe that has produced man cannot be indifferent to his highest good.

Any process is intelligible in view of the end it aims at achieving. The character of the different stages and their qualities are determined by the end. In the cosmic process, we find that life uses matter for its instrument. Similarly mind uses the living organism. The highest order of being called spirit which is mind illumined by the ideals of truth, goodness and beauty is rooted in human intelligence and grows from it. The universe attempts to realise these ideals and cannot be understood except in the light of them. They are not only the goal of the universe in the temporal sense but are the timeless principles in the light of which alone the universe becomes intelligible.

Professor Alexander is prepared to concede that "deity" which is the next higher quality to emerge is the explanation of the world process, though for him it is yet non-existent, though the world is striving for its existence. It is yet an ideal and an existent only in so far as the tendency is operative in the world. It is always to come but never comes. It is the name of the next higher quality which is to emerge but which has not yet emerged. In a sense, Alexander's "deity" is not the creator but the created. It cannot serve as the explanation of the world, if it does not exist and operate in some sense. It does not yet exist in the temporal sense. It must therefore exist in a timeless way. This world has meaning and value only in so far as it realises in time and existence that which transcends time and existence. No explanation of the cosmic process is possible without a transcendental reference.

The cosmic process is sometimes traced to an experimenting life force with which Bergson has made us familiar. The advocates of life force are impressed by the inadequacy of purely naturalistic explanations. They hold that life will continue to produce higher types of existence. They have sufficient faith in the trustworthiness of life force and its responsiveness to our deepest aspirations. Bergson suggests that it discovers original solutions to the problems set by external conditions and overcomes obstacles in an intelligent way. If we are so certain that the life force will behave in a reasonable and purposive way, it is not fair to think of it as an unconscious agency. If it is the operative principle of the cosmic process and contains, as Bergson suggests, the essential characteristics developed in the different lines of evolution in a state of reciprocal implication, "instinct and intelligence being mere views, taken from two different points, of that simple reality," then it is unmeaning to call it vital impetus or life force. In his latest work on *The Two Sources of Morality and Religion*, Bergson argues that the creative energy, the principle of life in general which inward intuition reveals, is to be defined as love and is God Himself.[1]

God is the timeless spirit attempting to realise timeless values on the plane of time. The ideal of the cosmic process which at the same time is its goal and explanation is real in one sense

[1] E.T. (1935), p. 320.

though wanting to be realised in another. The ideal is the greatest fact in one way and a remote possibility in another. The values which the cosmic process is attempting to achieve are only a few of the possibilities contained in the Absolute. God is the definitisation of the Absolute in reference to the values of the world.

There are aspects in religious experience, such as the sense of rest and fulfilment, of eternity and completeness, which require the conception of a being whose nature is not exhausted by the cosmic process, which possesses an allfulness of reality which our world only faintly shadows. This side of religious experience demands the conception of the supreme as self-existence, infinity, freedom, absolute light and absolute beatitude. On the other hand there are features of our religious experience which require us to look upon God as a self-determining principle manifested in a temporal development, with wisdom, love and goodness as his attributes. From this point of view God is a personal being with whom we can enter into personal relationship. Practical religion presupposes a God who looks into our hearts, knows our tribulations and helps us in our need. The reality of prayer and sacrifice is affirmed by the religious life of mankind. It assumes the reality of a concrete being who influences our life. To leave the Absolute in abstract isolation dwelling in Epicurean felicity is to reduce it to an ornamental figurehead who lends an atmosphere to an essentially agnostic view of the cosmic process. The permanent reality beyond the transient world of struggle and discord is also here and in everything. In religious experience itself there is no conflict. The supreme satisfies both sets of needs. But for philosophy of religion, the central problem is to reconcile the apparently conflicting views of the supreme as eternally complete and of the supreme as the self-determining principle manifesting in the temporal process.

In Greek thought, Plato and Aristotle conceived the Divine being as self-sufficient in His own perfection and undisturbed by any changes of the world. Plato sets up a hierarchy of Ideas with the Idea of Good at its apex. For Aristotle, God is the unmoved mover, a thought thinking itself, self-enclosed, operative only by the appeal of its own perfection. The God of the Hebrews is of a different type. He is personal and active in history and interested in the changes and chances of this developing world.

He is a being who holds communication with us. Christianity represents a blend of the Hebrew and the Greek traditions, though it has not yet succeeded in reconciling them.

The Hindu is aware of this fundamental problem and as early as the period of the Upaniṣads we find attempts to reconcile the doctrine of the changeless perfection of the Absolute with the conviction that God is also responsible for this changing world.[1]

The way in which the relation between the Absolute and God is here indicated is not the same as that either of Śaṁkara or of Bradley, though it has apparent similarities to their doctrines. While the Absolute is the transcendent divine, God is the cosmic divine. While the Absolute is the total reality, God is the Absolute from the cosmic end, the consciousness that informs and sustains the world. God is, so to say, the genius of this world, its ground, which as a thought or a possibility of the Absolute lies beyond the world in the universal consciousness of the Absolute. The possibilities or the ideal forms are the mind of the Absolute or the thoughts of the Absolute. One of the infinite possibilities is being translated into the world of space and time. Even as the world is a definite manifestation of one specific possibility of the Absolute, God with whom the worshipper stands in personal relation is the very Absolute in the world context and is not a mere appearance of the Absolute.

When the Old Testament says, "Before even the earth and the world were made, Thou art God from everlasting, and world without end," it is referring to the Absolute and not to God who is organic with the world process. The Absolute is joy: God is love. Joy is a self-existent reality, an absolute which does not depend on objects but only on itself. The divine power of love spends itself on the objects of its love without expecting any return from its self-expenditure. In the course of the cosmic process, God accepts an element of the given, certain necessities which His will does not approve, though He is struggling to transform them through His creative effort. God appears to be finite in the process though His infinity reveals itself when the world plan reaches its fulfilment.

[1] For the views of the Upaniṣads, the Bhagavad Gītā and the great teachers, Śaṁkara, Rāmanuja and Madhva, see the writer's *Indian Philosophy*, vols. i and ii, second edition.

In a famous passage of the *Microcosmos*, Lotze repudiates the objection to the personality of God, which affirms that the distinction between self and not-self is essential for the existence of personality and as the divine self is infinite and therefore has no other, it cannot be personal. Lotze's answer to this difficulty is that while the contrast between self and not-self is an invariable accompaniment of personality as known to us, it is not an essential quality of it. The contrast is characteristic of human personality but not of the Divine. But if the being of God is a positive activity, this activity has meaning only when it is opposed or limited by conditions which are not created by itself. Whether or not the contrast of self and not-self is essential to personality, human or divine, life of a personal being is not possible except in relation to an environment. If God has no environment on which He acts, He cannot be personal. If God is personal, He cannot be the Absolute which has nothing which is not included in it in every possible sense of the world.

God can only be a creative personality acting on an environment, which, though dependent on God, is not God. Though the acting of God is not forced on Him from without, still it is limited by the activities of human individuals. The personality of God is possible only with reference to a world with its imperfections and capacity for progress. In other words, the being of a personal God is dependent on the existence of a created order. God depends on creation even as creation depends on God. In the sphere of thought, being and non-being are opposites. The being of which we have experience is not absolute being. Whatever falls short in any degree of absolute reality has in it an admixture of non-being. In the world of experience, we have a conflict between being and non-being. In and through their mutual hostility, the world exists. If there were no non-being, there would be no being. Each presupposes the other. The two are not related to each other as the carpenter to the wood or as the potter to the clay.

The world exists in and through an act of self-assertion. The self which asserts itself and which says "I am" is the divine self. Over against this self, this will to be, is the infinitude of non-being, the passive resistance which has to be met and overcome. The spirit of God moves over the waters, the formless matter, the totality of possible existence.[1] Vital impetus and raw matter are, for Bergson, the complementary aspects of creation. We cannot eliminate the dualism between subject and object, between God and the given in the process of the universe.

At the beginning, God is merely the knower with ideas and plans, which are realised at the end when the world becomes the express image of God. The difference between the beginning and the end is analogous to the difference between the "I" and the "me." The "me" becomes an adequate representation of the "I" at the end. All things move towards the creator. When the creator and the created coincide, God lapses into the Absolute. Being in a sense which both attracts and eludes our thought is the ideal goal of becoming. In attaining this goal, becoming fulfils its destiny and ceases to be.

Creation marks the beginning of this world with time, though not in time. The Newtonian conception of time as a prior framework within which events happen, which is said to flow on at an even pace without cessation and without end, is now given up. Time has no existence apart from events. It is a conceptual construction from the experience of successive events. The universe though unbounded is said to be finite. It has a beginning and an end. If we give up this view we will be committed to the belief in the eternity of this world. A dualism of God and the world where one of them will have a precarious, illusory existence will result. The ideal of the world is not an ever elusive perfectibility, working ineffectively above the world of the actual but what is most real and decisively operative in it and will one undated day be achieved.

Evolution and history belong to the world and are real and not mere appearances or illusions. God is not absolutely timeless, though He is not in time in the sense that His whole being is subject to succession and change. Though God does not consist of a succession of states, succession is real for Him. The future has meaning for God who executes designs in the sphere of the created order. In a sense God Himself is subject to change. There is a stage in which He attempts to realise an ideal and another in which the ideal is realised. The contrast between the ideal aimed at and the actual is real for God.

[1] Cp. gahanam gambhīram . . . apraketam salilam. *Rg. Veda*, x. 129.

Again, what appears in subhuman forms as tendency or striving becomes in man conscious will which is guided by the idea of value. Men are active agents, not passive participants in the return of all things to God. They can work with God or turn away from Him. The religious soul who has direct contact with the Divine in an experience where the distance between the subject and the object, the lover and the beloved is overcome, identifies itself with the Divine will and participates in the creative work of God. When once the possibility of working out an evolutionary manifestation of values is accepted, God becomes the agent of creation achieving power, light and love through the overcoming of inertia, darkness and death. The self-existent Absolute becomes for this world with its resistance of finite things to the unity of the whole, God, compassionate, consenting, helpful, the soul of truth in all things and the saviour of mankind. He redeems the corrupt and reconciles the hostile, evolves rhythm out of chaos. God's work does not cease until He has fashioned immortal substance out of evanescent nothingness.

The Absolute transcends not merely its finite but also its infinite expressions taken singly or in a finite number. In its range of expression or degree of expressiveness, the Absolute transcends all finite limits. The question of immanence and transcendence does not arise with reference to the Absolute. For immanence implies the existence of an Other in which the Absolute is immanent. But the Absolute represents the totality of being and there is nothing other than it. The Absolute is in this world in the sense that the world is only an actualisation of one possibility of the Absolute and yet there is much in the Absolute beyond this possibility which is in process of realisation.

God is the Absolute with reference to this possibility of which He is the source and creator. Yet at any moment God transcends the cosmic process with its whole contents of space and time. He transcends the order of nature and history until His being is fully manifested. When that moment arises, the word becomes flesh, the whole world is saved and the historical process terminates. Until then, God is partly in *potentia*, partly in act. This view is not pantheistic for the cosmic process is not a complete manifestation of the Absolute.

So far as the Absolute is concerned, the creation of the world makes no difference to it. It cannot add anything to or take away anything from the Absolute. All the sources of its being are found within itself. The world of change does not disturb the perfection of the Absolute. "Though suns and universes would cease to be, Every existence would exist in thee" (Emily Brontë). We cannot say that the world follows from the nature of the Absolute even as the conclusion of the syllogism follows from the premises, as Spinoza would have us believe. The Absolute is the ground of the world only in the sense that a possibility of the Absolute is the logical prius of the world. The world would not be but for this possibility in the Absolute.

As to why this possibility arose and not any other, we have to answer that it is an expression of the freedom of the Absolute. It is not even necessary for the Absolute to express any of its possibilities. If this possibility is expressed, it is a free act of the Absolute. Hindu writers are inclined to look upon the act of creation more as the work of an artist than that of an artisan. It is *līlā* or free play. The world is the work of an artist whose works are worlds. His fertility is endless. Śaṁkara says that the world originates from the supreme without effort (*aprayat-nenaiva*), on the analogy of sport (*līlānyāyena*), like human breath (*puruṣânihśvāsavat*).[1]

VI. CONCLUSION

True religion is born of spirit, not of flesh and blood, not of codes and customs, not of races and nations. The life of spirit consists precisely in being free from these things and in penetrating into true being. Systems of theology and codes of conduct are elaborated for the sake of the large numbers who have no first-hand experience of religion and so require to be directed in the way of religion. So long as there are men who have not reached the spiritual level in which there is immediate contact with the divine reality and are therefore dependent on the experience of others, there is justification for authoritative religion.

Dogmas and codes are not an absolute embodiment of religious truth. They express particular stages in man's spiritual development. What is revealed is distorted and assimilated according

[1] Śaṁkara on *Brahma Sūtra*, i. 1. 3.

to the make-up and spiritual development of the persons receiving them. The intuitive seer understands the variety of theological doctrines and codes. They are but attempts to express the in-expressible, to translate into human words the music of the divine. In the face of the ineffable glory, nothing avails save the renunciation of the artist and the austerity of silence. The creed we adopt, the label we bear is largely accidental. We stay in the fold in which we are born simply because we are more at home in it than in any other. The dogmas and rites employed by religion for its expression and diffusion are only means for bringing about that elevation of the soul which can dispense with them all. To bestow a sacred character on racial traditions is to give a false turn to the life of spirit. To submit the infinite spirit to finite forms leads eventually to the enslavement of spirit.

Intellectualism admits the possibility of attaining a perfect system of divine knowledge. It refuses to see the super-being of God and denies the mystery of religion. It confuses the reflection of God in the mind of man with divine nature itself. It gives to the outward forms of the historical process an absolute justification. Intellectual religion pledges us to rigid definitions and obsolete dogmas. It encourages a hardness of belief almost mathematical in its rigidity. It does not believe in any half-tones between white and black, any fine shades between truth and falsehood. In its anxiety to bend all individual wills to the purpose of the group and establish social cohesion, it enforces rites and obligations peculiar to the group and ignores the claims of humanity. It declares that what it affirms is the truth, the whole truth and nothing but the truth. Different systems of theology acquire a sacred significance which is absolute and unchangeable and this leads to a quenching of the spirit.

The spirit in us is life and it resists death in all its forms, blind instinct, unthinking custom, dull obedience, intellectual inertia and spiritual dryness. A man's religion must be his own and not simply accepted on trust or imposed by authority. While trust and authority may put him on the way, it is his own independent search that will take him to the goal.

Religion is a manner of life dependent on the discipline of one's being, body and mind. It is to make oneself of a certain quality, to fashion one's being to a certain temper to reshape the stubborn world, to so change one's life as to enter the vital movement of the universe. Creative power of the spirit has not yet been seen in its widest scope. It has not yet achieved its full stature. Civilisation is in its infancy, and religion yet in the making. Human progress is to be defined as the process by which society is transformed increasingly in a spiritual way. The world is unfinished and it is the task of religion to go forward with the task of refining it.

On this view, religion is not quiescent but combative, exposing the hostility and hollowness of the irreligious principle. It means a profound dissatisfaction with the existing state of humanity and an active preparation for a new life, whether it be the kingdom of heaven on earth or beyond. Religion is an eternal revolutionary because no order of life can ever satisfy it. It demands the most radical transformation of man and society. It will not be content until a new social order with basic economic justice, racial brotherhood and equality, free intellectual and spiritual co-operation and true friendship among the nations is established. So long as man has to earn his bread by the sweat of his brow, he will spend his energies in the pursuit of food, but if society is organised with courage and vision so as to secure for all its members food, clothing and shelter, the individuals will be freed for the pursuit of the higher things of the mind and spirit. If a radical change in what may be called the mechanics of living is brought about, the art of living will receive a fresh impetus and the destiny of humanity will be achieved.

It is not enough to change outward forms and institutions. We must transform the feelings and passions of men. We require not a revolution in opinion but a revolution in behaviour. False intellectualism has led us to prefer in artistic life the supremacy of form to content; in politics, organisation to liberty; in morals, authority to personal experience; and in religion, orthodox systems to spiritual life. A discipline of our whole being including the emotions which are the springs of action is essential for restoring to the world the inspiration which it has lost.

PRINCIPAL PUBLICATIONS

The Reign of Religion in Contemporary Philosophy. Macmillan & Co.

Indian Philosophy, 2 vols. Second Edition. George Allen & Unwin.

The Hindu View of Life. Third Impression. George Allen & Unwin.

An Idealist View of Life. Second Edition. George Allen & Unwin

East and West in Religion. George Allen & Unwin.

Kalki, or the Future of Civilisation. Second Edition, Kegan Paul.

The Religion We Need. Benn.

The Heart of Hindusthan. Third Edition. Natesan & Co. (Madras).

Eastern Religions and Western Thought. Clarendon Press.

Religion and Society. Second Impression. George Allen & Unwin.

The Bhagavadgītā. Second Impression. George Allen & Unwin.

The Dhammapada. Oxford University Press.

THE INWARD ABSOLUTE AND THE ACTIVISM OF THE FINITE SELF

by Dr. P. T. RAJU

Born 17th August, 1903; B.A., Allahabad University; M.A., and Ph.D., Calcutta University; and *Sastri*, Sanscrit College, Benares.

THE INWARD ABSOLUTE AND THE
ACTIVISM OF THE FINITE SELF

I

MY interest in philosophy began during my jail life in Rajamundry, where I was imprisoned as a congressman during the first civil disobedience movement started by Mahatma Gandhi. I used to lead in prison a practically solitary life, somewhat aloof even from the other congressman, reading voraciously the works of Vivekananda and Ramatirtha. My interest in philosophy was from the beginning not merely academical and speculative. But it has taken nearly twenty years of intense study and meditative understanding for me to feel that the Indian philosophical concepts have to be correlated to inward experience. Indian Philosophy repeatedly proclaims this correlation; but minds which naturally look outward to see the truth, cannot easily appreciate it, which is therefore either accepted on faith or ridiculed as nonsense.

After my college course, I began my deeper study of the philosophical concepts from the stand-point of comparative philosophy. I had the unusual good fortune of studying Indian Philosophy on orthodox lines under great Sanscrit savants like Mahamahopadhyaya Pandit Vamacharan Bhattacharya and Mahamahopadhyaya Pandit Anantakrishna Sastri and of undergoing discipline in Western Philosophy under the well-known professors of philosophy in Calcutta like Professors Radhakrishnan, Hiralal Haldar and K. C. Bhattacharya. Particularly in my student days, the philosophical atmosphere in the Calcutta University was the best in India.

I knew from the very beginning that comparative studies had their risks, but also that they were absolutely necessary. I expressed both my fears and the necessity in *The Aryan Path* (June, 1934 and February, 1935). Western Philosophy is regarded as based mainly on reason and therefore as scientific. Hence the temptation is strong to discover all the philosophical doctrines of the West in Indian thought. But the result is that we present

Indian thought as a confused expression or a good copy of Western thought. Those that are particularly struck by the spiritual leaven and motif of Indian Philosophy are therefore rightly dissatisfied. My contention from the beginning has been that comparative studies should not only aim at pointing out similarities between Eastern and Western philosophies, but also their peculiarities, so that each will take proper notice of the other and progress by attempting new syntheses. It is really gratifying to note that this necessity is being recognised in the West also, particularly by some in America and by a few in England. The controversy still seems to be raging about the problem of interpreting one system in terms of another, because modern developments in semantics are emphasising the view that each system has its own philosophical language. But the truth seems to be that each system is dealing with the same facts, emphasising some aspect of them as more fundamental than the rest, and therefore failing in the final result to do real justice to one or more of the latter. The important problem in comparative philosophy therefore is that of the synthesis of the systems through the synthesis in thought of the facts and aspects regarded as fundamental by them, and not merely the interpretation of one system in terms of another. The latter will be useful if the systems deal with the same or cognate facts or aspects, but the former will be useful when they deal with different fields and realms of experience or treat them as primary. The Eastern and Western philosophical traditions seem, in general, to be concerned respectively with the inward and the outward approaches to the interpretation of the world (cp. my article "The Western and the Indian Philosophical Traditions," *The Philosophical Review*, March, 1947): and their comparison and synthesis as such will be more useful for understanding everything in which philosophy is interested than the discovery of common and similar doctrines and the invention of a common philosophical language.

II

As an example of what I plead for, I may narrate my first reactions to the study of the Sāṁkhya. The system advocates the doctrine of *pariṇāma*, which is generally translated by the word

evolution. In the West, Darwin first formulated it scientifically
and popularised it. The fact tempted many scholars to compare
the two. Then when the doctrine of emergent evolution was
expounded by Lloyd Morgan, some began to read it also into the
Sāṁkhya. But these doctrines are highly scientific and make an
outward approach; they are applicable mainly to the external
world. The consequence is that the Sāṁkhya is made to appear
as nonsense. For it preaches that *buddhi* (intelligence) evolves
out of *Prakṛti* (matter), *ahaṁkāra* (ego) out of *buddhi*, and *manas*
(mind), the organs of sense and of action and the *tanmātras*
(subtle elements) out of *ahaṁkāra*, and the gross world out of the
tanmātras. This process, in broad outline, is the reverse process
of natural evolution. Further, it makes out that the world of
concrete things comes out of what the West would think to be
pale mind. Even Prof. Radhakrishnan speaks of the obscurity
of this account (*Indian Philosophy*, Vol. I, p. 277). My first
reaction was to laugh at the Sāṁkhya within myself. It will
not be of avail to say that *Prakṛti* is matter, and so the Sāṁkhya
pariṇāma corresponds to natural evolution. This defence can
come only from one who isolates the Sāṁkhya from the rest of
Indian Philosophy. For even the non-dualistic systems of the
Āgamas, which treat Brahman and its energy (*śakti*) as non-
different from each other, advocate the doctrine of *pariṇāma*; so
that, according to them, the world ultimately becomes a *pariṇāma*
of Brahman, which is pure intelligence or consciousness.
The traditional Advaita of Sankara advocates *vivarta* (evolution
in which the effect is produced without affecting the cause)
instead of *pariṇāma*. Next, it should not be forgotten that
pariṇāma stands not merely for evolution but also for causality
(*kāryakāraṇabhāva*). I feel that evolution is logically a form of
causality for Indian thinkers and that we ought now to interpret
causality, taking both Indian and Western thought into consideration, as a form of evolution. Where there is no birth of a
new quality, there is no causality; and the emergence of a new
quality is evolution also.

The obscurity and the apparent absurdity of the Sāṁkhya is
due to our approaching the account from the outward or the
external point of view. From the inward point of view, it is quite
natural and reasonable. If God or the Absolute is to be discovered

within our hearts, if he is our innermost being and the whole world evolved out of him, then the Sāṁkhyan account or some account similar to it, would be the only rational one. There are three consequences to be drawn from this account: the discovery of God or the Absolute within our hearts is not to be taken as a sort of edification, but quite seriously and naturally; secondly, by the word heart we are not to understand anything physical; and thirdly, the Absolute is inward.

In Western Philosophy, the inwardness of the Absolute is most easily recognisable in the philosophy of Plotinus. But the form which the problem took, namely, how is the many related to the one or how does the many come out of the one, and the peculiar way in which it was understood by later philosophers, shrouded and obscured its true nature, and the inwardness of the Absolute was lost sight of. We can now appreciate why the philosophy of Plotinus has ceased to influence Western Philosophy and passed into Christian theology.

III

As the Absolute is inward, I am not very much in favour of calling it the World as a Whole, which makes one think of the external world, taken as a totality of objects placed side by side, and corresponds to Spinoza's concept of *natura naturata*. This is really the Absolute externalised and the result of our outward looking habit. Pantheism in the bad sense is the outcome of this conception. In my earlier writings, I did use the term, the World as a Whole, in place of the Absolute. But I did so, because, when the world as a whole—of which even thought, for which the world is a world, is a part—is taken into account, the world ceases to be the world of objects as such and becomes something inward by ceasing to be the "other" to thought. This is the teaching of Bradley, which most of the Indian idealists admire; for it involves the doctrine of the spiritual inwardness of the Absolute as an inevitable conclusion. True, the Advaita and the Mahayanists did speak of the world as identical with Brahman and the Sūnya; but the identity obtains even for them only in a sense, namely, in essence.

Thus Bradley's doctrine of the inevitableness of suicide which logic and thought have to commit if they are to grasp the Truth, confirmed me in the conviction engendered in me in my study of the Śāṁkhya doctrines, particularly as incorporated by the Āgamas and advocated by the *Kaṭha*. Naturally, I drew the conclusion that the inward Absolute is both psychological and metaphysical. If God or the Absolute is really our innermost being and is creative of both us and the world, in the study of his processes there should be no difference between psychology and metaphysics. This idea I expressed boldly in some of my articles ("Indian Philosophy: Its Attitude to the World," *The Vedanta Kesari*, Madras, November and December, 1944, "The Psychology of the *Bṛhadāraṇyaka* Upanishad," *The Journal of Oriental Research*, Madras, June, 1946, etc.).

IV

Due to the influence of Dr. Hiralal Haldar, I was greatly impressed by the Kantian and Hegelian methods, particularly as interpreted by Caird. In Kant's critical method I found the *arthāpatti* (postulation) of the Advaita. But did not philosophers prior to Kant know the method of postulation and did they not frame hypotheses? For instance, the metaphysical argument for the existence of God asks us to accept his existence for the reason that, unless he possesses existence, he cannot be perfect. Then where does Kant's greatness lie? He was able to postulate certain categorial functions of our inward being. That they belong to our inner nature is the contention of rationalism, which Kant concedes. He saw also that God, Self and the World as a Whole, the three Ideas of Reason, were ultimate postulates. The third he opposed to the second, and unified both in the first. But an important problem did not strike him: if the World as a Whole is a postulate of reason and works like other postulates through our inward being, should it be internal to us or external to us? The tendency of men in general is to look for the World as a Whole outside us: for, is it not treated even by Kant as the *gegenstand* of our Self? But if it is to work from within us, for organising our experience, in what sense can it be external to us? And if it is internal to us, in what way is it opposed to the Self?

Hegel tried to cancel this opposition and developed his imposing

R

dialectic. Its peculiar appeal to me lay in its interconnecting the categories left unconnected by Kant. Hegel contended that it was necessary to rise to the level of Absolute Consciousness in order to interrelate the ultimate with the lower categories; and that thought had the power to so rise. But he did not see that this rising of thought above finitude could be nothing more than thinking of infinitude, and that, by thinking that thought had become infinite by so doing, he was committing a fallacy involved in the ontological argument, namely, to think of the infinite is the same as to become the infinite. While thinking of the infinite, thought works its inferences as it conceives the infinite to work; but it still remains to prove that the inferences of thought and the workings of the infinite coincide. Thought at the higher level therefore means only a new method which the same thought adopts, but not that it actually becomes infinite, that its each and every idea comes to possess being, that it becomes the Absolute. If, at the lower level, it works on the assumption that the world is different from our selves, that being is different from thought; at the higher level, it works on the assumption that the two are identical. At both the levels, it is finite, and faces an "Other": at the lower level, the "Other" is what is assumed to be different from thought; at the higher level, it is what is assumed to be identical with thought. The difference between the two levels is the difference between the assumptions with which our thought works, but not that thought changes its nature and becomes its "Other." Hence the mistake of Hegel is that he completely denied the finitude even of our thought. True, we have to postulate the working of the Absolute Thought through our thought; but we have at the same time to acknowledge the difference between the two. Hegel's philosophy seemed to me to have cancelled this difference and therefore to have failed to do justice to religious consciousness, which does not accept that thinking of the workings of the Absolute is identical with experiencing its workings. Our thought is outward-looking; hence its finitude. For the Absolute Thought, there can be no "Other": the "Other" becomes inner to it and cancels itself. The merit of Bradley lies in seeing the former truth, though he did not see the full significance of the latter. Kant drew the latter conclusion boldly through the postulational method.

Such thought he called Intuitive Understanding or Intellectual Intuition, and said that it could belong to God only. If the Self and the World as a Whole are really unified in God, then both of them would be inward to him; they would be moments within his being. That is, for the finite self, the thought for which the world ceases to be an "Other," is still an "Other," though it is inward. It is too presumptuous to say that speculative thought is higher than religious experience and the former is able to overcome the "Otherness." Speculative thought is not the same as the Intuitive Understanding of God or the Absolute; it belongs to the finite self. That is why the real inwardness of the Absolute is lost in Hegel, who brings it down to the level of speculative thought, externalises and spreads it as a scheme or a network of abstract categories; Kant made no attempt to destroy its inwardness, though he treated the Ideas of Reason as only heuristic principles and did not work out how they were connected with the lower categories.

In this connection, Bradley seems to me to display greater originality and keener insight than Bosanquet, who is certainly more massive and constructive. What is the lesson we are to draw from thought's suicide for grasping truth and from the final difficulties in logic like the inevitable contradiction between the conclusion and the premisses in every inference, which Bradley has pointed out? No mystery need be attached to these logical difficulties. Even at the level of normal psychology, the prior connectivity of our experience is admitted in James' phrase "booming buzzing confusion" and Ward's concept of the "presentational continuum." Naturally thought arises by selection and abstraction; and so Bradley's criticism against inference has its point. The solution of the difficulty seems to lie only in the concept of the Intuitive Understanding of Kant.

Kant, peculiarly enough, compares his Ideas to those of Plato. Plato's Ideas are said to be dynamic, not passive but active agents. That is why they are creative. Now, if Kant's Ideas are only heuristic principles, they can hardly be active and do not deserve comparison to Plato's. But if they are to be active, they must be creative, that is, creative of the material they shape. So much is implied in the notion of God as inclusive of the Self and the World as a Whole. God, as giving a shape, through the Self, to the World, forms also its material. That is how he can be the Intuitive Understanding or Intellectual Intuition. The next conclusion would be that he is the Creative Understanding. For, this understanding, which gives shape, also creates the material to be shaped. So this Creative Understanding, of which the Self becomes the formative or the formal principle and the World the formed product or the shaped material, becomes the ultimate postulate of our experience. Here thought becomes identical with being and the universal loses its abstractness and becomes creative. This postulate belongs to our inward being and works through us.

Further, Plato's Ideas or universals should now be interpreted as belonging to the inward Absolute working through us. The universals cannot be dynamic and creative unless they belong to this Absolute, which is inclusive of both thought and being; otherwise, they would be abstract concepts or mere names. Plato's mythological narration of the soul's acquaintance with the Ideas has to be reinterpreted in the light of this development of the Kantian view. As the Absolute works through the soul, the latter, when not looking outward for experience, must have had knowledge of the Absolute's workings.

V

Thus the metaphysical developments necessitated by the epistemological problems as well as by the desire not to dismiss the accounts of the *Katha* and the Sāṁkhya as absurd led me to think that the Absolute could only be inward. This is what is meant by calling it spiritual. Very often it is said that the subject and object are correlated. But what is the experience in which they are correlated? It may be asked whether we should postulate an experience at all as the basis of this correlation. Is not the subject just the physical body which is the percipient and so an object among objects? The attitude behind the question is the stronger now that mind is regarded as the correlate of body or as a new emergent out of the bodily pattern or out of a physical synthesis. But it should not be forgotten that one's own physical body is also an object of one's own mind like any other object. In every act of perception, mind identifies itself with its body and says that "I, Mr. X, am perceiving the object"; but it can make its own body also its object. Thus two phases of experience can be distinguished in mind, the subject as identifying itself with the physical body and attributing to itself all the experiences of the body, and the consciousness that the subject is having such experiences. The history of the subject as such an agent and for this consciousness is thus built up. Thus mind in the latter sense is wider than the subject and is inclusive of both the subject and the object. The subject in the former sense is just the correlate of the object and is just an object among objects, though it is a privileged object by being the centre of experience. Such is the epistemological approach to the doctrine, in the *Muṇḍaka*, of the two birds sitting on a tree, one of which enjoys the fruit while the other watches on.

Because self-consciousness transcends even the subject, I am not much in favour of equating the distinction between *ātman* and *anātman* to that between subject and object. If we are to derive both the subject and the object from the *ātman*, then the *ātman* must include the object also. The *anātman* as such has really no existence. Hence what we call *anātman* is really all that is the result of our outward attitude. The same looked at inwardly is the *ātman*. Subject and object, being correlates, do not connote this significance.

Similarly, I am not very much in favour of approaching the *ātman* through the subject excluding the object. The *ātman* is all-inclusive; but the subject, as a correlate of the object, cannot be the whole truth. In epistemology, it will perhaps be said that the subject is self-revealing while the object is revealed only by the subject. This only shows that, as thought and for the purpose of knowing, the subject, appearing after the division of an original unity into subject and object, has gained an advantage over the object. But it has lost in being; that is why it is not sure of the existence corresponding to its ideas and, though we have an idea of God, we doubt whether God exists. We even doubt the existence of mind apart from matter. The subject posits itself and knows itself only while positing the object. Those who approach the *ātman* through the subject have no answer to this objection. Secondly, as the subject comes into being only after the division of the *ātman* into the subject and the object, the approach to the *ātman* through the object should be as much possible as the approach through the subject. In terms of Spinoza's philosophy, if the approach through the attribute of consciousness is recognised, the approach through being also should be recognised and is equally necessary. Without being, consciousness is a pale and valueless vacuum, a flame disconnected from its wick. Being is as much an attribute of the *ātman* as consciousness. Thirdly, even in the history of philosophy, though Spinoza felt that mind overlapped matter and not *vice versa*, he felt also the need to treat them differently. We may even add that matter as being overlaps mind, which is overlooked by Spinoza. It will of course be said that being is common to both mind and matter and that, according to Spinoza, both are attributes of being or Substance. But for modern philosophy in general, matter is being without consciousness and the being of consciousness is even questioned by it. The *ātman*, for Indian Philosophy, is a peculiar unity of being (*sat*) and consciousness (*chit*), and bliss (*ānanda*) is added to the two as a third attribute. One influenced by the Sāṁkhya may say that the *ātman* is a state of equilibrium of the three attributes, just as Prakṛti is a state of equilibrium of the attributes *sattva*, *rajas* and *tamas* (knowledge, activity and stupor). Fourthly the approach through the subject and apart from the object, breeds the feeling of a necessity for escape from the values of the world and will encourage morbid pessimism. There are two kinds of pessimism, the healthy pessimism necessary for every religion consequent upon the dissatisfaction with the imperfections of the world, and the morbid pessimism appearing generally during religious degeneration and openly or tacitly encouraging escape from the world. The first appears when our personality finds the values of the world inadequate for its further development; but the latter is an admission of defeat in the endeavour to build up a wider and deeper personality and is therefore a search for a way of retreat. In the fifth place, the motive behind the modern tendency to treat the subject as an object among objects and behind Russell's doctrine of the neutral stuff and Whitehead's theory of the super-ject, is the disinclination to treat the subject as infinite, and deserves serious attention by the idealists. Sixthly, in the Āgamas the subject or Purusha, which is the *ātman* finitised, is depicted as being born along with time and *avyakta* (the world in its unmanifest stage). This shows that Indian Philosophy, on the whole, is not prepared to accept that the subject as such is infinite. Lastly, a philosophy that depends mainly on this approach can give no place to the principle of evolution, according to which the object also becomes conscious by what Whitehead calls intensification of individuality. If the object as opposed to the subject has no reality, then the consciousness it obtains through intensification of its individuality will also have no reality.

VI

I am influenced by the doctrines of pragmatism also. They have a peculiar tinge of subjectivism, which, when cornered, its protagonists are not prepared to acknowledge. Whatever forms the philosophical attitude behind their outlook might have taken, it is the result of a sound factual sense. There is a deeper consideration which makes us feel that the universe as experienced by man is being built up by him. Kant also advocated that mind makes nature. The pragmatists have an unreasonable aversion to metaphysics, which means fear of going the whole length our reason takes us; and so they practically put man in the place of mind and say that man makes nature. This is the humanistic attitude. But man, the empirical individual, is not able to make nature. Hence arose the hypostatisation of race and humanity, and the contention that evolution should be taken more seriously. But even accepting the idealist position, at least as developed here, we can take evolution seriously. Some peculiar correlation between human mind and nature is noticed by us, which made Kant start with the question how and why objects correspond to our ideas. Had he started with the question how and why objects exhibit utility for man, he would have ended with some sort of absolutist pragmatism. The general concept of correlation between subject and object, mind and matter, explains both epistemological correspondence and pragmatist utility. The concept of the Absolute Mind working through us explains the lack also, wherever it is found, of correspondence and utility. For if the finite mind or man is wholly responsible for making nature, then there would be neither lack of correspondence nor lack of utility, because man will always try to make what is useful to him. The conclusion seems to be that there is something in man or mind, which is more than man or mind.

To this kind of pragmatism, the Upanishads furnish sufficient support. The world of objects is created for enjoyment (*aśanāpipāsā*), not merely to perceive. Hence the categories of the enjoyer and the enjoyed (*bhokta* and *bhogya*) are more basic than those of the seer and the seen (*drashṭā* and *dṛśya*). The commentaries on the Upanishads and the *Brahmasūtras* use the former ideas more often. The latter ideas are more common in later and smaller treatises on the Vedanta. The Brahman divided itself into subject and object in order to enjoy. According to the Sāṁkhya, Prakṛti manifests the world for the enjoyment of the Purusha. For the Upanishads and the Vedanta, what is simply the witness and so only sees is not the finite mind but the deeper mind within (*Muṇḍaka*, III, 3, 1.). The *Bṛhadāraṇyaka* says that the *ātman* created the world for the sake of enjoyment (I, 4, 3.). Even the orthodox Advaita speaks of the empirical world as *vyāvahārika*, which is generally translated by the world empirical. But *vyavahāra* primarily means conduct and action and secondarily usage and business. The *vyavahāra* world is really the world of action. But as the Advaitins do not accept the pragmatic criterion of truth (*arthakriyākāritva*), it has become the practice to translate the word as empirical. Yet the truth seems to be that the Advaitin is prepared to treat the phenomenal world as the world of action and enjoyment. But as he was predominently interested in the noumenal world, he made no attempt to construct the phenomenal world and was satisfied with showing that the phenomenal world was only relatively true. So my feeling is strong that pragmatism contains an important element of truth, which no constructive philosophy should ignore, namely, that the being of the world of plurality is connected with our practical life and not merely with our life of imagination or of consciousness abstracted from our life or action. Hence pragmatism should not be opposed to coherence or correspondence. If man or mind makes nature, continuously constructs it, then he or it would construct it coherently, though the application of the criterion of coherence would lead to infinite regress; and the finitude of man and his mind creates conditions justifying correspondence, though this criterion, in its turn, involves its own inapplicability. Similarly, the upholders of coherence and correspondence should acknowledge the truth of pragmatism. For mind or man that constructs the world constructs it with a purpose; and that purpose can have meaning only when it is concerned with our practical life.

VII

The problem how the finite individual can finally determine whether an object exists or not, has not yet been solved, though epistemology is some four centuries old. In practical life, we do not indeed wait for the final solution. But the question has been raised in theory, and philosophers have been struggling hard to solve it. We now find that we are in principle incapable of solving it. All the three important epistemological theories—correspondence, coherence and pragmatism—suffer from inherent defects. But all are based upon some basic facts: the first upon the otherness of the world to thought, the second upon the constructive nature of thought in apprehending the world, and the third upon the fact that man or mind does not work without a purpose. We see both the defects and merits of each. Yet we are still unable to solve how to determine existence. Why?

First, can thought determine existence? If it can, it would have been unnecessary for Spinoza to treat matter as a separate attribute from mind. Secondly, Bradley tells us, and the whole of his logic is devoted to prove, that thought must commit suicide before it can grasp existence. When we apply a test to know truth, we do nothing but use thought in order to determine existence. In the third place, we say it so often that no amount of intellectual analysis can exhaust the nature of any concrete particular and that we cannot therefore analyse the nature of a particular exhaustively into universals, whatever be their number. In the fourth place, does not this prove that the subject cannot know itself except while knowing the object, that is, that it knows its being or reality only when it knows the being of the object? The subject by itself has no being; and so whatever be the number of universals it can apply, it cannot produce the being of the object. The inherent defect of every epistemological criterion is ultimately due to the natural incapacity of thought to determine being.

What then is the lesson we are to draw? The existence of the object must be self-revealing. Thus, it is not merely mind that is self-revealing but existence also. This is an important truth of idealism, particularly of Sankara's Advaita, which should never be ignored, if we are not afraid of using the postulational method in order to solve the problems raised by epistemology. We should rather say, after the discussion in the earlier section, that it is existence that is self-revealing, and that the subject reveals itself while revealing the object. To be still more precise, the existence of the subject is revealed while the existence of the object reveals itself. This is what is implied in the Advaita doctrine of *svatah-prāmāṇyatā* (self-revelatory nature) of truth. The subject posits itself only while the object is posited. The being of the subject cannot be otherwise grasped. When the subject is apart from the being of the object, the consciousness of the subject gets divorced from being itself and so becomes abstract and empty in a sense. That is why abstract thought and universals are devoid of being. The being of the subject and the being of the object are somehow intertwined into one. This peculiar relation of the two explains the epistemological difficulties.

If the relation between the subject and object is such, then what is it that posits itself and affirms itself as the subject and object? We have seen that it is being or existence. But what is merely being cannot be the subject also, much less can it be self-revealing. So it must be conscious also and hence the Self, in which thought and being, *sat* and *chit*, are identical. Thus, we have come back to the position held by the Sāmkhya, more clearly developed by the Āgamas, and indicated by the *Katha*. that *manas* (mind) and the organs of sense and action on the one side and the world of objects on the other, issue out of the *aham* (the ego or self). That is, the ego is comprehensive of both the subject and the object, the "I" and "my object." The "I" alone is not the ego, the "mine" also is part of it.

Then how are we to account, as there is a plurality of selves. for the commoness of experience? The Sāmkhya tries to preserve the commonness of the world by postulating oneness of Prakṛti.

But the Advaitins ask: If Prakṛti is one and yet be different for different Purushas, why not treat the Purusha also as one and yet as being able to be many egos or *ahams*? The Śāṁkhya has no reasonable answer. Thus each ego can be the centre of synthesis of its own thought and being, and the commonness of the world can be preserved by postulating a deeper ego, which is the Absolute and in which the finite egos participate. So far philosophers are acquainted with the idea of finite minds participating in the infinite mind. But the view developed here necessitates the idea of the worlds of the finite minds participating in the world of the infinite mind and the new point of view which treats the ego (*aham*) as inclusive of both the subject and the object. The vagueness of the connotation of mind in Western Philosophy makes the word unsuitable for the development of this line of thinking.

One important point should be noted here. The Śāṁkhya views Prakṛti as inert matter and not as being and also as opposed to Purusha. But we need not leave the opposition unsolved. The Āgamas in fact removed the opposition and spiritualised Prakṛti by treating it as the Śakti (energy) of the Absolute. Spinoza treated matter as an attribute of Substance and not as having an existence of its own. Its existence is the existence of Substance. But how are the attributes related to each other? Is their relation like the relation between the smell and colour of a flower? A relation of juxtaposition and so of indifference? The relation seems to be much more intimate. Matter is matter for mind and for the subject. So they are not indifferent to each other but interdependent. Now we find, and modern Western Philosophy makes it clear that mind divorced from matter is abstract and hence lacks being. Hence the split in the original Self should now be interpreted more fruitfully as that into thought and being, *sat* and *chit*, and not into mind and matter. How is it that we have now greater assurance of the being of matter than of the being of mind? It is time for developing a system of idealism with consciousness and being, and not mind and matter, as the basic categories.

It may be asked whether the object of illusion posited by the ego exists even during illusion: and if it exists, how its existence differs from the existence of real objects. The answer certainly is that it exists during illusion; but its existence is cancelled after the truth is known. The truth that cancels the existence of the illusory object is a truth of the phenomenal or empirical (*vyāvahārika*) world, which is constructed of truths not cancelled. Further, this cancelling does not mean the cancelling of the experience itself, but the cancelling of the illusory object in the phenomenal world. Thus the existence of the phenomenal world is a limited category compared to existence as such, and is to be derived from the latter. The existence of the illusory object is a proof of the privacy of our experiences, which do not sometimes coincide with the experience that is an "Other" to them and belongs to the Absolute within us.

We have thus three kinds of existence: the existence of the Absolute, which is identical with thought; the existence of the illusory object, which is private to the individual; and the existence of the phenomenal world which is constructed by the finite individual for *vyavahāra* or action and which is the being of the Absolute split into subjects and objects.

VIII

Indian Philosophy, on the whole, showed very little interest, in the construction of the phenomenal world. Even those systems which regarded the material world as independent of God or spirit give us no clue as to how conceptually we are to build it up. The interest of all was centred in the inner spirit. It was really incumbent on the upholders of the *vyāvahārika* existence of the phenomenal world, as they themselves mooted the problem, to say how the phenomenal reality is built up through *vyavahāra* or action. They did not develop their thought here; but the need for developing it at this point should now be met. *Vyavahāra* involves purpose, causality and coherence, all of which should really be included in the idea of *arthakriyākāritva* (production of the anticipated effect), which is somehow identified with pragmatism only. If the effect is concerned with the subject, then both causality and purposiveness are involved; if not, only causality. Here for the construction of the phenomenal world, all the information that can be supplied by the special sciences, physical, biological and social, has to be used.

If the phenomenal world is thus the result of construction, we have to understand the phenomenal subject also accordingly. The ego posits itself as the subject and object simultaneously. Every object perceived is an object thus posited and the phenomenal world is constructed out of such objects. By every act of positing the object, the subject is posited and obtains phenomenal content. So the subject is not a static and fixed fact. The activity of this continuous positing brings content to the ego and becomes the apperceptive mass in subsequent positing. Thus the ego, which is inclusive of both the subject and the object, and the subject which is posited by it, obtain more and more detail. This is the truth contained in Leibnitz's theory of monads, which are not merely subjects but worlds inclusive of both subjects and objects, each monad, as a microcosm, containing the whole world within itself from its own point of view. But Leibnitz has not seen that our experience of a common world and the moral and social interaction of selves involves the cancelling of their finality or absoluteness, that is, that we have to postulate an absolute experience which ultimately becomes the "Other" to the experiences of the finite selves. It is the postulation of this "Other" that can reconcile the idea of our constructing the phenomenal world with the idea of our discovering it. And this "Other", as already indicated, should be treated as inward to the selves. An important result is that we should no longer picture even the finite self as confined to the physical body and as only the subject. Nor should it be thought of as empty consciousness devoid of its own being and depending on the being of physical things.

Thus what Leibnitz calls God is not a monad among monads but their truth or inward reality, the ground of themselves and of their common world. It is really the Self within Selves, controlling their activities and reminding them, as it were at every moment, of the presence of the "Other" in their experience. Each finite self is a centre of phenomenal construction, which takes place by division into subject and object and by making physical body the main instrument. The subject readily identifies itself with the body, because it acts through the body. The construction of the phenomenal world takes place according to forces acting through the centre, which are dynamic universals, the

Ideas of Plato. That is, it is really these forces that live and act through us, and it is not we that make use of these forces. This is implied by their spontaneity, pointed out by Kant. This is what the Upanishads mean when they speak of the *hṛdayagranthi*, the knot of the heart. (By *hṛdaya* they do not mean the physical heart but the metaphysical *buddhi*). The finite self is a knot (*granthi* or complex) of these forces. That is why the Buddhists thought that they could not find any residue after analysing the self into the five *skandhas* (aggregates) or the twelve *āyatanas* (the bases of phenomenal existence), which really constitute the phenomenal world of subject and object, produced by the activity of the living universals, and which account for the correlativity of the subjective and objective forms. These dynamic universals belong not to the body, not to the subject as opposed to the object, but to the self, which includes both the subject and the object. Rather, the subject belongs to them. The finite self is their knotted unity (*hṛdayagranthi*) and is the centre of their constant activity, without which the self-identity and the continuity of the world cannot be maintained for the subject. When they cease to be active, the world would cease to exist for the subject, which no longer partakes of the world of the Absolute Self, to which these spontaneous forces really belong, and which thought is identical with being and intellect with intuition. It is at this level that things can be created at will. As thought is identical with being, to will a thing confers being upon idea. Where thought is different from being, the thing willed should first be held in idea, and being should be given the form of the idea.

IX

Reference has already been made to the inadequacy of the Western concept of mind. Because of the correlation between mind and body, which is its primary instrument, the tendency has become strong to pay all attention to body and even to ignore mind. The scientific attitude, which is rightly impersonal, has been wrongly identified with the physical, non-mental and non-spiritual. This is also called the objective attitude, which, even in empiricism, accepts only whatever is given to the outward-looking consciousness as true and is prone to regard what is given

to the inward-looking consciousness as illusory and untrust-
worthy. It is not recognized that both the inward-looking and
the outward-looking consciousnesses may be illusory and that
even the inward-looking can give us truths, which have to be
patiently differentiated from illusions. The subject is rightly
treated by realism as an object among objects, but the full
significance of its being a privileged object is overlooked. It
seems to realism absurd that the self, whose seat is treated as the
physical body, can include the object also, which is outside the
subject. But the mistake lies in thinking that the self is in the
body or is the subject. The opposite is the truth. The self is not
in the body; it includes both our body and the other objects
concerned with it, as for instance in dreams, in which our minds
create their bodies and the objects perceived by them. The
emancipation of the self from the confines of the physical body
and the subject is a necessary principle at this stage of the
history of philosophy.

Another such necessary principle is the recovery of self for
philosophical explanation. It is the vogue now to explain self in
terms of space, space-time, time, or matter. But the inward or
spiritual experiences have thereby become unimportant and lost
their metaphysical value. They are rather explained away. Our
intellectual outlook therefore has lost its spiritual leaven. The
difficulties in the earlier philosophies from the stand-point of the
self were due to equating it to the subject, and can be overcome
by placing it, as it were, outside the subject. In truth, the self
is what is inward to both the subject and the object and is their
underlying unity. There are several reasons why the self should
be recovered for philosophical explanation. First, it is necessary
for the explanation of the inward and the spiritual. Secondly,
the problem of the one and the many, where the one is an all-
pervasive category, cannot be solved without treating it as a
dynamic factor in a unity that includes both the subject and the
object. Thirdly, it follows from the second that the interrelations
between the factors cannot be worked out except by postulating
the self. They must be the functions of a unified consciousness.
In the fourth place, though the subject can be understood from
the external point of view as an object among objects, there is
no reason to prevent understanding it from the inward point of

view. If we are mere superjects emerging out of peculiar pre-hensions, the problem how the prehensions themselves can be objects of their own superjects and how the superjects can have a life distinct from that of the prehensions, cannot be explained.

X

Philosophy therefore should not hestitate to take seriously the idea of the self. It is a postulate of our experience. Kant used the postulational method with a success that was the wonder of the time. But he went only half way in its use, did not postulate the interconnections between the ultimate postulates, and thought they were not constitutive of our experience. He could not see how they could be experienced at all. He could not see the possibility of pushing our experience, usually limited to the phenomenal world, beyond those limits through the process of inward realisation. Hegel's mistake lay in thinking that thought as such could do so. Here is the place for religion in its essence. Western Philosophy, in not seeing this truth, failed to give religion its proper place. Had it done so, it would have approached Indian Philosophy and recognised its spirit long ago. That is why not a single Indian philosophical concept has so far entered Western thought, which begins to feel uneasy the moment it is asked to take the inward into serious account. But the postula-tional method of Kant, in trying to take a synthetic view of both the subject and the object, does inevitably lead to the inwardness of the ultimate truth. That is why in his philosophy can be found the foundation for a philosophy, which would also be a philosophy of life, necessitating an experiential living of what is speculatively postulated. But this necessity and the inwardness of truth were not given due recognition by Western thought, which therefore does not advance beyond the speculative level, claiming generally the satisfaction of mere intellectual curiosity as its aim.

In science, what is hypothetically postulated is experimentally verified. Verification generally takes two forms: direct observa-tion and, where it is not possible, the observation of its being implied by other accepted hypotheses. When neither is possible, the simplest hypothesis, applying Occam's Razor, is accepted.

Now, how are the ultimate postulates of philosophy to be verified? What were really postulates for Kant, namely, God, Self and the World, were practically treated as premises by Spinoza and Descartes, who did not therefore feel the need for verification. Kant felt the need, but thought that it was impossible to verify them, which is the same as saying to experience them; for experience for him was always outward. But if outward experience cannot verify them and some experience is to verify them, then that experience should be inward. To verify the ultimate categories, there is no other experience and no other method. Ultimates are *ex hypothesi* not implied by other hypotheses; and the principle of Occam cannot go farther than postulating a unity of the three in the Intuitive Understanding of God. Here is the necessity for postulating religious experience.

It has been observed already that the Intuitive Understanding should be understood as Creative Understanding. Philosophy should be presented as a consistent description of the workings of the Creative Understanding. The chain or system of pure forms belongs to it. But which forms are we to accept? Can we derive them from the concept of the Creative Understanding itself? Certainly not. Here is the place for the empirical methods and sciences, which correct mere speculation when it accepts fanciful categories. We cannot *a priori* say what forms and how many of them there should be. Each empirical science starts with observations, develops its postulates, and then becomes a hypothetico-deductive system with axioms and theorems. When the special sciences discover their indispensable axioms, it is the task of philosophy to connect them and present them as a system helpful for life to form its ideals. The empirical sciences furnish categories of our outward experience. Philosophy connects them with the help of the method of postulation and develops the categories of our inward experience, without which the categories of our outward experience would fall asunder. The genetic method, where the idea of time is involved, belongs generally to the systematisation of our outward experience. Mere analysis, which refuses to postulate, leads nowhere: the analytic method by itself involves an endless and aimless process; the attempt to reconstruct leads necessarily to postulation.

XI

Indian Philosophy has often been criticised for giving no place to social and ethical thought. Its chief interest was in the inward reality and so it tried to give an account of the outward reality accordingly. Unlike the early Greek systems of Plato and Aristotle, Indian Philosophy showed no interest in society as such. A very rigorous system of self-discipline was preached; but it was oriented towards the realisation of the inner reality, but not towards the realisation of the best society. Here is found the basic difference between the Greek and the Indian stand-points. Christianity was intensely inward and other-worldly; but Augustine's *Civitas Dei* is an example of the influence of the Greek outlook on Christian thought. The tribal origin of the Jewish religion is also responsible for the social-mindedness of Christianity, for Catholicism claims to be universal.   Similarly Kant's philosophy is not merely Christian theology; and his conception of the kingdom of ends is another example of the same attitude. Similar conceptions are lacking in Indian Philosophy. It would be in vain to meet this criticism, though we may point out that self-control, which is the essence of moral activity, is not limited to its bearings to society, but has a deeper significance. It is control of one's thought and activity according to the Dharma or the Law of the Universe, which is greater than society, but certainly includes society. Yet its significance with reference to society is the most useful for ethics and other social subjects.

Now, the development of the outward attitude to its extreme has cut the very roots of social and ethical thought in Western Philosophy also. What is perceived by the senses in their outward activity is not self or mind but matter with its qualities. The subtle question, what is matter, need not be raised. What is perceived may be matter or qualities: it is the physical body, but not the self or mind. Hence the problem of our knowledge of other minds or selves has become poignant. Even the worship of humanity advocated by the positivism of Comte suffers ship-wreck here. How can I worship humanity if I cannot directly know other selves, but have only to infer them? And this infer-ence is to be, and can be nothing more than weak analogy based

on my experience of my own body and mind. The very foundations of ethics are destroyed now, for there can be no morality for
a Robinson Crusoe but only for man in society, and there can be
no social consciousness without direct knowledge of other selves.
Even Fichte, who was so anxious to lay a sure and secure
basis for moral philosophy, seemed to have overlooked this
difficulty. The ego, according to him, itself posited the non-ego,
which should therefore conform to the moral activity of the
former. But he did not insist that the non-ego should be another
ego. He was more concerned with removing the difficulty created
by Kant, namely, of reconciling the freedom of the will with the
determinism of nature; and was therefore content with postulating
nature as posited by the ego and as therefore conforming to its
activity and thereby making morality possible. But there is
another condition of morality, namely, that the object of moral
activity should be another ego and not merely nature. It would
be difficult to apply Kant's principle that we should treat other
persons as ends in themselves, unless we know them as selves
directly.

That we know other selves at least as directly as material
things is therefore an indispensable postulate of the ethical and
social sciences. Social consciousness is *a priori* like the consciousness of the categories, and can be made explicit only in inward
realisation. Here also, just as we do not identify our self with our
body, we should not identify other selves with other bodies.
Other selves also treat their bodies as their instruments. The
second reason for this postulation is that the experience of the
child and the savage shows that even inanimate objects are not at
first material for them, that the objects are for them what they
are themselves, which is confirmation of the view that the self
posits other objects first as it posits itself. The idea of matter or
life is a later growth. It is wrong to suppose that human beings
know material reality first and later derive their knowledge of
biological and psychological reality. Because of the determinism
ruling material reality, we may be more sure of objectivity and
of the absence of fanciful and illusory constructions in our
knowledge of it. But this surety belongs to the later stages in
the race and the individual; in the earlier stages, man sees, not
merely infers, every thing as he is—a fact which we now

stigmatise as anthropomorphism. Man's critical reflection later introduces the distinctions between matter, life and mind, but commits the mistake that we *see* matter only. Matter is as much a hypothesis as mind and can only be as much or as little perceived. It is not impossible to be aware of other selves as we are aware of substances. Our awareness is sometimes an illusion ; but we have illusions even with regard to material objects ; and everywhere illusions have to be distinguished from truths. The fact that we distinguish what a thing is in itself and what it is for us shows that we concede privacy even to material things, not merely to minds. Thirdly, if we are conscious of ideas and images, which are mental, we can be conscious of minds also. Some constructive imagination may be involved in this perception. But the same is involved in the perception of any material object. Fourthly, there is every justification for the ethical and social sciences declaring their autonomy, just as the biological sciences declared their independence from the physical. The axioms of one class are not workable in the other. The fifth reason is to be found in Jung's analytical psychology, wherein he speaks of the projection of the anima by man and the persona by woman. This projection is akin to the working of the Kantian categories, and shows how we can be conscious of other selves. Sixthly, this principle should be generalised, and we should say that no self can have adequate assurance of itself as a self and can therefore posit itself as a subject, unless it posits other subjects. That is why we are more sure of our self-hood in company of men and women than in company with animals and material objects. In the seventh place, the Upanishads support this view by declaring that the one felt lonely and created the many, which are selves. Loneliness can be removed only when a self is directly conscious of other selves, but not of material objects only. The Agamas also, which have an authority independent of the Vedas, declare the same truth, and treat the original unity as that of man and woman, Śiva and Śakti, or Vishṇu and his consort, and the world as being due to a split in that unity.

For these reasons, I believe, we have to postulate an *a priori* knowledge of other selves. The first act of positing or the act of self-externalisation of the Absolute Self should therefore be understood as of the form, "I and Thou", and not merely as the Agamas maintain, of the form, "I and That". If the split is into "I and That", there would be no morality. The world would only be the world of the animal and its food, not of man and his ethical environment, though both may be *bhogya* or objects of enjoyment. There can be love, not between the I and the That, but between the I and the Thou. Both the Upanishads and the Āgamas are indifferent to this distinction, though they treat the original unity as that between God and his consort, thereby emphasizing the intense bliss of love characteristic of that unity. In the light of the emphasis we have thrown, the maxim, "Love thy neighbour as thyself", gets a significance deeper than the moral. In love only is one the most sure of one's self as well as of the other's. The categorical imperative should be love's command.

Here I feel Indian Philosophy is left undeveloped, and here is scope for further development. It is not a mere speculative consideration, but a consideration for a philosophy of life. The mere neutral That, unless it develops into a personal Thou, cannot offer itself as an object for moral activity. This development, science tells us, does happen by evolution. When the subject perceives a material object, it is conscious of itself more as a material body ; but when the subject is aware of a person, it is aware of itself more as a person. In ethical consciousness, where man feels the command from within, he is nearer the inward reality than in any other form of social consciousness, which therefore presupposes it. Without the voluntary self-control of the individual, social laws are unworkable. Hence, ethics is higher than any other social science. It leads to the science of inward life or religion.

Incidentally we may observe that scientific studies, as they are so far developed, should be classified into six kinds : material sciences, biological sciences, mental sciences, social sciences, and the sciences of inward life, which belong to the field of religion or spiritual realisation. Religion is not to be left to sentimental treatment. Its essential nature has not so far been systematically studied in the West. The so-called science of religion studies only the externals ; and philosophy has been content with speaking of mysticism, though sometimes appreciatively. I am not in favour of the word mysticism ; for it is associated with the idea of clouding our intellect, whereas true religion should result in enlightenment. Buddha did not renounce the world in order to cloud his intellect.

Social consciousness remains so long as the I and the Thou last. Even in the ethical consciousness, which is more inward than the other forms of social consciousness, the distinction would remain. But religion begins with removing this distinction. When the Thou disappears, the I also disappears. The subject, it is already observed, is a knot : modern psychology would call it a complex, the Upanishads call it *hrdayagranthi*. The Buddhists thought that the resolution of the knot meant *nirvāṇa* and *śūnya* (peace and void), that there would be no residue after the resolution. But the Upanishads and the Āgamas maintained that the knot was only a form (*rūpa*), and that the resolution was only the removal of the form and so did not result in utter nothing. If form disappears, the result need not be mere nothing but something formless or beyond form. However, both religions preach the surrender of the I. The same spiritual principle is involved in the idea of faith in, and surrender to Christ. Thus religion, for epistemology and metaphysics, is the recovery of pure being or existence—not bare existence, which is only an abstraction—existence which is self-conscious and sure of itself. For when the distinction between subject and object is removed, self-revealing existence, which so far has taken on the form of that distinction, shines in its purity.

It is not possible, within the limits of this paper, to discuss the blissful nature of the inward Absolute. Existence, we said, is always self-revealing; the Absolute, therefore, is self-revealing existence. In it consciousness has recovered being and has ceased to be abstract. In it idea is not divorced from existence. Pleasure, happiness, and bliss lie in the fulfilment of desire, in conferring being on idea, in materialising idea. In the phenomenal world, striving and activity are necessary, because idea is divorced from existence, consciousness (*chit*) from being (*sat*). Where there is no such divorce, there would be eternal bliss (*ānanda*). That is why the Upanishads declare that the nature of the Absolute is *ānanda* also, and that in it everyone gets whatever one wants (*yo yad ichchati tasya tat*).

PRINCIPAL PUBLICATIONS

Thought and Reality: Hegelianism and Advaita, with a Foreword by
J. H. Muirhead. George Allen and Unwin Ltd., London.

"The Hegelian Absolute and the Individual". *Philosophy*, London,
July, 1934.

"The Message of Sankara Vedānta to Our Times". *Proceedings of
The International Congress of Philosophy*, Prague, 1934, pp. 804-12.

"The Reality of Negation". *The Philosophical Review*, New York,
vol. 1. No. 6.

"The Western and the Indian Philosophical Traditions". *The
Philosophical Review*, New York, vol. lvi, No. 2.

"Coherence and the Moral Criterion". *The International Journal of
Ethics*, Chicago.

"The Need for Transcending the Concept of Organism as a Principle
of Explanation". *The Philosophical Quarterly*, Amalner.

"The Idea of Superposition and the Sphere of Mind". (Presidential
Address to the Logic and Metaphysics Section, Indian Philosophical Congress, 1938).

"Negative Judgment and its Relation to Reality". (Indian Philosophical Congress, Symposium, 1939).

"Identity in Difference in Some Vedāntic Systems". *Festschrift
Sir Denison Ross*.

"Our Knowledge of the Universal". *Sir C. R. Reddy Commemoration
Volume*.

"Indian Philosophy: Its Attitude to the World". *The Vedānta Kesari*,
Madras, November and December, 1944.

"Perceptual Individuation" *The Indian Journal of Pscyhology*,
Calcutta, September-December, 1942.

"The Direction of Universalisatiou". *The Indian Journal of
Psychology*, Calcutta, September-December, 1943.

"The Buddhistic Conception of Dharma". *The Annals of the Bhandarkar Oriental Research Institute*, Poona, vol. xxi, parts 3-4.

"The Buddhistic and the Advaita View-points". *The New Indian
Antiquary*, Poona, May, 1941.

"Research in Indian Philosophy: A Review" *Journal of the Ganga-
natha Jha Oriental Research Institute*, Allahabad, February, May
and August, 1944.

"Indian Philosophy: A Survey" *Progress of Indic Studies*, Silver
Jubilee Volume, Bhandarkar Oriental Research Institute, Poona;
and several other articles published in the proceedings of the
Indian Philosophical Congress; The All-India Oriental Conference;
and periodicals.

THE EVOLUTION OF MY OWN THOUGHT

by R. D. RANADE, M.A.

Born July 3, 1886; Professor of Philosophy, University of
Allahabad

THE EVOLUTION OF MY OWN THOUGHT

I. INTRODUCTORY

WE cannot prize too highly the endeavours which Professors Muirhead and Radhakrishnan have been making to give Indian Philosophy its proper place in the World's Thought by arranging for a volume dedicated to Contemporary Indian Philosophy in the Series in which have already appeared the volumes on British and American thought. India glories in her philosophic past, but on account of her new relationship with Western Philosophy and Western Science, she has to incorporate many new ideas into her old scheme in order to make it workable in the modern world. Various methods have been hitherto followed by the writers in the Series above referred to ; some have had a perfected system of their own, which they only summarise in their essays; others cull out a chapter from their general contribution to thought; others give mainly biographical details with an interspersing of reflection. Not having published hitherto any completed system of my own, I am obliged to seek another method. In the small contributions that I have hitherto made to Indian and European Philosophy, I have followed the method of construction through critical exposition, and even though a perfected system of my own has not been in print, I thought it might not be irrelevant to take certain portions from my writings in order to show what line a completely systematised philosophy would take for me. This method may not exclude altogether some little biographical detail, in order that it may give to my philosophic thought a certain background on which might be seen the rough outlines of the picture I wish to draw.

As I have been looking at the evolution of my own thought from my early years, I cannot but wonder how the pendulum has swung exactly to the other extreme. I definitely remember the day, when, as an Undergraduate, in the year 1905, who had as yet hardly passed his teens, I was inducing my nephew not to offer Philosophy as one of his optional subjects at the B.A.

I was myself going to offer Mathematics, and why any Science which was not as precise as Mathematics was entitled to any serious study was to me beyond comprehension. On a deeper consideration, however, of the reasons which might have led me to take such a hostile attitude towards Philosophy, I have now found that this dislike of Philosophy was not due to the subject itself, but to the books which were prescribed in the University in those days, as well as to the method of teaching of the subject adopted in my college. The only books which students were asked to study in the Bombay University in those days were Mill's *Logic*, Aristotle's *Nicomachean Ethics*, Wallace's *Kant*, and Martineau's *Types of Ethical Theory*, and this was to me no very tempting intellectual fare. Nor had the teacher, who had been teaching the subject for about thirty years, any relieving feature in his method of exposition which could attract and inspire a young ambitious student. Dislike for the books and for the method of teaching, therefore, it seems, was transferred, in modern psychological terminology, to the subject itself, and the result was that if small things could be compared to great, I hated Philosophy, as Saul did Jesus before the enlightenment came.

II. AN EARLY SPIRITUAL MONADISM

Unconsciously, however, the impulse of Philosophy was strong within me, and even though I took my B.A. in Mathematics, even while I was a Fellow at the Deccan College, Poona, and when, as yet, I had made no systematic study of Philosophy at all, and had not even heard that Leibniz was the founder of Monadism, while I was once observing a cricket match for about six hours on the college grounds, the thought came to me powerfully that the whole Universe might be regarded as full of Spirit ; and as soon as I went to my room I began to put down on paper the thoughts which had struck me in that great day-reverie. It was inevitable for me, however, to start with a Pluralistic conception of Spiritual Reality, because that was the conception which was likely to give satisfaction to the enquiring mind in its earlier stages; and the result was my unconscious philosophising in a monadistic-spiritualistic vein. I take the liberty of quoting the following excerpt from one of my earliest writings on "The

Centre of the Universe" (1908), because it gives in an auto-biographical manner the starting-point from which my thought was to proceed in succeeding years. It will be evident to any scrutinising reader that I was at that time under the spiritual influence of Carlyle, and was philosophising after the manner of Teufelsdroeck:

"Our Professor was generally supposed to be an eccentric man. Careless in his dress, unmindful of the manners which the fashion of his time imposed on him, indifferent to his equals, and heedless of those who posed as his superiors, he nevertheless manifested his precious soul to those fortunate few who, after a long apprenticeship, had come to win his confidence. To those who judged him from what he seemed to be, he appeared more or less a lunatic; and they were encouraged in this belief by the doctrine of our Professor that 'all Greatness is Lunacy.' Our Professor steadily maintained that all great men must be lunatics, and that it was these lunatics who were the salt of the earth. Our Professor was thus known by the humorous title of the 'Apostle of Lunacy.'

"The present writer was one of the fortunate few who had won his confidence, though it must be admitted that he only brought up the rear among them. Long would he listen, and with ever-increasing interest, to what his master would impart to him. He has seen him pouring out his soul in those fits of fantasy when, like a lunatic, he seemed to be 'of imagination all compact.' His lectures were never given regularly; for regularity was not a word to be found in his dictionary. If he was regular in anything, it was only in his irregularity. 'Why bind ourselves by the fetters of Time and Space,' he used to exclaim, 'let us succumb to their power if they at all force us, but what is the use of courting voluntary imprisonment?' Rolling in a fine frenzy, the eye of our Professor glanced from Heaven to Earth, from Earth to Heaven. In the searchlight of his criticism, not the smallest or the darkest cranny of the Universe remained unilluminated.

"The present writer has been fortunate enough to hear him on several topics, and his great wish has been that what was in his thought should not die out. He must make apology to his master for having published his thoughts against his will; for it must be remembered that the Professor, following the bent of his eccentricity, is very averse to having his thoughts published. If, in doing so, the present writer has disobeyed the Professor, it is only because the consideration of the spread of Truth has weighed with him more than that of disobedience. And it is in the animation of this thought that he strings in the following pages his master's reflections on the Centre of the Universe.

"One day while he was in a pensive mood, with his mind focussed on a transcendental thought, I happened to sit at his feet, expecting every moment that his long and deep meditation might bring forth something worth hearing, when he suddenly began to think aloud in the following strain: 'The Centre of the Universe! Will not a discussion of this Centre lead to important truths? Is not the Centre of anything supposed to have peculiar properties? And are not people tempted to find out the Centre of anything, even when there is none? The fact is that people want to find unity in diversity, and order in chaos. Are they not hopelessly tempted by their "idol" of regularity? As in geometry, they know that a circle has got a centre, as in geography they assume that there is a centre of the Earth, as in astronomy they look upon the Sun as the centre of the planetary system, so do they try to find the Centre of the Universe. As in the former cases, they give the centre a definite position in space, even so do they consider that the Centre of the *Universe* is restricted by space. And herein they are mistaken. The Centre of the Universe is either Nowhere or Everywhere.'

"You will now ask me what is my own philosophy of the Centre of the Universe. The old Archimedes said that if he could get a fulcrum for the Earth, he could lift its whole weight with the least effort. I say, in a similar style, that if we can come to know the Centre of the Universe, we shall have solved the Problem of Problems! The questions that can be asked about this centre are the 'where' and the 'what'; and the 'where' determines the 'what'. *Where* is the Centre of the Universe?

"I summarily answer Everywhere. Man is but a speck when compared to the Earth, the Earth is but a speck when compared to the Solar system, and the Solar system vanishes before the Universe! How ridiculous would it then be to suppose that the centre of this infinite Universe is restricted to any place! Men had rather die with shame than entertain such a foolish idea! Where then is the centre of the Universe? Everywhere! Every particle of this infinite universe is its centre! Every particle of water, every particle of wind, every particle of matter is its centre, or, we had better say, hides its centre. The centre is rather *in* particles than the particles themselves! The particles may perish, but the centre does not! It is indestructible, imperishable; without end, and without beginning! Weapons cannot pierce it, fire cannot burn it! In Geometry, they speak of the centre of a circle as the *one* single point from which the distances to the circumference are all *equal*. And is this not true of the centre of the Universe, namely, its Presiding Element, that it is only *one*, and equally near to all? Again, they endow the centre of the Earth with the power of attracting everything on its surface—with the power of Gravitation. How far, then, would this be true of the centre of the *Universe*? How powerful would the Gravitation of *this* centre be? Conception fails to make an estimate of the Force with which all creation gravitates towards the Presiding Element! The Presiding Element is Everywhere! The Universe is but an Infinite Circle, with its Centre Everywhere, and Circumference Nowhere!"

This excerpt will suffice to show how I was already full of a spiritual idea even though I did not know how to philosophise about it. The early hatred of Philosophy had now given place to a new search, and I was thus brought to think that I must study my own Indian Philosophy, especially as I had been taking an acute interest in the Sanskrit language, and was full of respect for one of its greatest philosophers—Śaṁkarāchārya. I also feel myself bound to mention at this place that when I happened to pay a visit to Benares from Poona in October, 1908, I had been to see the remnant of the Mutt of Śaṁkarāchārya at Benares, when on a cool evening I happened to hear the devotional songs of Śaṁkarāchārya recited in the Mutt, which made me pause and think how a so-called Advaita Philosopher could at the same time make room for devotional songs in his philosophical teaching. That to me was a crux, which impelled me to study Indian Philosophy all the more. Just at this time I suffered a physical breakdown in my health which took some time to disappear, during which my mind turned definitely spirit-ward. As a consequence, the problem became all the more insistent for me how to justify spiritual experience in terms of philosophic thought. I definitely recollect that after that date I began a serious study of European Philosophy, with the intent of finding in Eastern and Western philosophic thought a justification for the spiritual life.

III. BRADLEY AND ŚAMKARA; WARD AND RĀMĀNUJA; MCTAGGART AND SĀMKHYA

One of the first things I noticed in the course of a few years of my study was that in Philosophic thought the East was East, and the West was West. This was not a thing which I supposed was desirable. The problem of philosophy to me was one and identical all the world over, and there was no distinction of country or race in the world of thought. I felt it, therefore, necessary to say that Indians should not remain content with the study of Indian Thought, but should study European Thought also; and that the Europeans should not remain content with the study of their European Thought, but should study Indian Thought as well. In fact, I advocated a definite correlative study of Indian and European Philosophy. It was thus that I wrote an article "On the Study of Indian and European Philosophy" in 1914, in which, among other things, I said :

"It is with the view of showing that Indian Philosophy is as rich and varied as European Philosophy that we wish to enter here on a brief correlation of different types of philosophy in India and Europe. It is not until we have shown that Indian Philosophy has such great similarities with European Philosophy that we can understand the importance of our own Philosophy: it is not until then that we can understand the significance of Deussen's words 'Indians, keep to your philosophy.' The correlation must necessarily be brief, and in order that this brevity may be attained, we shall devote more attention to the similarities than to the differences.

"To begin with, we might note the great resemblance between the ancient metaphysical systems of India and the present metaphysical systems of the West. The Absolutism of Bradley has numerous points of contact with the Advaitism of Śaṁkarāchārya. Both suppose that the Absolute is the only ultimate real. With both, God is different from the Absolute. With both, God is unreal compared to the Absolute. Both consider that our souls, our bodies, the worldly objects that we see, are ultimately appearances. And both hold that Space and Time are only phenomenal, and are transcended in the Absolute. Such a dictum involves that the Absolute be supermoral, beyond good and bad. And we find that with Śaṁkara and Bradley, the Absolute transcends moral relations. Moreover, with regard to the content of the Absolute, both Śaṁkara and Bradley hold that it is of the nature of intuitive experience. It is usual to speak of Śaṁkara's Absolute as being of the nature of the unconscious, but those who will think deeper will find that Śaṁkara's Absolute is Sat, Chit and Ānauda, that is Being, Thought and Bliss. Royce points out that though Bradley talks of a personal Absolute as being an intellectually dishonest conception, still Bradley's Absolute 'despite all Mr. Bradley's objections to the self, escapes from self-hood only by remaining to the end a self' (*The World and the Individual*, i, p. 552). and if this interpretation be correct, Śaṁkara's Absolute Consciousness, Bradley's Absolute Experience and Royce's Absolute Person differ, if at all, only in names. . . . Nor is Śaṁkara a determinist, as is ordinarily supposed. He does allow freedom to souls in the sense that they are free so far as they express the eternal purposes of the Absolute, and in this he is on a par with the other Idealists. The great difference between Royce and Śaṁkara is that while the former says that the soul comes into existence in time, Śaṁkara says that, seen from one point of view it is eternal, while seen from another and higher, it is merely an appearance as compared with the absoluteness of the Absolute, which is Bradley's position. This, as the reader will see, is not determinism in the ordinary sense. What we have tried to represent is that Śaṁkara's Philosophy may be best described as an Absolutism, or a Spiritual Monism, but not as a mechanistic, deterministic Pantheism.

"Other philosophers we must treat more briefly. Rāmānuja's system, which is a numerically pluralistic but a qualitatively monistic system, has its best parallel in the theism of Professor James Ward, and in Personal Idealism generally, represented by such writers as Rashdall. Rāmānuja's Absolute is God and the world, the world including souls. Such is also the Theism of James Ward (*The Realm of Ends*, p. 242), and of Protestant Christianity generally. William James has a clever remark in his *Pragmatism*, where he talks of the 'pantheism' of the Anglo-Hegelian school 'having influenced the more studious members of our protestant ministry, and having already blunted the edge of the traditional theism in protestantism at large' (*Pragmatism*, p. 17).

"Coming to other systems, we find a great resemblance between the plural souls of the Sāmkhya without a ruling God, and the 'system of selves or spirits, uncreated and eternal, forming together a unity but not a conscious unity' of the non-theistic Idealist, McTaggart. Both of these differ from the theistic monadism of Leibniz, who postulates a God, as pre-establishing the harmony between one monad and another, and between microcosm and macrocosm. And it is curious to find that while McTaggart's philosophy is non-theistic, Sāmkhya is also *nirīśvara* (God-less).

"There are many other correlations between Indian and European Philosophy, into which we do not here enter for want of space. Not only is metaphysical correlation possible, but also epistemological, logical and ethical. We can easily find parallels in European Philosophy for the nihilism of the Mādhyamikas, the subjectivism of the Yogāchāras, the Representationism of the Sautrāntikas, and the Presentationism of the Vaibhāshikas (Cowell and Gough: *Translation of Sarvadarśanasamgraha*, p. 15). The resemblances between the Aristotelian Logic and the Logic of Gautama are written in such 'text and capital letters that he who runs may read them.' The Hedonism of the Charvakas may be paralleled by that of the Epicureans; the rigorism of the Bauddhas by that of the Stoics; and the threefold ethical ideal of the Bhagavad Gītā, namely, its activism, its ideal of duty, and its self-realisation by those of Eucken, Kant and Green respectively."

s

IV. RELATIVISM AND TRUTH

After these early essays the first definite period in my work on philosophic subjects was connected with Greek Philosophy. One of the great Greek Philosophers who was the first to catch my attention was Herakleitos. It was well known how he propounded the law of Relativism. He said there was no absolute distinction between night and day, between life and death, between good and bad. The sea, he said, was both purest and foulest water. It was purest for fish, but foulest for men, thus pointing to the conclusion that there was no absolute nature of sea-water. In my discussion of Herakleitos' philosophy (1916), however, I saw that there was a point at which my Relativism broke, namely, at God, a fact which was acknowledged by Herakleitos himself:

"If we ask Herakleitos whether his law of Relativism holds good in the case of God, he gives two different answers at two different places. Once he says that the law of Relativism holds good even about God: the First Principle, he says, is willing to be called Zeus, and unwilling to be called Zeus: λ γεσθαι οὐκ ἐθέλει καὶ ἐθέλει Ζηνὸς οὔνομα But he says elsewhere that the law of Relativism stops at God, even though it holds good about men: to God, he says, all things are fair and good and just, but men hold some things unjust and some just: τῷ μὲν θεῷ καλὰ πάντα καὶ ἀγαθὰ καὶ δίκαῖα, ἄνθρωποι δὲ ἃ μὲν ἄδικα ὑπειλήφασιν, ἃ δὲ δίκαια. The conclusion at which Herakleitos arrives is that 'God is both day and night, war and peace, surfeit and hunger; but He takes various shapes, just as fire, when it is mingled with spices, is named according to the savour of each.' In short, says Herakleitos, every one gives Him the name he pleases: ὀνομάζεται καθ' ἡδονὴν ἑκάστου."

The upshot of such a doctrine is that Relativism has no application to Divine Life, while its proper sphere of application is only to the phenomenal and ephemeral sphere. In this, I heartily concurred with Herakleitos.

Protagoras failed to see this inapplicability of the law of Relativism to God. He applied it to the phenomenal and ephemeral sphere, and he supposed that Herakleitos' philosophy gave him sufficient justification for this. Aristotle, who saw this point cleverly, in his criticism of Protagoreanism first tried to take away the Herakleitean bottom from Protagorean relativism. It It well known how he tells us that the nemesis of the

Herakleitean doctrine of flux was reached in the extreme doctrine of Cratylus, who did not think it right to say anything, but only moved his finger, and who rebuked his master for having said that it was impossible to step twice into the same river, for he thought that this could not be done even once, for, he said, "in the very process of your stepping into the river, the waters have run off" (*Metaphysica*, 1010. a. 10-15). Then again, Aristotle said, exactly like Kant, that it was only the permanent that could change, and that it was only from a pre-existing thing that change or motion could take place ; and in addition that the process of change could not go on *ad infinitum*, and that there-fore there is no meaning in the idea of incessant change : "If a thing is coming to be, there must be something *from* which it comes to be and something *by* which it is generated, and this process cannot be *ad infinitum*" (*Metaphysica*, 1010. a.20-22). The last criticism that Aristotle passed on the Herakleitean doctrine of flux was that its author had unduly extended the sphere of application of the idea of change from his immediate surroundings to the whole universe. Granted that what immediately surrounds us is always in process of destruction and generation—this is, be it remembered, not even a fraction of the whole—it would thus be juster to acquit this part of the world because of the other part than to condemn the other because of this. So that, says Aristotle, it is evident that there is something whose nature is changeless, and if we were given the only alternative between "rest" and "change" as predicates of the Cosmos, we had rather decide for "rest" than for "change" (*Metaphysica*, 1010. a.28-36). Protagorean Relativism was attacked by Aristotle also for other reasons than its Herakleitean origin. Percipients, according to him, were not all on the same level. The judgments of different people were not equally valid; e.g. the judgment of the physician and the judgment of the ignorant quack were not equally decisive in regard to a disease (*Metaphysica*, 1010. b. 12-14). Finally, the most important criticism that Aristotle passed upon Relativism was that it did not take any account of "Differences of Value" and that it had no adequate theory of "Truth." I heartily con-curred with Aristotle in his view of Absolute Truth, when he said that so far from there being any question of Degrees of Truth and Error, there were only Degrees of Error. Truth is one, absolute, and immutable, and that is in God. To quote from my essay on *Aristotle's Critique of Protagoreanism* (1916):

"The most important criticism, however, which Aristotle passes on the relativistic sceptic is where he says that the sceptic does not recognise difference of worth among thiugs. If opposite courses are equally welcome to our opponent, asks Aristotle, 'why does he not walk early some morning into a well or over a precipice, if one happens to be in his way? Why do we observe him guarding against this, evidently not thinking that falling in is alike good and not gocd? Evidently he judges one thing to be better and another worse.' It is in this last remarkable sentence δῆλον ἄρα ὅτι τὸ μὲν βέλτιον ὑπολαμβάνει τὸ δ' οὐ βέλτιον (*Metaphysica*, 1008. b. 18-19), that Aristotle shows an insight that is wonderful. It is the argument from differences of value among things which is the final answer to the relativistic sceptic who would say that to be or not to be is to him equally welcome. Aristotle does definitely say that there is a more or less in the nature of things: τό γε μᾶλλον καὶ ἧττον ἔνεστιν ἐν τῇ φύσει τῶν ὄντων (*Metaphysica*, 1008. b. 32-33). He who thinks that two and two make five is, according to Aristotle, less wrong than he who thinks that they make a thousand (*ibid.*, 1008. b. 34-35). The absolute truth in such a case is that two and two make four. The nearer a thing is to the norm, the less of an error it would be. Thus it follows that while there is an Absolute Truth, there are various degrees of error. It would be wrong according to Aristotle to say that there are degrees of Truth. In his very original theory of Truth, Aristotle would say that Truth is one, but error infinite. This would in fact be necessitated by the metaphysical consideration that while, according to him, all the sublunary things are capable of motion and so are emblems of infinite error, the First Mover is himself unmoved and so is the emblem of Absolute Truth."

V. IDENTITY OF THOUGHT AND BEING

In pursuing my studies on Greek Philosophers, I was once greatly astonished to see how Parmenides, the great Greek Ontolocial philosopher, and Śamkarāchārya, the great Indian Vedāntist, had made exactly similar attacks on the conception of the Idea or the Universal. The question, which both had raised, was—Is the Idea or the Universal fully immanent in the Particulars, or not? If it is fully immanent, it is distributed in so many Particulars. If it is partly present in the Particulars, then it is divisible. It is, therefore, either many or divisible, and hence is not entitled to the name of "Universal." This was the criticism which Parmenides and Śaṁkarāchārya alike passed on the conception of the Universal; and this led me on to the closer study of Parmenides himself. His identification of Thought and Being seemed to me to be quite analogous to the Indian identification of "Sat" and "Chit." Zeller and Burnet had interpreted Parmenides in a materialistic fashion, and I could not sympathise with their interpretation. I went, therefore, to study Parmenides from the Sources, and I found there was a fallacy lurking in the materialistic interpretation, which I criticised as follows in my Essay on *Aristotle's Criticism of the Eleatics* (1919):

"The merging together of substantival and adjectival existence has, for Parmenides, not merely a logical significance, but a metaphysical significance as well. As, from the logical point of view, Parmenides asserted the unity of subject and predicate, so, from the metaphysical point of view, he asserts the unity of thought and being. τὸ γὰρ αὐτὸ νοεῖν ἐστίν τε καὶ εἶναι, said Parmenides. This very thought he reiterates in his *Poem* once more when he asserts, ταὐτὸν δ' ἐστὶ νοεῖν τε καὶ οὕνεκέν ἐστι νόημα: 'thinking and that by reason of which thought exists are one and the same things' (Fairbanks, *First Philosophers of Greece*, p. 90, l. 40, and p. 96, l. 94). Plato and Aristotle understood these expressions quite correctly as implying an identification of the real and the rational. Some modern critics, however, have rejected this interpretatiou, and have found in Parmenides' philosophy a crass materialism. Burnet thinks it a mistake to call Parmenides the father of Idealism; on the contrary, he says that all materialism depends on his view of reality (*Early Greek Philosophy*, p. 208). He asserts that it would be a Platonic anachronism to regard Parmenides as having made a distinction between appearance and reality (*ibid.*, o. 209, m. 2). We find Zeller also crediting Parmenides with the idea of a mere globular form of ultimate being, 'a fixed and homgeneous mass, symmetrically extended from its centre on all sides' (l. 589). Zeller, however, admits a little further on that we would be justified in rejecting this description as metaphorical, only if we could otherwise find any indication that Parmenides conceived Being as incorporeal (*lbid.*).

"The fundamental mistake of Burnet and Zeller and other similar interpreters of Parmenides consists, in the present writer's opinion, in their fallacious identification of analogy with fact. Shutting their eyes deliberately to the general tenor of Parmenides' *Poem*, which is unmistakably ontological, these critics have pinned their hope on a single passage which is as follows:—αὐτὰρ ἐπεὶ πεῖρας πύματον,

τετελεσμένον ἐστὶ πάντοθεν, εὐκύκλου σφαίρης ἐναλίγκιον ὄγκῳ
μεσσόθεν ἰσοπαλὲς πάντῃ.

"Now anybody who will take the trouble of interpreting this
passage will see immediately that Being is here 'compared' to a
sphere, and not 'identified' with it. It must be remembered that
Parmenides here uses the word ἐναλίγκιον which implies that he
regards being as 'resembling' a sphere. It is gross injustice to the
spirit of Parmenides to pin one's interpretation of him on a single
passage without looking to the tenor of the whole, and then to
distort it in such a way as to make him self-contradictory. Once
the foundations of a materialistic interpretation are laid, Burnet
has no difficulty in raising an equally materialistic edifice on it:
the Being of Parmenides is 'a finite, a spherical, motionless, corporeal
plenum' (*Early Greek Philosophy*, p. 208), and later he adds the
word 'continuous' (*Thales to Plato*, p. 68). If Parmenides regarded
Being as *finite* it was partly because he had not yet risen to the
sublimer conception of Melissos who regarded Being as infinite,
and partly because he was yet under the thraldom of the Pythagorean
identification of finitude and goodness. As a matter of fact, all the
epithets which Burnet interprets materialistically could also be
interpreted in an idealistic sense. To crown all, the following excerpts
from Parmenides' *Poem* should be eloquent enough to support our
interpretation: 'Being is without beginning, and is indestructible.
It is universal, existing alone, immovable, and without end. Nor was
it, nor will it be, since it now is. . . . Powerful necessity holds it in
confining bonds. . . . Therefore Divine Right does not permit Being
to have any end. It is lacking in nothing; for if it lacked anything
it would lack everything' (Parmenides' *Poem*, ii, 59-89)."

Other commentators on Parmenides were not affected by this
materialistic jaundice. Adamson understood Parmenides to have
at least risen to the conception of the Non-corporeal, if not to
that of the In-corporeal, that is, mental or psychical existence.
Gomperz interpreted Parmenides' philosophy in a Spinozistic
fashion. The Material Being of Parmenides was incontestably a
Spiritual Being as well: it was universal Matter and universal
Spirit at once. This was at least not an unfair interpretation.
A Spinozism is much more of an Ontologism than a crass Materialism could be. It is unfortunate that Burnet did not see that the
identical meaning which he later found in the two questions
"Is it, or is it not?", and "Can it be thought, or not?" (*Thales to
Plato*, p. 67), laid the axe at the root of his early materialistic
interpretation.

VI. THE STATIC PHILOSOPHY AND THE PHILOSOPHY OF THE INFINITESIMALS

Even though, therefore, Parmenides and his school carried my full sympathy, I could not explain how Zeno's plausible arguments could hold the field for so long a time, and no adequate answer be given to them. Zeno had proved by a sleight-of-hand that motion was inconceivable; but experience forbade such a false view of the universe. Equally false was the explanation of motion which Plato and Aristotle had themselves to offer as due to the initiation of the Soul: it was no less mythological and crude. Plato and Aristotle had played out their cards; Zeno had remained unbeaten; the problem was what trump-card could modern Mathematics and Science show?

"The fact is that Zeno could not be finally answered until it comes to be definitely realised that motion is a spatio-temporal relation. It is neither a purely spatial, nor a purely temporal, function. It consists of a correlation between places and times. As a modern mathematician has cleverly put it, 'there is motion when different times . . . are correlated with different places; there is rest when different times . . . are correlated with the same place. . . . Motion consists broadly in the correlation of different terms of t with different terms of s.'[1] In his arguments against motion Zeno with his right hand shows the card s and then withdrawing his right hand, with his left shows the card t; we must compel him to show the cards simultaneously. All the Sophisms of Zeno against motion, the flying arrow, the Achilles and the rest, depend upon a promiscuous huddling up of s and t and the clever passing off of one for the other. To put the whole thing mathematically, motion must be understood as defined by the differential co-efficient ds/dt; it is neither mere $\delta\sigma$ nore mere $\delta\tau$; it is a correlation of the two, different from either, and qualitatively new. It is this fact which has been urged upon us by the Neo-Herakleitean French philosopher, Monsieur Bergson. Time and again in his books he has urged that movement is indivisible: 'Motionless in each point of its course, says Zeno, the arrow is motionless during all the time that it is moving! Yes, if we suppose that the arrow can never *be* in a point of its course. . . . To suppose that the moving body *is* at a point of its course is to cut the course in two by a snip of the scissors at this point, and to substitute two trajectories for the single trajectory which we were first considering. . . . . The other three arguments all consist in supposing that what is true of the line is true of the movement . . . which is regarded

[1] Russell, *Principles of Mathematics*, p. 473.

as decomposable and recomposable at will' (Bergson, *Creative Evolution*, pp. 325-8. Also *Time and Free-will*, p. 113, and *Matter and Memory*, p. 250). It may be easily shown that Zeno's arguments could be disposed of by giving to motion the things which are motion's.

"We must not forget, however, to take account of certain Neo-Zenoist tendencies of modern thought. As we have a rehabilitation of Herakleitos in Bergson, so we have a rehabilitation of Zeno in Mr. Bertrand Russell. He preaches a philosophy of what he is pleased to call 'static change' (*Principles of Mathematics*, p. 350). With an eloquence which comes out of intense appreciation, he expatiates on the capriciousness of posthumous fame: 'One of the most notable victims of posterity's lack of judgment is the Eleatic Zeno. Having invented four arguments, all immeasurably subtle and profound, the grossness of subsequent philosophers pronounced him to be a mere ingenious juggler, and his arguments to be one and all sophisms. After two thousand years of continual refutation, these sophisms were reinstated, and made the foundation of a mathematical renaissance, by a German professor, who probably never dreamed of any connection between himself and Zeno. Weierstrass, by strictly banishing all infinitesimals, has at last shown that we live in an unchanging world, and that the arrow at every moment of its flight, is truly at rest' (*ibid.*, p. 347). At rest, indeed, and with a vengeance! For does not Mr. Russell say that all such conceptions as velocity, acceleration and force, which may to the slightest extent imply the existence of a changing, moving world, are mere fruitful fictions (*ibid.*, pp. 473, 482) of the scientific imagination? Is not Mr. Russell a fit associate of Weierstrass in banishing the conception of the infinitesimal, and in urging that there exist 'no infinitesimal differences at all'? For are not infinitesimals 'an attempt to extend to the *values* of a variable, the variability which belongs to it alone'? And finally, does not Mr. Russell justify the sophism that the flying arrow is always at rest, as being merely an illustration of a very widely applicable platitude that 'every possible value of a variable is constant'? (*ibid.*, p. 351). But the Nemesis of a static philosophy soon overtakes Mr. Russell. He bethinks himself that Zeno may probably have erred: he may have erred 'in inferring (if he did infer) that, because there is no change, therefore the world must be in the same state at one time as at another' (*ibid.*, p. 347). And, to crown all, he is in the end compelled to reject the Achilles argument (*ibid.*, p. 359) and favour the Tristram Shandy even though both are equally ridiculous, forgetting all the while that the rejection of the Achilles takes the bottom off the philosophy of rest!

'The fact is that the Infinitesimal Calculus cannot be so slightngly treated, as has been done by Weierstrass and Russell. The

Infinitesimal Calculus has come to stay, and mathematicians can ill afford to despise its rules. If the notions of infinity and continuity are to any extent valid—and that they are valid must be recognised by every thinker—the Infinitesimal Calculus must hold its own in spite of the Casca-like thrusts of Herr Weiestrass. Well might we say to Mr. Russell 'Et tu, Brute?' His attack on the Infinitesimals is the unkindest cut of all. The Infinitesimal Calculus supplies us with the only possible answer to Zeno's sophisms."

When we have once understood how Zeno's arguments can be disproved by the help of the Infinitesimal Calculus, we may know how Reality may no longer be regarded as a mere block universe, but that it may conceivably make room for motion and change.

VII. THE EPISTEMOLOGY OF SELF-CONSCIOUSNESS

After my studies in Greek Philosophy, I gave myself to a consideration of Indian thought. In one of the volumes hitherto published on the subject, *Constructive Survey of Upaniṣadic Philosophy* (1925), I discussed certain problems which might have a bearing on several subjects discussed in Contemporary Thought. One of the important questions which the Upaniṣads discuss is the epistemological significance of "Self-consciousness." The consideration which I gave to this question in *Upaniṣadic Philosophy* may be set down as follows:

"Epistemologically, we are told in various passages of the Upaniṣads, it would not be possible for us to know the Self iu the technical meaning of the word 'knowledge.' Our readers might bring to mind the fact that Kant equally regarded Reality, as consisting of God and the Self, as technically unknowable. These were, he said, merely matters of faith. The Upaniṣadic answer is that it is true that God and the Self are unknowable, but they are not merely objects of faith, they are objects of mystical realisation. Then, again, the Upaniṣads do not regard the Self as unknowable in the agnostic sense of the word, for example, in the sense in which Spencer understands it. Rather, it is 'unknowable' from the standpoint of philosophic humility.

"(i) The Ātman, say the Upaniṣadic philosophers, is unknowable in his essential nature. 'That, from which our speech turns back along with mind, being unable to comprehend its fulness, is the ultimate reality,' says the Taittirīya Upaniṣad. 'Of that, to which the eye is unable to go, which neither speech nor mind is able to reach—what conception can we have, except that it is beyond all that is known, and beyond all that is unknown?' asks the Keno-panisad. The philosopher of that Upaniṣad says in an Augustinian mood that he who thinks he knows does not know, while he who thinks he does not know does really know. *Cognoscendo ignorari, et ignorando cognosci.* The Kaṭhopaniṣad in a similar vein says that 'the Self is not in the first instance open to the hearing of men, and that even having heard him, many are unable to know him. Wonder-ful is the man, if found, who is able to speak about him; wonderful, indeed, is he who is able to comprehend him in accordance with the instruction of a Teacher' (v, sec. 13*a*). We see in all these passages how the Ātman is to be regarded as unknowable in his essential nature.

"(ii) There is, however, another side to the subject of the unknow-ability of Ātman. The Ātman is unknowable, because he is the Eternal Subject who knows. How could the Eternal Knower, ask the Upaniṣads in various places, be an object of knowledge? 'The Ātman is the Great Being,' says the Śvetāśvatara Upaniṣad, 'who knows all that is knowable; who can know him, who himself knows?' In the Bṛhadāraṇyakopaniṣad in various passages, we are put in possession of the bold speculations of the philosopher, Yājñavalkya. 'That by whom everything is known, how could he himself be known? It is impossible to know the knower.' 'It would not be possible for us to see the seer, to hear the hearer, to think the thinker, and to apprehend him by whom everything is apprehended.' 'He is the eternal seer without himself being seen; he is the eternal hearer without himself being heard; he is the only thinker without himself being thought; he is the only comprehender without anyone to comprehend him; beyond him there is no seer, beyond him there is no hearer, beyond him there is no thinker, beyond him there is no being who comprehends' (v, sec. 13*b*). We thus see that the question of the unknowability of Ātman has another aspect also, namely, that he is unknowable because he is the Eternal Subject of knowledge, and cannot be an object of knowledge to another beside him.

"(iii) But this raises another fundamental question. Granted that the Self is the eternal knower of objects, granted also there is no other knower of him, would it be possible for the knower to know himself? This very subtle question was asked of Yājñavalkya in another passage of the Bṛhadāraṇyakopaniṣad, and here again we see the brilliant light which the sage Yājñavalkya throws on the problem. It *is* possible, he says, for the knower to know himself. In fact, Self-knowledge or Self-consciousness is the ultimate category of existence. The Self can become an object of knowledge to himself. According to the philosophy of Yājñavalkya, nothing is possible if self-consciousness is not possible. Self-consciousness is the ultimate fact of experience. We see here how boldly Yājñavalkya regards both introspection and self-consciousness as the verities of experience. We also see the nudity of the doctrines of Kant and Comte when they try to deny the fact of introspection. Introspection is a psychological process corresponding to Self-consciousness as a metaphysical reality. Self-consciousness is possible only through the process of introspection. The Self is endowed with the supreme power of dichotomising himself. The empirical conditions of knowledge are inapplicable to the Self. The Self can divide himself into the knower and the known. It is wonderful how Kant should have posited the 'I am I' as the supreme metaphysical category, which he called the transcendental, original and synthetic unity of apperception, and yet should have denied the reality of the corresponding psychological process of introspection. The answer of Yājñavalkya is that Self-consciousness is possible, and is not only possible, but alone real. King Janaka asked Yājñavalkya what was the light of man? Yajnavalkya first said that the light of man was the sun. It is on account of the sun that man is able to sit and move about, to go forth to work, and to return. 'When the sun has set, O Yājñavalkya,' asked King Janaka, 'what is the light of man?' Yājñavalkya said that then the moon was the light of man. For, having the moon for light, man could sit, and move about, and do his work, and return. 'When both the sun and the moon have set,' asked King Janaka, 'what is the light of man?' 'Fire indeed,' said Yājñavalkya, 'is man's light. For having fire for his light, man can sit and move about, do his work, and return.' 'When the sun has set, when the moon has set, and when the fire is extinguished, what is the light of man?' asked Janaka. 'Now, verily,' says Yajnavalkya, 'you are pressing me to the deepest question. When the sun has set, when the moon has set, and when the fire is extinguished, the Self alone is his light' (v, sec. 13c). Yājñavalkya is here cleverly positing what Aristotle called 'νόησις,' the act of pure-self-contemplation in which the Self is most mysteriously both the subject and the object of νοήσεως, knowledge."

VIII. SELF-REALISATION: ITS ETHICAL AND MYSTICAL ASPECTS

Closely allied to the metaphysical problem of Self-consciousness, we have the ethical and mystical sides of what may be called Self-realisation. The question is not merely of the perfection of the various faculties of man, but of the realisation of the Self within. The Upaniṣadic seers understand that what is meant by Self-realisation is the unfoldment and realisation of the Ātman within us, instead of the insipid and soul-less realisation of the various "faculties" of man, such as the intellectual, the emotional and the moral, in which sense Contemporary Moralists understand it. Self-realisation, according to the Upaniṣads, is invariably connected with the enjoyment of bliss. This bliss cannot be measured in terms of pleasure and happiness. It is an experience of its own kind:

"Indeed, there cannot be any physical scale for the measurement of spiritual values. The bliss of Self-realisation is entirely of its own kind, absolutely *sui generis*. To cavil at the theory of Self-realisation by saying that the Self 'is realised' already, and that therefore there is no necessity of 'realising' the Self seems to us to be merely a listless evasion of the true significance of Self-realisation. When Canon Rashdall says that the Self is realised already, he is speaking about a metaphysical fact. On the other hand, when it is said that the Self is to be realised, we are asked to take into account the whole ethical and mystical process by which the human being is gradually weaned from the allurements of the not-Self, and the Self to be realised in its native purity and grandeur. It is in the doctrine of Self-realisation that the ethical and mystical processes meet, a fact to which we shall have to allude presently. It need hardly be said that by Self-realisation, as the Upanisadic seers understand that expression, is meant the unfoldment and the visualisation of the Ātman within us, instead of the insipid and soul-less realisation of the various 'faculties' of man, namely, the intellectual, the emotional and the moral, in which sense Bradley and other European moralists have understood that expression. The Bṛhadāraṇyakopaniṣad tells us that the Ātman, who constitutes the Reality within us as without us, is and ought to be the highest object of our desire, higher than any phenomenal object of love, such as progeny, or wealth, or the like, because, the Upaniṣad tells us, the Ātman, being the very kernel of our existence, is nearmost to us. 'If a man may say there is another object of love dearer to him than the Ātman, and if another replies that if there be God overhead he shall destroy his object of love, verily it shall so happen as this man says. Hence it is that we ought to meditate on the Ātman as the only object of desire. For him who worships the Ātman in this way, nothing dear shall ever perish' (vi, sec. 12*a*).

"The ethical and mystical sides of Self-realisation are fused together nowhere better than in that celebrated passage from the Chāndogya Upaniṣad, where having started an enquiry as to what it is that induces a man to perform actions, and having answered that it is the consideration of happiness which impels him to do so—for, we are told, had he experienced unhappiness in his pursuit, he would not have taken any action at all—the author of the

Chāndogya Upaniṣad comes to tell us that real happiness is the happiness which one enjoys in the vision of the Infinite, and that every other kind of happiness is only so-called, and of really no value whatsoever as contrasted with it. It thus comes about that, according to the author of that Upaniṣhad, there are two radically different kinds of happiness, namely, what he calles the Great and the Small. Great Happiness consists in seeing, hearing and meditating upon the Ātman. Little happiness consists in seeing, hearing, and meditating upon other things besides the Ātman. Great happiness is immortal; little happiness is perishable. If the question be asked, in what this Great happiness consists, the answer may be given, in Herakleitean fashion, that it consists in its own greatness and possibly not in its own greatness! People say that cows and horses, elephants and gold, servants and wives, lands and houses—these constitute greatness. No, says the author, these rest in something else, but the Infinite rests in itself. Great happiness is experienced when the Infinite is seen above and below, before and behind, to the right and to the left, and is regarded as identical with everything that exists; when the Being, that calls itself the 'I' within us, is realised above and below, before and behind, to the right and to the left, and is regarded as identical with everything that exists; when the Ātman is seen above and below, before and behind, to the right and to the left and is regarded as identical with everything that exists. He who thus realises the triune unity of the Infinite, the I and the Ātman, and experiences the truth of the Upaniṣadic dictum *So'ham Atmā*, is alone entitled to enjoy the highest happiness. One who comes to see this, and think about this, and meditate on this, really attains Swarajya; he loves his Self, plays with his Self, enjoys the company of his Self and revels in his Self (vi, sec. 14). In this way, according to the Chāndogya Upaniṣad, the ethical *Summum Bonum* consists in the mystical realisation of the triune unity as the goal of the aspirant's one-pointed endeavour."

IX. INTUITION, THE MYSTICAL FACULTY

The question may be raised as to whether there is any faculty in man by which this realisation of the Self is to be attained. Indian Seers have always said that there is such a faculty, and that it is the faculty of Intuition. It is not merely an artistic or poetical faculty. It is not the mere sense of life, as some modern philosophers have understood it. It is the faculty of Mystical realisation. It lies at the back of all the faculties in man which ordinary psychology recognises. Instead of contradicting Intelligence, Feeling or Will, it lies at the back of them all. I have discussed this question in my recently published work on *Indian Mysticism* (1932) :

"Mysticism denotes that attitude of mind which involves a direct, immediate, first-hand, intuitive apprehension of God. When Mysticism is understood in this sense, there is no reason why it should be taken to signify any occult or mysterious phenomena as is occasionally done. It is an irony of fate that a word which deserves to signify the highest attitude of which man is capable, namely, a restful and loving contemplation of God, should be taken to signify things which are incomparably lower in the scale of being. Mysticism implies a silent enjoyment of God. It is in this sense that mystical experience has often been regarded as ineffable. It is not without reason that Plato, in his 7th Epistle, which is now regarded as his own genuine composition, says: 'There is no writing of mine on this subject, nor ever shall be. It is not capable of expression like other branches of study. . . . If I thought these things could be adequately written down and stated to the world, what finer occupation could I have had in life than to write what would be of great great service to mankind' (341 *c-e; vide* Burnet, *Thales of Plato*, p. 221).

"The ineffable character of mystical experience is closely linked with its intuitional character. It has been very often supposed that for mystical experience no separate faculty like Intuition need be requisitioned, but that Intellect, Feeling and Will might suffice to enable us to have a full experience of God. Now it is a matter of common knowledge that even for heights to be reached in artistic, scientific or poetic activity, a certain amount of direct and immediate contact with Reality is required. Far more is this the case in the matter of mystical realisation. It is thus wonderful to see how people like Dean Inge contradict themselves when once they declare that 'the process of divine knowledge consists in calling into activity a faculty which all possess but few use, what we may call the seed of the Deiform nature in the human soul' (quoted by Selbie: *Psychology of Religion*, p. 257); and yet again that 'there is no special organ for the reception of Divine or spiritual Truth' (*Philosophy of Plotinus*, i. 5). People who would otherwise openly side with Intuition, yet declare that Intellect alone is sufficient for the reception of Divine knowledge; but their real heart-beat tells us that they believe that not mere Intellect is sufficient, but that a higher faculty is necessary. Intuition, so far from contradicting Intelligence, Feeling or Will, does penetrate and lie at the back of them all. Intuition would not deny to Mysticism a title to Philosophy if Intellect requires it. As it connotes a determinative Effort towards the acquisition of Reality, it implies a definite, prolonged and continuous exercise of the Will. Mysticism, *pace* Dr. Inge, necessarily makes a place for Emotion in a truly mystical life. It is strange that Dean Inge should fight shy of emotions, and deny to them a place in mystical life, when he says that Mysticism consists only in 'seeing God face to face' (*Philosophy of Plotinus*, i. 3). We may venture to suggest to him that unless the emotions are purified, and are turned towards the service of God, no 'seeing of Him face to face,' of which he speaks so enthusiastically, is ever possible. Thus it seems that Intelligence, Will and Feeling are all necessary in the case of the Mystical endeavour; only Intuition must back them all. It is this combined character of mystical experience, namely, its ineffable and intuitive character, which has served to make all God-aspiring humanity a common and hidden Society, the laws of which are known to themselves if at all. We may even say that they are known only to God, and not even to them!"

X. THE MORAL CRITERION OF MYSTICAL EXPERIENCE

It has, however, been a debated question as to how far Mystical experience is linked with Morality. In my opinion the answer is absolutely definite (*Indian Mysticism*, Preface, pp. 27-9). There would be no mystical experience and no development in it, unless there is a corresponding heightening of the moral sense. To try to achieve Mystical experience without a corresponding development of Morality is to enact the drama of *Hamlet* without the Prince of Denmark :

"The chief criterion of the reality of mystical experience is its capacity for the definite moral development of the individual and the society. It has been urged by critics of Mysticism that it tends on the one hand to a life of amoralism, and on the other, to a life of passivism. Dean Inge has said that those schools of Philosophy which are most in sympathy with Mysticism have been, on the whole, ethically weak; and he instances as a case in point what he calls Oriental Pantheism—as if it stands in a category apart—which regards all things as equally divine, and obliterates the distinction between right and wrong (*Studies of English Mystics*, p. 31). It is to be remembered that he also points out that there are two dangers to which such a mysticism is liable—Antinomianism and Quietism. Antinomianism teaches that he who is led by the spirit can do no wrong, and that the sins of the body cannot stain the soul; while Quietism teaches a life of contentment with anything whatsoever by sitting with folded arms (*ibid.*, pp. 30-1). Now it is to be remembered that this criticism of Mysticism comes from Dean Inge, who is more of a mystic than anything else; and a Mystic, saying that Mysticism starves the moral sense, is only attempting to throw stones at a glass-house in which he is himself living. On the other hand, we find that a true life of Mysticism teaches a full-fledged morality in the individual, and a life of absolute good to the society. We can scarcely find in the world's ethical literature anything that would come up to the very clever and accurate analysis of the different virtues which Jnanesvara makes in his Jnanesvari (M. M., pp. 71-107) in point of excellence of analysis, boldness of imagination or accuracy of portrayal. A Mystic like Jnanesvara who insists on these virtues can scarcely be regarded as teaching the 'effacement of all distinctions between right and wrong.' If we go to Plotinus, we find the same perfection of moral virtues in mystical life insisted on. 'The vision,' he tells us, 'is not to be regarded as unfruitful. In this state the perfect soul begets —like God himself—beautiful thoughts and beautiful virtues' (Enneads, 6. 9. 9). St. Teresa also speaks of the peace, calm and good fruits in the soul attained by contemplation on God, and particularly of three graces: 'The first is a perception of the greatness of God, which becomes clearer to us as we witness more of it. Secondly, we gain self-knowledge and humility as we see how creatures so base as ourselves in comparison with the Creator of such wonders, have dared to offend Him in the past, or venture to gaze on Him now. The third grace is a contempt of all earthly things unless they are consecrated to the service of so great a God' (The Interior Castle, 6. 5. 12). St. John of the Cross teaches that 'in a truly mystical life, a knowledge of God and His attributes overflows into the understanding from the contact with Him, and the soul is admitted to a knowledge of the wisdom, graces, gifts and powers of God, whereby it is made so beautiful and rich' (Cant. 14. 16. 24. 2). Ramadasa also tells us the same story when he speaks of the moral results produced in a mystic by contemplation on God (M. M., pp. 394-5). Then, again, so far as the utility of the mystic to Society is concerned, we may almost regard it as a truism of Mysticism that a Mystic who is not of supreme service to Society is not a Mystic at all. It is true that here again there are temperamental differences among mystics. One mystic may choose more or less to be of a quietistic, and another more or less of an activistic type. But the fact remains that in either case he is of supreme value to mankind by calling their attention from moment to moment to the vision and greatness of God. Thus Dean Inge's denial of the title of a Mystic to Thomas à Kempis, because the latter teaches Quietism, can hardly be justified. There have been mystics who, like Aristotle's God, have moved the world by their divine contemplation. They might be called, what a psychologist calls them, men of a world-shaking type. St. Ignatius is a case in point, and James speaks of him assuredly as 'one of the most powerfully practical human engines that ever lived. Where, in literature,' he asks, 'is there a more evidently veracious account, than in St. Teresa, of the formation of a new centre of spiritual energy?' (*Varieties of Religious Experience*, pp. 413, 414). Plotinus also tells us that 'Those who are inspired, those who are possessed, know this much, that within them they have something greater than themselves, even if they do not know what. From what they feel, from what they speak, they have some conception of that which moves them as of something higher than themselves' (*Enneads*, 5. 3. 14). Rufus Jones narrates how mystics have their consciousness invaded by the in-rush of a larger life: 'Sometimes they have seemed to push a door into a larger range of being with vastly heightened energy. Their experience has been always one of joy and rapture. In fact, it is probably the highest joy a mortal ever feels. Energy to live by actually does come to them from somewhere. The universe backs the experience' (*Studies in Mystical Religion*, p. xxx)."

XI. CONCLUSION

One can see from what has been said hitherto what my opinions are in regard to some of the main subjects which are on the anvil of Contemporary Thought. It is clear that I have given only a rough outline of my views through a critical exposition of some of the problems attempted in Ancient and Modern European and Indian thought, and that I have not stated them deliberately, and on my own behalf. To have given a full account of my opinions on various philosophical subjects within a short compass would have been impossible ; to have given only an aspect of my thought would have been like doing injustice to the whole. I hope, however, that my readers may forgive me for this. One can see, nevertheless, how I was inclined from early days to spiritual life ; how I thought that a correlation between Indian and European Philosophy was not only possible but necessary in the interest of the development of Philosophy in general; how I sympathised with the doctrine that Relativism failed at God; how I regarded "Truth" to be One, and its existence to be only in God, while all other things were full of error; how the onto-logical strain of thought interested me; how I thought that a place must be made for motion and change even within a static philosophy; how Self-consciousness was not only possible, but alone real; how there were ethical and mystical sides to the problem of Self-realisation; how Intuition was the only faculty by which this Self-realisation could be attained; and how, finally, mystical experience had no meaning apart from moral development. These were the problems which affected my thought until I took up my position in the Allahabad University in 1928. I am much indebted to the opportunities which I have had at the Allahabad University to widen my philosophical horizon during the last few years of my stay there. These years have opened out a new intellectual vista before me, enabling me to define more accurately to myself my own position in philosophy from the side of contemporary developments in Metaphysics, Ethics, Psychology and Religion. I only hope it may please Providence to enable me to place my views on these matters before the philosophical world in course of time. Spiritual life has been my aim from the beginning of my philosophic career; let me hope that it would be its culmination also.

DIALECTICAL MONADISM

by M. M. SHARIF, M.A.

Professor of Philosophy in the Aligarh Muslim University.

BIOGRAPHICAL

I was born in a humble home at a small village near Lahore. Though well-connected and counted among the village nobility, my father, far from being financially well off, was a man of small means. He had no ambitions and he neither earned nor cared to earn his living. To maintain his family he had to depend entirely first upon an allowance from my grandfather and then whatever share of property he received as one of nine brothers and sisters. Therefore my University education meant a great sacrifice for him and a great struggle for me. His main interest was a life of mysticism. My mother was profoundly religious, deeply affectionate, intensely devoted to her children and in spite of her meagre income, most generous to all those who approached her for help or whose pecuniary difficulties came to her notice. She was the daughter of the Kazi of the village. I believe I have something of my father's lack of ambition and my mother's religious mindedness, love for humanity, and devotion to the family.

The date of my birth is doubtful, but according to school records it is February 28, 1893.

I received my education first in the village school, then in the Islamia and Model High Schools of Lahore and the famous M.A.O. College, Aligarh, and finally in the University of Cambridge. I took the Bachelor of Arts degree from the Universities of Allahabad and Cambridge respectively in 1914 and 1916.

I had only joined the Secondary School when I lost my mother, a brother and a sister, all from plague, within a short period of two years. That gave an extremely pessimistic outlook to my early life. This pessimism is reflected in a quatrain in Urdu that I then composed. Its English rendering would be as follows :

> There was no autumn, no spring.
> Life alone knew the secret of life.
> What a life of ectasy in *not!*
> All that *is* would rather be *not.*

But for the effect on my mind of the beauty that surrounded my little village, I would have long remained in this gloomy state of mind. Roaming in the fields around the village in those sorrowful days used to make me sad; but gradually that sadness began to be mixed with faint rays of joy. The famous Shalimar Garden of Lahore, built by the Emperor Shah Jahan, was situated close to the village school. The vast Terraces of this magnificent garden became veritable play-grounds for me. Swimming in company in its canals and tanks and bathing under the silvery showers of their fountains raising their heads in rows and rows, playing on its velvety turfs studded with flower-beds of variegated colours, watching the play of butterflies and glow-worms in its bushes and groves, reading for hours under its shady trees and gazing at the moon or the starry heavens sitting on its benches or lying on its marble throne—these became in course of time the sources of unmixed delight to me. The most impressionable period of life spent in these surroundings of superb beauty gave me an abiding taste for beauty and fine arts. Thus love, sorrow and the joy of beauty characterised my early life. They have remained important elements of my mental make-up even to this day.

While at College in Aligarh, I regarded the life of a College student or teacher as ideal; and I had a strong desire to becaome a teacher of the main subject of my study, philosophy, in my own college; and live in a particular house the large grove of which had long fascinated me. On my return from Cambridge I realised my goal of joining the teaching profession and started living in the house of my choice. After eighteen years' stay in that house, I was forced by circumstances to leave it. But if I have a choice, I should like to live in the same house to my last day.

About four years after my joining the staff of the M.A.O. College, this institution was raised to the status of a University. For twenty years I combined my work as a Reader or Professor of this University with the Provostship of its Premier Hall, the Sir Syed Hall; and for nearly three years I acted as Pro-Vice-Chancellor of the University. Since my administrative duties hardly left me time for studies I resigned the Provostship in 1938, and have since been engaged in purely academic work. I was Chairman of the Department of Philosophy from 1921 to 1928 and have held that office again since 1945, the year in which I was elected by the Indian Philosophical Congress as its General President.

The precincts of a university are supposed to be a haven of peace and of refuge from life's storms. But I found that even in this ideal sphere of life one may have to struggle against satanic forces—forces that arise from the unholy alliance of high intellect and low character. Since the evil wrought by these forces in this sphere takes deeper and longer roots, the struggle for the victory of human values may sometimes be even harder here than elsewhere.

As an undergraduate at Aligarh I was an empirical idealist. At Cambridge the influence of Professor G. E. Moore and Bertrand Russell made me a realist. On my return to India, after passing through a period of indifference to metaphysics and interest in social sciences, I have gradually come to a position which may be described as dialectical monadism but I do not claim to have arrived at a system free from all difficulties. During the course of my studies I have read both Muslim and Indian philosophies, but, though I regard them of immense historical value, a value often ignored by Western historians, it is not with these but with the achievements of modern thought that all future enquiry must begin. Though we are rooted in the past, it is only our present that can bear fruit in the future.

DIALECTICAL MONADISM

I

(A)

I believe that all our actions spring from what in most general terms may be described as a natural urge to break through our limitations or a thirst for self-completion, and this urge or thirst manifests itself in a struggle. In activity in general this struggle consists in an effort to realise more and more the ideals of life in science, which is an intellectual activity, it consists in the attempt to apprehend more and more of truth in a chosen sphere of reality, and in philosophy, which is the same intellectual activity *par excellence*; it lies in the attempt to apprehend reality as a whole—or to apprehend its nature, meaning and value at least in broad outline. Since philosophy tries to understand the whole, it essentially has to be a complete system itself. It is a magnificent undertaking ; its triumphs are sublime and so are its tragedies.

In its system-making, philosophy cannot ignore the results of science. On the contrary it has to make a genuine effort to find a place for them in the systematic whole of knowledge. Nor can science disregard the fundamental basis of our knowledge and its nature and procedure—matters with which philosophy is primarily concerned. Each has to contribute something to the other and each ignores the other at its own peril.

To achieve its aim, philosophy has not merely to apprehend what things in general are in bare abstraction. It has to interpret them, to understand their meanings, to read them in the light of their relatedness, their origin, their value and their purpose. Even the barest outline of reality which philosophy aims at knowing is concrete and rich with content.

Philosophy must begin its enquiry with a study of experience. All our experience is complex and its elements are known only by analysis. It is always the experience of some object. It consists of at least two elements, (1) our *apprehension* of an object and (2) an *object* apprehended. To assume that objects are independent of thought or thought is independent of objects is wrong, and to study one without paying any regard to the other is worse.

But while philosophical study begins with experience, it does not spring from experience and does not end with it. It might find the ground of experience in something totally unexperienced. When it does so, it either refuses to describe this ground or describes it only symbolically by analogy from experience.

To study a part of experience as it *is* is science, as it *was* is history, as it *shall be* is prediction based on history and science, and as it ought to be is axiology. To have a synoptic view of experience as it *is*, *was*, shall and ought to be—even to know whether is, was, shall and ought are genuine, distinctions at all —and to know its ground is philosophy. And not only to know, but also to *be* in a more intimate relation with this ground is religion.

But knowing is itself experiencing. An unknown experience is no experience. Therefore what philosophy aims at is not mere knowing, but understanding, penetrating deeply this knowing and its known, and their relation, significance, value and ground. Its aim is deepest knowledge and fullest experience.

Experience is nothing fixed, rigid and static. It is dynamic. It is a process. It grows in all dimensions. With the growth of our knowledge our experience grows. Its movement is from concrete comparatively limited and undifferentiated experience to wider, deeper and more and more differentiated experience. It is an accumulating, forward-looking, forward-going, ever-expanding and ever-growing process. Both our knowledge and our experience are recorded partly in our being and partly in agreed symbols and are thus handed down for further advance from species to species in the first case and from individual to individual and generation to generation in the second.

Experience is the direct and immediate apprehension of that which is thought (a complex of thought and thought-object). That which is apprehended directly, or to use Bertrand Russell's expression, by *acquaintance*, may be a sensation, percept or object; an image, hallucination or illusion ; an idea, judgment or inference ; an urge, will, wish, desire or action ; a feeling, senti-ment, emotion, or mood ; an element or a complex of these ; or a

self. Whatever is apprehended indirectly may later be apprehended directly and then become experience. An act of perceiving,
willing, judging, etc., is different from what is perceived, willed
or judged or otherwise apprehended directly ; though this act
can itself be directly apprehended and become experience.

That which is directly or indirectly known and known truly is
real or factual or simply *is* ; and since in all judgment what is
known is *taken* to be known truly, it is *taken* to be real. If the real
is known to be in time and place it is existent ; if in time alone,
it is temporal; if out of time and place, subsistent. According to
these distinctions not only objects are real, but our volitions,
feelings, thoughts, etc., are also real. But reality in this sense is of
different orders and different planes, subsistent, existent, temporal, or again, sensuous, perceptual, objective, etc. Whatever
is real in one order or plane is unreal in another order or plane.
That which is real or factual may be shortlived or it may be
eternal. Subjectivity and objectivity are distinctions within the
real.

Whatever is indirectly known and known truly may be known
by inference or testimony. Before we take it to be real by testimony, regard has to be paid to errors of memory, capacity,
conditions of observation, integrity, etc. ; for ultimately the
truth-value of all testimony depends upon direct knowledge and
correct report. Before we take a thing as real or factual by inference, care has to be taken against fallacious reasoning. Hence
the need for methodology.

Although for us reality is that which is truly known, nevertheless "being truly known" is only an external mark of it, not
its essence. Considered in isolation from thought, whatever is, *is*
real or factual. But since we can truly know, i.e., can form true
judgments about, our knowledge, our hallucinations, illusions,
errors and even ignorance, *these when truly known to be such* are no
less real or factual than any other reals—only they are reals of
different orders.

If these distinctions are true, it follows that reality can be
known. Not only that. It is in fact known ; for in fact I know
truly, say, my ignorance of higher mathematics, my error of
judgment in measuring a distance by sight, my seeing a yellow
disc called the sun rising in the east and setting in the west,

hydrogen and oxygen in a certain proportion and at a certain temperature combining into water, and two and two making four.

Reality, therefore, is knowable and known, but whether ultimate reality is known or knowable is a different question.

(B)

I have said that knowledge must begin with experience and have defined experience as a complex of thought and object thought of. Of all the objects thought of, the simplest, though not the basic, experience is sensuous experience. In and through this experience the subject directly apprehends a sensation, and if he is an advanced subject, some qualities of this sensation, intensity, brightness, extensity, etc., as well. Beyond this he directly knows nothing. Sensations like smell, taste, sound are undoubtedly modifications of the subject himself; and a little reflection shows that the same is true of colour. Therefore if a person could apprehend only one sensation in its rudimentary or complete form, he would apprehend nothing besides, though the fact that the sensation is not created by him, and it comes and goes independently of his will would prove inferentially to him that, though he is the base for the sensation, its basis or ground is something different from him. The sensation may be said to be the response of the subject to the action of *another*. The case of such sensations as bulk, figure, number, situation and motion and rest—Locke's primary qualities—seems to be different ; but Berkeley's contention that it is not really different is irrefutable. Therefore all that we know directly through sensuous experience, we mediately know to be our own response to the actions of something other than ourselves.

The perceptual situation is not very different. It consists in a subject's apprehension of a sensation-complex.

Thus sensations and perceptions are emergents or qualities issuing from the action of one entity upon another entity.

If the subject is the *base* for sensations and sensation-complexes, their *basis* is another entity that acts upon him. Yet when he is non-responsive, e.g., when asleep or absent-minded, it fails to produce them in him. Therefore the subject's conscious attention is also an essential condition for their emergence. A sensation or a perception, a sensation-complex, is polar in its origin. On the one side it is the directly apprehended quality of the action of another entity on the subject ; on the other side it is a reaction-quality of the subject. Like a seal impression it is *in* or *on* the wax but *of* the seal. Being born of the action of the basic entity and reaction of the base-entity, the same sensation or sensation-complex can be viewed in two ways—as an action-quality of the basic entity or the reaction-quality of the base-entity. Those who are blind to the subject's part in its emergence are materialists, those blind to the part played by the basic entity, i.e., the entity other than the subject, are Solipsists ; while those who ignore both are presentationists. Those who falsely give the sensation or sensation-complex the place of the basic entity are dualists ; and those who divorce sensations or sensation-complex from their elements of apprehension, call them sensa, sense-data or something similar, and give them the place of the basic entities, are realists.

The matter becomes slightly complicated when we come to the question of our apprehension of the so-called external object. This is experience at a higher level. Locke and some modern realists regard those objects as consisting of the primary qualities, but I find it difficult to agree to that view on grounds similar to those given by Berkeley. For me the object is also a kind of sensation-complex. The differences between this and a sensation-complex *qua* sensation-complex are two. Firstly, it is this that the latter can be apprehended by a subject without his apprehending himself ; but he can apprehend an object only when he can apprehend himself as distinct from the sensation-complex, when a sensation-complex is regarded or can be regarded by the self as other than itself. But this other (the object) is different from that other to which it is my response-quality, which is the basis and together with me the co-ordinate ground of its being.

Secondly, this response-quality is not so simple. It is at this level a spatio-temporal sensation-complex having certain quality, quantity, relations, etc. Kant divides these new elements of experience at this higher level, space, time, quality, quantity, relation and modality into two classes: (1) pure intuitions by which physical objects are perceived or received passively by a faculty of the subject called the sensibility, and (2) pure concepts or categories by which the objects are thought, that is to say, their representations are spontaneously created, by a faculty of the subject called the understanding. His analysis is vitiated by his false faculty psychology. The apprehension of spatio-temporal sensation-complexes is indeed psychologically prior to the apprehension of quantity, quality, relation, contingency and necessity, but the apprehension of space and time *qua* space and time is as much thought as the apprehension of quantity, quality, etc.

Now these elements—space and time on the one side and the categories on the other—which have the same epistemological origin and status are the characteristrics of physical objects, i.e., of the response-qualities of the base-entity and at the same time of the action-qualities of the basic entity. Which of these two, the base-entity and basic-entity, is responsible for their appearance in the sensation-complexes ? There are only three alternatives which do not allow the presence of these elements to be left unexplained ; and these are that the responsibility falls either on the first, or the second or both ; i.e., either on the base-entity or the basic-entity or both. Kant accepts the first alternative ; Aristotle, the second. But each takes an extreme view. Contributions of the basic entity alone they are not, for they are found to have universal and necessary manifold of their own which can be apprehended by the base-entity, the subject, independently, without reference to the experience of physical objects. They cannot be contributions of the base-entity alone, because as characteristics of physical objects they are relatively independent of its will. I, as a base-entity, can think of a mathematical or logical manifold whenever I choose, but I cannot apprehend physical objects — the spatio-temporal sensation-complexes, having qualities, quantities, relation, etc., when I like, where I like and whichever I like.

Kant holds that since universality and apodeictic necessity of space, time, quantity, quality, etc., cannot be *derived* from the experience of physical objects, they must be contributions of the mind alone. But while the universality and apodeictic certainty of these cannot be apprehended through the experience of physical objects, has this experience ever contradicted their necessity and universality ? In fact if there has ever been a contradiction between the thought manifold of, say, Mathematics, Geometry or logic and the physical world, the fault has been on the side of thought—as an error in mathematical calculations or logical conclusions, general hypotheses or faulty apprehension, and never on the side of the physical objects. Kant explains this by saying that we see them in the physical world because we have already put them into it ; and this explanation seems plausible; but it is not true because, as said in the last paragraph, if they were entirely subjective they would not as features of the physical world be independent of the subject's will.

It is therefore more reasonable to accept the third alternative and hold that space, time and the categories are contributed to physical objects both by the base-entity and the basic-entity. They are found by the subject—the base-entity—in his thought as universal and necessary manifolds, and in the physical objects as suggestive of and never contradicting these manifolds and as completely independent of his will ; and they are grounded in him as well as in the basic-entity. They first emerge into consciousness from the convergence of both.

But since both the basic-entity and the base-entity are also subject to them, because they inhere in them as much as in the phenomena, they are over-individual and their ultimate ground must also be over individual.

Sensation-complexes may be produced in me as a response to the action of another entity through a third basic-entity as in a photograph, or through a third, fourth or even fifth agency as in movies. They are of course directly apprehended by me, but the other pole consists of several basic entities in a co-operative relation.

Although these existents, these physical objects, i.e., spatio-temporal sensation-complexes having quality, quantity, relation, etc., cannot emerge from me alone, some of them are more intimately connected with me in as much as they, relatively speaking, obey my will. Some of these again become media of my apprehension of the rest of them and of physical objects other than themselves. These I consider as parts of my body and their totality as my *body*. But these are no less partly grounded in basic entities than those objects which show greater independence in their behaviour and inter-relations. Since these are relatively pliant and obedient to my will, the basic entities behind them must also be viewed to be so, and, since these are apprehended by me as an organic whole of physical parts, the totality of the basic entities behind them must also be regarded as an organic whole of parts.

But this organic whole of basic-entities behind my body is not identical with me, for if it were so, I should be able to create my body at will. It must be taken to be a system of entities which in spite of being my co-workers in creating my body, are yet subordinate to me. The systems of basic-entities behind other bodies do not show such subordination to me, and when they do so, it is not of the same degree.

Our knowledge of basic entities is entirely inferential, but what about our knowledge of ourselves as base entities ? As stated before, the knowledge of objects from which the knowledge of basic entities is inferred, is impossible without our knowledge of ourselves—without self-consciousness. This self-consciousness is direct apprehension or knowledge by acquaintance *par excellence.* I become conscious of myself directly. "I am the self-same *I* in spite of the differences of content" is an immediate piece of knowledge. Here the subject to which the differences of content appear is *identical* with the object to which these differences belong, the self known and the self knowing are the *same*—the self-same identity. Al-Ghazzali tries to prove his being from his willing ; Descartes from his thinking ; but actually neither my thinking nor my willing can prove my being. "I am" cannot be derived from "I will" or "I think". Nor even "My thinking *is*" or "My willing *is*" can be legitimately derived from these judgments, for each involves a separate category. The category involved in "I think" or "I will" is action, and in "I am", subsistence. "I am" and "I think" (or "I will") are independent judgments and each is direct, intuitive and synthetic.

Now the base-entity, the knowing subject, is called by Kant the Transcendental self, for, according to him, it cannot be known. Only its experience, i.e., the self as it appears, the empirical self, and its mental states can be known.

That this position is untenable is clear from the fact that this supreme protagonist of the unknowability of the self knows so much about it that he can say, expressly or by implication, that it is a *self* as distinguished from a *thing*, that it is the self-in-itself as opposed to the empirical self, that it is a unity and a unity of appreciation, that it has the faculties of sensibility, understanding and reasoning, that it has free-will, and that it is higher than phenomena in worth, for it is an end in the realm of ends.

This distinction between the transcendental self and the empirical self has therefore to be rejected. When we discard this distinction we readily see that the categories are applicable to the self no less than they are applicable to the physical world. Whatever else I may know about myself, I know at least this much by direct acquaintance that I am a self-identical, persistent and resistant unity, an active and responsive, conscious and self-conscious centre of energy, having a free will working within the limits of the categories and their manifold, and, after due development, capable of apprehending the *a priori* manifold as well as its own response-qualities in various degrees of discernment.

But what about the basic entities ? Kant calls them things-in-themselves, transcendent and unknowable ; and yet he seems to know that they *are*, are plural and distinct from the transcendental *self*, are different from sensations and are their active grounds, It is more reasonable to think that, though not directly knowable, they are yet inferentially known to be the centres of energy that act upon the base-entities.

Now I find in the objective world some bodies similar to mine, and by analogical inference I conclude that they must have base-entities apprehending phenomena even as I am a base-entity apprehending phenomena ; and just as certain phenomena (my body) and the basic entities behind these phenomena are mine, similarly their bodies and the basic entities behind them must be theirs. That is to say, just as I as a subject, as an energy centre, am base for the phenomena called my body, and the centres of energy behind them are subordinate to me, likewise the bodies similar to mine have subjects or responsive energy centres (other human beings) as their base-entities which claim these bodies and the basic-entities (the active energy centres) behind these bodies as theirs. Similarly from myself as a *basic*-entity and my relation to objects, I infer the nature of the *basic* entities *behind* them.

To communicate with these entities I devise symbols by manipulating my pliant body and other relatively less pliant phenomena (written words) and I find to my delight that these symbols can communicate their thought to me and mine to them. This gives me a deeper conviction of their subsistence.

By similar devices, instruments and symbols, I discover the animal minds and the minds or base-entities of a still lower order, i.e., the base-entities behind plants and inorganic objects.

Each centre of energy when responsive to the action of another centre of energy is a base-entity for the phenomena as response-qualities and the same energy centre when active to create a response in a base-entity is a basic entity for the same phenomena as action-qualities. Actually it is the same entity playing two roles, the role of the base-entity and of the basic entity ; and the same phenomena when viewed from the side of base-centre of energy appear as response-qualities and when viewed from the side of their basic energy-centres appear as action-qualities, and when just viewed without any further reference appear as individual objects. Following Leibnitz who followed either Bruno or his own contemporary, Vol Helmont, I would designate these energy-centres as monads. It is evident that these monads are not existents, but subsistents, while these phenomena are existents.

Since certain phenomena other than my body even in their relative independence are pliable and can be controlled and manipulated by me, these I regard as the action-qualities of *lower* monads.

If our view is correct then reality primarily consists of active and responsive monads and their action-response qualities, the physical phenomena, the first as subsistents and the second as existents.

There are layers and layers of phenomena arising from the interaction of monads—sensations, perceptions, objects, systems of objects. The phenomena apprehended by the lowest monads consist in some vague, just discerned sensation ; of higher monads, a combination of sensation—a percept ; of monads higher still, the phenomena called objects. This last stage is reached by the monads which are self-conscious—whose direct experience is not only of objective phenomena, but also of themselves as the subjects experiencing these phenomena.

From ourselves as base-monads and our relation to our bodies we infer by analogy the nature and function of other monads as base-entities ; and from ourselves as basic-entities and our relation to objects, we infer by analogy the nature and function of other monads as basic-entities.

The monads behind the phenomena known as my body being subordinate to me are organically related to me and to one another. Each body is an organic whole of monads behind it. But the organic wholes of monads, both as base-entities and basic-entities are immanent in the phenomena and yet go beyond the phenomena and are therefore also transcendent, even as the wax and the seal are immanent in the seal impression and yet both transcend it, or as water vapours and the perceiving mind are immanent in the rainbow and yet each of them transcends it. Not only are monads immanent in and yet transcending the phenomena, but the same relation subsists between the higher and the lower of them. The higher monads are immanent and yet transcending the lower ones. I am immanent in the subordinate basic monads of my body and yet am more and beyond. The objects, though response qualities of myself as a base-monad, are characterised by unity, identity, persistence, existence. These, unity, identity, etc., are the characteristics of my self as a basic-identity, and therefore I conclude that similar basic-entities are immanent in them and just as I transcend my action-qualities, I regard these basic-entities as transcending their action-qualities.

Kant thought that things-in-themselves are the ground of phenomena, but they cannot be known. Leibnitz denied their being the grounds of phenomena, but admitted their knowledge. I hold that they are the grounds of phenomena and they can be known by analogy.

The phenomena seem to influence one another, but actually it is the monads inherent in them that influence one another. It is not phenomena that cause other phenomena, but the monads in them that cause modifications in and create other monads. Causality only means this modification or creation of monads by monads, appearing in the phenomena as causes and effects.

All phenomena have a certain degree of relativity to their contexts and yet each has an identity which is only affected by the context. To regard the phenomena as entirely relative is a mistake, even as to regard them as totally discrete and isolated is a mistake. Both the relativity and self-identity of the

T

phenomena are of course ultimately grounded in the inter-relation and self-identity of the monads inherent in them.

We have so far concluded that the apprehended physical phenomena are categorical spatio-temporal sensation-complexes arising from the action and response between two monadic entities which both are immanent in them and yet transcend them. But this is not a complete account of their nature. There is a further function of the base-monads (the percipient minds) which makes the phenomenal content still richer. This is its function of apperception by which it stitches the gathers of past experiences to the present ones and dyes them with the hues of anticipations in the light of the knowledge already gained.

(c)

Our analysis has so far shown us the presuppositions of the intuitive or direct apprehension of objects. But this direct apprehension supplies us only with the apprehended objects or implicitly known objects, not with the *explicit knowledge* of objects. The unit of explicit knowledge is judgment. But a judgment is not possible unless the base-entity performs four functions of a still higher order. These are : (1) reproduction, (2) recognition, (3) identification, and (4) ideation. By the first a content is repro-duced in the mind as a distinct representation ; by the second we get a sense of familiarity ; by the third the object is taken to be the same as experienced before in spite of changes, and by the fourth the common elements of objects are held in thought as distinct entities with a reference to their *status* as elements in the objects. These thought products with this special reference are called empirical ideas. These empirical ideas are also directly and intuitively apprehended, though their intuitions are as likely to be confused as the intuitions of objects.

The above four functions of the base-entities, these processes of synthesis, are preconditions of not only our knowledge of objects, but also of our knowledge of the *a priori* manifold of the categories (including space and time) with this difference that in the case of the latter type of ideation, the reference is to contents which are themselves universal and necessary realities of a different order. But since the categories also are constituents of the categorised experience, this reference may be to them *as found* in the physical objects.

Without ideas explicit knowledge or judgment is impossible.

A judgment is the mental act of affirming or denying a certain content of a certain other content. And this is possible because we have ideas to stand for the contents to which they refer even when these contents are partly or wholly absent from our immediate apprehension. The common elements for which an idea stands can never be in immediate apprehension in their *completeness*, though one instance of these is always present in the judgment of perception. In "This is red", the red I am seeing is one *instance* of the red which is shared by several objects and not the whole content of red so shared. Since an idea has reference to a content with its status in the *a priori* or phenomenal manifold, it does not interfere with our knowledge of the content. We use words to stand for our ideas and ideas to stand for contents. So long as words bring to the mind the ideas for which they stand, and the ideas bring to our minds the contents for which they stand there is no interference with our knowledge and no confusion arises, but since this does not always happen, our judgments are often infested with confusion and error.

When a complex *idea* is analysed and as a result of this analysis one element in the idea is affirmed of it, the judgment is analytic. The laws of identity and contradiction permit us to do so, and the need for doing so arises from the desire to emphasize logical consistency and to keep an idea free from incoherence. These judgments, however, do not advance our knowledge . All other judgments are synthetic and they advance knowledge, for they affirm or deny a new content to a content already known. They are made on the *discovery* of a content in or related to the subject. The laws of identity and contradiction alone do not warrant these judgments. The content on the discovery of which these judgments are possible may be a complex of several relations and qualities. Judgments are synthetic *a priori* when on the basis of direct apprehension they affirm or deny an element of the *a priori* categorical manifold of another element of the same manifold. Although judgments about the categorical manifold are *a priori*, yet because the categories pervade through the phenomena as well, they can also be made on the basis of the experience of these

I*

phenomena. But then they are only probable. On that basis alone they cannot have any universality. Synthetic judgments are *a posteriori* when the content affirmed or denied is empirical, is a quality or relation (or a complex of both) in the physical phenomena, or in the secondary formations called mental states (images ; ideas, impulses, feelings, etc.), the phenomena arising in the basemonads from their working upon physical phenomena. The physical phenomena are called external, because their existence depends on the activity of the basic monads as well as that of the base-monads, while the secondary formations called mental states are the result of the activity of the latter alone. In no other sense is the distinction legitimate.

A judgment does not refer to the entire wealth of a content in all its relatedness and in all respects, but only in one aspect interesting to us, though it may be a complex one. Judgment is essentially selective. Full knowledge is the name of a complete self-consistent system of judgments.

Inference is the derivation of one judgment from other judgments. Passing from one judgment to another judgment necessarily implied in it, is immediate inference. Deriving from at least two judgments another judgment which necessarily follows from them is deduction. Syllogism is one valid form of deduction. It *involves* no *petitio principii*, even if extensionally interpreted. The function of syllogism is to see what new cases by virtue of certain characteristics fall under the law given in the major premise. Although each individual man's mortality is included in the major "Man is mortal", John's mortality is not; for we do not yet know if John is a man. When by empirical evidence John has been discovered to be a man and the minor has thus been formulated, and then mentally apprehended together with the major, only then do we arrive at the judgment "John is mortal". Symbolic representation of syllogism conceals the concreteness of the minor and lays the process open to the charge of *petitio principii*. Being *ex hypothesi* universal, each individual man is *ex hypothesi* covered by it and yet the syllogistic procedure, as a concrete inference, is, as just explained, free from the charge of *petitio principii*.

As a purely formal process, it is not really a mediate inference at all, for in "All S is P" any one S's being P or this S's being P is implied and directly apprehended. It consists in the analysis of the S P idea and therefore does not advance our knowledge.

But the major is a concrete universal only in the field of the *a priori* manifold. In the *a posteriori* field it is always probable. The angles of a triangle are necessarily equal to two right angles, but man is not necessarily mortal. The later judgment is merely probable. It is only assumed or *taken to be universal*. The judgment being *ex hypothesi* universal each individual man is *ex hypothesi* covered by it, and yet the syllogistic procedure as a concrete inference needs the supply of the minor from direct experience by what may be called *de facto* analogy.

Explicit analogy is a syllogism in the second figure, in which form the fact that some object (or objects of a certain kind) has (or have) a certain quality, we conclude that the same quality characterises also other objects of the same kind, that is to say, other objects having similarity or partial identity with that object (or those objects). The conclusion is only probable and the degree of its probability depends on the degree of similarity. The analogical conclusion, being a mere probable hypothesis, has to be supported by facts, if they are, under natural or artificial conditions, observable at all. If not, then it gains strength only by its success in making knowledge a coherent whole.

Passing from judgments of facts to judgments of laws is induction. Its procedure is collection of facts, making an hypothesis by analogy or conjecture, deducing conclusions from it, and then taking it to be a law or universal judgment, if its conclusions and conclusions of no other hypotheses are borne out by facts. If some difficulty still remains in its explanation of facts, it is accepted provisionally as a working hypothesis, till it is overthrown by a better one.

Since phenomena are never pure sensation-complexes for a thinking human being, but categorised sensation-complexes, the *a priori* necessity and universality of the *a priori* manifold of identity, number, space, time, relation, etc., are inherent in them. And that is the reason why conclusions arrived at by pure mathematical calculations from a lucky hypothesis supported by facts are borne out by subsequently observed facts.

The degree of approximation to necessity and universality in the laws discovered by induction depends on the degree of the dominance of the categorical manifold inherent in them over their non-*a priori* contents. The law that two oranges and two oranges are four oranges is as certain as $2 + 2 = 4$; but the law that life depends on oxygen has a low degree of probability, for there may be a world where living beings, having different organisms, may thrive on some other gas. If we ignore the necessity of the categorical manifold, then on the basis of a purely sensuous experience we can never arrive at anything nearing necessity and universality.

Thus all *a priori* judgments of law (universal judgments about the *a priori* manifold) and the conclusions following from them are necessary; and all empirical judgments (judgments about phenomena) of laws and the conclusions following from them are only probable hypotheses, approximating to necessity and universality, if the *a priori* elements dominate the sensuous elements.

The conception of the *succession* of cause and effect seems to be nonsense to me. Cause is the name of several forces (conditions) converging, and the effect appears simultaneously with their convergence. Some of the converging forces may be present long before the event, but so long as even one is missing, the cause is not yet present, and the moment that appears and the cause is completed, the very moment the effect appears.

Causal conditions individually may (and I believe some of them always do) precede the effect in time, yet their totality functioning as a totality never does. The appearance of the last one condition and so of the effect may be gradual, but from each completed section of the conditions simultaneously emerges each completed section of the effect.

When the behaviour of certain objects is unpredictable by causal laws, it still falls under the *a priori* manifold of the calculus of chance, and therefore the laws of its probable occurrence can still be discovered. No phenomena are completely free from the necessity of the *a priori* thought pervading through them. Of course, there are degrees of our success in apprehending this necessity through judgments and reasoning.

(D)

Each judgment, whether intuitive or inferential, supplies us with a fresh idea, for an idea is nothing but a condensed judgment.

As judgments increase our ideas increase ; and, since ideas stand for objects (real or taken to be real), in the multitude of ideas we accumulate our knowledge of the multitude of objects. If the word physical object be used, as I have used it, for the monad-inferred-categorised-sensation-complexes, then their manifold of qualities and relations may be called their meanings. On the apprehension of these meanings, and meanings within meanings depend the extent and depth of our knowledge. A particular flower does not mean the same thing to a little girl playing in the garden as to an expert botanist. The same is true of meanings in the *a priori* field. A triangle does not mean to a rustic what it means to a trained geometrician.

The objects of thought in general (whether physical or monadic or *a priori*), have not only meanings, but also value-qualities. They are true or false, useful or harmful, beautiful or ugly, good or bad, lower or higher, and so on. Value concepts are as *a priori* as the categories and the objects are informed with them just as they are informed with the categories.

(E)

In so far as objects are described, truth-value of the judgments about them depends on correspondence with facts. I may judge a distance, in terms of the yardstick, to be 10 or 12 yards, but when actually measured by the yardstick it may turn out to be, say, 10 or 12 yards. I may judge that a certain bird belongs to a particular species, but when its characteristics have been closely studied, it may prove to belong to this or another species. In the first case my judgments would be true, in the second false. We directly know objects—the characteristics of our primary responses—and we also *directly* know our ideas—the characteristics of our secondary responses to these primary response-characteristics; therefore there is no difficulty in comparing them to see if they correspond with each other or not.

But in so far as objects are always within a context or relative to a context, the ultimate truth of judgments about them will rest on their complete coherence in the entire systematic whole of knowledge. Since one judgment only reveals one aspect of its object, the totality of judgments in their coherence alone can reveal all aspects of things. The complete whole of knowledge which can claim absolute truth must include in complete coherence all judgments of facts, all judgments of the *a priori* field of the categorical and value manifold, logical principles and those hypotheses, which we must postulate to explain facts. A single judgment will ultimately be true, if it is a constituent of the entire coherent whole of knowledge.

But such a whole is so far only an ideal. Only by degrees can we finite beings hope to have an approximation to it. Truth value of judgments and systems of judgments can therefore be achieved only by degrees. The degree of the truth of a system of judgments, say, of physics depends on coherence within itself and its coherence with other systems. This coherence must be concrete coherence, not merely logical coherence, for the latter can characterise even fiction. The system must have within it an important place for the *a priori* manifold, whether known intuitively or inferentially, *and* for all judgments tested by correspondence with facts. Complete knowledge is possible only for a perfect monad of whom we have a vague conception but of whose subsistence we have no proof. For us such complete knowledge is only an ideal which we can gradually but, owing to our finitude, only partially realise.

II

(A)

Let us for a moment go back to the opening remarks of the last section. There I said that all action springs from our natural urge to break through our limitations—an urge which manifests itself in a struggle consisting in an effort to realise more and more of our ideals of life. In the preceding pages I have explained the process of our realisation of truth and other related questions and, this I have done with the help of an hypothesis suggested by analogy. The same hypothesis helps us in the interpretation of other matters of philosophical significance.

Knowing is as much an activity as any other activity. It is a developed form of our impulse of curiosity directed to the goal of self-completion of the knower by truth-finding about things.

But the impulse of curiosity is itself a specialised form of the basic monadic energy. The goals of monadic energy, whether incipient or explicit, are, so to say, projectiles of a finite self (monad) thrown out into the not-self to catch or destroy it, and thereby to achieve its own fullness or freedom.

Monads being energy centres, are active, moving or dynamic; and their movement is dialectical. But though dialectical, it is not so in the Hegelian or the Marxist sense. It is not a movement from one idea, through its opposite idea to a synthesis of both ideas, as Hegel would make us believe. Nor is it, as Marx holds, a movement from something material, through its opposites (also material) to a material something which is the synthesis of both. It is not a movement of mere thought, nor a movement of mere matter, whatever that means. It is essentially a monadic movement, a movement of beings essentially like my *self*. It is a movement from the self through the complementary not-self or rather not-yet-self to the synthesis of both in a more developed self. It is still triadic, consisting of a thesis, anti-thesis and their synthesis, but the thesis is always a self, the anti-thesis, a factual or imaginary but always complementary not-self and the synthesis is their unity in the fuller self.

In all my conscious activity I find that I in my present state create from within myself an ideal (something other than myself which I do not possess) and then the synthesis of both occurs in my realization of the ideal in me. By analogy from my own behaviour, I regard this as true of other *human* beings and also, in a lesser degree, of *all other* beings. In man this dialectical process is explicitly teleological so far as the goal is consciously intended and realised; in animals it is incipiently teleological, for it seems to be consciously realised but not intended; in the inorganic monads the process is *de facto* teleological, for the goal is neither intended nor realised consciously. In man the triad of the process consists in his existing self (thesis), his deliberately chosen not-self as a goal (anti-thesis) and his achievement of this goal (synthesis). In animals the thesis is the animal itself, the antithesis the wanted and craved for not-self, and the synthesis its assimilation, sex union, etc. In the inorganic world the monads attract or repel, i.e., have a faint tendency or tension towards or against the not-self resulting in their self-fulfilment as noticeable in atomic structures, crystalline formations and chemical combinations.

The fact that below animal life only *de facto* teleology functions in animal activity both *de facto* and incipient teleology work, and in man's total activity all the three forms are present, not only in succession as he grows from the embryonic to the adult stage, but also simultaneously in the adult stage, is indicative of evolutionary formations within their nature.

The triadic movement of the dialectical process must go on till the finitude of a monad or monadic organisation is completely removed. But, since the finite can never cover infinity, the dialectical process of self-completion is an endless process, a perpetual chain of triadic links consisting of a self, seeking its end in not-self, and achieving this end.

In their teleological self-development the monads in the earliest stage act in one of two ways, either by attraction or by repulsion. The dialectical process consists of monadic self, its development into ideal assimilation or repulsion of the not-self (antithesis), and its self-fulfilment in the actual assimilation of incipiently idealised not-self by attraction or in freedom from it by repulsion. If direct assimilation by attraction, or expansion or freedom by repulsion is not possible, the monadic activity takes other forms such as tension for the achievement of domination, possession, submission, co-operation, interpenetration of itself and the not-self. This results in the monadic organisations (individuals or groups) of dominating, subordinated, co-operatiug, interpenetrating parts. It also leads to further differentiation in the forms of monadic energy within the individual monad, e.g., differences of impulses in animals and human beings.

Concrete monadic unity is preserved, maintained and developed by attraction and diversity by repulsion.

Cognition illumines the thesis, antithesis and the synthesis according to the stage of a monad's development; In the lowest monad this illumination is extremely dim, so dim that the materialists totally deny its existence. In the higher monads, such as human beings, the clarity it gives to the self in self-consciousness, to the not-self as a deliberately chosen and pursued goal and to the real achievement of this goal, is too well-known to be denied by any one but a narrow behaviourist.

The dimmer is the cognition of the dialectical triad, the simpler and more direct is the monadic activity, i.e. the more is it a simple, undifferentiated attraction or repulsion. The clearer the cognition, the greater is the differentiation in the monadic activity and the more are the ways of goal-formation and goal-realization. In man's higher life it functions as deliberate choice and determination.

It is for this reason that *de facto* teleology looks to be mechanical, incipient teleology as stimulus-response automatism and explicit teleology as freedom. But even what looks mechanical or automatic is basically teleological, and each monad, though partly determined by other monads, has an aspect of inner freedom. We are told that even the behaviour of electrons is partly undetermined.

Thus all activity is teleological and the emergence of every effect from the convergence of conditions is the result of the more primary function of goal-seeking. In our own case the meeting of conditions, whether natural or artificially brought about to create something useful, to discover a truth and so forth, is always clearly functional. Recent discoveries by analogy in the field of natural history show the same goal-seeking in the activity of all organisms. When we push the analogy further down to the inorganic world, the same goal-seeking appears in its simplest form as attraction and repulsion, leading to the creation of such wholes as atomic structures, crystalline formations and chemical combinations.

The opposition of thesis and antithesis in the dialectical process does not essentially involve a conflict. It may lead to the formation of such interactional organizations as the solar system, group life in insects and mammals, or societies and states in men. But whatever forms the behaviour of finite monads may take in the case of mutual interaction, repulsion or co-operation, it becomes rhythmic when the monads collide with one another and each becomes an obstacle for the other. When in this way the dialectical process is arrested, the monadic energy accumulates, regresses and returns with added force to meet the obstacles, In other words, it then moves in waves. In the monad-informed phenomena, the physical world, this rhythmic flow of energy is exemplified in radio waves, water waves, air waves, etc. Whether the dialectical process in chemical-structure formation or plant life is rhythmic or not is a matter for conjecture, for to my knowledge no study of these stages of evolution has ever been made from this point of view. But in animals and men the dialectical process when arrested does move in waves. In the face of an obstacle, the energy of an impulse, say, anger or love, accumulates, regresses for a time and then returns with added force to break through the sluices. Strong momentary tensions and high surges are created at intervals. Such an ebb and flow seems to be present in all mental activity which meets an obstacle. We work for some time, work harder in the face of difficulty, then regress in sleep or rest, and with renewed vigour, resume our activity to make our plans and achieve our goals, We want to remember a name, but if we fail to recall it at the moment in spite of concentrated effort, our energy regresses into the unconscious and when strong enough breaks through the obstacles and the name is suddenly recalled to our minds. We want to solve a mathematical problem, when difficulties arise we put in greater mental effort, and, if they are not resolved, we leave it off, and when the high surge returns, the solution suddenly comes up to consciousness. The same mental surges explain the sudden and spontaneous appearance of images in poets and artists, of hypotheses in scientists and philosophers and inspiration and revelations in saints and prophets. Such phenomena are the result of momentary surges that over-shoot their normal value.

B.

Each monad dimly or clearly values the triad of its dialectical movement. The self, the goal and its achievement are all three valued. The present self, though valuable itself, feels its lack of some further value, and the not-self, the object, possessing that value becomes its goal, finally to be realized. The objective is not merely the goal but the realization of the goal and the self in which, for which, and by which it is realized. Values are thus the qualities of objective—not the *tertiary qualities* of objects, as many have supposed them to be, but the qualities of *tertiary objects* (i.e., objectives as compared with the monads and the apprehended physical objects as such). Apart from its general reference to the self, each value has a special reference to some specific aspect of the self, e.g., truth to cognition, good to will, beauty to emotion and right to action. All hindrances in the achievement of these values are disvalues. Disvalues are not merely the formal opposites of values, but concrete entities and forces that conflict with values. The ultimate values are as intuitive and *a priori* as the categories.

The flow of monadic energy is thus dialectical, through and through teleological and informed with the categories and values. But all this is true of the finite monads. Since the categories and values are universally shared by all finite monads, they transcend each one of them; and since they are spiritual entities pervading through the finite monads and the phenomena arising from their interaction, their source must also be something spiritual or rather supra-spiritual. We have the conceptions of such a source in the idea of the Absolute or God, in the idea of a primary, infinite, eternal, self-sustained unity of all values in their perfection—a monad of all monads, immanent in all finite monads and yet transcending them all, just as the finite monads are immanent in and yet transcend the physical objects. Having nothing beyond Him, He has no goal beyond Himself to achieve. Therefore His activity cannot be conceived as dialectical and outward-directed activity, though with reference to the finite monads within Himself, it can be conceived as grace. But, as Kant argued, the presence of a conception is no prooof of the actual being of that of which it is the concept. Intellect does indeed supply us with this general concept. It is the highest synthesis of our imagination and it makes things intelligible to us. Therefore, rationally considered, the actual subsistence of the Absolute can at best be a plausible hypothesis. But since the Absolute is the highest ideal of our will and in His contemplation our feelings are fully appeased, we develop the *faith* that the Absolute is not merely a real on the plane of *thought* but is the ultimate real as *being*. To quote from what I have written in another context, "The testimony of the whole of our soul—the criteria of the intellect, clarity and consistency; the criterion of emotion, satisfaction or *rasa*; the criteria of our will, our highest hopes—all lead not to the knowledge (for the finite cannot know the infinite), but to the faith that such an infinite Absolute which is Perfect Knowledge, Perfect Beauty and Perfect Good, does exist"—i.e., does subsist as the Ultimate and Absolute monad immanent in and yet transcending all finite monads and the phenomenal world that comes into existence as a result of their interaction.

PRINCIPAL PUBLICATIONS

Aristotle's Theory of Tragedy. Asiatic Press, Lahore.
Beauty. Asiatic Press, Lahore.

MAN'S INTEREST IN PHILOSOPHY:
AN INDIAN VIEW

by V. SUBRAHMANYA IYER

Born 1869; President, Board of Sanskrit Studies
and Examinations, Mysore
and
Reader in Philosophy to His Highness
the Maharaja of Mysore

BIOGRAPHICAL

EIGHT of my direct ancestors devoted their lives *entirely* to philosophy. While at the Madras Christian College, as a youth, I commenced my studies under Dr. Charles Cooper, Professor of Logic and Philosophy, who kindled in me a passionate love for metaphysics. Then, after a course in Physiology under Dr. J. R. Henderson, Professor of Biology, in the same college, I felt a deep interest in Thomas Huxley and Herbert Spencer, which made me turn to Physical Science and Mathematics, under Dr. John Cook, at the Bangalore Central College. I next privately pursued a course in Natural and Social Sciences. Subsequently I spent a number of years in learning *Vedanta* under the *late* Swāmi, the Jagadguru, of Sringeri, who was held in the highest esteem as a most learned and genuine philosopher. As Registrar of the University and as President of the Board of Sanskrit Studies and Examinations in Mysore, I have had occasion to come into close contact with many distinguished Pandits and Professors of Eastern and Western thought, which was an education in itself. Among modern interpreters of Indian Philosophy or Life, no one can ignore the most outstanding figure of Sir S. Radhakrishnan, whose striking originality has often called up new vistas of thought in me. My knowledge has been considerably widened by my association with those who have studied and are still studying philosophy under my guidance, some of whom are among the leading members of the famous religio-philosophical body, the Sri Ramakrishna Order. Far greater is my indebtedness to an eminent royal personage, whose exceptional interest in philosophy reminds one of Marcus Aurelius. During the past fourteen years I have had the valuable privilege of being a Reader in Philosophy to His Highness Sri Krishnaraja Wodiyar Bahadur IV, Maharaja of Mysore, a ruler of remarkable metaphysical insight and attainments, who has been referred to, in contemporary literature, as a modern "example of Plato's conception of the Philosopher-King."

MAN'S INTEREST IN PHILOSOPHY:
AN INDIAN VIEW

I. WHAT IS PHILOSOPHY?

As is well known in India and as was acknowledged by many a scholar and thinker of the West, one of India's distinguished philosophers of our own times was the late Sri Sacchidānanda Sivābhinava Narasimha Bhārati Swami of Sringeri, in Mysore. It was while sitting at his feet as a pupil that I learnt some of the most valuable lessons in this subject. One of them is that Philosophy is Knowledge that rises above creed and scripture, vision and ecstasy, art and science, its sole object being a complete realisation of all that life implies. He used to say: whoever has wants physical or mental, and fears present or prospective, is impelled to satisfy the former and overcome the latter. Various are the attempts made to attain these objects, and various are the degrees of success attending them, all of which are comprehended under one or more of the heads: religion, art, science and their numerous developments. The endeavours of most men cease when they are satisfied with whatever they achieve. But to some men, remedies incomplete or tentative, or applicable only to individuals and groups of men, or of an ascetic character, or lastly of the nature of promises to be fulfilled after death, fail to appeal sufficiently. They ask whether all wants (including the craving for knowledge), and all fears, wherever found, cannot be perfectly satisfied or eradicated, *in this life*. They evidently aspire to an absolute or universal and verifiable solution to their question. For this purpose they seek a knowledge of all that exists. Exceedingly unpractical or unattainable as the quest may appear, those who pursue it nevertheless are known in India as philosophical enquirers.

But before the solution is finally reached and tested in life, doubts arise as to whether the enquiries are proceeding on right lines. And the disappointments in them, which imply error or ignorance, further stimulate the urge to get at truth, which seems to recede farther as men seek to approach it. The necessity, therefore, for a clear knowledge of it, is felt at every stage of the enquiries. So the Swami often said that the student of philosophy must first be able to distinguish between "*Tattvam*" and "*Matam*," i.e. between Philosophy on the one hand and Religion, Theology, Scholasticism, Mysticism, Art, Aesthetic experience and Science on the other, especially because the latter have often been mistaken for Philosophy. Philosophy is what seeks, as the *end* of all thinking, the truth that admits of no difference of views and of no doubts whatever. Or, as the Hindu thinker would put it, Philosophy seeks a complete eradication of ignorance, the cause of all error. And as two plus two are equal to four is true for all, so must the truth sought by Philosophy, as its aim implies, be universal and necessary. Contrariwise, in all matters of knowledge other than this, in so far as they are communicable, there always exists some actual or possible difference of view. Hence, the disagreeing views are known as *Matam* which is private or individual; whereas *Tattvam* is public or common.

Enquirers in general being eager to find satisfaction as quickly as possible, take satisfaction to be truth itself or the final test of truth. But experience shows that satisfaction often fails to reveal truth, which has therefore to be sought independently, though satisfaction invariably *follows* truth. For satisfaction is often found in error also. Hence its unreliability. Even the earliest Indian philosophers held that the highest satisfaction (*Anandam*) is but a cover (*Kosa*) that should be dropped before reaching *differenceless* truth. Those who seek truth by making satisfaction the test, like those who make satisfaction itself the ultimate goal, as do the mystics and others, belong to the world of *Matam*.

Philosophic enquiry naturally proceeds by steps which are by some termed "degrees" or "kinds" of truth, the goal—being denominated the "highest" or "ultimate" truth. Religions, revelations, ecstatic experience, intuitions, visions, opinions, hypotheses are all not merely valuable, but indispensable, as steps. What characterises the steps are various degrees of difference of view, actual or possible, in respect of truth. Among them truths of science rank highest, science being the nearest gateway to philosophy. For science, to a greater degree than all others, aims at differencelessness in its conception of truth, though *not absolutely*, as does philosophy. Even in the past, they who tried to reach the heights of Philosophy, through religious paths, had subsequently to pass through the gates of *Scientific method*, though they did not call it "Science."

Progress in philosophy does not mean in India the attainment of new concepts of ultimate truth, but the starting, as knowledge advances, at higher levels and the finding of less difficult approaches, if possible, to the *same* peak of *Tattvam*.

Lastly, in India the philosopher seeks "That knowledge which, if attained, makes everything known." Philosophy is, therefore, not only the "Science of Sciences" and the "Art of Arts," but also, as the Indian philosopher holds, the "Truth of truth," the "End of all knowledge." But this end means also the fulfilment of the purpose of life; for, to him nothing remains unknown, and nothing remains unattained in life.

Philosophy in India, therefore, does not subscribe to Fichte's view that "The kind of philosophy that a man chooses depends upon the kind of man that he is." This idea of philosophy is *matam*; for it is *matam* that so varies, not *tattvam*.

A FUNDAMENTAL ISSUE

To some philosophy is only "speculation" and *Ultimate* truth a chimera. It is argued by many, that if the highest knowledge of philosophy cannot remove wants and fears, its pursuit could be no better than an exercise—or a diversion in solving a problem in chess or geometry. Some say that philosophy yields only conceptual knowledge, whereas religion and mysticism lead to actual felt *experience*, and that therefore they naturally appeal to the largest number. They even declare that "truth" value with which philosophy is concerned is not of so much consequence as other values. They start with the belief that whatever idea or object they are most attached to must be ultimate and point to the absolute reality. But the fact that others do differ or may differ is proof that such values cannot be *ultimate*. Europe has felt the need for taking a higher step towards what it calls a "Trans valuation of Values."

A most marked tendency among the great scientists and

philosophers of our day, when they attempt to deal with ultimate facts, is to lose themselves in mysticism of some kind. That is due, as the Indian philosophers long ago observed, to a lack of the strength and courage needed to pursue truth to the end. To the Western speculative philosopher, his Eastern brother who avers the possibility of attaining ultimate truth and eradicating pain and want, is either a mystic, a religious fanatic, or a primitive, self-deluded being. But what constitutes philosophy, in India, is the *rational* knowledge, that directly results in the removal of wants and fears. It is *verified* only by appeal to life, *as a whole*. That knowledge and life are intimately connected is known to everyone. But what *complete* knowledge might reveal as regards their relation is not known to all. A fundamental issue, therefore, is whether knowledge is a means or an end or both in life. If knowledge be only a means to the attainment of some reality other than knowledge itself, is there any means of ascertaining whether knowledge reveals this reality *beyond all* possibility of doubt?

This is somewhat akin to the question of the relation between what are known in the West as "Thought" knowledge and "Sense" knowledge.

KNOWLEDGE

To many, knowledge seems to signify something different from what it means to the Indian philosopher. To the former it is what is "known" of the external or the internal world (matter and mind). To the latter, however, it implies something more, which can never be included in the "known." For the "known" cannot comprehend the knowing agent or factor, i.e. "awareness," which is something entirely different in character from everything known or knowable. Awareness is always the knower, which is distinguished from knowledge and the known. When we try to know or think of awareness, we only betake ourselves to a thought, which is only something known. We never get at awareness itself as the knower. Again, if there be more awarenesses than one, how is one to be distinguished from another? Nor is awareness known to have any limits like those of a body or an external object. Nothing can be outside of it. The West does not treat awareness as something distinct from the mental contents of which it is aware. Even the "I," the ego, the self[1] as generally understood, is only something thought of or "known." The latter changes, while the former perceives the change. It is therefore unique. The knower or awareness is not the same as the self. which is used in several senses.

Again, it is generally held that by knowledge is meant what is known or thought about in the waking state. The West, though it has specially studied dream and deep-sleep psychologically and physiologically, has not enquired into them metaphysically. Their reflections from the metaphysical standpoint are confined to the waking state alone. Whereas the Indian philosopher's metaphysics cover the whole field of the *three* states. The others consider all experiences, *assuming* the waking experience to be the standard of reality, the rest being treated as less than real. The fact, however, is that all the *three* states are on the *same* level, they being the known. And the objects of the waking state are as much ideal or real as those of the dream. The common distinction between what is internal (mental) or ideal[2] and what is external (material) or real, is of comparatively less philosophic consequence; for, "externality" and "internality" obtain with equal force in the mental world of dreams also. The argument that in the waking state others witness the same objects and contribute to our common knowledge has no special force, because this holds true of the experience in dreams also. As it is with objects, so it is with space in which they exist, or with time and cause by which they are bound. So long as the dream lasts, it is as real as the waking state. The distinction of real and ideal has value only so far as the waking state or, as it is called, the *practical* world, goes. But from the philosophical standpoint it is of less importance. When one starts with the assumption that the waking world is real, he is a realist. When one realises that the waking world is like the dream, an idea, he is an idealist. The idealist's view, or "mentalism" as some prefer to call it, is being reached by the modern scientific thinker also.

[1] In Indian Philosophy "Self" means the *common* factor or feature of all individual cognisers. To avoid ambiguity the word "awareness" is used here. "Contentless consciousness" is used by some writers.

[2] "Ideal" or "mental" comprehends *all* that is *known* as existing in the mind: thoughts, feelings, volitions, visions or intuitions.

But the Indian philosopher does not stop with the dream. When he proceeds to a consideration of deep-sleep he finds that all objects, external (material) and internal (mental) of both dream and waking states, disappear then. They being all *ideas* are refunded into or are absorbed by the mind. Even the body and the "I" to which one is so strongly attached, being but ideas, cease to exist as such. The "I" is a something of which "awareness" becomes cognisant, and which, therefore, belongs to the world of the "known" or object (mental). Next, it does not signify the same thing every time it presents itself to consciousness or awareness. The import of the notion "I" when one is doing business as a shopkeeper or a banker is not the same as he himself understands by it when he thinks himself a father or a brother. These different connotations change endlessly in life. The "I," therefore, instead of being a factor of the "greatest certainty," as some philosophers hold, is a most unreliable, nay an *unreal*, something.

This may appear ridiculous. For, it will be said that the universe does not consist of one man alone. Others see the material objects while one is asleep. But this is to forget that the entire universe is "idea." Unless one abjures one's love of truth and science, one cannot help recognising this fact. As for the "I" (personality or self) in particular, the phenomena of double and multiple personalities will bear out in the waking state itself what has been just said. All the states disappear into and reappear from that which in the waking state is called "mind," but which is really, by itself, indescribable. This is sometimes pointed to as the Fourth, inasmuch as it is that which is aware of the appearance and the disappearance of the other three states. *Here is no solipsism as will be evident from the sequel.*

At this stage the standpoint is neither that of the realist nor that of the idealist. The known is unreal or illusory. But though there is nothing of the known in deep-sleep, this does not imply absolute non-existence; for, non-existence is not known as such then. Here one must guard against the mistake of thinking that if this beautiful material world and the more beautiful world of thought or mind, which though called ideal or unreal, disappear every day in deep-sleep, one must be the greatest loser. But the

truth is, *"Nothing is ever lost."* The appearance and the disappearance of the universe only prove that it is made of the same
"stuff" or "essence" as that into which it disappears. As such
essence, the entire universe is ever indestructible. If one chooses
to call this essence of the all X or Y or reality, the all would be
X or Y or real. But truly it is beyond the reach of word and
thought.

The *rationale* of the three states is that in the world of the
known, totality of data gives us the whole truth, part of the
data gives only fractional truth. The waking or the dream state
or even both lead only to fractional truth. The three states which
yield fulness of data are what philosophy is concerned with. If
to this totality of the known be added the factor of the knower
or awareness, then this added totality, or what is more than
totality, is what reason is concerned with. It may be noted that
the term totality or whole implies parts which are found in the
known only. What knowledge implies in addition, is awareness
which has no parts.

That there is variety (many) in the waking state is universally
admitted. But the West appears not to note that there is non-
variety in deep-sleep.

REASON, INTELLECT AND INTUITION

Once again, it has to be pointed out that many in Europe and
America seem to confine reason to a part of what is really such.
It is confounded with intellect which is Reason *limited* to the
experience of waking and dream states. Reason is the highest
court of appeal in the world of thought. That intellect is Reason
working in a limited sphere is evident from the fact that logic, the
science of intellectual processes, invariably *assumes* universality
and uniformity, which the mind derives only from Reason.
Without this assumption, logical process can have little value.
Further, Reason reveals the limitations and contradictions of
not only intellectual processes but all knowledge based upon the
fractional data of single or double states. And the intellect,
whenever it rises to its original level as Reason, frankly admits
its inherent defects; nay, even points to a something unknown,
beyond itself.

Many a thinker when he becomes alive to this feature of the intellect, jumps to intuition which vainly seeks exemption from the criticism of intellect or Reason. Reason points out the vagaries and contradictions of intuition also. And knowledge based on it disappers like that based on intellect, in deep-sleep. Intuition being something "known," has validity only in the single state of either waking or dream. But those that know that "intellect" is only Reason cribbed or cabined, seek to free the intellect, instead of appealing to intuition. This freeing process is what is known in India as "purifying" the intellect, "sharpening" it, or making it "one-pointed." As this process brings the intellect nearer its original, Reason, it sees more of the ultimate truth, based on the oneness of life than either of the former. In India, therefore, philosophy is based finally upon *Reason*—not authority, tradition, revelation, intellect or intuition and the like, though all these with their data are needed for enabling one to rise from intellect or intuition to "Reason." The sole function of Reason is to detect and eliminate the cause of error whether of intellect or of intuition.

What is instinct at a lower level is intuition at a higher. Intuition is the natural or raw knowledge yet untested by intellect as to its truth-value. Intellect tests it by comparing intuitive experience with the experiences of the waking and the dream states. Intuition implies a something known and therefore implies a *duality* which is the filed of *intellectual* criticism. Whereas Reason, which comprehends deep-sleep also, rises above quality and compares intuition with deep-sleep experience as well. Reason declares intuition to belong to the sphere below the Ultimate Truth, i.e. to the world of *duality*. Reason negates all duality, in seeking the Ultimate Truth or Truth *beyond all doubt*.

OBJECTIONS TO THE DOCTRINE OF TOTALITY

1. The modern psychologist will tell us that it is only primitive infantile or insane minds that mistake dream objects for the real ones of the waking state. But what the Indian philosopher does is to label both "dream" and "waking" objects alike. If the dream world be not real, the waking is not real either. If the latter be real, the former also would be the same. Or again, both could be called ideal. Some of the sanest minds of the world have felt

the waking world to be no more than a dream. The Indian philosopher does not consider dream objects real and waking unreal.

2. Some critics think that idealism, when pressed too far, lands one in *solipsism* which, thought not a logical fallacy, is opposed to all common sense. Indian philosophy fully recognises the weakness of solipsism, and does not find it in its view of idealism. It is only in half-baked idealism that solipsism is met with. Once again it has to be pointed out that by idealism the West seems to understand only a part of what it means. Idealism fully understood points to the "Ideal" character or unreality of the "*I*" (ego) on the assumed reality of which solipsism depends. Solipsism is a warning against halting half-way in idealism. The "three-states" comprehend evidently more than one, the waking. In the waking, we take full account of *all* the experiences and thoughts of other men. To this are added our experiences of dream and deep-sleep. Indian philosophy does not omit anything so as to be liable to the charge of solipsism, which has a meaning in waking experience only. For in it alone it is possible to think of others and of ignoring others' knowledge.

3. The critic may say that what proves the reality of external objects of the waking world is the irrepressible sense of reality. But the same sense is equally forcibly felt in dreams while they last. In fact, the dream while it lasts is felt to be waking. There also exists the sense of "givenness" on which the realist so firmly relies. When the two states are compared, "givenness" is found to be no distinguishing mark of the reality of external objects of the waking. Should it be argued that the "givenness" of the waking world does not depend upon the mind's own creative power, whereas that of the dream is so dependent, the reply is, first, that the "givenness" of external objects in dreams is also felt to be non-dependent. Next, the "given" of the waking as well as the dream disappears alike in deep-sleep. The sense of reality, untested by reason, is no criterion of reality.

4. If the standpoint of the "three-states" proves the futility of the feeling or sense of reality, what does this feeling or sense signify? This taking the unreal to be the real is perhaps the greatest problem of life. There are two stages in understanding it. First, we ask what this material universe is. And we learn that it is

a mental construct (Idea or thought), like a dream, a conclusion confirmed by the latest scientific investigations also. Next we ask what an "idea" or "thought" is. And, as the Indian philosopher says, we learn that it is a non-entity inasmuch as it disappears or dissolves into the mind every moment, and beyond all doubt during deep-sleep. Lastly, we find that both the material and the mental universes are in themselves non-entities, illusions, therefore unreal. How then are we to account for the feeling or sense of reality? Since all ideas or thoughts are of the same stuff as the mind essence, the only reality existing, they are, as such stuff, real, and that always. The unreal therefore *appears* as real. When the states are analysed it is seen that the entire factor, the "known," is unreal, which is no theory, but fact.

5. If in deep-sleep all the "known" should disappear, including my own self, my own body and my intuitions of the highest realities, can there be any basis for ethical life? Is there any use in living? It has already been said that deep-sleep does not mean a blank (non-existence); it is that into which the universe, the *known*, is refunded. As the universe reappears, entity cannot come out of non-entity. So long as the existence of other men and beings is admitted, as it is, in the waking state, ethical life is indispensable and its value is fully recognised. Its significance will be further considered under Ethics.

6. If the entire universe (mental and material) be only ideas, and if they completely disappear in deep-sleep, what becomes of the eternal God and visions of Him, which are among men's dearest possessions? The ideas called God and Visions of Him are absorbed into that which is called "mind" in which no distinctions exist as in deep-sleep. If this is the truth and if even God Himself disappears, is truth higher than God? In answering, we have three alternatives before us: God is higher, truth is higher, or both are on the same level or non-different. That God is higher than truth and that truth itself cannot reach God but can only point to Him, is the view of religion. And it logically relies upon faith. That truth is higher than God is held by many a thinker who makes the Absolute, the Unconditioned, the Unknowable or the Supreme Existence, the truth. But there are other philosophers who say that Ultimate Truth is itself God, the two being non-different. Now, if God be something "known"

He does disappear iu deep-sleep. If He be not "known," He must be the knower; or, He does not exist at all.

TRUTH

We have proceeded till now assuming that we know what is meant by truth. For truth as commonly understood is one's knowledge of some item of experience, internal or external. In respect of truth also, as in that of knowledge, many thinkers seem to confine it to a part of it. They ignore the knower as something different from the "I" or other contents of the mind. The whole mind including its contents, such as the "I" and its acts, is the "knower" for them. Owing to this defect, though truth is admitted to be knowledge, whether all knowledge is truth is still a controversial matter. Further, so far as the Western conception goes, whatever meaning be given to truth, "copy," "correspondence," "coexistence," "coherence," "harmony," "pragmatic import" or any other, in all cases two factors are implied. The two are not the knower (awareness) and the known, but mind (as a whole) and matter. And if matter (the object) be considered mental, both the factors are mental. Whatever the nature of the factors their relation is still a subject of doubt, to remove which the Indian philosopher proceeds to his "Truth of truth" which takes him to awareness itself. The relation between awareness and the known, i.e. mind and matter, is also one of non-difference in their essence; for as "ideas" both mind and matter disappear into the distinctionlessness of deep-sleep and then reappear.

According to an Indian analysis all knowledge is not truth. Knowledge may be true or erroneous. And there are two stages in the interpretation of truth: first, the ordinary (empirical) in which the knower and the known are un-analysed, and secondly, the critical, in which the two are fully enquired into. In both, truth is a bridge sought to be thrown across the two factors to bring them together; the closer they come the less is the room for doubt or error.

Truth, as has been already indicated, like two plus two are equal to four, admits of no difference of view. Man, therefore, at every stage of making sure that his knowledge is true seeks agreement either by quoting authorities, ancient and modern, or by repeating his observations, or, as in religious proselytisation, by compelling others to hold his own view, so that he may have the satisfaction derived from non-difference, which is the essential characteristic of truth. But as it is not possible to find out what all men—past, present and future—think of any item of experience, the first necessary condition to be fulfilled in this quest is that the item of experience, knowledge of which is sought, in itself excludes all possibility of difference. This condition can be fulfilled only in "Non-duality."

Next, ordinarily (in the waking state) we find two sources of doubt or error: (*a*) the knowing mind and (*b*) the object sought to be known. The knowing mind has various capacities at different times. And there are many minds. The matter to be known appears to present various aspects and that at different times. Each mind sees some one aspect at a time. Hence arise doubts. *To be free from all possibility of doubt*, one's mind should comprehend at a given moment all minds and all their capacities, and the matter to be known should likewise comprehend all its aspects of all times and should present them at once. The existence of two such factors, the one knowing the other absolutely, is impossible, unless they be non-different.

Again, even when there are only two minds, one cannot know the other truly (beyond all doubt), unless the two be non-different. Similarly, no one can say that one knows God (who is not a material being) truly, unless one be non-different from Him. Similar is the difficulty of comprehending totality, whether the knowing mind be included in the total or excluded from it. Non-difference is a necessity in attaining truth beyond doubt. Absolute non-difference in thought or knowledge is the same as non-duality in existence or being. It must be absolute, for there may be two entities, non-different in all respects, excepting in regard to their location in time and space.

It is sometimes said that if the ultimate truth be non-duality, what is there to prevent the knower from undergoing change and knowing it himself? But how can change have a meaning, unless distinguished from changelessness, and unless change be known to something unchanging? The impossible feat of conceiving an entity remaining unchanged and at the same time undergoing change is attempted by some. But the problem disappears on deeper enquiry, which leads one to the second stage in which the knower is unchanging awareness only. The final problem, therefore, is how can the unchanging and indivisible awareness know the changing as non-different, so that truth may be attained. The appeal is made to life. All changes disappear in deep-sleep which is non-duality. Change, therefore, is unreal, being an idea appearing and disappearing. Change appears with the waking and ceases with it. And what constitutes the essence of ideas is non-duality, which is beyond change and changelessness. In non-duality all distinctions of knowledge (thought) and existence (being) cease to exist. There is no proof that the *known* —which is idea—exists or can exist apart from awareness. It is needless to consider the unprovable hypothesis that a third unknown entity produces all ideas.

Some philosophers make no distinction between "Monism" and "Non-dualism," but say that "Unity" is what they also seek in philosophy. But Monism and Non-dualism are poles asunder. They do not see this because they ignore the uniqueness of the knower. When one is conscious of the idea (concept) of Unity, the knower is one and the *known* (concept) is another; there are two. Unity here really implies duality. Non-duality only means that what is beyond duality cannot be characterised either as "Unity" or as "Non-existence." For unity has no meaning unless distinguished from multiplicity; nor can non-existence have a meaning apart from the notion of existence. They refer, therefore, to the world of duality, where no term can have a meaning without reference to any other. The Ultimate Truth negates all duality. But truth is no truth unless verified.

VERIFICATION

Is non-duality a mere word or sound, like the "Barren woman's son," or a mere concept? No; it is actually realised in life. In deep-sleep there is no known, no second, no duality. Nor is it absolute non-existence. But this is only an instance of non-duality in *one* state, which is enough to prove its possibility in actual life. What philosophy seeks is a Non-duality in all the three states. Now, into the distinctionless non-duality of deep-sleep disappears the entire known (universe). Then nothing else is known to exist to which could be traced the origin of the universe of ideas—the known, of the waking and dream states, in which (states) the universe reappears. It may be likened to the *water* of the sea, which remains the same whether the sea be waveless or full of waves. The waves, when they arise, cannot be said to be different from water in their substance. Whatever that non-dual distinctionless entity of deep-sleep be, that is what constitutes the substance of the waking and the dream states. Again the existence of the waking or the dream worlds is unthinkable unless distinguished from their non-existence, which is deep-sleep. Further, there is no memory either in deep-sleep; for memory implies something known, which is then absent. When therefore, non-duality is said to be known, it only means that in it there is no distinction of knowing and being. There, *to know is to be*. When some men think that they grasp non-duality, they only form a concept, a sort of dummy, and delude themselves by mistaking the imaginary dummy for what they vainly attempt to grasp. Similarly, when others say that non-duality is something attained in mystic ecstasy or vision, they only think of it from the standpoint of *intellect*, not from that of *"Reason."* For we have non-duality for instance in deep-sleep, which is common to all men and even to lower animals (and plants) which no one takes to be mystic realisation or intuition. For attaining the truth, i.e. the non-duality verfied in the three states, which philosophy seeks, Reason is needed—not intellect. To one confined to intellect, Reason appears mystical.

Were Non-duality not the truth beyond doubt, philosophy would be, as it is to so many men, mere chaff, mere words. It is so to those who talk the grandest conceptual philosophy, living at the same time the most unethical lives. With the absolute non-difference reached in knowledge, perfection is reached in life. They are non-different. In philosophy Non-duality is not only the Ultimate truth but also the Ultimate reality.

CAUSALITY

The importance of this subject to the philosopher in India may be measured by the fact that there it is the knowledge of its meaning that marks the qualification needed for one to enter the gates of philosophy.

The notion of cause and effect is found associated with all that is known, i.e. with the waking and dream states. Nothing in the world of science, religion, and even art in some aspects, has meaning apart from the idea of "cause." But as the entire universe is only an idea or mental phenomenon, cause also is of this nature. That stories of creation found in all the scriptures are but fairy tales or myths meant for children, and have a value only as such, was known thousands of years ago in India. Even the modern scientific theory of evolution is no more than a concept, useful for scientific or practical purposes. Nevertheless, causal relation even in the waking state itself is an enigma. Everyone knows that what at one stage is a seed, is a shoot at another, and a plant or tree with fruits, flowers and foliage at a third stage. But who knows how a seed transforms itself, or other materials, into all these? What kind of continuity or connection is there? Various explanations have been attempted in the West. But in India three are offered to suit different stages of thinkers. (1) The effect fully exists in the cause, though it manifests itself as effect subsequently, both being in essence the same. (2) The effect has new forms which did not exist in the cause but which spring out of nothing. (3) The effect is only an idea or concept superimposed on the cause, which remains unaffected by the effect. All these fail to satisfy Reason because of the contradictions in them and because the phenomena of the world of "cause and effect" disappear in deep-sleep. "Cause and effect" in the world of duality convey sense. But to talk of them with reference to what is beyond duality is meaningless. That God (the Absolute, Unmanifest, Unconditioned or Infinite) created, produced, manifested or in any manner became the universe, is from the standpoint of truth meaningless. From the waking standpoint, that is, of duality, mind cannot but think in terms of cause and effect. The mind when it posits a cause for this world, *imagines* it to be antecedent to the world as effect. Causal relation is only characteristic of the thinking process, which enables the mind to know the world of experience. This is well known to Europe also. The urge to seek a cause for the world is an urge to transcend the effect, because the unknown universe is unreal, or as it is sometimes said, "not self-subsistent." Considered from the standpoint of "substance," cause cannot be different from the effect, even in the waking state. But what appears significant now is that even modern science in its quantum theory is approaching the same truth. Seeing that all Ideas and concepts are wiped out in deep-sleep, they are, as such, unreal. This universe, when viewed as unassociated with the concept of causal relation, is neither produced nor destroyed.

Space and time which causality implies, share the same fate. Modern science has seen the old truth that the former two are inseparable. It will also see in the future that even "cause" is inseparable. It is not "space-time" but "space-time-cause" that really forms the fourth dimension of matter. Perhaps the meaning of cause will then be extended.

MEANING OF EXPLANATION

The greatest value of "causal relation" lies in the fact that it gives a meaning to the term "explanation." When an explanation of any fact is sought, it is the cause that is usually sought. But the need for the "cause" arises because the "effect" by itself is meaningless without its correlative. The two form a whole. In other words, it is the whole and its relation to the part, that "explains." The true explanation of life or existence, therefore lies in the knowledge of the relation of awareness to the three states, that is the whole of life to each of them.

SCIENCE, RELIGION, ETHICS AND ART

There being no field of experience that science does not study or attempt to study, even Religion and Art cannot be beyond its reach. As already indicated, all these do, but only in certain degrees, contribute to the attainment of ultimate truth. They also satisfy wants and remove fears in a measure. In indicating their trend or outlook, nothing more than a bird's-eye view, and that from the standpoint of philosophy alone, is attempted under this head.

Science, as knowledge, is concerned with the known only, not the knower (simple awareness), which can never be an "object" and cannot, as such, be studied. Psychology, physical and natural science, social and sociological sciences, which deal with "objects," mental or material, are all of unquestionable value in the waking state. But philosophy deals with the totality of the data of the three states. What interests the philosopher ultimately is not so much the conclusions or the applications of science, as its method and outlook. The conclusions of the scientists of to-day may be scrapped tomorrow, but their method and outlook continue.

The features of science that philosophy values are:

First, science aims at generalisation, which is a measure of differencelessness. Next, science has the great virtue of not accepting anything as truth till that is verified as far as possible, though the test be confined to the waking state alone. It makes the meaning of the term "explanation" clearer. Turning next to its conclusions, physical and natural sciences have now reached the stage in which it is recognised that all phenomena of the material world or the mental world imply not merely change but also exchange. It is a truism to say that the constituents of one form of existence become in part, or in entirety, the constituents of another and vice versa. Loss in or of one is gain to another, elsewhere. There is no absolute destruction of anything. This is the meaning of what are known as growth, decay and death, or transformation and whatever constitutes life. The food I now eat formed part of something different from me, and has now, after my eating it, become my body. Even so, what I give up from my body forms part of the world outside. This goes on continuously. No line can be drawn between my body and the rest of the world so far as the constituents go. The lesson of philosophical significance learnt here is that ultimately non-difference characterises the highest truths of the sciences of the world of matter and energy. What the world considers the most wonderful achievements of practical scientists is based upon the transmutability of one kind of matter or energy into another, which in turn points to Non-duality.

The case is not different with the objects or contents of the mental world with which psychology deals. As already indicated, all the contents of the mind, namely thoughts, volitions, feelings, including visions, intuitions and ecstasies, are only transformations of the stuff (if the word may be used) of the mind. No line can be drawn between the stuff of the mind and the stuff of the volitions or feelings and other phenomena. So psychology also points in the same direction.

Thirdly, the latest science is the most emphatic on the inference that mind and matter are not two different entities in their stuff.

The entire universe is resolvable into mind or a third common entity. Non-duality again meets us here.

Fourthly, science doubts the existence of causal relation as it does in its theory of indeterminacy and approaches philosophy in holding this relation to be a concept only.

Next, we turn to the science that answers the question: of what practical use is science to the growth of society or mankind as a whole? Men die, but man or society lives. What promotes its growth and life? This is what sociology is concerned with. The whole urge in the world of sociology is towards the gradual realisation of the *unity of interests, negating differences,* so that society may live. To take only a few instances. In politics, whatever the form of government, the struggle is to overcome the painful consequences of the failure to realise one's self as the *all* . . . The elimination of difference so as to lead to unity in interests is the goal, but not merely the changing of forms such as monarchy into democracy and so forth. Any political organisation or institution can give satisfaction only to the extent to which this truth is recognised. Political disturbances arise when difference is accentuated in any form. They are least where the feeling of difference is least. It is even so with all other sociological concerns. Social progress and stability are promoted to the extent to which the negation of differences is achieved.

It is the same with forms of Religion, whose number is legion. It is ever multiplying, and developing differences and distinctions. But this urge to seek spiritual satisfaction does not cease till in the mystic the individual is merged in the Absolute or God. In the lower stages he seeks to approach God or realise God in his thoughts and acts. But merging into Him is the goal. Even then the urge might continue for knowing or realising the *whole* of God. All doubts can cease only when man identifies himself with God. Though the science of religion teaches that religion in general seeks an Ultimate Unity called God, yet this Unity cannot be reached except by negating differences. Man comes nearer God by eliminating differences and realising that both are of the same stuff called "spirit" whatever significance that term may have. But so long as something known as satisfaction, hitherto unattained, is sought and for this purpose one has to depend upon another, *absolute* non-difference cannot be said to be contemplated in religion or mysticism.

The conception of God as a perfectly good Being is contradicted by the presence of evil in the world created by Him. He is saved from this inconsistency by the Hindus with the help of their doctrine of *Karma*. Philosophy indicates that one's body and personality (self) are, like the universe, only ideas or creations of the mind. Man is, therefore, said to be the architect of his misfortunes also. And the continuity characterising that into which all ideas are refunded, gives to the Hindu the closely allied doctrine of *re-incarnation*. These two are of great value, not only in religion, but also in ethics. They serve to check the impulse towards hatred, the curse of life, which only means the accentuation of difference. And what is more valuable still, is that they are powerful stimulants in making men seek an ethical life, which grows in strength as differences disappear.

In ethics the first rule of right conduct starts from the urge in the mother to identify herself with her child in pain or pleasure and to seek common good. It proceeds in ever-widening circles of such identification, till it includes the whole of humanity. The various ethical ideals find their final explanation in the Hindu doctrine that another is non-different from one. The goal is to see one's self as all and all as one's self. The all here comprehends even animals and plants. Hindu ethics enjoins not only the seeking of the common good but also the scrupulous avoidance of injury to anyone because by inflicting injury one not only ignores non-difference but also perpetuates the error of the conception that one's self or ego is a reality and that separate from the self the injured. The ideal in ethical conduct is to realise not merely the "non-difference" of ego and non-ego, but the fact that the ego or the individual self, as "idea," is unreal. The more one represses the ego till it is effaced as a separate entity the greater the virtue. This is not done by suicide or chloroform. For, beginning with self-restraint, ethics leads one up to self-sacrifice in life, which means the dissolution of the

U

ego in others or in the all. And this is the same as saying that the realisation of the all as the ego is the ideal or goal.

In Art and Aesthetics, which deal with the urge to derive pleasure from what is considered beautiful, two facts are noticeable. Art consists first in conceiving ideas and then in projecting them into the world of the senses. The artist finds in the world of ideas whatever pleasure the layman or he himself would find in the world of the senses. The artist often forgets his body and the material surroundings when he is engrossed in the ideas, which for him constitute everything. And when he expresses himself in sounds, words, stone, wood, on the canvas and so forth, he seeks only the realisation of his ideas there, emphasising the non-difference of mind and sense world. The other aspects of art which point to the realisation of time, space and cause as ideas cannot be discussed here.

Aesthetic enjoyment comes from what is considered beautiful, in the material or the mental world. The externally beautiful first produces in the enjoyer ideas, which have truth enough to give pleasure, and enable him to enter into the substance or life of the sense world and to realise the common mental character, indicating his essential non-difference from it. This is most evident from the feelings of sympathy evoked at the sight of forests, mountains, rivers, sky and the like; and especially when men feel impelled to address them as living beings.

When the artist seeks expression in the sense world, so that it may evoke similar mental states in other men, he realises himself in others. In all the processes of conceiving, expressing and communing there is a forgetting of one's self. This forgetting gives pleasure because the truth is then realised that individuality is unreal. The source of pleasure, the beautiful, is found everywhere to the extent to which one is able to look beyond the unreal limitations of appearances or to negate the sense of difference and duality.

Those whose feeling of reality is based most on external objects derive pleasure most from the *sense* world. Those whose real interest is greater in the mental world derive it most from conceptual or intellectual constructions. Those whose notion of the real rests on neither of these two, find satisfaction in ignoring them both as some mystics do. Those, however, who seek to rest on that which is the stuff of all existence find delight in feeling themselves to be one with the all. But they have first to know the meaning of the all, which is the philosopher's aim.

In religion, ethics and aesthectis, not to say sociology in particular, the highest significance is attached to what is known as "LOVE," which only means the realisation, though in different degrees, of "NON-DIFFERENCE."

ULTIMATE TRUTH: HOW ATTAINED

A bird's-eye view of religion, art and science points to the fact that while they imply truth-values they do not aim at *Ultimate* truth. They stop at the stages where they find the satisfactions they seek, which are no criteria of philosophic truth.

The very fact that philosophy seeks the truth *common* to *all*, is proof that it can be no construction of any human mind or minds. Truth is there already and it has only to be "discovered" or as the Indian thinker says "uncovered." Philosophic effort only aims at removing the cover of ignorance, the cause of error and doubt.

Some men reach it quickly and others slowly, often with considerable effort. This labour is needed only to remove mental or material obstacles, such as are implied in personal predilections, temperaments and limitations of the power of observation or of intellectual capacity. When the mind is not strong enough to remove all obstructions, it seeks satisfaction by imagining the ultimate truth (as in Religion), or the immediately next higher degree of truth (as in Science). But philosophy does not stop till the end is actually attained and therefore it strictly pursues the path of science to the end in freeing the mind of all its errors. In it, as in science, only verified facts count. For eliminating error, Indian philosophy lays down certain conditions as indicated below, which, excepting the last, are common to both philosophy and science.

1. To know that there is something more than appearances for one to seek.

2. To eliminate all personal predilections or preconceptions regarding the object of enquiry.

U *

3. To possess calmness, self-restraint and patience, concentration, and an absence of religious bias.

4. To possess the supreme determination to eradicate all doubts and their possibilities and all causes of error and all ignorance.

The scientist does not admit the last (No. 4); for, he does not seek ultimate truth, which he presumes to be unattainable.

The most important of the conditions common to both philosophers and scientists is "Depersonalisation" or "Self-elimination" leading to the detachment of awareness, which is a *sine qua non*. But scientists admit it only to a limited extent. This item and a few others, however, show to what extent moral discipline is needed for removing the cause of error and for sharpening the mind. Philosophy insists upon an unqualified fulfilment of the moral condition. Egoism within limits does not seriously obstruct the pursuit of truth in the intellectual field; but attachment to the ego, which is unreal, is a positive hindrance of the greatest magnitude in the world of Reason. Religion lays emphasis on moral discipline, and Science on intellectual, but Philosophy upon both, in the highest degree.

Doubt and possibilites of error can never cease so long as one confines oneself to waking experience. And there can be no end to philosophies springing up so long as men build solely upon waking experience ignoring the rest. Reason alone leads to truth beyond all doubts. Philosophy based on Reason, therefore, is, and can be, only one.

Theology, Scholasticism and the like do make use of logical or intellectual arguments in interpreting authorities, scriptures and so forth. They are no doubt valuable as disciplines. But as they do not appeal to Reason in its universal character, they can never lead directly to truth beyond all possibility of doubt. Nor can authority and scripture or their interpretation constitute philosophy.

LIFE

The touchstone of philosophy is life. As shown above, all life's activities comprehended under science, religion and art tend towards the realisation that not only the universe is an idea, but that there ultimately exists no difference between thought and being, knowledge and existence or life. The past years that one has lived enjoying or suffering, achieving or failing, waking or sleeping and the past world of one's childhood and youth, all so real then, are now no more than ideas or knowledge. Such is also the past history of man and his past world, so real while they lasted. Everything known resolves itself into knowledge or idea. The man of knowledge, feeling, thought or intellect, be he scientist, artist, theologian or whatever else, to the extent to which he rises above the gross world of the senses, is, and is held, superior to others. Every man, whether he likes it or not, converts according to his capacity all experience or life into knowledge, something known in the mind, that he may value it.

Philosophy rises above distinctions of creed, caste, colour, race, calling, age or school of thought. Its most distinguishing feature is that the philosopher seeks the supreme realisation of himself as the all and the all as himself. This perfection is either for all or for none; for to the philosopher individually there is no perfection inasmuch as the universe as an idea is in him and of him. Till one realises this existence by eradicating ignorance one thinks life, world or God to be different from "knowledge." And one will not have realised "Non-duality."

But for the man who has not attained perfection, who has not realised himself as the all, the many with differences exist; and for him, no one has attained the truth of non-difference. Absolute non-difference or non-duality has no meaning when the thinker excludes or differentiates himself from another or the rest. To the imperfect, therefore, the so-called perfect man is imperfect or less imperfect than others. Perfection looks most like mysticism to the man of mere intellect. But to the man of perfect reason nothing is more real, more universal.

Philosophers do not seek to distinguish themselves from the rest of mankind in any manner, for all distinctions are but ideas and therefore unreal. Philosophers discharge, like their fellow-men, all duties, pleasant or unpleasant, and all functions in society as well as they can. Whatever the circumstances in which they are placed, prosperity or adversity, on the battlefield or in the parlour, with a crown of diamonds or of thorns, in the mountain caves or in market places, whether praised or con-demned, they remain ever balanced, resting on the Ultimate

Truth. They only strive to help others to reach the goal that they have themselves reached. Their sole object in life is to make others reach this perfection. The philosopher is he who in various ways seeks to realise himself in the all and the all in himself, their joy being his joy and their sorrow his sorrow. When all ignorance is dispelled, when everything is found to be of the same stuff as that which is labelled knowledge, when there is no second or other, and when there remains nothing unattained, then there can be no room for "want" or "fear" of any change or even of death which is unmasked by truth.

Why do men not reach this goal easily? The failure is due to the inability to see that the external world including the body and individuality are mental, that the body and the universe are not outside the mind but all is idea.[1] The inherited and almost ineffaceable prejudice or preconception that these are what they appear, in spite of the everyday experience of deep-sleep, is erroneous knowledge which mankind is most reluctant to give up. Even the thought of death fails to teach this lesson. Men with preconceptions cannot hope to attain, as Indian philosophers say, even scientific truth, much less philosophical truth. Divesting the mind of its preconceptions is a gradual process, which takes the mind through the disciplines of religion, art and science.

The supreme test of Philosophy or supreme verification of Ultimate Truth lies in life, i.e. of the three-states, but not in any intellectual solution of the problems, nor in weaving conceptual webs called "systems" of thought, which must be interminable. Philosophical enquiry based on Reason, therefore, leads one beyond vision, intuition—however unique—intellect and concept. Reason, which with a view to removing the *intellectual* misgiving that such a goal may be non-existent or unattainable, names it Non-duality. It is nothing but awareness together with the three-states, in which, like the water of the sea, with the waves (as in waking and the dream states) or without them (as in deep-sleep) the distinctionless Non-duality is never non-existent, to which has been given the name *Atman*.

[1] This difficulty increases when the question is raised as to the relation of mind to its contents (ideas, thoughts, etc.). But that is beyond the scope of this essay.

In India, Philosophy is sought for the sake of the one and only lesson it teaches man: How to attain and live the life in which is realised the all as himself and himself as the all. It is sought only by him who pursues the truth that admits of no doubt or possibility of doubt, which reveals the absolute non-difference of complete knowledge and perfect life. Such a man (*dhira*) will not stop, come what may, till he reaches the end, in which Reason makes absolutely sure that there exists nothing unknown and unattained.

To what extent mankind attains to this truth, to that extent does it approach perfection, known as *Brahman*, and to that extent is it philosophic. When perfection is reached, there is none imperfect, no imperfection anywhere. When perfect knowledge is attained, perfection of life in all its aspects is attained, which is "the highest good comprising all possible good in itself."

PRINCIPAL PUBLICATIONS

Avasthātraya: the three States (Mysore and Leipzig, 1931).

The Final Test of Truth (Calcutta, 1927).

Modern Vedānta (Leipzig, 1928).

Anubhava: The Criterion of Truth (Baroda, 1920).

Śaṁkara and His Modern Critics (Madras, 1932).

Reason or Revelation (Poona, 1915).

Introductions to *Dṛg Dṛśya Viveka* and *Māndūkya Upaniṣad* (Mysore, 1931-6).

PRAGMATIC IDEALISM

by A. R. WADIA

Born 1888; Educated at Wilson College, Bombay, Oxford
and Cambridge
Professor of Philosophy, University of Mysore

BIOGRAPHICAL

POETRY is fundamentally imaginative, and philosophy fundamentally logical. But I have always believed that in the last resort both are born of intimate personal experience. A man's thought can be appreciated in its true perspective only in the concrete setting in which it takes its birth. If my thought has any interest for anybody, a brief account of its genesis will not be out of place.

The Wadia family is an old Parsee family that has played since 1735 a great part in the civic life of Bombay. It has been very wealthy, but I was born at a time when the fortunes of our branch of it were at their lowest ebb, and perhaps it was not altogether a disadvantage that I was not brought up in any luxury. I had to live rather on the tradition of wealth than actual wealth, and stories of past luxuries merely whetted my imagination, and in course of time made me deeply introspective as I heard of old friends of the family and rich relations gradually turning their backs on us. The sense of injustice was burning into my soul, and even as a boy I became thoughtful and found it difficult to believe that a just God could exist with so much misery and evil in this world. I should have assuredly drifted into atheism but for the Hindu belief in Karma. This belief does not find any sanction in Zoroastrianism, but centuries of contact with the Hindus have made it a part and parcel of the Parsee faith. The experiences of my childhood have left me the legacy of an odd mixture of shyness and pride, which persists till the present day. Temperamental aristocratic feeling has gradually yielded place to a reasoned-out democratic sympathy. I have not failed, however, to notice within myself a conflict due to the fact that though an aristocrat by temperament I have grown to be a democrat by conviction.

Bred up in more or less orthodox traditions I early imbibed a great reverence for all the old forms and rituals and prayers, but more than anything else I imbibed a passionate sense of duty, a firm belief in morality as the highest good in life. My mother never tired of impressing on us that she did not care whether we learned or not, whether we earned much or not, but that she wanted us to be good. Ever since those days nothing appeals to me except in so far as it can stand the test of morality. My main philosophic interest has been predominantly ethical.

As I grew up and took to English I became a voracious reader, a tendency accentuated by the fact that under medical advice at the age of twelve I was prevented from taking any part in sports. My reading comprised all branches of literature, history and religions. There were leanings towards philosophy, Though I read no distinctively philosophical books till 1908, when I took up philosophy as my optional in the B.A. Class. Till that year all my high-school and intermediate education has been in Jesuit institutions: St. Xavier's High School and College. I learned method and discipline from them, and for the late Father Devine, an Englishman, I shall always cherish deep affection. The college authorities were against teaching philosophy, but for more reasons than one I was bent upon taking up the subject, and so I preferred to leave my old college for Wilson College, where the Professor of Philosophy was the Rev. J. R. Cuthbert, a very earnest and clear-headed teacher.

In 1910 I left for England. For a year I studied in London and attended lectures of Professor Carveth Read, perhaps the most interesting teacher I have ever come across, and Dr. William Brown. In 1911 I joined Oxford University. My plans were somewhat uncertain. I was not sure if I could continue long enough at Oxford to take any degree. So I studied for the Diploma in Economics and Political Science and secured it with distinction. Along with it I continued to study philosophy without any reference to examinatiou requirements. This was an advantage, as it made my study more spontaneous and untrammelled. I was able to read books an average Oxonian, burdened with the examination curriculum, would not worry about. I attended the lectures of Professor J. A. Smith, Mr. C. C. J. Webb, Mr. A. L. Smith, Dr. A. D. Lindsay and Professor A. G. Adams. I particularly came into contact with my tutor, Mr. C. C. J. Webb, who later became the First Oriel Professor of the Philosophy of the Christian Religion. My weekly meetings with him were a most valuable experience and made me appreciate the tutorial traditions which have made Oxford great. My contact with Professor Webb still continues to be a living one, as even to-day I can count upon him for sympathy in my difficulties.

At Oxford, oddly enough, more than anywhere else I began to feel an Indian as I had never done in my life before. The traditions of my family had been almost ultra-loyalist, and I had been far more interested in Queen Victoria and in Gladstone than in Dadabhoy Naoroji or Tilak. It was my inordinate admiration for Gladstone that had made me hanker after Oxford. When this ambition came to be satisfied, I found the centre of gravity of my interests shifting slowly but surely from England to India. At Oxford I had the good fortune of coming into contact with some of the choicest spirits, both Hindu and Muslim, among my fellow-Indian students. In their company I felt more and more proud to be an Indian. A wanton attack on India in the pages of *The Varsity*, run by under-graduates, put the coping-stone on my nascent patriotism, the most priceless legacy of my Oxford days.

Circumstances made it possible for me to stay a year longer in England so that I could take a degree, but Oxford in those days had no degree in Philosophy except as a part of the Literae Humaniores course, and I found it necessary to migrate to Cambridge in 1912. There I graduated in 1913 in the Moral Science Tripos.

Cambridge represents the traditions of British empirical philosophy, and for that reason the philosophic teaching of my learned teachers did not touch my soul. I became conscious there of a tendency to reduce philosophy to mere logic or to mere science. In the former case one always appears to be hovering about the portico, never entering the main building itself. In the latter case one tends to deny the genuine philosophical categories. Even the Cambridge Idealists like Ward and McTaggart and Professor Sorley did not go far enough in their idealism to satisfy me. But I dare not deny the intellectual value of Cambridge training. If Oxford tends to soar too high, Cambridge tends to make us cling more closely to the hard soil of facts. Without Cambridge English philosophy would be too dreamy; without Oxford it would be too soulless. Real thought would be a mixture of both: true to facts; but steeped in ideals, for only ideals make life worth living.

In 1913 I was called to the Bar. I had no particular taste for practising as a lawyer, but I enjoyed the study of Roman Law and Constitutional Law and developed a taste for Jurisprudence.

My stay in England was of a peculiar type. I was for a year at each of the three great centres of learning. It brought me into contact with a large number of men and introduced me to varying standpoints in philosophy. But I was not long enough at any one place to strike root there. On the whole I must admit that the teachers whose lectures I attended did not influence my thinking as much as might have been expected. I did learn a lot from them, but in developing my own thought I have been influenced far more by the books I have read and digested than by the lectures I attended.

My reading has always been of a very varied and heterodox kind. Among European philosophers I have learned most from Plato, Kant and Hegel, and even more fundamentally from T. H. Green's Ethics and Politics. Fichte was perfectly right in his idea that "The kind of philosophy that a man chooses depends upon the kind of man that he is." I could never be anything but an Idealist, but the Absolute Idealism of Bradley-Bosanquet type I could not accept. Their static Absolute left me cold. My fundamental philosophical problem, the problem of evil, was not satisfactorily solved. My thought drifted in a direction which gained great impetus from Bergson and Croce. I have learned from many, but I have never been able to give a whole-hearted allegiance to any one thinker so as to justify my being labelled as a follower of this or that particular thinker.

My approach to philosophy has been from the side of literature and religion with Ethics as the fulcrum. Science did not have any direct appeal for me till comparatively late. I fully appreciate its value for life, but science can never be a substitute for philosophy. In this conviction I am confirmed by scientists and mathematicians like Einstein and Sir James Jeans, Whitehead and Eddington. Metaphysics is not an end in itself with me. I value it as giving a background to our life. My main aim in thought is the life of man. This has led me on to a study of politics and in recent years my best endeavours have been making for a study of Sociology with particular reference to Indian social institutions. My interest in Indian Sociology has driven me to a more intensive study of Indian metaphysics and Indian Dharma Sastras. What my thought has come to be I have given expression to in my scattered writings and lectures, many of which I have not had time to reduce to writing. Conditions of work in Indian universities—except where only postgraduate classes are taken—unfortunately do not give one as much time to write as one would wish.

I shall now proceed to give a brief résumé of what I believe to be the essence of philosophy, and I can but trust that this brief biographical note will make it more intelligible to all who may happen to be interested in what I think.

PRAGMATIC IDEALISM

"WHY this injustice?" This was the question that very early in life thrust itself on me and it started the train of thought which has culminated in a view which I can best speak of as Pragmatic Idealism. Why should evil exist? Can it be justified? Can it be transcended? These questions revolved through my mind and clamoured for a solution. The traditional reply that a pious Zoroastrian could give is that evil is all the work of Angra Mainyush, the conceptual ancestor of Satan in Judaism and Christianity and of Iblis in Islam. But a rival to God who could nullify his work appeared to me highly unsatisfactory. Even assuming that Angra Mainyush could spoil the work of God, God should have ultimately the power of undoing the work of his rival, and traditional Zoroastrianism seeks to solve this problem in terms of heaven and hell. But how can a just God abandon even a wicked man to the tortures of hell till the day of Resurrection? What parity can there be between the wickedness of a man in the short span of a life, which does not cover even a hundred years, and his punishment for centuries and millennia? The whole thing appeared to me mythical, at best merely symbolical, having a certain moral value, but no truth.

Why should one person be so different from another in his looks, in his abilities, in his circumstances, in his character? To these questions I got a satisfactory answer only from the Karma theory of the Hindus. If one man is born a king and another a beggar, it must be due to their past Karma: actions in a previous birth. All my subsequent reading and thought have not dislodged this principle from my thought. In European philosophy I do not find any serious or successful attempt to grapple with the problem. The story of the Fall is only a myth and no just God can be expected to visit the sins of the fathers on the heads of their innocent children millennia after millennia. It has always been a puzzle to me why European thinkers—apart from the old Pythagoreans or the modern Theosophists—have not been attracted by the Karma theory. The main reason assigned against it—that it breeds fatalism—is not entirely justifiable. For Karma has not merely a retrospective aspect, it has also a forward look. It is not merely effect, but it is also cause. I cannot deny that fatalism has taken a grip of most Hindus, but that is because of their petrified caste system, which is repugnant to the highest thought of all world religions, and I believe even to Vedānta. Our past Karma determines the *kṣetra*, the field of our life. It is our duty to make what we can of it, and that will determine our future life. Suffering may be the effect of our past, but *doing* is our most precious privilege. This is not a mere dogma, nor a mere matter of faith. The whole history attests its truth. Success does not necessarily attend the palaces of kings or the mansions of the rich. It comes as often to the cottage of the poorest, and men who make history are often those who have no distinguished pedigree behind them. Their genius is their success. The world is open to him who dares.

The problem of evil raises two questions: why does it exist? and what is the way out of it? Neither of these questions receives adequate treatment at the hands of the great European thinkers, while theologians are apt to lapse into mythological dogmas. The Hindu doctrine of Karma has answered the first question quite convincingly. The second has occupied the highest thought of India since the day, nearly 3,000 years ago, when the Upaniṣadic seers produced the highest metaphysical wisdom that the world has ever seen. But the doctrine of mokṣa has been variously presented by the different schools of Hindu thought, and therefore no cut-and-dried solution is ready to hand, and each thinker has to pursue his own path of thought.

Armed with the theory of Karma I came to look upon morality with fresh interest. Here I have all along been a sincere follower of Zoroaster, and I believe that there can be nothing higher in life than morality. If a man finds that he can grow only in society, it follows that the means of maintaining and developing society is the paramount concern of man, and that can be nothing but morality. Truth and purity are fundamental personal virtues; justice and benevolence, fundamental social virtues. The ethics of Zoroaster has passed into all later religions and it stands firm today as much as it did in the age of Zoroaster himself. To a Zoroastrian evil is not merely a negative possibility, it is something which has to be continually overcome. Evil negates the best in man and it has to be fought and vanquished. By evil is meant what harms mankind or wantonly injures other living creatures. Merely different modes of thought and worship are not necessarily evil and hence were not persecuted. That is why Isaiah was in raptures over the Persian Cyrus and even Hegel was constrained to admire the tolerant spirit of the ancient Persians. Persian symbolism has centred round fire from times immemorial, and it represents the purifying spirit of knowledge. The Persian spirit has always encouraged the conquest of *Druj* or Lie and the Behistun inscriptions of Darius the Great have borne witness to it through the ages.

The spirit of justice, of benevolence, of independence, of the will to do has always appealed to me and that explains my interest in history and heroic literature. It also explains my deep and abiding interest in social reform. Caste with its pride, its repression of women, its outcasts, its rigidity, its spirit of exclusiveness has always repelled me, and that is why, till my stay in England, political movements had no interest for me. I used to feel that there were other questions, predominantly social in character, which were far more vital and urgent.

Morality is the greatest thing in life. What are its foundations? This is the question that has engaged my thought for a number of years. Three alternatives suggested themselves: religious, metaphysical and psychological. The last explains the growth of morality as conscience, as the result of the conflict between our egoistic and gregarious impulses and motives. Recent Psychology has certainly deepened our knowledge of moral conflicts. It has made for a humane treatment of criminals and wrong-doers generally. But it has not carried us very far. Psychologically, morality remains a subjective phenomenon, and ethics as a science cannot emerge out of mere subjectivity. The ultimate significance of morality Psychology is not thus competent to explain.

Ethics raises certain ultimate questions which can be either dogmatically answered by religion or rationally answered by metaphysics. If God is perfect in Himself, why did He create the world? If He created it, why could He not have created it better? If He could not have created it better, what becomes of

His omnipotence, His justice, His mercy? These are difficulties which Kant's God does not answer. The theism of Lotze has appeared to me to be a bold attempt to give a rational account of God and I have naturally admired the theistic philosophy of my own guru, Professor Webb of Oxford. But doubt has always waylaid the theistic emphasis on a personal God. Books on mysticism apparently ally themselves with religion, but in fact they are usually double-edged. For theistic mysticism may appeal to all who have faith, but to others it merely points to the purely subjective psychological origin of all such phenomena.

The merely religious foundations of morality appeared to be crumbling before my very eyes and recourse to metaphysics became inevitable. The process of thought has been easier in this matter, as I have always been an idealist by temperament. Never for a day have I been attracted by Realism as understood in contemporary European philosophy. To set up mind against matter, to look upon mind as merely emergent out of matter, to look upon philosophy as a mere appendix of science, crossing the t's and dotting the i's of scientific categories, or to soothe one's metaphysical conscience by erecting the Unknowable as the highest metaphysical entity—all these have engaged my attention only to be discarded as unsatisfying both logically and ethically. Idealism as emphasising the supremacy of mind or spirit has been my philosophy from the earliest years. On the metaphysical side of Idealism I have learned most from Plato and Hegel, on the ethical side most from Kant and T. H. Green. The concept of the Absolute is the logical culmination of the inter-relatedness of things and I have been most impressed by the close interdependence of all things in the universe. Consciousness of this has made me believe in the doctrine of Internal Relations and no system of pluralism has appeared to me to be logically consistent or even true to our normal experience. The Absolute as the unconditioned or the self-conditioned is the logical presupposition of all our experience. Within it we have our being and within it we grow. But for me the Absolute itself is also growing, and if the past associations of the term preclude its use in the sense of growing, I would much rather sacrifice the term than the facts which make me believe that it is not a closed system.

My study of Hegel makes me think that the Absolute in his philosophy is not a closed concept. In his Logic that interpretation is possible, but a philosopher's thought is to be gauged in terms of his whole thought and not only in sections. His Logic represents pure philosophy as an attempt to study the movement of thought in abstract and the Absolute becomes the culminating point epistemologically. Metaphysically, too, it becomes the prius of all existence. The core of his philosophy, however, comes out in his Philosophy of Spirit, which I look upon as his Applied Philosophy. In this we find an emphasis on growth and evolution, and the reality of time is implicit in it. The growth of the parts cannot but affect the whole—the Absolute—if there is a real organic relationship between the whole and its parts. It is from this standpoint that what is usually known as Absolutism, as developed in the writings of Bradley and Bosanquet, is logically defective. For there the Absolute is above all change and is the same from age to age. This would be possible, if we could look upon the Absolute as a huge box within which all sorts of things may be churning in endless forms of different permutations and combinations without in any way affecting the size or the nature of the box. But this reduces the worth of human effort to nothingness. Genuine Absolutism implies an organic relationship between the Absolute and its parts. It is inconceivable that any change in any part of an organism within our experience, say a human body, should not affect the organism as a whole. The Absolute as Spirit *par excellence* cannot be indifferent to the efforts of finite spirits like human beings to express themselves in higher and higher forms of beauty, truth and goodness. From the orthodox religious standpoint a God that is not interested in the salvation of a human soul, however high and omnipotent he may theoretically be, is not worthy of human homage and worship. Similarly, the Absolute which does not gain in worth through the increased worth of finite spirits forfeits its right to be called spirit at all; it can only be fit to be called matter—dead and inert.

This position is repudiated by orthodox Absolutists, as they repudiate change as an ultimate category and consequently also the reality of time. Bradley does at times make admissions which go to show that the Absolute is real only in the experiences and feelings of concrete beings, but on the whole his emphasis falls on the changeless Absolute and the reconciliation of these two ideas is brought about, if at all, by recourse to his notoroius mystic term "somehow." His metaphysical genius is undoubtedly great, yet in recent years he has been partly responsible for the contempt into which metaphysics has fallen. The unsatisfactory character of his metaphysical thought is to be found in the unreconciled dual tendency of his thought: a helpless scepticism seeking solace in the arms of religion. These tendencies we see corroding the work of several orthodox idealists. The latter-day Absolutism marks the decay of the great Idealistic philosophy initiated by Kant and Hegel. Bradley's greatest service to philosophy was that he provoked thoughtful reactions and facilitated by contrast the vogue of new philosophers: Bergson and William James, Croce and Gentile, and even the Realists. If they have done any service to philosophy in our times it is that they have raised a note of warning against a metaphysics too much in the sky and too little on terra firma. I have learned a good deal from Bergson and the Pragmatists and the great Italian Idealists, but I differ too radically from many of their fundamental teachings to describe myself as a follower of any one of them.

If the Absolute is the ultimate category of thought, can it be identified with the concept of God? If not, has religion any place in the realm of truth? These are vital questions for me, for I have always had a great interest in religion, especially in view of the fact that while metaphysics is the possession of but a few, religion has found its home in the hearts of millions of men and women. Orthodox theism with its emphasis on the omnipotence, omniscience and perfection of God can rest secure on dogma, but not on a critical examination. Lotze's attempt to found theism on rational grounds has been most noteworthy, but even he does not succeed in solving all the difficulties latent in the theistic position. Personal Idealists have succeeded in giving a new lease to Theism only by sacrificing the omnipotence of God to His goodness, but to the ordinary religious consciousness a limited God sounds like a contradiction in terms.

I have felt that the problem of evil is the rock on which theism flounders. Evil cannot be the expression of a righteous God. Therefore either evil is real and falls outside God, or it is unreal, a mere illusion, and therefore needs no explanation. In the former case we lapse into some type of dualism and God can only be one of the ultimate concepts and not the only one as genuine theism demands. In the latter case we get a very ostrichy metaphysics: an attempt to solve a problem by denying its existence. I can admire Spinoza for his denial of evil as unreal *sub specie aeternitatis*, but I cannot bring myself to deny the existence of evil. Nothing is more real in human experience. All religions have flourished because they point out paths of redemption to achieve freedom from evil. Evil exists as the counterpart of good. Good is real only because of the potentiality of evil, because it is shadowed by evil. Failure to do what we ought to do is evil and may bring us face to face with physical evil, the evil of the body, or moral evil, the evil of the soul. Evil can not be ultimate for then the world would be fundamentally irrational. It is just a stage to be transcended on our onward march. In the very finiteness of our nature evil is inherent, but it has to be overcome. That it has a place in the scheme of existence and that it can be overcome is the presupposition of all Ethics, as it is the presupposition of all knowledge that the world is intelligible. The presupposition of Ethics has to be justified by metaphysics. Theism with its emphasis on a personal God does not do it. Can Idealism in any form do it?

It is at this stage that I have found Indian philosophy much more helpful than European philosophy. Indian seers do not deny evil. In fact they have often been charged by Western scholars of Indian philosophy and religion with being so very conscious of it as to become "pessimists." But no Indian seer, not even Buddha, has allowed himself to be overpowered by the sense of evil. One and all of them teach that it can be overcome in the life of each individual, that *nirvana* or *moksa* is the right of everyone, if not in one birth at least through birth after birth, when a soul purges itself of evil bit by bit and ultimately shines in the full glory of freedom from birth and death. This is accepted by the Jain and the Buddhist as much as the Vedāntin, whether he be an Advaitin, Visistādvaitin or Dvaitin. Karma and the transmigration of soul are the common inheritance of almost every Indian. Even when he changes his religion, in some form or another these beliefs linger in him and consciously or unconsciously mould his life. The spirit in man must be the ultimate victor, and the Indian is not daunted even if the prospect of victory is to come to him in ages beyond computation.

My agreement with Indian thought ceases as soon as the question has to be faced: how is this evil in us to be overcome so as to attain *nirvāṇa* or *moksa*? The orthodox Indian answer to this question invariably takes the form of some type of ascetic ethics. It aims at an increasing simplicity of life so that the man who has neared or attained the goal should have nothing to call his own. That is why the extreme Jaina Digambar rejects even clothing and the Jain muni insists on moving about naked, unmindful of the presence of men and women alike. This extreme attitude is not taken up by all the sadhus in India, but they all aim at having nothing of their own so that ultimately they have to be dependent on public charity even for their barest needs of life. The notorious beggar problem in India has its roots in this application of Indian thought, and making allowance for a few genuinely advanced souls, the majority cannot escape the charge of being social parasites on one of the poorest communities on earth. Sometimes this asceticism even takes the form of a claim that a liberated soul rises above all social ties. He is said to have no moral duties — a doctrine extremely dangerous in itself. Sometimes it is even claimed that such a soul can do no wrong and that is made an excuse for doing every wrong. Luckily such cases are exceptions, but they essentially point to the perversions that are likely to arise when any school of thought imagines that a man under any circumstances can possibly be above morality.

As I have noted previously, I have never felt it necessary to give up my ethical Zoroastrian inheritance. The spirit of Zoroaster's teaching is anything but ascetic. It has been noted even by non-Zoroastrian students of the old Persian faith that it is the only religion which eschews asceticism in every form. It does not advocate fasts or celibacy. It does not look upon life with sickly eyes. It has faith in a righteous God and believes that in order to succeed, man has but to try courageously to rise above all evil temptations. From my own metaphysical standpoint, too, I see no justification for asceticism. Like the ancient Greek and the Persian I believe that man is most natural when he is most developed and he is most developed in the life of civilisation where arts and literature, science and industry flourish. If the Absolute Spirit lives in all its parts there is nothing which it need repudiate as alien to itself except the evil which hinders its life of harmony. What is needed is the recognition of the oneness of Spirit and therefore the real life of the Spirit is to be found in the interplay of individuals rather than in a studied exclusion from the life around us. Such exclusiveness is justifiable only as a stage of preparation for a fuller manifestation of the life of the Spirit, never as an end in itself.

If Theism breaks on the rock of evil, a very perplexing question arises: what becomes of the great religious teachers, who spoke in the name of God and who have undoubtedly taken mankind to a great ethical height, whatever mess their followers may have been responsible for? This question has certainly caused me a good deal of heart-searching for, as noted before, I approached philosophy through literature and religion, and the highest literature in the last resort is also religious and ethical. The first suggestion of a possible solution of this problem came from Stewart's *Plato's Doctrine of Ideas*. An original distinction is sought to be made here between Plato the philosopher and Plato the artist and man of religion. While the former is led to the impersonal Idea of the Good, the latter is led to personify it for artistic and religious purposes. It was a case of psychological necessity in the case of Plato. May not the same need exist in the case of every man? I have never got over the conviction that man in his heart of hearts is profoundly religious. The animist as much as the monotheist responds to the same needs of his nature, though their beliefs take different forms according to the varying standards of their culture. The case of Comte has struck me as a pathetic example of an intellectual who would fain deny God, but is driven to raise a new God: Humanity, in order to give vent to the rich emotional cravings for worship harboured in his heart. Soviet Russia is another instance of how the worship of Lenin may take the place of the worship of Christ, if not with the same paraphernalia, at least with as great intensity of feeling.

Śaṁkara's famous distinction between Nirguṇa Brahman and

Saguṇa Brahman has also contributed its quota to the development of my own thought in this respect. The orthodox interpretation of Śaṁkara's philosophy generally takes the form of characterising it as abstract monism as contrasted with the concrete monism of Rāmānuja or Hegel. *Nirguṇa* literally means without qualities. If taken literally, it would amount to Hegel's pure being, which is as good as nothing. I find it difficult to believe that such a meaning could have been intended by so keen a thinker as Śaṁkara. The single legitimate meaning of *nirguṇa* can only be that no quality we human beings can possibly conceive of can be an adequate description of Brahman, which in its infinity must necessarily transcend all human categories. I am also driven to agree with him as with European Absolutism that the highest category cannot be a person without sharing in all the limitations of personality. *Saguṇa Brahman* is *Īśvara* or God, who has qualities, but even he is a part of the world of Māyā, which is usually translated as illusion, but may more appropriately be translated as appearance. So *Īśvara* is not ultimately real. He may be worshipped by the masses, but for the *Jñāni*—the sage—he does not exist in the sense in which the highest religious consciousness conceives him. No wonder if the orthodox Brahmin of the rival schools looks upon an Advaitin as a *nāstika*, an atheist.

In this connection I may also refer to the phenomena of mysticism. Mystic poetry has had a great appeal for me. But the study of the psychology of mysticism has modified my old naïve enthusiasm and forced me into a fresh interpretation of mystic phenomena. William James's Gifford Lectures on the *Varieties of Religious Experience* I found very suggestive, but Leuba's writings have produced on the whole a more destructive effect. One cannot be blind to the fact that the trances and other paraphernalia of mysticism are found as much in the lowest types of shamanism as in the highest monotheisms. Even in the highest religious mystic experience would have an ultimate value if it not merely speaks of the ONE, but conceives the ONE in an identical manner. In actual fact we find that Christian mysticism centres round Christ, Vaishnavite mysticism round Vishnu, Saivite round Śiva and Kāli. This clearly shows the purely personal origin of many of these mystic experiences. Faith is strong indeed, but its strength is the strength of the human will behind it, as shown abundantly by Couéism and other similar phenomena. No wonder if a real devotee who has the name of Christ or Rām continually on his lips sometimes sees visions. As psychical phenomena they have worth, but whether they have any ontological value is certainly open to question. Mysticism at its highest can lay claim only to one great uniformity: the sense of oneness that the mystic feels with the whole universe and this is philosophically consistent with pantheism as much as with theism. There is a type of mysticism, not perhaps logically deduced, but intuitively felt and intellectually understandable which we find in the Upaniṣads and in Sufism, in the Stoics and the Neo-Platonists, in Spinoza and in Kabir. Leuba's crusade, so thorough in its onslaught on theistic mysticism, does not touch the deeper form of intellectual mysticism.

What then is the value of religion? *Consolatio religionis* implies a personal God to whom we can pray and ask for boons, on whose justice and mercy we can rely in our darkest moments. But if the ultimate reality is conceived as an It, what possibility is there for an intimate communion between God the Father and ourselves as His children? This has proved a very perplexing question, for my old theistic faith in its orthodox garb does not square with the logic of my thought. A God that could respond to the innermost wishes of my heart is indeed a God that my heart, anybody's heart, can eagerly yearn for. But Kant was devastating when he said that the idea of a hundred dollars is not the same as a hundred dollars actually jingling in one's pocket, and that the idea of God does not necessarily imply the reality of God. A wish of my heart, however intense, cannot be mistaken for an objective reality. Is religion then nothing but an idea, an emotional craving of a lonely and oppressed heart?

Religion has been too priceless a possession of mankind to be so lightly discarded as the atheists of the Bolshevik type seek to do. In what form can it be harmonised with the Idealistic metaphysics? and that is the only metaphysics stamped with truth so far as I am concerned. Religion involves a way of living, essentially practical, but if it is not to dissolve into waves of mere emotions, it must be based on truth, which is fundamentally an intellectual or philosophical category. Religion must in the resort be Applied Philosophy. Even a fetichist has a philosophy, but a philosophy so crude as to be mere mythology. This applies as much to polytheisms, whether found in India or Babylonia, in Greece or in Egypt. The monotheistic prophets from the days of Zoroaster down to the last of the prophets, Abdul Baha, have brought mankind at least to a consciousness of the unity underlying the whole universe, a consciousness of the brotherhood of men and lastly to a consciousness of the moral government of the world. I regard these as the most important contributions of the great religious geniuses to human civilisation, and none of them can be denied without loss to the spiritual worth of men. The insistence on prayer and worship is only of secondary importance as aids to spiritual development. The subjective or psychological need for prayer and worship may give rise to the necessity of personifying the ultimate unity of the world as God, anthropomorphical and very human in His passion for being worshipped and appeased and propitiated. But I feel that the great prophets who have been really responsible for the moral uplift of mankind have not cared for this God, in whose name countless human beings have been sacrificed. Not human sacrifices, not animal sacrifices, not vestal virgins, not even fruits and flowers, not fasts, not mere prayers are in the last resort pleasing to God. He only demands that men shall be righteous and the only offering that He will accept is a pure and contrite heart. This is the gist of the teaching of Zoroaster, of Isaiah, of Christ, of Mahomed, of Kabir. Love and service embody the most precious legacy of the prophets. Idealism by its very emphasis on the fundamental unity of nature in general and mankind in particular links itself with moralism and that is why the particular brand of Idealism that I accept I speak of as Pragmatic Idealism. I do not find the traditional Pragmatism of James or Humanism of Schiller to be intellectually satisfactory, but I do believe with them that a metaphysic which does not ultimately bear on life and make our life better is not worth worrying about.

Religion is fundamentally an attitude, an attitude of reverence reacting to Reality as Truth, in every fibre of which there breathes the fire of Life. This may be called God, not a person one among many, but a living presence that unites each to all. God is the personified aspect of the Absolute, the mind in which everything

lives and moves. Prayer and worship are but mere instruments
to put us into a *rapport* with this all-pervading presence. God is
within us as He is all around us. Kabir gave a lofty expression
to this idea when he said: "There is musk within the deer and
yet it imagines that the fragrance comes from without and hunts
and hunts for it in the forest. So, too, God is within us, but we
mortals pass Him by."

Similarly the man was a true mystic who when blamed for
sitting with his feet towards an idol said: "In all directions there
is God. Where am I not to stretch my legs?" Religion therefore
properly viewed is an attitude of reverence and an emotional
realisation of what thought discovers as truth in the field of
philosophy. The practical realisation of the harmony of life is
morality. In the man who transcends his narrow self and merges
it in the life of the whole, philosophy as truth, religion as devotion,
and morality as goodness meet. Religion in short is the emotional
aspect of philosophy. In this sense it is not opposed to philosophy,
rather is it the complement of philosophy. For philosophy without
religion would be barren, and religion without philosophy would
be blind. In short, for me the ultimate reality is Spirit. It does
not live in a transcendent world, but within everything that is.
It is the life and soul of everything. It is essentially living and
growing. Religion as applied philosophy is life in harmony with
the purpose of Spirit. And what is the ultimate end of man?
To live in the life of the Spirit till life's work be done in a birth or
a series of births, and the individual soul finally merges in the
Spirit that pervades all.

It is from the practical standpoint that the attitude of the
average educated Hindu of to-day leaves me cold, even dissatisfied. The high metaphysics of the Upaniṣads and the ethics
of the Gītā have been reduced to mere words by the tyranny
of the caste. Emphasising the unity of the whole world animate
and inanimate, India has yet fostered a social system which has
divided her children into water-tight compartments, divided
from one another from generation to generation for endless
centuries. It has exposed her to foreign conquests which have
left her poor and weak, and worst of all she has become the home
of untouchability and unapproachability, which have branded
her with the curse of Cain. I am not unaware that with many

educated Indians philosophy has come to be looked upon as a subject to be eschewed and treated with contempt. Much against my grain I often think that if metaphysics is merely a matter of intellectual jugglery and religious pride, as it has come to be in India, it would be good for India to take a metaphysical holiday. But it would be far better for India if her sons did not take their social intitutions as divinely ordained, which no man dare touch. Rather the great need for India today is a new Social Philosophy. It was with this purpose that I attempted a new departure in my presidential address to the All-India Philosophical Congress in 1930. I was prepared for criticism, but I got it much less than I expected, and this only from a few metaphysical highbrows.

Having secured a certain metaphysical standpoint, for the last seven years my main interest has drifted into sociological channels. This has led me to make a more intensive study of Indian socio-logical problems. If philosophy is not to end merely in talk and endless bandying about of quotations from the Upaniṣads and the Gītā, and still more endless quotations from the numerous commentaries on them, we in India must break loose from the shackles of the past, retain all the good that we can and merci-lessly discard the rest. The garden of Indian life and thought has been choked with weeds, in the midst of which a few beautiful flowers may grow and give us the illusion of life, but as a matter of fact there is a certain deadness of outlook in the millions of Indians, hardly redeemed by the political activity of the educated classes. We have yet to learn that political democracy cannot grow on the basis of an antiquated system of a rigid social hierarchy with its twain attendant satellites: a superstitious womanhood and an ignorant priesthood.

Philosophers in the West have always shown great vitality. They have allowed themselves to be influenced by the great currents of thought around them whether in the political field, as e.g. in the days of the Reformation, the French Revolution or the Russian Revolution, or in the scientific field, as e.g. the Copernican Revolution, Darwinian Evolution or Einsteinian Relativity. Sufferings of people have produced in them new vital rejuvenating ethical reactions. In India the dogma of a changeless Brahman has produced lethargy and elevated philosophy above the cares of life only to make it a game for the learned and a butt of ridicule for the irreverent. Philosophy will grow when we think and write and do in the spirit of the poet:

If nobody listens to thy call,
Then march thou, all alone.

Consistency may not be a virtue in a politican, but it is an imperative necessity in a thinker. The demand for consistency is the sole justification of a "system" of philosophy. Some thinkers in the West tend to display a suspicion of what they call "system-mongers" and pride themselves on resisting the temptation to produce systems of philosophy. But philosophy is nothing if it is not systematic in the sense that its various parts hang together in some sort of logical cohesion. Absence of this implies loose thinking and vitiates the worth of a man's thought. It is from this standpoint that I distrust a philosophy, Eastern or Western, that teaches universalism in metaphysics and particularism in ethics. I have been anxious to see that the unity or system of a man's thought also permeates his life. It is from this standpoint that the question of the relation of philosophy and religion looms large in my thought. Among the Hindus there has been a tendency to take it for granted that there is a unity of thought in their philosophy and religion, which has not been present in the history of European thought since the days of Xenophanes and Socrates. But I believe that in India, too, there has been more a juxtaposition of religion and philosophy than a real unity, for while Vedānta as the philosophic contribution of India to the thought of the world is marked by a high universalism, Brahminism as a religion has hardly risen above the level of a national religion, as admitted by so conscientious a thinker as Professor Hiriyanna. Popular Hinduism revolves round caste, which in its exclusiveness is a denial of the catholicism of Vedānta. India needs today a reorientation of thought, realising in practice what has only been taken for granted in thought: the unity of life, the all-pervasiveness of Brahman.

"Philosophy as a human pursuit ought to be no barren speculation but an illuminating vision of truth which inevitably prompts to self-culture and social service. 'An unexamined life is worth nothing' and 'nothing human can be alien to man' are perhaps the two aspects of your teaching which have been the spur to self-development and the awakener of the social conscience in us." On a certain occasion these words were used by an old pupil of mine, now a colleague, to summarise my thought. They so truthfully express my aim that I cannot better them and that is the only excuse for reproducing them at the end of a statement, which is expected to be an account, in the words of the editor, stating my "convictions on the ultimate problems of philosophy and the processes of thought" by which I arrived at them.

INDEX

Abhedānanda Swāmi, 49–63
Absolute, the, 191, 310, 426, 427,
   496–502, 511–516, 524, 534,
   589–590
Adamson, Robert 315, 316, 550
Adhikari, Professor P. B., 431
Advaitism, 239, 520, 522, 523
Agnosticism, 423
Alexander, Professor S., 85, 89,
   340 n., 347 n., 400, 496
Al-Ghazzali, 574
Appearance and Reality, 414–417
Arcesilaus, 479
Aristotle, 141, 151 n., 497, 540,
   546–548, 549, 551, 555, 560,
   572
   his *Metaphysics*, 547
   his *Nichomachean Ethics*, 540
Arnold, Matthew, 489
Art, 37–46, 371–375, 460, 488–
   490, 614
Augustine, St., 156, 162 n., 166
   his *Confessions*, 151
   his *Civitas Dei*, 530
Aurobindo, Sri, 400, 403, 404
   his *The Life Divine*, 387
Avenarius, 89

Bacon, 489
Baha, Abdul, 638
Bain, Alexander, 316
Beauty, 91
Behaviourism, 261–262
Belief and Knowledge, 233–236
Bergson, M. Henri, 95, 141, 296,
   383, 384, 401, 495–496, 500,
   551–552, 632
Berkeley, 14, 136–137, 298, 315,
   317, 318, 320, 438—444, 570,
   571
Bernard, St., 171 n.
Bhāgavata, 224 n.
Bhagavadgītā, 49, 158 n., 167 n.,
   179, 182, 322, 328, 395, 545

Bhandarkar, 182
Bhātpara, 67
Bhattacharya, Haridas, 67–100
Bhattāchārya, Professor K. C.,
   105–125, 232, 457, 509
Bhattacharya, Pandita R. S., 67
Bhattacharya, Pandit V., 509
Böhme, 165
Bosanquet, Bernard, 75, 185,
   291, 316, 515, 631
Bradley, A. C., 351
Bradley, F. H., 89, 136, 138, 257,
   316, 321, 326, 391, 400, 401,
   498, 512, 514, 515, 521, 543–
   545, 556, 631, 632
   his *Appearance and Reality*,
   129, 390
   his *Principles of Logic*, 389
   his *Ethical Studies*, 397
Bréhier, 165 n.
Brentano, 298
Brontë, Emily, 502
Browning, 191, 495
Bruno, 576
Buddha,-ism, 181, 476, 526, 534,
   545, 633
Burnet, John, 549, 550
   his *Early Greek Philosophy*,
   549, 550
   his *Thales to Plato*, 486 n., 550,
   558
Byron, 482, 489

Caird, Edward, 315, 316, 449,
   513
   his *The Critical Philosophy of
   Kant*, 380
Calkins, Miss, 184
Carlyle, 541
Caste, 629
Caturvyūhavāda, 383
Causality, 582, 608–610
Chandra, Rasick Lal, 49

Chārvākas, 545
Chatterjee, Bankim Chandra, 25, 49
Chatterji, Professor G. C., 129–148
Chiplunkar, Vishnushastri, 180
Christianity, 498, 627–628
Clement of Alexandria, 158 n.
Commonsense Realism, 239–243
Comte, 181, 530, 555, 635
Consciousness, 233, 295–297, 452
Coomaraswamy, Dr. Ananda K., 151–171
Cratylus, 547
Croce, 90, 481, 632

Damle, N. G., 175–194
Daṇḍin, 489
Dante, 30, 158 n., 160, 169 n., 170
Darwin, 511
Das, Professor Bhagavan, 197–227, 431
Das, Ras-Vihary, 231–248
Dasgupta, Professor S. N., 13, 251–285
Datta, D. M., 289–310
Descartes, 437–438, 440, 441, 485, 529, 574
Deussen, Paul, 52
Dharma, 530
Dialectical Process, 585–589
Driesch, 72
Duperron, Anquetil, 182
Durkheim, 481

Eckhart, 150, 158 n., 160, 163, 168, 170, 171 n., 190, 485
Ego, 420–426, 428
Ehrenfels, 386
Einstein, 252
Emerson, 55
Empiricism, 434, 437, 445
Epicureans, 545
Epistemology, 521
Erigena, 160 n., 170
Eucken, 545

Evolution, 73–75
Emergent, 141–143
Existence, 304, 305

Fairbanks, 549
Farid, Ibnu'l, 170
Fawcett, 192 n.
Fichte, 57, 182, 191 n., 531
Förster, Georg, 182
Freedom, 246
Freud, 181, 183, 264, 296, 372, 479

Gadādhara, 185
Gandhi, 15, 17, 21, 180, 509
Gaṅgeśa, 185
Gautama, 545
Gentile, Giovanni, 90, 452, 632
Goethe, 31
Gomperz, 550
Goodness, 92
Green, 315, 316, 545, 630
Guénon, Rene, 160 n., 164 n., 168 n.

Haeckel, Ernest, 58
Haldane, Lord, 316
Haldar, Professor Hiralal, 315–331, 431, 509, 513
Hartmann, Nicholai, 83, 395, 397–398, 401
his Ethics, 387, 393, 396, 397
Hastie, Dr. W., 315
Hebrews, 497–498
Hegel, 56, 57, 94, 132, 136, 137, 205, 252, 263, 290, 315, 316, 324–326, 380–382, 384, 400, 513–515, 528, 585, 629–632, 636
Heine, 30, 31
Helmont, Vol, 576
Heracleitus, 167, 380, 546, 547, 552
Hering, 71
Hilbert, David, 293
Hinduism, 475–478
Hiriyanna, Professor M., 335–352

Holt, 299, 300
Hügel, Baron von, 494
Hume, 85, 86, 133, 137, 300, 444

Idealism, 239, 245–248, 298–301
Ignatius, St., 560
Illusion, 412–414, 417–419
Imagination, 375
Individual, the, 371
  and Society, 357–362
Induction, 581–582
Inference, 580
Inge, W. R., 558, 559
Instinct, 301–302
Integral Idealism, 188–190
Intellect, and Intuition, 191, 401,
  483–487, 558
  and Morality, 74, 76
  and Will, 85–88
Intuition, 411, 419–422

Jahan, Emperor Shah, 565
Jainism, 181, 252, 293, 328, 634
James, William, 52, 129, 305,
  515, 632, 638
  his Pragmatism, 545
  his Varieties of Religious Ex-
  perience, 561, 636
Jesus, 490
Jñāneśvara, 175, 560
Joad, C. E. M., 185
Joachim, Harold H., 431, 433
John, St., of the Cross, 560
Jones, Professor Henry, 178, 316
Jones, Rufus, 561
Joseph, H. W. B., 431
Judaism, 627
Jung, 532
  his Modern Man in Search of a
  Soul, 164 n.

Kabir, Humayun, 357–375, 637.
  639
Kanāda, 49
Kant, 13, 55–56, 57, 78, 84, 86,
  90, 91, 93, 105–106, 116, 182,
  240, 274, 324–325, 380, 416,

Kant—continued
  431, 436, 437, 440, 445, 447,
  481, 487, 513–515, 519, 526,
  528–531, 545, 547, 571–575,
  577, 589, 637
  his Critique of Pure Reason,
  315, 553, 555, 630, 632
  his Religion Within the Limits
  of Reason, 481
Kapila, 50, 58
Karma, 63, 93, 255, 457, 627–628
Kathopanishad, 394, 395
Knowledge, 410, 411
  and Belief, 233–236
(Knowledge)
  Theory of, 295–301

Lacombe, 154
Landor, 484
Lao Tse, 494
Leibnitz, 74, 85, 136, 181, 296,
  328, 525, 545, 576, 577
Lenin, 481, 635
Leuba, 636, 637
Lipps, Theodor, 488
Literature, 39–44, 460
Lloyd Morgan, 142, 511
Locke, 137, 437, 438, 441–444,
  447, 570, 571
Logic, 459
Logical Positivism, 185, 289, 290,
  458, 459
Logos, 484
Lotze, 136, 630, 632
  his Microcosmos, 499
Love, 246
Lovejoy, 299

Mādhyamikas, 463, 545
Maitra, S. K., 379–405
  his The Spirit of Indian
  Philosophy, 394
Mālavikāgnimitra, 488
Malkani, G. R., 409–428
Malory, 158 n.
Martineau, 540
Marx, 585

Mathematics, 261–262, 459
Max Müller, 13, 52, 56 n.
Māyā, 37–38, 59, 61, 418
Mazoomdar, Protap Chandra, 49
McDougall, 182
McTaggart, 129, 130, 252, 543–545
Meinong, 386
Mill, J. S., 143–144, 540
Molière, his Le Bourgeois Gentilhomme, 389
Moore, 129, 130, 144, 252, 270, 290, 298, 299 n., 301, 566
Morality, 74, 76, 307, 308
Morris, G. S., 316
Muhammad, Prophet, 225
Muirhead, Professor J. H., 13–17, 539
Mukerji, A. C., 431–453
Münsterberg, 386, 389, 398
Murti, T. R. V., 457–471
Myers, F. W., his Human Personality and Its Survival of Bodily Death, 316
Mysticism, 557–561, 636–637

Naturalistic Fallacy, 144
Nicholson, 165, 167, 170 n.
Nimbarka, 51
Nyāya, 185, 214–215, 269, 328, 340 n.

Occam, 528–529
Old Testament, 498
Otto, 182

Pal, Bipin Chandra, 380
Pāṇini, 51
Pantheism, 154 n.
Parmenides, 380, 548, 550
Patāñjali, 50
Perry, 301
Personality, 77–78
Pessimism, 518
Pfleiderer, 85

Philosophy, as Critical Reflection 236–238
function of, 289–292
Philosophical Differences, 292–295
Plato, 55, 56, 62, 179, 324, 368, 374, 483, 486, 494, 497, 515, 516, 526, 549, 551, 558, 635
his Republic, 486
his Symposium, 486
Plotinus, 166, 169, 487, 512, 560, 561
Practical Idealism, 245–248
Prabhākara, 340 n
Pragmatism, 338
Prakāśānandās, Siddhāntamuktāvali, 151, 169 n.
Pringle-Pattison, Professor A. S., 316, 431
Protagoras, 546
Pythagoras, 62

Radhakrishnan, Professor S., 13, 21, 457, 475–504, 509, 511, 539
Raju, Dr. P. T., 509–534
Rāmadāsa, 177, 560
Rāmakrishna, 50, 51, 52
Rāmānuja, 51, 157, 319, 543–545, 636
Rāmātirtha, 509
Ranade, R. D., 178, 179, 539–562
Rashdall, Hastings, 545, 556
his Theory of Good and Evil, 397
Rationalism, 368–369
Realism, 298–301
Commonsense, 239–243
Reality, and Appearance, 414–417
nature of, 301–308
as Value, 385
Reason, 411
Rebirth, 62
Reid, 318
Religion, 308, 309, 409
Ṛg. Veda, 59, 166, 169 n., 500 n.
Rickert, 386, 389, 398

Ritchie, D. G., 316
Robertson, George Croom, 57–58
Ross, 182
Roy, Raja Rammohan, 25
Royce, 544–545
Rūmī, 165, 170
Russell, Bertrand, 129, 130, 138, 262, 290, 293, 298, 300, 518, 551–553, 566, 568
Saccidānanda, 385
Saddharma Puṇḍarīka, 159 n., 168 n.
Śāṁkara, 49, 51, 157, 160, 193, 318–319, 347 n., 476, 483, 498, 502, 522, 543, 544–545, 636
Śamkarāchārya, 548, 549
Sāṁkhya, 181, 182, 254, 255, 328, 510, 511, 513, 518, 520, 522, 523, 545
Santayana, 300, 480
Sarvadarśanasaṁgraha, 545
Sastri, Pandit A., 509
Sautrāntikas, 545
Śāyaṇācarya, 34
Scepticism, 243–245, 444, 445
Schiller, 182, 638
Schlegel, Friedrich, 182
Schopenhauer, 56, 83, 182
Science, 188, 403, 404
Seal, Dr. B. N., 232, 380, 382, 383
Sen, Keshab Chandra, 49
Shakespeare, 349, 490
Sharif, M. M., 565–590
Shastri, Pandit Harihar, 431
Shrinivasachavi, 182
Society, and the individual, 357–362
    and revolution, 362–368
Socrates, 489–490
Spencer, Herbert, 55, 57, 90, 181, 402, 553
Spinoza, 55, 56, 179, 182, 263, 321, 502, 512, 518, 521, 523, 529, 633, 637
Spirit, 465–471
Sribhāsya, 51

Śrīmadbhāgavata, 394 n., 404
Stephen, Professor Henry, 68, 380
Stewart, his Plato's Doctrine of Ideas, 635
Stirling, 315, 316
Stoics, 545
Stout, 89
Subrahmanya, Iyer, Mr. V., 593–619
Syllogisms, 580–581

Tagore, Rabindranath, 17, 25–45, 179, 379, 380, 381
Tarkachudamani, Pundit Sasadhar, 49
Taylor, Professor A. E., 138, 184
Teresa, St., 560, 561
Thomas à Kempis, 560
Thomas, St. 153 n., 155 n., 156 n. 163, 164, 165, 166, 168, 485
Tilak, 179
Time, 190
Triads, 211–214
Trivedi, Ramendra Sundar, 381
Truth, 90, 192–194, 246, 419, 427

Ueberweg, 316
Underhill, Miss, 191
Unknown, the, 309, 310
Urban, 393
    his Valuation : Its Nature and Laws, 386, 392

Vaibhāsikas, 545
Vairāgya, 200–202
Vaiśeṣika, 328, 340 n.
Vallabhāchārya, 51
Values, 81, 82, 385–390, 391–399, 401–405, 457, 588, 589
    emergent theory of, 399–401
Vedānta, 187, 297, 305, 464, 465
Vedāntavāgish, Pandit Dinanath, 431
Vedāntavāgish, Kalibara, 50
Vivekānanda, 50, 51, 52, 177, 509
Voluntarism, 82, 83

Wadia, Professor A. R., 623, 642
Wallace, William, 182, 316
  his *Kant*, 540
Ward, James, 129, 136, 252, 515,
  543–545
Watson, Professor 183, 316
Webb, Professor Clement, 630
Weierstrass, 552, 553
Whitby, 154 n.
Whitehead, A. N., 185, 298, 368,
  370, 518, 519
  his *Process and Reality*, 85, 86
Will, and Intellect, 85–88

Wilson, his *History of India*, 49
Windelband, 386, 389, 390, 391,
  398
  his *Präludien*, 390
Wordsworth, 40, 489, 492

Yoga, 181
Yogāchāras, 182, 545

Zeller, 549
Zeno, 551–553
Zoroaster, 628–629, 638
Zoroastrianism, 627, 634